PEOPLE OF THE BOOK

Wisconsin Studies in American Autobiography

WILLIAM L. ANDREWS
General Editor

PEOPLE OF THE BOOK

Thirty Scholars Reflect on
Their Jewish Identity

Edited by

JEFFREY RUBIN-DORSKY

and

SHELLEY FISHER FISHKIN

The University of Wisconsin Press

The University of Wisconsin Press
114 North Murray Street
Madison, Wisconsin 53715

3 Henrietta Street
London WC2E 8LU, England

1   3   5   4   2

Printed in the United States of America

Library of Congress Cataloging-in-Publication Data
People of the book: thirty scholars reflect on their Jewish identity /
edited by Jeffrey Rubin-Dorsky and Shelley Fisher Fishkin.
520 p.   cm.—(Wisconsin studies in American autobiography)
Includes bibliographical references and index,
ISBN 0-299-15010-0 (cloth: alk. paper).
ISBN 0-299-15014-3 (pbk.: alk. paper)
1. Jews—United States—Identity.   2. Judaism—20th century.
3. Jews—United States—Intellectual life.   4. Jewish college
teachers—United States—Biography.   5. United States—Ethic
relations.   I. Rubin-Dorsky, Jeffrey.   II. Fishkin, Shelley Fisher.
III. Series.
E184.J5P335   1996
305.892'4073—dc20   95-44454

This book is dedicated to
our grandparents, Z"L

Lily and Max Dorsky
Anna and Morris Taubman
Sadie and Samuel Fisher
Yetta and Charles Breger

and to our contributors' grandparents:
Progenitors all.

CONTENTS

Contents

PART V. MEDITATIONS

ACKNOWLEDGMENTS

We wish to express our deepest gratitude to Milton Fisher, who supported this project with creative and sage guidance from its inception to its conclusion, and who gave us the title, *People of the Book: Thirty Scholars Reflect on Their Jewish Identity*. We also owe special thanks to Lillian Robinson, who played a critical role in helping us assemble our stellar group of contributors, and to Julie Greenblatt, who believed in this collection from the outset and urged us to push ahead despite obstacles.

We also wish to thank Susan Brienza, Jim Fishkin, Fannie Fishkin, Joey Fishkin, Bobby Fishkin, Carol Fisher, Helen Dorsky, Lucien Zahendra, Dr. Stanley Wagner, Dr. Renée Rabinowitz, Rabbi Kerry Baker, Rabbi James Ponet, Carla Peterson, Geoffrey Hartman, Richard Yarborough, and Gordon Hutner for their encouragement, help, and advice during the book's production.

Thanks to Ervin Nussbaum for allowing us to reproduce his fine watercolor that graces our cover, and to Louis Cicotello, Matthew Kees, and Teresa Caldarez for their assistance in designing and producing the cover.

We wish, too, to express our appreciation to Wisconsin editors Mary Elizabeth Braun, Raphael Kadushin, Carol Olsen, and to marketing director Sheila Leary, for their loyalty to this project, and for their expertise. In addition, we are pleased to acknowledge the wisdom and support of the Wisconsin Studies in Autobiography series editor, Bill Andrews.

The memory of Reuben Dorsky, Renée B. Fisher, Joseph Fishkin, and Bertha Plaine, and their sense of what mattered most in life, helped sustain us as well.

PART I

INTRODUCTION

In each generation every person must act as if he or she
personally had gone forth from Egypt.
                              —Mishnah (Pesahim 10:5)

Reconfiguring Jewish Identity in the Academy

Jeffrey Rubin-Dorsky and Shelley Fisher Fishkin

EVER SINCE THE Prophets' first thunder, Jews have been hearing of their wandering from the ways of righteousness, and the last several years are no exception, having brought powerful critiques aimed at Jewish apathy and alienation. Like late-seventeenth-century Puritans, who were harangued by their elders about loss of religious purpose at the moment they were most enjoying the fruits of their New England labors, late-twentieth-century American Jews are being warned by self-chosen (though highly credentialed) prophets that their spiritual and cultural community may perish at the time of their greatest comfort and prosperity in this promised land. The authors of these lamentations may well be right that traditional forms of Jewish identification and community are growing weaker. But rather than mourn the loss of unambiguous, uncomplicated identification and community—which, when they existed, were usually (but perhaps not always) forged in response to powerful external threats—the contributors to *People of the Book: Thirty Scholars Reflect on Their Jewish Identity* ask whether the commitment and creativity that has enabled the Jewish people to survive for five thousand years may be reconfigured anew at the end of the twentieth century.

In *The Jews in America: Four Centuries of an Uneasy Encounter* (1989), the historian-rabbi Arthur Hertzberg chronicled the decline of American Jewry as a "community of faith." "After nearly four centuries," he concludes, "the momentum of Jewish experience in America is essentially spent." The obvious accomplishments of Jews in all forms of American life, including the learned professions, will not substitute, in Hertzberg's formulation, for the loss of religious belief. "Jews who cared about being Jewish knew," he says, "if only in their bones, that they had to turn to religion." But there is little hope of this happening; while "the embers of the classic Jewish faith still smolder," Hertzberg predicts that they will die "among the mainstream of American Jews."[1]

In 1992, historian and Orthodox Jew Edward S. Shapiro published *A Time for Healing: American Jewry since World War II,* the fifth and final volume of *The Jewish People in America,* a series sponsored by the American Jewish Historical Society. Shapiro's overall complaint echoes Hertzberg's: American Jewry's hunger and drive for material and professional or vocational success have subverted religious observance, communal feeling, and ethnic identification. But where Hertzberg emphasized the abandonment of Judaism (as opposed to Jewishness), Shapiro seems most worried by the diminishment of the Jewish population itself through intermarriage, which he terms an "insoluble dilemma." With 52 percent of Jews now marrying out of the faith, Jewish "peoplehood" is doomed, and this is especially true, since Shapiro rejects the Reform movement's 1983 decision to include as Jews the children of Jewish fathers and non-Jewish mothers. (The problem, he says, is that "non-Reform Jews could never be sure that potential spouses were in fact Jewish.") Shapiro's despondency over acculturation and assimilation leads him to conclude that "Jewish survival" matters only if the "quality of that life was worth preserving"—with "quality" being achieved only through Orthodoxy.[2]

A different kind of book about Jews was also published in 1992 by Harvard-trained Ph.D.'s (in comparative literature and philosophy) Sara Bershtel and Allen Graubard, who characterize their backgrounds as "intensely Jewish" ("Orthodox in one case, secular, socialist, and Yiddishist in the other") and yet their personal and professional lives as having "no explicit connection to Judaism, Jewish culture, or the Jewish community." In *Saving Remnants: Feeling Jewish in America,* they describe and analyze the interviews they conducted with all kinds of contemporary American Jews, ranging from Orthodox, Zionist, and Marxist, to Reform, newly observant, and unaffiliated. Asking these Jews to explain what, in a thoroughly American context, being Jewish means to them, and what role it serves in their lives and their "sense of themselves," they conclude that not only has modern life thoroughly and irrevocably destroyed old forms of "Jewish peoplehood," but it has also prevented newer ones from taking root in what remains of a recognizable Jewish community. All these new forms or attempts at constructing a Jewish life, they claim, "no matter how vivid and compelling, cannot escape the fragility that modernity imposes on any enterprise essentially dependent on individual choice and commitment." For Bershtel and Graubard, the emphasis on self (self-consciousness, self-aggrandizement, self-doubt), which is modernity's enduring legacy, precludes the reinvigorating of vital, cohesive communities.[3]

The recent jeremiads may not be new, but they are serious, and accordingly they have received thoughtful, though frequently negative, responses. Labeling Arthur Hertzberg a "pulpit bully," Robert Alter, professor of comparative literature at the University of California, Berkeley, and author of several books and many articles on Jewish themes and topics, took him to task in the *New Republic* for being a disillusioned rabbi, "despairing of the whole enterprise of modern Jewish existence because he can no longer hope for the resurgence of faith to which he has been exhorting." While acknowledging the essential correctness of Hertzberg's claim that American Jews have, for the most part, strayed from religion, Alter nevertheless sees as absurd the idea that the "partial displacement of religion by a more secular consciousness of peoplehood means the end of Jewish life." In fact, he insists, "ever since the late eighteenth century, quite apart from the special circumstances of America, a return to the secular realm has been one of the most powerful forces of Jewish history," producing, among other achievements, the "German-Jewish scholarship known as *Wissenschaft des Judentums,* modern Hebrew literature, Yiddish literature, Zionism, and more than one variety of Jewish socialism," as well as a "spectrum of Jewish communal, cultural, and service organizations, many of them still vigorous." "Secular Jewish existence," Alter says, "is embattled in Israel, and it is always threatened with dilution and erosion in this country, but it is far from giving up the ghost."[4]

Also writing in the *New Republic,* David Brion Davis, Sterling Professor of history at Yale, author of influential studies of violence and slavery in American history, and a convert to Judaism, argued that Edward Shapiro was far too pessimistic in his discussion of the "supposedly rapid erosion of Judaism and the loss of a separate Jewish identity." Shapiro's despair, in fact, would have been mitigated by a "less rigid definition of religious observance and a more open-minded interpretation of Jewish history"; he might, for example, have recognized the significance of the extensive efforts of both Reform and Conservative Judaism to bring the offspring of mixed marriages into the Jewish community as well as to "convert non-Jewish spouses." Moreover, Shapiro ignores the proliferation of adult education classes in Hebrew, Talmud, biblical exegesis, and Jewish history, which have attracted "large numbers of women, who were long excluded from such intellectual excitement." Citing his own experience among converts who have become "expert in Hebrew, *halakah,* and Jewish history," Davis claims that Shapiro's "essentially racial view of Jewishness" closes off the very possibilities for survival that he desires—"vigorous outreach programs to the children of Jews, to the 1.35 million gentile adults who live with Jews and to the estimated 3.5 million 'core Jews' who are not affiliated with synagogues or other Jewish institutions."[5]

Arthur Waskow, fellow at the Institute for Jewish Renewal, director of the Shalom Center, noted author of books on Jewish spiritualism, and 1960s counterculture leader, wrote in *Tikkun* that although Bershtel and Graubard introduce readers to a wonderful array of "newly creative Jews"—Jews attempting to remake Jewish social and political life and discover new depths spiritual engagement—they refuse to believe what they see, retreating instead to their "modernity" thesis. Worldly Jews committing to Jewish prayer, activist Jews developing new Jewish approaches to progressive politics, radical Jews struggling to reconcile Judaism and feminism, Judaism and gay liberation, nonethnic and converted Jews reshaping their environments to accord with their faith: all these ways of being Jewish Bershtel and Graubard take as evidence of the "decomposition of the old Jewish community" rather than as verification of efforts to imagine a meaningful life beyond assimilation. According to Waskow, Bershtel and Graubard therefore neglect "a crucial source of cohesion and strength in the Jewish world: a *movement* for Jewish renewal . . . a diffuse, multicentered shift in consciousness that flows under all the usual barricades of Jewish life and runs into the different arenas of the Jewish community." This movement has produced, Waskow says, "new forms and new geographic centers of Jewish creativity in music, prayer, Torah study, art, fund-raising, and social action." Unfortunately, by mistaking "diffuseness for dithering, experiment for ephemerality," Bershtel and Graubard fail to recognize, argues Waskow, how Judaism is becoming a "spiritual/religious community of choice rather than an ethnic community defined by birth."[6]

The editors of this volume align themselves with the positions taken by Alter, Davis, and Waskow, believing that Hertzberg, Shapiro, and Bershtel and Graubard have failed to acknowledge the ways in which Jews and Jewish communities have been meaningfully constituting (and reconstituting) themselves. Our vision of contemporary Jewish life is not of "erosion"—the metaphor used by Alter and Davis to characterize the worries of Hertzberg and Shapiro that the rich, productive soil of Jewish history is being washed away—but of "flow"—Waskow's metaphor for the water of replenishment. While we are aware that modernity has brought destruction and upheaval, the Holocaust and the return of anti-Semitism in Eastern Europe, we also know that it has witnessed resurgence and renewal, the birth of Israel, and the emergence of a politically powerful American-Jewish constituency, as well as the striving toward equality for women in Jewish life. The fundamental issue here, as we understand it, turns on whether or not what Davis calls "Judaism by choice" truly has a future; that is, whether Jews who have come of age in an era where recognizable ethnic patterns have not been the defining factor of their lives can, as Waskow suggests, actually *choose* a "community and spirituality that fit their individual needs" and sustain that choice in the face of modern disintegrating forces. If, except for small pockets of Orthodoxy, the old forms of "Jewish peoplehood" are vanishing, can new Jewish paradigms take their place? Moreover, can those who are constructing the new paradigms pass them on to succeeding generations? Can they create an enduring legacy that will nurture their biological and spiritual offspring?

Along with Alter, Davis, and Waskow, and many other American Jews, we are not ready to say Kaddish for Judaism—and being Jewish—in America. Or, to paraphrase Mark Twain, rumors of its death are greatly exaggerated. These prophecies of doom, however, do serve a useful purpose (as do, of course, the rebuttals they have compelled), since they highlight a historical moment in which third- (and even fourth-) generation American Jews, grandchildren (and great-grandchildren) of early-twentieth-century immigrants, have discovered that, in Alter's phrase, "the special circumstances of America," as liberating as they have been, do not by themselves produce a satisfying life. Somewhere between the sharp alternatives of absolute faith and thorough assimilation lie other options, and what we are seeing around us are attempts to reconfigure American-Jewish identity. "Identity," in this respect, involves something one *does,* not something one *has.* (Orthodox Jewish identity has always been defined both by belief and by the performance of the *mitzvot,* or commandments.) It consists, as we envision it, of an exploration of origins, an engagement with the past, and a willingness to ask difficult questions and confront hard, sometimes painful, answers about our professions and purposes. It seeks legitimacy through commitment to the aspirations, symbols, and meanings embodied in Jewish history.

The historian Marcus Hansen said many years ago that we could expect a revival of interest in their origins by third-generation children of immigrants, which he attributed to the luxury of assimilation. But in spite of what we editors are arguing here, some observers have devalued the content of this interest; Martin Peretz stated the objection most succinctly when he wrote in the *New Republic* that, to the extent such a revival exists, it is "more sentiment than substance," and has tended to express itself as a nostalgic enjoyment of a Yiddish phrase or the rediscovery of the food rejected at Grandma's table.[7] This leads to the commodification of Jewish identity by those Leonard Fein calls "inertial Jews," for whom being Jewish means playing out "patterns of affiliation and association," rather than an examination of "values and beliefs and ideas."[8] These Jews may pay attention to traditions, but more for the immediacy of communal gathering than for an appreciation of ritual purpose or the experience of spiritual transcendence. We do not deny that such trivialization occurs, but what we have been seeking are imaginative expressions of awakened Jewish consciousness, and we believe that the essays gathered in this volume provide just such examples: thoughtful, engaged, Jewish intellectuals probing their disciplines, their pasts, and their beliefs in an attempt to locate themselves more fully on the map of Jewish subjectivity.

Some years ago, the two of us met at a professional meeting and asked each other whether we who spend the greater part of every day operating in the secular realm of the academy as scholars and teachers dealing with texts and issues that (seemingly) have nothing to do with being Jewish might, in fact, be incorporating our Jewish backgrounds into our work without quite realizing it. At first, the answer we gave one another was direct and simple: No. How could it be otherwise? The two of us wrote books and essays—but not on Jewish topics. We taught classes and gave seminars—but not on Jewish themes. We discovered that we shared a love of the phrase "People of the Book" to describe the Jews—but we understood that the sacred book referred to was not the one we assigned in classrooms or read late at night. We were Jewish, but not in the academy.

We both knew, however, if only in our bones (to borrow Hertzberg's wording), that we were supported by Jewish traditions of intense, passionate intellectual engagement. We felt proud (albeit an unannounced pride) that our ancestors valued knowledge and wisdom, loved studying texts and debating interpretations, honored the search for truth. Yet what right did we have to claim this history of scholarship and learning—so pointedly Jewish in its focus—as our own? Rabbi Nachman of Bratslav is reputed to have said, "Whoever is able to write a book and does not, it is as if he has lost a child."

We understood that idea profoundly, especially as we juggled caring for the families we did have and trying to write the books we knew we could write but had not yet written. Yet we couldn't help asking ourselves, "Was Rabbi Nachman talking about people like us?"

In the face of our doubts—in fact, in spite of our fears that the question of our Jewishness in the academy was both preposterous and pretentious—we continued to ask it; finally, albeit tentatively, we began to ask it out loud. When, at meetings and conferences, we would encounter fellow Jewish scholars also working on non-Jewish subjects, we would inquire if their examinations of literary or cultural issues had been shaped by dimensions of their Jewish heritage. Or, conversely, we asked if their scholarly work had influenced their sense of themselves as Jews. We were both surprised and delighted when, time and again, our colleagues responded, "Yes, but how did you know?" Each of these Jewish scholars, it seems, had believed that he or she was the only person in the profession thinking along these lines.

Hoping to make public what had heretofore been private, and to sustain the delicious sense of community we felt when several of us would share and debate our ideas, we solicited essays on the ways in which Jewish-American intellectuals inside (and in one case, outside) the academy were considering, evaluating, and shaping—or *re*considering, *re*evaluating, and *re*shaping— their identities as Jews in American society. The response was overwhelming. The collection we assembled from those submissions addresses the following questions: How have we, through our scholarly endeavors, become conscious of, or altered our awareness of, ourselves as American citizens of Jewish origin or affiliation? How do Jewish values, themes, and patterns, of thought shape our work, and how did we become aware of their role? How does our Jewish background influence our artistic tastes, choices of texts, scholarly projects? How does it inform our relations with non-Jews in particular, and our role in American culture in general? What kind of dialogue, questioning, negotiations do we pursue with ourselves to arrive at an understanding of our Jewishness?

Since we asked our contributors to consider the complex nature of their relationships to the subjects they study, their essays would have to be simultaneously analytical and autobiographical, personal yet professional, a dynamic but difficult mode for academics accustomed to scholarly rather than introspective inquiry. Some plunged boldly into the task, making autobiography the very structural principle of their essays; others proceeded firmly if a bit cautiously, using autobiographical reflection as a framing device for cultural observation and/or literary analysis; a few waded in tentatively, with self-reflection emerging on occasion to link their presentations to subjective experience. The stylistic result is eclectic, often entertaining, and even the essays that are not fully autobiographical still attain a voice and a freedom of expression rare in academic writing.

The volume that has emerged from all this reconfiguring celebrates the diversity of American-Jewish culture by highlighting its multifaceted dimensions. For example, by exploring the ways in which their analysis of particular texts, tropes, writers, and cultural figures have opened a path for them into their Jewish-American identity, our essayists assimilate such Jewish writers as Gertrude Stein, Hélène Cixous, Lenny Bruce, Henry Roth, Cynthia Ozick, Walter Benjamin, Harold Bloom, Woody Allen, and Anne Roiphe, as well as confront such non-Jewish authors as Fyodor Dostoevsky and T. S. Eliot. By analyzing Jewish-American communities in the contexts of others with which they intersect and overlap—feminist, academic, African-American, Israeli, lesbian, activist, survivor, and so forth—our scholars dissect such subjects as cultural pluralism, social justice, dissent, sexism, anti-Semitism, ethnicity, memory and the Holocaust, homophobia, and the place of Israel in the American imagination. *People of the Book* also underscores the multivocal richness of American-Jewish experience in the academy by bringing together scholars from Departments of English, American Studies, French, Slavic, Comparative Literature, Romance Literature, Women's Studies, Judaic Studies, History, Anthropology, and Philosophy at universities in the United States and Israel. Contributors, half of whom are men and half of whom are women, include white Jews and black Jews; Orthodox, Conservative, Reform, and totally secular Jews; Jews by birth and Jewish converts; heterosexual and homosexual Jews. If a homogeneous Jewish community is no longer a possibility, there nevertheless are, as our collection indicates, varied and vital ways of being Jewish in America.

As editors of a book with such a diversity of viewpoints, beliefs, attitudes, and approaches, we took it as our goal to ask of each individual essay clarity of expression, coherence of structure, and consistency of style—but not conformity to any ideology or overarching point of view. As a result, we do not agree with everything that appears here. Although we argued and debated with our contributors (and argued and debated with each other), we would not dream of censoring them, and in the end accepted their essays, no matter how controversial or iconoclastic. We also allowed them to stake out their own position in regard to the question of a hyphenated identity. Jews, we take comfort in pointing out, are no strangers to controversy.

While we, the editors, may have ceded authority in regard to content, we asserted it where organization was concerned, grouping the individual pieces in this collection, not just for easier access by readers, but more for the resonances that would emerge through the arrangement of each section. The four major divisions represent, generally speaking, the four categories of personal experience our essayists illuminate. Part 2, "Transformations," demonstrates how Jewishness has prompted our authors to work for change in the academy or in the world beyond their institutions of higher education. Part 3, "Negotiations," presents the various ways in which our contributors have discovered the importance and contours of their Jewishness through contact with both Jewish and non-Jewish communities. Part 4,

"Explorations," shows our scholars seeking the proper relationship of Jewishness to the different branches of learning—anthropology, art history, literature, philosophy, history, and French—to which they have devoted their intellectual lives. Part 5, "Meditations," shows our critics reflecting on their own lives by examining the means other creative Jews have adopted for self-reflection through art and cultural critique. We freely admit that the placement of an essay in one section or another may not always fit the neat divisions described above, but an essay's ability to find a home as well in some different section shows the very overlap, indeed convergence, of these four categories of experience.

Editing this volume has brought wonderful rewards. The poet Muriel Rukeyser once wrote, "To be a Jew in the twentieth century / Is to be offered a gift. If you refuse, / Wishing to be invisible, you choose / Death of the spirit."[9] Visibility, we editors have discovered, is its own gift, enlivening the spirit and animating the intellect. We also have been given the gift of community; we know that in many cases the bonds we have formed with our contributors will be deep and lasting. What we don't know, of course, are the answers to many of the questions that concern American Jews at the end of the century. Who is a Jew? Who has the right, privilege, and responsibility to speak as a Jew? Can "Judaism by choice" provide continuity and sustenance? Nobody knows what it will take to keep a "Jewish peoplehood" alive in the twenty-first century. All we can say with certainty is that it will take Jews; and so it follows that, for each of us, finding a way of being Jewish, either alone or together, becomes imperative. The essays gathered in this collection show thirty of us struggling to do just that.

The doomsayers will not disappear. But as we share our efforts to transform ourselves and our world, negotiate our identities, explore as Jewish scholars a multitude of disciplines and discourses, and meditate on how other Jews dealt with similar challenges in the past, the future seems less bleak. The combination of *sechel, chochma,* and *chutzpah* that brought our ancestors through far more difficult times than our own may yet come to our rescue. After all, if a one-night vial of oil managed to burn for eight nights, who can tell for certain what it will take to sustain the Jewish people?

NOTES

1. Arthur Hertzberg, *The Jews in America: Four Centuries of an Uneasy Encounter* (New York: Simon and Schuster, 1989), 386, 387, 388.

2. Edward S. Shapiro, *A Time for Healing: American Jewry since World War II,* Vol. 5 of *The Jewish People in America,* gen. ed. Henry C. Feingold (Baltimore: Johns Hopkins University Press, 1992), 191, 253.

3. Sara Bershtel and Allen Graubard, *Saving Remnants: Feeling Jewish in America* (New York: Macmillan/Free Press, 1992), 7, 8.

4. Robert Alter, "Pulpit Bully," *New Republic* (March 5, 1990): 39.

5. David Brion Davis, "The Other Zion," *New Republic* (April 12, 1993): 31, 36.

6. Arthur Waskow, "Sewing Jewish Remnants into a New Tallit," *Tikkun* (March-April 1992): 70, 71, 72.

7. Martin Peretz, "Identity, History, Nostalgia," *New Republic* (February 6, 1989): 43.

8. Leonard Fein, *Where Are We? The Inner Life of America's Jews* (New York: Harper and Row, 1988), 171.

9. Muriel Rukeyser, "Letter to the Front," in *The Collected Poems of Muriel Rukeyser* (New York: McGraw-Hill, 1978), 239.

PART II

TRANSFORMATIONS

If I am not for myself, who will be for me? If I am for myself
alone, what am I? If not now, when?
                                    —Hillel

1

Eating the Bread of Affliction
Judaism and Feminist Criticism

Susan Gubar

AT MOST PASSOVER celebrations, participants make a Hillel sandwich: matzoh, the unleavened bread taken in haste by the ancient Jews on their flight from slavery, is eaten with *maror*, a bitter herb, usually horseradish. Sometimes, to set teeth further on edge and to dramatize the paradox of a feast commemorating the misery of slavery as well as the joy of liberation, the matzoh is topped with *maror* and *charoset*, a mixture of apples, honey, and cinnamon that represents work (the mortar and bricks made for the pharaohs) but also the exhilarating relief of release: deliverance from bondage in Egypt. While the sharpness of the horseradish brings stinging tears to the eyes, the tongue tastes intense sweetness.

Eating the bread of affliction had nothing to do with nutrition, appetite, or taste—not health, not need, not desire—or so I thought, as if I could detach all three from my Jewish identity. If anything, my scholarly commitment to feminism only further convinced me that my health, my needs, my desires depended on being a Jewish non-Jew, a secular Jew. It took some time for me to feel anything but bitterness about Judaism as a religion. Yet I have come to believe that Jewish experience has profoundly shaped the evolution of feminist thinking in our times. Still, even now the vexed relationship between Judaism and feminism seems to mean that the pleasure I and many of my contemporaries can receive from our heritage will always be mixed with sorrow, the pride with grief, the joy with anger, sweetness with bitterness, honey on the tongue with tears in the eyes.

The First Seder

The first time I put together a seder of my own must have been in the late 1970s or early 1980s, because the girls were quite young. Figuring time the way parents do, say 1980, and that would mean Simone was three, Molly seven. Why would an assimilated nonbeliever attempt this kind of event? Perhaps it was related to the fact that as Jews we were such a tiny minority in our midwestern college town that I had to explain Chanukah at all the day-care centers and elementary schools my children attended, getting *dreidels* through the mail from my mother in New York and handing around jelly beans for the bets. Maybe it was because the little one, Simone, wanted to grow up and become not Christian but, in her own language, "Christmas." Or that the older, Molly, had insisted on enrolling in Sunday school at the only synagogue in town, a conservative *shul* where she learned all about customs never practiced at home. Could the motivation have come from a rebellious determination to resist conforming to an overwhelmingly *goyishe* society, to affirm family roots? If so, the nostalgia was a fictive one for what had never been. Neither my husband nor I came from religiously observant families.

Yet there we sat, a jar of Manischewitz gefilte fish in the refrigerator, matzoh-ball soup simmering on the stove, chicken roasting in the oven, red wine and grape juice on the table, and a copy of the Maxwell House Passover Haggadah, deluxe edition, at each place setting.[1] Of course, I had participated in other seders: in my Brooklyn childhood, just a particularly good meal with matzoh passed around the table along with rye bread; during City College days, with Israelis who smoked, drank, and argued politics throughout the prayers; in graduate school, with Orthodox friends whose rigorous adherence to Hebrew made the whole event incomprehensible to me. But at this seder, I was reading with skills related to my newfound involvement in feminist criticism. Sandra Gilbert and I had just published *The Madwoman in the Attic;* we were beginning to think about the possibility of a sequel, examining the achievements of women writers in the twentieth century; and, because we had collaborated successfully on selecting the essays for another book, *Shakespeare's Sisters,* we were also deciding to continue working together as editors, though the idea of compiling a *Norton Anthology of Literature by Women* would not arrive till the next year.

What did it mean to interpret the Haggadah by taking on the role Judith Fetterley had just called that of "the resisting reader"?[2] Not merely a confirmation of my earlier estrangement from Judaism, this experience actually fueled more indignation than I had thought possible, given my noninvolvement, my life as a Jewish non-Jew. Sandra and I had begun *The Madwoman* with a discussion of the interrelatedness of ideas about authority and masculinity in the history of Western culture, and the Haggadah seemed to dramatize the spiritual, social, ethical, and political repercussions of that connection. The God of Maxwell House was a "King of the Universe," "our Father" (34), "the Ruler in His kingdom" (52), blessed be "He," who witnesses and then punishes the pharaoh's cruel decree. The Egyptian tyrant had commanded, "Every son that is born ye shall cast into the river, and every daughter ye shall save alive" (17). Was the God of the Jews enraged by the death sentence against the boy babies or the survival rate of the girls? The text leaves itself open to such a scandalous question not only because its God is presented in terms of male domination but also because his followers in the Bible, his interpreters in the past, and his celebrants in the present function together as an exclusive men's club.

Thus, the Maxwell House God's anger causes him to "smite every first-born in the land of Egypt, both man and beast," when he vindictively demonstrates his superiority to all other gods: "On all the gods of Egypt I will execute judgment I, the Eternal" (17). With "a strong hand" and "an outstretched arm," this God takes revenge out of regard for his covenant with Abraham, Isaac, and Jacob, for he is "our God, and the God of our fathers" (45). His ancient interpreters include only the male of the species: the wise rabbis Eliezer, Joshua, Elazar, Akeebah, and Tarphon. And his newly inducted followers, whose four questions the seder leader must answer, consist of the "wise son," the "wicked son," and the "simple son," along with "him who hath no capacity to inquire." Male god language, the preservation of an exclusively male genealogy both in the Bible and its interpretive community, and the assumption that normative Jewish presence in the present time is masculine: how could these surprise me? Yet they took on new meaning unfolding before the eyes and ears of my girls, because this Haggadah metaphorically casts every daughter into the river, even as it saves alive the sons and their lineage as the only liturgical and historical Jewish reality.

The authority of that reality seemed grounded not only in assumptions of male superiority but also of Jewish—and only Jewish—righteousness. I was dismayed watching Molly and Simone dip their fingers into their cups to sprinkle grape juice on their plates while they lustily shouted out the ten plagues visited on the Egyptians: "blood, vermin, murrain, hail, darkness, frogs, flies, boils, locusts, and the slaying of the first-born." We had an Egyptian friend; the plagues, followed by the drowning of the Egyptians in the Red Sea, seemed a bit grisly or ghoulish, sort of like overkill. What if the idea of the Jews as a chosen people was as vexed as the idea of masculinity as a chosen gender? Was chosenness a form of self-righteousness? of sanctimoniousness? an ideology of racial or ethnic superiority? If the Maxwell House Haggadah was right, moreover, God "brought us forth from" bondage "that He might give us the land which He swore unto our ancestors" (25). We were supposed to exclaim, "The Following Year Grant Us To Be In Jerusalem" (53). "Grant Us To Be In"—not felicitous phrasing. In any case, though, did teaching the kids about Jewish ceremonies necessarily induct them into a Zionism I had always questioned? The same year as our seder, some thirteen years after Israel's occupation of the Golan Heights, the West Bank, East Jerusalem, and the Gaza Strip, the Copenhagen International Women's Conference served as the setting for a diatribe delivered by the PLO representative Leila Khaled. To the consternation of many Jews on all sides of the Zionist issue, Khaled highlighted the injustices suffered by Arab refugees, heralding the idea—tragically illuminated two years later during the invasion of Lebanon and the massacres at Sabra and Shatila—that the Palestinians were the Jews of the Middle East.[3]

17

MA NISH-TA-NAW HA-LAI-LAW HAZEH MEEKAWL HA-LAYLOS?
(Why is this night different from all other nights?) Indeed, why is this God, this religion, this version of the past different from all other patriarchal cultural constructs? After the gefilte fish, the matzoh-ball soup, and the roast chicken, with some snickering the adults sitting around the table agreed not to read aloud the line "Gentlemen, let us say Grace." After opening the door for Elijah, we refused to ask God to "pour out thy wrath upon the heathen who will not acknowledge thee. . . . Pursue them in wrath and destroy them" (38). Enough is enough, I thought, so we all sang "Dayenu" while the kids found the hidden piece of matzoh, the *afikomen,* using it to mop up the remaining *charoset.*

Although at the time I did not know it, my personal anger at this particular seder resembled the responses of a generation of women writing during the 1970s, 1980s, and now in the 1990s, feminists reacting to gender assymetries in the legal, liturgical, and spiritual traditions of Judaism. From Rachel Adler and Cynthia Ozick to Judith Plaskow, Jewish women have explored their bitterness about their secondary status in their own heritage. In "The Jew Who Wasn't There: *Halakhah* and the Jewish Woman" (1973), Adler documented the ways in which women are categorized with children and slaves in Jewish law—excluded from the *minyan* (the community of prayer) and exempt from the commandments that shape the Jewish man's life (praying, hearing the *shofar* [horn] at the New Year, wearing such sacred symbols as *tallitot* and *tefillin*)—and she therefore asked, "Are women Jews?"[4] In "Notes toward Finding the Right Question" (1979), Ozick admitted with some pain, "My own synagogue is the only place in the world where I am not named Jew," attributing the problem to the Torah itself: "The relation of Torah to women calls Torah itself into question. Where is the missing Commandment that sits in judgment on the world? Where is the Commandment that will say, from the beginning of history until now, *Thou shalt not lessen the humanity of women?*"[5] More recently and most extensively, in *Standing Again at Sinai* (1990) Judith Plaskow has confronted the ways in which "the central Jewish categories of Torah, Israel, and God all are constructed from male perspectives," only to find herself wondering, "What can we claim that has not also wounded us?"[6]

Countless other scholars have analyzed particularly vexed areas of Judaism for women,[7] but I did not read them. By an accident of birth, I was a Jewish feminist, but by virtue of that very fact I could not conceive of becoming a feminist Jew, a label that would have struck me as a contradiction in terms. In the catalogue of quintessentially misogynist sayings listed under "Know Your Enemy" in *Sisterhood Is Powerful,* I underlined the daily Orthodox prayer: "I thank thee, O Lord, that thou hast not created me a woman."[8] As a literary critic supplied with at least a cursory biblical background, I understood how difficult it is to reclaim what has wounded the imagination. The linking of the covenant between God and Abraham with circumcision (Genesis 17:10); the maxim that a woman who bears a male child is unclean for seven days, while she who bears a female baby remains contaminated for two weeks (Leviticus 12:2–5); the law "Do not lie with a male as one lies with a woman; it is an abhorrence" (Leviticus 18:22)—how hilarious this sounds if we suppose it to be meant for a female reader; the punishment allotted a man raping a virgin, which consists of a fine paid to her father and the rapist having to marry the woman without the right to divorce her (Deuteronomy 22:28–29): how could the Torah seem like anything but an anachronistic, wounding *patrius sermo?*

In these same years, the essayists and scholars I did read—Adrienne Rich and Carolyn Heilbrun, Florence Howe and Annette Kolodny, Alicia Ostriker and Nancy K. Miller—wrote about androgyny, marginality, and maternity; about women's experience and metaphors of the feminine in the works of American colonists, British poets, and French psychoanalysts. Like me, they examined many different aspects of what we were beginning to call the cultural construction of feminity, a virtual cornucopia of femininities except, oddly enough, the one manifest in the quite startling fact that so many of our peers in this undertaking were Jewish.[9] Why did the enormous energies of feminist critics derive so frequently from Jewish women who sometimes explicitly, sometimes implicitly denied their Jewishness or its impact on their feminism? Did my own sense of alienation and anger reflect the feelings of the others, feelings that might explain these silences-even-in-the-midst-of-speech? Throughout this period of time, my collaborator was composing a series of eloquent, evocative poems and essays about being an Italian-American, but even that didn't inspire any comparable undertaking by me or my cohorts.[10]

Indeed, some time ago, on setting out to draft this essay, I felt so unnerved that I decided not only to engage in the usual background reading, in this case looking for recent meditations by feminist critics on the relationship between their Jewishness and their feminism, but also to raise the subject directly by surveying a number of my contemporaries, knowing full well how very different—in degrees of Orthodoxy, geographical origins, attitudes toward assimilation and native languages, as well as economically—our backgrounds were bound to be.[11] Curiously, both publicly in print and privately in correspondence, many expressed a sense of estrangement not unlike my own.

Writing retrospectively about her sense of herself amid a tumultuous feminist movement that throughout its beginnings "claimed universality," Adrienne Rich explained in her essay "Split at the Root" that she "saw Judaism, simply, as yet another strand of patriarchy; if asked to choose I might have said (as my father had said in other language): *I am a woman, not a Jew.*"[12] Carolyn Heilbrun, also invoking her parents' severing of their roots, found that "being Jewish was for me altogether unreal."[13] Like Rich and Heilbrun, many feminist critics came from assimilationist and highly secular Jewish backgrounds: Elizabeth Abel describes her family's household as "vehemently atheistic" while Rachel Blau DuPlessis remembers being brought up as "an explicit secular humanist (in the Ethical Culture Movement)." Indeed, Judith Gardiner and Nina Auerbach depict the religion of their girlhoods not as traditional Judaism but, in Auerbach's phrase, as "its New York offshoot, Freudianism."[14]

Rich's title "Split at the Root," then, may refer explicitly to her sense of herself as "neither Gentile nor Jew" because born of an interfaith marriage, but implicitly it describes many other women's sense of estrangement, ignorance, and indignation about a Jewishness in early life shared but often denied, derided, or diluted by parents or at a later time split off in antagonism from feminist aspirations. Thus, one anonymous respondent to my queries confides that, though her identity and ideals are "very specifically those of a firmly secular, highly assimilated person of Jewish-diaspora descent," these same identity and ideals depend "on an intimate loathing of Judaism as a religion." For her, the "unthinkability" of this "too unstructurable and ungroundable set of issues . . . feels like the very Abject." In a fascinating analysis of the ways in which her Jewishness has also "always been defined through contradictions," Annette Kolodny recalls her grandfather taking her to an Orthodox synagogue on High Holy Days, at the same time teaching her that religion is the opiate of the masses: "It wasn't until I was in my teens," Kolodny wryly admits, "that I realized the statement . . . wasn't an original insight of my grandfather's."

Significantly, Kolodny and her beloved grandfather stopped going to temple when she reached puberty and would have been segregated from the men in an upstairs women's section of the synagogue: "We rejected my rejection, together," she writes. Less fortunate in this respect, Florence Howe—recalling her childhood education in Hebrew and Yiddish from a "*zaida*" who feared he was "wasting" his time on a girl—summarized "the lesson that orthodox Jewry had taught me": ". . . there are rewards for good women students, but to get them they must keep their place. Education prepares women well for submission or stupidity."[15] Just as ambivalent about Judaism as Kolodny and Howe, Alicia Ostriker, who terms her grandparents, her parents, and herself socialist Jews and atheists, begins a meditation entitled "Entering the Tents" with the sentence "I am and am not a Jew" and later elaborates:

> . . . to Judaism I am marginal. Am woman, unclean. Am Eve. Or worse, am Lilith. Am illiterate. Not mine the arguments of Talmud, not mine the centuries of ecstatic study, the questions and answers twining minutely like vines around the living Word, not mine the *kabbalah,* the letters of the Hebrew alphabet dancing as if they were attributes of God. These texts, like the Law and the Prophets, are not-me.[16]

Published in 1989, this piece would have been inconceivable earlier when she was working on *Writing Like a Woman* and *Stealing the Language: The Emergence of Women's Poetry in America,* paradoxically at least in part because the problem it addresses (women's marginality in Judaism) had made Judaism seem marginal to Ostriker's feminism.

Similarly, when Sandra Gilbert and I found in Lilith the prototypical madwoman in the attic, I remained almost willfully ignorant of any connection that might have existed between our ideas and those that began appearing in *Lilith: The Jewish Women's Magazine.* Like the rebel Lilith, defiantly inhabiting a liminal zone outside the Jewish community, and like the disobedient, stiff-necked Jews who had escaped Egyptian pursuit only to find themselves in the wilderness unable to drink the bitter waters, many scholars in the so-called second wave of feminism felt themselves embittered, hopeless about receiving spiritual sustenance suited to our desires. In our revulsion toward "the terrible past" and "in the bitterness of youth," we could only forget, deny, distance ourselves from our Jewish backgrounds; yet, as Adrienne Rich intimated in one of her poems about being split at the root, for some there may have been an awareness even then that such denial was an aspect of "the task of being ourselves," a task that would eventually require or enable us to heed her prayer: "May the taste of honey linger / Under the bitterest tongue."[17]

The Second Seder

By the mid-1980s, my family and friends sat down to the seder with a mimeographed, revised Haggadah at each place setting and with *kepot* (no longer called *yarmulkes*) available for female as well as male heads. Actually, I was far too dispirited to create such a liturgy. We owed it to our Catholic friend, Mary Jo Weaver, who was wrestling with her own recalcitrant tradition and who had adopted the girls as her honorary nieces, thereby rather bizarrely taking responsibility for their further induction into their own heritage. Say it was 1986: Molly, getting ready for her bat mitzvah, had searched through the Torah for a nonsexist portion and was learning to read her passage in Hebrew, although the visiting student rabbi had refused to change gender-specific pronouns in the translation, had prohibited Mary Jo from participating in the service, and had discouraged Simone from performing a cello solo at the service; Shabbat was a day of rest and no amount of argument would persuade him that music was played, not worked. The youngest child and therefore the one who was supposed to ask the four questions, Simone had found sometime earlier that her most disturbing questions—whether people could be counted on to die in their birth order, whether they could find each other after death—remained unanswered at temple so she overslept most Sundays and now scornfully let her older sister recite her part.

Many photocopied Haggaddot like ours exist, and quite a few have been privately circulated or published.[18] They celebrate the *kiddush* and the Washing of the Hands by calling on *shekhinah,* the female aspect of divinity, as a "Presence, Source of Life." The four questions are asked by daughters now, not sons. The story of the liberation from Egypt includes legends about the prophecies of Miriam, the savior of Moses, as well as accounts of the heroism of two midwives, Shiphrah and Puah, both of whom refused to obey the pharaoh's command to kill male babies, and of the pharaoh's daughter, who circumvented her father's law by adopting Moses. We named the plagues in sorrow over the pain that exists in the world, sprinkling wine on our plates to diminish Egyptian suffering, and consecrated sips from our cups to those strangers in many lands who suffer the grief of oppression. "This year we are slaves," all at the table proclaimed at the blessing of the matzoh, "but next year we shall be free women and men." We opened the door for Miriam and filled a cup of wine in her name to commemorate the joyous dance with timbrels she performed in the desert with other women. When we made the bittersweet Hillel sandwich with *maror* and *charoset,* we recalled that Hillel had asked, "If I am not for myself, who will be for me? And if I am only for myself, what am I? And if not now, when?"

What did it mean to read the Passover story in relation to the injunction "In every generation it is the duty of each woman to consider herself as if she had come forth from Egypt"? My Sabbath *goy,* my *schiksa* friend, had reproduced from a feminist Haggadah a passage entitled "Remembering" about Pesach in 5703 (1943 C.E.) when the uprising of the Warsaw Ghetto began. "Blessed is the heart with strength to stop its beating for honor's sake"—a poem by Hannah Senesh, a resistance fighter, was accompanied by an account of her tragic dilemma. Her mother would be killed by the Nazis if Hannah did not reveal the names of other members in the movement, but Hannah knew she could not betray the resistance. Her mother replied that, by not informing, Hannah proved her love. Though seated at the head of the table (I was supposed to be in charge), I found my eyes filling with tears, unable to read the words on the page. "If I am not for myself, who will be for me? But if I am for myself only, what am I? And if not now, when?"

My husband's family was from Russia and Poland, mine from Germany. We are both first-generation Americans, but his parents had arrived right after World War I, while mine had miraculously come forth on the brink of the second, only some five decades ago, just a few years before my birth. In fact, my mother's father was drafted as a doctor in the Great War on the German side—I had a photo of him in uniform and on horseback to prove it—and during the depression my father had recited the poetry of Heine to himself when he was sent with bushels of money to buy an apple at the market in Hamburg. Only later did those who were able to leave disperse: to Israel, to England, to Central and South America, to New York. *Das einzige amerikanische Kind,* the only American-born child, I was not to dwell on these uncertainties. Instead, I was supposed to be happy, have fun, live the normal life the others had abandoned, remain mystified by the German spoken only when the kids were not meant to understand. Along with German culture and their history and their property and most of all the community of each other, the immigrants in my family relinquished what little faith they had. *"Quatsch,"* my father would call Judaism. Rot. Nonsense. Yet my mother had seen to it that her German- and her American-born children received at least a minimal education in a Reform congregation so we would "know what it means to be Jewish."

They were not exactly "survivors" because they had not been incarcerated in the concentration camps. Yet like many survivors, they and the tiny circle of relatives in our vicinity would never again be the people they had been.[19] First hiring herself out as a maid and then keeping house and sewing gloves until midnight to sell to visiting customers and neighborhood stores, my mother mourned her youthful ambitions for college in Nuremberg. Hammering out dents in the fenders of cars, my father never worked less than nine hours a day, six days a week, haunted by the deaths of the parents he had left behind, his abrupt descent into the working class, his inability to attain in English the fluency he had enjoyed in *Hochdeutsch*.

The atmosphere of dread and humiliation, of grueling work and social isolation, made itself palpable on their hands—in the dark, dead callous from a crochet hook in my mother's palm; in the tenacious dirt beneath my father's scrubbed fingernails. *"Alt und arm und krank und Jude, ein vierfach Elend!"*— a variant of Heine's line, the source of the inscription on the Jewish hospital in Hamburg where my brother had been born, became their self-mocking motto: old and poor and sick and Jewish, a fourfold misery.[20] During the McCarthy hearings, my parents intently watched the television screen to see if "it" would happen again, but the fragmentary, allusive stories they rarely recounted to my brother and me left us mystified about what had actually happened to grandparents, aunts, uncles, and cousins. We were our parents' hope, just as they had been their families' and Molly and Simone were mine. Yet, as one scholar of the Holocaust has put it, "a resurrected hope is not like a hope that never died."[21]

When the murder of Jews became national policy in the homeland of Bach, Beethoven, and Brahms, when the "Aryan"–"non-Aryan" polarity organized a great divide into which all Jews were to be thrown and, dead or alive, buried, many people besides my father believed themselves to be witnessing what Martin Buber called the "eclipse of the light of heaven, eclipse of God."[22] But for my parents, as for many other highly assimilated European Jews, a shattered faith in a religion that had never really shaped their imaginative or practical lives was itself eclipsed by a shattered faith in virtually any social group or political party or economic coalition or geographical assembly or national identity. What trust they had left they placed in relatives and close friends, personal ties that had provided the tenuous, fragile umbilical cord to a new world which they inherited warily. Reading from the feminist Haggadah about the egg, hard-boiled to signify how an oppressed people harden (their resolve? their hands? their hearts?) under slavery, I began to decipher in my own commitment to feminism a response if not to Judaism then to Jewish experience that turned out also to inform the feminist criticism of many contemporaries. While we had documented the influence of civil rights on the women's liberation movement, we never understood the impact of our own past. Despite the antagonisms between Judaism and the women's movement, Jewish history may have served as a leavening for the second wave of American feminism, especially in the academy.

Clearly, those of us who grew up Jewish during the postwar years inherited a mistrust of national authorities and a reliance on private bonds that anticipate the feminist imperative to interrogate (male) institutions of authority and to valorize (feminine) networks of reciprocity. Just as important, we had been served up a monitory lesson about conformity and acquiescence: living through debates over the immorality of "blaming the victim," some of us nevertheless harbored suspicions about a generation of adults blind to the writing on the wall because of their belief that they had integrated successfully into mainstream European culture. These were suspicions that I, for one, was discouraged from expressing, but they nevertheless persisted. Why hadn't our parents left earlier, organized more effectively, saved their families? Or if they had to remain in Europe, why did their survival depend on risky evasions, tenuous lies, grievous sacrifices?

Typical of the children hidden from the Nazis, Susan Suleiman, provided with false papers, a false name, and a false faith during her escape from occupied Budapest, attributes to her wartime "adventure" a lapse in memory and a reconceptualization of history: after the time spent hiding out in the countryside, "I could not remember my name," she explains, and she began to think "of history as a form of luck."[23] Typical of the children brought up by parents who fled Europe, Naomi Schor finds her Jewishness "bound up with the Holocaust": "When I was a teenager I thought I was Anne Frank," she explains. "Her diary probably had a more profound impact on me and my sense [of myself] as a subject of writing (as well as history) than any other book I read during adolescence." Typical of the children brought up by American-born parents, Andrea Dworkin recalls "the first time" the "earth moved" for her when, at ten years of age, she visited a "shaking, crying, screaming, vomiting" cousin caught in the vise of a terrible anniversary, the month "her youngest sister had been killed in front of her, another sister's infant had died a terrible death, their heads had been shaved. . . ."[24] In multiple ways, what our Jewish backgrounds foregrounded was the problematics of hyphenated identities—German-Jewish, Polish-Jewish, Hungarian-Jewish—or, to put it another way, the dangers of difference. Repositories of otherness, Jews in European history had been forced to dramatize for the entire world the deadly double bind of integration and separatism when played out within a hostile dominant culture, the stranglehold of anti-Semitic stereotyping that could not fail to produce hatred as well as self-hatred.

Of course, precisely the category of alterity and the consequences of its attendant stereotypes form the basis for feminist investigations of women's situations in male-dominated societies. Beginning with an analysis of woman as other, two stages in feminist literary criticism developed to examine, first, the ways in which misogyny generates disabling gendered images that operate to silence, marginalize, or demean women and, second, the strategies by which female aesthetic traditions provide unique tropes to empower women's efforts to escape a secondary, subordinated, or self-subverting position. More recently, in a logically inevitable phase inaugurated by postmodernist theorists as well as by scholars of African-American and gay studies, both the "ghetto-ization" of women's worlds or works and the "universalizing" of generalizations about them have become suspect, for such critical moves could reinstate debilitating stereotypes or might naively discount differences between women or could underplay the significance of the interactions of men and women in a particular historical, aesthetic, or ethnic context. Even in this third stage, however, the project has continued to depend on refuting what Elaine Showalter has defined as the prefeminist "assimilationist" position taken by women writers, namely, the view that their achievements—being "as good" as those produced by men—should be judged as qualitatively no different from those created by men.[25]

Both the category of "other" and the repudiation of "assimilation" depended on insights not only achieved directly after World War II but also framed in the context of the history of anti-Semitism. Simone de Beauvoir's *The Second Sex* (1949), which introduced the crucial notion of female alterity, evolved out of her work in the French resistance and negotiated between, on the one hand, her assertion that "the biological and social sciences no longer admit the existence of unchangeably fixed entities that determine given characteristics, such as those ascribed to women, the Jew, or the Negro" and, on the other, her belief that "to decline to accept such notions as the eternal feminine, the black soul, the Jewish character, is not to deny that Jews, Negroes, women exist today—this denial does not represent a liberation for those concerned, but rather a flight from reality."[26] Even more pointedly (and disturbingly, to some readers), Betty Friedan's *The Feminine Mystique* (1963) relied on a comparison between the housewife in the home and the prisoner in a concentration camp; in a chapter that alludes to Bruno Bettelheim's work on the "zombies" who inhabited Nazi camps, Friedan argued that "the comfortable concentration camp that American women have walked into, or have been talked into by others, is . . . a frame of reference that denies woman's adult human identity."[27]

Similarly, exploring Hitler's assertion in his 1934 Nuremberg speech that "woman's emancipation is a message discovered solely by the Jewish intellect," in *Sexual Politics* (1969) Kate Millett argued that "as in the case of the Jews (why persecute your finest talents?) the Nazi method with [gentile] women was hardly practical," and she therefore interpreted sexual politics as an ideology that shapes all psychological and emotional facets of existence, rather than an isolatable political or economic phenomenon.[28] No wonder, then, that Naomi Weisstein's touchstone essay elaborating the ways in which "psychology constructs the female" was resonantly titled " 'Kinder, Kueche, Kirche' as Scientific Law" (1969).[29] As vexing as the metaphorical conflation of woman and Jew has become for Holocaust historians, it continued to play a crucial role in the very influential poetry of Sylvia Plath, whose ferocious curses against "Herr God, Herr Lucifer" and the man with "a Meinkampf look" were articulated by means of her adoption of a Jewish mask that bespoke a sense of herself as a displaced, doomed victim.[30]

Behind the project of many feminist critics, propelling or motivating it, resides a distrust in official authority that can sometimes be traced back biographically to Jewish roots. Explaining her personal suspicions inside and outside the academy, Annette Kolodny remarks, "Somewhere lurking in my responses to everyone I meet is the unarticulated question, 'Would you hide me?' " According to Nina Auerbach, "the Holocaust and the blacklist were twin specters" of a youth in which she "grew up mistrusting society in general. . . . Official authority has always looked stupid and menacing. . . . I associate this sense of exile, mistrust, and damn-the-consequences pride in integrity with Judaism." Jane Gallop believes that Jewishness bequeathed "a 'negative' identity" of being "set apart from a larger culture." Her sense of herself as "an internal alien within American (Christian) culture"—"being proudly not-Christian"—has "analogies in my theoretical positions and in my implicit definition of woman as proudly not a man." Naming this sense of being set apart "productive alienation," Judith Frank explains that her own estrangement from Judaism does not stop her from feeling in certain spaces like Woody Allen in *Annie Hall* when he imagines himself as a Hasid at the dinner table of Annie's aggressively gentile family.[31]

None of the critics I have mentioned presents herself professionally as representing a Jewish community and not a few would (and have) disclaimed the association entirely.[32] Lillian Robinson, for example, came from a "freethinking" family whose "lexicon in the matter of the Jewish religion ran the gamut from 'fanatic' . . . to 'hypocrite.' " Yet this "freethinking tradition" trained her "to treat the very idea of a sacred text skeptically, which is a pretty good beginning for someone seeking to expand and enrich the literary canon." Similarly, Nancy K. Miller admits that she does "not always want to speak 'as a Jew' "; however, she concedes that "being both Jewish and a feminist is a crucial, even constitutive, piece of my self-consciousness as a writer."[33] Privately, she has explained that, in her New York childhood, "most everyone I knew was Jewish and yet the world seemed divided into who was and wasn't. (Perhaps this crucial division of the world into two was what predisposed me both to feminism and to structuralism)."

Miller's reference to structuralism, as well as her sense that "most everyone" she knew was Jewish, should remind us of the general influx of Jews into American, English, and comparative literature during the postwar years. Like Leslie Fiedler and George Steiner, Jacques Derrida and Geoffrey Hartman, some of these contemporary scholars are religiously observant or flauntingly ethnic, while others are self-confessed "terminal Jews," to use Fiedler's phrase for those with whom Jewish tradition dead-ends.[34] Clearly sharing a devotion to the book, which may have been fostered by a religion based on reading, interpreting, blessing, kissing, and parading classical Jewish texts, as well as an absorption with what Steiner calls "the unhousing" of language, many have extrapolated a career in letters from their own complex relationship to, say, German or Hebrew or Yiddish or Ladino or, for that matter, English.[35] Obviously, too, the orientation toward education in Jewish culture also brought many Jews into the academy

For Jewish daughters during the postwar years, teaching in the humanities became a viable means of advancement into the American middle class, since training in medicine, science, and law was generally assumed to be the prerogative of their brothers. For Jewish daughters of Eastern European background, a division of labor that defined men's spiritual role as intellectual and women's secular job as providing the material conditions to make men's holy work possible helps contextualize a paradox that may have shaped the evolution of a generation of feminist scholars: on the one hand, the strength and success of Jewish female immigrants—mothers and grandmothers—and, on the other, their exclusion from the intellectual fruits of their labor.

For many feminist critics, moreover, Jewish devotion to the text and to education has been supplemented by the equally long history in Judaism of a strong commitment to each individual's social responsibility. Indeed, precisely what Judith Kegan Gardiner considers the "habit" of "fighting for social justice," what Rachel Brownstein refers to as being "by definition and by blood on the side of the oppressed," reflects the ethical teachings of Judaism which insist upon personal responsibility for acting justly in this world. Annette Kolodny therefore attributes her own "powerful sense of wanting to live in a just universe," as well as her "passionate moral outrage at *in*justice," to Judaism. Similarly, Elizabeth Abel, considering a Jewish inheritance "deeply intertwined with the labor movement," sees her own feminism as "in part the extension of a political perspective that had to do less with thinking of myself as a Jew than with thinking of myself as positioned by my (Jewish) heritage already on the left." Yet exactly such a concern about social and political justice would underscore the exclusion of women from, in Ostriker's words, the "questions and answers twining minutely like vines around the living Word."

The jarring contradiction between women's liminality in Judaism and the lesson of, say, Passover—"You shall not oppress a stranger, for you know the feelings of the stranger, having yourselves been strangers in the land of Egypt" (Exodus 23:9)—may have spawned not only the feminist movement in Judaism but also feminism itself as well as feminist scholarship: not only the work of Adler, Ozick, and Plaskow, but also that of Bella Abzug, Shulamith Firestone, and Gloria Steinem as well as Blanche Wiesen Cook,

Natalie Davis, Estelle Friedman, Linda Gordon, Linda Kerber, Ruth Rosen, and so forth.[36] Thus, according to Naomi Schor, though the "rush" to establish "ethnic credentials" after "years of assimilation" seems "spurious and opportunistic," a pattern of "working on the underdog (aesthetically), the victim," is "connect[ed] to being Jewish."

At the same time, these jostling terms—"credentials" and "assimilation," "victim" and "Jewish"—raise issues related to what Nancy Miller calls "the shifting line between poignancy of self-representation and the didactics of representivity."[37] Her insight reminds us that the tensions between Judaism and feminism result in an acute awareness of the interlocutionary setting within which language reverberates, the atmospheric change that accompanies the shift from "I am" to "You are" syntax. In the mid-1980s, several incidents jolted me into the realization that, regardless of any personal disavowals, others would embed me in the history I was only just beginning to comprehend. First, at a retreat for American and Continental feminists in upstate New York, a participant from Amsterdam turned to me and cheerfully, even benevolently, remarked, "Your type doesn't exist anymore in Europe." Then, several years later at a speaking engagement in London, an audience member waiting behind me in line at the drinking fountain commented with some astonishment, "I didn't know you weren't Caucasian." Despite Sandra Gilbert's subsequent and hilarious etymological riffs on the terms "type" and "Caucasian," we were both struck by how "You are" sentences inundate "I am" sentiments.

"Why did he call me a Keek?" Simone asked about a hostile paper boy. "He meant Kike," I explained, wondering again about what Miller calls "the didactics of representation." Or, "How could she say that in front of me? 'Jew him down . . . I'll just Jew him down?'"—a phrase that clearly outraged Molly, used by a respected, devoted music teacher. In the absence of Jewish efforts at self-definition, would Jewish identity be shaped by prejudiced, non-Jewish stereotypes? Had I too quickly rejected a self-representation that might have seemed credentializing or indulgently poignant? If my earlier feminist reaction to the Haggadah had involved me in worries about reclaiming what has wounded the imagination, now I wondered about the effects of disclaiming such traditions altogether.

Couldn't the idea of chosenness be interpreted as a safeguard, a warrant—complete with rights and responsibilities—for survival under hostile circumstances? Given the history of the Holocaust, how can one deny the need for a safe place for Jews, a refuge from the wilderness? What does it mean to suggest that Judaism is so constituted as to silence or marginalize women, when Jewish mothers and their children were criminalized and murdered as non-Aryans? And if Jewish feminists had been in the vanguard of deconstructing patriarchal authority, couldn't it be said that they did so precisely because they saw—stamped on the bodies and minds and spirits of their fathers—the disabling effect of marginalization, dislocation, and emasculation on men?

In her verse-sequence *Sources,* Adrienne Rich writes, "I saw the power and arrogance of the male as your true watermark; I did not see beneath it the suffering of the Jew."[38] But it may have been precisely the unnerving mixture of arrogance and suffering in Jewish history that enabled a generation of us to see a shadow of ourselves in the figure Sandra Gilbert and I have called the "no-man." In our most recent work, the three-volume *No Man's Land: The Place of the Woman Writer in the Twentieth Century,* we focused on maimed, unmanned, victimized male characters created by modernist men of letters haunted by a dream of aesthetic potency. Perhaps I had seen in the Jewish "no-men" of the twentieth century the root of my bitterness but also, para-doxically abiding in a memory straining against the impulse to forget, the sweet anticipation of a hope resurrected.[39]

The Third Seder

The third seder is always in the future, or so it seems to me. Yet, marking solidarity with the dead, it brings the past into the present. How odd that this time—the late 1980s, the early 1990s—has been transformed by the coura-geous tenacity of Jewish women more religious and, in some sense of the word, more conservative than anyone sitting around the dining room table.[40] A microcosm of sorts, Bloomington's congregation Beth Shalom (House of Peace) has a resident rabbi now, a feminist named Joan Friedman, whose cantor, Deborah Gordon, serves as Simone's tutor for a bat mitzvah preceded by a Mozart trio and centered on her chanting of the Torah portion. Al-though Simone may harbor private doubts about death-order and death-loneliness, she has been attracted back to Judaism by the neat rankings of the degrees of *tzedakah* (charity) enumerated by Maimonides, a fitting conver-sion for a daughter of the commandments (a bat mitzvah). When Molly is called up after my mother to recite the blessings, to receive an *allyah,* and when Mary Jo appears on the *bema* to hold the scroll, we are looking at a community of women who have passed over the resentments of contradic-tions and tensions not so much through resolution or transcendence as by dwelling within them in a postmodernist collage that resembles the Jewish heritage itself. No doubt Passover, too, will become such a collection of competing, checkered, even incongruous rituals dedicated to loss in the past, renewal in the future.

It is pointless to ask if we have adulterated the tradition to such an extent that we have lost touch with Jewish roots, for both the Passover meal and the bat mitzvah are paradoxically more conventional than the Reform equivalents with which I had grown up. Nevertheless, our participation—as well as this sort of writing about it—does pose problems related, at worst, to political correctness and, at best, to ethical insensitivity. Does a return to even a modi-fied form of Judaism involve substituting the metaphysics of identity for the materiality of history and thereby capitulating to a faddish, retrograde identity politics, as Jenny Bourne has recently charged? That is, has "What is to be done?" been replaced by "Who am I?"[41] In our efforts to examine the dynamics of anti-Semitism, have Jewish women been guilty of eliding the differences between our history of oppression and that of other peoples and in the process eclipsing the struggles of those others? Or, worse yet from some points of view, in our appreciation of the need for Israel as a Jewish refuge from anti-Semitism, have we ignored, again in Bourne's terms, "the exclusionist basis of Zionism and the racist practices of Israel"?[42] Both American and Israeli racism have been used recently to qualify the trajectory traced here, a progress admittedly eccentric and consciously meant as nonteleological, for many have traveled between its two poles (using feminism to critique Judaism, viewing Judaism as constitutive of feminism) in an opposite direction from mine and still others continue to oscillate between them.

To take the charge of American racism first, clearly all claims about parallel oppression threaten to involve Jews and women of color in a "competition of victimization" that can only trivialize the complexities posed by two quite distinct histories.[43] Indeed, any equation of anti-Semitism with racial persecution could be said to backfire against Jewish and African-American proponents, with the former committed to resisting analogies to the Holocaust which rob that event of its catastrophic singularity as a rupturing of civilization and the latter dedicated to redressing a grievous inheritance of slavery and colonialism that continues to deny black people economic, political, educational, and social equality. Yet analogies between white and black experiences have always haunted women's imaginations, dating back to the writings of Margaret Fuller and Olive Schreiner in the nineteenth century and forward to the crucial scholarly work on African-American culture done by such historians and literary critics as Gerda Lerner, Florence Howe, and Elizabeth Abel, many of whom resemble Lillian Robinson in her attributing a commitment to multiculturalism to an "awareness of the existence of anti-Semitism as a form of racism."[44] Elizabeth Abel, confronting the "problematic displacement of [her] Jewishness," describes "a preference for dealing with other, more unambiguously virulent forms of racism than with . . . anti-Semitism." Rather than allowing our attempts to deal with our various backgrounds and allegiances to splinter the feminist movement, these scholars try to keep in focus the problems and ambiguities of cross-racial, cross-cultural identifications.

Has so-called Holocaust blackmail—the justification of Israeli actions on the basis of a history of genocide—led us to defend the indefensible sexism, homophobia, and imperialism of the Israeli government? Here one can only point to a chorus of voices—including those of Grace Paley, Evelyn Torton Beck, Elly Bulkin, Melanie Kaye/Kantrowitz, Irena Klepfisz, Letty Cottin Pogrebin, and many others publishing in the new *Bridges: A Journal for Jewish Feminists and Our Friends*—that addresses the necessity of distinguishing between the various populations of Israel and a government that too often speaks in the cadences of the Maxwell House God as well as the need of supporting Palestinian and Israeli peace activists whose efforts are dedicated to the proposition that military occupation cannot be countenanced as a safeguard against past or present anti-Semitism.[45] Although we Americans have been taught that only the Jews in Israel will suffer the consequences of a rash trust in Arab coalitions proven capable of terrorism or dedicated to the elimination of Jewry, we have also been admonished to accept our responsibilities to a homeland there for those of us in need. Since we are deeply implicated in Israeli policy, in the eyes of others and in our own eyes, what is to be done except to translate our personal efforts to negotiate between rivalrous commitments into an admittedly controversial politics of cooperation that respects differences, for anything else constitutes a diminishment or, as our own history shows us, a tragic loss. Yet, as Judith Gardiner points out, such a stance will "involve us in difficult controversies . . . with members of our own families and communities as well as with segments of Israeli opinion."

Writing about the loss of Jewish lives in her own time, Muriel Rukeyser mourned the double bind posed by European history:

> To be a Jew in the twentieth century
> Is to be offered a gift. If you refuse,
> Wishing to be invisible, you choose
> Death of the spirit, the stone insanity.
> Accepting, take full life. Full agonies:
> Your evening deep in labyrinthine blood
> Of those who resist, fail, and resist: and God
> Reduced to a hostage among hostages.[46]

Poised between "death of the spirit, the stone insanity" and the "full agonies" of "labyrinthine blood," throughout her life Rukeyser herself chose to associate with resistance, failure, and resistance again. Today, at least in part because of the existence of Israel, we Jews need not choose "the stone insanity," for like Moses wandering in the wilderness, we can find nourishment in the desert, suckling "honey from the rock."[47] Yet, unless we too align ourselves with those who resist, fail, and resist again, the gift will be poisoned by an "evening deep in laybrinthine blood" and by the bitterness of those to whom we deny full humanity, thereby dehumanizing ourselves.

Blood on the lintel, a signpost to stay destruction, the blood of a sacrificed lamb to save the blood of a child. Will the ceremonies of innocence at Pesach be drowned each year in a doomed sense of bad faith, inauthenicity, ignorance, and anger? Or will we continue to eat the bread of distress, hoping that—bitter with *maror*, sweet with *charoset*—it will speak to the bittersweet experience of those who have come to hunger for coexistence between feminism and Judaism, between women and men, between Jew and Gentile, between Palestinian and Israeli? When the hidden piece of matzoh is found by the child, and should the broken *afikomen* fit like a jigsaw puzzle piece into the other half of matzoh on the seder plate, could we almost taste a spring in which kindness endures forever? Or is the concealed *afikomen* called *tsafoon* (that which is hidden) because it always eludes us?

NOTES

This essay is dedicated to my dear friend Mary Jo Weaver. As always, I am indebted throughout to my collaborator, Sandra M. Gilbert, whose meditations on her own origins have served as an impetus as well as a model. I also received helpful suggestions and encouragement not only from Mary Jo Weaver, Jeffrey Rubin-Dorsky, and Shelley Fisher Fishkin but also from Shehira Davezac, Luise David, Molly and Simone Gubar, and Donald Gray.

1. The Passover Haggadah, Deluxe Edition, Compliments of the Coffees of Maxwell House (New York: General Foods Corporation, 1964) has been used for many years by many synagogues and families. According to Burton L. Visotsky, a professor at the Jewish Theological Seminary in New York, "Maxwell House has probably done more to codify Jewish liturgy than any force in history" (in Allen R. Myerson, "Editions of the Passover Tale: This Year in Profusion," *New York Times,* April 4, 1993, Sec. 4, pp. 14–15). All subsequent page references in the text pertain to this edition of the Haggadah.

2. Judith Fetterley, *The Resisting Reader: A Feminist Approach to American Fiction* (Bloomington: Indiana University Press, 1978), xx–xxii. My colleague Alvin Rosenfeld has pointed out to me that my phrase "Jewish non-Jew" deviates from Isaac Deutscher's "non-Jewish Jew"; however, I have kept it here to emphasize through the adjectival an inescapable history, not a claimed identity.

3. For a very different reaction to Khaled, see Letty Cottin Pogrebin, *Deborah, Golda, and Me: Being Female and Jewish in America* (New York: Crown Publishers, 1991), 158–59.

4. Rachel Adler, "The Jew Who Wasn't There: *Halakhah* and the Jewish Woman," in *On Being a Jewish Feminist,* ed. Susannah Heschel (New York: Schocken Books, 1983), 12–18.

5. Cynthia Ozick, "Notes toward Finding the Right Question," in *On Being a Jewish Feminist,* 125 and 150.

6. Judith Plaskow, *Standing Again at Sinai: Judaism from a Feminist Perspective* (San Francisco: Harper, 1990), 3 and 1.

7. See, for example, Charlotte Baum, Paula Hyman, and Sonya Michel, *The Jewish Woman in America* (New York: New American Library, 1976); and Elizabeth Koltun, ed., *The Jewish Woman: New Perspectives* (New York: Schocken Books, 1976). Many of the authors included in these anthologies and in *On Being a Jewish Feminist* discuss exclusionary aspects of Judaism: the partition separating women from men in the synagogue, for example; the prohibiting of women from saying Kaddish at the grave; the injunction of *kol ishah,* whereby a female singing voice is considered sexually arousing to men and thereby forbidden in worship; and perhaps most alarmingly, the discussion in talmudic tractate *ketubot* of whether a woman should be considered a

virgin for the purposes of her marriage contract if a man had intercourse with her when she was under three years old.

Others examine disturbing Torah passages: the episode in which two strange men under threat of sexual molestation by the male inhabitants of Sodom are offered by Lot his two virgin daughters (Genesis 18:4–8); the law that a jealous husband who suspects his wife "has defiled herself" may require a priest to administer "the water of bitterness"—sacral water mixed with earth from the floor of the tabernacle—that will distend her belly and make her "a curse among her people," unless she miraculously remains unharmed, thereby proving her innocence (Numbers 5:11–28); the description of the war with the Midianites, in which the Israelites' booty amounts to "675,000 sheep, 72,000 head of cattle, 61,000 asses, and a total of 32,000 human beings, namely, the women who had not had carnal relations" (Numbers 31:32–35). To be sure, as Alvin Rosenfeld has pointed out to me, such proof-texts may place the feminist critic in the role of a fundamentalist, for any interpretation of them as constituting Jewish thought omits the entire corpus of the oral Torah.

More recently, *Twice Blessed: On Being Lesbian or Gay and Jewish,* ed. Christie Balka and Andy Rose (Boston: Beacon, 1989), provides crucial insights on the contradictions between Jewish traditions and homosexual existence, as does Eve Kosofsky Sedgwick, *Epistemology of the Closet* (Berkeley: University of California Press, 1990), 75–82.

8. Robin Morgan, ed., *Sisterhood Is Powerful* (New York: Vintage, 1970), 31.

9. At the time, at least one commentator noticed the disparity between the number of Jewish feminist critics studying literature and the paucity of Jewish woman writers: see Carole Zonis Yee, "Why Aren't We Writing about Ourselves?" in *Images of Women in Fiction,* ed. Susan Koppelman Cornillon (Bowling Green, Ohio: Bowling Green University Popular Press, 1972), 131. Lillian Robinson has pointed out to me that "the cover of Showalter's *The New Feminist Criticism,* where your collaborator is the only gentile on the list, is an especially striking example" of how many feminist critics are Jewish. She adds that "another cover, this one listing the five co-authors of *Feminist Scholarship: Kindling in the Groves of Academe,* includes four Jewish women and one Gentile. (It may be of some sociological interest that the four Jews are named DuBois, Kelly, Kennedy, and Robinson, and the only Gentile, Carolyn Korsmeyer, is married to [a Jewish scholar].)"

10. See Sandra M. Gilbert, "For the Muses," "The Dressmaker's Dummy," and "Anna La Noia," in *Emily's Bread* (New York: Norton, 1984), 17, 21, and 50; the section entitled "The Summer Kitchen," in *Blood Pressure* (New York: Norton, 1988), 51–85; and "*Piacere Conoscerla:* On Being an Italian-American," in *From the Margin: Writings in Italian Americana,* ed. Anthony Julian Tamburri, Paolo A. Giordano, and Fred L. Gardaphe (West Lafayette, Ind.: Purdue University Press, 1991), 116–20.

11. In an eccentric and nonscientific manner, my questionnaire went out to feminist critics who had not established their professional identities on any Jewish scholarly subject. I am grateful throughout this chapter for the wonderful responses sent to me by Elizabeth Abel, Nina Auerbach, Rachel Brownstein, Rachel Blau DuPlessis, Judith Frank, Jane Gallop, Judith Kegan Gardiner, Annette Kolodny, Nancy K. Miller, Alicia Ostriker, Adrienne Rich, Lillian Robinson, Naomi Schor, Susan Suleiman, and several respondents who wished to remain unnamed. All undocumented quotations from these critics were taken from these questionnaires.

12. Adrienne Rich, "Split at the Root," in *Nice Jewish Girls: A Lesbian Anthology*, ed. and rev. Evelyn Torton Beck (1982; Boston: Beacon Press, 1989), 89.

13. Carolyn G. Heilbrun, *Reinventing Womanhood* (New York: Norton, 1979), 23. Earlier in this essay, Heilbrun admits, "Having been a Jew had made me an outsider. It had permitted me to be a feminist," but she goes on to explain that "if Jews were outsiders, women were outsiders among Jews" (20–21).

14. Judith Kegan Gardiner, who grew up in Chicago, writes, "My father used to tell me bedtime stories about Freudian theory."

15. Florence Howe, "Feminism and Literature," in *Images of Women in Fiction*, 255–56.

16. Alicia Ostriker, "Entering the Tents," *Feminist Studies* 15 (Fall 1989): 542.

17. Adrienne Rich, "At the Jewish New Year," in *The Fact of a Doorframe: Poems Selected and New, 1950–1984* (New York: Norton, 1984), 190.

18. I would like to thank Deborah Reichler for providing me with copies of several such feminist Haggadahs. Also see E. M. Broner, "Honor and Ceremony in Women's Rituals," in *The Politics of Women's Spirituality: Essays on the Rise of Spiritual Power Within the Feminist Movement* (New York: Anchor Press, 1982), 234–44; Penina V. Adelman, *Miriam's Well: Rituals for Jewish Women around the Year* (Fresh Meadows, N.Y.: Biblio Press, 1986), 60–66; and Aviva Cantor Zuckoff, "Jewish Women's Haggadah," in *The Jewish Woman*, ed. Koltun, 94–104.

19. This is one of many themes running throughout Helen Epstein's excellent book *Children of the Holocaust: Conversations with Sons and Daughters of Survivors* (New York: Penguin, 1979).

20. It wasn't until reading Sander Gilman that I knew this phrase to come from Heine's "The New Jewish Hospital in Hamburg" (composed in 1842):

> A hospital for poor, sick Jews,
> for people afflicted with threefold misery,
> with three evil maladies;
> poverty, physical pain, and Jewishness.
>
> The last named is the worst of all the three:
> the thousand-year-old family complaint,
> the plague they dragged with them from the Nile valley,
> the unhealthy faith from ancient Egypt.
>
> Incurable, profound suffering! No help can be looked for
> from steam-baths, showerbaths, or all the implements
> of surgery, or all the medicines
> which this house offers its sick inmates.

See Gilman, *Jewish Self-Hatred: Anti-Semitism and the Hidden Language of the Jews* (Baltimore: Johns Hopkins University Press, 1986), 384.

21. Emil L. Fackenheim, *The Jewish Bible after the Holocaust* (Bloomington: Indiana University Press, 1990), 69.

22. Martin Buber, *Eclipse of God* (1952; New York: Harper Torchbooks, 1957), 23.

23. Susan Rubin Suleiman, "My War in Four Episodes," *Agni* 33 (published at Boston University).

24. Andrea Dworkin, *Our Blood: Prophecies and Discourses on Sexual Politics* (New York: Harper and Row, 1976), 5.

25. Elaine Showalter, "A Criticism of Our Own: Autonomy and Assimilation in Afro-American and Feminist Literary Theory," in *The Future of Literary Theory,* ed. Ralph Cohen (New York: Routledge, 1989), 350 and 359.

26. Simone de Beauvoir, *The Second Sex,* trans. H. M. Parshley (1949; New York: Knopf, 1953), xiv. Also see pp. 118–19: "Just as in America there is no Negro problem, but rather a white problem, just as 'anti-semitism is not a Jewish problem; it is our problem'; so the woman problem has always been a man's problem."

27. Betty Friedan, *The Feminine Mystique* (1963; New York: Dell Publishing, 1983), 308.

28. Kate Millett, *Sexual Politics* (1969; New York: Avon, 1971), 223 and 221.

29. Naomi Weisstein, " 'Kinder, Kueche, Kirche' as Scientific Law: Psychology Constructs the Female," in *Sisterhood Is Powerful,* ed. Morgan, 205–29.

30. Sylvia Plath, "Lady Lazarus" and "Daddy," in *The Collected Poems,* ed. Ted Hughes (New York: Harper and Row, 1981), 246 and 224.

31. Judith Frank, who describes herself as "bitter" about Judaism and Israeli culture, says of this feeling identifiable as a Jew in a gentile context: "[It] gives me a certain amount of wry pleasure, but also a certain belligerence about my style of talking and arguing: I'm prone to a kind of aggressiveness, even vulgarity, when speaking among my genteel colleagues."

32. In other words, I did not send my questionnaire out to self-identified Jewish feminists like Evelyn Torton Beck, Melanie Kaye/Kantrowitz, or Irena Klepfisz. However, their books are essential background reading on the subject of women and Judaism: see Beck, *Nice Jewish Girls,* as well as *The Tribe of Dina: A Jewish Women's Anthology,* ed. Kaye/Kantrowitz and Klepfisz (Boston: Beacon Press, 1989).

33. Nancy K. Miller, *Getting Personal: Feminist Occasions and Other Autobiographical Acts* (New York: Routledge, 1991), 97.

34. Leslie Fiedler, *Fiedler on the Roof: Essays on Literature and Jewish Identity* (Boston: David R. Godine, 1991), 179.

35. George Steiner, *Extraterritorial Papers on Literature and the Language of Revolution* (New York: Atheneum, 1976), 3–11.

36. Esther Ticktin proposes a "new *halakhah*" on the basis of this Passover text; see "A Modest Beginning," in *The Jewish Woman,* ed. Koltun, 129–35.

37. Miller, *Getting Personal,* 95.

38. Adrienne Rich, *Sources,* in *Your Native Land, Your Life* (New York: Norton, 1986), 9.

39. Sandra Gilbert and Susan Gubar, *No Man's Land: The Place of the Woman Writer in the Twentieth Century* (New Haven: Yale University Press, 1988–94); see especially volume 1, *The War of the Words,* 43–53, and volume 2, *Sexchanges,* 258–69. To be sure, the "no-man" made impotent by, say, the Great War cannot be equated with Jewish men's experience during the Holocaust; however, the crisis of virility Sandra Gilbert and I study in relation to modernism clearly shaped Jewish history throughout the late 1930s and 1940s.

40. Melanie Kaye/Kantrowitz, Irena Klepfisz, and Grace Paley make a similar point in "An Interview with Grace Paley," in *The Tribe of Dina,* 329.

41. Jenny Bourne, "Homelands of the Mind: Jewish Feminism and Identity Politics," *Race and Class* 29 (1987): 1.

42. Bourne, "Homelands," 7. For a critique of Bourne, see Asphodel P. Long, "Anti-Judaism in Britain," *Journal of Feminist Studies in Religion* 7 (Fall 1991): 130.

43. See Elly Bulkin, Minnie Bruce Pratt, and Barbara Smith, *Yours in Struggle: Three Feminist Perspectives on Anti-Semitism and Racism* (1984; Ithaca, N.Y.: Firebrand Books, 1988) for extended analyses of "competition for victim status" and "oppression privilege" (75 and 99). About the "relative silence among Jewish feminists about Jewish oppression," Bulkin argues it must be seen in the context of self-hatred or assimilation, both of which define "any visible Jewish presence as 'too much' " (145).

44. Elizabeth Abel explained on the questionnaire: "I do think that my current attraction to black women's writing is shaped by my Jewishness; there's some identification at work here that's only starting to become clear to me."

45. See Irena Klepfisz, "*Yom Hashoah, Yom Yerushalayim:* A Meditation," in *Nice Jewish Girls,* 260–85. I am indebted to Adrienne Rich for sending me several copies of *Bridges,* which is published by New Jewish Agenda and is committed to combining "the traditional Jewish values of justice and repair of the world with insights honed by the feminist, lesbian and gay movements" (Editorial Mission statement).

46. Rukeyser, section 7 from Letter to the Front, in *The Collected Poems of Muriel Rukeyser* (1944; New York: McGraw-Hill, 1982), 239.

47. See Moses' poem in Deuteronomy 32:7, 10, 13.

2

Strange Identities and
Jewish Politics

Paul Lauter

By what sends
the white kids
I ain't sent:
I know I can't
be President.
                    —Langston Hughes, "Children's
                    Rhymes"

IT WASN'T THAT I ever wanted to be president. Crown prince might have fit
my upbringing as only son—only child, in fact, for nine years. It was the feel
of being different, evoking even now a child's pride and terror. Different: a
mother who worked, even in the depression 1930s. Preschool, a private kin-
dergarten, unusual in that era. P.S. 88, down across 170th Street, when all the
other kids in my part of Sheridan Avenue went to P.S. 64, across the Grand
Concourse. The Little Red Schoolhouse for a miscellaneous year. Different,
too, at some point in sexual identity, whatever it was—and who to ask?

What was *common* in that Bronx world was Judaism, or rather Jewishness,
which wasn't really the same. Not that it was clear what either involved. In
the beginning, there wasn't the state of Israel with which to identify. And
then, when there was, it was still long before the Israelis had mounted a
conscious policy of fostering second-hand nationalism to substitute for
Jewish-American identity. At any rate, identity for me did not primarily have
to do with the nation-state to which one belonged, vicariously or even by
birth; rather, it involved how one acted toward others and they toward you,
whether one might assume comfort and acceptance or had best anticipate
enmity or even violence. Much later, I found a theoretical basis for this idea of
identity in Sartre's *The Anti-Semite and the Jew*, and in the equation of
"chosenness" with progressive social action.

I struggled over identity—for "authenticity," as Sartre called it. Surely it was
more than going after school to chant literally meaningless foreign words with
seven other unruly boys in a *shul* basement; there, Judaism was reduced to the

ability to make the sounds of Hebrew, but to know nothing about its meaning or traditions. It was more, too, than the occasional visits to *shul* itself—mostly on the High Holidays, mostly to satisfy my grandfather, always with an intense sense of boredom at the chatter and the chanting to which people—men mainly—subjected themselves for reasons no one ever explained. Clearly it had something to do with the shouted hatred of neighborhood Micks, somehow linked to the overseas hatred of Nazis and Poles and Ukranians I read about, along with equally tiny accounts of Chinese rural reformers, buried in back pages of the *New York Times*. Perhaps its mystery resided in the blue and white can I shook—probably to compete with the other boys for the rabbi's grunt of satisfaction—outside the 171st Street subway exit: "Please give to the Jewish National Fund." The proceeds bought trees—or it might be, I later learned, the Irgun's guns. But then again, what was Yisrael to me? Whatever constituted that identity, I knew I couldn't be president.

Still, it was not being Jewish in my world that made me different; quite the contrary. Later, much later, Jewishness gave a social dimension, a public shape, to my elsewise quite personal experience of otherness, that malaise I found expressed in Whitman: "Hours of my torment—I wonder if other men ever have the like, out of the like feelings?" ("Hours Continuing Long, Sore and Heavy-Hearted"). The political definition of Jewishness with which I emerged into my teens seemed to me natural, but may well have been idiosyncratic, since there were plenty of apolitical nodes for Jewish identity in those pre-Israel days:

The *horah*—but the folk dancers at Ethical Culture seemed to have another agenda, and nimbler feet as well.

Borscht—but Leslie Fiedler told us at the 1954 dinner I'd brewed up for him and my wife's WASP professor of Russian history that surely there was more to Jewish culture than strange foods.

Talmud—but I was no *yeshiva-bücher*, though we lived down the block from Yeshiva University; for in Hebrew school, where I'd been sent to get up to bar mitzvah speed, I'd never really moved beyond the issue of why one had to substitute Adonai for the name Yahweh (which, in any case, sounded to me like a football yell).

Buber—but I couldn't really make out how he differed, when you came down to ethics, from Tillich; and what was the use, then, of being persecuted?

Chused—now that began to fit a Jewish son—chosen! Forget by whom—mother, say. But for what? That became the question worth asking, especially then, before and during World War II. If Jews were in any sense "chosen," it seemed to me then, and has seemed to me since, surely that had to do with implementing the decent values I heard every day expressed around me in the liberal, middle-class ghettoes where I grew up. "Do unto others . . ." had too Christian and individualistic a ring for me. "Do the right thing" might have been closer. The formulation I came to, some years later in preparing for a course on "The Origins of Christian Civilization," was Hillel's: "If I am not for myself, who will be for me? If I am for myself alone, what am I? If not now, when?"

Hillel's phrases gave expression to the link I had *felt* as early as I could remember between the Jewish idea of "chosen" and its enactment in progressive politics. What Hillel could not do was subdue the danger of this link in late-1940s America. To be chosen for social commitment was to step precisely into that kind of activism then being plowed under by Harry Truman, Joe McCarthy, my high school social studies teacher, and the other "cold warriors" of that post-Hiroshima moment.

When I went away to college in 1949, as green a child of New York as any immigrant of fifty years before *to* New York, I joined the NAACP. Ted Poston, a reporter for the then-liberal *New York Post,* had come to Rochester to talk about the "Little Scottsboro" case in Florida,[1] and I, enraged by what his narrative said about my country, took what seemed the altogether natural next step of supporting the organization which defended a persecuted race. My parents were shocked—not opposed, to be sure, for their liberalism was the source of my politics. Yet they feared that my father would lose his state job as a court reporter. Worse could happen. Especially to Jews. Years later my mother told me that the Rosenbergs lived three blocks away. Just whose country was it, anyway?

Back the following school year at NYU, as much a citadel of secular Judaism as Bronx Science had been, I moved into English and music from physics and bombs. The academic cold war and the Korean hot war were in full swing. Edward Berry Burgum, whose rather innocent novel classes I had been auditing, was, with a few other professors, being fired for refusing to rat on his fellow Communists. A committee was set up; meetings were held; our English honors class voiced some ineffectual protest; I expected to be drafted and sent to the wilds of Oklahoma, where, the novels I'd been reading told me, Jew-boys would be the butts for every red-neck corporal. I set out to become 4-F—a more practical form of resistance, I finally concluded, after the Korean War began on my eighteenth birthday.

But difference seemed both inevitable and unsafe. It closed in upon me, even as I tried to accommodate to 1950s America by an honors thesis on e. e. cummings, marriage, and graduate school in Indiana. Wasn't I as American as the next kid in the Indianapolis selective service physical? Only I wasn't: I'd had queer diseases—and dis-eases—the examiner didn't even want to know about. I seemed to share them with a few others in the university—New Yorkers, we called ourselves delicately—moving uncertainly, a first generation, into this gentlemen's profession of literary study. Later, much later, having read W. E. B. Du Bois, I could recognize a version of what he described as "double consciousness," but for me, then, Du Bois was only the name of a Tennessee Williams heroine. In any case, my problem, as I perceived it in graduate school, was to "leave" New York, not to smuggle it along with me into the decidedly Anglo-Saxon, occasionally Germanic, and almost, wholly male, white, and relentlessly heterosexual business of literary study. Lionel Trilling and a few others notwithstanding, success in the literary profession seemed to demand that one scrub away New York. I succeeded, learning irony—as someone phrased it—before I quite knew what there was to be ironic about.

I emerged from my graduate education, which had been consummated in New Haven, trimmed in tweed and about as safe-seeming as my church-going classmates. It did not *seem* to matter—it certainly didn't to me—that I was, so far as I could tell, the first Jew in Dartmouth's English department; my indifference to snow seemed more problematic. But then I started teaching the Bible as literature, *The Dartmouth Bible,* in fact. And I began dimly to sense that my relationship to the text was somehow different from that of almost all the undergraduates maneuvering as best they could through the freshman requirement. I had been looking in it for what it might explain about *me;* they were looking through it for what they had to explain *to* me. Was I getting *too* intent on their grasping what I was trying to learn? Ironic distance was, after all, at the heart of my New Critical training, and genteel appreciation at the center of a Dartmouth education. I was teaching a critical skill, close reading, was I not? If I read as a Jew, could I also read as a critic? Where had that odd, half-articulated question come from? Did it arise, like the ghost of my Hebrew teacher, from the fact that I could pronounce as well as explicate the *Sh'ma?* Was the ever-so-light touch of the language sufficient to mark me?

I looked harder at Judaism—the Reconstructionist version thereof,—not just at Jewishness . . . as a few undergraduates sought me out for bagels at Hillel. Bagels in the Protestant wilds of New Hampshire circa 1958 were comforts, to be sure. Still, my ethical home drifted closer to the radical pacifism of my Quaker friend and Yale classmate Allan Brick, who began to reawaken the sense of social justice I had so carefully jacketed. He precipitated considerable agitation in Hanover by bringing A. J. Muste, the septuagenarian radical and pacifist, to speak and by posting signs directed to men of draft age about "conscientious objection"—words as remote from the Dartmouth as from the New York vocabulary. Could there be a Jewish pacifism (after Hitler?), I asked myself through my next two jobs?

The second of these, at Hobart and William Smith, colleges of some vague affiliation with the Episcopal church, involved teaching the massive Western civilization course required of all first-year students. I sometimes think it was here that my own education really began, for the weekly staff meetings, the long written briefings, the challenge of teaching not only biblical but Greek and Roman and then later key modern texts like the *Communist Manifesto* forced me to think through a whole set of social, ethical, and education issues, altogether beyond the scope of my own education. Having been fired from the previous job at the University of Massachusetts for my political activities—I opposed ROTC on campus, handed out antinuke leaflets at showings of *On the*

Beach, and joined the nascent faculty union—I was finally ready to be educated in the way that few of my adolescent undergraduates then were.

I came to question the subtitle of the course, honest if discomforting: "The Origins of Christian Civilization." Its narrative was clear enough: from the Hebrew Bible we moved to the birth of Western culture in Greece, through its trials by fire in Rome, and to the triumph of culture and spirit in the New Testament. Now, I was not much of a historian, but it did seem to me that there was something of a gap between the final books of the Old Testament and the advent of Jesus. And about three years into my time at Hobart I raised this problem, an increasing problem given the larger number of Jewish students beginning to make their way through "Christian Civilization." My senior colleagues were serious, judicious: perhaps, yes, we should have a lecture on that intertestamental period. "Perhaps you should take responsibility for it, Paul, as the one, ah, most concerned in it." Chosen again.

I thus learned the first principle of multicultural education: if you are it, you are *it*. What you "are," by ethnicity or race (or gender), predicts for many people what you are supposed to know. The library contained what seemed to me many hundreds of texts, books, and articles from or about the intertestamental period, and I came forth from that immersion experience with two hours' worth of lecture for the fifty minutes which had been made available. That allocation seemed reasonable, of course, for these were (don't you agree) neither canonical texts nor the classics of our civilization (whatever it was which defined "our" or "civilization")— "classics" we thought we had a handle on. And so I told the four or five hundred students to put down their pens and simply listen while I speeded up my sound track, hoping mostly that they would pick up the historical continuity of the "New" Testament with the "Old," the way familiar New Testament phrases like "do unto others" so often echo "intertestamental" verses. Perhaps some did, perhaps some heard special pleading, perhaps "do unto others" came to be a more usable piece of ideology—and rhetoric—to my Jewish students, even as the Vietnam War heated up and the question of Jewish pacifism came to be less and less an abstraction.

For *me,* the experience first raised doubts about the "literary canon," although we did not then refer to it as such. If so much of such interest was left out, what confidence could we have in the narrative we were presenting? Perhaps Napoleon (Derrida had not yet arrived on the scene) was right that history is "a lie agreed upon." What did that say about what we ought to be offering our students, *all* our students? Were we really teaching them the best that had been thought and said or only the good news that seemed to fit? Some of it, after all, didn't seem to fit *me* all that well. But I then had no conceptual framework, no vocabulary, no intellectual community to be able to regard the curriculum, much less "our cultural heritage," as contested ground, historically contingent, socially constructed. If such terms even existed, they were no part of my training. Yes, Judaism had historically placed great value on commentary, dispute, interpretation, but the core texts, beliefs, even many distinctive practices were—or so it then seemed to me—quite fixed: *"Sh'ma Yisrael, Adonai Eloheynu, Adonai Ehod."* Nothing in my Jewish upbringing prepared me for such destabilizing cultural questions, questions that brought the entire underlying project of my graduate education into question.

Still, the social values which my Jewishness had reinforced led me to think a lot about my work as a teacher in the 1963–64 school year, during which I served as director of Peace Studies for the American Friends Service Committee and spent some time in the freedom schools of the Mississippi Summer project. Moving into political work and out of the academy, even for a year, was enormously liberating. It opened my mind to the implications of earlier experiences, to ideas which it would take me many years to clarify, but which were then being placed on educational and political agendas by the movements for social change.

First, it was perhaps not my *problem* but my *virtue* that texts like the Old Testament, which others approached as an assignment or an opportunity for critical display, felt like an interrogation of family history. The emotional valence of a work might not be determined by the grand abstract reader speaking through the pages of *Understanding Poetry*,[2] but might depend upon who and what you are, "reader, holding me now in hand," as Whitman put it. Such a queer notion began to explain the doubleness of my perceptions, the divisions between my coat of tweed and the circumcised body I carried under it, between the cadences of Cleanth Brooks's voice, which I kept forever in my ear, and the inflections of my own New York speech, always lurking beneath how I'd learned to sound.

Second, it came to seem almost reasonable, almost to feel not even quite irritating, that I was omitted from the underlying cultural narratives that informed curricular structures. If I were here—and I was, though I was not given to shouting that in seminar rooms—why was I left out? By the end of the 1960s, of course, questions like "Where are the blacks?" and "Where are the women?" became central to rethinking curriculum. And discomfort, a queer sense of malaise, was transmuted into demand, a politics of identity.

And third—a conclusion forced on me by the power of my freedom school classes on Richard Wright's *Native Son*—literature courses are about people and values, not just metaphor and irony. Otherwise they are as much empty forms as the Hebrew lessons I'd endured en route to my bar mitzvah. Having learned sufficiently the disciplines of formalism to enter the profession, I had to unlearn that dominant lesson, together with most of what my graduate education had taught me about canon and value. In particular, I had to stop chanting in the language of intellectual irony and embrace the partisan activism that Jewishness had once again in the 1960s come to mean for me.

The first two of these ideas—about what we might now call subject position and about inclusion—came to me specifically from the marginalization I experienced and explained as Jewishness in the literary profession. The third, the question of connecting our values and our work, seemed to me the constant among the many Jewish volunteers with whom I would exchange smiles across the hymns in the back of one or another black church of a 1964 Mississippi Sunday morning. We were teachers, more and less experienced, finding for the first time that what we did might matter enough to die for it. That was "chosen" with a vengeance.

It seemed to me altogether natural that so many of the white Mississippi volunteers were Jews. Where else should a Jew be, after the Nazis, but on the front lines in the struggle against racism? Modern American progressive movements, about which I knew very little, seemed to feature alliances between blacks and Jews. Besides, Jews played prominent roles in every liberal organization or institution I knew, from the governorship of New York to Students for a Democratic Society, from the magazines I read to the teachers' union I'd joined. Changing not only how we understand the world but also how we live in it seemed to me the baseline of the Jewish contribution to history. These were not lessons I had learned in some Sunday school, but the warp and weft of the culture in which my New York childhood had clothed me. Without the slightest sense of dissonance, I wrote about my activism in the mid-1960s for a Jewish audience (in the *Reconstructionist* and *Conservative Judaism*), about the ways in which the civil rights movement seemed to me a fulfillment of the responsibilities and the opportunities Hillel's phrases posed for us: "If I am for myself alone, who am I?" I loved writing to that audience, for it seemed to me I had, really, to explain very little about why I did what I did. To be a Jew, or so I thought, was already to understand why Andrew Goodman and Mickey Schwerner had been buried in that Mississippi earthen dam with James Chaney. "Which side are you on?" was no question, but an affirmation. What else *could* "chosen" mean?

Ironically, however, and probably not surprisingly given the innocence of my beliefs, my political trajectory and that of the Jewish audience to which I thought I wrote were, within a short time, to hurtle in opposite directions. It was 1967. I stood on a Chicago street corner reading the latest reports from the Middle East and talking, seriously, about whether Israel might need volunteer defenders in the war then just begun: "If I am not for myself, who will be for me?" In a day or two, of course, I recognized how little my services were required there. What I didn't see was how radically for most American Jews the question of Jewish identity would shift—shift away from the ethical imperative that had brought me to that discussion of volunteering as well as to Mississippi, away from the childhood New York assumptions that had, for me, made Jewishness a badge of commitment to principled action: "If not now, when?"

It may be hard to recollect—or, for younger people, even to imagine—but a quarter-century ago, few Jewish-American intellectuals, wherever they located themselves on the political spectrum, saw Israel as central to their political, much less personal, identity. Within a year or two, however, the state of Israel had launched its quite successful effort to convert American-Jewish identity into Israeli nationalism. And with the onset of the Nixon administration, the fragmentation of the Left, the widening division between blacks and Jews, and the emergence of a new religiosity across America, the sharply secular Jewishness that had shaped my conscience flagged before the revival of an organized piety generally linked to a fevered Zionism. I observed the gulf between the Jewishness to which I adhered and this new right-wing form opening, particularly in the magazines I read and had written for. The *New Republic,* from which, as an adolescent, I had learned much of my liberal politics, and in which I had published one of my first articles, was taken over and turned toward the Right primarily by Martin Peretz, one of the main financial backers of the wildly disastrous National Conference for New Politics (NCNP). Designed as the "rainbow coalition" of its time, NCNP turned into a fountainhead of acrimony, especially between liberal Jews and militant blacks; it seemed to "prove" to many of its Jewish participants that the key middle term of Hillel's troika—"If I am for myself alone, what am I?"—would inevitably be squeezed into liberal impotence between the insistent self-interest and the impetuous immediacy into which the two other terms could be distorted. Likewise, the *New York Review of Books,* which had printed a diagram for a Molotov cocktail on one of its 1960s covers, no longer featured dissident voices like that of Noam Chomsky or, indeed, my own. By the early 1990s, it had sunk to promotional reviews of such right-wing journalistic twaddle as D'Souza's *Illiberal Education.* OK, I thought—to the extent that it seemed worth thinking about in the 1970s—if Menachem Begin, Henry Kissinger, and Saul Bellow were to be models of Jewish success, well then, give me Tom Paine, Elizabeth Cady Stanton, and Ho Chi Minh.

Judaism and I parted company. But in the rush of events, for years I was not aware of how far in opposite directions I and so many of my *landsmen* had traveled. When in 1988 I began teaching at Trinity College—a return to New England, private education, and a Protestant venue—I was tempted to lunch at the college's Hillel House. Two students were reporting on their summer activities at American-Israeli lobby organizations' work camps in Israel—much as, twenty-five years before, I might have heard their parents reporting about Quaker work camps in the Dominican Republic or in Alabama. "We went to the northern border," one of them said breathlessly, "and there, not a hundred yards away, was the enemy." "Whoa," one of my colleagues interrupted, "whose enemy?" The student caught herself, for the moment; but amplified by the Israeli posters and propaganda that dominated the building, the moment crystalized for me how altogether different were her concerns as a Jew from those with which I had struggled. For her, it was clear, the twentieth-century disease, ethnic nationalism, had buried the questions that had obsessed me: how we who were "other" could convert into power the strangeness with which we felt marked, and could give practical social content to the historically charged idea of being "chosen." For me, her secondhand nationalism, her unconsidered obliteration of Arab people as "the enemy"—the Other, the *schwarze* , the menace—seemed a betrayal of precisely what Jewish consciousness in the time of the Holocaust had come to mean to me.

For many of these students, as for an increasing number of my former comrades, what defined difference seemed not to be the kind of doubleness on which I agonized and thrived. Rather it had to do with Shabbat candles, *yarmulkes,* and *mikvahs*—with the triumph of ritual over reason and, more darkly sometimes, of born-again fanaticism over whatever it is that links us as humans. As Tillie Olsen's Eva says of her daughter's Sabbath candles in "Tell Me a Riddle": "Superstition! From our ancestors, savages, afraid of the dark, of themselves: mumbo words and magic lights to scare away ghosts."[3]

I want to be offensive here, otherwise why write in a book about Jewishness at a time when it no longer means "progress," as surely as it did in the world where I grew up. A few years ago I heard chuckles at Tammy Bakker's hairdo, at Jimmy Swaggart's sex life, at Marilyn Quayle's literalist theology. But I had to wonder at the silence before the born-again Jewish pieties that, as surely as other fundamentalisms, have helped underwrite ayatollahs across the face of the earth. During the last presidential election campaign I read with enthusiasm the come-lately denunciations in the *New York Times* by A. M. Rosenthal and William Safire of Pat Buchanan's venom toward anything (to him) queer, and, less frequently, of Pat Robertson's politics of Christian exclusion. But what I did *not* read is how the rightward stampede by such Jewish intellectuals beginning about 1967 and accelerating in the 1970s helped cradle these Leonard Jeffries of Republicanism. Even as I began drafting a piece to suggest how voting patterns in the 1992 election showed the dissolution of the liaison (it had never been a marriage, I proclaimed) between mainstream Judaism and the American Right, the Jewish Right in Crown Heights was noisily trying to demonstrate the opposite.

After fifty-some years of conscious exploration, it has finally occurred to me that my identification of Jewishness with progressive social activism is as much a historical construction as the messianic intolerance of Gush Emonim. Jewishness, or even Judaism, is what it always has been: what people acting in history have chosen to make of it. Our story is filled with contradictory evidence of idealism and barbarity, of religious aspiration and secular action, of hope defeated, exile transformed, difference avoided, flaunted, denied, idolatrized. It has long been evident that there is no "Judaism"; there are Judaisms. And even more clearly, there is no "Jewishness," but an array of secular and religious cultures contesting for title and authority. In the 1950s, I learned to speak a professional tongue that masked the Jewish origins I could—or would—not deny. In the 1960s, I learned to reembrace my strangeness, Jewish and otherwise, because it allowed me to see what the conventions of America had been hard at work hiding: the realities of segregation and want in a land of plenty, the horrors of warfare in a world of poverty, the arrogance of Western civilization in a universe of difference. It allowed me to believe that a better world was in birth and to act on that belief. In the succeeding decade, I left the struggle for Jewish legitimacy to comrades (I honor them here) willing to contest the piety and nationalism which had become dominant. Now, in writing this chapter, I add whatever voice I have to the insistent chorus of those who pose Jewishness not as a ritual bath or a parochial nativism but as a record of human hope and a badge of commitment to human progress.

NOTES

I wish to express my appreciation to the editors and to Ann Fitzgerald for their very helpful comments, and especially to Selma Burkom, without whose devoted criticism this piece would never have come into being.

1. As in the *Scottsboro* case, a group of young black men was being railroaded to prison by what then passed for justice in the South.

2. Cleanth Brooks and Robert Penn Warren, *Understanding Poetry,* 3d ed. (New York: Holt, Rinehart and Winston, 1960)—probably the best-known and most influential text by which the formalist ideas of the New Criticism were translated into classroom practice.

3. Tillie Olsen, *Tell Me a Riddle* (New York: Delta, 1971), 81.

Changing the Story

Shelley Fisher Fishkin

Rabbi Zusya said, before his death, "In the world to come, I shall not be asked: 'Why were you not Moses?' but 'Why were you not Zusya?' "
—Hasidic saying

I AM HAVING lunch in a cafe in Berkeley with a colleague who is in town, as I am, to do research at the Mark Twain Papers. "What got you interested in all this?" he asks, referring to the issues involving Mark Twain and race that have absorbed me passionately for close to a decade. I stare at him for a moment to decide whether he wants a real answer or is just being polite. To my surprise I find myself saying, "I suspect it has something to do with my being a Jew and a woman."

I

> Mein Yiddishe meydele
> Zie is azoy sheyn
> Mein Yiddishe meydele
> Mit a Yiddishe cheyn

This was the song my grandmother often sang to me. Softly stroking my forehead, she would sing in Yiddish, "A Jewish little girl is so beautiful, a Jewish little girl with her Jewish charm." I was that *Yiddishe meydele* I would think, as I drifted off to sleep, beautiful, important, cherished. In those days, premature babies born as small as I was usually didn't make it (my parents even waited a few months to send out the birth announcement, and when they did they gave my weight in grams rather than pounds); when the babies survived, more often than not they ended up blind. Healthy and strong, with 20/20 vision and a passion for books, I became a walking, talking miracle as far as my family was concerned. As a child it never occurred to me that being Jewish and female was anything but wonderful.

Jewish, female, American. All these terms described me, and I was happy to "claim" them as well. Being Jewish was hearing my father and grandfather tell witty stories and jokes in "Yinglish." It was learning Yiddish songs and proverbs from my grandmother, hearing my mother play *freylachs* on the accordion and piano, helping my grandmother make flaky *rugelach* and fragrant *chalupses,* getting a new outfit for Rosh Hashanah and on Chanukah a guitar and a dollhouse and a tool chest and eight days worth of books and Chanukah *gelt* besides. Dancing *horas* to exhaustion at big, joyous weddings. Watching the dancing in the streets on Simchat Torah. Chanting flawlessly the "four questions" I'd memorized in Hebrew at Pesach and wolfing down *hamentaschen* at Purim.

Being female was being surrounded by strong, capable, happy women who told me stories about how my great-grandmother baked elaborate wedding feasts in the Old Country for girls too poor to afford even a simple one; of how my grandmother picked out my grandfather at a party on the Lower East Side soon after they had met and boldly announced to him that he could have the next dance; of how my other grandmother learned to drive when she was widowed in her sixties; of how my mother graduated at the top of her class in college. Being female meant not getting kicked out of the kitchen. It meant being part of this group of special women.

Increasingly, however, I became aware of complex and often disturbing attitudes toward both Jews and women in American culture, and similarly complicated and troubling attitudes toward women in Jewish culture. How do you respond to a culture that doesn't fully recognize your worth, your potential to contribute, your right—as much as anyone else's—to consider yourself central to what that culture is and what it means?

There seemed to be two options, separatism and assimilation, neither of which struck me as particularly appealing. I could celebrate my marginality and forgo any claim to the mainstream, or erase my "difference" and aim for the top. Both options had their proponents; I found the idea of choosing either course depressing. It was not until I delved into the lives and experiences of two people who were neither Jewish nor female that I became aware of a third option: that of changing the story, of transforming fundamental dimensions of a culture that previously excluded or circumscribed "people like you." This essay is about Warner McGuinn, Mark Twain, and me.

II

". . . Clark and his extremists who made up the team admitting students . . . turned down scores of sons of Yale men who richly deserved to succeed their fathers and scoured the ghettos of New York and elsewhere to recruit freshmen. That is what has today made Yale a Jewish University. . . . The place we knew and loved has been wrecked by . . . the lack of foresight of the Corporation and the willfulness of three men [Kingman Brewster,

William Sloane Coffin and Inslee Clark], who have made Yale a Jewish haven."

—alumni letters cited in "Class of
1912S Notes," *Yale Alumni*
Magazine 36 (April 1973), quoted
in Dan Oren, *Joining the Club: A*
History of Jews and Yale

"You know what the Hebrew letters in the Yale seal mean?" a Jewish friend asks me soon after I arrive at Yale College in 1969, a member of the second class to be admitted after Dean Inslee Clark abolished the quota on Jews. I don't know. He grins: "Ten percent."

An incredulous assistant chaplain is overheard saying to his neighbor at a freshman dinner the year the quota is lifted, "Did you know that 29 percent of the freshman class *admit* to being Jewish?"

On a campus boasting no fewer than seven replicas of the chapel at Kings College, in which even the main library was built to look like a Gothic cathedral, it is easy to feel like an interloper. No Jewish writer nor any reference to anything Jewish ever creeps into my literature syllabi or class discussions as an honors English major.

Only once during my years at Yale did I merge the world of the classroom with the Yiddish voices of my childhood. In a graduate folklore course taught by Bill Ferris, I studied the use of Yiddish proverbs over three generations, doggedly pursuing every three-generation Jewish family that we knew. *Der verm in chreyn denked as is ziess* (The worm in horseradish thinks his life is sweet). *Is zeyhr shveyhr tsu tantzen auf tsvay chassenes mit eyn tuches* (It is very hard to dance at two weddings with one behind). *As tsvay zuggen du bist shikeh, gay shlufen* (When two say you're drunk, go to bed). I considered expanding my research paper into my dissertation. My folklore professor was encouraging but others were not. "You want to do *what?*" was a typical response. Choose something more mainstream, less esoteric and narrow, I was told: my interest in Yiddish proverbs had to be discarded if I wanted to make it as a well-rounded Americanist. In effect, they were saying, "As a scholar, look more like us."

There was talk throughout my childhood of people who changed their names and fixed their noses in order to appear "less Jewish," but I could never understand why; it was simply one of the mysteries of the adult world. I was probably six or seven when I noticed the blue numbers tattooed on the arm of a family friend. My parents gave me a short history of the Holocaust, sanitized for a child, but shocking nonetheless: not only had Jews not been valued, they had been thrown away—by a culture that had prided itself on being consummately "civilized." For the first time I understood why, despite all the stories about cousins and aunts and uncles my grandparents had left behind in the Old Country when they came to America, we had no relatives left now in Europe (years later I found the name of my grandmother's town, Delatyn, engraved in stone at Yad Vashem at the memorial to the destroyed communities). But it still all seemed terribly remote.

Then one Sunday when I was ten my parents and I followed the Connecticut Turnpike from Brooklyn in search of a new home. The drive out to the Connecticut town my mother had fixed on as the most likely place for us seemed terribly long, particularly since the plan was for my father to continue commuting daily to the city. "What's wrong with *this* town?" I inquired about the town we were then passing through. It was obviously closer to the city than the one to which we were heading. "Jews aren't welcome there," my mother said flatly.

When I went to see the house we were making plans to move into, I was excited by all the activity a few hundred yards down the road. In a lush, fenced-in green field the most beautiful horses I'd ever seen jumped over white barricades; a short distance away children were playing in an attractive little playground. Surely being so near a wonderful place like this was one of the great benefits of our new home. "What's *that?*" I asked in happy anticipation. "Oh. That's the Hunt Club," my father said, without enthusiasm. "Can I use the playground?" No. You have to be a member." "Will we become members?" "No. They don't admit Jews."

New variations on this theme played out as I lurched through adolescence. At fifteen, walking down the street with my friend Josh after a movie, four young toughs whom he knew yelled "damn kike" at him and threatened to beat him up. We crossed the street to avoid them and quickened our pace. Josh was profoundly embarrassed. Should he have stood up to them? No, he did the right thing, I insisted. But he avoided me from then on.

Physically, I realized somewhere in my adolescence, I already did "look like them." "Passing" was the last thing I wanted to do, but I seemed to do it by default unless I somehow "declared" myself. My strawberry-blonde hair and freckles, and the New England tones that had replaced the Brooklyn ones in my speech could derail even a *maven* like the Henry Higgins of American ethnicity, Daniel Patrick Moynihan. After spending two days with my husband and me when he came to Yale under the auspices of a program that I ran, he gave us his "take" on us: "You're Jewish, but Shelley's not," he said to my husband. "She's Irish. Your family had trouble with it at first, but they've gotten used to it, right?"

Sometimes my confusion drove me to showy subversive gestures, like the time I took a van load of mainly *goyish* Yalies to Crown Heights on *Simchat Torah* to watch the dancing in the streets, something I had done with my father each year of my childhood. I *kvelled* when I saw in print the headline I had written for the New Journalism–style account of the trip I had given to the *Yale Daily News*: "*Freilach* Means Joy in Brooklyn." It was the first Yiddish to grace the pages of the Oldest College Daily. Deep down, however, I knew that the world in which "*freilach* means joy" was much further from what Yale was all about than Brooklyn was from New Haven.

The simple joy I had taken in things Jewish during my childhood was now tempered by my awareness that the mainstream was content to marginalize Jews and dismiss Jewish traditions as insignificant and irrelevant. What probably upset me most was that all this didn't upset me more. Most of the time I was happy. I felt "at home." That scared me. Had I gotten the equivalent of an intellectual "nose job"? Would I never find some middle ground between separatism (an option I never took seriously) and total assimilation to the purveyors of prevailing paradigms, complete with their omissions and exclusions, their disdain for people who didn't look, act, and sound just like them?

III

Oyfn pripetshik brent a fayerl
Un in shtub iz heys.
Un der rebbe lernt kleyne kinderlach
Lernt dem alef-beyz.
> —Yiddish song

I loved the song about teaching the little children the alphabet in the warm cozy kitchen. An incantatory hymn to learning and reading, it provided a soundtrack to my studies, connecting me to the long line of scholars of which Jews were traditionally so proud. I chose to ignore the fact that those scholars had been only men, that throughout the ages intellectual life had been largely closed to Jewish women.

In 1969 Yale College abandons its 268-year-old policy of admitting only men. Someone could make a fortune selling maps to women's restrooms in classroom buildings (it is usually safe to check in the basement, behind the boiler, but not a sure bet). Women have not yet made it into the curriculum. Or the faculty. One woman writer appears on the reading list for one class; otherwise there are none. All my teachers are men.

But I am glad to be here, happy to be a "Yalie." I'm not quite sure what that means, but I suspect it has something to do with feeling at ease in cavernous, fake-gothic dining halls and knowing the words to "Boola Boola."

That spring my friend Peter, a Yale law student who graduated from Yale College, invites me to be his guest at his prep school reunion, which is being held at the Yale Club of New York City. We sail into the Yale Club and head for the elevators across the lobby. A blue-uniformed guard peremptorily blocks our path. "You'll have to go around the perimeter," he announces. We stare uncomprehendingly. He explains, "Ladies are not allowed in the lobby."

The following spring I call the chairman of the board of Mory's, the famous Yale eating club where most important university business is conducted, to interview him for a news story about why Mory's continues to refuse to admit women as members two years after women had been admitted to Yale College. He hangs up on me.

Senior year I knock on a professor's door to request an application form to be a Carnegie teaching fellow. He stares at me coldly and then says, "I think 'female fellows' is an oxymoron, don't you?" "No," I respond, silently seething.

Truth be told, being dismissed peremptorily as a woman does not upset me seriously until it happens within organized Judaism. After we join the local synagogue in Austin in 1985, invitations to "Sisterhood lunches" appear but the lunches are always held when I'm scheduled to teach. If I can't relate to "Sisterhood," I resolve to get involved in local Jewish activities in some other way. I volunteer for the organizing committee for the rally for Soviet Jewry, since it meets at night. I am the only woman. The committee is planning to present its first annual award to a political figure who had worked hard on behalf of Soviet Jews. They want the award to be memorable and special. I volunteer to contact my friend Roe Halper, a distinguished artist from the East Coast who specializes in dramatic woodcuts addressing the theme of liberation. Two of her large woodcuts in a series titled "Freedom" hang in the Martin Luther King, Jr., Museum in Atlanta, and she frequently holds exhibits on Jewish themes. Roe gives us the rights to use one of her woodcuts on the award and as a logo for the rally, and sends us a camera-ready copy, which we then reproduce on the framed certificate, in the newspaper, and on the program.

The rally is a huge success. At the end of the day, the members of the organizing committee sit on the *bima* of the local temple, and the chairman of the committee introduces each of us to the assembled crowd, which is by then several hundred strong. As he introduces the other members of the committee (all of whom are male), he waxes eloquent about the important contributions they have made and continue to make both as valued professionals in the community and as active members of the Committee for Soviet Jewry. Then he gets to me. It is my first public appearance in Austin, my first formal introduction to the Jewish community. "Shelley Fisher Fishkin," he begins, "is new in town, but she is already a very important member of our community." Will he tell them I had come to Austin from Yale, that I taught at the university, that I'd just published a book? Or will he focus on the role I played in getting a nationally known artist to donate a stunning work of art to our cause? "She is a very important member of our community because she's in our carpool, and gets our daughter to nursery school religiously every week." The crowd has had a long day, and they welcome the excuse to laugh. After the program, no one comments on how the introductions had been handled.

How dare that *schmuck* erase me like that? Angry and humiliated, I recall other times and other places when I felt erased, as a woman, in the stories we tell about who we are and where we've come from as Jews. Every Pesach during my childhood, as the youngest in the family, I had read the part of the "four sons," whose questions play such an important role in the Passover seder. How come daughters never asked questions? Were they stuck in the kitchen making matzoh balls? And why weren't there any women mentioned anywhere else in the Haggadah either? Where were those two *chutzpahdik* Hebrew midwives, Shifrah and Puah, who led the first spark of resistance in Egypt? Where was Miriam, who put the music and dance into the celebration when her people got across the Red Sea? How come in the Shabbat service we praise the fathers—Abraham, Isaac, and Jacob—but not the mothers—Sarah, Rachel, Rebekah? How come God says to the Jews gathered at Sinai waiting to receive the Commandments, "Be ready for the third day, do not go near a woman"? Weren't there women at Sinai, too? Or were they off driving carpool?

I continue to drive carpool, but I avoid any contact with organized Judaism for years.

IV

December 24, 1885

Dear Sir,

Do you know him? And is he worthy? I do not believe I would very cheerfully help a white student who would ask a benevolence of a stranger, but I do not feel so about the other color. We have ground the manhood out of them, & the shame is ours, not theirs, & we should pay for it.

If this young man lives as economically as it is & should be the pride of one to do who is straitened, I would like to know what the cost is, so that I may send 6, 12, or 24 months' board, as the size of the bill may determine.

You see he refers to you, or I would not venture to intrude.

Truly yours,
S. L. Clemens

On February 18, 1985, exactly one hundred years after *Huckleberry Finn* was published in the United States, an antiques dealer from Hamden, Connecticut, wakes me with a phone call at 6:30 A.M. and says she has to see me immediately. She has just read an op-ed piece I wrote for the *New York Times* about Mark Twain's use of irony to attack racism. She says she has a letter by Mark Twain that no one has ever examined; she is sure I will know what to do about it.

I drive out to her house. The handwriting and paper certainly look like Twain's (later I am able to authenticate it completely). But what excites me most is the rare, nonironic condemnation of racism the letter contains. While scholars knew that Twain had expressed such ideas privately (his friends reported them), this letter is the only direct statement on the subject from Twain himself.

The reply to Twain's letter, which I locate in his papers at Berkeley, and an article by literary scholar Philip Butcher make it clear that Francis Wayland, dean of the Yale Law School, is the addressee, and that the student to whom Twain refers is a Warner McGuinn.[1] But McGuinn himself is still largely a mystery.

Most of the law school's nineteenth-century archives have been discarded. Sitting in the Yale Archives room in Sterling Memorial Library, I devour whatever records I can find. A handful of registers and rosters. Some committee meeting minutes. A record book of awards and prizes. I hear lights flipping off around me. "I'm sorry," says the librarian. "We're closing. You'll have to go now." Frustrated, I begin to close the book. Then I see his name under the listings for 1887, the year he graduated: "Warner McGuinn, Townsend Prize." "Just a minute more," I plead. The librarian is unmoved. He turns off my light. Damn. I make note of the page number, return the book to the reserve cart, and walk out through the thick, double, Gothic doors to a now-dark Wall Street, planning my next step. The university registers. Try to find out where he lived. No sitter tomorrow, I think to myself. But Bobby will be in nursery school until noon, and then I can grab two hours in the library before I have to pick him up. I do a U-turn at my front door: I have forgotten to pick up the milk we need for breakfast. When the chill winter air cuts through my thin sweater, I realize that I have left my coat on the library coat rack. I take extra care crossing the street; I know that the present has pretty tough competition for my attention. I am deliciously, dangerously, possessed by this fragment of the past.

V

"He was one of the greatest lawyers who ever lived," said Thurgood Marshall, Associate Justice of the Supreme Court of the United States. Justice Marshall, who as a young lawyer in Baltimore shared adjoining offices with McGuinn, said yesterday that McGuinn enjoyed the respect of the entire bar and judiciary. "If he had been white, he'd have been a judge," Justice Marshall said.

> —Edwin McDowell, "From Twain, a Letter on Debt to Blacks," *New York Times,* March 14, 1985, pp.1, C21.

Dean Clark addressed the Corporation on the changing trends in his admissions policy. Following the presentation, one Corporation member who had "hemmed and hawed" throughout the report attacked Clark's modern ideas: "Let me get down to basics. You're admitting an entirely different kind of class than we're used to. You're admitting them for a different purpose than training leaders." Clark responded that the America of the 1960s was different from what it once had been and that more national leaders would be coming from more groups, including women. The Corporation fellow was unsympathetic: "You're talking about Jews and public school graduates as leaders. Look around you at this table. These are America's leaders. There are no Jews here. There are no public school graduates here."

> —Dean Inslee Clark recollecting the mid-1960s, in Dan Oren, *Joining the Club: A History of Jews and Yale*

Warner McGuinn was one of the first black students in the Yale Law School when he arrived in New Haven in 1885. Eighty-four years later I was one of the first women in Yale College, and also a member of the second class to enter after Inslee Clark abolished the quota on Jews. We were here, as women and as Jews, but we were surrounded by reminders of the fact that the institution had functioned happily for hundreds of years without us. As a friend of mine quipped, "A place that's kept people like you out for over two hundred years takes a little while to get used to letting people like you in." What had it been like, I wonder, for Warner McGuinn?

I return to the library the next day, and each day after that for weeks, intensely following McGuinn's elusive trail. Fortuitous "finds"—a scrapbook McGuinn kept that someone sent to the library after his death but that no one ever looked at before; a microfilm copy of the newspaper he edited after graduation; his 1937 obituary in the Baltimore *Afro-American*—gradually reveal the contours of a truly distinguished career. Born in Virginia during the Civil War, McGuinn attended Lincoln University in Pennsylvania, and then read law in Washington, D.C., with Richard Greener, the first black graduate of Harvard. In 1885 he was admitted to study law at Yale. McGuinn supported himself as a waiter, accountant, and bill collector during his first year in New Haven. He met Twain when the author came to the law school to lecture. Shortly thereafter Twain wrote to Dean Wayland and arranged to pay McGuinn's future expenses. Once relieved of the burden of all his part-time jobs, McGuinn achieved a stellar academic record. In 1887 at his Yale commencement, an eminent group of judges that included Chief Justice White of the U.S. Supreme Court and U.S. senator William Evarts judged his oration the best of the day, and awarded him a hundred-dollar prize. After graduation he served as editor of the *American Citizen* in Kansas City, Kansas, and then set up law practice in Baltimore, where he won a major civil rights victory in federal court, helped found the local branch of the NAACP, served as counsel to the *Afro-American,* was elected to the city council, and became a mentor to Thurgood Marshall.

I soon come across another fact: during his time at Yale, Warner McGuinn had to board with the college carpenter, "an excellent colored man," as the dean put it.[2] (Dean Wayland made the arrangements himself, as he noted in a letter to Twain.)

The college carpenter and his family were probably glad to have this hardworking, intelligent college man as a border. The arrangement may have suited McGuinn, as well. But I was struck by McGuinn's lack of choice in the matter. Obviously the thought that he might live among his fellow white students was deemed out of the question. I poke around Sterling's map room until I find a map of New Haven from the 1880s and locate where the carpenter had lived. The street names have changed but I am able to narrow the area down fairly precisely. Later that afternoon I wander over there. A hundred years later it is (still?) a black ghetto.

The afternoon I search for McGuinn's house, I recall my own first encounter with Connecticut. I had dismissed that town which didn't welcome Jews as probably a very dull place to live. And I lost all interest in the Hunt Club the day that a dozen shouting, sweaty WASP's on horseback chased a beleaguered little fox across our driveway into the woods behind our house. But while these experiences may have been inconsequential in and of themselves, they began to fit into a larger mosaic forming in my consciousness. Within a few of years I had read Arthur Miller's *Focus,* and seen *A Gentleman's Agreement.* I had read *The Diary of Anne Frank,* and other books on the Holocaust, and understood more fully the meaning of the blue numbers tattooed on our friend's arm. The exclusions I had experienced personally were relatively trivial, but they bore witness to the process by which the dominant group in a culture defined a minority as undeserving of inclusion and respect. I had come to view being kept out of certain neighborhoods and clubs as the relatively benign end of a continuum of discrimination and oppression rooted in the process of "othering" that included, in its most horrific forms, murder and genocide as well. I sensed that Warner McGuinn understood an analogous continuum in the same way; his efforts to dismantle it excited and inspired me.

VI

Once the negroes began to join, it was declared, the Southern white boys would stay at home.

The suggestion was made that some scheme might be devised by which the two races may be organized and trained at different camps, so that there would be no racial intermingling

—Baltimore *Sun,* morning edition,
June 15, 1916, extract from a
clipping in Warner McGuinn's
scrapbook

Tonight Mr. Trickett Giles, of Somerset, one of the prominent young members of the House, a protege of former Congressman Joshua W. Miles, introduced two "Jim Crow car" bills. The most significant fact was the applause by the Democratic members and spectators which greeted the reading of the title of the bill. One of the bills provides for separate compartments on steam passenger cars, and another makes a similar provision for steamboats.

—*Baltimore American,* June 16,
1916, extract from clipping in
Warner McGuinn's scrapbook

Reading Warner McGuinn's scrapbook is a disorienting experience, since many of the pages are covered with pages torn from a volume titled *Vital Statistics,* on top of which are pasted the newspaper clippings McGuinn saved. Like a curiously postmodern palimpsest, mortality and disease statistics in specific wards and districts in Baltimore and the District of Columbia broken down into "white" and "colored" columns frame stories about disenfranchisement, discrimination, segregation, and racially motivated violence. McGuinn had run precisely the same kinds of stories when he edited the *American Citizen* in Kansas City, Kansas, some thirty years earlier.

In his scrapbook, above two dense columns headed "city ordinances," McGuinn had scrawled "Segregation Law" in thick black letters. A few pages later I see why those columns had been so carefully clipped and preserved. In federal court in the autumn of 1917 (several months after he had clipped the extracts quoted above from local newspapers) McGuinn challenged that law. Baltimore's white establishment lined up against him, confident in their ability to maintain the status quo. According to newspaper reports, he thoroughly bested his opponents. McGuinn's obituary in the Baltimore *Afro-American* described it like this:

> Arguing the celebrated Baltimore segregation case in 1917, before Judge John C. Rose in the Federal Court, Mr. McGuinn objected frequently to the points of law made by opposing counsel and finally asked the court to have him argue the case at issue.
> Judge Rose in a squeaky voice replied: "Leave him alone, Mr. McGuinn, he's doing the best he can." Baltimore *Afro-American*, July 17, 1937, reprinted Baltimore *Afro-American*, March 23, 1985.

When the case was decided, the *Philadelphia Tribune* ran McGuinn's picture under the headline "The Attorney Who Knocked Out the Baltimore Segregation Ordinance." The victory discouraged Baltimore and other southern cities from passing further segregation ordinances, and played a major role in the eventual legal (if not de facto) desegregation of American cities.

How had McGuinn felt about the implication that white Yale students would be contaminated by too-close contact with him outside class? How had he felt, after graduation, writing, editing, and reading story after story, year after year, about blacks who were marginalized, trivialized, excluded, lynched, simply because of the color of their skin? What rage must have simmered under what the press referred to as his gentlemanly, almost patrician, demeanor? What part did festering hurt over incidents of his own marginalization play in galvanizing him to attack the problem head-on in court?

How do you respond to a society that marginalizes "people like you"? Do you leave? (Marcus Garvey urged McGuinn's contemporaries to do just that.) Do you stay? If you stay, do you remain uncomplainingly on the margins, at a safe remove from the mainstream, as his teachers at Yale probably expected him to? Warner McGuinn chose a different path. Rather than accept segregation, he challenged the law itself. By inspiring a young lawyer in the office next door, a lawyer named Thurgood Marshall, he helped change history as well.

McGuinn's response to those who would erase him and people like him was to break their erasers. I was fascinated by that subtle alchemy of empowerment and disempowerment that sparked McGuinn to challenge and change the system itself. Here was a new response to being written out of the story: change the story. Such *chutzpah!*

VII

> When Israel was in Egypt
>   land,
> Let my people go.
> Oppressed so hard they
>   could not stand,
> Let my people go
>   —"Go Down, Moses"

> Calves are easily bound and
>   slaughtered
> Never knowing the reason why,
> But the man who cherishes freedom
> Like the swallow will learn to
>   fly.
>   —"Dona"

For as long as I can remember, "Go Down, Moses" was a part of our Passover seder. As a child, I was sure it was a Jewish song. I believe it was not until I was in high school that I learned it was a Negro spiritual. It seemed fully as Jewish as "Dona," the Yiddish-Russian song we sang alongside it at family seders. The two meditations on freedom in a haunting minor key flowed into one another. Accompanying our singing on guitar, I recall being able to get through entire seders, at least up to "Dayenu," without having to play any major chords. Today we still sing "Go Down, Moses" and "Dona" at our seders. My sons read the "four questions" that had been my task to read as a child. I still use my grandmother's recipe for matzoh balls. But (with the aid of the modern miracle of desktop publishing) I've made some changes in the story.

I've added women. Women like the Hebrew midwives Shifrah and Puah, who risked death by defying Pharaoh's command to kill newborn Jewish boys at birth. When Pharaoh asked them to account for all the living children, they claimed, "The Hebrew women are lively, and give birth before we arrive!" I like having Shifrah and Puah, and other women as well, in my Haggadah. I first encountered them during the years I spent avoiding *shul* except for driving carpool. During this period the only Judaism I could bear to deal with was in books—Susannah Heschel's *On Being a Jewish Feminist,* Irena Klepfisz and Melanie Kaye/Kantrowitz's *The Tribe of Dina,* and Judith Plaskow's *Standing Again at Sinai.* Through these books I came to understand that the sense of erasure that had driven me out of *shul* a few years earlier resonated with the invisibility of women in Jewish history and theology throughout the ages—in the stories our people tell of who we are and where we come from. Reading Plaskow, Klepfisz, and others helped me suspect that I might be able to come back in some day, but on my own terms, in my own way.

Shortly after my eldest son's bar mitzvah I enrolled in an adult bar and bat mitzvah class myself, determined to learn some of what I'd missed in my Reform Temple childhood. I enjoyed studying Torah and Hebrew with others as ignorant, ambivalent, and curious as I was. Our class—mainly women, but a few men as well—wrote a group sermon, which we all delivered, each of us reading a paragraph. In it we affirmed the element of "choice" in the commitment that had drawn us to this occasion, emphasizing that, on this day, we were actively and publicly choosing to identify ourselves as Jews. "But," we went on,

> there is a difference. We will not allow women to be erased from our people's present and future, as women were so often erased from the record of our people's past. The Torah portion we read today contains some words that are still painful for many of us to hear. Preparing for the revelation at Mount Sinai, Moses says in Exodus, chapter 19, verse 15, "Be ready for the third day, do not go near a woman." At the very moment when Israel stands waiting for God's presence to descend upon the mountain, Moses addresses the community as only men. Over the past year we have struggled to understand the invisibility of women in our history. Today we affirm our commitment to a Judaism that is egalitarian and inclusive. Remembering the sting of erasure and exclusion that *we* felt, we are committed to preventing Judaism from inflicting that pain on others. We recognize that female and male, gay and straight, white and black, hearing and deaf, are all needed—for the repair of the world.

The rabbi, who checks out all bar and bat mitzvah speeches before they're delivered, asked, "Do you really want to say that? Don't you think you might tone it down a little? Isn't 'invisibility' too strong a word, and 'erasure'?" Yes, we did want to say that; no, we didn't want to tone it down.

VIII

> Many ethnocentric judgments about blacks stem from the white man's inability to understand or appreciate the creative aspects of living in an oral atmosphere. He neither understands nor remembers the ways in which an effective talker-performer may strongly influence our attitudes. He does not value words effectively used in speaking events enough to confer high social status on the effective speaker.
>
> —Roger Abrahams, *Deep Down in the Jungle*

> Although the literary culture devalued black speech, made it appear infantile alongside the matured mode of literate expression, the oral culture Africans brought with them to the New World flourished.
>
> —John Edgar Wideman, "Frame and Dialect: The Evolution of the Black Voice in American Literature"

One afternoon in November 1991, on a bus to the Baltimore airport after the American Studies convention, I listened to two Jewish friends engage in a particularly spirited display of *kibbitzing,* a verbal duel that combines insult and humor in what might best be understood as a Jewish version of the "dozens." How different this exchange was from the academic papers we had sat through during the past weekend. I was aware that I was hearing something special, something familiar, something I valued but had not been exposed to for some time: a vital *oral culture* that bristled with wit and energy. All of us were literature professors. We spent our working lives writing about and holding forth on that which was written down, the culture of books. Yet here were voices from somewhere else—oral traditions that years of graduate school and generations of assimilation had not succeeded in eradicating—a delicious, virtuoso performance to which I felt a deep sense of connection.

The delight I took in that afternoon of *kibbitzing* swam into my consciousness for days afterward, as I researched the book I was writing on Mark Twain and race. Gradually I understood the connection: Twain and I were both deeply affected by oral traditions that had nothing to do with books. Intuitively I sensed that my own response to the oral performance I witnessed that afternoon paralleled Twain's responses to a number of oral performances he heard throughout his life.

When I moved to Connecticut at age ten, the formal, decorous tones of New England speech replaced the spirited Yiddish-inflected *kibbitzing,* curses, proverbs, jokes, and storytelling I recalled from my Brooklyn childhood; but the memory of those "other voices" was never entirely erased. Similarly, when Twain moved to Connecticut soon after his marriage, the tonalities of the Yankee gentry replaced the rhythms and melodies of the southern speech of his Missouri youth; but in his case, as well, the memory of those "other voices" persisted. These other voices had no place in mainstream literary culture, but they were important to Twain, and to me, nonetheless. Each of us simply needed a catalyst to bring back the sounds we could so vividly recall.

Soon after returning to Austin, I reread a posthumously published essay by Twain in which he referred to an "impudent and delightful and satirical young black man, a slave" named Jerry as "the greatest orator in the United States." I also reread an obscure article Twain had written in the *New York Times* in 1874 about a ten-year-old black child named Jimmy who had impressed him as "the most artless, sociable, exhaustless talker" he had ever come across, someone to whom he had listened "as one who receives a revelation." If black oral traditions and vernacular speech had played such an important role in shaping Twain's art, why hadn't anyone noticed it before, given the thousands of books and articles on Twain that had appeared? Literary scholars had denied any African-American influence on mainstream American texts, much as linguists had denied any African-American influence on southern speech and American speech in general. All of them, I became increasingly convinced, were wrong.

"Let me ask you one question," a friend said, when I laid out my tentative theory. "Do you have tenure?"

I went to the Mark Twain Papers at Berkeley and set a record for photocopying; back in Austin I mined published and unpublished fiction and nonfiction by Twain, folklore and linguistic studies, history, newspapers, letters, manuscripts, and journals. I didn't come up for air all spring.

As I knew from my first encounter with the book in high school, critics had long viewed *Huckleberry Finn* as a declaration of independence from the genteel English novel tradition. Something new happened here that had never happened in American literature before. *Huckleberry Finn* allowed a different kind of writing to happen: a clean, crisp, non-nonsense, earthy vernacular kind of writing that jumped off the printed page with unprecedented immediacy and energy; it was a book that talked. I now realized that, despite their having been largely ignored by white critics for the last hundred years, African-American speakers, language, and rhetorical traditions had played a central role in making that novel what it was. Rather than stifle those voices from "somewhere else" that were ringing in his ears, Twain stifled the forces that said they had no place in great art, changing our very definitions of literary art in the process.

Ralph Ellison had his number. "The black man," Ellison wrote in 1970, was the "co-creator of the language Mark Twain raised to the level of literary eloquence."[3] But literary historians ignored Ellison's insight, and continued to tell us that white writers came from white literary ancestors and black writers from black ones. I knew that story had to change if we wanted to do justice to the richness of our culture.

I now understood my earlier moment of "possession." Like Warner McGuinn, I knew that "people like us" (people possessing the "wrong" skin color or gender or religion or ethnicity) had somehow not really been a part of the story our culture told about who and what it was. McGuinn's accomplishments in the legal realm dwarfed my own in the literary realm, but some curious resonances remained. Empowered by our education and training, yet disempowered by our awareness that mainstream American culture marginalized people and traditions we respected, we responded by channeling our energies into changing the structures themselves—desegregating American cities, desegregating the American literary canon.

IX

When the Czar had issued the infamous May Laws against the Jews in 1881, three Jews in a little Ukrainian town gave vent to their indignation.

"He is an idiot, a nitwit!" jeered one.

"He guzzles vodka like a swine!" sneered another.

"Not only that, but he's a thief! He collects taxes and puts them in his own pocket!" raged the third.

No sooner had he said this than a gendarme appeared as though he had sprung out of the ground.

"Seditious Jews!" he roared angrily. "Just wait—you'll pay dearly for insulting our Holy Czar! Come with me—you're under arrest!"

So the three Jews, trembling with fear, went with the gendarme to the police station.

"How dare you insult our beloved Czar?" shrieked the commissioner of police.

"Who was talking about the Czar?" replied the Jews innocently. "We were talking about Kaiser Wilhelm, that enemy of Israel!"

The police commissioner softened.

"Oh, in that case—be more careful the way you talk next time. How was the gendarme to know? When you said 'idiot . . . drunkard . . . thief' . . . he naturally thought you meant the Czar."

> —*A Treasury of Jewish Folklore,* ed.
> Nathan Ausubel

Jewish folklore is filled with *meychelach,* with delicious stories like this one (my youngest son's favorite) that show Jews triumphing over those who would grind us down. Like many African-American trickster tales, it is a story of *sechel* triumphing over strength, of wit over weapons. Like the stories of the slave "John" outwitting his master, stories of poor Jews outwitting the czar's police are a source of hope for those at the bottom. They are stories of empowerment.

I want my children to take pleasure in stories like these, in Jewish folk songs, in *klezmer* music, in *freylachs,* in Jewish humor, in the rich oral tradition of *yiddishkeit* that loses something but not everything in translation. I also want them to have a sense of pride in the courage and creativity Jews have shown throughout history.

This sense of empowerment is crucial. But it is not enough. I also want them to understand what it means to be disempowered, to understand that continuum of "othering" that runs from stigmatization to exclusion to murder and genocide. My sons know the story of their great aunts, first forced to wear yellow stars, finally seized by the police from a movie theater and summarily sent to their deaths. I want my sons' Jewishness to be a lens through which they can sustain a clear-eyed view of the nature of prejudice and erasure wherever it may occur in our world. I want them to understand how ready mainstream Western culture has been to devalue, dismiss, and trivialize out of existence Jews themselves and Jewish vernacular traditions. I want that awareness to help them identify sufficiently with the marginalized and oppressed and their traditions to feel viscerally and personally moved—as Warner McGuinn was, as Mark Twain was, as I was—to change the paradigms that write them out of the stories our culture tells about where it has come from, what it is, and what it can be. As Jews we know that stories—texts, lives, and cultures—are always being rewritten; millennia of commentary on the Torah teaches us that. And as Jews we know what it's like to be written out of the story.

Driving home from the university in Austin I am happy to hear on the radio that First Street is being renamed Cesar Chavez Boulevard. Then an Anglo city councilman explains why. He says he thinks it's important, when Mexican-American parents take their children downtown, for them to be able to take them to a street named for a Mexican-American of whom they can be proud. I am caught in traffic and can't call up the station to respond. Can't *my* kids be proud of Cesar Chavez, too, I want to ask him? The councilman's myopic vision—in which whites are supposed to be proud of only whites, blacks of only blacks, and Chicanos of only Chicanos—saddens me. I recall Mitsuye Yamada's poem "Mirror, Mirror":

> People keep asking me where I come from says my son.
> Trouble is I'm american on the inside and oriental on the outside
> No Doug
> Turn that outside in
> THIS is what American looks like.[4]

Why is it that we can change the names of city streets but we can't seem to change the story we tell about who we are as Americans?

X

Rabbi Zusya said before his death, "In the world to come, I shall not be asked: 'Why were you not Moses?' but 'Why were you not Zusya?' " How do I become the person I was meant to be? Throughout most of my life that question has obsessed and tormented me. Jew in a Christian culture. Woman in a man's world. Granddaughter of immigrants. Privileged, educated, angry, confused. Caught in the cracks. Not quite fitting. Proud and defiant. Hurt and cowed. Not wanting to retreat into a cocoon of difference with others who "don't fit." Not wanting to erase what makes me different to gain admission to a mainstream that has use for only some parts of myself but not others. Warner McGuinn, that Yale-educated defier of Jim Crow who prodded America to live up to its promises, and Mark Twain, that white man who refused to banish from his imagination black voices and traditions that his culture dismissed and devalued, serve as my guides.

NOTES

As I reconfigured this essay more times than I care to remember, I benefited greatly from criticism and comments from David Bradley, Emily Budick, Joel Dinerstein, Carol Fisher, Milton Fisher, Joey Fishkin, Paul Lauter, Jane Marcus, Carla Peterson, Lillian Robinson, Jeffrey Rubin-Dorsky, David Smith, and Richard Yarborough. The depth of my debt to them is exceeded only by the breadth of their generosity.

    1. The article is Philip Butcher, "Mark Twain's Installment on the National Debt," *Southern Literary Journal* 1:2 (Spring 1969) 48–55.

    2. Francis Wayland to Samuel L. Clemens, Dec. 30, 1885. Courtesy, the Mark Twain Papers, the Bancroft Library, University of California, Berkeley.

    3. Ralph Ellison, "What America Would Be Like Without Blacks," *Time*, 6 April 1970; reprinted in *Going to the Territory*, by Ralph Ellison, 109.

    4. "Mirror, Mirror," quoted in Amy Ling, "I'm Here: An Asian American Woman's Response," *New Literary History* 19 (Autumn 1987): 160. Ling notes that "Mirror, Mirror" is the final poem in Mitsuye Yamada's chapbook, *Camp Notes* (San Lorenzo, Calif., 1976).

4

Back to the Garden

Reading the Bible as a Feminist

Alicia Ostriker

I

What in fact I keep choosing
are these words, these whispers, conversations
from which time after time the truth breaks moist and green.
—Adrienne Rich, "Cartographies of
Silence"

November 1985. I come home from work on a stormy night, take off my wet things, pick up a notebook and pen, and start to jot some notions about the Book of Job. I have no particular purpose in mind. I had not especially planned to do any writing on this subject. The idea I'm toying with is that the God of the Jews seems to like being challenged and called to account, and even rewards those who most boldly interrogate him. Throughout the paradoxical encounter between Job and God, in which Job's challenge to God's justice is first scorned, then affirmed, Job signifies the human mind at the moment when it becomes possible—necessary—to question the divinity in which it believes. Similar moments exist elsewhere, I suppose; there is the skepticism of Euripides, or Lucretius' representation of the gods as neither benevolent nor malevolent but indifferent to the created world and to human life. Yet only among the Jews does a man rage against God's injustice, demand a divine response, and receive that response. Only among the Jews is protest divinely sanctioned. Only among the Jews does this tormented insistence on justice seem to run as a central thread. And surely nobody but the Jews maintains this intimate sort of relationship with God, this covenant about which we keep asking if he's keeping up his end.

Jews argue. Two Jews, three opinions, as the saying goes. We argue not only with each other but also with God. Long before Job, we have Abraham bargaining with God at Mamre, Jacob wrestling, Moses facing off with his maker on Sinai after the Golden Calf, the anguished Jeremiah begging to know why the way of the wicked prospers. With Job, we have the oddity of the frame structure which gives us the two closures. First the end of the poem, when the Voice from the Whirlwind has thundered and Job has humbled himself. Then, back in the folktale frame of the story, God tells Job he was right all along, and rewards him. It is as if God was embarrassed by Job. I conclude that God must be reminded about justice, even teased into it, by his own children, in a sort of ratchet effect. First he demands goodness of us, then we demand it back of him, and the stakes get steadily higher.

Setting these cogitations down is pleasant, relaxing, not particularly different from other journal jottings; I am clarifying thoughts recognizably my own. Then something else happens. I find myself writing, without forethought and at astonishing speed, as if someone else were directing the pen, about Job's wife—that nameless woman. When her husband is afflicted with boils yet remains patiently submissive, Job's wife has a single thing to say: "Dost thou still retain thy integrity? curse God, and die" (Job 2:9). Obviously she knows perfectly well that justice is not to be expected of God. Her husband's response is to tell her she talks like one of the foolish women. How would a woman capable of that one-liner feel about having her ten children, who had been casually slain in order to test the man's devotion to his God, replaced by ten new children? How would any woman feel about that?

Some years later I will read Stephen Mitchell's Introduction to his translation of the Book of Job, which finds the "most curious detail in the epilogue" to be the naming of Job's new daughters, Dove, Cinnamon, and Eye-Shadow, who receive a share of Job's wealth as their inheritance along with the seven anonymous new brothers. For Mitchell, "the story's center of gravity has shifted from righteousness to beauty," and "the whole yin side of humanity . . . has finally been acknowledged and honored."[1] I enjoy Mitchell's idea that the Voice from the Whirlwind resembles the voice of Lord Krishna speaking the *Bhagavad-Gita* to Arjuna, elevating us to a sense of divinity beyond good and evil. But the epilogue does something else. It hooks us back, back to the issue of God's moral responsibility to his servant Job. In that frame "the yin side of humanity" is all very well, but it elides the little matter of Job's wife and the dead children.

I am a mother. I write as a mother. That is my identity. I know perfectly well how Job's wife would feel. There is a scream unrolling in my mind that is three thousand years old. And what if Job's wife were to find the courage to challenge God as her husband did? What would she—what would we—say to God if we dared? What will we say, when we, the collective mind of woman, at last become so inflamed with rage and outrage that we too call God to account? We are far from that moment. However angry some of us believe we are, we are far from angry enough. What will we say, boiling over with the putrescence of our own boils as we will then be? And how will God respond? Will he be embarrassed by us, as by our husband Job? And what recompense will we demand for his abuse of us and his killing of our children?

By the time my pen stops, I dimly understand that I am on a train I cannot get off. The results so far have included a volume of revisionist *midrash* entitled *The Nakedness of the Fathers;* a set of feminist essays on biblical hermeneutics, *Feminist Revision and the Bible;* a graduate seminar, "The Bible and Feminist Imagination"; workshops on the Bible and women's *midrash* at the Havurah Institute; numerous lectures, readings, conversations; and a preoccupation amounting to obsession with Judaism, the Bible, God.

II

To you I'm an atheist. To God I'm the loyal opposition.
—Woody Allen, *Stardust Memories*

What right have I to write? I come to the Bible as a third-generation Jewish atheist socialist, raised to believe that religion is the opiate of the people. Jewishness in my family meant reverence for books and intelligence. It meant the superiority of knowledge to ignorance, kindness to brutality. It meant that you had sympathy for anyone who suffered, because Jews suffered, and that you fought against bigotry. It meant Einstein and Heifetz. None of this do I recall doubting as a child, for both my parents were working-class, voracious readers, and tender-hearted to a fault, so that I never had the opportunity of seeing moral hypocrisy at close quarters. Nor do I dispute those early teachings today. For my money, the lefty, secular Jews are still the best ones. Yet the notion of God always had some sort of meaning for me—quite apart from anyone's organized religion, or perhaps because religion seemed to fall ridiculously short of whatever God might be. When my grandfather died I prayed every night, in case God existed, that he would let my grandfather into heaven even though my grandfather didn't believe in him, because he was a good person. I was nine then. In high school I read Emerson and William James's *Varieties of Religious Experience,* and had some transcendent flashes myself.

After marriage I became a twice-a-year Jew like my husband's family. For thirty-five years I have fasted on Yom Kippur while cooking the pot roast. For Passover we invite my husband's siblings and their families, using the wine-and-gravy-stained Reconstructionist Haggadot of my husband's childhood, dated 1942, with their folkloric illustrations, their half-blushing one-paragraph treatment of the Plagues, and their elaborate reminders that Passover signifies the struggle against all tyranny, all cruel and heartless rulers:

> And that is why Pesach means more than that first emancipation. . . . It means the emancipation the serfs in the Middle Ages won from their masters; the freedom the common people of countries won when their kings were overthrown; it means the guarantee of the sacred rights of life, liberty, and the pursuit of happiness.

We always smile over that innocent text, quarrel about it, pay it an homage which is in fact an homage to my husband's parents.

It was my husband who first suggested that I read the Bible, back in college when we were courting. I read it cover to cover one summer, experiencing a sustained shock of recognition. These stories belonged to me, were mine, were myself. In art class I did an etching of Jacob and the Angel, entitled "I will not let thee go except thou bless me." The characters with whom I most identified were Jacob, Moses, Job, David. The story of Saul was the most exquisite tragedy I had ever read. The Psalms ravished, the Song of Songs melted, the Prophets exalted, the plagues and battle scenes sickened me, and I skipped most of Leviticus. The women made little impression, though I applauded Eve's decision to eat the apple and Sarah's triumphant laughter. Ruth was a nice girl but not interesting. Esther, the spoiled beauty queen who saved the Jews only because Mordecai twisted her arm, had no appeal for a bookwormy poet. I preferred proud Vashti. Thanks to my secular upbringing, I was unaware that rabbinic tradition excluded women from the life of intellect. Was I a male-identified woman? Or merely a language-identified girl? For it was the language of the Bible which took me. The language in which divinity communicates with us, and demands response. The incomparably magnetic language which enabled my people to survive for two millennia without a land.

September 1982. The weather is deliriously balmy this Rosh Hashanah afternoon. I sit outdoors with my son during a break in services. A year ago, at age eleven, he decided that he wanted a bar mitzvah, after rejecting Hebrew school, like his two older sisters, years before. Why? We had no idea. He is our dreamer, shy, inward, nonmaterialistic (so he's not doing it for the presents), not fond of study. But he nagged until we went to the Princeton Hillel, where Rabbi Eddie Feld found him a student tutor on condition that we attend Sabbath services during his time of preparation. What I like best is the weekly discussion of the Torah portion.

We are listening to the fountain play. My son asks what you have to do to be a *real* Jew. I remind him that we have just finished reading a handout from an essay of Martin Buber's which explains that there is no single correct way to be a Jew, but that each individual has his or her own right path to God. He asks, reasonably, how you find out what the right path is for you. You listen, I tell him, to your inner voice, through which God speaks to you. He looks puzzled, as well he might. I am on the spot. Then I get it. Your inner voice, I tell him, is what made you want the bar mitzvah, and what made you *nudge* Dad and me until we took you seriously. He looks blank a moment longer, then he nods, yes. And yes, in the absence of any more plausible explanation, I too suppose God instructed Gabe.

In the Hillel discussion when we were doing the *akedah,* attackers and defenders interrupted each other vehemently. Where was Sarah when her son was being brought to the sacrifice? Why did nobody ask her? Why should God want to test Abraham in such a terrible way? I am among the attackers. Then Merle Feld, the *rebbitsin,* remarks that God, who speaks to Abraham so often and so intimately before this episode, never speaks to him afterward.

Perhaps, Merle says, it was indeed a test of Abraham, but Abraham failed the test. Perhaps God hoped Abraham would refuse. If he had refused, all of human history would be different.

III

> For the God who does not include her is an idol made in man's image.
> —Judith Plaskow, "The Right
> Question Is Theological"

I read the Bible as a poet, a critic, a feminist. Possibly this move was inevitable. The poets whose visionary company I first loved were the great spiritual rebels Whitman and Blake. William Blake, quintessential radical, was my hero and guru for ten years after graduate school, until I became aware of the misogyny which coexisted with his protofeminism. When I came to write on women's poetry, it was the female wrestling with/against the dominant literary culture which I attempted to trace. Gradually I perceived that women's voices, issuing from female experiences hitherto excluded from literature, were spiritually as well as politically and personally subversive. If the personal was the political, it was also the spiritual, the mythic, the visionary. The final chapter of my book *Stealing the Language: The Emergence of Women's Poetry in America* explores what I call revisionist mythmaking by women poets as a means whereby we invade the treasuries where Western civilization stores its deepest meanings for "male" and "female," and emerge with potentially transformed definitions of gender and much else.[2] Most of my subsequent writing constitutes an extension of that work.

The Nakedness of the Fathers is an invasion of the patriarchal tent, a speculative gaze at the dangerous (to women) body of scriptural narrative, an attempt to discover, through the act of writing, what these stories burned into my own brain and my culture's collective brain mean to me and I to them, what I love/hate in Judaism, its deity, its patriarchs, its Book.[3] Beginning in a revisionist Garden, the work tracks God's relationship with his chosen men, including pieces on Abraham, Isaac, Jacob, Joseph, Moses, Joshua, David, Solomon, and Job, and some of their adjacent females, chosen and otherwise. My Eve is a demoted Great Goddess who remembers presiding over her own garden accompanied by her own snake and consort, where they spoke together with the birds and animals. What breaks her heart is that Adam remembers nothing. My Noah suffers survivor guilt like Primo Levi in *The Drowned and the Saved* (1988). Isaac, fighting trauma with comedy as Jews learned early to do, is the ancestor of Lenny Bruce and Woody Allen. Moses is God's pack animal, the unloved Nursing Father. Joshua is racked by contradictory divine messages about neighboring tribes, whose cities he must destroy while remembering the commandment never to oppress the stranger. David in my reading is history's most charismatic politician, artist, and public relations genius. A consummate sign of Solomon's wisdom is the permission he gives the women of Israel to worship their goddesses.

And God? What can one say? God is a sublimely unpredictable being, a source of overwhelming creative and destructive energy, never-to-be-grasped, never-to-be-tamed, who seems to incorporate all possible ideas of divinity within himself; is unutterably remote yet nonetheless behaves intimately and uncannily like a person, demanding that we be persons in response. The God who identifies himself to the patriarchs as El Shaddai, conventionally rendered in English as "Almighty," derives from the Akkadian *sâdû* (mountain) and the Hebrew *shad* (breast), so that his proper name is God of the Breast-Hill-Mountain, a biological-geological pun like the Grand Tetons, appropriate for a nomadic people. His compassion, *rachmones,* is his womb; his wisdom, *hokhmah,* who dances before him, is like the Greek Sophia, a woman. Since *ruach* is another feminine noun, perhaps we should say, when we read Genesis 1:2, that God the Mother moved on the face of the waters. When named Elohim, a plural form, God is plainly a collective being, a remnant of polytheism. Yet he is also the monster of egoism who swallowed the Great Goddess and then denied she ever existed; he is the ultimate patriarch whose demand for worship is the model for all structures of domination, oppression, and tyranny. No other gods before me, he says, and he has been able to make it stick down the centuries, thanks to his language, his magnificent language. Or perhaps his power derives from the tremendous notion of a single God who incorporates all possible notions of divinity within himself: perhaps monotheism is a force field whose primary function is to contain contradiction.

I try, as I meditate on biblical texts which both are and are not mine, to remember when my own name was wisdom, woman of valor. Like the Bible, *Nakedness* slides across categories, mixing analytic commentary with dramatic monologue, fantasy, comedy, autobiography, poetry. Like the Bible, it includes metaphor, wordplay, contradiction, transgression (more on this topic below). The book looks to the eye like prose, but I have written it the way I write poetry—seized and commanded to write, without knowing beforehand what it will say, permitting something which I do not quite control to traverse and employ me to articulate its own intentions. The penultimate section of *Nakedness* describes what seems to be a death-of-God scene taking place under the TV lights in an intensive care room. Two women reporters named Chloe and Olivia, stolen from Virginia Woolf's *Room of One's Own,* speculate that perhaps he is not dying, only pregnant. The last piece in the book, then, is a prayer to the *shekhinah,* that figure out of *kabbalah,* that Jewish equivalent to the swallowed, repressed, immanent, once-and-future feminine being to whom so many Jewish women today have turned their attention: though she delay, we believe she will certainly come.

Intimately connected to this writing is my work as a critic, reading other women's rewritings of biblical narrative along with biblical criticism, and attempting to rethink certain customary assumptions about feminism and the

Bible. Here, to begin with, I have found it tremendously reassuring to discover that I belong within a long tradition of interpretation and reinterpretation. Modern biblical criticism recognizes that Scripture has at no moment in history been a unified, monolithic text, has always been radically composite, multiply motivated. Numerous poetic portions are rooted in archaic Sumerian, Egyptian, Babylonian, and Canaanite myth and poetry; the written narrative stems from long oral tradition; the wisdom literature lies under the long shadow of Hellenism. Compiled over a thousand-year period, comparable to the period between Beowulf and T. S. Eliot, its editing, redaction, and canonization process stretches from the time of Ezra to the composition of the Mishnah, c. 400 B.C.E. TO 200 C.E. When we speak of the J text, E text, P text, D text, R the redactor, we invent tidy designations for an untidy canon, filled with fractures and inconsistencies which may resist the seeker after unitary meaning but stimulate the literary critic. Geoffrey Hartman describes enjoying the "fault lines" of scriptural texts and proposes that biblical writing is "a fusion of heterogeneous stories . . . layered" like Lévi-Strauss's bricolage in myth, or Bakhtin's heteroglossia in novels. Critics such as Roland Barthes, Robert Alter, Frank Kermode, and Harold Bloom take similar stances.[4]

That biblical texts not only can but must be read plurally, and that no single interpretation can ever be definitive, have become commonplaces of contemporary biblical criticism. Nor is this notion confined to secular readers. Rabbinical tradition itself tells us to expect that the process of understanding Torah will and should continue until the coming of the Messiah. According to the sages, all commentary on Torah—past, present, future—is an intrinsic part of Torah itself. As the scholar Gerald Bruns argues, the effort to establish an originary meaning is not merely futile intellectually but fallacious spiritually, since Scripture addresses itself not to the past but to "the place where the interpreter stands. . . . If the text does not apply to us it is an empty text. . . . We take the text in relation to ourselves, understanding ourselves in its light, even as our situation throws its light upon the text, allowing it to disclose itself differently, perhaps in unheard-of ways."[5]

Among male scholars, these insights have seldom been applied to issues of gender. With the exception of Harold Bloom, no major biblical critic treats questions of gender and sexuality as problematic. And Bloom's provocative notion that the J author was a woman in the post-Davidic court produces something more like a preemptive strike against feminism than a feminist analysis.[6] Mainstream feminist theory, on the other hand, with few exceptions treats "patriarchal" texts as uniformly antagonistic to women and femaleness. From Kate Millett and Merlin Stone to Mieke Bal, feminist commentary on the Bible typically foregrounds biblical misogyny, critiquing the pain, suffering, oppression, and silencing of its women characters, or showing how systematically rooted in gender polarization and hierarchy biblical imagery is.[7] I do not disagree, yet something is missing from such analyses as well.

In *Feminist Revision and the Bible* (1994), I try to demonstrate that, precisely because the scriptural text is layered and laced with fruitful inconsistencies, women writers can and do relate to it in complex ways. The book contains two linked essays. In the first, using the burials of Sarah and Miriam as exemplary episodes, I trace a recurrent pattern in biblical narrative: the repression of female power and agency as condition and consequence of an exclusively male covenant. I argue that this pattern encodes the (never complete) erasure of the goddesses widely worshiped in Canaan and throughout the Middle East before the advent of monotheism, and underpins biblical misogyny. This is not simply a question of blaming Eve (and female sensuality) for all our woe, as Milton puts it. The *akedah*, in a woman's reading, represents the overthrow of matrilinearity and the binding of the sons to potentially murderous human and divine fathers. The death and burial of the first matriarch, Sarah, immediately following the *akedah*, confirms the defeat of female power, as does the humiliation in the desert of the prophetess Miriam. Eve, Sarah, Rebekah, Rachel, and Leah, Judah's daughter-in-law Tamar, Potiphar's wife, the virtual conspiracy of women who act across class and ethnic lines in the opening of Exodus to defy patriarchal law, Zipporah, Miriam, the mother of Samuel, the mother of Samson—all are significant figures at the outset of stories, and all vanish before the closures, which reinscribe God's relationship to his people, which is to say his beloved males.

Moreover, from a feminist perspective the story of Exodus and the promised land appears disastrous. Certain core values of family life as we see it in Genesis—peace, prosperity, a closeness to biological experience, and a lively relationship between husbands and wives—are replaced by the values of nationhood, which are military, priestly, and legal. Women almost disappear as personalities, becoming objects under Jewish law. Both before and after the law, to be sure, abuse of women either is sanctioned or becomes a pretext for male violence: witness the stories of Abraham's exploitation of his wife's beauty (Genesis 12:10–20, 20:1–18), Lot's daughters offered to the mob of Sodomites (Genesis 19:1–8), Dinah's rape (Genesis 34), Jephthah's daughter (Judges 11:29–40), the murder and dismemberment of the Levite's concubine (Judges 19), the rape of David's daughter Tamar (2 Samuel 13).[8] Women in the Bible are valued as procreators; they are not kings, judges (with the exception of Deborah), priests, prophets, or warriors.

Yet the story of women's repression and oppression—and the story of the law that enforces that oppression—is not the whole truth of scripture. In the second essay of *Feminist Revision and the Bible* I propose that the Bible invites as well as resists transgressive readings of itself through narratives which privilege challenge and transgression. Abraham bargains, Jacob wrestles, Job questions. Exodus supports political rebellion. The Prophets attack monarchic and priestly power in the name of social justice. The Song of Songs and the Book of Ruth are countertexts which offer eroticized and gynocentric versions of covenant, while (not coincidentally) implying the acceptability of negotiating ethnic boundaries. King Solomon makes treaties rather than wars with Israel's potential enemies, and as a concession to his foreign wives allows the worship of the goddess "on the high places" and even in the temple. All such texts have been inspirational for women writers, as they have been valuable throughout the history of religious and political dissent. In the rest of this essay I survey revisionist biblical poetry by women from Emily Dickinson ("The Bible is an antique volume / Written by faded men") to Lucille Clifton ("I am the bush / I am burning / I am not consumed"),[9] who tacitly or openly rescript both Hebrew and Christian scenarios for female purposes.

Clifton's work is part of a burst of religious revisionism by post-1960s women poets. Not surprisingly, these poems are often political. Sylvia Plath's line "Herr God, Herr Lucifer" summarizes her opinion of generic male authority. Ursula Le Guin's "She Un-Names Them" is an ecological counterparable in which Eve gives the animals back to nature. Lot's wife, in a powerful poem by Celia Gilbert, chooses not to survive the destruction of Sodom because of her horror both at God's cruelty in destroying it and at Lot's offering their virgin daughters to the mob. The poem splices her monologue with an account of another utterly destroyed "wicked" city, Hiroshima. Eleanor Wilner's Sarah in the title poem of *Sarah's Choice* urges Isaac to set forth with her in the desert to reclaim Hagar and Ishmael, warning him that if he does not, he and his half-brother will be at each other's throats. Wilner's Miriam, as horrified at the murder of firstborn Egyptians as of firstborn Hebrews, sees herself as leaving "one ruler / for another, one Egypt for the next."[10] To my ear, all such writing illuminates a split between the biblical values of global compassion and the equal and opposite values of exclusionary (self-) righteousness. Which side are we on? Both are "Jewish." Both are mandated scripturally. More than any other group of Jewish writers I can think of today, women stress the imperative of choice.

Of the multiplication of revisionist books by Jewish women there is no end. Sometimes they defuse biblical misogyny by foregrounding those women who are treated positively in the Bible—Ruth, Judith, Deborah, Hannah, Esther, and so forth. The contemporary explosion of new gynocentric rituals, of feminist *haggadot,* and of women's *midrash,* alter the emphasis and sometimes the substance of biblical narrative and poetry, in ways which encourage women's dignity.[11] At times the idea is to pursue—reading between the lines of those very texts which exist in part to erase the memory of polytheism—traces of the goddess who flourished in Canaan before the arrival of Jahweh. When women today imagine a goddess they usually make her simultaneously spiritual and sensual. The heroine of Rhoda Lerman's *Call Me Ishtar* is both a bread-baking Jewish wife and a lawgiving goddess who mocks the dualisms of patriarchy. In E. M. Broner's *A Weave of Women* a communal set of American-English-German-Israeli heroines invents a new set of rituals corresponding to the births, deaths, struggles, failures, and rebirths of their lives; finally the women are able to say, "How goodly are thy tents, thy reclaimed ruins, O Sara, O our mothers of the desert." The modern heroine of Deena Metzger's *What Dinah Thought* is inhabited by the biblical Dinah, according to whom "the daughters of the land" were teaching her Goddess-religion and Schechem was not her rapist but her secret husband; when her brothers massacre the town of Schechem, it is Dinah's curse that dooms the sons of Jacob to a history of bloodshed with their neighbors until and unless Jew and Palestinian enter into remarriage at the site of the murder. (Schechem is the modern Nablus, presently in the occupied territories.) Enid Dame's raunchy and philosophical Lilith notes that "the names they call me / haven't changed in 2000 years." Julia Vinograd's Jerusalem resembles both the cruel goddess Kali and a neglected lover. Rachel Adler's "Second Hymn to the Shekhina," ironically recognizing that the "Daddygod" defines the female principle as "nothing," addresses her nonetheless:

> Nothing is my own mama and
> I am nothing myself . . .
>> hollow in the pot   nothing
>> hole in the flute   nothing
>> rest in the music   nothing
>> shabbat in the week   nothing[12]

It is obvious that biblical reinterpretation is a risky matter, especially for a woman, and especially when that woman stands deliberately outside Orthodox traditions of interpretation. Yet many women today must stand here. As Adrienne Rich observes, "Revision—the act of looking back, of seeing with fresh eyes, of entering an old text from a new critical direction—is for women more than a chapter in cultural history; it is an act of survival."[13] Survival, let me add, not only for ourselves but also for the ongoing life of Judaism. What may seem outrageous, blasphemous, or irreligious about women's reimaginings of Scripture (my own and others') is in fact the inevitable outcome of Jewish tradition. For are we not told that "there is always another interpretation" of Torah? "Turn it and turn it," say the rabbis, "for everything is in it." Jewish tradition has been a tradition not of stasis but of continual reinterpretation of Torah in response to changing social and political needs and realities, not only after but even before its canonization.[14] If we require a sacred tradition that will be sacred indeed to that half of the Jewish people who have been oppressed and excluded by it, women must look to their own spiritual imaginations just as men have looked to theirs. As a woman, I feel acutely that the Bible as we have it is an overwhelmingly male document in which femaleness has been buried—but not killed. Half-erased, yet not without a trace. Reading between and through the lines of Scripture, I and other women perceive a wide range of female meanings, both in human figures and in God. And if we question prevailing dogmas and pieties, do we not have Job on our side?

IV

> If your philosophers insist that the world is a dichotomy, tell them that two plus two don't make four unless something brings them back together. The connection has been lost. But I'm back. Don't worry.
>
> —Rhoda Lerman, *Call Me Ishtar*

The longer I read the Bible the more impressed I am by how it eludes the doctrines that have been built on it. There is a joke in which God tells Moses, "Thou shalt not boil a kid in its mother's milk." "You mean I shouldn't eat meat and dairy at the same meal?" Moses asks. "Thou shalt not boil a kid in its mother's milk," God repeats. "Oh, you mean I need two separate sets of dishes for *fleishig* and *milchig*?" "Thou shalt not boil a kid in its mother's milk," God repeats yet again. "Ah, I see, you mean I should have two kitchen sinks and two racks for the washing machine." "Have it your way," God sighs. When I think of the supposed thirteen (no more, no fewer) attributes of the Holy One, Blessed be He, or of the supposed 613 *mitzvot* required of Jewish men, I think of Solomon's confession to God upon the completion of the temple: "Behold, the heaven and heaven of heavens cannot contain Thee; how much less this house that I have builded" (1 Kings 8:27). Would to God that all the Lord's people understood as much.

Because the Bible is the founding text of Western patriarchy, women sometimes wonder why I should want to read it at all, much less hold it sacred. A Jewish woman writer who is a heroine of mine (lefty, secular) once berated me furiously after I gave a talk about rescuing the Bible for feminism. For her, there was nothing redeemable there. But I remember that most of the values I love as well as the ones I hate originate in the Bible. Beating swords into plowshares wasn't invented by the Unitarians. Besides, we do not change a system by denying it. Growth comes from what is already alive and rooted, extends and transforms what is present. And then there is the language to which I am addicted. But shouldn't women be worshiping the Goddess? Yes, of course, for the divine being which is the source of the universe must be female as well as male, must be everything— kangaroo, bacterium, quasar, electron. Raphael Patai argues that Judaism has always had a goddess in some (usually disguised) form. Numerous Jewish theologians, including Judith Plaskow, Rita Gross, Arthur Green, and Arthur I. Waskow, have already argued for the necessity of female God-language, and numerous women's spirituality groups and *havurot* in this country already use it.[15] If God the Father swallowed God the Mother in prehistory, it's the job of the Jews to deliver her from his belly, however long it happens to take.

On the other hand, I get berated for blasphemy. An Orthodox woman scholar once mentioned the possibility that I was inspired by demons. That took me aback, though I don't believe in demons. Once after I lectured at Notre Dame University on my theory of the triple hermeneutics, a divinity student asked why I didn't include a hermeneutic of *faith*. For Jews, I said, doubt *is* faith; but I don't think he got it.

When I tell people I write feminist *midrash*, they usually assume I'm resurrecting "biblical women." Why do I pay so much attention to biblical men? The fact is that those men are there and will not go away, in the Book or in reality. Nor are they all alike. No other major culture I can think of has a founding epic in which men can be heroes without being warriors, men for whom negotiation rather than violence is normal behavior. My personal favorites are Jacob and Solomon. But I desire to know them all; to understand them all. How else can I understand myself? I *am* my fathers as much as I *am* my mothers. On the other hand, many a rabbi has sincerely wanted to know why what's good enough for Mother Sarah and Queen Esther isn't good enough for me. Were I to answer while standing on one foot, I would say that, if monotheism is an intellectual and spiritual necessity, patriarchy is a spiritual and intellectual abomination.

Sometimes I am asked if I am afraid to do this writing. Yes, I am. I feel quite unqualified to do it. Nonobservant, heterodox, lacking credentials (desire is not a credential), an illegitimate daughter, one of the foolish women: I am very like Job's wife. Still, many a Jew before me has found that the margin is a firm place for an intellectual to stand. Yes, I work in fear and trembling. But if not I, who? And if not now, when? To read the Bible as a feminist is a task I cannot complete. Neither am I free to give it up.

NOTES

1. Stephen Mitchell, Translation and Introduction, *The Book of Job* (San Francisco: North Point Press, 1987), xxx.

2. My major work on Blake consists of *Vision and Verse in William Blake* (Madison: University of Wisconsin Press, 1965) and my annotated edition of Blake's *Complete Poems* (New York: Penguin, 1977). After the breakup of our romance I wrote "Desire Gratified and Ungratified: William Blake and Sexuality," *Blake Quarterly* (Winter 1982–83), reprinted in Hazard Adams, ed., *Critical Essays on William Blake* (Boston: G. K. Hall, 1991); and "The Road of Excess: My William Blake," in Gene Ruoff, ed., *The Romantics and Us: Essays on Romantic and Modern Culture* (New Brunswick: Rutgers University Press, 1988). For my work on women's poetry, see *Stealing the Language: The Emergence of Women's Poetry in America* (Boston: Beacon, 1985).

3. Alicia Ostriker, *The Nakedness of the Fathers* (New Brunswick: Rutgers University Press, 1994).

4. Geoffrey Hartman, "The Struggle for the Text," in *Midrash and Literature,* ed. Geoffrey Hartman and Sanford Budick (New Haven: Yale University Press, 1987), 111–13. Roland Barthes, "The Struggle with the Angel," in *Image, Music, Text,* trans. Stephen Heath (New York: Hill and Wang, 1977), 140. Robert Alter, Introduction, *The Literary Guide to the Bible,* ed. Robert Alter and Frank Kermode (Cambridge: Harvard University Press, 1987). Alter states the case for the inconsistency of biblical texts, suggesting that "the selection was at least sometimes impelled by a desire to

preserve the best of ancient Hebrew literature rather than to gather the consistent normative statements of a monotheistic party line. In fact, the texts that have been passed down to us exhibit not only extraordinary diversity but also a substantial amount of debate with one another" (12–13).

5. Gerald Bruns, "Midrash and Allegory: The Beginning of Scriptural Interpretation," in *Literary Guide,* ed. Alter and Kermode, 633.

6. Harold Bloom and David Rosenberg, *The Book of J* (New York: Grove Weidenfeld, 1990).

7. Kate Millett, *Sexual Politics* (New York: Simon and Schuster, 1979), 51–54, and Merlin Stone, *When God Was a Woman* (New York: Harcourt Brace Jovanovich, 1976), represent views which have influenced the subsequent course of feminist writing on the subject; Mieke Bal, *Lethal Love* (Bloomington: Indiana University Press, 1987), and Judith Plaskow, *Standing Again at Sinai* (San Francisco: Harper and Row, 1990), effectively represent contemporary feminist literary theory and theology. An exception to a monolithic view of the Bible's phallocentrism is Phyllis Trible's *God and the Rhetoric of Sexuality* (Philadelphia: Fortress Press, 1978), which attempts to "rescue" the Bible for feminism by interpretations of Genesis and other texts designed to demonstrate the original androgyny of both God and Adam. Ilana Pardes, *Counter-Traditions in the Bible: A Feminist Approach* (Cambridge, Mass.: Harvard University Press, 1992), also examines a series of "counter-texts" representing gender in a variety of non-normative ways.

8. Adrien Janis Bledstein makes the interesting proposal that Tamar is the author of the J text, in "A Feminist Response to *The Book of J,*" *Lilith* (Summer 1991): 28. As a courtly woman who enters seclusion after her violation, Tamar might well have become a scribe; but of course there is no historical evidence either to support or refute such a hypothesis.

9. Emily Dickinson, *Complete Poems* (Boston: Little, Brown, 1960), 644; Lucille Clifton, "To a Dark Moses," in *Good Woman: Poems and a Memoir* (Brockport, N.Y.: Boa Editions, 1987), 127.

10. Sylvia Plath, "Lady Lazarus," in *Collected Poems* (New York: Harper and Row, 1981), 244; Ursula Le Guin, "She Un-Names Them," in *Buffalo Gals and Other Animal Presences* (Santa Barbara: Capra Press, 1987); Celia Gilbert, "Lot's Wife," in *Bonfire* (Cambridge, Mass.: Alice James Books, 1983), 65–71; Elinor Wilner, *Sarah's Choice* Chicago: University of Chicago Press, 1990), 11.

11. See, for instance, the essays by Cynthia Ozick and Grace Schulman in *Congregation: Contemporary Writers Read the Jewish Bible,* ed. David Rosenberg (New York: Harcourt Brace, 1987); the varied and provocative essays in Christine Buchman and Celina Spiegel, eds., *Out of the Garden: Women Writers and the Bible* (New York: Ballantine, 1994); Judith Kates and Gail Twersky Reimer, eds., *Reading Ruth: Contemporary Women Reclaim a Sacred Story* (New York: Ballantine, 1994).

12. Rhoda Lerman, *Call Me Ishtar* (New York: Holt, Rinehart and Winston, 1973); E. M. Broner, *A Weave of Women* (Bloomington: Indiana University Press, 1985), quotation from p. 294; Deena Metzger, *What Dinah Thought* (New York: Viking Press, 1989); Enid Dame, *Lilith and Her Demons* (Merrick, N.Y.: Cross-Cultural Press, 1986), quotation from p. 10; Julia Vinograd, *The Book of Jerusalem* (Julia Vinograd, c. 1984); several poems from this rare book are in Janine Canan, ed., *She Rises Like the Sun: Invocations of the Goddess by Contemporary Women Poets* (Free-

dom, Calif.: Crossing Press, 1989); Rachel Adler, "Second Hymn to the Shekhina," in *The Divine Feminine: The Biblical Imagery of God as Female,* ed. Virginia Ramy Mollenkott (New York: Crossroad, 1984).

13. Adrienne Rich, "When We Dead Awaken: Writing as Re-Vision," in *Of Lies, Secrets, and Silence* (New York: W. W. Norton, 1979), 83.

14. Alter (Introduction in *Literary Guide,* 13) compares the self-reinterpretiveness of biblical texts, where "what is repeatedly evident is the abundance of authoritative national traditions, fixed in particular verbal formulations, to which later writers respond through incorporation, elaboration, debate, or parody," with the pervasive allusiveness of Eliot's *Waste Land* or Joyce's *Ulysses.* Two major kinds of reinterpretation within the canon are described by Robert Polzin, writing on Deuteronomy (in *Literary Guide,* ed. Alter and Kermode, 92–101) as a narrative which both reinforces and undermines the Mosaic doctrine of God's unconditional covenant with the Israelites; and Mary Callaway, *Sing, O Barren One: A Study in Comparative Midrash* (Atlanta, Ga.: Scholars Press, 1986), which describes the transformation of the figure of the barren woman from Genesis to Judges, Deutero-Isaiah, and the Apocrypha in responses to historical change.

15. See Susannah Heschel, ed., *On Being a Jewish Feminist* (New York: Schocken, 1983) for articles by Plaskow, Gross, Green, and Waskow defining this position.

5

Apologetics and Negative Apologetics; Or, Dialogues of a Jewish Slavist

Gary Saul Morson

... the decisive part in the subjugation of the intelligentsia was played not by terror and bribery (though, God knows, there was enough of both) but by the word "Revolution," which none of them could bear to give up. It is a word to which whole nations have succumbed, and its force was such that one wonders why our rulers still needed prisons and capital punishment.
—Nadezhda Mandelstam, *Hope against Hope*

... there is no alibi [for everyday responsibility].
—Mikhail Bakhtin, "Toward a Philosophy of the Act"

Witnessing and Judging

In ways that are often quite unexpected, many Jewish-American scholars have found themselves listening to a Jewish voice within them that they had long neglected. The result is often a resurgence of some sort of Jewish consciousness, a dialogue of their ethnic or religious heritage with their professional training, which may be quite distant from Jewish concerns. Like all true dialogues, these may have surprising results and may yield insights that neither voice would have reached on its own. Identity acquires a new meaning and tonality, while professional commitments may achieve greater depth and moral force.

The invitation to contribute to the present volume led me to reflect on this process, which has, I think, intensified over the past few years. I recalled that during my career my Jewish voice has spoken to me many times, often deflecting me from some conclusions and redirecting me to others. One can, it appears, be ambushed by tradition. The present volume testifies that in this experience I have not been alone, especially in recent years. In other respects, however, I imagine I differ from most Jewish-American scholars, because the insights at which I have arrived seem to be outside of today's academic mainstream. Whether these differences are to be attributed to my specialization in the small field of Russian literature, to a particular way of being Jewish, or to the particularities of my own moral development, they do not disturb me. Disagreements, if they grow out of real conviction, are what real dialogues are made of, after all. A taste for passionate and open intellectual debate is itself, of course, an important part of the Jewish tradition.

Shortly after graduating from college, I lived for several months in Poland, a country that held great interest to me as a budding young Slavist. It was less than two years since the 1968 student uprising against Communist party rule, an uprising put down by blaming it on the Jews. Matzohs were renamed "dietetic biscuits." The number of Jews left in Poland by then was negligible, and I remember a widely circulated mot that, "if there were no Jews, they would have to be invented." And in fact some were invented when the government declared that several non-Jewish agitators were Jewish. The earnest Poles I met were gratified to have an American witness of what was going on, and for me it was pleasant—too much so, probably—to play that moral role, so gratifying to intellectuals and to the young. Detached study of others, after all, is what most cultural scholarship is all about, so it all felt like an exciting kind of training.

Scholars often imagine themselves as history's witnesses, as its organs of memory and conscience, and therefore as somehow in a distinct position within society to see clearly what others, immersed in their interested daily concerns, overlook or distort. I remember how young scholars of my generation liked to quote the messenger's line from Job used to powerful effect in *Moby Dick:* "And I alone am left to tell the tale." Slavists remembered Ivan Karamazov's occupation of "collecting" stories of child abuse and his practice of signing his articles with the pseudonym Eyewitness.

But another experience led me to reflect on the morality of "witnessing" itself. While in Poland, I spent a day as a tourist—there is no other word for it—at Auschwitz. Years later, my troubled reflections about the ethical ambiguities of such a visit, in which I viewed in comfort that scene of unimaginable suffering, led me to write an article about the morality of tourism. Using a story by Tolstoy as a springboard, I discussed the ethics of vision, the moral problems involved in the detached viewing of horror, and the complexities of occasions in which one must *"bear* witness." Looking, I decided, is also an action that can be performed morally or immorally, and the stance of detachment, though sometimes necessary, carries great risks, especially if it is assumed habitually.

That little settlement near Krakow was not explicitly mentioned in my article but, for me, it was silently present. So, for that matter, was the morally voyeuristic pleasure I had taken in my visits with Polish students. I began to wonder whether scholarship itself, in which one views and passes judgment upon the sufferings of humanity from the comfort of one's study, might not lead to an unconscious dulling of one's moral sense at the very moments when one feels most morally secure. Since visiting Auschwitz and writing that article, I have never been able to shake the sense that our activity, especially when we make ethical pronouncements, should provoke more self-reflection than it usually does.[1]

A few years after my time in Poland, I wrote a dissertation on Dostoevsky's *Diary of a Writer,* a "new literary genre" that combined fiction, notebooks, autobiography, and articles on current events in monthly issues of a one-man periodical. Trained by New Critics, I was concerned primarily with the Russian tendency to produce formally anomalous works. As Tolstoy included nonfictional essays by himself (not just his narrator) within his great fiction *War and Peace,* so Dostoevsky's *Diary* attempted an even more inclusive synthesis of diverse material. I wanted to arrive at a poetics of such combinations and thereby to achieve a better understanding of formal anomaly in Russia and elsewhere.

But I found myself increasingly drawn to the *content* of the *Diary's* journalism, which included, among other things, predictions that the world was literally about to end, accusations of a "universal Catholic conspiracy" to take over the world, descriptions of "the Yid" Disraeli as bent on destroying all humane feelings because they are Christian, and truly blood-curdling anti-Semitic tirades. "I sometimes imagine," Dostoevsky wrote,

> what if there were not three million Jews, but three million Russians in Russia, and there were eighty million Jews? Well, how would they treat Russians, and how would they lord it over them? What rights would Jews give Russians? . . . Wouldn't they turn them into slaves? Worse than that, wouldn't they skin them altogether? Wouldn't they slaughter them to the last man, to the point of complete extermination, as they used to do with alien peoples in ancient times?[2]

I was thankful that Dostoevsky did not know the part of the Passover Haggadah that prays: "Pour out Thy wrath on the nations that know Thee not, and upon the kingdoms who invoke not Thy name. . . . Pursue them in wrath and destroy them from under the heavens of the Eternal"—lines that I always omit reading aloud, and not only when non-Jews are present at our seder.

The *Diary's* anti-Semitic (and anti-Polish and anti-Turkish) passages forced me to consider a number of troubling issues, moral, aesthetic, and historical. For a Jew who had visited Auschwitz, it was hard to be *only* a formalist. It was about this time that I first read, and read extensively about, what I suppose must be the most widely circulated work of Russian thought, *The Protocols of the Elders of Zion.* A forgery that purports to be the transcripts of Jewish conspirators plotting to dominate the world, the *Protocols* was concocted by the tsarist secret police, published in 1903 by a Russian Orthodox priest (who seems to have believed it genuine), widely disseminated within Russia, brought to the Nazis by Rosenberg (a Baltic German from the Russian

Empire), and since then circulated around the world, without interruption and claiming new readers every year.[3] It struck me that the Russian origins of this document were significant and that it was in some disturbing respects a characteristic document of the Russian intellectual tradition. Its forecast of an imminent total upheaval, its fanaticism, and its ready acceptance of conspiracy logic were all characteristic of the Russian intelligentsia, Left and Right; its anti-Semitism was, alas, all too common in Russian culture generally. I recall writing somewhere that anti-Semitism is the only product that Russia has ever been able continually to export without creating a shortage at home.

And yet my literature teachers avoided this theme, which is—so I believed—one of the important currents in Russian thought. Although it would be nice to think that only fools or madmen, but not intellectuals, become anti-Semites, the history of European thought reveals such a sunny view of intellectuals to be a sentimentality. It would therefore seem to be important to study, and so to comprehend from within, this tradition.

I understood why my teachers, mostly Jews and liberals, did not want to spend time on the *Protocols,* which, to put it mildly, hardly constitutes a major work of Russian literature. Indeed, if the *Protocols were* a work of literature—a fiction rather than a forgery—it would not have been so harmful. It was actually a work of imagination that had been repackaged (not by its author) as literal fact: it was fabricated by taking a fictional philosophical dialogue, transforming it, and offering it as a transcript. Awareness of this peculiar textual history has always left me rather suspicious of the theoretical position that holds all "texts" to be equally "fictions." This sort of reasoning blurs some key distinctions, which we lose at our peril.

Unlike the *Protocols,* the writings of Dostoevsky are indubitably great literature, and it disturbed me that almost no one talked about his anti-Semitism. Books on Dostoevsky's life and works would usually treat even his minor stories, but not the gigantic *Diary* that was his primary occupation for better than three years. In a review of one such study I spoke of this strategic omission as "negative apologetics."[4] But how should we respond to this material?

One reason that many sensible people preferred not to raise the question became evident from a book called *Dostoyevsky and the Jews,* a translation from the French.[5] The author, David Goldstein, evinced both earnestness and crudeness in studying, or rather denouncing, Dostoevsky's attitude toward the Jews, and his book provoked some quite distinguished scholars to answer the challenge of his denunciations. I decided to sort out my own views through a lengthy review article of this material ("Dostoevsky's Anti-Semitism and the Critics"). I soon became even more concerned with the sort of hypocrisy, false apologies, or easy, sanctimonious judgment practiced (in publications, conversations, and probably also in private thought) by Dostoevsky's critics, myself included. My essay, which is part autobiographical, contained some rather painful self-reflection on my own attempts to apologize for my favorite writer, but for whose works I might not have become a specialist in Russian literature. What are the obstacles to intellectual integrity in dealing with such a morally charged issue?

Goldstein seemed to me to be an object lesson in what not to do. In retrospect, he also seems an avatar of many later condemnations of great writers by critics who are sure they are wiser for having been born later, and sure they are more moral because they belong to a persecuted group. At the time, I wrote:

> Reading this book, I was frequently reminded of that (probably apocryphal) headline and sub-head in a London Jewish newspaper: "5 DIE IN TOKYO AIR CRASH / Fifty-three non-Jews also killed." Goldstein is also able to state, without irony or qualification, that "At all times the attitude toward the Jewish question has been the acid test of liberalism." Blacks, trade-unionists, feminists, Poles, Irishmen, newspaper editors, censored writers, and non-Europeans might see the matter differently (Goldstein, 305).

I was struck by how Goldstein handled the fact that earlier in his life Dostoevsky wrote *in defense* of the Jews. For me, such a turn of events raised the question of what made Dostoevsky change his mind, but for Goldstein, who began with the assumption that anti-Semitism is innate and that Dostoevsky was an anti-Semite *"a priori,"* the articles on behalf of the Jews were dismissed as hypocritical, a devious attempt to appeal to liberals. Goldstein's model of anti-Semitism as a sort of congenital disease, to which people of certain groups are subject, itself seemed perilously close to prejudice.

As for Goldstein's ready-made dismissal of Dostoevsky's earlier views, it seemed to me that this sort of reasoning, which makes counterevidence impossible in principle, transformed a complex question—How did Dostoevsky become an anti-Semite?—into a simple activity, an occasion for condemning. Curiously enough, it was also an example of the same conspiracy logic—which typically makes evidence out of anything, even counterevidence—that of course also underlies the very anti-Semitic propaganda that Goldstein disputes. I began to see why my wise teachers, who must have foreseen this sort of analysis, had avoided the question altogether. One might naively think that the more important the moral question, the more responsible the analysis would be; but in practice, the more serious the charge, the greater the temptation to crude moral posturing. Such an outcome is to be expected. And this is itself a moral problem.

When I visited Auschwitz, I now recalled, I was dismayed by how the Soviet government had used the exhibit as an occasion for vulgar Communist propaganda about the life-giving Soviet doctors who rescued inmates—as if the Soviets did not have their own Gulag, as if Soviet citizens rescued from German death camps were not promptly sent to Russian ones as a matter of course, and as if there had been no Hitler-Stalin pact to divide up Poland in the first place. Above all, they seemed so inured to condemning anyone but themselves, whose morality was guaranteed by History itself, that they had never entertained the suspicion that perhaps Auschwitz should not be treated as just another occasion for a political diatribe. There are many ways to desecrate the dead.

On the other hand, I was no less disturbed by the attempts to fabricate *ad hoc* apologies for Dostoevsky. One prominent critic suggested that, inasmuch as Dostoevsky hated Poles and Turks (and many other peoples) as well as Jews, he was not anti-Semitic, only xenophobic. I marveled at the logic that makes hatred of many people an extenuation for hating any one of them. It was also suggested that Dostoevsky's hate-filled writings of the 1870s do not make a mockery of his plea for human kindness because, although he vilified the Jews, he felt *guilty* for doing so, as most anti-Semites do not.

Here I was struck by the ways in which critics (for I was answering the very best of them) who study famous writers may become their defense attorneys, seemingly forgetting the loyalty owed to the truth rather than to the writer in question. I was all the more disturbed because in my own private thoughts I had myself formulated *ad hoc* apologies. It may have been only an accident of my youth (I reasoned) that those private apologies had not found their way into print. My reply, to myself and others, was that I did not see any evidence that Dostoevsky felt guilty, and that, if this were indeed guilt, it was of a Dostoevskian kind—the sort that, as Dostoevsky himself brilliantly analyzed the emotion, is often a cause of, not a response to, shameful behavior, and is the very opposite of repentance.

Most defenders of Dostoevsky tried to separate his anti-Semitic journalism from his great novels, in which anti-Semitic passages are both rare and relatively mild. The impulse behind this strategy, not to throw out the baby with the bathwater, is obviously sound. For what writer has not been guilty of some moral sin, some transgression against some *-ism*? For that matter, each of us is probably violating the *-isms* of tomorrow. We would impoverish ourselves terribly if we, like Soviets with their sanitized but shallow socialist realist criticism, were to read seriously only those works written according to currently acceptable moral standards. But if the impulse not to condemn too readily and too easily was sound, the arguments that supported it generally were not.

A typical formulation distinguished "two Dostoevskys," one who appealed to humane and liberal values, and another who propagated reactionary or anti-Semitic views. The former (it was frequently argued) was responsible for the artistically successful novels (or parts of novels); the latter, for the artistically unsuccessful journalism (including the *Diary*). One is all baby, the other all bathwater.

There are many problems with this formulation, but the most important is that it is untrue. Very often, the reactionary, and even anti-Semitic, passages were remarkably successful artistically. In this sort of argument I detected vanity and a certain sentimentality in the unspoken assumption that all great writers must be nice liberals and that somehow great art always endorses what decent people like us already know. Dostoevsky himself was wiser than that, and wrote about how good and evil, "the beauty of the Madonna" and "the beauty of Sodom," are terribly intermingled in art and in the soul. "Beauty is a terrible and awful thing!" says Dmitri Karamazov.

> It is terrible because it has not been fathomed, for God sets us nothing but riddles. Here all shores meet and all contradictions stand side by side. . . . I can't endure the thought that a man of lofty mind and heart begins with the ideal of the Madonna and ends with the ideal of Sodom. What's still more awful is that a man with the ideal of Sodom in his soul does not renounce the ideal of the Madonna, and his heart may be on fire with that ideal, genuinely on fire. . . . Is there beauty in Sodom? Believe me, that for the immense mass of mankind beauty is found in Sodom. Did you know that secret? The awful thing is that beauty is mysterious as well as terrible.[6]

I reached the following conclusion: ethical criteria do belong in literary evaluation, and we may properly take them into account in assessing a writer. But they are not everything; the sources of artistic value are complex and multiple. I wound up thinking that Dostoevsky's anti-Semitism did indeed make him less of a great writer, but that the philosophical depth and psychological complexity I discovered in the course of examining this issue made him more of one. How these positives and negatives balance out I could not say.

In his haste to condemn, Goldstein appeared to have blinded himself to what he could learn; in their desire to defend, Dostoevsky's apologists in effect compromised themselves. Ethical criticism involves more than passing judgment, but must be, like all criticism, an occasion for learning and self-reflection. I did not and do not see why such conclusions would not arise from a study of other authors as well.

Paul de Man and the Critics, and Other Horrors

I had occasion to reexamine these ideas when the Paul de Man affair raged. I say "raged," because so much of the discussion seemed shallow and morally simplistic. I was struck first by the same old "defense attorney" response of de Man's supporters when his pro-Nazi writings surfaced—the automatic reaction of engaging in "damage control." On the other hand, it was disturbing to see an unseemly rush to win political points against deconstruction on behalf of newer, more radical ideologies—the moral obtuseness of using the Nazi horrors for professional ends. One might think (I reflected) that the last people to assume the high moral tone would be Marxists, since, after all, Marxist regimes in our time have themselves much blood to answer for, even more than the Nazis, and one might therefore expect more soul-searching on their parts, especially before they condemned the thought of someone who had justified the ideology of a bloody regime. But that was not the case, I saw.[7]

With de Man, as with Heidegger, Pound, Céline, Dostoevsky, Shaw, Sartre, Lukács, and so many others, it does not follow that obnoxious politics necessarily discredits all other work, I reasoned. It may, and it may not, as I knew from my earlier thinking on Dostoevsky. One needs carefully to examine the texts in question, sort out what is useful from what is not, what is tainted from what is untainted, and perhaps to see something of value in what is tainted. These are not questions one can judge a priori. It is, of course, easier and more comforting just to condemn. But comfort and ease are themselves suspect on such occasions.

I had no stake in the de Man controversy, having never been much impressed with his work or much agitated by it. But the various reactions of my fellow literary critics were disappointing. Most disappointing of all was the response of the deconstructionist establishment. In my view, what finally discredited that movement much more than de Man's early articles was the fact that virtually every prominent deconstructionist (including Jews) defended the articles. Indeed, they deconstructed them, and invented spurious arguments in their defense. The most loathsome of these arguments contended that, since deconstruction was itself thoroughly antifoundationalist and therefore antitotalitarian, anyone who criticized de Man's early articles was himself abetting totalitarian oppression. If essentially all the influential deconstructionists reacted this way, and did so on the basis of deconstruction itself, then surely such actions did discredit the movement, even if it should turn out that Paul de Man's Nazi articles did not.

On the whole, both sides of the de Man controversy—even more than both sides of the debate on Dostoevsky's anti-Semitism, which was not so shallow—left me with a sense of unease at their moral obtuseness. The second controversy seemed more significant to me, not only because it engaged a much larger proportion of the profession, but also because something crucial seemed to have changed in literary studies in the interim. By the time of the de Man affair, literature professors had begun to claim a special insight into the nature of politics and ethics, and were reshaping their discipline accordingly. Their usual moral shallowness was therefore all the more disturbing. (Of course, there were some exceptions.)

The more politicized the profession of literary studies became, the more I began to notice equivalents of what I had examined years before, especially apologetics and negative apologetics. Here a brief digression is necessary, and the fact that it *is* necessary—that the information I need to convey is known to few outside of Russian studies—is already part of my point. From 1929 to 1933, the Soviet regime conducted a war in the countryside. There were several phases to this war: In "dekulakization," millions of peasants were exterminated or sent to Arctic labor camps, ostensibly because they belonged to the wrong class of peasants (were economically better off), but in practice often because they were recalcitrant, or were expected to prove recalcitrant, to Communist party plans. Forced collectivization of agriculture followed.

85

These two phases cost millions of lives, but do not compare with the horror that came next.

In 1932–33 the world witnessed, or rather failed to witness, what has come to be known as the terror-famine. Basically, what happened was that for large areas, especially in Ukraine, *all* the food was requisitioned, the peasants were left to starve, and measures were taken to make sure that no food from the outside got in. Armed Bolshevik officials were stationed in the area to enforce the state-induced famine. The number of people who slowly starved to death in this deliberate extermination campaign is still debated, but it is clear that the figure runs to several million. The most widely respected scholar of this war on the countryside calculates that in its three phases more lives were lost than in all the countries that participated in World War I, that is, well over ten million.[8] Remember that this was only one of the mass killings that took place under Soviet rule; for instance, it was not until a few years later (1936–38) that the better-known Great Terror took place.

The obvious parallel of the terror-famine to the Nazi death camps was not lost on one Russian-Jewish writer, Vasily Grossman. Grossman was a well-known journalist, who during the war reported on Nazi atrocities. He was the author of a documentary work entitled *The Hell of Treblinka* and a coeditor (with Ilya Ehrenburg) of *The Black Book* on Nazi horrors during their occupation of Soviet territory. After his death, two novels that Grossman wrote, but knew he could not publish in the Soviet Union, came to light. One of them, *Forever Flowing,* contains a harrowing and lengthy account of the terror-famine, narrated from the perspective of a well-fed Bolshevik official who had helped enforce the famine.[9] A particularly horrifying moment is her description of starving peasants lining up along railroad tracks in the vain hope that passengers in passing trains might toss food out the windows; but the windows had been sealed to prevent just such "sabotage." It is not surprising that Grossman, reflecting on the two great European exterminations of our time—one of millions because they had been born Jews, and the other of millions because they had been born peasants—should have concluded that Marxism is racism by class.

And yet, the very fact that I have just had to recount these events indicates that they are not widely known. Whenever I have mentioned them to American intellectuals and college professors, almost none outside Slavic studies had ever heard of them; and very few had heard about Soviet genocide of some two dozen small nationalities, even though that was a central point of Nikita Khrushchev's speech against Stalin in 1956. I recalled reading that the Nazis used to taunt their victims by saying that their sufferings would never be widely known. That proved false for the Nazis, but has proved largely true for the millions of Soviet peasants, as well as for the exterminated Chechens and Crimean Tatars and Volga Germans. And this raised troubling questions for me, as a scholar and as a Jew who understood the importance of *remembering.*

Why, I asked myself over a period of years, are these horrors not a central fact in the consciousness of American intellectuals and college professors, especially those who insist that political liberation and the exposing of tyranny is central to their very purpose as scholars? What about Jewish scholars, for whom the remembrance of Jewish oppression has supported this redefinition of scholarly purpose? I eventually arrived at three answers, one benign, but the other two profoundly disturbing and, it turned out, important for my understanding of moral judgments in practice, for my Jewish self-consciousness, and for my identity as a professor.

The benign explanation first: The Nazis lost the war, and so their atrocities came to light rapidly, whereas our Soviet allies (as they then were) won, and so access to information was limited for some time. But this could not be the whole story, because information about the terror-famine and related horrors has been widely available for some time now, yet it is never spoken about, and is virtually unknown, except among specialists. There must be more to it, I reflected.

Rather uncomfortably, I arrived at a second contributing factor. Jews have long played a central role in the American intelligentsia, and have therefore (both understandably and correctly) made sure that the Holocaust is widely known. But how many Chechens are there in the American intelligentsia? Until very recently, who even knew what Chechen is? As for the starved peasants: we have no peasant intellectuals to write about the suffering of other peasants. Moreover, most of the starved were Ukrainians, and although Ukrainians are relatively numerous in North America, they hardly constitute a significant portion of the intelligentsia. To be sure, Ukrainian organizations have tried (quite unsuccessfully) to disseminate knowledge of their Holocaust, but curiously enough their efforts have, if anything, been counterproductive. Eyewitness accounts in large numbers were dismissed because they came from Ukrainians, whereas no one would think of dismissing eyewitness accounts of the Nazi camps because they came from Jews. Most telling for me were a number of experiences I had in narrating these events to Jewish intellectuals, who often replied that Ukrainians are anti-Semites anyway, as if that somehow meant that the mass starvation of millions of people were therefore unreal or not of concern.

I cannot adequately express how disappointed I became when I realized how widespread this attitude was. My fellow Jews, people telling non-Jews they must "never forget," were willing to justify and abet the forgetting of others' suffering. Those who appealed to Gentiles to care about the murder of Jews often resisted what they properly recommended to others. Why was that? What should be a Jewish scholar's response to this attitude among many Jews? These were questions that were to ramify for me over the years. In a sense, the present chapter constitutes one result of such meditations.

When I arrived at the third factor contributing to lack of knowledge about the terror-famine, I was, if anything, even more troubled. I realized from experience that to mention Soviet atrocities, or those practiced by other Marxist regimes, was to elicit from my fellow literature professors a reaction similar to the one I got when, as a graduate student at Oxford, I mentioned politics or religion at the dinner table. It was a faux pas. When my colleagues did not accuse me of red-baiting, or of being a "cold warrior," they made haste to change the subject. If a response was unavoidable, I would hear absurd comments such as: it is really Henry Kissinger who is to blame for the Khmer Rouge. It became readily apparent that criticisms of right-wing regimes or of the United States were always encouraged, but that left-wing regimes must be discussed rather selectively. I was again encountering negative apologetics and apology by silence, this time on a truly grand scale. I had learned how such apologetics have served anti-Semitism; was I, as a Jew and a scholar, to be less disturbed by the practice when the question did not primarily concern Jews?

I reflected further that this reaction was *not* usually the result of Marxist sympathies—it was typically good liberals who practiced such obfuscation— but of a sense of unease at criticizing the Left. For these liberals, their very identity was somehow bound up with being on the left, and they were evidently profoundly uncomfortable at any action that could be construed as an attack on it. Of course, that is not always true of liberals, some of whom correctly recognize that the difference between liberalism and the radical Left (especially Marxism) is not one of degree; that is the sort of liberal I myself aspired to be. But it too often seemed to be the case that liberals, having become used to opposing conservatives and to rejecting ideas *because* they were less "progressive" or further "to the right," had neither the inclination nor the habits of thought that would allow them, without great reluctance, to criticize those to the left of them. They seemed to betray a fear, often explicitly voiced, of being considered, or—still worse—considering themselves, conservatives. Since it was right-wingers who usually brought up the horrors of Marxist regimes, liberal intellectuals resisted being put in a position where they might have to agree with those who were not just regarded as opponents but also *defined* as opponents.

And this was truly terrible. For think what it means (I told myself): Rather than be called conservative or think of themselves for a moment as agreeing with conservatives, too many professors and professed intellectuals were willing to overlook, and so implicitly apologize for, the deaths of millions of people. And yet such people always (and properly) condemn all attempts to deny, minimize, overlook, or impugn the integrity of those concerned with the Holocaust. Since we know that all these forms of Holocaust revisionism are morally loathsome—are truly unspeakable—then how can anyone condone or overlook what I came to think of as "Gulag revisionism"?

I began to feel less than proud to be a professional intellectual. We have properly interrogated Heidegger, de Man, and other Nazi or Fascist sympathizers, it occurred to me, but we do not do the same for all those countless apologists for Stalin, the Soviet Union, Mao.

I considered: here we are at the end of the century that has been dominated by totalitarian regimes and millenarian ideologies, from the Thousand-Year Reich to various Marxist people's republics around the world. And it may now be added: we have seen most of these regimes rot from within and fall at the hands of their horrified citizens. As Ceaușescu and Hoenecker and Mengistu have been, so Kim Il Sung junior and Castro may soon be. The first time a secret ballot governed Russian voting, Communists running unopposed lost overwhelmingly. Pieces of what the East German regime used to call the Anti-Fascist Protective Wall (ostensibly put up to keep Westerners *out*) have glutted the souvenir market. St. Petersburg has returned. The toppling of Lenin statues has become an international pastime. Even Albania—which, unlike the USSR did not just discourage but actually illegalized the practice of religion—has opened churches and mosques. The Baltic states, whose continued recognition by the United States long seemed an absurd anachronism, have regained the independence lost as a result of the Hitler-Stalin pact. Lech Walesa became president of Poland and Vaclav Havel of Czechoslovakia. Almost everywhere except in American and British departments of literature, Marxism has ceased to be a danger and has become, instead, a joke.

A specter is haunting English departments: the specter of ridicule.

The fall of these regimes surely constitutes the most dramatic and morally significant political event of our times. And yet literature professors who insist that their discipline must be political, must deal with social and political upheaval around the world, and must be concerned with human liberation, *have not made this rise and fall of totalitarianism a central topic of their discussion*. People instead still speak without irony of late capitalism. When in question periods after lectures I mention the lack of serious thought among politicized literature professors about what is obviously the most far-reaching political story of our times, I almost always get a stunned and uncomfortable silence, except from Slavists. If, like my former teachers, they had not defined their discipline politically, one would not be moved to ask why this reaction is not a form of hypocrisy.

Why were Jewish scholars, whose identity was so strongly shaped by the need not to forget, so selective in their memories? How did I account for my own reactions to twentieth-century history, so different in some crucial respects from those of most other academic Jews?

Thus my questions about the terror-famine, which had themselves arisen in part as a result of the habits I developed while thinking about Auschwitz, had led me to view the mentality of my profession with suspicion and also to wonder about the mental habits of my fellow Jewish literary scholars. Was it just the literary studies of my time that I was questioning, or did the phenomena I had encountered have deeper implications?

Anti-Intelligentsialism

I had arrived at the following quandary: if Jews, like myself, want the non-Jewish world to remember the Nazi horrors, if they want Auschwitz to be on the moral map of the whole world, if they want it to be a searing issue not only for Jews, then they must frame their moral questions in such a way that people care about horrors practiced on groups other than their own. This was what I had decided so many years before when visiting Poland. Moreover, Jewish scholars have long understood that if memory is to have any meaning, then facts must be preserved and considered. Neither the denial that there are facts (a common position among literary scholars) nor the selection of only facts favorable to one's political position or ethnic group would allow scholarship to *remember* what really did happen and what must not be forgotten. I had applied these lessons to other people's suffering, which, like the suffering of the Jews, had taken place on an unimaginable scale. But I had found that fellow scholars, including Jewish scholars who called on others never to forget the Holocaust, developed a deaf ear to atrocities committed by Marxist regimes. It was as if their very status as intellectuals did not allow such judgments. As a Jew and as a scholar, what was I to make of this disturbing complex?

For a number of reasons, I began to suspect that there was something about intelligentsias that led them, not inevitably but too often, to forms of thinking contrary to their proper role and contrary to the moral position involved in *remembering*.

At this point in my thinking, three statements—two by Eastern Europeans, and one by a Jewish-American literature professor—led to more systematic inquiries about the intelligentsia (about which I have since written a good deal):

Statement #1: In 1989, Northwestern University Press sponsored a conference ("Writing under Totalitarianism") of Eastern European writers and artists who reflected on their own experience under repressive regimes. As you can imagine, none of the participants equated Marxism with human liberation, and their unabashed and unqualified preference for Western democracies disturbed a large part of the audience. During the question period, someone asked a Polish artist to comment on the idea, widely held among American literary critics, that the regimes that fell in Eastern Europe were never really Marxist to begin with, and that therefore it was now time to build truly Marxist societies. After musing for a few seconds at this (to her) unexpected way of looking at things, she replied: suppose someone were to say that Hitler's regime was not really National Socialist and that now was the time to build the real thing? And I remember thinking: *that* absurd argument would still be stronger than its Marxist equivalent, because, after all, national socialism produced horrible results in only one case, but there have been some eighteen Marxist regimes, from Cuba to Ethiopia to Cambodia and

North Korea, and all have produced variations on the same dismal result. And yet we are asked to believe that the nineteenth will be different, or at least to regard the proponents of these regimes as nothing worse than misguided idealists.

Statement #2 belongs to the prominent literary theorist Tzvetan Todorov. It appeared in the *TLS* as one of "two very different analyses" of the de Man controversy. Across the page, in parallel columns, it was opposed by J. Hillis Miller's essay. The contrast could not have been greater, in intelligence, in profundity, and in moral sensitivity.[10]

Miller's piece is remarkable, even in the context of the deconstructionists' damage control, for its moral and intellectual lapses. Reflecting on the massive publicity occasioned by the discovery of de Man's wartime writings, Miller remarked, "It is as though these professors had somewhat abruptly discovered the power of the Press in this area, just as the young de Man discovered the power of the press in wartime Belgium"—an amazing equation. All this publicity, Miller opined, betrayed "a suspicion of any new and difficult mode of thought . . . a general hostility to critical theory"—as if there could be no one interested in new ideas and critical theory who might still be horrified at what de Man wrote. Miller insisted: "The real aim is to discredit that form of interpretation called 'deconstruction,' to obliterate it, as far as possible, from the curriculum, to dissuade students of literature, philosophy, and culture from reading de Man's work or that of his associates, to put a stop to the 'influence' of 'deconstruction' " and beyond that of feminism, "the so-called 'cultural criticism' " and other innovative critical modes as well (676). It does not take a course in deconstruction or rhetoric to see that Miller was attempting to appeal to readers' reluctance to align themselves with anything that might be considered conservative in any way. By this method, he apparently hoped to deflect attention from de Man's pro-Nazi and anti-Semitic writings.

Todorov's commentary, printed on the same page, proceeded quite differently. It stressed the sorry tradition of intellectuals, both before and after the war, of advocating and apologizing for totalitarian or otherwise undemocratic regimes. Todorov then asked whether there might not be something wrong, not just with this or that thinker, but with the intelligentsia itself:

> The Heideggerians of the Nazi period were enthused by extremist political ideas. However, they were clearly not the only ones: both before and after the war, probably more intellectuals committed themselves, body and soul, to political Marxism in one form or another (Stalinism, Trotskyism, Maoism, Castroism). If we add to this list a number of isolated cases—such as Michel Foucault's support, however ephemeral, for the Khomeini regime—and then calculate the sum total of these different tendencies, we must then acknowledge that it represents, not all intellectuals, of course, but a large proportion of them. This raises a very thorny problem: whereas over the past two centuries Western countries have embarked on the path of democracy, their

intellectuals—theoretically the most enlightened segment of the population—
have systematically opted for violent and tyrannical political systems. If, in
these countries, the franchise had been restricted to intellectuals, we would
now be living under totalitarian regimes, and there would no longer be any
franchise. (684)

What is it about intelligentsias that leads them, time and again, to embrace
such loathsome political solutions? Whether or not one likes Todorov's
answers—and I found them only partly satisfying—it is this *question* that has
played an important role in my thoughts about the Holocaust, Gulag, and
other twentieth-century horrors ever since.

Todorov suggests that intellectuals like to define themselves in opposition
to prevailing values, which in democratic societies tempts them to one or
another antidemocratic ideology. Perhaps more important to Todorov, intellectuals tend to judge culture by how aesthetically exciting it is, which means
that political programs, no less than art, have been assessed "by their degree
of originality, by how radically innovative they are, by the intensity of the
experiences they promise" (684). Workaday democracies fare less well by
these criteria than aspiring utopias. Utopianism thrills with its fearful symme-
try, but "bourgeois" democracies bore with their messy moderation.

Todorov's stress on moderation accorded well with another part of my
ongoing research. I had long been working on an approach to literature and
culture, largely inspired by Tolstoy, Chekhov, and Bakhtin, which I came to
call prosaics. (A book by Martin Buber and reflections on Jewish daily life also
played a role in my thinking.)[11] Prosaics, as I defined my neologism, has two
interrelated meanings. As a theory of literature, prosaics stresses the special
importance of novels, which tend to be misunderstood when approached
using the terms and categories derived from poetry or drama (poetics).

More important for our purposes, prosaics names a general view of the
cultural world that is deeply suspicious of all grand systems (including all
total relativisms). Skeptical of the possibility of historical or cultural laws, and
keenly aware that chance and choice make the claims of all-encompassing
Theory untenable, prosaics insists on the fundamental messiness of the cultural world and the precariousness of all human-made order. On these
grounds, Tolstoy rejected Hegel and all others who thought they had found
the hidden key to history; Bakhtin argued against what he called the
"theoretisms" of our century, structuralism, Freudianism, and Marxism; and
both were keenly sensitive to the dangers of all forms of utopianism.

Prosaics also suggests that the most important events of life may not be the
dramatic events and crises that so occupy our attention, but the sum total of
all the *prosaic* ones. To paraphrase Abe Lincoln, God must have loved the
ordinary events because he made so many of them. We usually overlook such
occurrences precisely because they are familiar. Cloaked in their ordinariness,
they remain hidden in plain view. In short, prosaics sees the world as governed by small particularities that resist formalization into laws. Since such a

view of experience governs the great realist novels, prosaics as a theory of literature and prosaics as a view of culture are closely linked. That linkage is traced in Bakhtin's studies of the novel, a genre whose form conveys "prosaic wisdom" and "prosaic intelligence."

Viewed from this perspective, Todorov's warnings against the mental habits of the intelligentsia seemed to echo those of Tolstoy and Chekhov, both of whom were deeply hostile not only to grand theories but also to the class of people given to such theorizing. "I have my knife out for professors," Chekhov once remarked, a comment I found both threatening and illuminating (and cited in my article on Chekhov). In my thoughts, prosaics and Todorov's essay were soon to encounter the third statement to stimulate my reflections on the intelligentsia, this one a letter from another Jewish-American professor of literature, whom I prefer not to identify.

Statement #3: At the time, the book that Caryl Emerson and I wrote, *Mikhail Bakhtin: Creation of a Prosaics,* had not yet appeared, so one professor, writing for an audience of Bakhtin scholars, chose to review my article on prosaics as a foretaste (or warning) of the book to come. He was kind enough to send his remarks to me in advance, but the review itself was anything but kind. In most cases, I could see the point of the reviewer's objections, but I did not understand his description of me as "anti–intellectual." Since I knew him, I wrote to ask what he meant. His prompt reply clarified my thinking. He explained that, since I had said in so many words that I was opposed to the dominant trends of the intelligentsia (especially its addiction to a certain sort of theory), I was *by definition* anti–intellectual.

It had always seemed to me that *non*conformity of thought was what made one an intellectual; and here I was being told that unless one's thought conforms to that of the intelligentsia, to the fashions of the moment, one *can not* be an intellectual. Two more radically divergent views of intellectual values could scarcely be conceived. I reasoned that it is important to draw a distinction between *anti-intellectuality* and what I have since come to call *anti-intelligentsialism*. Not to draw this distinction is, in effect, to play into the hands of those who would equate the two, thus defining intellectuality as conformity to the dominant beliefs of the intelligentsia at any given moment. It seemed to me that the concept of anti–intelligentsialism, which might bespeak real intellectuality, was sorely needed.[12] I realized that over the years, my reflections on anti-Semitism, on Dostoevsky, on de Man and the theory establishment, on Gulag revisionism, on prosaics, Buber, and Bakhtin, had, bit by bit, alteration by tiny alteration, turned me into an anti-intelligentsial.

I will always be grateful to my harsh reviewer, because this was the insight I needed to give shape to a book on which I had long been laboring. In its initial formulation, this book sought to trace the development of "prosaic" thinking in Russia, from Alexander Herzen to Tolstoy, Chekhov, and Bakhtin (plus a few others, less famous). I now saw clearly that this tradition in fact constitutes a *countertradition* to the dominant Russian tradition, that of the intelligentsia.

"Intelligentsia" is a word we get from nineteenth-century Russia, where it meant something quite distinct from thinking people or educated people or intellectuals. Rather, the intelligentsia was identified, and identified itself, by a complex of attitudes and beliefs to which its members subscribed. For decades, if one did not believe in socialism, atheism, and a mystique of Revolution, one could not, almost by definition, be an *intelligent* (a member of the intelligentsia). Codes of behavior—for example, bad manners of a specific sort—were also defining. A person who never read a book or had an independent thought but who held the right beliefs and lived a properly sordid (antibourgeois) life would be accepted as an *intelligent* much more readily than, let us say, Count Leo Tolstoy, who used his title, believed in God, and insisted on defying the fashionable intellectual trends of his day.

It is not surprising, then, that Russia generated a countertradition of thinkers deeply suspicious of the intelligentsia and its habits of thought. That countertradition produced the overwhelming proportion of Russia's greatest literary works as well as a handful of its most remarkable critics, including Bakhtin. As one countertraditional thinker remarked, without too much exaggeration, "In Russia an almost infallible gauge of an artist's genius is the extent of his hatred for the intelligentsia."[13]

Countertraditional intellectuals above all despised the intelligentsia for its intolerance and intellectual conformity. (As a result, they often found themselves caught between government censorship and the "second censorship" of journals controlled by *intelligenty*.) They also pointed out the moral lapses and political dangers of people willing to apologize for anything done in the name of the proper ideals. Asked to join a typical intelligentsia circle, Chekhov replied with contempt for intelligentsial "solidarity" and stressed the conformism those groups enforce. Shocking the *anti*bourgeois, he recommended prosaic virtues, for which "you've got to be . . . just a plain human being. Let us be ordinary people, let us adopt the same attitude *toward all,* then an artificially overwrought solidarity will not be needed."[14]

In lines that seem prophetic, Chekhov warned that, if *intelligenty* should ever actually attain the power they seek, they would surely turn out to the worst oppressors of all: "Under the banner of science, art, and oppressed free-thinking among us in Russia, such toads and crocodiles will rule in ways not known even at the time of the Inquisition in Spain."[15] If this was intended as a rhetorical flourish, it proved to be a gross understatement. In another letter widely quoted after his death, Chekhov contended that the mentality of the intelligentsia was uncannily like that of the secret police and bureaucracy that it opposed: "I do not believe in our intelligentsia, which is hypocritical, false, hysterical, ill-bred, and lazy. I do not believe in it even when it suffers and complains, for its oppressors come from the same womb."[16] Joseph Conrad, of course, was to make much the same point in *Under Western Eyes.*

The Russian tradition would seem to be admonitory. To the extent that thinkers anywhere identify themselves as members of a group based on shared ideas, they are likely to succumb to the same faults as their Russian predecessors: intellectual conformism, an unearned sense of superiority to the rest of society, the habit of "refuting" ideas by labeling them conservative or unfashionable, and a whole series of moral compromises tainted by hypocrisy and *ressentiment*.[17] Todorov, it will be recalled, attributed the intelligentsia's shabby romance with totalitarianism to a longing for an oppositional stance and to an infatuation with judging politics in aesthetic terms. It now seems to me that these tendencies will be pronounced to the extent that people think of themselves *as* members of an intelligentsia and seek their identity from shared views. Real intellectuals do not do that; they do not allow the pleasure of agreeing with the right people, or fear of being taken for one of the wrong people, to dictate their conclusions. They do not succumb to the syndrome of "no enemies to the left" (or to the right).

If in addition to intellectual independence they also have a concern for moral issues, then both imagination and ethical sensibility will profit by their ongoing dialogue with each other. One may hope that such people will succumb less frequently to false apologetics and negative apologetics. Politics is grounded in ethics, to be sure, but it must never be identified with ethics; for if the moral does not have the relative autonomy to serve as a *check* on one's favorite convictions, they are likely to lead to monstrous results.

I recall that in the secular Jewish culture in which I was raised, it was thought to be characteristically Jewish to be both intellectual and, still more, heterodox. Of course, as the example of Chekhov demonstrates, the idea of an intellectual who diverges even from the intellectual herd is not *only* Jewish, but, unless my own upbringing was unique, it at least represents one important Jewish value. No less Jewish, I imagine, is the idea of recognizing the misfortunes of other groups, even when it is uncomfortable for us—whether as Jews or as intellectuals or as people of particular political commitments—to do so.

In my own case, the dialogue between my professional voice and my Jewish voice keeps drawing me to conclusions that, even a few years before, I could not have expected. I must therefore anticipate that my present beliefs may change again. Neither voice, I am sure, has said its last word.

NOTES

1. The article is Morson, "The Reader as Voyeur: Tolstoy and the Poetics of Didactic Fiction," *Canadian-American Slavic Studies* 12 (Winter 1978): 465–80; reprinted in full in "The Reader as Voyeur," in the Norton Critical Edition of *Tolstoy's Short Fiction*, ed. Michael Katz, 379–94 (New York: W. W. Norton, 1991), and in part in *Modern Critical Views: Leo Tolstoy*, ed. Harold Bloom (New York: Chelsea House, 1986). I have recently reexamined the distortions caused by the comfort of scholars in "Coping with Utopia" (review of Andrei Sinyavsky's *Soviet Civilization*), *The American Scholar* (Winter 1992): 132–38.

2. This citation from *The Diary of a Writer* was one of my epigraphs to "Dostoev-

sky's Anti-Semitism and the Critics," *Slavic and East European Journal* 27 (1983): 302–317. A new and superior version has appeared in two volumes: *A Writer's Diary: 1873–76* and *A Writer's Diary: 1877–81,* both ed. and trans. Kenneth Lantz (Evanston, Ill.: Northwestern University Press, 1993–94).

3. The authoritative work on the *Protocols* is Norman Cohn, *Warrant for Genocide: The Myth of the Jewish World-Conspiracy and the "Protocols of the Elders of Zion"* (1966; New York: Harper, 1969). *The Protocols* continue to circulate around the world, and not only in Arab countries. They have enjoyed success in Japan, for instance. In "Black Demagogues and Pseudo-Scholars," an op-ed piece in the *New York Times,* Henry Louis Gates, Jr. noted that "U.C.L.A.'s black newspaper, Nommo, defended the importance of The Protocols of the Elders of Zion. . . . Those who took issue were rebuked with an article headlined: 'Anti-Semitic?' Ridiculous—Chill" (*New York Times,* July 20, 1992, p. A11).

4. Morson, "State of the Field," *Slavic and East European Journal* 22 (Summer 1978): 206.

5. David I. Goldstein, *Dostoyevsky and the Jews* (Austin: University of Texas Press, 1981).

6. Fyodor Dostoevsky, *The Brothers Karamazov,* trans. Constance Garnett (New York: Random House, 1950), 127, translation amended.

7. One reader of my chapter in this volume observed in a marginal note to this paragraph: "Is there a difference between theoretical Marxists and political Marxists? Does it matter? Would it be part of your critique, in fact, that intellectuals believe they can profess Marxist ideology (or use Marxist ideology as an underpinning for literary theory) without being committed activists?" This objection is often made, so it is worthy of reply. I would answer as follows:

(a) It cannot be that practice is irrelevant to a theory grounded in and directed toward politics, economics, and cultural practice. For what is a social theory that is immune to actual evidence of its performance in practice? Here the failure of Marxist economics, its extraordinary and often repeated political repression, and its terrible effects on culture (from Soviet socialist realism to the Chinese cultural revolution to Khmer Rouge's treatment of intellectuals) cannot be irrelevant, just as Marxist theorists themselves do not regard as irrelevant the actual conditions of capitalist or liberal democratic regimes when analyzing them.

(b) This is an especially strange argument for Marxists to advance (or to be advanced on their behalf) inasmuch as Marx himself explicitly rejected such a view of theory. See, for example, the *Theses on Feuerbach:* Thesis 2: "The question whether objective truth can be attributed to human thinking is not a question of theory, but is a *practical* question. . . . " Thesis 8: "Social life is essentially *practical*. All mysteries which mislead theory to mysticism find their rational solution in human practice and in the comprehension of this practice." Thesis 11: "The philosophers have only *interpreted* the world, in various ways; the point, however, is to *change* it" (Karl Marx and Friedrich Engels, *Basic Writings on Politics and Philosophy,* ed. Lewis S. Feuer [New York: Doubleday, 1959], 243–45).

(c) A rallying cry for current Marxist theory is "Always historicize!" Marxist critics historicize other theories and ideologies. The refusal to let themselves be historicized therefore seems disingenuous, a defense the possibility of which is admitted only when the wolf is at the door.

(d) If it were really true that Marxists were such only as an underpinning for literary theory, then one would expect Marxist literary theory to be free of political judgments. But it is typically filled with condemnations of various "bourgeois" positions and practices. The defense therefore would again seem to be either disingenuous or unevenly applied.

Whenever I hear a version of this defense, I recall what an Eastern European intellectual once observed about it: what if there were in America a respected tradition of National Socialist literary theorists, and they offered the same defense to insulate themselves against criticisms of Nazi practice?

8. The classic study of these events is Robert Conquest, *The Harvest of Sorrow: Soviet Collectivization and the Terror-Famine* (New York: Oxford University Press, 1986).

9. Vasily Grossman, *Forever Flowing*, trans. Thomas P. Whitney (New York: Harper, 1986; first Russian edition, Frankfurt am Main: Posev, 1970).

10. The two articles appeared in the *TLS*, June 17–23, 1988. An introductory statement by the editors took the place of article titles: "Two current debates, one in France over Heidegger's affiliation with the Nazi Party, and the other, in the United States, over the collaborationist journalism of Paul de Man, raise important questions about the significance of the political allegiances of philosophers and literary critics. Below, two critics, one from France and the other from the US, offer very different analyses." The critic from France, Todorov, also identifies himself as someone brought up in Stalinist Bulgaria. His essay appears on pp. 676 and 684, Miller's on pp. 676 and 685. The subsequent page references in the text pertain to these two essays.

11. On prosaics, see especially Morson, "Prosaics: An approach to the Humanities," *The American Scholar* (Autumn 1988): 515–28; Morson, "Prosaic Chekhov: Metadrama, the Intelligentsia, and *Uncle Vanya*," *TriQuarterly* (Winter 1990/91): 118–59; and Morson and Caryl Emerson, *Mikhail Bakhtin: Creation of a Prosaics* (Stanford: Stanford University Press, 1992). I first used the term in Morson, *Hidden in Plain View: Narrative and Creative Potentials in "War and Peace"* (Stanford: Stanford University Press, 1987). The book by Buber is *Two Types of Faith,* trans. Norman P. Goldhawk (New York: Harper, 1961). Buber's view of religion as tradition (as opposed to dogma) is essentially the view at which Levin, the hero of *Anna Karenina*, arrives.

12. On anti–intelligentsialism, see Morson, "Prosaic Chekhov," and Morson, "Prosaic Bakhtin: *Landmarks*, Anti-Intelligentsialism, and the Russian Counter-Tradition," *Common Knowledge* 2 (Spring 1993): 35–54.

13. Mikhail Gershenzon, "Creative Self-Consciousness," which appeared in the scandalous volume he edited, *Signposts: A Collection of Articles on the Russian Intelligentsia* (1909; English translation by Marshall S. Shatz and Judith E. Zimmerman [Schlacks: Irvine, 1986], 60.

14. Letter of May 3, 1888, as cited in Ernest J. Simmons, *Chekhov: A Biography* (Boston: Little Brown, 1962), 165.

15. Letter of August 27, 1888, as cited in Simmons, *Chekhov,* 165.

16. Letter of February 22, 1899, as cited by Gershenzon, "Creative Self-Consciousness," 58.

17. On *ressentiment* and intellectuals, see Michael André Bernstein, *Bitter Carnival: "Ressentiment" and the Abject Hero* (Princeton: Princeton University Press, 1992).

6

Terrifying Tales of
Jewish Womanhood

Riv-Ellen Prell

Learning about Jewish Women

Something about Jewish women made me uncomfortable when I became an adolescent. I cringed at the thought of them. Once I basked in the pleasure of Jewish women. My mother and her sisters were soft women. Since I lacked grandmothers, these were the women whose job it was to indulge me, even while my mother also had to discipline and raise me. I felt especially loved as the youngest of all their children. Every holiday was filled with wonderful kitchen smells and a dining-room table overflowing with dish after dish and course after course of special foods completely different from nightly American fare. They cooked to please, and the pleasure of children mattered fundamentally. In my world women gave consistently and generously, and I counted on their gifts of food and affection.

Although during my childhood I enjoyed the sensuous pleasures of my aunts' large bodies and enormous meals, when my own womanhood approached I began to sort out who I was in earnest, what sort of girl I might be, what manner of teenager, and what type of Jew. Jewish women seemed large, noisy, and domineering, altogether too excessive for my 1960s adolescent sensibilities. Jewish mothers were a joke; my mother was a fierce version of one. By this point I didn't even like the things Jewish women did when they were being Jewish. I never wanted to be in the kitchen. I preferred a place at the table right next to my father, especially at the seder. Words were better than soup. I wanted to eat the food, not prepare it. What I really desired was to offer clever opinions and spellbinding answers to the seder questions and anything else I could imagine that would captivate a listener or a reader. I wanted to fill a room with ideas and leave the food preparations to someone else.

My very self became a staging ground for conflicts over what it meant to be a Jewish woman. There is no easy way to tell the story of "traditional" Jewish gender roles. Jewish women stayed in the kitchen, left the work of the Jewish religion—study, public prayer, and Torah—to men. But who knows if that was how it "really was." European-Jewish women ran businesses, hired domestics, deferred to patriarchy, and at the same time often controlled money and power in the realm of ordinary, nonreligious life. This division of labor differed if a person were wealthy or poor, secular, socialist, or religious. Poor women always worked; wealthy women were not as likely to be in business. Socialists wanted equality; the religious Jews insisted on the divine origins of separate spheres for the sexes. Women did not study sacred knowledge, but some were educated. What is certain is that the trip across the Atlantic changed everything, and beginning in the 1900s affluent Jewish women modeled themselves on the "womanly" virtues of the American-Protestant elite.[1] American-Jewish women became guardians of the home and family. Domesticity was their domain. Yet, being brainy and undomestic seems so familiar and quintessentially Jewish for my generation that I wonder what powerful and ambivalent messages both the fathers and mothers of the newly affluent Jewish suburbs sent to their daughters.

I did believe that I was different from other girls because I rejected the "classic" postwar suburban woman's interest in clothes, hair, women's organizations, and kitchen that constituted the female domain. I also remember all my friends who were rebellious as well. The apparently entrenched assumptions about "what women do" seemed to topple without too hard a fight. The world of men, nevertheles, remained my image of what was desirable. Men had prestige in the world. They commanded authority. We listened to my father. He knew what was what in his business, in the Torah, in politics, and in the newspaper. He sat at the head of the table. If I did not like the world of the kitchen, then it was his world I wanted.

As a very young child I remember the pleasure of my father's silky *tallit* brushing against me in synagogue, and the games I played with its fringes to pass the time on our yearly visits there. I remember little else from our infrequently attended synagogue services other than the men, and particularly my father. They filled up that space as my mother and aunts filled up the house. But I do have a vivid, if partial, memory of another woman from an early New Year's encounter at the synagogue. She wore black gloves with a large gold and pearl ring over her gloved finger. When I described her to my mother she told me that wearing a ring over a glove was in terrible taste. Sometimes I think that I imagined that woman. Sometimes I think it was one of my aunts. But whether or not I invented her, her hand is as vivid to me as my father's holy fringes. I was too young to know what "taste" was, but I was as fascinated by my mother's definition of it as by the woman's hand. For here was a taste lacking in the sensuous pleasures of soup, meats, and cakes. This taste rendered some women as excessive and others as proper, determined what was beautiful and what was dangerously vulgar. This faceless memory, in contrast with the sensuality of the bodies of the important women in my life, lurked behind my adolescent sorting of what type of girl I was to become. The vulgar, bejeweled hand seemed to define a Jewish womanhood that filled me with uneasiness. My childish understanding of the hand, glove, and ring was, as I now reflect, remarkably like my adolescent discomfort with Jewish women—remote and secondary. My mother defined what was unacceptable about that fascinating hand, and in parallel fashion others taught me what was unsavory about Jewish women, particularly the ones I did not know.

I believed that I had ample opportunity to observe those undesirable Jewish women from whom I was separating myself. They appeared to surround me in the bakeries, supermarkets, homes, and synagogues of my West Los Angeles neighborhood. And I didn't want to be one. I didn't want to get my hair "done" every Friday, live in large new houses decorated in pale and golden tones. I didn't like shopping, and I came to feel that my large frame did not need anything else added to it, particularly gaudy jewelry, which seemed to be the quintessence of Jewish women's adornment as I saw it or imagined it on the gloved hand of a woman at prayer. When I learned words like "bourgeois" and "nouveau riche" it became much easier to process what was distasteful, ridiculous, and embarrassing about Jewish women. I intended to avoid all such things in my life. I would never be defined by that taste, demeanor, or those values. I was not going to be a Jewish woman. But since I wasn't a Jewish man, by the time I turned eighteen I was simply not sure what I was.

When I think of how uncomfortable Jewish women made me feel I realize that I am not by any means simply describing my mother. Through one set of lenses she embodied those women, and through another she resembled them not at all. My mother cared immensely about good manners, good taste, and decorous behavior. She hated excess. But she also admired it, and often she was unsure on which side of the line her desires or possessions fell. It was not only my mother or the Jewish women I knew whom I feared. I was much more repulsed and horrified by the ones I did not know, who threatened me because I never wanted anyone to mistake me for one of them.

My older brother, three years my senior, taught me a lot about Jewish women. He showed me how young Jewish women grew into the older ones surrounding us. He told me that girls he knew didn't like to sweat and they didn't like sex. Jewish girls were interested in money, "used" boys like my brother to take them to expensive places, would even take the boys' last dimes to buy cokes. Often these girls didn't even care about a guy. By the middle of college he was so fed up with Jewish women that he rarely dated one again. I took my brother's stories as morality tales. I would never do that to a high school boy. I would never want things if wanting was something Jewish girls did.

Over the years I learned about Jewish women from a great many Jewish men—from comedians on "The Ed Sullivan Show," from humor books, from boys and then men, from novels, from a few films and an occasional television sitcom, too. A paucity of media images of Jews made every one count in larger-than-life terms, and all of them portrayed Jewish women. These descriptions and dramatizations of Jewish women seemed to resonate with my West Los Angeles youth. I was sure that I knew the Brenda Patimkins, Marjorie Morningstars, and Lila Kolodnys of literature in person. I knew, I later told myself, Sophie Portnoy. I was quite certain that around the corner, or in the next class-room, at the other library table, or as someone's date in the car next to mine were those demanding, whining, excessive, sexless Jewish girls on their way to a house on my mother's block in the Jewish neighborhood where I would not even be caught dead. I had bigger plans in mind, although remarkably unspe-cific ones. I wanted "more." I wanted to do something interesting, to be differ-ent, and not to live the life I saw around me with its deadening normality.

In high school in the early 1960s I noticed that the interesting people were the smart ones, so I began to discipline myself, working hard to achieve success. To that point I had lots of opinions and never bothered much with academic rigor. Neither of my parents had graduated from high school; my father began to work when he was twelve and finished school in the eighth grade. Of course everyone went to college in my neighborhood, but as I became interested in the pleasure of ideas and achievement, pursuing a doctor-ate, and having a career, I moved further and further from any world my parents or their friends and family understood. I was creating my life out of a cloth as alien and unpromising to my family as the new fabrics that con-fronted my father's dry-cleaning business during the same period.

My mother's ambition was never to work, to leave behind the constant anxieties over money that beset her family when her father died shortly after their arrival in Los Angeles from Montreal in 1923. Marriage in 1934 prom-ised my mother the opportunity to create a real American life. The hard times of the depression delayed that promise. But by the 1950s she had a house, a young son and a daughter, and a husband with a growing business. She looked forward to ease and "nice things" for herself and her children. Why would her daughter want something different from that life? I imagine she and her entire generation asked themselves this question daily.

"All you ever wanted for me was to live down the block from you and get my hair done on Friday," I shouted at my mother on a visit home from graduate school. I was raging at her for not valuing me for who I believed I was. "That's ridiculous, Rivie," she said with exasperation. I never knew who was right, and it never came up again. It certainly did not seem important enough to discuss with her nearly two decades later in the last months of her life while pancreatic cancer rapidly consumed her. In those months all I wanted to know about was who she was through her own eyes, her memories of being young, of being a mother, a wife, a woman. I wanted some guide ropes to hold on to after she left me. I was in my early forties then. I had stopped believing that I was not a Jewish woman.

The Iconic Jewish Women

I thought a great deal about my mother a year after her death when, in 1991, I spent a month at the American Jewish Archive seeking to understand how gender and gender relations shaped Jewish immigrants' Americanization. It dawned on me while I read through English-language Jewish newspapers, novels, magazines, and a few sermons from early in the twentieth century that I was glimpsing the world of my mother's childhood.[2] I refocused on the publication dates of this or that article thinking, "She was eight in 1920, ten in 1922, twelve in 1924." These articles defined what a young Jewish woman should aspire to be. I don't know if Yiddish women's magazines ever found their way into her home, but their sentiments did, because I recognized them from my own childhood. The women's pages of the Yiddish-and English-language Jewish newspapers from throughout the nation reflected mainstream, middle-class ideas of American womanhood. Women were to be ladies, well mannered, modulated, and oriented toward creating domestic bliss. They were in charge of the moral as well as physical health of their families. They shouldered responsibilities for germs, wild children, and the family's lack of piety. They were arbiters of what was proper, far better suited to these tasks than men, especially immigrant men, who financed the family's ascent to the middle class but had no idea how to occupy it, caught up as they were in the world of work.

My mother absorbed those lessons well from American culture as the youngest daughter of Rumanian immigrants. She learned them in public school, from American magazines she read, and from movies. She learned them from her Jewish peers at their dances and social events, and from the more acculturated Jewish women she would have admired from afar. The gulf between the American world of movies, books, and school, and her own childhood in the home of immigrant parents seemed immense. My mother experienced a constant disjunction between the idealized Protestant-American womanhood of gentility, domestic management, and quiet grace, and her own home filled with the intense emotions of a widowed mother, unable to speak or read English, who managed the family economy and everyone else besides. What my mother experienced at home was a powerful, authoritative, and competent woman, who by painful and bitter necessity learned to live without a husband she dearly loved, first when he immigrated to Canada seven years before her, then when his business required travel, and finally when he died. This competence was linked to foreignness in every sense. My mother's mother was large when American women were slender, loud when she should have been soft, an observant Jew who did not fit into the mainstream of American life because of the food she ate and the Sabbath she observed. My mother's task was to become simultaneously an American and a woman. Her mother could be of little help in either pursuit. She was the child of an immigrant in the 1920s, when Americans found difference dangerous and womanhood explosive. Power was the last thing she needed; propriety and normality were her paths. She appeared to learn the lessons of Americanization all too well.

Indeed, my mother never acknowledged any uncertainty about her role as moral arbiter of womanhood and all other family matters. In fact, it was her very hyper-certainty, constantly routing us on a collision course, that leads me to suspect her deeper anxiety about what she proclaimed was the right way, the best way, the only way to be a woman. The prescriptive literature that I read, catching the feverish pitch of its time, made it clear that women believed that, if they were not vigilant and diligent guardians of their families, their children would fall prey to the evil lurking all around.

For immigrants, that danger seemed to be of a very specific type. These Americanizing ethnic newspapers not only described ideal Jewish womanhood; they also characterized the Jewish women who were to be scorned, ones who threatened the whole Jewish community's ability to Americanize by their vulgarity and excess. Social workers, popular Jewish writers, and journalists throughout the first decades of the twentieth century commented on a young Jewish working woman they called the Ghetto Girl. Though I have been unable to find another soul—librarian, historian, or literary critic—who has heard of her, she was an altogether too familiar image of Jewish womanhood. As I read about this "girl" the voices of my brother and all those other commentators on the perils and terrors of Jewish women began to sound like echoes of a distant time, rather than fresh observations of the world around them. And I began to understand who it was my mother feared when she insisted on modest clothing, decorous behavior, and aspirations for domestic life for both of us.

The Ghetto Girl embodied the vulgar Jewish woman for immigrants just as the nouveau riche Jewish woman did for acculturating Jews after World War II, and as the Jewish-American princess did for the post-1960s generation. She was overpainted, overdressed, and overjeweled. She was loud, socially unacceptable, and obsessed with surface appearances. Those who described the Ghetto Girl lamented her false values and misunderstanding of true Americanization, just as later generations would berate the suburban mothers and daughters who endangered Jewish male development, and made Jews look silly in the eyes of Americans. The Ghetto Girl was an object of fear and scorn. Would she slide into prostitution as a result of her love of fine clothes?[3] Would others assume all Jews were this way, ostentatious and crude, even if more affluent or educated? In 1916, for example, Mrs. Marion Golde, who wrote for a New York Jewish newspaper, expressed chagrin at the Ghetto Girl:

> I do not know whether a hardened New Yorker will notice it, but plant a stranger from out-of-town on Avenue A, One Hundred and Sixteenth street to Pitkin Avenue, on a Friday and Saturday night, and if he is of a sensitive turn of mind he will be first astonished and then disgusted at the appearance of the girls who pass by. If he is a Jew he will also be angered and hurt, for the girls he sees are all of his own race. It is lovely to dress in fashion, charming to wear your hair in a graceful little dip; and a touch of powder and a little familiarity with rouge-stick does bring out nicely that atmosphere of elegance and coquetry so dear to the hearts of girls and so enticing to the minds of men; but the fashionable dress of the East-side girls shrieks its cheapness and mimicry of the real

thing. . . . Her exaggerated coiffure, with its imitation curls and soaped curves that stick out at the side of the head like fantastic gargoyles, is an offense to the eye. Her plated gold jewelry with paste stones, bought from the Grand Street peddlers on pay-day reveals its cheapness by its very extravagance.

What is the matter with this girl? Is this bad taste acquired? Is it inherent in her character? Or is it simply a transient mood of the immigrant? Or perhaps is the East-side girl quite normal in taste and all this talk just prejudice? These questions I have heard wrangled and argued so often.[4]

All the things that had made me queasy about Jewish women, all the negotiating my mother did about what was and was not proper or excessive, were contained in this image, which I found in fiction, journalism, and social worker reports.

What is most striking about this description of the Jewish working girl is its sheer absence from other portraits of New York's Lower East Side by people other than acculturating Jews. Hutchins Hapgood's 1902 sketches of East Side Jews in *Spirit of the Ghetto* report a great many types of Jewish women: housewives, intellectuals, political activists, and Americanizing women, but no Ghetto Girls.[5] Eastern European Jews' descriptions in memoirs and newspaper accounts often praise their own young Jewish working girls for introducing fashion to the East Side. The only ones who cringed seemed to be those closest to "making it"—the new professionals, the better educated, and the more established Jews. The recently arrived working-class immigrants appear to have repulsed those Jews who saw in the clothing of these young women a threat to their safety. Middle-class Jews feared that, when Americans saw this personification of bad taste, they would be confused with these gaudy creatures.[6]

When more affluent American Jews saw "common," "vulgar," and "excessive" Jewish women on the streets of New York City, they saw Jews whom the popular press and "good society" delighted in ridiculing as Jews, not merely as immigrants or, specifically, as Russian Jews. Many of these Jewish observers, whether they found extravagance a moral failing or an inevitable stage in the evolution of a new American, were themselves not far removed from the immigrant past of their parents. Others might well doubt their authority to dictate the style of Americanization the Ghetto Girl should emulate. Nevertheless, whether crusading Progressives, wealthy philanthropists, or Jews firmly committed to the maintenance of a moral American Judaism, they knew what needed to be done. If the larger American society refused to distinguish between vulgar and proper Jews, then it was obvious that those of privilege must transform these young Ghetto Girls into acceptable Jewish women.

Creating Gender Boundaries

These middle-class Jews defined themselves as "not being Ghetto Girls" just as I had defined myself as "not being a Jewish woman" like those in the supermarket, in another classroom, or with some other boyfriend. The vulgar

Jewish woman is a boundary marker. By standing away from her I placed myself in a territory in which it was safe to be Jewish, in which no one assumed that I was incivil or demanding. I wanted to be the Jewish woman who bore no resemblance to what my brother, and a host of Jewish men, saw when they recoiled with disgust from the horrors of Jewish women.

If my mother had perfected a 1920s model of American-Jewish womanhood—modest, domestic, and cautious—I was aiming for a countercultural womanhood that allowed for an unlimited range of possibilities, other than ones that appeared "too" Jewish. The irony was that it didn't matter. Even without makeup, bright colors, coiffed hair, or jewelry made of either paste or authentic stones, I was the Ghetto Girl's sister. We Jewish women are potentially dangerous to any Jew for whom difference is a threat to membership in American society, but particularly so for Jewish men.

The Ghetto Girl and I share the same long history of providing such markers for what is or is not acceptable to American culture. If men have been the target of anti-Semitic stereotypes, condensing hate for the outsider in images of exaggerated body parts and fantasies of avarice and wealth, Jewish women's bodies and fashions have allowed Jewish men and affluent Jews to project their fears of difference on images of excess and display.[7] Each generation constructs a Jewish woman who speaks to the anxieties of the time, to the failure to Americanize, to the demands of upward mobility, or to the deadening workplace.[8] Each of these generations can find women to point to, real women whose faces are whitened, whose jewelery hangs heavily, and who lie by swimming pools never considering wetting their hair or exerting themselves by a vigorous lap. These features' inscription as "Jewish," the discussion they cause among Jews, and the need I feel to guard against such behaviors for fear of what people might assume about me, all speak to a pervasive cultural anxiety. Do Jews wear more jewels than Italians or WASPs? Are these jewels a strategy for making wealth easy to carry, or do Jews have more relatives in this business, or, as Marion Golde asks, do they just lack good taste? These questions might have less to tell us about the image of the "tacky" Jewish woman than ones concerned with why minorities in America remain outsiders, and why those who dominate the culture also define taste, generally advocating a minimalism which opposes the flesh. The sisterhood of dangerous Jewish women is located in a minority's anxiety about being different.

When I told a historian friend of mine about Ghetto Girls, she asked, "Why, in the early twentieth century, when Americans were obsessed with young women's sexuality, were Jews concerned about how women looked?" Perhaps all the worry about vulgarity and cheapness was a code for young women's unregulated sexuality. Jewish newspapers with columnists who embodied proper womanhood might have demurred from making more straightforward statements about Jewish girls' sexuality. Yet sexuality itself might signify a greater anxiety about who has the right to define, to see, and to judge.

Looking is a privilege when it allows the viewer to define and objectify whomever is seen. Being seen and defined is the burden of the weak. Men look; women are seen. The rich look; the poor are seen. Obviously the Jews newly comfortable with America worried that they were indistinguishable from Jews who were "seen." They looked at other Jews through the eyes of those they emulated. Women came to embody the dangers of being visible.[9]

All newcomers to American society first purchased new clothing. A hat, a suit, shoes, or an entire outfit marked the transition to membership in a new culture. How one appears is the first defense against being looked at. Poor Jewish women were not the only ones who served as icons of difference. In the 1920s Anglo-Jewish newspapers and magazines exhorted wealthy women to be careful about the loudness of their voices and the propriety of their manners. They were repeatedly told that good clothes were not enough. They were constantly in danger of being exposed as crude, undesirable, and unfit for the elite society to which they aspired. Wealthy Jewish women were dangerous because their loud voices (a sign of their commonness) could betray their obvious social climbing on behalf of their families. Whether working-class or wealthy, whether appropriating popular style or exercising discerning taste, Jewish women were mapped as a boundary between "good" society and the common one, or between what was desirable and what was repulsive for Jews in the United States. There is no time that American-Jewish women do not appear to require transformation to assure Jews that they will be acceptable to this society.

When most American Jews had become fully middle-class, when a Jewish immigrant was the exception and not the rule—in short when I was growing up—I still had reason to fear Jewish women. Ironically, to be desirable to Jewish men, to marry one—the script I was given at birth—I had to appear not to be a Jewish woman. To pursue a life full of uncharted cultural possibilities I had to deny that I was one. Perhaps my brother's opinions weighed too heavily on me. Perhaps I exaggerate. When I graduated from high school in 1965 there were no vicious stereotypes like Jewish-American princesses. We called one another Nice Jewish Girls, which indicated a desire to get married and a certain reticence about the physical world. But there was always that edge of distaste, anger at Jewish mothers, and an admiration for blondes swirling around the very Jewish world in which I lived. Did I imagine a longing in the boys I dated for a woman who would never be like their mothers? Why did these boys' fundamental sense of themselves as American men seem to depend on attracting women unlike me and my friends? Perhaps my brother's words seemed so powerful because he gave voice to something I noticed, but never quite grasped.

Strategies of Neutrality

So I devised a strategy to negotiate the complex avenues of young adulthood, to have aspirations for a life beyond the success of nouveaux riche women, to foreswear excess, and to continue to attract men. I became neutral—not a

Jewish woman, not a Jewish man, yet still Jewish: gender deemphasized. The oppression was not so weighty that I had to become invisible, just neutral. The neutrality did not render me genderless. I simply chose to minimize it, to achieve some new state for a heterosexual woman. I hedged my gender bets; I appeared to be a woman, but just barely. I cut my hair short. I was drawn to clothes that were baggy and dark. I remained outspoken in classes and on the debate team. By the middle of my college years I became less and less interested in what I wore or how I looked, and kept myself running night and day from classes to political activities to student committees. I cringed as girls lined up for dates in the dormitory, not understanding what we had in common as almost-women. I drew a fuzzy line between boys who were friends and the objects of romance. I was perched on the cusp of the sexual revolution, waiting to decide whether my body would vote for propriety or liberation. I felt ambiguous in all relationships. I tried to want or expect nothing from the material world. I was a woman, and yet I found that fact constantly confusing. Because of the fear that I could find myself back at home, dressed in pink waiting for my prom date to arrive at my door, I searched for a womanhood that could never be confused with my past, a journey that led me awkwardly to reinvent myself in opposition to a femininity that really never existed in me or my mother.

None of these expressions of a neutral self were unusual in the mid-1960s. This compelling historical moment was generated by a passionate desire among the people I knew for liberation from the confines of parochial expectations. We sought to change the rules, to rebel against middle-class niceties, and to expose the corruption beneath the surface of American benevolence. Assumptions about gender fell a little later, but those definitions were as open to revision as any other. Courtship rituals, gender-coded clothing, and ideas about how men and women behave and look, all took on new meanings, creating new possibilities for relationships and intimacy. It was easy to abandon the markings of femininity from only a few years previous. It felt revolutionary to imagine something other than "just" marriage and family for my life.

The neutrality around me created a sense that only the future mattered. Personal histories might be affectionately remembered, but they had no guidance to offer for the future. My own sense of my past was not so easily dismissed. My feelings about my "parochial" Jewishness swung between rage and affection. I was always drawn to Jews who were activists, especially the boys, just as I despised the bourgeois Jews on campus, especially the girls, who forever embarrassed me. I enjoyed trading stories about families with other Jews, and always stood ready to wince if non-Jews commented on how clannish we were. I could not exactly explain why, in my very WASP university, I always felt safer with Jews. I was undeniably a Jew, but it seemed to have so little to do with the future or our vision for a transformed world.

I wanted to abolish gender and global inequality, race oppression, and all forms of injustice, and I wanted to do it as an anthropologist who could use the classroom to launch thousands of students into a heightened awareness of both cultural relativism and a respect for differences. I wanted to empower students to rip away the masks of "truth" and convention in order to reveal the arbitrariness of culture, and with that revelation to realize the need to liberate people from their oppressors and colonizers. En route to anthropology I had a similar romance with religious studies, where I had learned to distrust one religion's claim of superiority over another; I also discovered the striking similarities among the myths and beliefs of religions that held their truths to be sacred and unique. I felt a deepened respect for the diversity, rather than authority, of culture and religion as a result of my studies. I was particularly drawn to scholars who penetrated their mysteries unlike those who clung to their tenets, naively believing they were seeking the truth.

I had established neutrality all around me, even as I passionately pursued the ideas I learned in the classroom and in the limited political arenas of my conservative undergraduate college. So it surprises me that as I look back on my undergraduate days the novel that I remember most vividly, the one whose words I quoted in order to explain my history to others, is *Portnoy's Complaint,* published in 1969, my senior year in college, by the bad-boy novelist of American-Jewish life, Philip Roth.[10] I never took a literature course in college, though I read avidly for pleasure. I remember with excitement the social science and social theory texts I studied. Their impact was great; they restructured my world and provided the intellectual moorings for the political and cultural life I was creating for myself. But no book resonated as powerfully as *Portnoy's Complaint*. It had such a strong effect on me that shortly before I married in 1970 I told my partner-to-be that he would understand my family much better if he would simply read this one book. At this moment of great neutrality, of my universalist self-definition, I found truth in a work of masculine American-Jewish identity—funny, ironic, full of rage, a withering critique of American-Jewish life through the eyes of a beloved and perverse son who recoils in horror at Jewish women, personified by his mother.

Me and Portnoy

Alexander Portnoy, Roth's outrageous antihero, is a divided self careening through a psychoanalytic monologue. He is, on the one hand, the soul of virtue, the culmination of everything immigrant Jews dreamed of for their children. Intellectually gifted, he enters college at sixteen, attends law school, and devotes himself to alleviating New York City's injustices as a commissioner in John Lindsay's government. Such virtue and achievement are anticipated by Portnoy at his own bar mitzvah. While he retells the event he imagines that he might have replaced the holy scroll in the Torah procession around the synagogue. Portnoy, not the Torah, would merit the respect and adoration of the congregation usually reserved for the sacred book. Alexander's high IQ and commitment to racial equality, dutifully recounted by the rabbi, embody the goals of second-generation American Jews as concretely as the sacred scrolls do. But, on the other hand, the former bar mitzvah boy is full of shame over the very thing that fills him with frantic energy. His sexuality, personified by his penis, dominates Portnoy's life. By adolescence he is a relentless masturbator and, when he enters college, an equally relentless pursuer of women and sexual encounters that never fully gratify.

Portnoy's self-division begins, as his monologue does, with his mother. A nurturer who threatens Alexander with a bread knife if he will not eat, Sophie is at the root of his problems. She fills Alexander with fear and anxiety of the world around him, particularly of Gentiles, despite Jews' moral superiority. She introduces a Judaism so pointless that its dietary laws depend on nothing other than who is watching the family when they violate the rules, and she fawns over a rabbi who is the height of banality. Sophie's demands for Alexander's perfection are limitless. His father, Jake, is a hardworking insurance agent constantly defeated by an anti-Semitic corporation. Diminished by the world and Sophie, Jake lives with continuous constipation. Thus, Portnoy is attached by guilt to the world of Jewish particularism, and driven by the burden of his mother's excessive affection for him in the face of a father who has been unmanned by her and the world. His insatiable penis provides the only way out from under his family's pressures.

Portnoy inverted my solution for neutrality. I attempted to diminish gender in search of a meaningful cultural identity. Portnoy inflated his gender and sexuality to behemoth proportions in order to neutralize his sense of difference. His idiom for that neutrality was his pursuit of *shikses:*

> O America! America! It may have been gold in the streets to my grandparents, it may have been a chicken in every pot to my mother and father, but to me, a child whose earliest movie memories are of Ann Rutherford and Alice Faye, America is a shikse resting under your arm whispering love love love love love! (164–165)

The high school women that Portnoy describes to his analyst in detail—their thighs, their skirts, the curtained windows of their homes, their polite conversations with their parents, and of course their small noses that can emerge unscathed from drinking cups of hot chocolate—embody a mainstream America that he wants to embrace in order to free himself from the world of his family, a world that is apparently driving him mad. That family is inseparable from his American-Jewish life:

> The hysteria and the superstition! The watch-its and the be-carefuls! You musn't do this, you can't do that—hold it! don't, you're breaking an important law! What law? Whose law? They might as well have had plates in their lips and rings through their noses and painted themselves blue for all the human sense they

made! Oh, and the milchiks and flaishiks beside, all those meshuggeneh rules and regulations on top of their own private craziness? It's a family joke that when I was a tiny child I turned from the window out of which I was watching a snowstorm, and hopefully asked, "momma, do we believe in winter?" . . . Do you get what I'm saying? I was raised by Hottentots and Zulus! (37)

Portnoy's capacity to experience democracy in the beds of non-Jews will save him from the life of savages. Yet, he cries out to be free from taking account of what is Jewish and what is *goyishe,* and his *shikse* strategy fails him, leading him to Dr. Spielvogel's couch to deliver his oratory. The *"shikse* strategy,"* successful or not, nevertheless bears the mark of mid-twentieth-century American-Jewish life. Although Portnoy may excoriate the Gentiles, his masculinity is really counterposed to women, beginning with his mother, since Portnoy defines himself as the victim of her perverse power. His sister Hannah is caricatured as "sallow," "oozing melancholy at every pore" (85). And the *shikses* that he pursues in the end never please him. In fact he only glimpses the ideal world of Jewish masculinity when he accompanies his father and friends to the sweat bath, where through their "oys" of pleasure Portnoy discovers the Jewish man's natural habitat, "a place without goyim and women" (40). Jewish women are boundary markers; their knives and pores outline the undesirable world. They are mired in particularity, unliberated enough to miss the importance of neutrality. And since I, Portnoy's reader, could not have his masculinity, how could I embrace his search for liberation without it?

I found some resonance with Portnoy by identifying with him as a Jew even though I was forced to efface my own womanliness in the process. Like Portnoy, I wanted to bomb the sexual landscape whose edges were defined by Jewish women, especially since I didn't want to be a "knife wielder" or a "melancholy oozer." That is why I did not wince at his descriptions of American-Jewish life as I do now upon rereading the book. Roth was, after all, not lining up with the Gentiles. He took every anti-Semitic memory of his New Jersey childhood and transfused them into Portnoy's youth. Portnoy wanted to be not-Jewish and not not-Jewish at the same time. He wanted freedom, and unsuccessfully used his penis to find a way out of his conundrum. Roth was surely conscious of a long tradition of European images of the Jewish male as highly sexed, corrupting non-Jewish women.

I had no anti-Semitic stereotypes with which I could refashion an outrageous liberation. If my generation wanted to neutralize the past, then as an American Jew it seemed natural to try to alter myself as a woman and a Jew, two quintessential parochialisms. I tried to shape and reshape, to twist and refashion, that combination of Jewishness and womanhood into a cultural identity that could liberate and free me. Yet, it was not Philip Roth's attack on Jewish women alone that could have so indelibly etched *Portnoy's Complaint* on my memory. Though extreme, Roth was still safely within a genre of self-parody. I believe that, in retrospect, I was drawn by the book's sheer outrageousness. Roth ripped open the window sashes and let anyone who pleased look in on the foibles of Jewish family life; no anxiety about the *goyim* here. Roth's Jewish comic writing was built on oral language, a language that was both familiar and funny. I was drawn to a shared vocabulary that, in the end, made neutrality pointless. I do not know how I screened out Portnoy's penis, but in doing so I attached myself to a narration of American-Jewish life in a medium that bristled with the vernacular and asked its readers to think again about being a Jew in America. I saw the glimmerings of a world worth exploring, full of embodied people with senses of humor that made me wonder what place I might have in a New Left utopia free of histories. These savages that Portnoy feared, Jews as Hottentots, presaged my own interest in an anthropology of American-Jewish life, the study of a living, complex culture.

Another Way

American life of a little more than twenty years ago, the era in which I completed college and went to graduate school to study anthropology, is now the subject of films, television documentaries, and enough books to fill a library. Understanding that time is understanding how America, not to mention the world, was reshaped from the bottom up. My neutrality, born from the cultural consensus of the 1950s and supported by the New Left vision of a world without difference, unraveled on the woof of feminism and the warp of what is now called cultural pluralism.

The anthropology that initially supported my neutrality also challenged the possibility of dwelling in such a world. While I learned about the particularity of culture, I began to wonder about the foundation of my own life. While my friends in graduate school went in search of the "other," I sought to understand those people and that culture that I had made other. In exploring American-Jewish life I comprehended what had drawn me to the comparative study of culture—how religions change, how rituals allow people to articulate their conflicts and their dreams, how symbolic systems shape the multiple values of a people, and how men and women construct their experiences in contrast and in cooperation with one another to create a culture of contradictions. In the process I claimed this American-Jewish culture, choosing to embrace it from within, not just from without.

In all the settings in which I pursued these questions I found myself reflecting on the choices that my parents had made, both the ones that troubled me and the ones that touched me. In my thirties I listened in a new way to my mother's stories about her childhood in Canadian-Jewish society, and about her family's move to Los Angeles at the insistence of her older sister. Her recounting of her mother's courage and power took on a new meaning when I heard her describe her own yearnings to be different, to Americanize, to be feminine, and to have "nice things" after years of poverty. My mother wove together stories of all those ancestors I never knew and of a world I could never see, and made her tapestry so sensuous and vivid that it became mine finally to experience rather than to scorn. As I once had struggled to understand what it meant to be a Jewish woman, I now began to wonder what it would mean to be a scholar of American-Jewish life. Was this subject parochial, of marginal interest to scholars, an exercise in romanticized ethnicity? Occasionally, my research evoked the vulgar hand in the synagogue linked to the pleasure of my father's *tallit* strands. Was I pursuing authentic culture entwined in the memories of the prayer shawl? Or was I attracted again to the mirage which evoked the gloved and jeweled hand? Could second- and third-generation American Jews ever be more than gauche and failed imitators of either a real (but lost) Judaism, or middle-class (but inauthentic) ethnics? Was American Judaism and Jewish life no more than a grotesque imitation masquerading as tradition? Was I doing *research,* or was I simply on a personal journey of discovery? I was asked these questions by some colleagues and teachers. I was constantly reminded of the need for distance, disinterest, of the importance of a significant research area. I was warned that my work would be read only by Jews and I would be forced to the margins of academia. These questions and dilemmas frighten and challenge me still as I struggle to fathom the partial culture of a people—my people—whose experiences speak to me about the partial cultures most Americans inhabit.

It was not anthropology alone that undid utopian neutrality. Far more important were the feminist lessons that taught me why I found Jewish women dangerous. Feminism created a sisterhood of women who could feel a deep stake in one another's lives. As a Jewish woman I never believed that all women share the same experiences, but I found an important truth in women's common struggles, which necessarily take many different forms. Through feminism's indictment of a politics that excluded women I learned that difference is the crucial foundation for a just society, and an important alternative to an American culture which homogenizes its minorities, those who have the privilege of European ancestry and those who have not. I claimed the richness of a cultural heritage in relationship to those others whose heritages also ask us to expand the narrowness of the America of my childhood.

Through my research about American-Jewish women, about why Jews have negotiated their lives in America continually through relations between men and women, I have discovered that those who stand outside the dominant norms of American culture (and that is most of us) learn to reject our cultural siblings. Portnoy's distorted masculinity and my neutrality, my brother's wariness of Jewish women and my mother's longing for rules of femininity, are the ways we fantasize that others will not see us as outsiders, and therefore as failures. Our ability to write outrageous novels, or to study what some take to be parochial, and to find a way to speak across canyons of fear and discomfort assures hope for an affectionate reunion with those whom we once fled in anxiety. I no longer fear Jewish women.

NOTES

I appreciate the very thoughtful comments I received on an earlier draft of this chapter from Rachel Buff, Maria Damon, Sara Evans, Shelley Fisher Fishkin, Steven Foldes, Elaine Tyler May, and especially Jeffrey Rubin-Dorsky. I appreciate the contribution of a helpful conversation with Anna Geyer Heinrich.

1. For a discussion of this process, see: Susan Glenn, *Daughters of the Shtetl: Life and Labor in the Immigrant Generation* (Ithaca, N.Y.: Cornell University Press, 1990); and Charlotte Baum, Paula Hyman, and Sonya Michel, *The Jewish Woman in America* (New York: Dial Press, 1975).

2. For a fuller discussion of Americanization and its particular impact on gender relations in the Anglo-Jewish and Yiddish press, see Riv-Ellen Prell, *Fighting to Become Americans: Jewish Women and Men in Conflict in the Twentieth Century* (New York: Basic Books, forthcoming).

3. Viola Paradise, "The Jewish Immigrant Girl in Chicago," *Survey* 30 (September 16, 1913): 699–704, esp. 702–3.

4. Marion Golde, "The Modern Ghetto Girl: Does She Lack Refinement?" *American Weekly Jewish News,* March 22, 1916, p. 11.

5. Hutchins Hapgood, *Spirit of the Ghetto* (1902; rpt., Cambridge, Mass.: Harvard University Press, 1967).

6. Recent scholarly attention has turned to nineteenth-century working-class culture of women, which parallels the ethnic Ghetto Girl. See Christine Stansell, *City of Women: Sex and Class in New York 1789–1860* (Urbana: University of Illinois Press, 1982).

7. For a discussion of anti-Semitic stereotypes of the Jewish male body, see Sandor Gilman, *The Jew's Body* (New York: Routledge, 1991).

8. Riv-Ellen Prell, "Why Jewish American Princesses Don't Sweat: Desire and Consumption in Postwar American Jewish Culture," in *The People of the Body: Jews and Judaism from an Embodied Perspective,* ed. Howard Eilberg-Schwartz, 329–60 (Albany: State University of New York Press, 1992).

9. John Berger (*Ways of Seeing* [London: Penguin Press, 1992]) develops this concept in his analysis of European painting.

10. Philip Roth, *Portnoy's Complaint* (New York: Random House, 1969). The subsequent page references in the text pertain to this source.

PART III

NEGOTIATIONS

Rabbi Zusya said before his death: "In the world-to-come I shall not be asked, 'Why were you not Moses?' but 'Why were you not Zusya?'"

—Hasidic saying

7

Visiting Bubbe and Zeyde
How I Learned about American Pluralism
before Writing about It

David A. Gerber

MOST SUNDAY MORNINGS when I was growing up in Chicago in the 1950s and 1960s, I sat alongside my father and brother and numerous aunts, uncles, and cousins and visited my immigrant grandparents at their modest apartment in one of the city's older, Jewish neighborhoods. Conspicuous by her absence, my mother had few relations with my father's people. Her parents were American-born Jews. She was raised in southern Arizona on the Mexican border, where her father had managed a small store for his uncle. Her mother's favorite recipe was chili con carne. Whatever the long outstanding problems in interpersonal relations might have been, for her my father's people were greenhorns, possessed of exotic, unpredictable, and embarrassing ways.

My father's parents shared the apartment with one of their three daughters, Golda, her husband Irv, who was a shoe salesman in a fashionable downtown store, and their two children, so close in age and resemblance, and so indelibly associated in family consciousness, that their names merged in conversation into one (usually problematic) entity. Upstairs lived Aunt Tessie, with her husband, Jake, who seemed to do little but read Colonel Robert McCormick's reactionary *Chicago Tribune* and gossip about obscure figures in local politics, and their two children. This large, complex household (for in countless ways they lived as one unit) was always in tumult. So frequently was it described by that particular word that for many years I thought "tumult" was Yiddish. The aunts were always agitated about their children's safety, choice of friends, career prospects, or, later, marriage prospects. Or, there was the suspicion some loved one was on the verge of a health crisis. My father, brother, and I usually attempted to make ourselves comfortable amidst this ceaseless fretting, which now mingles in my memory, in a kind of Proustian revery, with the smell of freshly brewed coffee, mothballs, and the faint traces of an oniony brisket cooked days before, to set the place off as singular, symbolic, somehow even historic.

In a rumpled housedress, her hair in an old-fashioned bun, her thick glasses slightly askew, and her teeth sometimes not yet in her mouth, Bubbe (Grandmother) was frequently in the center of the household's agitation, sometimes attempting to spread calm, but more often stirring up the pot. Zeyde (Grandfather), however, sat on the couch, imperturbable, at least for the moment, and slightly disgusted, reading the *Freiheit,* his left-wing slant to the news that his son-in-law upstairs got from the *Tribune.*

My grandparents, Sam and Miasha, came to America in 1910. They were from the same *shtetl* (town), Ruzhany, in the Jewish Pale in Byelorussia, but had met and married while working in a garment factory in Bialystok. They were radicals, and had once been arrested by the tsarist police in a roundup of members of the Bund (a Jewish radical organization). Jewish life in the Pale was precarious, economically and politically. The next arrest would mean Siberia—or worse. They had three children in rapid succession, but saw no future for them in Russia, so like millions of Russian Jews, they came to join *landslayt* (people from the same region) and kin already in America.

For all her many decades in America, Bubbe still mangled what little English she knew. When she attempted English at all, and when she was agitated (which was frequently), she put her syllables in the wrong order or attached syllables from one word to another. But more than anything else her poor English was the product of years of secure isolation in the bosom of a Yiddish-speaking household and community. After coming to America she never worked outside her home. Her social life was shared exclusively with family, kin, *landslayt,* and the wives of men who, like my grandfather, belonged to their secular temple, the Workmen's Circle. A fraternal organization with leftist politics and a strong Yiddish cultural orientation, which many former Bundists joined after coming to America, the Workmen's Circle was ambivalent about Zionism because it was hostile to nationalism of any sort and antireligious to the point of holding its meetings on Friday night. For years it was one of the principal reference points in my grandparents' lives.

Under any circumstance, Bubbe only happened to live in America; she was hardly an American in any but the formal status that came with her citizenship papers. She understood little of the America that lay beyond her ethnic communal associations. She was certain only that America was a dangerous, unpredictable, crazy place, a conviction that was confirmed by everything she saw through her thick glasses on television. Football was proof, above all: when she glanced at the TV as she walked through the room where the uncles and cousins were watching the Chicago Bears some Sunday, she couldn't see the ball on the screen. All she saw were grown men dressed like gladiators, colliding ferociously. Clearly America must be a *gonef* (thief) to exact such a sacrifice in the name of even a well-paying job. What, she asked, was left of these men for their wives and children when they went home at the end of a day of this violence? Yet the radical sentimentalist in my grandmother mixed unpredictably with more deeply embedded, premodern habits of thought that were even less at home in postwar America. Folkish superstitions randomly entered her conversation. She often threatened to return from the grave to haunt us if a certain beloved granddaughter were still not married when she departed from the earthly *gehenna* (hell) of capitalist America.

My grandfather, who avoided emotional discussions unless they involved politics, responded to all catastrophic speculations about family matters by burying himself more deeply in the *Freiheit*. Transported beyond his living room by news of heroic resistance to some injustice perpetrated by the bosses, he sat surrounded by his family, but refused to surrender himself to their fixation with disease, death, and the perils of the American streets. Never a patient man, however, he would eventually put down his paper and, with a dismissive gesture of the hand and an emphatic "*Genug* [enough], already!" he would signal the end of the discussion. When particularly perturbed, the gesture, pointed at Bubbe, was accompanied by an emphatic "Sher up!" Usually, however, he treated her with an almost courtly respect, and called her Mrs. Gerber, just as she referred to him as Mr. Gerber.

He did not accept the notion shared by my grandmother and her daughters that America was a deranged place, full of menace. It was often unjust, unfair, and filled with greed, certainly; yet he recognized that one could have a secure life here on reasonably ethical terms. Not even that was guaranteed Jews in the Europe he had left. With the exception of a nephew, who barely survived the war, living an impoverished refugee existence in Soviet Central Asia, the Holocaust had claimed everyone of the kinfolk he and Bubbe had left behind. A lifelong Communist, though too devoted to *yiddishkeit* (the secular culture of Yiddish-speaking Jews) to join the Communist party and embrace its internationalism, he nonetheless had been affluent for a time. He spent the last three decades of his near-ninety years living comfortably on investments my father had made for him out of what remained of Zeyde's money. Could Paul Novick, the anarchocommunist who edited the *Freiheit* in New York City, have known that the contributions Sam Gerber of Chicago made to buoy up the paper, as its elderly Yiddish-speaking readership declined, were ultimately financed by IBM and AT&T?

Zeyde's story was indeed filled with bicultural ironies. Orphaned at an early age and practically expelled from the land in which his people, after a millennium, were still contemptuously regarded as foreigners, he had left the tsar's domain gladly. He went by himself; the three daughters and Bubbe were to join him when he was employed and settled. Years later, he still spoke of this period of solitary travel and then of resettlement with great enthusiasm. He was a tailor and, as a husky, strong fellow, also worked as a presser. His skills were in demand in America. He followed the trail of his earlier-emigrated acquaintances, to Denmark, then Philadelphia, and finally Chicago, where *landslayt* got him a job in a dress factory. Somehow he soon managed not only to send for his family, but in a few years to open his own small dressmaking shop, which for an all-too-brief moment in the 1920s and 1930s became one of Chicago's larger women's clothing factories.

Sam Gerber was a Communist, but he knew that, although there were risks, he could make more money going out on his own than working for someone else. He was charming and canny, and, like Abraham Cahan's fictional, immigrant, garment entrepreneur David Levinsky,[1] he skillfully dealt with the gentile clothing buyers from the big retail houses. Without formal education, he was nonetheless well-read and a lover of fine music, a self-taught, cultivated artisan-intellectual of the type then common to the ranks of European socialism. For him socialism meant nothing if it failed to hold out the promise of opportunity for workers to live a cultured, dignified life rather than a beastly existence of unremitting toil and fearful insecurity. If America could promise him such a life, and he did not have to violate his conscience to get it, why not do the best he could for himself? So he patiently built up his business until he had about a hundred workers, his own designer, and several salesmen. The workers, some *landslayt* and most Jews, though there were also Italians and Poles, formed one of Chicago's first International Ladies Garment Workers Union locals—with their employer's support.

His success was premised on the unlikely combination of his radical sensibility, competitive entrepreneurial tactics, and canny intuitions about American culture. Alongside his designer, he walked down State Street in Chicago, and once or twice a year Fifth Avenue in New York City, making sketches of the fancy styles that the retail fashion giants displayed in their windows. He then returned to the shop to produce something that looked like the same item, but sold for much less money. During the desperate early years of the depression, when everyone else in the industry was filled with gloom, he reasoned that the consumerist passion of Americans would lead many of them to attempt to brighten their days by shopping, if they could get a good bargain. Besides, he felt sorry for the hard-pressed wives of wage-earners who could never justify spending any money on a dress in such terrible times. So he brought out a line of $6.95 polka-dot "copies," and while other businesses collapsed and the leaders of American capitalism jumped to their deaths from their offices above Wall Street, G & G Clothing prospered. Sam, Miasha, the three daughters, and the American-born son (my father) enjoyed a middle-class life style—a big apartment far from the proletarian neighborhoods, piano and violin lessons, and even a rented summer home on Lake Michigan in the Indiana dunes. During the depths of the depression, my father grew up in relative affluence, attended college away from home, lived at a fraternity, and entered law school. All the while, his parents continued to attend meetings of their *landsmanshaft* (an association of *landslayt*) with their proletarian friends and, with them, continued right up to the war to sponsor the immigration of their kin and friends. When the war was over they patiently sought, mostly without success, to find the survivors of the Final Solution. Zeyde also remained active in the Workmen's Circle. When it split in 1929 over whether to criticize the Soviet

Union, Sam affiliated with the pro-Soviet fragment of the Yiddish Left; gradually it, too, became critical of the Soviet Union, especially when the extent of anti-Semitism there was discovered.

The demise of G & G had many of the elements of ethnic family drama. On the basis of Bubbe's appraisal of one fond relation's indifferent prospects as a provider, Sam brought the genial, unambitious man into the business and then promoted him to second-in-command. The business suffered. Other, more distant relations, to whom he had given work in sales, stole a little here and a little there from him. On the eve of World War II, when the American economy was rapidly reviving, Zeyde was close to bankruptcy and in poor health from worry. He sold out, managing to take some of the remaining assets with him. His dignity intact, however, he then returned to work as a wage-earner in someone else's factory. When Zeyde retired in the late 1940s, my father invested the old man's savings in some high-yield instruments, which allowed these immigrant Communists to spend their last decades wintering in California and Florida, attending their political meetings, and devoting themselves to guiding the destinies of *landslayt* and family members. New causes and emotions entered and enriched their lives in these decades. By the time I began to know them in the 1950s, they had finally made some peace with Judaism, partly influenced by the example of their Americanized son, for whom synagogue membership was a sign of the middle-class respectability they had never sought. Out of their anti-religious principles, they had decided that my father would not have a bar mitzvah. Now they participated in my bar mitzvah and those of my cousins with pleasure, though one had the feeling they were never entirely at home with religion. For many years they had been ambivalent about Zionism. But when they came to understand that their hopes that the solution to anti-Semitism would emerge in the USSR had been betrayed, they became supporters of Israel. Here, too, they were influenced by their son, a tireless worker on behalf of Israel during its precarious early decades.

Seated uncomfortably in a heavy, straight-backed, living room chair covered by thick plastic, my successful father, a powerful presence in the Chicago legal profession, spoke to his parents in a loving Yiddish he probably used only on such occasions after leaving home in 1932 for the University of Illinois. Simultaneously there would be a running translation, with commentary by Uncle Irv. A sly ironist in his own right, Irv's response to the fretting was heavy sarcasm, which artfully shaped his translation.

Every Sunday we walked in on tumult. But for my father's sake the family eventually made an effort at cordial conversation, usually beginning with commentary on the headlines. The tumult, so lacking in conventional decorum, I believe actually embarrassed them in front of my respectable, accomplished father. But efforts to speak about current events usually ended up pitting Paul Novick against Colonel McCormick. We were soon back to tumult. The moral claims of individualism and capitalism were set off against

those of human solidarity and socialism, and when the inevitable philosophical impasse was finally reached, both world views were then measured by that
no more reliable, even if more emotionally satisfying, yardstick: Is it good for
the Jews? The conversation lacked propriety. It was animated by vast, puzzling inferential leaps and massive misconstruals of what one's adversary said.
Most of the time you could not anticipate what side anyone was going to be
on, with the exception of my Republican father and his Communist father.
Though Zeyde was very proud of my father's American success, and indeed
depended for his comfort on my father's ability to manage his investments,
they were often antagonists. The aunts and uncles, warm and generous people, were neither educated nor thoughtful in any systematic way, and their
arguments were particularly inchoate and unpredictable. I barely understood
the conversation, and Uncle Irv proved an unreliable guide because he was
often busy putting me on for his own amusement. But to me it seemed vital
and utterly exotic, especially in the bland political climate and middlebrow
culture of Eisenhower's America. Gentile families never behaved like this—or
at least so I thought from watching "Ozzie and Harriet," "The Stu Erwin
Show," and "My Little Margie," for I did not really know any Gentiles. The
public schools I attended did not encourage speculation about the worthiness
of the American experiment or a debating style built on retorts such as, "Do
you think you're still in Bialystok?" and "Only a *narr* [fool] would believe
what the *Tribune* says about Russia!"

They would go on like this for perhaps an hour, stop for coffee and
Bubbe's rock-hard *mandelbrot* (an almond loaf made of cookie dough), the
remains of which would go home with us in an old shoebox to be thrown
away untouched after a decent interval. Then the conversation would turn
from politics to practical family matters. My father would be asked to sort out
everyone's problems in dealing with the perplexing American environment. A
nephew needed a summer job, preferably one in which he wouldn't have to
work, because he had a bad back. Maybe my father's old fraternity pal, who
now sat on the county board of commissioners, could be approached about a
job in the park system? A niece was assigned to teach at an inner-city public
school where there were now Puerto Ricans. Couldn't she be reassigned?
Gradually the problems became even more intractable. A nephew had flunked
the CPA examination. Another niece still wasn't married and all the men these
days had only one thing on their minds. But among the already married, there
were misunderstandings and possibly even infidelities. And yet another
nephew, who had broken his father's heart by refusing to go to medical
school, was in California trying to find work in the movies. The list of
grievances, difficulties, and vexations would grow. Like some combination of
a Mafia don and an embassy consular in a hostile country, my increasingly
hard-pressed father promised this, recommended that, expressed sympathy
here, begged forbearance there. But, like his own father, he lacked patience.
He soon crossed some threshold of disgust and frustration, and announced

that he was leaving to return to the quiet of his den, where he worked on legal papers and watched golf on television.

There before me on these occasions, with me as a participant and an observer, lay the developing bicultural experience of the Jews in their American diaspora, neatly ordered by generations. It was history-in-the-making, an early lesson in the culture of ordinary people whose lives had been and were being transformed by epic events and processes.

But I cannot claim these highly symbolic occasions had anything directly to do with my decision to become a historian of American pluralism. The culture, memory, and self-understanding I acquired on these Sundays were so deeply embedded in my consciousness, I would not know them in myself for years. On the practical level, furthermore, a series of decisions having to do with getting the best possible higher education for which I was qualified led me to almost wholly gentile environments and produced a profound discontinuity in my experience. Yet I did, quite consciously, turn away from the world of my grandparents. That world seemed parochial and defensive, closed to and suspicious of the worlds beyond itself at a time when America—the gentile America personified by the tough, confident, commanding figure of John Kennedy—seemed especially cosmopolitan and hopeful and thus so enticing.

Certainly writing about the history of the Jews in America, one of the several projects I eventually undertook as a scholar,[2] was the furthest thing from my conscious mind when, after graduating from Northwestern, I went to Princeton in the fall of 1966 to pursue a doctorate in American history. I remember telling a good friend, a fellow graduate student with roots in colonial New England, about my family and these Sundays, delivering ethnographic detail, as if I were relating data acquired by an expedition among the hill tribes of Papua New Guinea, with the comic timing and tone of Myron Cohen. My friend responded wisely, "History happened to you when you were there on Sundays, and you'll never forget it. It once happened to WASPs like me, but we've forgotten it. You're fortunate." I have only come to see his point in the last few years, as the contingencies that shaped my vocation as a scholar and teacher have become clearer to me. Meanwhile that world of Sunday mornings slowly dissolved, when first the grandparents and then the aunts and uncles passed away. My cousins grew up and formed their own families. My parents moved to Arizona, and my brother and I left Chicago, and in our chosen fields became American professionals.

I had little to guide me when I embarked on my journey into the historical profession. There were no role models from the immediate cultural environs in which I had grown up. Indeed, our comforting mythologies about the Jewish love of knowledge never proved so shallow as when held up against the reality of those environs, where material prosperity, comfort, and security were worshiped just as vigorously by postwar generations as they were everywhere else in America. Not unlike their fathers before them, my neighborhood friends were, at the time I made the decision to go to graduate school, becoming druggists, accountants, and gym teachers, marrying their high school sweethearts, and finding an apartment not too far from their parents. Moreover, as much as I myself was fleeing from that neighborhood ethnic culture of *alrightniks* and from the Jewishness and Judaism I had experienced within it, and embracing some sort of American identity, there wasn't much in the scholarly understanding of the American past to guide me on my journey. I had to come to link my identity to America and the American past. But little in the American history books I read helped me to understand, let alone gain confidence from, the Americanness of the Jewish diaspora in the United States—its rightness in the place it had established for itself here. American-Jewish historiography shared with other ethnic historiographies tendencies toward ancestor-worship, the point of which was ultimately to place a Jew at Plymouth Rock, or at Yorktown when Cornwallis surrendered, or at Atlanta when Sherman set it on fire. My own people, however, had not charged up San Juan Hill with Teddy Roosevelt, and anyway I was too "critically minded" to gain pride, let alone self-understanding, from the knowledge that Jews had fought in, not to mention financed (for that seemed *too* Jewish), the Revolution or any other war.[3]

The Jews hardly appeared at all in the great tradition of American historiography that was descended from the work of Bancroft, Adams, Turner, Beard, Parrington, and others. When they did, like other immigrants arriving in massive numbers at the turn of the century, they were not perceived as a source of strength or creativity, or as a formative element widening the American mainstream. Instead, the Jews appeared as a *problem,* a context for the development of either American decency (the narrative of Progressive social work and political reform) or American intolerance (the narrative of American racism and nativism).[4] We were the confused, alien, huddled masses, worthy of scholarly compassion now that anti-Semitism was no longer respectable in the historical profession, but seen as the objects, not the subjects, of history. Jewish historians, such as Oscar Handlin, who were our first representatives within this historiographical tradition, generally accepted this schema. These historians chose to orient their work on the history of American Jews around developing the themes of compassion for and acceptance of Jews and explaining away anti-Semitism as a marginal phenomenon originating with fringe groups and enemies of progress, who were essentially un-American in their intolerant beliefs.[5] They had little interest in the complex bicultural life of American Jews, especially in the ways that I had experienced it as a part of my grandparents' rich, active lives.

Yet, after 1945 their interpretation of the American-Jewish experience certainly appeared to be plausible. There had been no American Holocaust. The thinning ranks of American anti-Semites were on the defensive. Jews were sharing in postwar prosperity, and opportunities were opening to us throughout the economy. Judaism had even become the "third faith." Politicians courted the Jewish vote and vowed to protect our embattled kin in Israel. If we were objects, "refuse" from foreign shores, as Emma Lazarus would have it, we were daily becoming less wretched.

It was the compassionate, tolerant side of the reform tradition, personified by the abolitionists and the early social workers such as Jane Addams, that inspired the moral purposes I was pursuing in becoming a student of the American past. It was the 1960s, and the nation was in the midst of the civil rights revolution. Along with every young Jewish intellectual I knew, I was in wholehearted sympathy with the African-American struggle, not only on the merits of the case, but also because I vaguely saw the historical ordeals of my own people, about which I actually knew surprisingly little, recapitulated in the long travail of African-American experience. If I had any clear purpose in going to graduate school, it was certainly not to understand the communal world I had left behind. Rather, it was to study the history of American race relations and to find in it positive, universalistic political traditions that might provide an ethical direction for my own scholarship and teaching about race and racism.[6]

Yet, politically engaged as I believed myself to be, my work was not undertaken to empower, in any direct or explicit way, a movement or ideology. In the late 1960s, because of my opposition to the Vietnam War and all the domestic cultural and political forces that appeared to have brought it about, I came to identify with the New Left. But something still held me back from taking the leap that would have allowed me to say, as some of my friends did, "I write for the Left." That "something" was a vaguely felt sense that I could not unify my life or my identity by subscribing to a political manifesto, let alone by writing one. I felt within me two people simultaneously. I lived at once in two cultures that refused to be easily reconciled, and according to two codes, one of them public, cosmopolitan, and hopeful, and the other, private, ethnic, and nourished by a sense of being an outsider. At Princeton I felt sometimes as if I were "passing." According to my undergraduate sociology textbooks, such feelings were supposed to be bad for one. Sociological theory, from the writings of Robert Park in the early twentieth century on, told me that what I felt was nothing less than alienation, and that it was an inevitable, mostly debilitating part of the life of the person caught between cultures. Yet I craved this tension, which I dimly recognized as a source of energy, imagination, and even wisdom in personal relations, conversation, and intellectual discourse.[7]

My early work as a scholar in African-American history now provides me with a retrospective illustration of these centrifugal forces. If I had been asked in 1967 why I chose to do a dissertation on the history of northern blacks in the nineteenth century,[8] I would have responded that I sought to spread knowledge of wrongs and of the struggle against them, in the service of decency. But what I now think actually fascinated me about the history of the relatively obscure black politicians, teachers, ministers, lawyers, and artisans I studied was the dualism that W. E. B. Du Bois identified in his own character, and described so compellingly in 1897, two years after obtaining his doctorate at Harvard. "One ever feels his two-ness—an American, a Negro; two souls, two thoughts, two unreconciled strivings; two warring ideals in one dark body."[9] Like Du Bois, many of these men and women were not really comfortable in either of the worlds they inhabited, and somehow, I thought, in spite of this—later I came to feel *because* of it—they attained enormous self-awareness and understanding of the world around them. One of them, Peter Clark, a brilliant teacher and school administrator in Cincinnati, haunted my thoughts for years after I finished a book based on this research. A man of mixed racial ancestry, Clark believed deeply at one and the same time in integration and in the maintenance of separate, soul-sustaining, black cultural traditions and institutions. I returned to Clark in the mid-1980s and once more sought to understand the dilemma posed by this "two-ness" in his life.[10] During those years of thinking about Peter Clark, I now believe I was slowly working my way back home, writing an autobiography, at the heart of which was my own two-ness.

Meanwhile there were other young historians and social scientists who were able to merge their scholarly work and the political aspirations of the New Left. Prominent among them, more as symbols of the intergenerational continuity of radical politics than because of their numbers, were Jews, both "red diaper babies" (the children of former or current Communist party members) and others who had grown up in some leftist Jewish environment. For them, and many others who identified with these political traditions, scholarship was conceived as an extension of a family, as well as a Jewish, mission to the world. One became so used to hearing expressions of the self-righteous, humorless, and ideological side of this mentality that it was all too easy to miss what was compelling in it. There was, of course, considerable idealism. A great deal of romantic sentiment also informed this state of mind, reminding one at times of the beneficent sensibility of religious missionaries who experience personal joy in the good news they seek to spread.[11]

I could accept most of the message, but I never wished to celebrate it in my work. With my Republican father and mother, I was a poor candidate to be a red diaper baby. But I also could not create a political lineage for myself through my grandparents. Sam and Miasha were not romantic figures whose lives inspired a political mission in me. When I tried to think of them as such, it seemed utterly contrived, somehow both an indulgence in a fantasy of the historic significance of their political role and a refusal to take them seriously enough. They were "role models" only in the much more general sense of devotion to family and concern for others. The political message of their lives was, if anything, pretty confused. Of course, there was the matter of the investments that financed their retirement, and seemed somewhat to qualify their commitment to political principle. Their lingering though ambivalent affection for the Soviet Union, moreover, was something I could never share.

As it actually existed in the world, communism seemed—*was*—bleak, totalitarian, and sustained by force and lies. Eventually I came to sense that what remained of their feeling for the USSR was a desire to retain faith in the idea of socialism, a world without scarcity and the desperate hatreds it breeds. Moreover, compared with the cultural richness of their lives, which had many dimensions, their politics was a shallow standard for evaluating them. I was proud of their ethical stance toward the world, but had spent too many Sunday mornings in their presence to believe that the best or only way to think of them was simply as "radicals." If anything the ironies, accidents, and twists and turns of fate that marked their lives served to distance me from determinism and dogma, sensitize me to the role of unintended consequences, and deepen my resistance to the simple-minded and insidious politicizing of such aspects of daily life as one's affection for grandparents and for family traditions.

My tempered enthusiasm for the New Left impulses in the new historiography aside, there cannot be any doubt that those impulses, as well as ones from such other democratic insurgencies of the 1960s as the civil rights movement and the new feminism, did remake American historiography.[12] Indeed, the "New Social History" was a revolution in the writing of the American past that put ordinary people and daily life at the center of the American narrative. Immigrants, slaves, housewives, Chinese railroad laborers, Chicano farm workers, proletarianized foreigners on the assembly line were no longer to be conceived condescendingly as part of the agenda of past social work, but rather as active and creative agents in the formation of alternative cultures and in resistance to capitalist power and ideology.[13] Not only did this new history differ greatly from our classic American historical works, but also the contrast to the dominant interpretive schema of the immediate postwar decades themselves could not have been more profound. American historiography in the 1950s was informed by consensus social theory, which stated, in effect, that liberal capitalism, by virtue of its productivity and political flexibility, did away with the need for conflict and confrontation in ordering society and politics. Read back into the American past, consensus had it that there had never really been any basic disagreements among Americans on the shape and purposes of society. Everyone had always believed in capitalism and democracy. Radicalism, consensus contended, was to be understood as a backward-looking response of those temporarily inconvenienced by the confusion of the industrial revolution while they were, unbeknownst to them, on their way to consumerism and to the suburbs.[14] The New Social History turned these contentions upside down, offering a narrative of the American experience that looked not very different from the histories of the European capitalist countries—a story of cultural diversity, class conflict, social fragmentation, and sharp ideological clashes, the outcomes of which, well into the twentieth century, were said to be always in doubt.[15]

I certainly identified with the moral purposes of this scholarship and have defended it for two decades against its conservative critics, who have wished to rehabilitate American history as the study of high politics within a narrow ideological consensus and eliminate the little people once again. But I retained gnawing doubts about the conception of America in the new history. The gap between the new history's view of the American past and America in the 1970s and 1980s was fairly considerable. Why did a past that was accurately described as replete with conflict always seem to take a path into consensus and accommodation of diversity, whether ideological or cultural? Some leftists spoke of repression, police violence, subtle manipulations, and paper reforms. But, with its recognition of unions, welfare policies for the poor, and safety nets for the middle class, the New Deal–crafted social order, in which I grew to political consciousness, hardly seemed to me to be a mask for exploitation, even if it were not exactly the advanced welfare state that I favored. I saw no police state in America, however stupid, venal, racist, and reactionary local police and the FBI could be at times. Under any circumstances, the politics of law and order had great drawing power among working- and middle-class people, whose votes helped to bring about the long period of conservative politics ushered in by Richard Nixon's call for a return to traditional values and safe streets in 1968. The exodus of these average Americans from the Democratic party greatly profited Ronald Reagan in 1980 and 1984, and he sought to dismantle the social subsidies for which the working class had fought years before. And, my scholarly reasoning aside, I simply could not see my own family history within the narrative of American society that the New Social History had inspired, though one would have thought our story would be central to it. But I could not see our past in consensus history either. The former view threatened to make one-dimensional, political symbols of my grandparents and misconstrue their relationship to and influence upon their children and grandchildren, while the latter seemed to refuse to take seriously what was different about us— and it was this difference that I came increasingly to treasure most about my family and my past.

So I began to take a direction in my own work that diverged from that of many of my contemporaries. I remained concerned with the same problem of the interaction of class and ethnicity that preoccupied many of them in their search for radical political traditions. But increasingly I came to think of the American experience less in terms of conflict than of pluralistic accommodation and integration. For some years I worked at explaining to myself the nature of American pluralism, by which I mean the organization of that spectacular diversity of groups, identities, memories, and cultures that has characterized American history and been one of the great singularities of our historical experience.[16] I came to understand that the genius of American pluralism lies in the way in which Americans in the nineteenth and twentieth centuries have maintained a differentiation between public and private life. Essentially they have created processes for grafting pluralisms onto the bifurcated character of modern social existence long ago recognized by the German sociologist Ferdinand Tönnies, who posited the familiar distinction between *Gemeinschaft* (community) and *Gesellschaft* (society) in describing the contrasting worlds of urban industrial social relations.[17] Since the rise of urban-industrial society and European mass immigration in the nineteenth century created new metropolitan living spaces, populated by a broad diversity of peoples, Americans have departed from the traditional model for organizing life. In that model the family, often the extended family, was not only an affectional and communal household but also the basic economic and political unit in a society of small, homogeneous agricultural villages, in which there was no sharp distinction between public and private. During the nineteenth and twentieth centuries in America, however, public and private have come to be much more separated. In public life—government, politics, and the economy—where diverse peoples have been mixed together, there are both demands for cultural homogeneity and quite clear, if largely unstated, codes of respectable conduct and belief that have ultimately determined who would have access to power, status, and influence, and who would be excluded. In the private realm of family, kinship, neighborhood, and community, however, one has had the liberty to attempt to maintain one's own codes, which have been shaped historically by religion, ethnicity, and gender, but now increasingly also by age, sexual orientation, and marital status. Here one has had the opportunity not only to be different but even to hold in contempt the pretensions and demands of the public, mainstream culture. I have come to believe that American society has been free of revolutionary upheaval over the structure of wealth and power, because whatever the insults born in public by the successive waves of displaced newcomers, there have always been the sustaining consolations of a communal existence, forged out of common memory, tradition, experience, kinship, and the warm embrace of family.[18]

This is hardly a cause for national celebration, since in ordering society around cultural diversity rather than around social class, American development exchanged one set of conflicts for another, which has had to do with the especially volatile issues of manners, morals, and the boundaries of private and communal life. Moreover, in a democratic society of cultural islands, forging a sense of common purpose from a national ideology crafted by elites and an array of ambiguous patriotic symbols has never proved easy, even in the midst of our most dangerous crises. So my thinking establishes America, not as better, but instead as different from other developed Western nation-states.

But I must acknowledge, too, that lately I have come to understand that my warmest memories and desires have to do with personal experiences of the communal bonds it has been possible for Americans to forge within the pluralistic patterning of our social life. In recent years I have come consciously to cultivate a bicultural life. I have endeavored to become more Jewish. Jewishness in America has become a part of my scholarly project. To the extent my skepticism about religion allows, I have reembraced some of the central rituals of Judaism, lighting Sabbath candles, taking pleasure in the celebration of Jewish holidays with family and friends, and anticipating with emotions more powerful than I could ever have imagined my own son's bar mitzvah. I identify strongly with that segment of the Israeli peace movement that bases its politics upon an understanding of the Jewish ethical tradition. I have also allowed myself simultaneously to become a kind of American patriot. While rejecting nationalism and militarism, I have come to believe in the possibilities that this democratic society, with all its great and abiding imperfections, holds out for ordinary folk, Jews among them, to participate at once in improving the social order and in maintaining a grip on those things in their communal pasts that are most dear to them. These manipulations of the practice and meanings of politics, work, family, friendship, and community are the negotiations and renegotiations of American Jewishness and Jewish Americanness by which in adulthood I have been inventing a memory and cultural lineage to deepen the identity I received as a child and allowed to lie dormant as a youth. In its general outlines, this process of invention is really not very different for me, in the third generation, from what it was for my grandparents and then my parents when they undertook in the middle years of their own lives to situate themselves simultaneously within Jewish and American time and space. America makes such inventions possible, indeed legitimate; an abiding feeling for Jewishness, amidst the pressures of change and growth that tempt one to the loss of memory, makes them necessary.

I cannot claim that sitting in my grandparents' living room led automatically to my conception of American pluralistic society or of the place I myself wished to occupy within that society. Surely there was evidence there of the difference between the codes that have governed private and public life, of the frustrations and confusions that result when circumstances lead to the interpenetration of these spheres, and of the importance people attach to communal ties, which somehow lose little warmth in the presence of those quite real, abiding difficulties. The view of American pluralism at which I finally arrived does seem at the least to have been overdetermined by my own identity and past. To be sure, historians of other ethnic groups, whose ancestral migrations coincided with those of the Jews at the turn of this century, could certainly advance the same argument about the bicultural bases of American pluralism as the result of their own experiences, and some have done so.[19] But it takes nothing away from their claims to say that Jews have often made the case most forcefully, whether in the novels of Phillip Roth, or in the scholarly works of Herbert Gutman, Aileen Kraditor, and Ira Katznelson, from whom I have learned a great deal.[20]

In the Western experience Jews have been the archetypical masters of the tactics of social marginality and of cultural improvisation and invention, because for centuries in the diaspora, as a people apart and often powerless and vulnerable, we have found it necessary to master two codes of behavior and belief. Jews have anticipated great penalties throughout much of the history of the diaspora for being ignorant of the rules governing the public and the private or for confusing the two realms. Threatened continually with physical or cultural annihilation, people learn quickly to understand what competitors and enemies demand. The dangers and opportunities that mingle paradoxically in Jewish experience in the diaspora have forced us to sharpen our knowledge of ourselves and others. (It is not an accident that Jews, with their strong intuitions about what others wish to believe about themselves, have always been prominent in the United States in the movies, broadcasting, and advertising.)[21] Indeed it is a tribute to the paradoxes of life in the diaspora that we have known not only great tragedy there but also great bursts of bicultural creativity.[22] I speak not simply of the obvious: the work of many gifted people in the arts, scholarship, science, business, and the professions. I refer to those who are less well-known—ordinary people like my own extended family, whose cultural work has been creating a daily life along the frontiers of two realms of existence that brought them, though not without cost, a measure of dignity, security, and the pleasures of community. Perhaps there is no cure for the "two-ness" that is part of bicultural experience, or for the tensions and losses that seem inherent in that experience. Yet in light of what we have gained through our efforts in bonding Jewish and American identities, are we really sure we would take the cure if it were offered to us?

NOTES

I wish to express my gratitude for the suggestions of Art Efron, William Freehling, Rose Glickman, Alan M. Kraut, Georg Iggers, Orville Murphy, and Bruce Travis.

1. Abraham Cahan, *The Rise of David Levinsky* (New York: Harper, 1917).

2. David A. Gerber, "Cutting Out Shylock: Toward A Reconceptualization of the Origins of American Anti-Semitism," *Journal of American History* 69 (December, 1982): 615–37; David A. Gerber, *Anti-Semitism in American History* (Urbana: University of Illinois Press, 1986); and David A. Gerber, "Of Mice and Jews: Cartoons, Metaphors, and Recent American Jewish Experience," *American Jewish History* 77 (September, 1987): 159–75.

3. The concerns of American-Jewish historiography during its long primary period are well-summarized in Howard Rabinowitz, "Writing Jewish Community History," *American Jewish History* 70 (September, 1980): 119–27. Also see William Toll, "The 'New' Social History' and Recent Jewish Historical Writing," *American Jewish History* 69 (March, 1980): 325–7, 340–1.

4. Richard Hofstadter, *The Progressive Historians: Turner, Beard, Parrington* (New York: Random House, 1968), 37–8, 41, 52, 60, 188–9, 122–3, 156–7; Edward Saveth, *American Historians and European Immigrants, 1875–1925* (New York: Russell and Russell, 1948). At its best, this tradition could produce excellent histories, whatever its ultimate failures were in providing immigrants with a voice and with agency in their own behalf; see, e.g., Barbara Miller Solomon, *Ancestors and Immigrants: A Changing New England Tradition* (Cambridge: Harvard University Press, 1956); and Allen F. Davis, *Spearheads for Reform: Social Settlements and the Progressive Movement, 1890–1914* (New York: Oxford University, 1967), both of

which I encountered in graduate school and were part of my introduction to the study of immigrants.

5. Rabinowitz, "Writing Jewish Community History," 127; Jonathan Sarna, "Anti-Semitism and American History," *Commentary* (March 1981): 42; Oscar Handlin, "American Views of the Jew at the Opening of the Twentieth Century," *Publications of the American Jewish Historical Society* 40 (June, 1951): 323–45; and Oscar Handlin, *Adventure in Freedom: 300 Years of Jewish Life in America* (New York: McGraw Hill, 1954). In sharp contrast, see Michael N. Dobkowski, *The Tarnished Dream: The Basis of American Anti-Semitism* (Westport, Conn.: Greenwood Press, 1979), an example of recent revisionist scholarship that typically sees anti-Semitism as pervasive in every level of American society and present throughout the entire sweep of the American past.

6. Jews, particularly Jews of my generation, who came of age in the 1960s and 1970s, have been prominent in the writing of African-American history and the history of black-white relations; see August Meier and Elliott M. Rudwick, *Black History and the Historical Profession, 1915–1980* (Urbana: University of Illinois Press, 1986), 107–9, 143–44, 163–67, 179–80, 184–85, 294–95.

7. Park's was the notion of the ethnic as "Marginal Man"; see his "Human Migration and the Marginal Man," *American Journal of Sociology* 33 (May, 1928): 881–93; and thereafter, Everett Stonequist, *The Marginal Man: A Study in Personality and Culture Conflict* (New York: Scribner's, 1937); Arnold W. Green, "A Reexamination of the Marginal Man Concept," *Social Forces* 26 (December 1947): 167–71. The marginal man idea, as it was popularly understood, implied a negative view of ethnics, which led to criticism, especially from Jewish scholars; see, for example, David I. Golovensky, "The Marginal Man Concept: An Analysis and Critique," *Social Forces* 30 (March 1952): 333–39. In fairness to Park, however, a less well-understood and well-known aspect of this thesis concerned the positive, creative possibilities of marginality, as some other Jewish scholars also understood. For expression of the creative possibilities in "marginality," also see Georg Simmel, "The Stranger," in *The Sociology of Georg Simmel*, trans. and ed., Kurt H. Wolf, (Glencoe: Free Press, 1950), 402–8; David Reisman, *Individualism Reconsidered* (New York: Free Press, 1954), 153–78. Reisman's and Simmel's formulations of marginality clearly speak to the point I am making here.

8. Later published as David A. Gerber, *Black Ohio and the Color Line* (Urbana: University of Illinois Press, 1976).

9. W. E. Burghardt Du Bois, "Strivings of the Negro People," *Atlantic Monthly* 80 (August 1897): 194; Dickson D. Bruce, Jr., "W. E. B. Du Bois and the Idea of Double Consciousness," *American Literature* 64 (June 1992): 299–310.

10. David A. Gerber, "Peter Clark: Of Hope and Despair, Commitment and Ambivalence in the Life of a Black Leader," in *Black Leaders of the Nineteenth Century*, ed. August Meier and Leon Litwack, 173–90 (Urbana: University of Illinois Press, 1988).

11. Arthur Liebman, *Jews and the Left* (New York: Wiley, 1979), 559–87; Kirkpatrick Sale, *SDS* (New York: Random House, 1973), 88–90 and passim; Stanley Rothman and S. Robert Lichter, *Roots of Radicalism: Jews, Christians and the New Left* (New York: Oxford University Press, 1982). Kenneth Kenniston, *Young Radicals: Notes on Committed Youth* (New York: Harcourt, Brace, and World, 1968), providing the most intense psychological portrait of New Left activists, found Jews disproportionately

engaged (pp. 11–12) in radical politics, but did not develop a cultural dimension to its interpretation of the bases of activism. Also see n. 12, below.

12. Much of an entire issue of the *Journal of American History* is devoted to documenting and commenting upon these influences, the Jewish presence in which is easily detected; see the group of essays under the collective title "A Round Table: What Has Changed and Not Changed in American Historical Practice?" *Journal of American History* 76 (September 1989): 393–478, and among the essays represented therein, see especially Jonathan M. Weiner, "Radical Historians and the Crisis of American History," 399–434.

13. There was a variety of roots, disciplinary as well as political, of the New Social History, but the political ones gave not only much of the energy that the new history possessed but also many of the questions it addressed. See James B. Gardiner and George Rollie Adams, eds., *Ordinary People and Everyday Life: Perspectives on the New Social History* (Nashville: American Association for State and Local History, 1983); and Henry Abelove et al., eds., *Visions of History* (New York: Pantheon, 1984), as well as the collection "A Round Table: What Has Changed and Not Changed in American Historical Practice?"

14. John Higham, "The Cult of the 'American Consensus': Homogenizing Our History," *Commentary* (February 1959): 93–100; John Higham, "Beyond Consensus: The Historian as Moral Critic," *American Historical Review* 67 (April 1962): 609–25; John Higham, "Changing Paradigms: The Collapse of Consensus History," *Journal of American History* 76 (September 1989): 460–66.

15. In no single area of historical inquiry was this clearer than in labor history, and particularly in regard to the recent attempts to formulate a response to the time-honored question, Why is there no socialism in the United States? which has often been the point of departure for explaining the uniqueness of American historical development. See Eric Foner, "Why Is There No Socialism in the United States?" *History Workshop* 17 (Spring, 1984): 57–80; Sean Wilentz, "Against Exceptionalism: Class Consciousness and the American Labor Movement, 1790–1920," *International Labor and Working Class History* 26 (Fall, 1984): 1–4.

16. This project culminated in my writing *The Making of an American Pluralism: Buffalo, New York, 1825–1860* (Urbana: University of Illinois Press, 1989).

17. Ferdinand Tönnies, *Community and Society,* trans. Charles P. Loomis (New York: Harper, 1963); Thomas Bender, *Community and Social Change in America* (Baltimore: Johns Hopkins University Press, 1982, paperback).

18. Bender, *Community and Social Change in America,* 61–78; David J. Russo, *Families and Communities: A New View of American History* (Nashville: American Association for State and Local History, 1974), 14–51; Lawrence H. Fuchs, *The American Kaleidoscope: Race, Ethnicity, and the Civic Culture* (Hanover, N.H.: University Press of New England, 1990).

19. Michael Novak, *The Rise of the Unmeltable Ethnics* (New York: Macmillan, 1976); Richard Gambino, *Blood of My Blood: The Dilemma of the Italian American* (New York: Doubleday, 1974); John Bukoczyk, *And My Children Did Not Know Me: A History of Polish Americans* (Bloomington: Indiana University Press, 1986); John Duffy Ibson, *Will the World Break Your Heart? Dimensions and Consequences of Irish-American Assimilation* (New York: Garland Press, 1990).

20. Philip Roth, *Goodbye, Columbus and Five Short Stories* (Boston: Houghton

Mifflin Company, 1959), all of which stand as important testaments to bicultural dilemmas and opportunities, even after three decades. Herbert G. Gutman, "Work, Culture and Society in Industrializing America," *American Historical Review* 78 (June 1973): 531–88; Aileen Kraditor, *The Radical Persuasion, 1890–1917* (Baton Rouge: Louisiana State University Press, 1981); Ira Katznelson, *City Trenches: Urban Politics and the Patterning of Class in the United States* (New York: Pantheon, 1981).

21. Neal Gabler, *An Empire of Their Own: How the Jews Invented Hollywood* (New York: Crown Publishers, 1988); Daniel Pope and William Toll, "We Tried Harder: Jews in American Advertising," *American Jewish History* 72 (September 1982): 26–58; Frederick D. Sturdivant and Roy D. Adler, "Executive Origins: Still a Gray Flannel World? *Harvard Business Review* 54 (November-December 1976): 127.

22. The dean of Jewish history in the United States, Salo Baron, contended for many years against the "lachrymose conception" of postbiblical Jewish history as "a protracted nightmare of trial and suffering," and invited us to see the wide variety of Jewish accomplishments in the diaspora; see Baron, *Social and Religious History of the Jews,* rev. ed. (New York: Columbia University Press, 1957), 6:232–34; and Baron, *Historians and Jewish History* (Philadelphia: Jewish Publication Society, 1964), 88–89.

8

Circumscriptions

Assimilating T. S. Eliot's Sweeneys

Rachel Blau DuPlessis

WHERE WAS I positioned as a [Jew]? Where did I stand? A little atheist, a reader, whose difference—in the contexts in which I grew up—was intellectualism (that was the religion), was secular humanism (as the positive vanguard). The universalism of ethics, the promise of assimilation of all differences (unseemly disequilibriums) made any particularity theoretically unmarked, although all were covertly active—class, race, religious culture, gender. I had no temple, no Hebrew, no Jewish holidays (one rare Pesach), no mandated joys or despairs of a traditional spirituality—to be a Jew was too normal, too (I hesitate here) déclassé.

Class narratives infected both sides of the family. My maternal grandmother identified with the Hapsburg Empire; three of her four daughters became Christian. My paternal grandfather, Joel Blau, the rabbi, the elegant Hungarian, quipped, when someone's necklace of pearls broke in synagogue and rolled toward his sermon, that he thought he was "the only one casting pearls." Such a man would not have lasted long at any one congregation; he did not, and then he died, in 1927 at forty-nine, having wandered among congregations in New York City, Trenton, Rochester, and finally, briefly at West London Synagogue. He was eulogized in the *New Palestine* as "the Hebrew Aristocrat"; his essays in modern Hebrew helped point to its literary possibilities during debates about the "national" language for Palestine.[1] He was absolutely disdainful of *yiddishkeit* for its class connotations, as was my British-Jewish grandmother, Rachel Woolf, who referred to the Yiddish-speaking, Eastern European, Jewish immigrants to London in the 1890s as "those foreigners."

Still, about a hundred Yiddish words floated through my childhood on my mother's lips, including phrases which I hear now as shadowy comments on the Holocaust—*gunnish hilfin* (*gornisht helfin*—can't do anything about it); *chaserei* and *tsuris* (filth and trouble), *gefeyrlach* (dangerous, terrible), and *mishigas* (madness, craziness). The Holocaust was the great shadow; I developed my own relationship with it, with Anne Frank's the first dead hand I clasped. I later walked, in lightly falling snow, up the single line of train tracks to Dachau.

My father was a scholar of American philosophy and religion who weaned himself from traditional or even Reform Judaism for reasons to some degree involved with family narratives and interior exile, to some degree from a lack of conviction in Jewish beliefs and practices, but to a large measure from a principled intellectual commitment to transcendent liberalism. He, however, read Hebrew, was conversant with and wrote on Jewish history, philosophy, and religion. He was, in fact, a secular rabbi. He was, his obituary says, "one of the first Jews in the emerging field of [university-based, academic] religious studies"; a number of his books were explicitly on American Judaism. Yet Jewish identity (in a familial or personal sense) existed for him, I think, only as a thick burden from the past; he was a utopian, a Deweyan; he wanted new social practices. He still wanted to be one of the Chosen People, but differently.

Thus (yet it does not really follow) I was brought up as an explicit secular humanist in the Ethical Culture movement, and this produced a marginality even more astonishing than Judaism might have. With my father's encouragement, I acted against the aggressive (right-wing Christian) religiosity that afflicted the 1950s, in principled struggle. My ten- and eleven-year-old child-self refused to say grace in school, refused school prayer, when little heads were bowing right and left all around me. To this day, I cannot say "under God" in the Pledge of Allegiance, a phrase added during that sanctimonious time.

The conjunction of two aspects of the Jewish Enlightenment marked me: intellectual mastery and reason in the hegemonic world, and nonparticipation in Jewish particularism. The ugly furor of the McCarthy era I could decode at the time as involving anti-Semitism as well as antiprogressivism. The Rosenberg executions, the imagination of volts of electricity searing, were like a personal displacement of the Holocaust. I am still only a [Jew], although I would identify only *as* a Jew. Or, as I say in a poem, a "J–w." In fact I have repeatedly questioned my place in this anthology. Except that the struggles around social justice, tolerance, and especially feminism were brightened, for me, by a light, an aura from Judaism. Except I have a post-Holocaust identity as confronting (though one never can) an ineffable enormity that Happened (with many Agents) to many persons, some just like myself. Post-Holocaust writers—Paul Celan, Edmund Jabès, Primo Levi, George Oppen—I read as a significant core of my cultural and ontological identity. My current poetry makes many allusions to Jewish materials—Yiddish words, Old Testament narratives like Jacob and the Angel, midrashic form, self-commenting questions, as well as allusions to the concentration camps. I take it that the only apt cultural ambition is to speak from a posthumous site, to speak as if yours were the only shard that would be rescued, to speak in the medium "anguage." This poetics clearly bears the marks of its origins.

Certain questions about Jewishness confronted with liberal culture were activated for me in a peculiar, repressed, and embarrassing moment at the height of New Criticism, in college (the approximate date is 1961; the site is an urban women's college with a high proportion of Jews attending). I was being taught how properly to consume T. S. Eliot's work. Which was, in brief, to discount as inappropriate certain questions (I think I tried to ask them) about the very words which were most disturbing to me. It was Eliot's line from "Gerontion," a meditative poem spoken by an old man in a "decayed house," a "rented house," that awakened me the most. He said, "And the jew squats on the window sill, the owner, / Spawned in some estaminet of Antwerp. . . . "[2] What was the shock? Was it the small *j* on "Jew," a habit which only much later Eliot gave up?[3] Was it the insult of "squats" (because "merds," a nearby word, and other refuse are very much at issue)? Or was it the slimy and animalistic "spawned"? You understand, there are still all sorts of ways to justify these and similar lines in early Eliot. It might be said that the poem is spoken from a "persona": the poet "does not necessarily mean" what "the mask" is saying. But the words, once spoken, enter into the cultural airwaves. And some kind of cultural diagnosis is absolutely at issue here and throughout early Eliot. He certainly means something by what he invents or marshals about Jews. Or—another justification—if some specific anti-Semitic remark is acknowledged as present in these lines, it is said to be local, not constitutive, and anyway, if prejudice existed, it was given up, in the main, when Eliot turned to a formal Anglican confession.[4]

Yet even these helpful, embarrassed arguments were not adequate to this task. For this task of reading demanded the repression of my uneasy, suspicious sensations of his unfairness, of his prejudice, of my being fingered for something of which I thought I was innocent. Sheer difference. Does not a Jew (as does a Christian, a Buddhist, even an atheist enlightenment [Jewish] womanish-girl reading) squat, spawn, also bleed, and so forth? In the loss of particularities, differences, and markers, would we not find what joined us as human? Could we not then unite? This was the noble one-world ethos in which I was raised. "[Emanicipation] strove to eliminate the provincial particulars of Judaism and to discover those elements of rational religion upon which all reasonable men could unite."[5] So it didn't matter because it wasn't supposed to matter; such a word, such a little word with a little letter on it was buried there, and couldn't possibly evoke or mean to Eliot all the suspicions and estrangements I brought to the reading and then, as quickly, repressed. Insofar as I am a daughter of the Jewish Enlightenment, I had a stake in certain values—Learning, Aestheticization, and Self-realization: the modernization of the individual, the acquisition of "Western aesthetic norms in literature as in daily behavior." Benjamin Harshav speaks of the years in which Enlightenment was embraced (as a means of struggle against prejudice and social hatred) as a "watershed in the history of Jewish culture and consciousness."[6] It certainly was such for a female; one cannot imagine finding consolation of any kind in the texts and practices of Jewish misogyny.

Liberal humanism fused with Jewish Enlightenment and emancipation bore me; New Criticism undid me. My questions about Eliot were tamped down, "What should I resent?" But there was still a residue left over, a smudge whose trace I want here to pursue. The smudge is in myself, and it is still palpable, though long repressed. In assimilating T. S. Eliot, there was certainly a flare of embarrassment for him, this enormous cultural hero (as we then saw it). Such heroes have to be protected—and most emphatically by young women trying to be good—from the ravishments of their announced hatreds. And literature under the heroic aegis of the great men Yeats and Eliot and James served us as secular cult: the objects of yearnings for certainties, the objects, in brief, of religious yearnings. Thus we did not question Culture; it was our most compelling form of monotheism. We lived in the florid assertion of one-ness—one world, one nation, one time—thus missing and suppressing discontinuities, margins, double determinations. Genius was also "one": the promulgation of the artist as isolated, unique, asocial, total, and intact.

Further, New Criticism, the pedagogic movement that isolated the literary artifact for its formalist values, did not easily bend to accommodate traces of social meaning within poetry, or indeed, even within fiction; it discredited as lesser those literary materials most tied to social representation (the realist novels of Howells or Wharton, as opposed to the more aestheticized James, for example). No doubt it was a way of not seeing or not saying the 1930s, or any kind of Marxist reading of literature. Context, polemic, rhetoric, social force fields, and cultural production were all zoned, bleached; we mainly treated art as received wisdom, produced by artists about whom an occasional, and folkloric, biographical fact was admitted, usually a disparaging and acontextual one—Yeats believing in spirits, that kind of thing. Silly biography was a displacement from a sense of rich social context as a determinant. It was a funny time, frozen with unexpressed fear.

Were New Criticism and our carefully received reading strategies in some way complicit with the ravishing loss of Jewish particularity? My reading strategy of induced repression might even be a version of what Sander Gilman has called Jewish self-hatred. This is the displacement to "another Jewish Other" of the negative stereotypes and prejudices attached to Jews in general. A Jew faced with "jews squatting" might accept the charge and assimilate herself to the powerful speaker of the insults, while the powerless object of the insults is distanced, displaced to another Jew—to the speaker of Yiddish, to the immigrant from Eastern Europe (Poland and Russia rather than Germany), to the others as snarling reeking parvenus, as materialist and grasping.[7] There were certainly more than traces of Jewish self-hatred in what I can reconstruct from certain members of my family (though three of the four grandparents had died before I was born; direct access was sealed). But in fact, the family ethos was more a transcendent sense of moral and intellectual superiority tied precisely to the overlooking of prejudice, taken as a sign of other people's inferiority. I have heard this strategy noted, as well, by people of African descent.

What happened in college to my reading manner confirms Gilman's analysis of the "secret language" or the bilingualism of groups "othered" in various ways. All "others" therefore are at pains constantly to stress their ability to understand, to write, on levels more complex, more esoteric, more general, and more true than do those treating them as " 'inarticulate Jews.' "[8] While I do not feel that little "me" was overtly self-hating—perhaps because I was more a [Jew] than a Jew—I understand the response as consistent with the self-hatred that Gilman probes: "claiming special abilities in the discourse of the reference group. . . . "[9] One repressed information discontinuous with New Criticism as the "discourse of the reference group."

Liberal culture was an agreement. If Eliot, if Pound violated it, if "jews squat" in their works, this fact drew from us a compensatory allowance, a genteel tolerance which was disinterested to the point of self-effacing magnanimity. Proving that we were better than the very cultural figures in whom we invested—we might even, by that tolerance, offer that culture an example of its own ideals.[10] Proving that we could be trusted with their invective, using reading strategies to filter and sweeten these letters. Tolerant— to the point of what? of ignorance? of innocence of what those words might really mean in other contexts? Tolerant, in any event, to a fault. Such an act of forcible repression, the recoil *in* noticing, and then the recoil *from* noticing "the rat is underneath the piles / the jew is underneath the lot" bespeaks, perhaps, a hyperexaggerated mimicry of Arnoldian premises of sweetness and light while we were being treated to one dingy erosion of its promises.

The mechanism of prejudice Eliot used in several notable, much-anthologized poems bears examination. "Sweeney Among the Nightingales" and "Burbank with a Baedeker: Bleistein with a Cigar" from his *Poems 1920* were termed "intensely serious," and "among the best that I have ever done."[11] Sweeney and Bleistein are part of the human menagerie of humeral creatures whose traits and interactions Eliot was anatomizing in early works, with their propensity to the deeply parodic.[12] *In toto,* Eliot's characters are animated by something like the impulse of Sinclair Lewis in his 1922 *Babbitt:* satiric social anatomy.[13]

> Apeneck Sweeney spreads his knees
> Letting his arms hang down to laugh,
> The zebra stripes along his jaw
> Swelling to maculate giraffe.

I am going to start with a primerlike simplicity. Sweeney is an Irish name, and he evokes an Irish stereotype. In both England and America in the latter half of the nineteenth century, the Irish had passed, in popular consideration, from depictions making them into simple peasants, feckless, sometimes witty drunks, to—apes. They were depicted visually as simianized figures with flat nose, long projecting lip, sloping forehead, and forward jutting jaw. In "historical physiognomy," the angle of the forehead (high versus sloping) and the jutting of the jaw offer visual coding for intelligence and superiority or the opposite, stupid inferiority—something based loosely on a sense of species evolution. As "species" went, the Irish were subhuman, "white chimpanzees." This mid-Victorian stereotype of the savage or simian Irishman, "the gorilla metaphor[,] cropped up often after the outbreak of rebellion in 1916, followed by the Anglo-Irish guerrilla war of 1919–21."[14] So Sweeney seems like a postrebellion emergence of long-standing cultural materials involving threats to hegemony.

But ape-necked, spotted or freckled, and therefore perhaps "Irish" as Sweeney is, he is also spotted or polluted, animallike, a giraffe or a zebra. With his apish posture—or is it a strained vision of a vaudeville singer, a Charleston dancer, a minstrel?—and with the geographical origin of these animals in mind, it seems equally likely to see him as "African." Houston Baker has alerted us to the encoded presence of blacks in this kind of ape/animal metaphor.[15] Sweeney may then allude to the African and African-American presence in early modernism, ambivalently viewed: the Harlem Renaissance in America; the use of African art as an inspiration for cubism and artistic innovation; jazz clubs and the sensual license that any new popular music encodes. Sweeney's guarding of "the hornèd gate" may even draw upon the debate over black troops used in World War I, their presence as the barbarian within the gates parallels the image used by Eliot at the poignant, elegiac climax of his poem. This suggestive convergence of despisable groups I take to be a very significant moment, both ideologically for Eliot and critically for us. By the use of these evocations, Eliot builds a shimmering undertext, constructing an interplay of veiled and tacit social suggestions which also have a way of being self-denying—the figure is not "really" Irish, not "really" African.

This personage is surrounded by a set of lowlifes out of Rick's in *Casablanca* or the cabaret scene in *Star Wars:* drunk, out of control, sinister. Many of these folk are sexualized female characters, whorish and slattern. A woman falls off Sweeney's lap, into a revealing tarty pose. Another Jewish woman trying perhaps to "pass" as non-Jew—one "Rachel *née* Rabinovitch"—is spotlighted as piggish and aggressive; her "murderous paws"—exaggerated in their object, a bunch of grapes—continue the animal motif and the sense of threat.[16] New woman–Jew woman–lewd woman are peculiarly intertwined. Here as elsewhere in Eliot, insurgent females, rank sexuality, and the cunningly animalistic are fused. The "silent vertebrate in brown," an onlooker, is attracted and yet withdraws; his back-and-forth movement forms the center of the poem: tempted by the two whorish women, yet declining the "gambit"; exiting, yet found "leaning in" at the window with a "golden grin."[17] This one—a peculiar fusion of "brown" man (with the "grin" of stereotyped representations of Negroes) and the poet himself—seems to be deciding whether to be an animal or a distanced, but implicated, voyeur. In fact, Eliot here produces an image of himself as a minstrel, if not in blackface (as his characters are in *Sweeney Agonistes*) at least in brown suit. This zoo is apparently, by its creatures' very obliviousness, dishonoring triumphant moments of high culture: the Convent of the Sacred Heart, Agamemnon's sexualized vulnerable death, the traditional heroic and martyred. "Dishonored" is the word that Eliot proposes at the end of the poem for the fate of the European tradition.[18]

What is encoded? The question demands a plural answer. Sweeney is a white Negro, or a "maculate" (stained/blackened) white, offering some intertwining of two commonplace simian stereotypes for the primitive louts that are somehow, barbarously, at—or inside—the gates. The sexual triumph (like that of "Sweeney Erect") is apparent and posed in the most degrading terms: sex is coterminous with a low drunkeness, prostitution, and strange positions. The social triumph may be in destabilizing imperial claims (the Irish Sweeney) or in displacing Eurocentric culture (the Christian Church and Agamemnon figure displaced by black Sweeney).

Thus Sweeney is a multiracialized figure with sexual-social implications. He is a figure who encodes attitudes toward threatening races and groups who are (in terms the poem proposes) beneath Culture in one sense while exhibiting a lurid, complete, and tempting culture of pleasure, avariciousnes, and sadism. In yet another poem, the simian has achieved a Darwinian and sexual "ascent."[19] Sweeney is then also a lowerclass Englishman—"Sweeney Erect"—in ambiguous sexual-social triumph.[20] So while any Sweeney is clearly "white" in Eliot's poems, this male lout has been coded in both a class and also a multiracialized fashion.[21] In the playlet *Sweeney Agonistes*, the Sweeney figure is one of the businessmen who visit the British demimondaines; these Babbitts break into a minstrel show as "Tambo and Bones" and sing a primitivizing song, as whites in blackface. Sweeney further speaks of a lurid cannibal urge to kill and dismember women in a ritual manner, a primitivizing image which slides over to cartoon African.[22] It is clear that the Sweeney figure embodies Eliot's terrific and mobile *ressentiment*—and admiring jealousy. The primitive is admired and deplored; it destroys and revitalizes. It is sexually potent and culturally active.

But the balance shifts when Jews are added. I bring in Jews via the second poem under consideration, finding the figure of Bleistein an extension of the Sweeney figure by comparison of their postures of presentation. In the one poem, we have seen how "Apeneck Sweeney spreads his knees / Letting his arms hang down to laugh." There is a matching posture in "Burbank with a Baedeker: Bleistein with a Cigar": Bleistein's "saggy bending of the knees / And elbows." The posture (similarly apish and minstrel) also makes him *krum*, or crooked and bent, a stereotype of the Jew.[23] One might argue that Sweeney is the black and Irish Bleistein; Bleistein is the Jewish Sweeney. In the main figures of these two poems, poems linked in his own mind as important work, Eliot has made metonymies, linked chains of stereotype.[24] These chains are fused through gender fears: whether erect or *krum,* this sexualized lout triumphs over women. Like the lout and his crew in "Sweeney among the Nightingales," in this poem "Jew" is proposed as the antonym of real culture (classical, sacred, invested with magnificence) by virtue of beast-like, cosmopolitan, and rootless qualities.[25] Eliot's erasure of Jewish learning *as* culture (there is no Jewish Burbank here) is especially rankling. Bleistein may suggest the fullest development of Sweeney, in a continuum of urban horrors. Or the Bleistein figure may embody far worse cultural suggestions of real decay and destabilization. T. S. Eliot can circumscribe and even admire elements of Sweeney, but he is circumscribed by Bleistein and his denizens.[26]

Our British or American gentleman, the plain Jamesean tourist Burbank, has fallen into the sexual and/or cultural clutches of a Venetian and venereal "princess," voluptuous and wolfish Princess Volupine, while the poem makes sounds which resemble the barge scene in *The Waste Land:* "Her shuttered barge / Burned on the water all the day." Sexual deregulation of women, impotence of men, and failing historical hegemony are linked. Indeed, the regulation of women and gender to achieve male potency and social health is a point that will be repeated numerous times in many modernist texts.

The poem has a pastiched epigraph whose exaggerated, feminized, "gay" language contrasts with the stolid quatrains of the poem.[27] A homosexual turn of language (campy pastiche), filled with an exciting and mysterious het-eroglossia, seems to offer but brackets another position besides that of the onlooker Burbank from which this material could be judged—the position of gossipy scandalmonger. This position, it appears, does not lead to cultural critique, but to a renewed complicity. Eliot, in contrast, proposed the poems critically. "Logopoeia"—a rhetoric of heteroglossia, ironic swings, combined social levels and registers, esoteric diction—is used by Eliot in these quatrain poems to signal a critical rupture of poetic practice from debased romanti-cisms and from sexualities considered debased. Logopoeia can function in his work as an attack on the effete and the feminine.[28]

The paralyzed observer, Burbank, is contrasted with the tourist Bleistein.

> But this or such was Bleistein's way:
> A saggy bending of the knees
> And elbows, with the palms turned out,
> Chicago Semite Viennese.
>
> A lustreless protrusive eye
> Stares from the protozoic slime
> At a perspective of Canaletto.
> The smoky candle end of time
>
> Declines. On the Rialto once.
> The rats are underneath the piles.

The Jew is underneath the lot.
   Money in furs. The boatman smiles,

Princess Volupine extends
   A meagre, blue-nailed, phthisic hand
To climb the waterstair. Lights, lights,
   She entertains Sir Ferdinand

Klein.[29]

The female predator, and possibly prostitute, Volupine is located between two horrible Jews—an American immigrant ("Chicago Semite Viennese") so low in the evolutionary scale that he mimics "protozoic slime," and a European ("Sir Ferdinand Klein"), perhaps a banker and certainly a Rothschild figure.[30] This double Jew displaces Burbank sexually, economically, and culturally.[31]

Bleistein does not possess anything in a directly sexual way (though his -ay rhymes take over Volupine's), but his posture, protrusions, and slime defile a depiction of Venice by his very gaze. Mr. Bleistein and his "slime" is another kind of Sweeney; he is the classic stereotyped "sheeney," economically and sexually parasitic.[32] For slime, swampiness, fungus, and other things that are somehow overfertile and verminous at once are all affiliated, in many representations, with the Jew. Robert Casillo has traced this set of images in his study of Ezra Pound, for whom the Jew became, finally, an "ultimate contamination."[33] Casillo notes (in a chapter about the regressive sexuality of slime/swamp) how slime indicates sexual promiscuity, borderlessness, and the rejection of "patriarchal restriction and authority."[34]

Our Chicago Jew, taxed with both evolutionary (protozoic) lowness and apishness, is also, as slime, a figural representation of the (tainted) spermatic discharge of a marked or circumcised penis.[35] His prop, the cigar, one is amused thereupon to notice, is a smoke that has had its tip cut off. Despite Burbank's attempts at sexual-cultural possession and assertion, he is circumscribed by the circumcised. Venice/Volupine has, in both forms, been whored, and by Jews. Her immorality and decline and Burbank's belatedness in visiting her seem peculiarly intertwined. Sexual contact with Volupine (which Burbank apparently has had) opens him to a taint, a disease, an infection both sexually and culturally destructive.

For if Burbank has been unmanned by indulging in sensual bliss, he has also been frightened by fears of infection. The poem seems to be a late reflection of a discourse surrounding syphilis, which was a social and medical issue in the 1890s, "at the precise moment," as Elaine Showalter reminds us, "when arguments over the future of marriage, discussions of the New Women, and decadent homosexual culture were at their peak."[36] In European literatures, syphilis had different discursive nodules. Eliot's poem reflects two: Fear of the foreign prostitute as carrier of the disease and scapegoat for male sexual anxieties; in Eliot's poem the prostitute is displaced upward to a diseased princess. And the second was the metaphor of the Jew as carrier. As Jay Geller tracks this, "historical, structural, and representational connections are drawn between Jews and syphilis, usually through the mediation of representations of the prostitute. . . . ; in the early twentieth century syphilis became indelibly associated with Jews."[37]

The Sweeney/sheeney Irish ape, black or blackface vaudevillean reaches the climax of horror as an animalistic Jew. For the Jew has been seen throughout popular and literary representations as prone to crimes of indecency, filth, and immorality.[38] Sexual offenses and offensiveness were central to early twentieth-century conceptions of Jewishness. Jews had, it was alleged, a peculiar propensity to sexual crimes such as pimping; the 1909 Dillingham Commission in America reported on the white slave crimes of Hebrews—"offenses against chastity and in connection with prostitution." This specific American provocation is superadded to the centuries-long sexualized discourse concerning circumcision, blood taint, syphilis, the cosmopolitan, and the blurring of binary sexual difference; Jews are the center and collection point of these materials.[39]

Princess Volupine herself is fundamentally diseased. The rare word "phthisic" literally means "tubercular," and her disease is consumption in several figurative ways. She consumes, with her interest in acquisition (which explains her alliance with Jews and bankers), and she consumes men. But in her diseased state she is also a displaced symptom of the blood poisoning and syphilis, widely represented as related to Jews and constituting their primary ineradicable taint. Again and again (as in the veiled metonymy sick-phthisic-syphilitic), Eliot works by rhetorical and connotative displacements and slightly refigured versions of cultural materials (stereotypes, "prejudices," etc.), building an ideological undertext by veiled traces, trailers, or tacit suggestions. When Burbank falls into Volupine's clutches, he will have been tainted by all her diseased former consorts. He will be Jewified: diseased, unmanned; like Agamemnon, given a mortal blow in the most intimate place. Syphilis, or sexual (consuming) disease, is part of Eliot's analysis that cultural and historical decay enters through the lower body, the lower orders or classes, and less-than-human people.

The Venetian lion itself has been fleeced and "flea'd" (verminized) by association with Jews. And "The smoky candle end of time / Declines." The pun on Klein, who is one de-kleining conjugation of the verb "to jew," is made textually. And it is also made by boxing the rhyme word "Declines" and the rhyme word "Klein" in a rich and strange prosodic position at the very end of a sentence, but doubly enjambed over a line break and at the very beginning of a new quatrain. These are the only two words to be so treated in all of Eliot's contemporaneous quatrain poems: decline and the Jew are prosodically fused in the deep poetic texture.

To the other Jew, Sir Klein, a (be)knighted person, the word "piles" is attached. Now "piles," of course, means "the posts driven into a marshy (slimy) part of a river, or supports for a dock," and offers a sinister waterfront scene compounded of vermin and commerce. But "piles" magnetizes an array of other interesting definitions, from "spikes, darts, shafts"; to "heaps of things"; to "heaps of money"; to "minting (money-making) apparatuses"; to "downy hairy wool," itself a pubic trope (recalling, in Woolf's *The Years,* the epiphany around the hair of the Jew in the bath). Finally, one understands "piles" as a disease of the lower rectum, or hemorrhoids. Money and lower body materials are hereby allied. The fascinating and disgusting Jewish body, activated by the deep connotations of a word, offers figures through which Eliot made a statement about the slimy, verminous control by Jews of "the lot," that is, of everything. This is again familiar material in anti-Semitic discourse.

For during the late nineteenth and early twentieth centuries, Jews had a heavy discursive burden even beyond the sexual crimes of the circumcised penis: they were seen as swindlers, as criminal, crass, aggressive, dishonest, parasitic: their economic deceit and their tribalism, coupled with their inexplicable (animal or intuitive) energy, led to the endlessly deployed working postulate of their transnational economic conspiracy. For instance, the list of cities and cultures, nouns and adjectives, in apposition around Bleistein ("Chicago Semite Viennese") uses metonymy, and the lack of commas, forcefully to represent the stereotyped rootlessness and shifting allegiances of the Jew. Depictions of Jews—in James, Norris, Wharton, by early social scientists, as well as in the theater and in popular novels—showed Jews as financial manipulators, hook-nosed vultures, unproductive and opportunistic middlemen, ignorant consumers and exploiters of culture, philistine yet cosmopolitan.[40] In the poem, both the Shylock allusion to the Rialto and the hemistich "Money in furs" stand for this; Eliot draws upon the sexual and somatic and the economic tropes constructing Jews.

Eliot's Jew "underneath the lot" is also a double political statement. The Jew is the lowest of the low, scurrying around in that low space with rodents, beneath contempt. Yet "underneath the lot" intimates the most controlling, basic and primary, a prime-mover. That strange lowest-highest image of inexplicable power is one with which we are familiar from analysis of the representations of women; the fact that it seems self-contradictory does not mean it is self-canceling.

"Underneath the lot" might also have had some particular suggestiveness in 1920, and in the years just before. For it was in that year that *The Protocols of the Elders of Zion,* a notable forgery, achieved English translation and wide circulation. These documents inform their readership that a secret Jewish conspiracy called the Kahal threatened the world. This set of materials, variously translated into the European languages between 1903 and through the 1940s, suggests that there is a secret Jewish government with a well-articulated plan to achieve world domination, taking over gentile states by fomenting political unrest, subverting morality, and inciting to class warfare.[41] Norman Cohn points out that "in Britain there had been talk of a Jewish world-conspiracy for a couple of years before the Protocols appeared [translated in 1920]"; it was fueled by a very literate and presumably informed response to the Bolshevik revolution.[42] Thus it is more than plausible, as J. A. Morris argues, that the impact of this conspiracy theory on Eliot is registered in the poems he wrote in 1918 and 1919.

Again, as with the Irish and black materials, the poem works a condensation of a long-standing or chronic set of stereotypes with a recently triggered activization of the materials in the post–World War I period.[43] It was Eliot's "seriousness" to offer, in metaphor, metonymy, prosodic choices, and deep connotations, a condensed social debate drawing on discourses of the Semite, prevalent in the United States in Eliot's youth in every site from dime novels for boys to sociological analysis and scholarship, and present in the England of his chosen residence. He may, indeed, have been condensing two distinct periods of anti-Semitism—the period of his youth, which had a certain anti-Jewish sentiment expressed as a wariness of teeming hordes of immigrants (and in American discourses, syphilis was linked to the rising tide of such immigrants); and the interwar period with its anti-Semitism of the European other, scapegoat for the pain and disorder of that time, focus of political anxiety about failing hegemony and social change. As I have already shown, this "Semite" does not stand alone, but is part of Eliot's multistranded depiction of a composite social figure. Jews are very much at stake in the Sweeney-Bleistein material, but they are not the exclusive recipient of animus.

Eliot's subtle uses of ideologically charged materials and chronic cultural stereotypes in the poetic texture (by allusion, metonymy, prosodic placement) create what I am calling circumscriptions. I mean by this not only a pun on circumcision, or observations about the euphemism and circumlocution (evasive writing) with which liberal culture greeted this material, but also Eliot's tactic, his way of rejecting "ideas" in poetry by appealing to a concatenation of ideology sometimes pitched too low for ears to hear. Eliot was, in his early work, trying to find and to negotiate a line between poetry of ideas (which he rejected) and poetry of ideology (which he embraced): overt espousal versus subtle deployment.[44] Circumscriptions would be the enclosure of "ideas"— disparaging tropes about race, gender, class, religious culture—in poetic texture in such a way as to deny their existence by means of a subtle undertext involving prosodies, metonymies, displacements, and refigurations.

The fusing of racialized, ethnic/nationalistic, and Semitic tropes in one figure or in a compound Sweeney-Bleistein made an ideological amalgam which could not be taxed with the imposition of one capital-letter idea, such as "The Jew." Hence even the charge of anti-Semitism was mystified and intermittent in commentary on T. S. Eliot. When Jews, the Irish, and other immigrants gained access to America, when the northward migration of blacks began, their presence appeared dangerously and damagingly destabilizing. Former inheritors imagined themselves entering a diasporic space. Eliot used a Protestant hymn stanza and a logopoeic diction of intellectual superiority to suggest the shift of his lot from inheritor to disinherited, displaced by some metonymic amalgam of difference which is greedy, murderous, and female; vacuous, diseased, and subhuman; phallic, simian, and triumphant: the Sweeney-sheeney, the Irish ape, the maculate African, the grasping Rachel, the Hebrew slime— all these representations bound and connected by the summary "The Jew is underneath the lot," in which the Jew functions not only in and for himself but also as a rude characterization of Semiticized, racialized, ethnic, class, and gender materials. The erosion of a "pure" America or a "pure" Europe by Jews and other peoples in diaspora radically displaced the Burbank figure into or as the shadow Jew, parallel to that figure haunting Henry Adams or Ezra Pound.[45] Burbank is wandering, expatriated, disenfranchised; he has become nomad, or no man. Eliot rejects the "powerlessness" of this figure, its call to refigure boundaries, its minoritization. His intention is to culture "us" to assimilate him. Culture—and especially religious culture—was indeed, as I have argued, the site of struggle. But his interests and mine cannot be made the same. Caricature has to be ruptured; diaspora embraced, with all its contradictory pulls, including the ironies of enlightenment and particularism. Willy-nilly, I become one version of that Rachel, tearing, after a murderous pause.

NOTES

I want to express my gratitude to various members of my father's family, particularly my uncles Clarence and Raphael, for telling me some of the stories for which I belatedly appealed. They are not responsible for what I have written here. In addition, this chapter was heard by The Columbia Seminar in American Studies; there, Jack Diggins, Louise Yelin, and Laurie and Barry Goldensohn contributed insights. Carl Schorske honored me by reading this with the lambent illumination for which he is famous and offering his own memories of assimilating Eliot. And at Temple, Miles Orvell, my colleague in American literature, made some piercing remarks challenging my (possible) recuperation of Eliot in this chapter

1. Reuben Brainin, "The Hebrew Aristocrat: An Epitaph on the Grave of Joel Blau," *New Palestine* (November 18, 1927): 394 and 406.

2. This is the opening poem in Eliot's *Poems 1920*. "Estaminet" means "small, somewhat nasty, café."

3. Eliot began using capitals for "Jew" only in the 1940s; see Christopher Ricks, *T. S. Eliot and Prejudice* (Berkeley: University of California Press, 1988). This is an important and frustrating book. Ricks deplores Eliot's anti-Semitism, yet his essential attitude is an ironized, hurt tolerance: "let he who is without sin [in this case, prejudice] cast the first stone." Eliot, he argues, makes you think about your own collusions with prejudice. Ricks traces rhetoric, nuance, undertexts, allusions, but does not link these to social debates and discourses endemic in European and American culture.

4. Eliot's racial and anti-Semitic prejudices are fully visible in the notorious *After Strange Gods,* whose arguments, made to a southern audience in 1933, support homogeneous populations and "blood kinship" as crucial for effective tradition, and dismiss "excessive tolerance." His overt attack on "free-thinking Jews" matches a covert attack

on blacks, who may "adulterate" the desired homogeneity. The book was never republished after its initial appearance in 1934. *After Strange Gods: A Primer of Modern Heresey* (New York: Harcourt Brace, 1934), citations on 20 and 19.

5. Joseph L. Blau, *The Story of Jewish Philosophy* (New York: Random House, 1962), 261.

6. Benjamin Harshav, *The Meaning of Yiddish* (Berkeley: University of California Press, 1990), has a succinct analysis of the paradoxes of Enlightenment Judaism (120–22), citations from 120 and 122.

7. I draw, of course, on Sander L. Gilman, "What Is Self-Hatred?" in *Jewish Self-Hatred: Anti-Semitism and the Hidden Language of the Jews* (Baltimore: John Hopkins University Press, 1986).

The snarling and reeking is a veiled citation from *The Education of Henry Adams: An Autobiography* (New York: Random, 1990). " . . . [Adams] had become an estray; a flotsam or jetsam of wreckage; a belated reveller, or a scholar-gipsy like Matthew Arnold's. His world was dead. Not a Polish Jew fresh from Warsaw or Cracow,—not a furtive Yacoob or Ysaac still reeking of the Ghetto, snarling a weird Yiddish to the officers of the customs,—but had a keener instinct, an intenser energy, and a freer hand than he,—American of Americans, with Heaven knew how many Puritans and Patriots behind him, and an education that had cost a civil war" (In chapter 16, called "The Press," 938). When Adams wants to characterize late nineteenth-century greed and capitalist expansion, he says that in their worship of money they were worse off than the ancient Hebrews (1020).

8. Gilman, "What Is Self-Hatred?" 15.

9. Gilman, "What Is Self-Hatred?" 19. I will mention another charge that could be levied: that assimilation itself is a symptom of Jewish self-hatred. This seems wrong because it compels participation in religious practices as the only proper sign of nonassimilation.

10. I am modeling this argument on Carl Schorske on Freud, "To The Egyptian Dig: Freud's Exploration in Western Cultures," a paper presented at the Conference on Psychoanalysis and Culture, Stanford University, January 11, 1991.

11. "Burbank" immediately follows "Gerontion" as the second poem in the book; "Sweeney Among the Nightingales" is the final poem. This book also contains a third "Sweeney" poem, "Sweeney Erect," and four poems in French. All the English-language poems, with the exception of "Gerontion," are written in elegant rhymed quatrains. A third of the work in *Poems 1920* is in French, Eliot thereby indicating his displacement from his own language, and a flirtation with becoming a poet in another language. To his brother Henry Eliot, February 15, 1920: "Some of the new poems, the Sweeney ones, especially 'Among the Nightingales' and 'Burbank' are intensely serious, and I think these two are among the best that I have ever done. But even here I am considered by the ordinary Newspaper critic as a Wit or satirist, and in America I suppose I shall be thought merely disgusting" (*The Letters of T. S. Eliot, 1898–1922*, vol. 1, ed. Valerie Eliot [San Diego: Harcourt Brace Jovanovich, 1988], 363). To Mary Hutchinson, about half-year earlier, soon after they were published, the same two poems, he says, are "meant to be *very serious!*" (311).

12. Eric Sigg, *The American T. S. Eliot: A Study of the Early Writings* (Cambridge: Cambridge University Press, 1989), 154–84, has an analysis of the caricature and parodic elements of these poems used for moral purposes.

13. In 1922 Eliot approved of *Babbitt:* "It has some good things in it" (*Letters* 618).

14. I am indebted in this analysis to a well-illustrated study of Irish stereotypes, L. Perry Curtis, Jr., *Apes and Angels: The Irishman in Victorian Caricature* (Washington, D.C.: Smithsonian Institute Press, 1971). The cartoonists Tenniel in England and Nast in America specialize in these depictions. The citations are from 100 and 105, respectively.

15. Houston Baker, *Modernism and the Harlem Renaissance* (Chicago: University of Chicago Press, 1987). See also Marianna Torgovnick, *Gone Primitive: Savage Intellects, Modern Lives* (Chicago: University of Chicago Press, 1990). There is some precedent for fusing blacks and Jews. Pound's 1930s doggerel fuses blacks, Jews, and sexy Christians in the "Yiddisher Charlestown Band"; see the letter of November 24 and 25, 1930, published in Ahearn's selection of letters 1928–30, *Montemora* 8 (1981): 173–74, which unfortunately is not available in *Pound/Zukofsky: Selected Letters of Ezra Pound and Louis Zukofsky,* ed. Barry Ahearn (New York: New Directions, 1987).

16. Christopher Ricks makes the ingenious suggestion that "Rachel" is "passing."

17. "Gambit," from the Italian *gambetto* (a tripping up) and *gamba* (leg), repeats the fallen woman/leg and stocking materials from earlier in the poem. "Gambit," a strategy, is sexualized.

18. The taint is affiliated with images about blood; this trails or traces a slight motif of sexual taint in a shimmering, hard-to-pin-down fashion. It suggests the blood taint of syphilis.

19. Stephen H. Clark, "Testing the Razor: T. S. Eliot's *Poems 1920,*" contains a startling line by line analysis of "Sweeney Erect," discussing "the violently repudiatory sexuality prevalent in these texts" and the "virulence of its misogyny . . . its capacity not only to shock and repel, but also to implicate" (in *Engendering the Word: Feminist Essays in Psychosexual Poetics,* ed. Temma Berg, Anna Elfbein, Jeanne Larsen, and Elisa Kay Sparks, 167–89 [Urbana: University of Illinois Press, 1989]).

20. Irishness, blackness, and class all fuse suggestively in a later description of the Sweeney figure by Eliot: "a man who in younger days was perhaps a pugilist, mildly successful; who then grew older and retired to keep a pub" (cited in Stephen Clark, as reported by Neville Coghill, in *T. S. Eliot: A Symposium,* ed. R. Marsh and Tambimuttu [London, 1948], 86). It is notable that Eliot needs to make a further, extrapoetic narrative to contain the discursive and social forces of the various Sweeneys.

21. Three comments: I thought I had invented the term "racialized" once while teaching; I was delighted recently to find the same term, with about the same meaning, in Mae Henderson's work ("Speaking in Tongues: Dialogics, Dialectics, and the Black Woman Writer's Literary Tradition," in *Changing Our Own Words: Essays on Criticism, Theory, and Writing by Black Women,* ed. Cheryl A. Wall [New Brunswick: Rutgers University Press, 1989]). Second, the ignoring of skin color in finding racialized materials is a certain way of responding to Gates on race in quotation marks: "race." Third, the discovery of racialized encodings occurs in my *Writing Beyond the Ending,* in the chapter on Schreiner, in which I read the white youth Waldo as a version of the black African, because of the imagery, materials, and meanings which Schreiner invests in this character.

22. By these examples of Sweeney, let me suggest a task for literary criticism: there are many more racialized figures in literature than one has superficially found. A

melanin-laden skin color is not the only marker of racialization; racialized materials can be disengaged by other clues or cues from cultural discourses.

23. I am indebted to Jay Geller for this identification (personal communication).

24. Sander L. Gilman makes the point that "stereotypes can be (and regularly have been) freely associated, even when their association demands a suspension of common sense"; see his Preface to *Difference and Pathology: Stereotypes of Sexuality, Race, and Madness* (Ithaca: Cornell University Press, 1985), 12.

25. This point is also made in J. A. Morris's "T. S. Eliot and Anti-Semitism" (*Journal of European Studies* 2 [March 1972]: 173–82), who notes several anti-Semitic moments in Eliot's poems of the 1920s including the ones I mention, and as well a passage about "the red-eyed scavengers" from "A Cooking Egg." The author especially notes the comparisons of Jews to animals, and their position in Eliot's writing as "parasites, maurauders, destroyers" (178). The author characterizes Eliot's opinions as consistent with the depiction of Jews in proto-Fascist and Fascist discourse.

26. I have seen only one argument that insists that the Semiticized materials pervade the poem: Hyam Maccoby ("The Anti-Semitism of T. S. Eliot," *Midstream* 19 [May 1973]) argues that "the whole poem thus contains a fairly complete anti-Semitic system," not a set of incidental metaphors (73). However, he concentrates on the economic and political tropes, not the gender-laden and sexual ones. Needless to say, neither he nor other commentators on anti-Semitism see the affiliations with representations of the Irish and of blacks. Despite the thoroughness of Christopher Ricks's treatment of Eliot's work, he backs off several times from a full examination of this poem, displacing to a full treatment of the "Bleistein" materials cut from *The Waste Land*.

27. George Williamson, *A Reader's Guide to T. S. Eliot* (New York: Farrar, Straus and Giroux, 1981), 101: a series of quotations from Gautier, James, Shakespeare's *Othello*, Browning, Marston.

28. Behind this bracketed voice of the epigraph which I have identified as "gay" may lie the culture of decadence, homosexuality, and the association of poetry with effeminacy, tracked by Richard Dellamora, *Masculine Desire: The Sexual Politics of Victorian Aestheticism* (Chapel Hill: University of North Carolina Press, 1990); and the questions thereby raised for gendering modernism, discussed by Cassandra Laity, "H. D. and A. C. Swinburne: Decadence and Sapphic Modernism," in *Lesbian Texts and Contexts: Radical Revisions,* ed. Karla Jay and Joanne Glasgow, 217–40 (New York: New York University Press, 1990).

29. "Entertain" means "to divert, to amuse (sexually or in society); to give parties"; also "to continue with, maintain, support (thus politically, economically)."

30. Max Horkheimer and Theodor Adorno are not alone in remarking that Jews serve as the scapegoat for capitalist relations: "The economic injustice of the whole [owning] class is attributed to them" ("Elements of Anti-Semitism: The Limits of Enlightenment," *Dialectic of Enlightenment,* trans. John Cunning [New York: Seabury Press, 1972], 174).

31. Many people have stopped to notice the anti-Semitism of this poem. Most have seen it as deplorable but local, limited to a few disgraceful lines. This is inaccurate. Note an example, from Eric Sigg: "Here the device [construction of an urban bestiary] sinks to its notorious nadir, comparing Bleistein to rats and then to protozoans, the lowest life form. The comparison, redolent with anti-Jewish overtone and

exposing Eliot's satire and its supposed ideal content to grave criticism . . . " (*The American T. S. Eliot*, 160).

32. Looking up "sheeney" in the *OED* gives, of course, "Jew," apparently from a pronunciation of a Slavic word for Jew. Miles Orvell notes that the Hebrew letter *sheen* appears on the windows of kosher butchers, and may be a source. When one looks up "sweeney," one gets a primary meaning "atrophy of the shoulder muscles of the horse" and the figurative "the stiffness of pride and self-conceit"—thus associating this name with the "stiff-necked people" found as a characterization of the Jews in Exodus 32:9 and elsewhere.

33. Casillo, *The Genealogy of Demons: Anti-Semitism, Fascism, and the Myths of Ezra Pound* (Evanston, Ill.: Northwestern University Press, 1988), a chapter called "Bachofen and the Conquest of the Swamp," citation from 327. Casillo notes Eliot's anti-Semitism, but does not see it structuring his work as it did Pound's (341).

34. Casillo, *The Genealogy of Demons*, 86. Casillo notes that the Hell Cantos of Ezra Pound, contemporaneous with this work of Eliot, never refer to the Jews, although the image package is thoroughly consistent with his later uses: "fragmentation, darkness, bogs, swamps, impotence, monstrosity, falsification, loss of origins, infection, plague, castration, organic disease, vermin, prostitution, filth, stench, sadism, and violence" are all characteristic of the Hell that is postwar England. This material is waiting to be galvanized by the centralizing conspiracy theory figure of the Jew (161).

35. Casillo makes an important remark about the noncapitalization of "jew" with reference to Pound; it is as applicable to Eliot (as in "Gerontion"). The lower-case "jew" is a cutting down to size, a castration motif, responding to the multiple threat to the phallus that Jews embody (circumcision as castration; syphilis, immorality) (42). A Bleistein poem cut from *The Waste Land* manuscript also represents this figure as diseased; the loss of this figure to the poem as completed may signal a further burial and diffusion of the suggestions around cultural decay, no longer as pointed to any one group.

36. Elaine Showalter, *Sexual Anarchy: Gender and Culture at the Fin de Siècle* (New York: Viking, 1990), 188. One does not want to make too much of the paternal mark here, but T. S. Eliot's father had a virulent attitude toward syphilis: as God's punishment, he felt it should not be tampered with. A cure should not be found. (Cited in Showalter, *Sexual Anarchy*, 189, from Lyndall Gordon.)

37. Jay Geller, "Blood Sin: Syphilis and the Construction of Jewish Identity," a brilliant synthesis in *Faultline* 1 (1992): 21–48; to be part of Geller's forthcoming *The Nose Job: Freud and the Feminized Jew* (Albany: SUNY Press). (Citations are from a typescript provided by Geller, 7 and 9).

38. Chicago and New York are particularly singled-out sites for Jewish sexual crimes. I am drawing heavily on the helpful, if horrifying survey of Michael N. Dobkowski, *The Tarnished Dream: The Basis of American Anti-Semitism* (Westport, Conn.: Greenwood Press, 1979). The citation is from 67.

39. Geller shows these linkages in detail. I am very grateful to Geller for sharing his work with me. Casillo's reading of anti-Semitic materials in *The Cantos* and in Pound's oeuvre as a whole also links castration, disease, especially syphilis, prostitution, parasitism, the swamp, loss of single, solid maleness, and identification with nomadic exiles—certain motifs of this Eliot poem appear throughout Pound.

40. See Dobkowski, *The Tarnished Dream*, for a survey of such materials.

41. See Morris ("T. S. Eliot and Anti-Semitism," 180), who mentions that the *Protocols* was serialized in the *Morning Post* in the summer of 1920; Norman Cohn, *Warrant for Genocide: The Myth of the Jewish World-Conspiracy and the Protocols of the Elders of Zion* (1969; rpt., Chico, Calif.: Scholars Press, 1981).

42. Cohn, *Warrant for Genocide*, 149.

43. These include the Irish uprising, the Harlem Renaissance with its literary flowering and the fascination of whites with blacks, the "theory" presented by *The Protocols of the Elders of Zion*, and the anti-Semitic Henry Ford campaign in America in 1920, itself based on a translation and dissemination of the *Protocols*.

44. Eliot, "Kipling Redivivus," *Athenaeum* (May 9, 1919): 297–98. Eliot has implicitly defined ideology as pervasive, extensive, and saturating, as if in Raymond Williams's terms in *Marxism and Literature* (Oxford: Oxford University Press, 1977).

45. *The Education* begins with the trope of the shadow Jew. When little Henry Adams is born, he is branded into his own patrician class and history. American history is seemingly the property of his own family; continuing that history seems his own destiny. Adams says he was scarcely less branded than if had been "born in Jerusalem under the shadow of the Temple, and circumcised in the Synagogue by his uncle the high priest, under the name of Israel Cohen." The bizarre "circumcision of Adams" is to be a marked patrician in a changed world to which he is, in his terms, never adequate, always lacking, always belated, and ironically never educated for what he must really confront. (Cited from Henry Adams, *Selections: Novels, Mont Saint Michel, The Education* [New York: Literary Classics of the United States; distributed by Viking Press, 1983], chapter 1, 723.)

9

Hadassah Arms

Nancy K. Miller

"I was a little safe, I had a coat and boots, so like a Gestapo wore when he was not in service. But Anja—you could see—her appearance—you could see more easy she was Jewish. I was afraid for her."
—Art Spiegelman, *Maus*

I. The French Connection

When I moved uptown a few years ago, I joined a health club called the Paris. Given my history as a Francophile, I might have chosen the club for the name, but its real appeal for me was the location: a two-block walk from our new apartment. Members were entitled to a free orientation session. The trainer assigned to show me around the daunting array of exercise machines aligned in front of the floor-to-ceiling mirrors was named T.W. I would have preferred one of the women trainers, or at least a man not known by his initials, but I didn't seem to have a choice. (Besides, once he had measured my thighs, what else was there to fear?) Midway through my initiation into the world of what the French call musculation, we arrived at a machine labeled shoulder press. As I arranged myself on the bench and attempted to raise the bar over my head at the first level of weights, T.W. explained: "This is for Hadassah arms." Responding to my blank stare, he pointed to my triceps. Hadassah arms. The image conjured by the expression came sharply into focus: the fold of soft flesh that lines the underarm of an aging female body. (In *Mr. Saturday Night,* a movie that unaccountably brought me to tears, the comedians' mother is fondly remembered for her arms heavily laden with "flaps," which, when thrown up in admiration of her sons' wit, seem to wave approbation.) I saw a large woman sitting at a banquet table at a generic Jewish event, wearing an expensive sleeveless dress, maybe a strapless evening gown in pale-colored chiffon that set off her jewelry but emphasized the vulnerable cast of her arms. She seemed self-satisfied, even smug, certainly oblivious to the state of her triceps. In retrospect, I suddenly understood, I had identified that look of complacency and privilege with a matronly style that I obscurely feared might someday be my own. Despite the fact that physically she was quite different from my own mother, who played tennis and never attended "functions," the woman with Hadassah arms represented a feminine incarnation I dreaded. Hadassah was, as we might say now, a floating signifier that for me had come to stand for the horrors of female destiny within the limited scenarios of middle-class Jewish-American life in the 1950s. With the effects of this unexpected reminiscence pressing in on me, I looked up and commented with a slight edge, gazing at T.W.'s not inconsiderable gut, surprising in a trainer: "Well, if you go around saying things like that, I hope you're Jewish." Actually, T.W. confessed, he wasn't; his ex-wife, who was, had taught him the expression. We completed the tour of the machines without further conversation. Swimming afterwards, I reviewed the episode with the obsessiveness brought on by doing laps. What kept coming back between strokes was less my lame reply than the thought of the figure I must have cut in his eyes, the image that had led him to make the association: a middle-aged Jewish woman who needed to work on her triceps. Looking Jewish.

My parents loved a certain number of jokes and stories that were told over and over again; in memory it seems as though they were repeated daily, usually to make a point. Mostly I retain the punchlines, which in some cases I spent a lifetime not getting. I can still see my parents doubled over in tears, unable to contain themselves as they retold with unflagging hilarity a joke they had heard, interrupting each other for corrections, anticipating the punchline, and invariably ruining the effect of the joke in the process. When they finally explained the joke to my uncomprehending sister and me, they added that you had to know Yiddish, which of course meant that the essence of the joke was lost, on us, in translation. This is one of their jokes I never thought was really funny, though I did smile at its aptness when I reheard it as an adult in French, in Paris. (By then I was willing to be Jewish.)

> Elderly lady on the bus to young man in the seat next to hers: "Excuse me, young man, are you Jewish?"
> Young man, politely: "No, I'm not."
> After a pause she asks again: "Are you Jewish?"
> "No, I'm not."
> This exchange is repeated several times. Despite the consistently negative answers she receives, the old lady asks one last time: "Are you *sure* you're not Jewish?"
> The young man, exasperated and hoping to put an end to the badgering, finally gives her the answer he thinks she wants: "All right, yes, I'm Jewish!"
> To which the old lady replies: "Funny, you don't look Jewish."

"Have a happy . . . " The attendant at the desk of the Paris Health Club started to say "Easter," then, realizing it was about to be Passover as well, caught herself: "We have to say 'holiday' around here."

I grew up in New York on the Upper West Side in the 1940s and 1950s knowing I was Jewish but without any conscious awareness of what Jewish

154

identity had meant historically in the world. Whatever I learned in Sunday school or absorbed through sheer repetition at the seders—the years in the desert, the Promised Land—was disconnected from contemporary history, of which I remained ignorant for a very long time: World War II, the Holocaust, the creation of Israel. I doubt whether these events were discussed in *When the Jewish People Was Young,* the only book we read in those weekly exercises in Reform Judaism for children whose parents could neither pass on the tradition themselves nor give it up. (Rereading *Memoirs of an Ex-Prom Queen,* I was enchanted to find a bond with Alix Kates Shulman's sardonic midwestern heroine: "If there was ever a possibility that I might have fallen for stories like Genesis or Moses and the Ten Commandments, it was destroyed by the ridiculous title of the textbook we used: *When the Jewish People Was Young*" [1972; rpt., Chicago: Cassandra 1985], 131). To assuage their twin anxiety about religious assimilation (moving away from the un-American constraints of Orthodoxy) and social mobility (out of immigrant insecurity into professional and business solidity), our parents insisted on the signs of a certain conformity to the tradition. Sunday school was the perfect solution. We would know what we were regardless of what we or they actually thought or did. From those years of enforced attendance I retain that title—the singular verb after "people" made an impression—and "Supersonic Purim": the holidays as theme park in the basement of Temple Israel.

Anti-Semitism seemed part of an archaic, European past. The famous pogroms, the high points of my grandfather's stories of what life was like for Jews at the end of nineteenth-century Russia, were part of family mythology: why they came to America. The couple that ran the neighborhood candy store had concentration camp numbers on their arms; and I knew that friends of my parents, Zionists—a term always uttered with a certain exasperation— gave money to plant trees in a place called Israel. Hadassah was doubly scorned: Zionism *and* women. But both the cataclysm of the Holocaust and the daily, ordinary forms of anti-Semitism that in fact crucially shape Jewish identity seemed to pass me by. Being Jewish was primarily a matter of local domestic strife: internal family policing (turning up at temple on the High Holidays, fasting at Yom Kippur, not eating bread at Passover, etc.) and intrafamilial comparison (invidious, of course, with the cousins who "kept kosher"—hypocritically, we thought—while we didn't). The world, we knew, was divided into Jews and non-Jews. The part of being Jewish that involved one's relation to the world, therefore, had primarily to do with knowing who was and wasn't Jewish. Why that mattered so much became clearer with puberty, which in my parents' apocalyptic sense of timing led directly, leaping through the years, to sex (the avoidance of) and marriage (the condition for the former): we had, they said, to marry one.

Who was and who wasn't. Not looking Jewish, I thought then, was more important than being Jewish. By junior high, when looks are all, I had come to understand that looking Jewish was bad, aesthetically. We idealized the counselors at summer camp. Blonde, long-legged phys-ed majors (our vulgar parents, to our horror and scorn, referred to our idols as *shiksas*), they embodied all that we intense dark-haired campers would never be. How did that deficiency of beauty square with what I had been told about being Jewish as something good—smarter, more talented, more sensitive? It didn't. Being smart and talented was taken for granted in the tracked classes and special schools which served as the alternative to private school for the children of the professional and artistic middle class, whose parents thought of themselves, however apolitically, as belonging to the Left. Being smart—and how smart could one be with "geniuses" everywhere (staggering IQ's were routinely alluded to and boasted about)—seemed a poor consolation prize in the perpetual popularity contest that passed for life.

The unfairness of the division marked the beginning of my problems with Jewish identity: what was so great about being Jewish if it meant you would never look like Sandra Dee? It's not that I honestly thought Sandra Dee was beautiful. It was that what she looked like was deemed beautiful and, of course, American. The power of those conventions in the 1950s for girls, especially in families where American identity was newly acquired, is not to be underestimated, even if at the same time we also resisted them in other areas, often covertly. Although I servilely wanted to look like everyone else, wearing exactly what the other girls wore (the same brands from the same stores), I sensed that this conformity was ethically wrong. The tension came in part from my parents' attempt to convince me that it was OK, even good, to be "different." I never fully believed their discourse on the subject, since it always felt like an attempt either to rationalize their refusal to buy me the coveted item they couldn't afford (the storm coat from Saks on Fifth Avenue, not S. Klein's "On the Square"), or to console me for what could never be acquired: golden thighs or, more simply, hair that moved.

This was the era for white girls of ironing one's already straight, long, blonde hair, glamorized in *Seventeen* magazine by the model Carol Lynley, to make it even more perfect. My father, whose kinky hair I had inherited, signed a promise to me when I was nine that at age twenty-five I would no longer hate my hair. I was of course unmoved by this prediction—would I still be alive at twenty-five?—and talked my mother into letting me have my hair straightened once, just to see. When I read *The Autobiography of Malcolm X,* I recovered through the vivid re-creation of his first hair straightening the sensation of exquisite burning that first experience had involved. At age nine, I thought the pain was worth it, but my parents refused to subsidize my masochism. In 1968, after years of being straightened, my "natural" hair was finally "in," just as my father had promised, and I jubilantly grew my hair into a huge "Afro." I was always a little miffed to hear it described as an "Isro." (The sense of a productive connection between blacks and Jews as common victims of discrimination was alive in the 1950s and 1960s in a way that identity politics has long since dissolved.)

Despite my abject acceptance of these aesthetic norms, whose historical significance I did not begin to suspect, like a George Eliot heroine I also nourished a nameless and secret wish for some way of being in the world outside conventions altogether; it would take feminism for me to discover what that was. In the 1950s girls like me obsessed about our appearance with a single-mindedness that closed out the larger world of history, politics, and, paradoxically, Jews. Our corner of the diaspora (a word I didn't know then) was a lonely place. We assimilated American girls, oblivious even to Anne Frank, managed not to know that looking Jewish could mean death.

Going to Europe for the first time in 1959, to France in particular, was a shock, and created a swerve in my ideas about identity—both feminine and Jewish—I haven't finished accounting for. I began by switching my college major from English to French. Under the alibi of perfecting my French, I returned to France as a student in 1961 and remained there for six years. This choice had everything to do with my visceral response to the style and overt sexuality of Paris. Inspired by the nouvelle vague movies I had watched with fascination in New York, and more generally by American postwar ideas of what Frenchness represented, I wanted to smoke cigarettes and have steamy love affairs with sullen young men. I memorized the faces and the walk of French women. I straightened my hair and wore stockings to school. (I was secretly thrilled when a "boy," walking up Broadway behind me, commented appreciatively on my legs. He was surprised and mortified when it turned out that he knew me: I was a classmate's girlfriend. I loved it.) But looking back now, it also seems to me that a less conscious but equally powerful current was at work: the escape from a New York Jewish female fate and voice. Speaking French, dressing French were not so much a way of "passing"— since it is impossible to pass as French—but displacing the more predictable intonations of identity; at least that was the fantasy.

My years in France in the late 1950s and early 1960s complicated the question of being different and being Jewish for me in unexpected ways. I discovered two surprising things: Jews who weren't American and ordinary anti-Semitism. I got to hear my first anti-Semitic remarks from French people who seemed to think that, because I was American, I wasn't Jewish. This had a double effect on my ideas about identity: I heard things that my life in the heavily Jewish community of New York had sheltered me from, and I flirted with passing. The frisson of passing came in response to French people saying: "But you don't look American. You look . . . What are you *really?*" In this version, not looking American (like Sandra Dee) was good; my French interlocutors were not thinking Jewish but something . . . different. Explaining that my grandparents came from Russia and Poland, though not mentioning the Jewish connection, I would add to my own pleasure by saying: "Oh, there are lots of girls in New York who look just like me." That no one seemed to believe me was the final touch of private gratification: my difference was unique.

Ordinary anti-Semitism, Paris, circa 1962:
Take 1:

"What's that heavy package you're carrying?"

"Oh, it's a rug I just bought."

"Why did you bring it with you tonight? Wouldn't it have been more convenient to leave it at the store and pick it up tomorrow on your way home?"

"Yes, but they're Jews."

This exchange took place in my presence over cocktails. I said nothing, in part because I was nonplussed, in part because I wouldn't have known what to say. "I'm Jewish. Don't say that in front of me"? To which there are two or three replies: "Oh, but you're different." "Oh, it's just a way of speaking." Or, "I'm sorry, I didn't know." Like "Hadassah arms," the rug-merchant stereotype seems to require a speech, but I never seem up to making it.
Take 2:

"I might have a chance to teach at Lyons. What's it like?"

"It's swarming with them" (translation of *Ça grouille,* complete with gestures).

This one was less clear. In fact, friends had to explain that there was a rather large Jewish population at Lyons. Had I understood the metaphorics on the moment, my reticence would have been the same.

Three decades later, it continues, there and here:

After a lecture in Spain, a young woman, having heard me speak about Spiegelman's *Maus,* remarks with some surprise: "I gather from what you were saying that you are Jewish. I didn't know that Jews had blue eyes." (My eyes are green.)

I'm eating in a fashionable downtown Japanese restaurant with two forty-something European friends. One says, "I've never seen you with your glasses. You look more Jewish." I ask if this is good or bad. Her companion answers, "Oh, good, of course. You look intellectual." She offers me a piece of her sushi with a delectable, bright pink shrimp hugging the rice. First woman deftly removes the shrimp from my plate and, looking accusingly at her partner, replaces it with an elaborate vegetarian concoction: "Don't you know, Jews don't eat shellfish."

At the dinner table my French, Catholic stepson-in-law observes that his friends tell anti-Semitic jokes, but that they (the friends) are not anti-Semitic. When pressed by me to explain why he says that he doesn't tell such jokes even though they are not "really" anti-Semitic, he concedes that they might be the "beginning" of anti-Semitism. The only Jew at the table, I vastly enjoy watching him sink into the mire of his contradiction.

Getting hooked on Europe and staying there was bound up with my desire to emancipate myself from parental authority. Having made the fatal error of living at home for my college years, I thought that putting an ocean between my parents and me offered the only hope for what they liked to call my independence. I desperately wanted to mark my distance from what I saw as their determination to control my life. This meant quite pointedly revolting against their ideas about being Jewish and what that implied for my destiny. The simplest solution for my rebellion was to marry a man who wasn't Jewish, but I didn't come up with it right away: announcing that I was no longer a virgin was one thing, "intermarriage" was another.

For a while, though, it seemed that I would meet only Jews in Europe. My first trip to Europe on the *S. S. Rotterdam* ended in a Dutch port where I took an overnight ferry to England. An English major at Barnard, I was going to study Shakespeare at Stratford-upon-Avon. I spent the night of the channel-crossing outdoors in a dark corner of the deck flirting madly with an incredibly handsome "older man" (he was twenty-five to my eighteen—the same age difference as my parents'!). I was crushed to learn at the end of my journey, many passionate embraces and declarations later, that he had a fiancée waiting for him in London; I had already married him (an English Jew) in my imagination.

Two years later, when I went to France to study, the Jewish connection continued to play itself out. In the dormitory room I was assigned at the Foyer International des Etudiantes, my roommate, it turned out, was Jewish. This took me some time to figure out, since she (a) put reproductions of Renaissance portraits on the wall, (b) came from North Africa (Africa?!), (c) spoke French, and (d) didn't Look Jewish. The choice of art seemed the most convincing evidence to me: the portraits of aristocratic women looked so much like religious subjects I somehow concluded they all were. Primitive as it may seem, my reasoning was that someone Jewish couldn't personally *like* Christian art; you could, of course, *study* it as a topic. In part because of our mutual commitment to smoking, sexual experience, and literature; in part because we were both Jewish and foreigners at the Foyer (even though French was her "native" language), M. and I became friends. In the spring of 1962 I found myself going to Tunisia for Passover. The following fall M. became romantically involved with a friend of her cousin from Tunisia, and I, in a gesture of mimicry that has often spelled disaster for me, moved in with *his* cousin J.-P. In the spring of the following year, I went home with him for Passover as his fiancée. Why did I imagine I really wanted to marry this insignificant young man? Mainly because he spoke French; also because he asked. When my parents came to Paris that summer, prepared to meet his parents, they played the ultimate authority card by appearing to be reasonable. "Are you sure you want to marry him?" they asked, whereupon I burst into tears of relief.

In the early 1960s the girls I knew still expected, 1950s style, to marry and have children. But we also had begun subconsciously to think of ourselves as heroines in quest of experience and adventure, which was an unnamed form of resistance to the marriage plot. My flip-flop over poor J.-P.

had something to do with the unspoken confusion produced in that cusp moment between generational styles when identities began to seem less fixed. It was not yet the 1960s, but no longer the 1950s. Some of us had begun to feel the winds of change, but we were still pretty timid. J.-P.'s Jewishness had mediated his North African difference, but then his North African difference turned out to be familiar: middle-class Jewishness. The escape was beginning to look like home.

When I decided, despite the fiasco with J.-P., to stay on in France, my parents announced that they had done with supporting me. They wanted me to come home and weren't going to finance a life they had begun to suspect was not driven purely by a passion for education. I had nonetheless, between affairs, gotten an M.A. in French and started a second M.A. degree in English. In order to earn some extra money I answered an ad for teachers of English in the *International Herald Tribune*. This was how I met my first husband. An Irish-American expatriate, T. seemed the perfect choice for my revolt: thirteen years older than I, an alcoholic (although I didn't fully understand this at the time), and, it turned out, a borderline psychotic (I chalked up his eccentricities to his Irishness). He was also utterly charming, brilliant, and above all, Not Jewish. He ran a language school out of his hip pocket, employing a whole circle of young Anglophones living in Paris, and spent most of his money—the company's expense account—on eating out in fabulous restaurants (I got the menu without the prices). This time, I decided not to consult my parents. One Easter vacation we drove to Geneva, got married in City Hall, and sent them a telegram. Having married not only a non-Jew but a Catholic—he had a cousin who was a nun!—and spent my honeymoon in Ireland, I set out to try to reproduce all the recipes for Jewish cooking I could remember. This is how I reconnected with my parents: they had to forgive me when I was making pot roast and what my mother, pre–Julia Child, called barley pilaf. My mother decided to tell her father that T. was half-Jewish (after all, he had a beard) and threw a party for us in New York. My cooking notwithstanding, the marriage collapsed, and I came back to New York, graduate school, and the construction of an identity, dependent this time neither on parents nor on a husband. I was out of the kitchen for good.

II. Feminism and the Jewish Question

With my conversion to feminism in the early 1970s, the aimless questing about "who I was" and "what I would do" shifted away from the marriage plot and moved into the new categories of "theory." Being "different" stopped being a matter of personal anguish and became a question about gender and sexual politics. Suddenly there was language for understanding the malaise of identity that I had tried to banish by living in France. At the same time, the Jewish question disappeared from the horizon. To the extent that it had always been tied to the wars with my parents, and that my prolonged adolescence seemed finally at a close, Jewishness no longer figured among my conscious concerns. My parents were relieved that I hadn't married someone black, as my sister had, and found my feminism a minor irritant by comparison. At least it meant I was back in school, doing something that didn't seem an assault on their values—like living in Paris—or a subject of embarrassment.

To my surprise, the Jewish question came back into my life in the next decade through two different doors, the first professional, the second familial (but not as a matter of parental authority). At a feminist conference in 1985, Evelyn Torton Beck, speaking as a Jew and as a feminist, dramatically challenged the feminists in the audience who were Jewish to "take back their noses and their names." When were we going to assume our identity and our responsibility to it? In women's studies curricula every minority or ethnic literature was taught except Jewish. Why, she wanted to know, no courses on women's Jewish-American or Yiddish literature? Beck's challenge was never answered on its own terms because it was immediately displaced into a violent exchange with another panelist, who argued that Jewish women could not consider themselves oppressed, since they could choose to pass, whereas black women did not have this luxury. Jewish women's writing did not belong to the alternative history, the history of the oppressed. I was profoundly disturbed by this debate, not only because it was ugly and classically divisive, but because it forced me to consider why I, a great partisan of "identity," had never thought to assert a Jewish or a Jewish feminist one.

In the aftermath of Beck's harangue, I added Anzia Yezierska's powerful novel *Bread Givers* to our introductory women's studies course at Barnard. I taught the book one semester, even though it made me intensely uneasy to do so. While Yezierska's depiction of immigrant life in New York seemed true to my inherited sense of the *shtetl* culture, against which my grandparents had invented themselves, it put Jews in a bad light: in Jewish-immigrant communities on the Lower East Side men were allowed, indeed authorized, to control and exploit women so that men could be scholars while women worked twelve-hour days to support their sublime contemplation. I produced a reading that worked effectively with the rest of the syllabus by making Sara Smolinsky the heroine of a protofeminist *Bildungsroman* in which she achieves autonomy by refusing patriarchal authority and an imposed marriage to become a teacher, but I never taught the book again. I couldn't figure out how to position myself in relation to the representation of "otherness." Neither the respectful reader of other others—say, Maxine Hong Kingston's *The Woman Warrior*—nor the identified witness of my "own" experience, I couldn't find the right distance. Neither "they" nor "we."

The second door through which the question of Jewish identity reimposed itself on my conscious concerns was, I said, familial. This return had two parts, both related to the question of legacy: the one emerging in the after-math of my parents' illness and death, the other as an effect of my French goddaughter's move to Israel. (Of course, technically, Jews don't have "god" children. But the concept, via the French signifier, which doesn't include any reference to god, seemed an attractive way to acknowledge the attachment I felt to this child from the moment I laid eyes on her.) A. was the daughter of my former roommate at the Foyer International, who had gone on to marry her boyfriend and make her life in Paris. We had stayed in touch and hers had become my second family. Born in 1967, the year I left Paris—the year of the Six-Day War—A. decided at age twenty-two to study philosophy in Israel, then at twenty-four to marry an Argentinian Jew. It was to visit her that I made my first trip to Israel; the second was to attend her wedding on a kibbutz outside Jerusalem.

I'm not sure why it took me so long to go to Israel. In part, I had inherited the resistance, not to say condescension, my parents expressed toward Zionism, and why go to Israel if you weren't a Zionist? When several years after visiting most of Western Europe they finally went to Israel in 1961 (combined with a trip to Greece, Turkey, and Yugoslavia, and ending up back in Paris), it seems to have been a disappointment. (In my father's travel diary, which typically records facts—the weather, shopping, people encountered—not personal feelings, the two-week visit is treated exactly like any other piece of tourism. The only experience in Israel to rank above "pleasant" was a trip to the New Hadassah Hospital described as "a fabulous excursion.") By the time I went to visit A. in Jerusalem both my parents were dead. They had, I remembered, stayed at the very fancy and historic King David Hotel. Forever poorer, I booked a room across the street from the King David at the YMCA. I rationalized my choice to myself by saying that it was the only hotel in its category the travel agents offered that had a swimming pool, but I also know that I got some perverse satisfaction out of the "C" in the address. I made the trip from Paris, where I was spending my sabbatical year, and didn't take El Al.

Despite these gestures of resistance, I was an enthusiastic tourist. I visited Yad Vashem, went to Masada, hiked in Ein Gedi, and, covered with black mud, floated in the Dead Sea. For six days I thought and talked constantly about BEING JEWISH, LOOKING JEWISH, and what it meant for there to be a JEWISH state. I found this exciting, even thrilling. But there was one image I could not endure, and it continues to haunt my reflection of what being Jewish could come to mean at this point in my life, or what would be at stake for me to write from an identification called writing "as a Jew." This was the spectacle of the gender divide at the Western Wall. A partition made of woven metal strips that left gaps to peer through separated the women from the men. Lined up against the partition was a row of plastic chairs upon which the women would stand to witness the events from which they were excluded. I, of course, knew that the division of the sexes was the bedrock of

Orthodox Judaism. But the sight of the men praying and celebrating in groups on one side of the line, and the women weeping into the wall and praying privately on the other, was an image that exceeded its message. It jarred me out of my growing sentimental adherence to the idea of a Jewish state. I confess, however, that moved by the spirit of the place I actually stuffed a little piece of paper into the cracks as though I believed in the power of the wall instead of my therapist. Nonetheless, no rescue operation of "Jewish Feminism" can ever make the foundational gender assymetry acceptable to me. The binaries do not stand alone, particularly in Israel, where they are politically intertwined in a logic of circularity: the division of the world into Jews and Others (the Dome of the Rock is adjacent to the wall); the support of the division through Orthodoxy (the internal Other that allows secular Jews their good conscience); the articulation and nationalization of Orthodoxy through institutionalized laws of gender.

(This performance of sexual differences gets to me every time. I was almost as shocked by a photograph in the *New York Times* bearing the legend: "Grand Rabbi of Lubavitch Sect Refuses the Messianic Mantle" [February 1, 1993]). In the foreground men and boys crowd together and strain to see Rabbi Schneerson during a telecast. In the back against the wall a row of women's eyes peer out from blank faces as though through a mail slot—or the opening in a prison door. In the far corner one little girl, shielded by her older brother who rests his hands protectively on her shoulders, stands out as an accidental tourist, a category mistake. I wonder about her fate: whether she, like Sara Smolinsky, will find her way out of there. And as if by the fatal power of juxtaposition that haunts life in America, directly below this photograph was a story whose headline read: "When Good Will Is Not Enough: Desegregation Project at Heart of Hartford School Suit.")

On my second trip to Israel for A.'s wedding, I had started writing this chapter and kept taking mental notes about how Jewish I was feeling at all times, alternately, how I felt about being Jewish. This emotional research was complicated by the fact that I was traveling with S., my second non-Jewish husband, who took the fashionable and irritating left French line that Israeli Jews are "racist" in their dealings with the Palestinians; *he* wanted to go to Bethlehem and also to Jericho in order, he said, to show support for the intifada. Whether as a counterpoint to his politics, or as part of my attempt to understand A.'s choice to live there, I found myself more attracted to Israel and Zionism than I had on the first visit. I wanted not only *to be* but also *to be seen* as Jewish. At the airport in Paris, the security guard began her interrogation by saying "shalom"; I nonchalantly replied "shalom." This led her to start a conversation in Hebrew. On seeing that I understood not a word, she apologized for assuming that I would know the language and I felt ashamed that I didn't. As we drove through the labyrinth of Jerusalem streets (the most important of which was not on our map), S. chided me for not being able to make out a word of Hebrew. What was the point of my being Jewish if I couldn't even read the signs. I thought back bitterly to the idiotic Hebrew classes we had sat through in Temple Israel; we learned to decipher the alphabet but not to understand what the words meant.

The languages of identity. Lost in Jerusalem, I walked into a shop, reminiscent of my grandfather's tailoring shop in the garment district, where two elderly men sat bent over their sewing machines making alterations. I asked for directions to our hotel. Neither of the men spoke English, as many Israelis do. But wanting to be helpful, they asked if I understood Yiddish. Hopefully, one of them asked: a *"bissel?"* To this I nodded assent, equally hopefully, but though the cadences were familiar, the way back to the Hyatt Regency in Yiddish continued to escape us.

I had in fact tried to repair my ignorance when I was living in Paris in the early 1960s by taking classes in Yiddish at the School for Oriental Languages. I'm sure I did this both to please my philo-Semite husband, and to emphasize my difference from him. In my attempt to reconstruct the legacy I had ardently refused, I reached the reading level of a Sholom Aleichem story. My mastery stopped there, and with the years, vanished; I still have my dictionary.

If I miss anything about what being Jewish meant to me when my parents were still alive, it's having access, albeit mediated, to a culture said to be untranslatable. I now can't tell certain jokes in two languages, one of which I never spoke. I normally either forget the punchline, or begin with it. With the jokes my parents told, I am doubly at a loss. When they said their jokes were funnier in Yiddish, I believed this, though I have no way of knowing whether that was true.

III. The *Tchotchke* Museum

At one time, so I am told, West End Avenue in New York had an inordinately high proportion of *tchotchkies* (plural).

—Leo Rosten, *The Joys of Yiddish*

Even unto them will I give in mine house and within my walls a place and a name better than of sons and daughters: I will give them an everlasting name, that shall not be cut off.

—Isaiah 56:5

When I moved into the new apartment, I also took out of storage what my sister and I had decided should be saved of my parents' possessions; I now had room for *tchotchkies*. Because I had gone to France on a sabbatical immediately after my father's death, and my sister had emptied the apartment, I had not examined in any detail many of the boxes. I piled them up in the maid's room—dubbed "The Tchotchke Museum"—for the duration. And so I found myself at age fifty unpacking the remains of my parents' classically middle-class, urban, professional life, a life I had despised when they lived it, and now was belatedly trying to relive. My sister had labeled the boxes "chackes" and had divided them by genre, or rather material: glass, metal, fabric, and so forth. These were, for the most part, souvenirs of my parents' travels (my mother was the Imelda Marcos of candlesticks), of dubious taste and no commercial value. There was nothing thematically Jewish, except for a menorah from Israel that seemed as though it had never been used.

Oddly, among my father's belongings I found not one but several embroidered velvet pouches containing phylacteries. Whose were they? Why did my father save them? Why in multiples? I had never seen him wear either *tallis* or *tefillin* and yet there they were, stashed away in a dresser drawer for safekeeping. What to do with them? In *Patrimony* Philip Roth offers a comic version of his father's decision to abandon his *tefillin* in the locker room at the local gym. My fantasy was to leave the pouches at the door of one of the many tiny synagogues in my neighborhood, where in the early morning men, carrying identical equipment, go to pray. I kept eyeing these men on my morning jogs but couldn't bring myself to ask for advice. Finally, one of my husband's colleagues, who also happens to be a rabbi, offered in the course of an e-mail exchange to take them off my hands and find them a proper home; I accepted with relief, since the contents of the suitcase were never meant for me. I kept one velvet pouch and two empty boxes as the souvenir of a vanished past and a paternal mystery. I'm still waiting to hear.

At seven o'clock in the morning I observe the men silently converging on their space. Dressed for work, carrying their pouches, they usually arrive alone; occasionally, when I approach the park at a trot, I cross a pair of old men. Each is wearing a tweed overcoat, with a muffler and a felt hat, the way my father did whenever he left the house. They are holding onto each other in the quiet streets, holding each other up. I don't know what I think of them, any more than I can decide what to make of the Sabbath parade of practicing Jews on West End Avenue: the groups of men of all ages in black or in business suits, some with extravagant hats; the women, especially the younger ones with their modern wigs (or fashion-proof hats), long skirts, and growing brood; the little boys with *payos* and *yarmulkes;* the girls in long dresses from another century. They seem unembarrassed by the spectacle they make. They have, after all, chosen it. Like the Hadassah ladies, I find them both alien and familiar, but not me. And yet who is to say? The trainer at the Paris gym couldn't tell the difference.

IV. Writing as a Jew?

I started thinking about this chapter in the summer of 1992 in Paris. The newspapers were full of Jews: the elections in Israel; Itzak Rabin's trip to Egypt. But the real news was closer to home. Vichy was on the agenda and why François Mitterand had been putting flowers on the grave of Marshal Pétain. Pressed by the Association of Children of the Deported, he stopped, without giving any direct explanation. It was the fiftieth anniversary of the

"Vel d'hiv," the roundup of fourteen thousand French Jews in Paris *by the French*. I wondered whether this renewed attention might represent the beginning of a French acknowledgment of their own participation in the Final Solution, of their official and not-so-indirect support of the Holocaust.

I gave up my French life in 1967 right after the Six-Day War, one of the few occasions when Jews and the state of Israel managed to penetrate, even surprise, French consciousness, and when French Jews themselves felt shaken in their commitment to assimilation. I think now that the general absence of Jewish identity as a visible social, cultural, or political force in Paris—as compared with New York—was part of what attracted me to life there in the 1960s. Although in an excess of cross-identification, T. would drag me to la rue des Rosiers to buy bread on Fridays, I enjoyed the evacuation of *yiddishkeit*. I was seduced by the intermittences of "passing," forgetting who I was.

Yad Vashem is about remembering. The museum offers staggering documentation about the Holocaust and monumentalizes the task of memory. The question, however, is not just what is remembered, but also what is to be *done* with it. The creation of Israel is one answer, and a dramatic one, to the attempt to erase Jewish identity. But as always, to affirm the logic of one people's identity—Chosen People, Diaspora, Holocaust, Promised Land, Israel—is also to affirm that of others': the necessity, for instance, of a Palestinian state as well.

One of the effects of identity politics, we know, has been an acute self-consciousness about differences. Unexpectedly, this has caused me to revert to one of my grandmother's most irritating activities: counting Jews. This took the form of noticing in any list of names which ones seem Jewish (in the list of accident survivors, for instance), or more broadly evaluating any event in terms of the consequences it might have for Jews. I startled myself a few years ago at the meeting of an editorial board where a small group of academics weighed a decision about the format of a research volume. Seeking to make a humorous point and expecting complicity, I asked, "But is it good for the Jews?" In the deep silence and blank stares that followed I realized that in fact there was only one other Jew in the room, and he wouldn't meet my eyes. Later, I could not figure out why I had ever said that, or thought it might be remotely amusing. What was going on? Had I added counting Jews to counting women? Perhaps I had never stopped.

Soon after that, in a paper devoted to identity politics and feminist theory, I tried on speaking autobiographically "as a Jew" by talking, before I had ever gone there, about Israel. I managed thereby both to irritate Edward Said and to find myself enlisted by others in Jewish feminism. That appropriation bothered me: I feel neither moved nor entitled to add "Jewish" to "feminist," even though, separately, I am both. Recently, in a seminar on autobiography and minority identities, I taught Vivian Gornick's *Fierce Attachments* (a book I adore) and listened to the students go on about how much they disliked the memoir; they were put off by all the complaining. I wound up telling them they sounded like a bunch of anti-Semites; that I did this without my heart pounding, despite a terrific anxiety attack afterwards, still amazes me. I've since written essays on Philip Roth and Art Spiegelman in which I deal with *their* Jewishness, though not explicitly with mine, not "as a Jew."

In an account of Art Spiegelman's brilliant cartoon of the Holocaust, *Maus,* one reviewer, describing an episode in which Spiegelman portrays himself leaning despairingly on his drawing board trying to rise to the challenge of his material, refers somewhat disparagingly but without further comment to the artist's project as "passing himself off as some kind of Jew." Part of the shock of visiting Israel for me was the realization that identity is not solely organized there along the Jewish–Not Jewish divide on which many of us were raised, but also constructed through divisions within diasporic populations. I find myself wondering again about those terms; am I not trying to write here as "some kind of Jew"? But what kind? I resist, while I'm obviously tempted by, the invitation to take on "Jewish" in some authenticating way. In my oscillation between wanting to have Jewish difference matter and yet feeling that I don't coincide with its dominant representations, I am perhaps at my most Jewish. I resist taking on "Jewish" as a fashionably nouveau identity, and yet don't I run the risk of doing that, even as I write this chapter about my resistance?

Had I married a Jew or had children of my own, I probably would have had to come to terms with Jewishness in a more coherent way. Now married to a non-Jew, whose children look like my camp counselors—blonde hair, long legs, and thin thighs—I get to insist loudly on the fact of my Jewishness, without taking any responsibility for my *shtick;* my ignorance stops with me. Though I've begun to light a *Yahrzeit* candle on the anniversaries of my parents' deaths and make *latkes* on Hanukkah, I'm not likely to become a practicing Jew in any more than an occasional dalliance with rituals performed by others, remembered from childhood. The vocabulary of regulation repels me: service, practice, observance. Nor can I imagine taking the equally unlikely secular course of joining, say, the New Jewish Agenda. What then? And why do I think there is something *to do,* that being Jewish entails a responsibility?

What's clear at this juncture is that for me what began in the family won't end there. My own idea of Jewishness, if it is to have a future, will have less to do with scenarios of immigration and assimilation than with the unfolding dilemmas of identity politics in postmodern culture. In my family history, as is true for many families of the great wave of emigration from Eastern Europe in the late nineteenth and early twentieth centuries, at the origin are *only stories, no places.* By this I mean that retrospectively where one came from is only a place one left: it is not a place to which one would ever return, even if it could be found on a map. I've often wondered whether the slightly fraudulent sense of Jewish identity I've always had wasn't bound up with the fact that my grandparents—three of whom I knew—seemed to come from places unreal to them. What counted finally were my maternal grandfather's endlessly re-told stories about the army and pogroms, but my grandfather could not fathom why my parents or I would go to Europe voluntarily. From my paternal grandparents' side there were no stories, but a few artifacts: silver serving spoons, and forks with family initials engraved in Russian letters. And yet no one seemed to have any hard information about ancestors; and no one seemed to care. One of my father's cousins told me recently that the silver came from their maternal family's tenure as caretakers on an estate in Kishinev. I contrast this with my husband's southern WASP family, where the family name coincides with a local place name, and heirlooms are handed down from generation to generation. My point here is that these scraps of information are utterly unverifiable and unusable in any real way as part of an autobiographical construction—unless, of course, one understands autobiog-raphy more modernly as a fiction of self-invention. I can be Jewish, then, as a story, not to say anecdotes about being Jewish, but not necessarily as a story with truth value.

Nonetheless, to the extent that as a critic and teacher I rely on the materials of the culture around me, even that story feels a little underrepresented. While Philip Roth, Woody Allen, and Art Spiegelman, for instance, have brilliantly pushed the questions of "writing as Jew" and Jewish subjectivity to the fore-front of popular consciousness, what their work acts out are the perplexities of Jewish men, and more specifically *sons* in the late twentieth century. There's a disturbing continuum between the spectacle at the wall and contemporary performances of the Jewish experience in which both the gender divide and the women's side of things are sublimely discounted. What a secular narrative produced by daughters—and feminist writers—will bring to our current sense of "Jewishness" remains to be seen.

As far as I can tell, one of the few benefits of middle age is the acknowledg-ment of one's limits, recognition of all one is never going to become, and with luck, acceptance of what one cannot help being. In that sense the answer to the question "what kind of Jew" I am remains caught for the moment in the logic of the old Groucho Marx jokes that have haunted me all my life: the kind of Jew who only knows what kind of Jew she doesn't want to be.

NOTE

This essay is part of a forthcoming book about contemporary memoirs, to be pub-lished by Oxford University Press. I'd like to thank Rachel Brownstein, Alice Kaplan, Michael Rothberg, and Jeffrey Rubin-Dorsky for their generous editorial advice along the way. It's not easy to write about being Jewish.

10

The Soul of Identity
Jews and Blacks

Laurence Mordekhai Thomas

DID I EVER tell you the story about the black man and the Jewish woman? Not only is it a wonderful story; it has the virtue of being a true story as well. Let me begin with it.

Once upon a time, there was this man who walked into a furniture store, where he was warmly greeted by a very cheerful salesperson. He was obviously black; she was obviously Jewish—whatever "obvious" is supposed to mean in these instances. They got along fabulously, and before long the conversation turned to his summer plans. Well, did he have a surprise for her. He was on his way to Israel. If she had been cheerful before, she was now absolutely ecstatic. For one thing, she had never been to Israel. For another, just who was this black man taking such a delight in heading off to Israel for, of all things, a wedding? When he told her that he, too, was one of them, the man went from being a wonderful and cordial stranger in her eyes to an absolutely adorable human being. Her name: Mrs. Harris.

She asked whether he would send her a postcard from Israel. Of course he would, so he requested her business card. Since he and she were perfect strangers, he had just assumed that he would write to her at her work. But she was not about to have her very first postcard from Israel handled in so mundane a manner, and insisted that he mail the card to her home address, which she gave him. As he departed, she paid him what was perhaps the ultimate compliment when she remarked, "I hope you find a nice Jewish girl in Israel to marry."

Now, that black man could have taken umbrage at the woman's use of "girl"; after all, he prides himself on being politically correct. Instead, though, he found himself more than a little moved by how utterly irrelevant his skin color had become. In a society where negative attitudes toward those with an abundance of melanin defies all logic, anything that manages to make skin color utterly irrelevant in a matter of seconds is extraordinary.

I should probably confess that I am the black man in that story, in case the thought has not already occurred to reader.

So often people ask me what they take to be the really tough question: Are you able to reconcile belonging to both groups—being both a Jew and a black? My first response is a rather cavalier one: most people, in fact, belong to more than one group, including most Jews. After all, most people have both an ethnic or racial identity and a national identity. Indeed, if the latest trend in America to hyphenate has any basis in reality, then there is not an American alive who does not belong to at least two groups.

I gather, though, that being Jewish and black is thought to raise special problems—that having both a Jewish and a black identity is rather like being engaged in a neverending internal tug of war over which identity shall have full sway in one's life. Further, this thinking is directly connected to two things: first, the fact that both groups have a history of having been systematically and horrendously oppressed; second, the reality that when a people have greatly suffered, then to that extent their suffering tends to be an ineliminable part of their self-identity. Surely, no Jew can be unmindful of the Holocaust, and no black (American or not) can be unmindful of American slavery. But why should this make being black and Jewish a problem? For no matter what her or his composition, no morally decent person can deny the horror of either American slavery or of the Holocaust, let alone that either occurred. Perhaps the thought is that the soul of a black Jew must be tormented with feelings of persecution. I wish that were the explanation for why people ask the question.

However, I fear that there is a much more invidious reason for why being black and Jewish is perceived to be a problem. There is the issue of who has suffered the most, blacks or Jews. And while it is polite to say that both have suffered sufficiently horribly that no good comes of trying to answer that question, the truth of the matter is that people often say one thing for the sake of politeness, yet believe another, namely: Our oppression was worse than theirs. By this line of thought the black Jew would be the very epitome of a divided self, with no hope of reconciliation in sight. For though gestures of politeness truly have a place in the world, even when they are not always heartfelt, being polite to oneself cannot get one very far.

Well, I may be something of a divided self, but the basis for my division has nothing to do with an internal war being waged in my soul over whether blacks or Jews fared worse in the case of American slavery or the Holocaust. I happen to believe that the nefarious institution of slavery and the equally nefarious event of the Holocaust had radically different aims, and that to focus on the number of deaths to which each gave rise is in fact to lost sight of those aims. While the number of people who died is a measure of the evil done, it is not definitive of it. As evil as both the institution and event were, neither was the complete embodiment of evil, because there were utterly atrocious evils in one not to be found in the other. The aim of slavery was the utter dependence of slaves upon the slaveowners; the aim of the Holocaust was the extermination of the Jews. As is readily apparent, these are such radically different matrices of evil that it can hardly be inferred that one was worse than the other merely on account of having more victims.

Whatever problems my self-identity might have, the question of who suffered more, blacks or Jews, does not exist for me. Nor am I much fazed by the reality that there are not many black Jews, or that I do not fit the stereotypical look of a Jew. Allowing that there is such a look, the truth is that not everyone who is Jewish, and unabashedly proud of it, fits that look. Besides I have interacted with enough Jews outside North America and, in particular, outside the United States, to realize that that so-called look has much more to do with being a part of American-Jewish culture than with simply being a Jew.

On an early Friday afternoon in Israel recently, I purchased a book on Jews and engaged the proprietor in a conversation about Jews, only to have him remark "Shabbat shalom" as I departed. All this occurred as naturally as if in the United States I had purchased aspirin at a drugstore. Yet, what occurred so naturally in that bookstore in Israel would not have occurred so naturally in the United States. In case the reader might be wondering, I was not wearing a *yarmulke,* and my nationality was obvious to the proprietor. In Israel, the simple truth is that Jews come in all shapes and sizes (certainly dark skin is no bar to being a Jew), and only a very obtuse Israeli individual would fail to appreciate that.

Of late, I have been spending a great deal of my time interacting with members of the Synagogue of Puteaux, as it is called (Puteaux being a village one metro stop outside Paris proper). Just about every Jew in that Synagogue is more French than distinctly Jewish in appearances and mannerisms. One member of the family which so beautifully welcomes me had this to say: "French Jews are French first and Jewish second, whereas American Jews are Jewish first and American second." And whenever I heard her say *"Viola!"* I mused to myself that surely there was truth in her remark. In both style and manner of speech, there is certainly no analogue in Paris to the New York Jew; and French culture does not reflect Jewish culture to nearly the extent, if at all, that American culture does. Bagels are fast becoming an American food item; Woody Allen is a piece of Americana as the ever-so-neurotic *Jew.*

Regarding the fact that there are comparatively few black Jews: that, too, is more an issue within the borders of America than outside them, since color just does not factor into the daily lives of people outside America in the insidious way that it often does within, as is clear from the bookstore story that I just told. This is true even if one simply goes next door to Canada. The most despicable racism I have ever encountered outside America, including in Israel, has been from Americans traveling abroad. Outside America it is simply being an American, rather than being black, that tends to dominate people's perceptions of blacks (though this may be changing as other countries view more and more American television programing).

Here is another story: On one visit to Israel, I said something to the hotel receptionist which invited the assumption that I am Jewish. She clearly had not thought so before. But without missing a beat, she changed her view of me. There was not that ever-so-familiar look of incredulity, followed by a barrage of questions. It was clear that from her perspective she had simply made a factual error in her assessment of me. The next day, feeling rather full of myself, I muttered some sentences in Hebrew, having gotten some clarifications from the other receptionist (who is male) the previous day. Well, the male receptionist was quite taken with how quickly I had mastered the few lessons he had given me, and commented on it. As an explanation for my supposedly phenomenal learning ability, the woman receptionist remarked: "It is his Jewish brain!" The day before I was simply an American in her eyes.

That story speaks to what I believe are some of the deep, deep, self-identity concerns that come with being a black Jew. For me the problem goes far beyond the stereotype of the Jew, which, while profoundly and disturbingly negative in many respects, is that of a person who is exceedingly capable intellectually, whereas the stereotype of the black, while negative in different ways, does not credit the person with any positive intellectual abilities. Blacks make for good dancers, singers (classical music aside), and athletes. None of these is thought to require intellectual talent as such.

As I shall argue, the problem is that the self-identity of American blacks as members of the black race is tied entirely and exclusively to their past history of suffering. By contrast, while the self-identity of Jews accords suffering a fundamental place in the Jewish experience, suffering is by no means the most central aspect of Jewish identity. There is, I believe, a rich historical narrative (to be explicated below) which is also a part of the self-identity of Jews. Nothing comparable exists for blacks—certainly not blacks in America. When that woman in the Israeli hotel invoked my Jewish brain to explain my apparent rapid success with the Hebrew language, it was the Jewish narrative which made that possible. There is no narrative available for blacks which would have made it reasonable to invoke my black brain with regard to mastering the Hebrew language or, for that matter, an African one. The claim that I am making, therefore, is that American blacks do not have a historical narrative. That claim should not be confused with a different one, namely, that there are no vestiges of African traditions in the lives of American blacks. I take this latter claim to be manifestly false.

By a narrative I mean a set of stories which define values and purely positive goals, and fixed points of historical significance, as well as various ennobling rituals to be performed regularly. A narrative yields a set of practices that cannot be readily appropriated by others. We may say that the narratives of a people define a fundamental part of their conception of the good, and thus what their aspirations should be, while providing significant fixed points of historical reference. A goal is purely positive only if it is not in any way defined in terms of avoiding some harm. Thus, simply eliminating racism, sexism, or anti-Semitism does not constitute a positive goal, as important as it is to do these things.[1] Learning Swahili, by contrast, can be a positive goal, even if this turns out to help one to avoid some harm, since the goal itself can be defined independently of avoiding harm. The two are certainly conceptually separate. The stories which constitute a historical narrative may very well be anchored entirely in facts, but they need not be. If a story constitutes a sufficient focal point in the lives of people by articulating a set of rituals which are to be performed regularly, then that story is part of the narrative of those people, though it is based upon few facts or none at all. For example, male circumcision is a fundamental part of the Jewish narrative, because Abraham is said to have circumcised himself in his old age as a sign of the Jewish covenant. Whether he in fact did so, however, is very nearly irrelevant nowadays, since being circumcised has come to be a defining feature of being a male Jew. Purely positive goals are goals that have intrinsic value.

The ennobling rituals of a narrative may either mark significant historical events or serve as an emblem of spiritual significance, or both. Eating matzoh during Pesach is an instance of the former, since a Jew may simply choose to consume neither leavened nor unleavened bread during Pesach. Wearing a *yarmulke* on a daily basis is an instance of the latter. By contrast, as much as bagels are identified with American-Jewish culinary traditions, consuming bagels does not constitute an ennobling ritual. Not all rituals articulated by a narrative need be ennobling. Participating in ennobling rituals generally serves as the most important way to reaffirm one's identity with one's narrative.

Now, I believe that without a historical narrative it is impossible for any people to flourish in a society that is hostile toward them. What is more, the narrative must be essentially isomorphic with respect to the people who are the object of the hostility. A historical narrative is essentially isomorphic when, taken in its totality, it cannot be shared with others; that is, there is a one-to-one relationship between the group and the narrative that defines them. Thus, we have two different narratives with respect to Muslims and Jews, although they have Abraham in common. It is for the following two interconnected reasons that I regard having a narrative as necessary for flourishing in a hostile society. The first is the obvious truth that genuine cooperation is necessary for the flourishing of a people who are the object of societal hostility. Second, there can be no genuine cooperation among people so situated in the absence of a narrative, for the narrative provides the basis for trust. There can be trust without cooperation, but not the converse; for cooperation is symmetrical, whereas trust can be both symmetrical and asymmetrical.[2]

To begin with, having a common enemy does not suffice to ensure cooperation among people, precisely because it cannot be a basis for trust. Nothing changes if in addition to a common enemy most members of the group are readily identifiable by some salient set of phenotypical features. If a member of an oppressed group has good reason to believe that she can avoid enough of the hostility without cooperating with others in her group, or can avoid hostility to the same degree whether cooperating or not, then there is simply no reason for her to cooperate if her only concern is to avoid hostility, regardless of her phenotypical features. While many may never have good reason to believe this, it cannot be insisted, as matter of logic, that no one ever has. More pointedly, if the only aim is to avoid a harm, then it is totally irrelevant whether one does so with one's group or on one's own when in either case one avoids the harm. And because avoiding the harm is the ultimate goal anyhow, then there will always be an incentive to avoid the harm on one's own, regardless of what might happen to the group. Thus, a common enemy makes for very unstable cooperation, if any at all, among a people. To be sure, people are sometimes moved by altruistic considerations to do for others. But to appeal to altruistic considerations is to appeal to something other than a common enemy. We can trust people only when they have given us good reason to believe that they will do their part even though they could refrain from doing so without bearing any loss whatsoever—in other words, when they do their part even though they are not being watched. Merely having a common enemy is not a good enough basis for mutual trust.

This is all quite ironic, for there can be little doubt that, when an oppressed people join together against the hostilities of society, the resulting good for the people as a whole far exceeds the good that comes from isolated individuals, taken together, avoiding the hostilities of society on their own. I have not, therefore, been arguing against cooperation; rather, I am insisting that cooperation among an oppressed people requires more than a common enemy.

By contrast, when a people are galvanized by a narrative many advantages occur. There is first of all a set of goals that is put forth independently of a common enemy, goals which are not readily achieved alone and which are not necessarily defined in terms of individual accomplishments. Second, there is what I should like to call contributory pride. Contributory pride is no more mysterious than pride itself and the delight we take, in general, in doing things that reflect well upon our talents. Even when alone and there is no chance of being heard by someone, a person who can play the piano well wants to do so. This is not just because it pains the ear to hear a concerto being played with one flaw after another; if this were the case, the person could easily put on a compact disk of the concerto. Rather, it is because she takes delight in playing up to her level of competence. Likewise, we want our lives to reflect those values and goals which are dear to us, and it is a source of pleasure to us when this is so. Thus, like pride proper, contributory pride has considerable motivational force. Just as pride can move a person to perform up to her level of competence, though this is of no consequence to anyone but herself, contributory pride can move a person to do her part in the realization of a goal, though the project's success is not contingent upon her contribution and her contribution or failure to contribute may go unnoticed anyway.

Because a historical narrative provides a basis for contributory pride, it allows for the possibility of genuine cooperation, in that people can be counted on to do their part even when no one is assessing their performance. In fact, people can be counted on to do their part even when they would be no worse off for not doing so (and actually better off, since they would have saved their resources) and, moreover, the goal would be realized anyhow. Thus, the contributory pride that comes with embracing a narrative gets us around the so-called free-rider problem of the person who aims to reap the benefits of success without doing his share, because such pride is a source of motivation in its own right.

The moral of the story, then, is this. There can be no genuine cooperation among people belonging to the same group simply on account of their having the desire to overcome the same problem, since this cannot be an adequate basis for mutual trust. What is needed is a set of values which define the self-identity of persons belonging to the group; for we know that values of this sort often have abiding motivational force in their own right. This, in turn, makes genuine cooperation possible, because shared values serve as a basis for trust—at least for a group which must contend with a hostile society.

(This moral has been lost on most of those working in game theory who have endeavored to solve the prisoner's dilemma, where the issue roughly is how to get two purely rational self-interested persons to cooperate, independent of any form of assurance, for a mutual advantage that is unattainable in the absence of cooperation, without either defecting for the sake of a smaller advantage that can be attained without cooperation. Owing to the absence of assurance, it invariably turns out to be rational for each to defect. As traditionally put, the dilemma systematically ignores several things. One is that human beings are not just creatures with self-interested desires, but that having values is a constitutive part of human life, and the successful pursuit or realization of values is what gives life meaning for humans. Another is that values need not be self-interested in order to have deep motivational force in the life of individuals. History reveals that historical narratives can be among the deepest values that individuals hold. What is more, otherwise perfect strangers who meet may have good reason to believe that they both deeply embrace the same historical narrative, and can thus display basic trust toward one another—trust being that psychological attitude which two people have toward one another without which cooperation between them is impossible.)[3]

Let me now apply the account of a historical narrative and its implications for group trust directly to the situation of Jews and blacks. First, I take it there can be no doubt that there is an isomorphic narrative for Jews. Even people who do not like Jews are prepared to acknowledge that the Old Testament is primarily about the history of the Jews. The ascendancy of Christianity has not changed that. What is more, there is a universal set of rituals the successful performance of which is relevant to being a good Jew, such as keeping kosher, being observant, mastering the Torah, or supporting Jewish life (which can be done in a myriad of ways). These ennobling rituals are defined by the narrative and are entirely independent of the culture in which Jews happen to find themselves (the state of Israel aside). What is more, they cannot be appropriated, at least not readily. A non-Jew who walks around wearing a *yarmulke* would be showing utter disrespect for the religious rituals of Judaism. And outside synagogues, non-Jews do not wear *yarmulkes*. A non-Jew who keeps kosher simply for the sake of keeping kosher would be so odd, since keeping kosher is extremely demanding, that his doing so would be more likely to garner disdain or contempt than respect. For unlike circumcision, which has been said to have health benefits, keeping kosher is not known to have any health or moral or spiritual benefits; hence, independent of being Jewish, there is next to nothing to recommend it.

When anti-Semitism was at a more virulent level in the United States, and all sorts of institutions rejected Jews, including Ivy League schools, Jews had a way of affirming themselves that was entirely independent of the oppressive society in which they lived. This is not to discount the self-hatred among Jews to which anti-Semitism has given rise. My concern here is simply to acknowledge an important reality, namely, that on account of having an isomorphic narrative, Jews have been able to affirm themselves in the face of social hostility. This truth is not defeated by the fact that Jews have, to varying degrees, been driven by the engine of assimilation. This is the truth I have in mind when I claim that it is impossible for a people to flourish in a society which is hostile toward them in the absence of a narrative.

Now, while avoiding anti-Semitism certainly has been important, it is manifestly obvious that there are also positive goals among Jews which are inextricably tied to the Jewish narrative. Most Jews see the existence of the state of Israel as a good. (Ultra-Orthodox Jews are still waiting for the "true" Israel to be realized.) Most Jews believe that it is a good thing that there are synagogues and that Judaism can be practiced. There are Jews who believe these things though they have no interest whatsoever in visiting Israel or in setting foot in a synagogue. The good of these things is part and parcel of the Jewish narrative. Of course, not all Jews view this good in exactly the same way.[4] Some argue that Israel cannot be criticized; others think quite differently. Many hold that Orthodox Judaism is more than just a little in love with outmoded rituals, to say nothing of the split between the major forms of Judaism in America: Reform, Conservative, Reconstructionist, and Orthodox. But if a people have a narrative only if all embrace it in exactly the same way, then no people can be said to have a narrative. For no other reason than that they are Jews, it turns out that, to varying degrees and in various ways, some of the values of most Jews are shaped by the Jewish narrative. This fact is no small explanation for the success of Jews in a very hostile world, since shared values among group members are indispensable to cooperation in such a context.

I do not deny that the existence of anti-Semitism is a galvanizing factor among Jews. It most certainly is. The Holocaust itself has been a reason for even the most secular Jew to be self-identified as a Jew, lest Hitler should be

handed a posthumous victory.[5] And modern times have seen no greater rallying point for Jews than the 1967 Six-Day War (during which Israel fought
Egypt, Syria, and Jordan). But none of this militates against the truth that
there are values and positive goals defined independently of anti-Semitism.
What is more, I maintain that it is precisely because there are such positive
goals that Jews are able to respond so successfully in the face of a common
enemy. It is one thing to know what to run from; it is quite another to know
where to run to. A common enemy can yield an answer only to the former; an
answer to the latter must come from values and positive goals. A historical
narrative determines the stakes and gives priority to activities; accordingly, it
yields an affirmation that cannot be had merely by avoiding the enemy.

Do American blacks have a narrative? I do not believe so. As I have said, I
should hardly deny that there are vestiges of African tradition in black American life. Blacks brought with them from Africa rich oral and rhythmic traditions,[6] which are manifested in the music and dance of blacks today. Nor
would I deny that these traditions have left an indelible stamp upon the way
many blacks practice Christianity. There can be no getting around the fact
that there is a most distinctive style to black gospel singing and to the cadence
of black preaching. No one hearing a speech of Martin Luther King, Jr.,
could think otherwise. This is form, though; it is not a narrative.[7] However
permanent an impression Africa may have left on black Christianity, the
message of Christianity is no different for black and white Christians. In
truth, there are probably fewer substantive differences, if in fact there are any,
between black and white Christian teachings than there are between the
Catholic and Protestant traditions. There certainly is no isomorphism between the Christian narrative and black people; nor, it seems, could there be,
since Christianity is a universalistic doctrine. Indeed, one wonders why the
very existence of slavery is not an outright indictment of Christianity. A
people coming to believe in the gods of their oppressors, as was the case with
American slaves, is perhaps as good a sign as one could want that the oppressed do not have a narrative of their own. And if the imprimatur of blacks
upon Christianity has yet to produce a black narrative, it is wildly implausible
to suppose that it will be found in some other walk of life, such as music or
dance. In the face of American slavery and the continued existence of racism,
blacks have been left without an isomorphic narrative to affirm them, one that
is entirely independent of the very society oppressing them.

Without minimizing it, I do want to insist that form cannot constitute a
narrative as I have defined this term. It seems reasonable enough to hold that
the very survival of American blacks during slavery was owed to the distinctive way in which they practiced Christianity. I have not denied this. I have
certainly not claimed that a people can cope *only* if they have a narrative. What
I am maintaining, though, is that a people can flourish in a hostile society
only if they have a narrative. Clearly, there is fundamental difference between
coping and flourishing. Children of sexual abuse often cope by forming

177

multiple personalities. This is not a means of flourishing on their part. To cope is to blunt the force of the harm that one has to endure, to render it less destructive than it would otherwise have been. To flourish is to go considerably beyond minimizing the harm, even if that is a first step. It is to apply one's history in ways that make for self-mastery and self-command.

To be sure, some people will flourish under the harshest of conditions, whereas others will flounder though all the world has been at their beck and call. Clearly, some American blacks have flourished in spite of slavery and racism. Frederick Douglass, Harriet Jacobs, and W. E. B. Du Bois come readily to mind. I never claimed that no blacks have ever flourished. My claim has been that American blacks as a people have not flourished, and that in the face of racism it is not possible for blacks as a people to do so without a historical narrative.

Lest there be any misunderstanding, I am no more blaming blacks for not having a narrative than I am crediting Jews for having one. Neither situation can be construed as a matter of choice. But as both birth and the character of the parent-child relationship show, our lives can be immeasurably affected by that which we did not choose.

As a way of making these remarks more concrete, let me return to the autobiographical mode once more. In traveling abroad, I have in two very different countries—Finland and France—been wonderfully befriended by families simply on the basis of showing up in a synagogue, not on account of being a famous Jew, but simply a Jew. I have been rather surprised by the fact that no comparable thing has happened to me on account of being black— not a famous black. To be sure, I have struck up conversations with black people in foreign countries, such as Israel and Poland, where encountering a black is something of a rarity. But I have never done so in Paris or London, where black people are common enough. I have, in fact, been a regular visitor to a bar in Tel Aviv frequented by blacks, but no special bonding has taken place between me and the blacks there. On one occasion in Tel Aviv, I was stopped by some black Americans who had been in Israel for nearly twenty years, insisting that they were entitled to Israeli citizenship on the basis of Israel's Law of Return, since Israel is a part of Africa—so they claimed. We had a discussion about that. But the discussion almost immediately turned to the topic of racism, and no less immediately did it become clear that we thought quite differently about a lot of things. Perhaps if I were to show up in a black church abroad, I would be treated as in synagogues abroad, with the exception of Israel. I do not think so, as I shall explain in a moment.

Needless to say, a foreign Jew visiting a synagogue in Israel is rather uninteresting. Sitting in the Great Synagogue in Jerusalem, I observed that just about every fourth person around me spoke a different language, A Canadian sat to my left; two French-speaking individuals sat directly in front of me; and some German-speaking people were behind me. The Canadian, who was a physician, thought it obvious that I was Jewish, for he said, "The *yarmulke* you are wearing is obviously yours and not one that they give a person who walks in without one." The American whom I encountered was too much taken by my black skin to be equally perceptive.

But to return to the argument I wish to make: Anyone claiming to be a Jew who shows up in a synagogue will be assumed to have certain values and beliefs and to be familiar with certain rituals. This is due to the historical narrative. There is an entire range of issues and things of amusement that can be discussed that are essentially Jewish which have nothing to do with anti-Semitism and which are not, strictly speaking, very religious. The conversation can begin there, even if it ends up being entirely about anti-Semitism. In the meantime, there have been interaction and expressions of good will, along with a delight in the differences and similarities. Showing up in a black church abroad would hardly be the same. There is simply no aspect of the Christian narrative that is isomorphic to blacks, no aspects of the Christian texts that blacks have interpreted as applying specifically to blacks and blacks only. Indeed, the very idea that parts of the Christian narrative could be isomorphic to a specific race or ethnicity borders on incoherency. And as I have indicated, if we do not find a black narrative in Christianity, as powerful an influence as Christianity has been in the lives of black people, then it is rather unlikely that we will find that narrative in other areas of black life.

Regarding Christianity, there is no one nation whose relationship to Christianity is such that the politics or religious practices of that nation are of special importance. I could ask the French family whether they think American Jews take themselves to have a special relationship to Israel. The question makes for great conversation without being threatening. There is no similar question that I could put to blacks abroad in a black church. I could, with amusement, ask the French family about the practice (in the Synagogue of Puteaux) of each person kissing his own hand after having shaken another person's hand. This is particularly amusing after the Torah reading, when the number of times which the reader ends up kissing his own hand is equal to the number of people whose hand he shakes, which is usually everyone's. It seems rather improbable that a like conversation would be occasioned by showing up in a black church; for no analogous set of rituals exists for blacks.

There just is no narrative that defines the personal identity of American blacks. The closest one gets to that, which is simply not close enough, is that of having the common enemy of racism. Furthermore, it is also true that blacks experience racial hostilities to widely varying degrees and in vastly different modes, as is the case with Jews experiencing anti-Semitism. More poignantly, if racism should cease tomorrow, there would be no common goals, no set of goods, which blacks could be said to want primarily on account of being black. Moreover, there are no universally recognized rituals, to be preserved or debated, which define being a good black, as there are ennobling rituals which define being a good Jew. There is nothing remotely close to wearing a *yarmulke* that constitutes widely shared ritualistic behavior among American blacks, such that it cannot be readily appropriated by other peoples.

And while, of late, much is made of Africa by American blacks, it is just not true that the relationship of American blacks or, for that matter, blacks born anywhere outside Africa is akin to the one embodied in Israel's Law of Return, according to which any Jew in the world is entitled to Israeli citizenship. There is no such policy regarding blacks with respect to any African nation. Let me mention, though, that I am most dismayed by the extent to which Africa is treated as a single unit.[8] How is it that the second largest continent on earth is regarded in such a homogeneous manner, when the smaller continent of Europe is regarded as teeming with differences? It might be supposed that the answer is the fact of shared blackness. But that just cannot be, since the equally evident fact of shared whiteness is no barrier to people seeing a multitude of differences among whites.

The irony of ironies, then, is this: As visibly black as I and many other black American people are, we are without a set of ennobling rituals and positive goals; we are without a conception of the good whereby we can affirm and identify with one another. This is due to the absence of a historical narrative among black American people. Perhaps there should not or cannot be one for all black people. But that is a different matter entirely. On the other hand, though at first glance I am an unlikely candidate for being Jewish, the ever-so-elusive Jewish look being what it is, I can literally traverse continents and be embraced by heretofore perfect strangers owing to the existence of a historical narrative for Jews.

Lest it be thought that I am making just a bit too much of the narrative as a unifying force among Jews, I am well aware that serious and perhaps irreconcilable differences exist among Jews, the narrative notwithstanding. But with the possible exception of life itself—that is, mere physical existence—the activity of living is rarely an all-or-nothing matter. The existence of deep and divisive differences among Jews does not in any way alter the fact that the Jewish narrative makes it possible for people who otherwise have nothing in common to affirm and identify with one another, albeit to varying degrees. For instance, Jews who could not imagine themselves keeping kosher can yet be united with kosher-keeping Jews on the importance of Israel. Nor does the existence of differences diminish the truth that the Jewish narrative has provided a source of independent affirmation in hostile societies. Jews need not be monolithic in their adherence to and interpretation of their narrative in order for these things to be true. Far more important than being monolithic is that we do not lose sight of the narrative and the often immeasurable good that it has wrought in our lives, sometimes in spite of our own doing. Our meaningful disagreement is perhaps as sure a sign as we could want that the narrative is very much alive. Better the cacophony of disagreement among a people over their narrative than a deafening silence.

Regarding blacks, it might seem that an adequate response here is that all blacks have their ancestral roots in Africa, which is a land rich in cultural traditions and narratives. I have not denied this. I have not done so even with the observation that blacks have no "right of return" to any African nation. The real issue, however, is the impact that the slave trade has had upon the descendants of those blacks who were forcibly removed from Africa and transplanted to a foreign and hostile environment. The plain truth of the matter is that being a descendant of a people does not entail maintaining the narratives of one's ancestors. It is possible for a people to be cut off from the narratives of their ancestors even though vestiges of their traditions remain a part of the lives of those people. Narratives are social constructs, not biological manifestations. Though, to be sure, biological lineage may entitle one to lay claim to an ancestral narrative, such lineage does not mean that the narrative is now operative in one's life.

I have claimed that American blacks, meaning descendants of those blacks forcibly removed from Africa, do not now have a historical narrative. I have not maintained that in the future they could not come to have such a narrative, be it a new one independent of Africa or the recovery of an old one steeped in African traditions. For American blacks, at any rate, the writings of Frederick Douglass, Harriet Jacobs, and W. E. B. Du Bois—to recall those mentioned earlier as having flourished in America—could acquire an elevated status forming an indispensable part of the liturgy in black churches during Sunday morning services.[9] And there could be ennobling rituals with respect to these writings. Indeed, some could attach greater value to one author than to another; hence, there could be ennobling rituals which identify blacks as Jacobsonians, or Du Boisians, or Douglassians. And there could be ennobling rituals identifying some blacks as pluralists if they regard these authors to be on an equal footing with one another. Again, I have not denied that there could be a black historical narrative. On the contrary, I have adumbrated the way in which American blacks could achieve a narrative which is independent of Africa. After all, there is no reason to insist that all blacks must share the same narrative, as no one supposes that all whites do.

Some would say that the very dignity of American blacks depends upon their acquiring a narrative. This I do not wish to dispute, though I hope it isn't so. For nowhere is it given that a people will inevitably come to have a narrative. And I should hope that, even in the absence of so profound a unifying focus, a people can yet have both honor and dignity.

Before concluding I wish to address the fact that the reader may very well have noted a measure of ambiguity on my part in talking about blacks. There are American blacks, and there are blacks throughout the world. And it would be hubris of the worst sort to suppose that claims made about the former apply *tout court* to the latter. The claim that blacks lack a narrative applies most forcefully and fully to American blacks. To varying degrees, blacks in other countries, especially blacks in predominantly black countries, may possess a narrative. In this regard, the Caribbean countries come readily to mind among non-African countries. On the other hand, there is nothing about the logic of a narrative from which it follows that a people must possess one by virtue of their being the vast majority of the population of their country. One has only to look at South Africa, where blacks outnumber whites by a ratio of nearly five to one, to see the truth of this statement.

These remarks bring me to a most interesting observation regarding the difference between blacks and Jews as it pertains to having a narrative. Since the occurrence of Kristallnacht in 1938 (taking that event as marking the beginning of the Holocaust), the Holocaust has henceforth been regarded as part of the Jewish narrative for all Jews throughout the world. That is, this event itself is to be regarded as part of the Jewish history of each and every Jew. (There is no inconsistency here because the Holocaust was an evil event; for it must be remembered that fixed points of historical reference can be part of a narrative. And there may be rituals which revolve around those points, as in the case of the rituals of Pesach.)

By contrast, we speak of American slavery and apartheid, the latter being a definite reference to South Africa. Yet, the very manner in which we label these two oppressive institutions against blacks prevents these institutions from being regarded as part of the history of each and every black. For all three instances, it is true to varying degrees that, but for an accident in history, any Jew living at the time might have been a victim of the Holocaust or any black a victim of American slavery or apartheid. Why the difference, then? I suggest that the idea of a narrative which I have offered has some explanatory power in this regard. The Holocaust was a threat to the continuing existence of a set of positive goals and rituals (defined by a narrative), which were more or less embraced by Jews who escaped (or by those who were somewhat geographically removed from the Holocaust, such as American Jews). Neither American slavery nor apartheid, however, threatened to destroy an overarching black narrative. To be sure, in the 1970s and 1980s, when apartheid was at the very forefront of the world's consciousness, any black living anywhere in the world other than South Africa could certainly look upon that country with utter moral disgust, and speak of the wrong being perpetrated against black people there. All the same, for most blacks living elsewhere in the world, apartheid was no threat to the continual existence of a set of goals and rituals defined by a narrative embraced by blacks worldwide, albeit to varying degrees.

Skin color alone cannot be the glue that makes a people one. But if I am right about the efficacy of a narrative, it is surprising just how little beyond that is needed. It is perhaps because so little else is required that many have been deluded into thinking that nothing at all is.

I should like to conclude this chapter, as I began it, with some autobiographical reflections. While I have no clue as to what my first interesting thoughts about human beings were, I am rather confident that understanding the major differences between blacks and Jews is something I wrestled with very early on in my life. I do remember, though, being terribly disappointed at the sort of pat responses that adults often give a child who asks a searching question to which they do not know the answer. I imagine that some thirty years ago it was considered impolite to be too concerned with certain questions. However, I never dreamed then that one day I might be attempting an answer to this question from my youth.

And if my readers assume from my answer that I am proud of being a Jew but ashamed of being a black, they are making an incorrect assumption. For I have drawn upon who *I am* to say something about the history of both Jews and blacks, examining my own experiences in order to determine the differences that are in contradistinction to one another.

Finally, I want to say that while it is true, strictly speaking, that the Torah attaches great weight to Jews helping other Jews, it does not in any way call upon Jews to diminish other peoples and traditions. Portuguese-, Moroccan-, Russian-, and Israeli-born Jews have very little in common culturally, save the Jewish narrative.[10] No one seems to think that any of the non-Israeli Jews are bound to experience an identity crisis on account of their cultural background. It is most unfortunate that ideological head winds would have it that being black and Jewish presents some special problem. Diminishing those head winds just a bit is a most affirming aspect of my Jewish identity, though doing so is far from being my *raison d'être* or *cause célèbre*—and I hope it never comes to that. It certainly need not, at least insofar as being a good Jew is concerned. And that, too, is very affirming to my Jewish identity.

My parental upbringing embodied the ideal that the success of individuals, whatever their walk in life, is never contingent upon their undercutting the endeavors of others. As I see it, this is a human good to which all can and should aspire. Inasmuch as I falter with respect to it, I am so glad that it has absolutely nothing to do with being Jewish and black.

NOTES

*I am grateful Alan Berger, Arlene Kanter, Steven Kepnis, and Yuval Steinitz for their criticisms and encouragement, and to the editors for searching comments upon this manuscript. The final draft of this chapter was completed in Israel. The hospitality of Aaron Ben Ze-ev, and conversations with him, on the kibbutz Ein Carmel made for quite salubrious conditions under which to rework this chapter.

This chapter draws upon my book, *Vessels of Evil: American Slavery and the Holocaust* (Philadelphia, Pa.: Temple University Press, 1993). For a partial account of how I understand the differences between American slavery and the Holocaust, see my "American Slavery and the Holocaust: Their Ideologies Compared," *Public Affairs Quarterly* 5 (1991).

The final version of this chapter was written more than three years ago; and in two important respects my views have evolved substantially since then. One is that I have now sharply distinguished between culture and narrative. It is my view that black

Americans have a rich culture or set of cultures, but not as of yet a rich narrative in the quite technical sense that I use the word in this chapter. See my "Narrative Identity and Group Autonomy," in *Blacks and Jews: Arguments and Alliances,* ed. Paul Berman (New York: Delacorte Press, 1994). The other is that I have tried to shed some light on the appeal of Louis Farrakhan in "Explaining an American Legacy: Tensions between Blacks and Jews," *Social Identities: Journal for the Study of Race, Nation and Culture* 2 (1996). What is more, since being black is not a sufficient condition for being a member of the Nation of Islam, I have argued that this supports my view that skin color does not a people make, but rather a narrative is required.

1. I take there to be a significant difference between anti-Semitism and racism, especially as racism applies to blacks. Anti-Semitism derives its energy from the view that Jews are irredeemably evil; racism derives its energy from the view that blacks are moral simpletons. See my "Evolution of Antisemitism," *Transition* 55 (1992); and chap. 6 of *Vessels of Evil.*

2. Interesting work is now being done on trust. See, for example, Annette Baier, "Trust and Anti-Trust," *Ethics* 96 (1986); Diego Gambetta, ed., *Trust: Making and Breaking Cooperative Relations* (Oxford: Basil Blackwell, 1988); and Laurence Thomas, "Trust, Affirmation, and Moral Character," in *Morality, Character, and Identity: Essays in Moral Psychology,* ed. Owen Flanagan and Amelie Rorty (Cambridge, Mass.: MIT Press, 1990).

3. For a searching discussion of game theory in the context of the prisoner's dilemma, see Martin Hollis, "Moves and Motives in the Games We Play," *Analysis* 50 (1990).

4. Here I am deeply indebted to Jonathan Sacks's most insightful work *One People? Tradition, Modernity, and Jewish Unity* (London: Littman Library of Jewish Civilization, 1993). But there is an important difference in our views. See note 9 below.

5. This is Emil Fackenheim's so-called 614th commandment. See his *Jewish Return in History: Reflections in the Age of Auschwitz and a New Jerusalem* (New York: Schocken, 1978). Tradition has it that the Torah issued 613 commandments.

6. See Sterling Stuckey, *Slave Culture: Nationalist Theory and the Foundations of Black America* (New York: Oxford University Press, 1987), who is concerned to show that American black culture is basically African at its roots. Stuckey suggests that, for example, the religious dance in black churches called the shout had great meaning in African contexts (88). No doubt the shout did. However, I dare say that most who participate in the shout today are clueless about its original meaning. This line of thought can be found in Melville J. Herskovits, *The Myth of the Negro Past* (New York: Harper and Brothers Publishers, 1941), chap. 8; and Lawrence W. Levine, *Black Culture and Black Consciousness* (New York: Oxford University Press, 1977). For further discussion of these matters, see chaps. 7 and 8 of my *Vessels of Evil.*

7. In order for Christianity to play the role that many would have it play in the lives of American black people, it is simply not enough that blacks put their own variation on Christian worship. Some substantial differences in reading the text are necessary. On this score, it is worth noting the way in which Islam distinguished itself from Judaism. Here I am indebted to Daniel Sibony, *Les trois monothéismes: Juifs, Chrétiens, Musulmans entre leurs sources et leurs destins* (Paris: Editions du Seuil, 1992). He writes of the Jewish religion: ". . . il n'a pas parlé des deux autres, et pour cause, ceux-ci n'étaient pas encore là quand il est apparu. Mais eux ont beaucoup parlé de lui. Parfois directement: en

parlant de leurs prédécesseurs dans les rapport avec ce Dieu, ils parlent des Juifs . . ." (13). Then he goes on to tell us that according to Islam, ". . . Dieu . . . a donné une première version [de la Bible] aux Juifs; . . . ceux-ci l'ont falsifiée—cela signifie surtout qu'ils ne l'ont pas repectée . . ." (53). Then, regarding the story of Moses killing some-one in Egypt, Sibony writes: "Dans le Coran c'est le même recit, mais cette fois Moise a tué un de ses <<adversaires>>. . . . [Alors], un homme est venue lui dire que les <<chefs des peuple>> voulaient le tuer. Cela peut désigner les chefs du peuple hébreu" (30). Finally, Sibony observes that ". . . contrairement à la Bible où la mission de Moise est de liberer son peuple d'Égypte pour lui donner la Loi, dans le Coran sa mission principale est de convertir Pharaon à Dieu" (110).

In other words (giving the sense of the French rather than translating it precisely): Because the religions of Islam and Christianity did not exist when Judaism appeared, the latter does not speak of them, although they speak of it in order to explain the relationship of their ancestors to the divine being. Unlike Christianity, however, Islam does not merely build upon the stories of Judaism, leaving the accounts of the actors and their performances essentially intact. Thus, Islam allows that the Jews were the first to receive the Bible, but maintains that the Jews nonetheless distorted it, thereby revealing that they did not respect it. And although both the Torah and the Koran maintain that Moses killed someone while in Egypt, a radical divergence follows. The Koran also has it that Moses repented, and identifies the person, not as an Egyptian, but as an adversary. And the man who tells Moses that the chief of the people wants him dead implicates the Jewish people rather than the Egyptians. Finally, while the Torah has it that Moses delivered his people from Egypt in order to give them the law, the Koran has it that the primary mission of Moses was to convert the pharaoh to the Almighty.

My point is simply this: Whatever changes there are in black Christianity, they do not even come close to being textual in the way that Islam is with respect to Judaism. (See note 10 below.)

8. Kwame Anthony Appiah's discussion of Alexander Crummel, in *In My Fa-ther's House: Africa in the Philosophy of Culture* (New York: Oxford University Press, 1992), indicates that this way of thinking would suggest that some very distinguished black thinkers, and some of the earliest Pan-Africanists, conceived of Africa and black people with a broad homogeneous brush (see pp. 3–11). Appiah uses the expression "African nationalism." Others do as well. Why isn't that expression an oxymoron, since there is no nation that corresponds to Africa?

9. Thus, in my view Cornel West is mistaken in his view that Christianity could have center stage in the black American narrative. At any rate, he is mistaken in not offering or pointing to an interpretation of Christianity that, at some level, gives it an isomorphic standing to blacks. (See West's *Prophecy Deliverance!* [Philadelphia: West-minister Press, 1982].) I do not claim that such an interpretation cannot be offered, though I suspect that any rich interpretation of Christianity that is isomorphic to blacks would result in a religious doctrine that is separate from Christianity. Form alone cannot yield such a separation, as the fundamental differences between Catholicism and Protes-tantism show; the two principal branches of Christianity are compatible with quite profound differences in both form and content. However, in all its forms, Christianity claims to be entirely universal; and therein lies the rub with an interpretation of Chris-tianity that is isomorphic to blacks.

185

10. For the record, let me mention what may already be obvious to some, namely, that as I am using the idea of the historical narrative of the Jews it is not coextensive with Judaism the religion—as constituted by Jewish law, *halakhah*. In *One People?* Jonathan Sacks maintains that *halakhah* is the "architecture of Jewish life" (21), the very basis for Jewish unity (97, 214). If his idea is that whatever unites Jews must be the same for all times, then Sacks and I differ radically on the nature of the social glue that binds Jews together. However, if he will allow that, in addition to *halakhah*, other things can come to unite Jews, then the difference between us turns of to be one of emphasis. My worry is that in Sacks's view, it is next to impossible to allow for the occurrence of watershed events in the history of the Jews which constitute a unifying force for them, but which do not owe their unifying energy to *halakhah*. The Holocaust, of course, is perhaps the paradigm example of such an event. There is simply no denying the importance of the Holocaust as an extraordinary unifying force among Jews. And, of course, Sacks hardly denies the moral significance of the Holocaust with respect to Jews. All the same, there is for him the question of the status of the Holocaust vis-à-vis *halakhah* as a unifying force among Jews. Sacks can be read as saying that, properly speaking, the Holocaust should not, even for a moment, ever have the same unifying force among Jews as *halakhah*, as any such results spell the demise of Jews as a people. For Sacks, *halakhah* is necessary and sufficient for Jewish identity and unity—or so it would seem; for me, *halakhah* is unquestionably necessary, but not sufficient. One cannot both take a people's history seriously and, at the same time, insist that their identity be exclusively defined in an ahistorical manner.

11

Stranger in Paradise

Encounters with American Jews

Susanne Klingenstein

I. Apéritif

"You have an accent. Where are you from?"

"Germany."

"Oh, I see. You were in the war?"

"No. I was born in 1959."

"But your parents—were they in the war?"

"My mother is from Switzerland; my father was adopted by Protestants in rural northern Germany."

"You're Jewish?"

"Yes."

"You don't look it."

"Schlötelburg. That's a difficult name."

"It's German."

"*Echt deutsch,* or Jewish?"

"German."

"You're not Jewish?"

"Yes, I am."

"How can you be Jewish? Are there still Jews in Germany?"

"Some. My mother is from Switzerland; my father was adopted by Protestants in a small coastal town in northern Germany. His adoptive mother could not have children, or did not want to bear them in her condition. She had had polio and was paralyzed from the waist down, but she wanted a child. My father was blond and blue-eyed. His parents, who lived in Hamburg, began looking for a safe spot for their son shortly after the Nuremberg Laws came out. Eva and Hermann Schlötelburg were willing to take the child should things get tight. And they did."

"What happened to your father's real parents?"

"I don't know. They disappeared."

"So, you're Jewish?"

"By whose definition?"

"Hitler's."

"Then the answer is easy. Yes."

"You don't look it."

"That comes in handy, sometimes. Though not in America."

"We see from your application that you are from Germany."

"Yes, rabbi."

"Why do you appear before the Rabbinical Court of Justice?"

"I would like to be accepted for a *halakhic* conversion."

"Our tradition does not encourage proselytes."

"I know, but my case is different, rabbi."

"Are you coming to atone?"

"For what?"

"The sins of Germany."

"No, I don't feel guilty. But I do come for the sake of history."

"We can only hear your case if you come for the sake of Torah."

"I am coming for the sake of the living Torah, *am yisrael*, to be confirmed as belonging to the Jewish people, *am avi ve-am avoteinu*, my father's people and the people of our fathers. My father was Jewish, but my mother was not. She gave me a choice when I grew up. I decided to be educated as a Jew. Between the ages of fourteen and twenty-two I received a traditional Jewish education: Hebrew, Torah, Mishna, Gemara, Rashi, Maimonides, Shulkhan Arukh, and later the writings of the *Rov,* that is, Rabbi Joseph Soloveitchik."

"Yes, we saw in your application that you are familiar with the sources. But you surely know that it is not essential for women to be learned. You are not obligated to study. But you are *mehuyev* all *mitzvot assey she eyn ha-z'man grama* [obligated to fulfill] all positive commandments not linked to time. You could begin with a *mitzvah* that has come to be taken on particularly by women, the *hadlik nerot,* the lighting of candles on Friday night to usher in Shabbat."

"You misunderstand. I know that you base your suggestion on a passage in tractate Shabbat, *perek bet, mishna vav* [chapter 2, *mishna* 6], that speculates why so many women die in childbirth. It concludes that they may have been remiss in observing the *mitzvot* of *challah, niddah,* and *hadlik nerot.* I know the *halakhot* for women; I have studied them. I am beginning to live them. I am coming to you to make sure that my children will be spared questions."

"Then you are seeing someone Jewish?"

"No. I am not seeing anyone."

"Are you coming for the sake of Ha-Kodesh Barukh Hu?"

"I am not sure. You see, rabbis, I am coming to you after the Shoah."

"You're from Germany! That's wonderful. Wherabouts?"

"Heidelberg."

188

"Marvelous little city. We were there for two years on a Fulbright. My wife and I loved it. Such clean streets, such nice people."

"We heard you are from Heidelberg."

"Yes."

"Then you must know Mannheim, the industrial city nearby."

"Indeed. I grew up there."

"We left it in 1938. I am Marianne, the daughter of Hugo Adler."

"The famous cantor? The last cantor of the Mannheim synagogue?"

"You know about him? Do you know his music?

"Absolutely. We used some of his melodies on Shabbat morning."

"You mean you're Jewish?"

"Yes."

"You don't look it."

"Camouflage; or, centuries of assimilation, whichever you prefer. I do take after my father though."

"What brings you to America?"

"I am doing research for a book on Cynthia Ozick; but mainly I am trying to live among Jews. It's hard, I didn't know they were so different in America."

"That's what my mother used to say, Selma Adler. Perhaps yours is simply a *yekke* [German Jewish] perspective? Some German Jews have problems adjusting to America."

"Maybe. There is something transformative, however, about America, something that has to do with the vastness of the country, and with sheer numbers. There are so many Jews here, but they don't feel like family. They are so free, so unburdened. I wonder if that's partly the freedom of ignorance. Being freed from history can be a blessing; it creates a living culture. And yet, American Jews make me feel like a stranger in paradise."

II. Hors d'oeuvres

"Keeping kosher has nothing to do with being Jewish." The man sitting across from me, an American physician in his early forties, delivers this state-ment with a sincerity that signals his inability to imagine a world in which his claim may not be true. In my old world, the book-filled universe of dead Jews in post-Shoah Germany, the observance of *kashrut* had everything to do with being Jewish; it defined Jewish life. Within minutes of our first meeting, while perusing the menu of an upscale restaurant in Boston, Bob and I have uncovered the vast chasm separating American and "four cubit" Jews. The latter are Jews who live anywhere, yet within the circumference of *halakhah*. Rabbi Ulla, a sage of an early talmudic period, taught: "Since the day that the Temple was destroyed, the Holy One, Blessed Be He, has nothing in this world but the four cubits of *halakhah*" (Berakhot 8a). *Dalet amot*, "four cubits," is an expression signifying the minimal amount of space that is legally one's own; it designates the circumference of one's possession as an individual. Figuratively, it is the amount of space Torah and talmudic learning take up when Jews are running from a pogrom.

What does Bob mean when he insists on the dispensability of observance in America? And why am I dumbfounded by a claim that seems to him as unexceptional as the air he breathes? Our attitudes toward being Jewish have been shaped by the same kind of fact: the experience of numbers. Bob, born in 1948, spent his early childhood in Washington Heights, a hilly enclave in northern Manhattan, populated so extensively by German Jews (among them twenty thousand refugees from Hitler's Germany) that it came to be called Frankfurt on the Hudson. Bob's father, Harry, left Germany in 1934, when his school friend, Erich Sachs, was shot by the SA,[1] and permission to open the casket was refused. Harry (Chaim ben Reuben), the son of an Orthodox cattle dealer in rural Unterfranken (Franconia), had planned to go to medical school, because he wanted to break out of his father's world. Hitler put an end to this dream when he closed medical schools to Jewish students. Having finished *Gymnasium* and being scared to death by the murder of his friend, Harry left home. In America he was snubbed by his wealthy relatives who had left Germany a generation earlier. So he entered the world of business with a vengeance. As Hitler was tightening the noose around the neck of German Jewry, the need to make money grew more urgent. Harry's family in Franconia was beginning to feel trapped. Yet in a gesture indicative of the mindset of German Jews, Harry set aside the first money he earned for his own burial so that the impecunious relatives with whom he was then living should not be burdened with the expenses of his funeral. Harry was then twenty years old.

In 1938, when Harry was twenty-three, he managed to bring his parents and younger brother to Washington Heights. His father, Reuben, a rough, tyrannical man, who had dealt competently with cows and peasants, and mastered the languages of God, the Germans, and the cattledealers, was lost in the cityscape of Manhattan. He could not adjust and fell into deep melancholy. The despot shriveled, relying increasingly on the mercy of a son who wanted nothing so much as to be angry at a father once perceived as omnipotent. Harry suppressed his anger but developed into a tyrannical father himself. His own son, Bob, would have liked to rebel against him during the furious 1960s, but did not do so because his father had been touched, however lightly, by the murderous persecutions of Nazi Germany.

Harry married Ida, a sixth-generation American, descended from German Jews, who had lost both her parents when she was eight years old. Ida understood her husband's desire for assimilation and integration and became his reliable guide to American social life. In the mid-1950s, when Harry's business prospered in the booming postwar economy, the family moved to Scarsdale, a formerly all-WASP New York suburb in Westchester County. Little Bobby, named Robert for his grandfather Reuben, grew up in environments populated largely by Jewish families like his own. He befriended boys who were mired in the same psychological and emotional problems, and propelled by the same dreams. Bob's world contained only Jews: the melancholy German Jews of Washington Heights; the brilliant, deeply self-conscious kids of Quaker Ridge and Scarsdale High; the bagel belt Jews in an Ohio college (displaced from the East Coast Ivy League by the enlightened admissions policy of geographic distribution, designed to limit the disproportionate influx of the "pushy" New York Jews); the medical students at New York University; interns and residents at New York's Mount Sinai Hospital; and finally the fellows and colleagues at the Harvard-affiliated Massachusetts General Hospital, the Matterhorn, so to speak, of academic medicine.

Wherever Bob went, he was surrounded by Jews like himself, ambitious young men (and a few women) eager to give their parents *nachas* (pleasure) by becoming the best possible doctors—dedicated, compassionate, successful. Many of them were "making good" by realizing careers that had been out of their fathers' (and certainly their mothers') reach. Some of these students, interns, residents, and doctors, often those with parents who had been emotionally crippled and psychologically scarred by the Shoah, hoped to win their parents' love and respect by becoming stars in their profession. They were often disappointed. But what mattered to Bob and his friends, regardless of their specific backgrounds, was brilliance, to have a "golden head." (To have a a *goyisher kop* was not so much a disgrace as simply inconceivable.) The heavy concentration of "golden heads" in the labs and on the floors of the top teaching hospitals in the country created, in a few places, the peculiar atmosphere of selflessness and understatement that reigns where no more peaks are left to climb. What mattered further to the generation of Jews born right after the war were love and politics, John Lennon, Kent State, civil rights, the Vietnam War, hatred of Nixon, difficult relations with distant fathers, Jewish girlfriends, and, in some cases, the tattooed numbers of the Holocaust. What didn't matter was observance. Jewish life was defined by the mere physical existence of Jews (their presence in American life in significant numbers), as well as by their intellectual achievements, recognizable behavior, and shared psychological traits. For that generation, being Jewish was first a cultural and then, increasingly, a biological thing; they thought of it as a genetic heritage, not to be acquired by outsiders, and a gut feeling for family.

My world could not have been more different. Imagine a country without Jews. Of course there were some fifty thousand Jews in West Germany (the figure has risen to sixty-five thousand after reunification), but they were about as visible as the spotted owl in California. Perhaps their closest analogue in the United States is the American buffalo, whose right to exist is guaranteed by the government. Such special protection belies any historical continuity of the government with the ruthless hunters and thugs of an earlier age. The rare buffalo are kept in clean zoos and parks, and exhibited on

191

certain ceremonial occasions. So with the Jews in Germany. They are now the government's Holy Cows. And cowed they are.

I never saw a Jew until I was fourteen. My parents, married in 1957, separated two years after I was born, while my mother was pregnant with my brother. Hurt to the marrow, my mother did not wish to speak about my father. But when I was about ten, I found out who he was by secretly reading, while my mother was at work, the huge folders with official papers and correspondence she kept in the living room wall unit. I did not reveal that I knew who and what my father was. Nor did it matter to me, until one day, in 1973, all students of my grade in an all-girl *Gymnasium* in Mannheim were assembled to attend a lecture on Judaism by the cantor of the local Jewish community. (The congregation, some four hundred people, was too small to have its own rabbi, a precious commodity in Germany.) None of us middle-class garden-variety German girls had ever seen a Jew, and we were ravished when the door opened and a young, Mediterranean-looking Frenchman walked in, and started his lecture with a swift, melodious: "*Bonjour, mesdemoi-selles*. I am a Jew. What do we mean by that? We mean that I chose and was chosen to live according to certain laws and principles, which I will now explain to you." At the end of his lecture Gérald Rosenfeld offered instruction in modern Hebrew to anyone who would come to the Jewish Community Center, stashed away in a posh part of town. A few days later, ten of us, an adolescent quorum, went to be instructed. A few months later, I was the only one who still sat and learned.

Over the years, "sat and learned" acquired its traditional meaning: the Jewish Community Center, where I was the only female student, became my *ye-shiva* (derived from the word *yoshev*, "sitting"). Here I sat and studied the classic texts that constitute the Jewish people. Between 1973 and 1982, I trudged to my *bet midrash* twice a week to immerse myself in the intense world of Jewish thought. At first it was Hebrew and Torah. In my third year I was allowed to read an easy book of the Mishna, *The Ethics of the Fathers* (*Pirke Avot*). In my fifth year, I was permitted to study Gemara, but I was not led through the traditional Baba Metzia (Middle Gate). I had to start with tractate Berakhot (Blessings), which opens with a discussion of when to say the *Sh'ma*.

It became clear to me then that I would not be getting anywhere with mere study. The principles of Judaism, its thought structure and ethics, were intellectually accessible, but being and thinking Jewish were not. The reason was that the classic Jewish texts (Torah, Talmud, Midrash) assume a parallel between study and life, thought and practice, between *talmud torah* (study of the law) and *derech erets* (ethical behavior). They assume that the way you think is mirrored in the way you live, and vice versa. The reigning principle in Jewish thought is chosenness, that is, the dedication of a small band of people to an idea, an abstract entity, YHWH, whose sole tangible reality is the enactment of "His" will (the personal pronoun is a deliberate anthropomorphism) recorded in the Torah. This "will" was translated by biblical and postbiblical interpreters into detailed prescriptions regulating the daily conduct of the Jews. The bottom line of the written Torah's 613 *mitzvot,* explained and updated in the *halakhah* of the oral Torah (the Talmud), is to separate the *goy kadosh,* the chosen people, from those not committed to Abraham's idea of God, and to the agreement (covenant, *brit*) first worked out between them, and later refined by Moses in his talk with God on Mount Sinai, on how to behave toward each other. To be Jewish, then, was to enact the terms of the Covenant, to practice discretion, to distinguish at every moment the holy from the profane, the allowed (kosher) from the prohibited (*treyf*), Jewish from gentile.

The absence of a single work outlining Jewish ethics, the moral theory behind ritual observance or orthopractice, has to do with the fact that ethical insights are regarded as an outgrowth of a specific discretionary form of behavior, which requires you to examine every act and action, to do nothing carelessly and thoughtlessly. Jewish moral thought emerged as a consequence of moral conduct, as is indicated in the answer the Israelites gave when they received the Torah at Mount Sinai: *na'asseh ve nishma,* "Let us do and hear [understand]" (Exodus 24:7). Jewish thought flows from the enactment of the *mitzvot,* since orthopractice, so the rabbinic argument goes, gradually leads to an understanding of the nature of Judaism born at the moment of Abraham's brilliant separation of transcendence from immanence. Hence there can be no theology of Judaism; and a Jud*aism* garnered from the study of texts remains a cripple. Jewish thinking derives from practice (which involves deeds like separating milk and meat in the kitchen, ox and donkey in the plow, cotton and linen in clothing, and distinguishing between rest and work, right and wrong, the hallowed and the ordinary). Being aware of differences shapes ethical conduct as well as one's knowledge and assessment of the world. (All medical diagnoses, say, involve acts of the minutest discrimination, distinguishing helpful clues from red herrings in an often inarticulate mass of complaints.) It became clear to me that I had started at the wrong end, with theory. Maimonides, lovingly called RaMbaM by observant Jews, wrote in *Moreh Nevukhim* (*Guide for the Perplexed*):

> Know that to begin with this science is very harmful, I mean the divine science. In the same way, it is also harmful to make clear the meaning of the parables of the prophets and to draw attention to the figurative sense of terms used in addressing people, figurative sense of which the books of prophecy are full. It behooves rather to educate the young and to give firmness to the deficient in capacity according to the measure of their apprehension. Thus he, who is seen to be perfect in mind and to be formed for that high rank—that is to say, demonstrative speculation and true intellectual inferences—should be elevated step by step, either by someone who directs his attention or by himself, until he achieves his perfection. If, however, he begins with the divine science, it will not be a mere confusion in his beliefs that will befall him, but rather absolute negation. (part one, chapter 33)

What Maimonides means is particularly appropriate after the Shoah and undermines Bob's single grudge against observance, its absurdity in a post-Holocaust world. Maimonides claims that you cannot begin your study with a divination of the nature of God. This will lead to atheism if you lack a proper foundation. The right approach is a *gradus ad parnassum*, beginning in practice and ending in the contemplation of God. Whoever was not ready for the ascent via philosophy should be prepared for it in nonintellectual ways, that is, by enacting the Torah's commandments. But the preparation can be even more basic than that, as Maimonides explains in his *Mishneh Torah:*

> A man should aim to maintain physical health and vigor, in order that his soul may be upright, in a condition to know God. For it is impossible for one to understand sciences and meditate upon them when he is hungry or sick, or when any of his limbs is aching. And in cohabitation, one should set one's heart on having a son who may become a sage and a great man in Israel. Whoever throughout his life follows this course will be continually serving God, even while engaged in business and even during cohabitation, because his purpose in all he does will be to satisfy his needs so as to have a sound body with which to serve God. Even when he sleeps and seeks repose, to calm his mind and rest his body, so as not to fall sick and be incapacitated from serving God, his sleep is service of the Almighty. (Book One: Knowledge, chapter 3)

Simply maintaining one's physical health was an act of worship or Jewish observance. That sounded easy enough; but there was a caveat. The RaMbaM's sleeper reposes in a *community* of Jews. In short, my years of study with Cantor Rosenfeld eventually led to one insight: thinking Jewish emanates from living Jewishly, and that is precisely what cannot be done in the absence of Jews. Even observance depends to some degree on the presence of a community. The Jews of Mannheim, many of whom had fled Hitler and come back after 1945, were an old, disheartened lot, somewhat enlivened by a few Israeli families. There were, of course, a large number of "half-Jews" in Germany; but most of them did not know who they were, and those who did tended to identify with the non-Jewish parent, because Jewish knowledge was exceedingly hard to come by in an essentially *judenrein* country.

I had chosen to live a schizophrenic life. The double and duplicitous existence in a physically German but intellectually Jewish world became a strain. I was a gifted student, and thus my personal eccentricities—a certain abrasiveness and lack of ease in social interaction—were condoned, at least by my teachers if not always by my fellow students. I functioned within German society, but conceived my intellectual identity, for which I had no communal basis, as Jewish, and as adversarial to post-Shoah German society.

In the late 1970s I began to study Yiddish with a survivor of Buchenwald. For years I lived according to a peculiar intellectual rhythm: three days a week I would immerse myself in the classical works of Jewish culture; on the other four days I would pursue my German passions: literature, fine arts, architecture. What one needs to know, perhaps, is that for the Germans of my generation the word "Jew," *Jude,* smelled of unspeakable death. We had been conditioned to link nothing with the word *"Jude"* but boxcar trains and the ovens of Auschwitz. To shuttle, as I did, between the cultural realms of the Germans and the Jews was to shuttle between what was alive and what was evidently dead. It seemed as if I needed to care about living German authors to bear so much death; but here I deceived myself. Gradually all German culture began to reek of murder, and I couldn't bear it any more.

I finished *Gymnasium* in 1978, and went on to study English, German, philosophy, and history at the Universities of Mannheim and Heidelberg, with brief academic interludes in Scotland and Massachusetts. I had been awarded a government scholarship to Brandeis University in 1982, which I accepted because the cantor, who had remained my teacher during all these years, went back to France, convinced that Jewish life in Germany could not be revived. I returned to Germany in 1983 because I missed my family and, in another way, the soft, warm voice of my Yiddish teacher. But he had ended his life while I was away; and my father, too, had died. He had been a writer of bleak but funny short fiction; he collapsed at his typewriter. We had just begun to be friends.

A job offer from the English department at the University of Mannheim in January 1986 gave me the opportunity to bring together the two halves of my life for the first time. I was hired to teach courses on American-Jewish literature and history. Before that I had been in a doctoral program in German literature at Heidelberg University specializing in Viennese culture around 1900; but I switched immediately when I learned that I would be able to write my dissertation on Cynthia Ozick. A new world opened up. Here was someone who had what I thought of as a similar problem: an intense commitment to Jewish thought, and a self that in its creative passion ran counter to the ethics of the fathers. I devoured Ozick's *The Pagan Rabbi* (1971), a collection of unmistakably Jewish stories in which the creative impulse, transcending all boundaries, is barely reigned in by the ethical imperative of the rabbis to establish categories and to keep them separate. The rabbis' insistence on "distinction-making," as Cynthia Ozick calls it, reflects a fundamentally rationalist and antitranscendental attitude toward the world. Keeping the divine out of nature gave the Jews of antiquity an edge over the pagan world, which suffused nature with divine spirits and thus allowed itself to be terrorized by natural phenomena. The Jews, in contrast, posited their God as a power that manifested itself intellectually, through words. God enters immanence in letters; their carriers were called prophets. For Jews, God is an intellectual presence in history, not a natural event. Rabbinic thinking, which informs Ozick's fiction, sees nature and history as antithetical. And yet, in Ozick's stories the victory of History over Nature is a narrow one at best.

These stories may strike an American audience as slightly bizarre, but for me they reverberated with deep truth. I understood immediately what Ozick meant when she claimed in her preface to *Bloodshed* (1976): "When I write in English, I live in Christendom."[2] In an exchange with the Israeli writer Aharon Megged (1975), she had argued: "The language a writer writes is synonymous with what he will write. A Jew writing in a diaspora language is by definition an 'assimilationist.'"[3] Here was what I had encountered in no other American-Jewish writer: an awareness of the possibility that Jewish intellectual culture is different from, or perhaps at odds with, the thought processes of the gentile majority; and an awareness, moreover, of a slight uneasiness when Jewish views were poured into a gentile language. (At one point in her career Ozick idealistically envisioned that the old wine would, if not transform, at least affect the new vessel, and a "liturgical literature" would come into existence.) Like few American writers Ozick was aware of the incompatibility between the intellectual parameters of Christianity, a culture that insists on fusing all differences in the mercy and promise of Christ, and the intellectual parameters of Jewish thought, which insists on upholding differences. Ozick's fictional characters are rarely observant Jews, but the ones she likes have a mental habit of discrimination. The ones that disappoint tend to be promiscuous, indiscriminate consumers with runaway appetites and sloppy mental habits; they are liars or enthused artists who forge illicit creations out of the marriage of the incommensurate. In Ozick's early fictions the creation of art appears as the opposite of the rabbinic command to maintain differences, to discriminate in all walks of life.

Observant Jews are not conscious of their mental habit of incessant "distinction-making" (which an exasperated Bob calls sheer obsessive compulsion). Hence we might say that the admonition to discriminate has seeped from the content level into the structure of their thinking, shaping what I call Jewish intellectual grammar. Was I deluded when I assumed that acquisition of this "grammar" might be accomplished through study as well as through observance? For Ozick, too, books were essential for Jewish self-preservation. In her famous essay "Toward a New Yiddish" (1970) she wrote:

> Especially as a Jew I am an autodidact: the synagogue at present does not speak to me, and I have no divine shelter other than reading; at the moment print is all my Judaism, and I crawl through print besotted with avaricious ignorance, happening here and there upon a valley of light. My reading has become more and more urgent, though in narrower and narrower channels. I no longer read much "literature." I read mainly to find out not what it is to be a Jew—my own life in its quotidian particulars tells me that—but what it is to *think* as a Jew.[4]

Here it was again, the insistence on an observant life, the arrangement of the quotidian particulars according to the specifications of the Torah. This arrangement propels Jewish life out of synchronization with gentile culture. To my disappointment, however, Ozick clearly put *being* Jewish before *thinking* Jewish, thus making observance the basis and starting point for Jewish thought. It dawned on me that I would not be able to live as a Jew on books alone. It was time to leave Germany.

Moreover, after three semesters in my job at Mannheim University, I felt reduced to a token Jew. I had to get out for reasons described by Cynthia Ozick in 1970: "Because of always having to be an ambassador to the goyim, speaking for myself, I am worn out by it, I am exhausted by it. I feel so spiritually, mentally, even physically drained by it that it is indescribable, and I know that I am not alone in this."[5] She wasn't.

In the fall of 1987, I accepted a postgraduate scholarship that placed me at Harvard University; I was hired by its English department in the fall of 1988, and taught there until the summer of 1992. I arrived in Cambridge full of plans for my dissertation on Cynthia Ozick, and a life arranged according to the specifications of the Torah in a community of committed Jews, because in America, surely, one was free to live somewhat out of synch with the majority culture without being pestered by questions or subject to ridicule and mockery. Living an observant Jewish life would feel natural and easy. I was in for some big surprises. Not the least of them was sprung on me by Bob when I replied to his suggestion for hors d'oeuvres: "You know, we can't really have anything with caviar. The sturgeon is not a kosher fish." Bob looked up from his menu. His radiant blue eyes became round with astonishment. "Nonsense," he announced, "keeping kosher has nothing to do with being Jewish. Not in this country."

III. Entrée

Bob was right: I knew nothing about American Jews. Which is not to say that I had not mastered the facts, their history and literature. I gaped at America: The sheer number of Jews, the richness of their living culture, their high visibility, were overwhelming. Jewish names were everywhere! And they weren't holy cows! To the contrary, they were just people, living their lives as best they could, as Zionists, atheists, leftist liberals, neoconservative, modern Orthodox, Reconstructionists, Hasidim, humanists, nothings; but Jews all. The urge to write a dissertation on Cynthia Ozick evaporated because the psychological drive behind it disappeared. In Germany, immersing myself in her fiction had insulated me; thus I had kept in touch with centrally Jewish thought. In America, I no longer needed to bury myself in another Jewish mind in order to maintain my hard-won identity as a Jew. Jewish life was all around me.

As a newcomer to paradise I had an immediate and not very original problem. How could I cope with the cultural diversity and centrifugal force of America? How had earlier immigrants maintained their hold on a tradition of learning that seemed to lose all substantiality in America? Jewish immigrant fiction showed that it was going to be an uphill struggle, but there had to be a way.

Then there were other things I did not understand. How, for instance, was it possible to *be* Jewish (with all the mental trappings that entailed) and be a leading specialist on Emerson or on Puritan literature? Technically, of course, that was no longer problematic. The universities had long overcome their reservations regarding Jews. At Harvard, for example, the leading Emersonian philosopher, Stanley Cavell, and the leading scholar on Puritan writing, Sacvan Bercovitch, were both Jews. But what did that mean intellectually—for the scholars themselves and for their scholarship? Both critics had fairly untraditional Jewish educations. Bercovitch, for instance, had grown up steeped in the world of left-wing Yiddish culture. Would such a critic produce readings of American literature that differed in outlook, attitude, analytic method from those of his WASP colleagues? Had the hiring of a significant number of Jewish professors since the early 1960s affected the course of American literary criticism in ways that could be attributed to the residual influences of Jewish thought? Or had these professors simply adjusted to the fundamentally non-Jewish thought structure of America? Had they adopted the dominant views? Did the language of the American Renaissance, for instance, handed down in the works of critical giants like F. O. Matthiessen, have the power to reshape the thought structure of its Jewish heirs? Did writing in academic English mean that one entered the refined Christian kingdom of the Concord transcendentalists? These are obviously questions of a puzzled outsider. You may want to dismiss them as absurd; but if you were to allow yourself to ponder them, you might find that they catapult you into the very heart of this book's subject matter: How *does* one think as an American Jew? If you live within the *dalet amot,* the four cubits, the answer is easy: you think in precisely the same ways you would think if you were to live as a Jew in France.

But in America? The country was founded on the uplifting ideal of equality—one nation under God with liberty and justice for all—an ideal that does not deny individualism and a certain amount of separation, but which has been understood by Jews as an unprecedented invitation to be like everybody else, to disappear indistinguishably into the great mass of mankind, into Whitman's catalogues and Allen Ginsberg's "allee samee." After a history of being singled out for persecution, disappearance into sameness was a relief. So how could one (and why should one) resist that call to melting and fusion, and keep on thinking (and living) as a Jew? Of course, after a generation in the melting pot, regret sets in and the search for "home" begins. But where do you start to retrieve and rebuild what previous generations were so relieved to give up? I don't know. I chose early to live within the four cubits. But was that the only possible way?

The attempt to find answers to these questions created what colleagues call my academic field. I began to reconstruct the history of Jews in the American academy, particularly the history of their integration into philosophy and literature departments. The first volume of my study, *Jews in the American Academy, 1900–1940: The Dynamics of Intellectual Assimilation* (1991), dealt mostly with newcomers like myself. I examined the ways in which intellectual Jews like Horace Kallen, Morris Cohen, Ludwig Lewisohn, and even Lionel Trilling, a second-generation American, negotiated between consent and descent (useful terms learned from Werner Sollors). I described how these men integrated the challenge of an open America into the firm structure of Jewish thought. What I learned from them loosened my own rigid perceptions of what Jewish life in America should be, namely, a reenactment of Old World Jewish thought in a country without pogroms. I began to consider other options and the possibility that, for Jews, America is different from the societies of Philo's Egypt, Maimonides' Spain, or Heine's Germany.

My second study, which is nearing completion, is more specifically about Jewish professors of English and American literature. It investigates what residues of Jewish thought and experience may have influenced their reading of American culture. From another perspective, my study presents itself simply as a history of Jewish professors in American English departments from the earliest visible appointments, those of Lionel Trilling at Columbia and of Harry Levin at Harvard in the late 1930s, to the symbolic apogee of Jewish integration, their ascent to and establishment in the mythmaking bastions of American academic culture. That apogee I would locate in the designation of Sacvan Bercovitch as editor of the prestigious *Cambridge History of American Literature* in the early 1980s. In 1983, Bercovitch was also named to a chair in American literature at Harvard University, where he was half expected to play the role of a second Perry Miller.

This appointment allows historians of the academy to measure the distance that Ivy League schools, Harvard in particular, have traveled since their founding for the education of Christian clergymen. In 1681, Cotton Mather argued, for his master's degree at Harvard University, the affirmative side of the question whether the vowel points in Hebrew are of divine origin. Forty years later, Judah Monis, a Jewish immigrant from Italy, offered his services as instructor in Hebrew to the Harvard Corporation. He was not employed until 1722, the year he converted in a public ceremony held in College Hall. It was not quite thinkable then that the Puritans would vanish like their foes, the Indians; and it was likewise difficult to conceive, in the 1930s, when Perry Miller began his groundbreaking work on Massachusetts Puritanism and the New England mind, that one day, fifty years later, the teaching of the Puritan legacy would be entrusted to a Jewish skeptic with scant knowledge of Hebrew but a persistent love of Yiddish literature.

Of course, one might just as well locate the apogee of Jewish integration elsewhere, in the stature accorded Stanley Fish, for example. He began his career in the 1960s with innovative books on seventeenth-century British poetry, he moved on to reader response theory, and from there to the advocacy of literary canon reformation. Asked cautiously whether he would consent to be interviewed for a book on Jewish professors, Fish shot back: "Absolutely. You can't understand my work unless you know I am Jewish." On the run from a conference session to a reception, Fish did not care to clarify his reply. Did he refer to his own dash and daring in dealing with John Milton and George Herbert, or to his pioneering spirit in literary theory and daredevil stance in the academy, or to his habit of playing the outsider despite the fact that he has long since become an academic trendsetter?

After years of study and scores of interviews with active and retired literary scholars, I am beginning to be able to describe the history of Jews in English and American literature since 1930 in terms of a clear generational pattern of consent and dissent, assimilation and dissimilation. The first wave of Jewish appointees (born in the 1910s) confined their work to main currents in American and English literature, even though many of them pioneered in new directions: the inclusion of the "Moderns," Joyce, Proust, and Mann, in the Harvard curriculum of the early 1940s, the establishment of American studies departments in the late 1940s, the shift from moral and cultural appreciation to a language-based literary analysis in the early 1950s, the highlighting of the (ethnic) Other in American fiction in the early 1960s. Men like Harry Levin, Daniel Aaron, Leo Marx, Charles Feidelson, M. H. Abrams, and Leslie Fiedler forced literary academe to think in new ways.

The second wave of Jewish appointees (born in the 1930s) started out by writing conventional books, most often on English or American romanticism. Once tenure was achieved during the late 1960s and early 1970s, this generation set out to rediscover the "other" aspect of their identity and to reorient their academic pursuits. Lawrence Langer and Alvin Rosenfeld wrote studies on Holocaust literature; Harold Bloom, a student of M. H. Abrams', discovered the hermeneutic uses of *kabbalah* and the modern Jewish heretics (Kafka, Freud, Scholem), preparing gradually his even more rebellious reconstruction of the biblical J-writer (a woman in the circles of the post-Solomonic court); Geoffrey Hartman, less flamboyant in his claims though equally creative, proposed nothing less than to revive the flagging energies of postdeconstructive literary criticism by infusing it with rabbinic hermeneutics, in particular with the playful principles of midrashic exegesis.

Robert Alter, by contrast, a student of both Lionel Trilling's and Harry Levin's, decided to bring his knowledge of Israeli Hebrew into the academy. After books on the picaresque tradition and the eighteenth-century British novel, Alter turned to modern Jewish writing and modern Hebrew literature, and in 1969, at the age of thirty-four, became the first American professor of secular modern Hebrew literature at the University of California–Berkeley. The distance traveled by American Jews in the forty years between Harry Levin's diffident arrival at Harvard in 1929 and his student's appointment to a chair in Hebrew literature in 1969 is enormous. But it is still too early to say whether there is a general trend in the writings produced by the emancipated sons and daughters of Alter's generation.

IV. Dessert

As an admiring, yet skeptic, chronicler of the lives and works of Jewish literary critics, and as a historian who is still steeped in the precepts of Old World Jewish thought, I am sometimes tempted to think of my subjects as orphaned Joseph in a magnificent Egypt. They make a living by deciphering its dreams, and rise to power through their wits. Joseph's position in the Egyptian establishment, however, was secured by his beginning to think as an Egyptian; it became his task to chart and administer the country's future. The Torah does not tell us whether or not Joseph then stopped thinking as a Jew. I am inclined to believe that he did, because I see it happen in his modern American counterparts.

The comparison of ancient Egypt and modern America is old and has often been drawn bleakly. That bleakness, reflecting concern for the survival of the Jews, is itself a Jewish tradition. I wish to conclude with a more lighthearted variant on the Egyptian theme. A stanza in the poem "November Ballad," by the Yiddish poet Itsik Manger, has always struck me as an enticing metaphor for the condition of Jews in America. In the prose translation of Sacvan Bercovitch the stanza reads:

> Midnight. The lady with red umbrella leads the way: behind her, incognito, comes the old king, and then His Excellency the fool.
> The king trips over the beggar-child asleep on the side-walk, dreaming pyramids of hot corn-bread.[6]

Clearly, the beggar-child dreams of satisfying its hunger. Yet the shape, in which the child sees the cornbread piled up, evokes the Egypt of death, of slave labor and exile. "Pyramids of hot corn-bread" is thus an oxymoron combining death (pyramids) and life (bread) that translates into the oxymoron "satisfying exile" (bread in Egypt), just as the beggar-child's dream is a satisfying exile from its real condition (being hungry in the streets). Indeed, any exile is satisfying at first because it stills the physical hunger. But then another hunger begins, a craving for freedom, which is to say for authenticity; there arises a longing for "home." Jews in America dream "pryamids of hot corn-bread." Most of them have achieved a satisfying life in a country that is now unequivocally theirs, isn't it? But what if their sense of safety turns out to be an illusion, a beggar-child's dream? Can we be so sure (if you will permit me now to join you in exile) that there is no "king" to awaken us? If and when we do wake up, we may discover that we are no longer regarded as sweet and innocent, that we are not accorded the harmlessness of Manger's beggar-child. This happened to the Jews of Europe. Their fate had been uncannily predicted in the first sentences of Franz Kafka's story "The Metamorphosis": When the Jews of Europe awoke one morning from uneasy dreams, they found themselves transformed into horrendous vermin. "It was no dream."

NOTES

1. According to *The Oxford Companion to World War II,* ed. I. C. B. Dear (Oxford: Oxford University Press, 1995), the SA (Sturmabteilungen, or Storm Detachment) was an "early Nazi paramilitary organization founded by Hitler in 1920, and destroyed by him in June 1934. The stormtroopers, known as Brownshirts from their uniforms in imitation of Mussolini's Blackshirts, were used by Hitler as an effective instrument of street terror in his accession to political power; but from mid-1933 their numerical strength and the increasingly political ambitions of SA leaders, particularly Ernst Röhm (1887–1934), made the SA a liability to Hitler" (974).

2. Cynthia Ozick, *Bloodshed and Three Novellas* (New York: Alfred A. Knopf, 1976), 9.

3. Cynthia Ozick, "Hadrian and Hebrew," *Moment* (September 1975): 77.

4. Cynthia Ozick, "Toward a New Yiddish," *Art and Ardor* (1970; New York: E.P. Dutton, 1984), 157.

5. Cynthia Ozick, "America: Toward Yavneh," *Congress Bi-Weekly* 38 (February 26, 1971): 57–58.

6. Itzik Manger, "Ballads," trans. Sacvan Bercovitch, *Moment* 3 (1978): 48.

12

The Challenge of Conflicting Communities
To Be Lesbian and Jewish and a Literary Critic

Bonnie Zimmerman

Memories

Chicago, 1958. On the news: Mike Todd, producer, impresario, husband of Elizabeth Taylor, is dead in a plane crash. My mother and aunt sit at the dining room table, discussing his death in hushed and sorrowful tones. My *bubbe,* probably sewing, although I have no concrete memory of her movements, pays no attention until one of them mentions that he is to be buried at Waldheim Cemetery. "Waldheim?" she asks. "He was Jewish?" Suddenly Mike Todd matters to her, belongs to her family. She mourns him like a long-lost son.

This is how I learned what it means to be Jewish. Family. Clan. Nation. The people you care for and care about. The people you can count on. If you are lost in a strange town, find the Jews. Jews will always take care of their own.

Chicago. I am probably about thirteen years old. I have never attended Hebrew school. I have not been bat mitzvahed. But I have discovered religion. I do not know why. Perhaps it is the music: I have begun to develop a love for classical music, and the ancient liturgical chants seduce me with their unfamiliar scales and sensuous cadenzas. Perhaps it is my identification with my grandfather: he is my special person, and Friday night temple is our special time. Whatever the reason, I am a regular attendee (and center of attention) at Temple Beth Shalom for a long time.

But my lack of a Jewish education finally has consequences: because I do not know Hebrew, I am bored during the long, noncantorial prayers and recitations. To amuse myself I read from the Old Testament that sits next to the prayer book. I usually skip the mind-numbing list of rules and regulations and search out the juicy historical narratives. One night—and I remember the sensation as clearly as if it were yesterday—I am struck with a profound realization. This sacred book is the record of war, violence, conquest, and insufferable arrogance. This is my people, my history—people "chosen" by God to be superior to all those idolators and sinners: the *goyim*.

I may not have stopped believing in God and Judaism that night, but it was not long after that I put such "childish" things behind me.

This is how I learned what it means to be Jewish. To be special, different, chosen. To be territorial, narrow-minded, militaristic, and above all patriarchal.

June 1965. I have left my comfortable Jewish enclave (family, school, suburb) to attend a large midwestern state university with, I learn later, a grand total of three hundred Jewish students. I leave home armed with warnings about anti-Semitism, which, I am told, I will confront at every turning. I do meet one anti-Semite—a roommate who (surely in jest) puts a cup on the toilet marked "Jews pay 10 cents here"—but everyone else is either pleasantly curious or simply indifferent.

September 1978. After years of attending a graduate school with a large Jewish student body and teaching at colleges in the Chicago area, I move to San Diego to take my first full-time teaching job. My first day in the classroom brings a shock: not since my undergraduate years in Indiana have I seen such a sea of pale faces and straight blonde hair. I have not felt this alien as a Jew in over a decade. As time goes on, I notice the little things: the constant assumptions that I am from New York, a student's complaint that I assign too many Jewish writers (two: Anzia Yezierska and Tillie Olsen). What is happening to me? Am I finally uncovering the anti-Semitism my parents warned me about?

This is how I learned what it means to be Jewish. No matter whether or not you believe in God, read Hebrew, fast on Yom Kippur, or support Israel, the anti-Semites know you are Jewish. They will come for you anyway.

I am probably about sixteen. The civil rights movement has been a force in this country for a decade. Martin Luther King, Jr., has brought the movement to the North with his march on Cicero, a gentile suburb of Chicago. I have been alert to political causes for two or three years, since the election of JFK. I have become a liberal on race issues. But all my life I have heard adults speak of the *shvartzes,* and not in liberal terms. I am ashamed of them, angry at them, act out my adolescent rebellion by calling them stupid and racist. They have betrayed me with their bigotry. I learn about a distant cousin (probably a Communist, but no one uses that word) who was run out of Alabama in the 1940s. I would like to claim him as my true kin, but he is too distant a branch on the family tree.

This is how I learned what it means to be Jewish. To resist, to be a fighter, to stake one's claim for social justice. To support the underdog, the victim, the oppressed. And to be racist, closed-minded, bourgeois, conservative. To turn your back on FDR and Adlai Stevenson and embrace Richard Nixon and Ronald Reagan.

Any family event, any time. So Bonnie, are you seeing anyone special? When are you going to make your mother a grandmother?

This is how I learned what it means to be Jewish. No matter what else a Jewish woman does in her life, it is her first responsibility to make her mother a grandmother.

Analysis

Joan Nestle, Jewish lesbian writer and archivist, began a review of *Nice Jewish Girls: A Lesbian Anthology* with the words, "I am not the Jewish Lesbian to write this review."[1] I have repeated those words to myself over and over again while I researched, planned, and wrote this chapter. Who am I to write about Jewish lesbian identity? I, who never went to Hebrew school or had a bat mitzvah. Who stopped believing in God at age thirteen and rejected organized religion shortly after. Whose only Yiddish is of the order of *sheyn meydele* and *oy vey*. Who does not belong to New Jewish Agenda and has not read *Tikkun, Bridges,* or *Lilith*. Who is not a member of the gay and lesbian *yachad* in her town. Who does not participate actively in the Jewish caucus of the National Women's Studies Association, and attended their Shabbat service only twice, the first of which raised confusing feelings of not being Jewish enough. Who has no settled (or rather a deeply unsettled and unsettling) position on the Arab-Israeli conflict. I am not the Jewish lesbian to write this chapter.

But, of course, I am Jewish and lesbian and, hence, as authorized to write as any other woman who is Jewish and lesbian. For the nature of my Jewishness (much more, I think, than my lesbianness) is precisely the ambivalence, questioning, and confusion that has shaped my ethnic identity over the past thirty years. This confusion, conflict, and, perhaps, contradiction, is what this chapter is about.

Like my grandmother, I have one eye open always for evidence of Jewish identity. I am proud that so many of the world's greatest intellectuals and artists have been Jewish. I am particularly tickled when I learn that someone I had never thought to be Jewish does, in fact, belong to the family (most recently, Nadine Gordimer comes to mind). I am pleased that so many of the founders and stars of the women's movement—Gloria Steinem, Betty Friedan, Bella Abzug, Andrea Dworkin—are Jewish. (I also have those waves of Jewish paranoia fed to me with my mother's milk: Are we too visible? Will our

Judaism discredit the women's movement? Will our feminism harm the Jewish community?) I remember when I first began to notice the disproportionate number of Jews in every feminist or lesbian group of which I have ever been part. We are a special people, I think: smart, creative, aggressive, over-achieving, committed to social justice.

But as a feminist and lesbian in the 1970s, it never occurred to me that being Jewish might mean something more than a cultural curiosity, that it might matter to my politics and my scholarly work. For the feminist move-ment, the 1970s were a decade to focus on the conditions that united women as a gender, or a sex class. Of course, that statement is too simple. Lesbians certainly raised the difference of sexuality, but we still assumed that all women, if they'd just free themselves of men or male influence, would dis-cover our commonalities. Racial difference was acknowledged, but women of color were expected (by white women) to choose their community—preferably that of women. Class differences, less prominently discussed, were articulated primarily in terms of attitudes and behaviors. Radical feminists and lesbian separatists argued that differences between women are the prod-uct of patriarchy and that if we could get rid of "the prick in our head" we could discover the female solidarity that would create a cultural revolution. Socialist feminists disagreed, and talked instead about racism and economics and a politics of materialism. But nobody was talking much about being Jewish. Judaism was just another patriarchal religion, so cultural feminists and lesbian separatists—many of whom were Jewish—dismissed it out of hand. Jewish women were all assumed to be white and middle-class, and so of little interest to socialist and antiracist feminists, many of whom were Jewish as well.

I began writing literary criticism in the mid-1970s, and not once did it occur to me that my Jewishness could or should be a factor in the content of or approach to my work. I wrote a dissertation and several articles on George Eliot, including my favorite novel, *Daniel Deronda,* and never once explored her handling of the Jewish question. I began reading and reviewing lesbian novels, like Elana Nachman's *Riverfinger Women* and Nancy Toder's *Choices,* and paid no attention to the fact that the authors and protagonists were Jews. Even when I began to write about identity politics, I concentrated on racism and racial identity, not anti-Semitism and Jewish identity. As I became more open and vocal as a Jew in the classroom, I did not translate that into print. I took it for granted, and assumed that everyone else would and, moreover, that "for granted" was all my Jewish identity was worth.

Looking back at two decades of lesbian feminist writing, I see that I was not alone in my indifference. Perhaps the reason I did not pay attention to Inez Bramanoi (in *Riverfinger Women*) or Sandy Stein (in *Choices*) as Jewish lesbian protagonists is that the authors did not emphasize their ethnic iden-tity, limiting it to a few descriptive phrases.[2] Just as author Nachman later changed her obviously Jewish name to the proudly lesbian Dykewomon, so she renamed the Jewish Inez, and every other female character in the novel, Jewish or not, the more evocatively lesbian Riverfingers. The unmistakable suggestion is that when women are baptized into the lesbian-feminist family (or, to use a more appropriately Jewish metaphor, dunked in the *mikvah* of dykedom), they leave the names of their fathers behind. But if these are *Jewish* fathers, what are lesbians leaving behind along with their names? Are we also leaving our Jewish mothers behind?

I was not asking those questions at that time. I had been evading my Jewish identity for over a decade, and I was not yet ready to take it up. To me, brought up in a strongly cultural, but not religious, Jewish family, Judaism represented the ties that bound me to family, the traditional role of women, compulsory heterosexuality, and the structure of patriarchy. To a certain extent, I had become a feminist and embraced my lesbianism in order to break those ties and establish my own adult identity. Judaism reeked of the past, of childhood, of strangling bonds and expectations. Judaism represented the secondary status of women, even more strongly when my brother introduced Orthodoxy into our family. Judaism was a religion, that superstitious, idealistic nonsense that Marx had aptly labeled an opiate. Judaism also brought back memories of family arguments over racial equality and Israeli politics, arguments in which I was always the odd woman out. In short, Judaism was the source—or symbol—of the world I wished to reject and reform. As far as I was concerned, Judaism and lesbian feminism were absolute contradictions, mutually exclusive worlds with no common borders, not even in my head.

Hence, the first time I mentioned being Jewish in a work of literary criticism was in *The Safe Sea of Women: Lesbian Fiction 1969–1989,* published in 1990.[3] The reference occurs on page 232, the last page of the text. That fact now seems very significant to me. Equally significant is the place where I do not mention being Jewish, specifically, on page xv of the Preface. It has become mandatory for lesbian feminist writers to locate themselves in relation to the lesbian community by including in their biographical notes every nuance of cultural identity available to them: for example, white, middle-class, forty-something, temporarily able-bodied, Jewish, feminist dyke. . . . At the beginning of my work, I identified myself and my critical stance solely in terms of race (white) and class (middle), with an offhand acknowledgment of the circumstances of my coming-out process (the women's liberation movement). By the end, I had added Jewish to the identity litany. What had happened to me (symbolically, of course) in the two hundred–plus pages in between? In the five years between the initial conception of the book and its final chapter? In the nearly twenty years between beginning literary studies in graduate school and coming out as a lesbian, and the present day?

Much had happened. Most significant, perhaps, was the 1982 publication of *Nice Jewish Girls: A Lesbian Anthology,* edited by Evelyn Torton Beck, a collection of essays, stories, poems, memoirs, and photographs by Jewish lesbians, many of whom had long been prominent in the women's movement. Here were Jewish lesbians asking the questions that I had been evading about the conflicts and common borders between Jewish, feminist, and lesbian identities, and asserting their (our) right to be "all of who we are."[4] Writing ten years later, I can look back at a number of additional texts that helped shape the way in which the lesbian and feminist movements were to incorporate cultural difference, and the way that Jewish lesbians and feminists, like myself, were to come to terms with their history. We now have unmistakably Jewish novels by Alice Bloch (*The Law of Return,* 1983), Sarah Schulman (*The Sophie Horowitz Story,* 1984), Ruth Geller (*Triangles,* 1984), and Judith Katz (*Running Fiercely toward a High Thin Sound,* 1992); *The Tribe of Dina* (1989), edited by Melanie Kaye/Kantrowitz and Irena Klepfisz, an anthology of Jewish feminist writing (originally a special issue of the lesbian feminist journal *Sinister Wisdom*); *Twice Blessed* (1989), an anthology of Jewish gay and lesbian writing; short stories and poems by many writers including Dykewomon, Kaye/Kantrowitz, Klepfisz, Lesléa Newman, and Adrienne Rich; and numerous essays in the feminist and lesbian presses that highlight how central identity issues had become to all movements for social and political change. All these happenings have left their traces on my self-concept and the way in which I practice my profession. It has become possible—indeed, necessary—to think in new ways about what it means to be Jewish and a lesbian feminist and an academic literary critic.

I tried to incorporate some of these changes in *The Safe Sea of Women* by focusing one chapter on the discovery and celebration of difference within the lesbian movement. Although I included analyses of Jewish novelists Schulman and Bloch, the bulk of the chapter is about the writings of African-American, American Indian, and Latina lesbians. I now think that I was unable to decide what stance to take in this chapter. Historically, it has been a challenging project for white women to learn how to write about the works of women of color. In so doing, we—I—have been vulnerable to conscious or unconscious racism, to appropriation or insensitivity. One way to have evaded those consequences might have been to situate myself as a Jewish woman writing about cultural diversity. By claiming *my* position on the margins, I could perhaps escape criticism. But such a stance seemed inauthentic to me because most Jews in the United States are accorded, however grudgingly, white-skin privilege by the dominant culture. No, I could not use my Jewishness as a shield; I would have to write as honestly and responsibly as I could without claiming any special dispensation for my Otherness. And, as a result, I overcompensated by not situating myself as a Jew in my text. Not even to raise the issue of anti-Semitism along with racism in lesbian literature, not even to reference the criticism Evelyn Beck had already raised in *Nice Jewish Girls*. When I think about that now, I consider it the most astonishing omission in the book.

Nonetheless, while I may not have wished to make my discussion of Jewish lesbians too central to my project, I was not entirely able to ignore it. I began to think, more deeply than ever before, about what it means to be a Jew who is a lesbian, a lesbian who is a Jew. As I write now, it is obvious that the feminist and lesbian communities have embraced cultural differences and that the current way we talk about identity does not mandate a choice between cultures, but embodies an ideal of wholeness in which all aspects of the self can be brought together in harmony and balance. But is it so easy? Contemporary Jewish lesbian writing (and the issues may be the same for Jewish feminist and Jewish gay male writing) suggests two ways of approaching the relationship between Judaism and lesbianism: one path leading toward the restoration of "wholeness" and the other to an acknowledgment of fundamental conflicts and, perhaps, contradictions. By the end of this chapter, it should become evident that I hold to the latter notion: that certain influences and traditions cannot be harmonized smoothly, that being lesbian is a decisive break with tradition that cannot be repaired easily, and that contradiction is a fruitful, if difficult, state in which to live.

As a literary critic, I always have tried to build my theories from the literary text, so I will begin my discussion of "fruitful contradiction" with an analysis of a Jewish lesbian novel. In the 1980s, a number of important texts, including Audre Lorde's *Zami*, Paula Gunn Allen's *The Woman Who Owned the Shadows*, and Gloria Anzaldúa's *Borderlands/La Frontera*, focused on these dilemmas of living with multiple identities, often illustrating a protagonist's movement from a condition of conflict and fragmentation to a state of integration and wholeness. Among these texts was Alice Bloch's autobiographical novel, *The Law of Return*, which follows the spiritual and geographical journeys of Ellen Rogin, a secular American Jew who, in 1969, immigrates to Israel under the Law of Return, which grants any Jew the immediate right to Israeli citizenship. Upon her "return" to the "motherland," Ellen takes a new name, Elisheva, a new language, Hebrew, and a new identity as a practicing Orthodox Jew. All she needs is a Jewish husband, she thinks, and she can live happily ever after, with "no contradiction, no inconsistency."[5] Her identity as an Orthodox wife and mother will be fixed, stable, and unencumbered by any messy tendrils escaping beyond the borders of self.

But the loud, explosive, untamed voices of rebellion and refusal erupt through the taut skin Elisheva stretches across her selfhood, like shellfire bursting through the "serene" kibbutz orchard (29). The repressed "returns" in dreams of erotic desire for women, and takes shape in the image of Lilith, the first woman who defied God and rejected male supremacy, and who now haunts patriarchal Judaism by preying upon men and children. Elisheva's attempt to fix a stable identity—analogous to her vision of a "reconstituted"

Jerusalem in which "every stone [was] restored to its rightful place"—is doomed to failure (50). As her religious and sexual identities crumble and change, she instead compares herself to "sheets of newspaper [that] slide together in a pathetic effort to reconstitute their original order" (197).

Since Elisheva holds to a totalizing notion of Jewish identity, in which she must claim all of Judaism or nothing, she begins to feel that she is "crouching at the edge" of the circle of Jews, with its "circumference pushing in on me, until I want to break out altogether" (196). If Elisheva is to be a Jew, she cannot be a lesbian; if she is to be a lesbian, she cannot be a Jew. To reconcile her dilemma, she forms a relationship with another Jewish woman, one which they construct as a feminist revision of Israel's Law of Return: "The power to return to the source. The Law of Return. We have returned to our Biblical names, to the origins of our Jewish female power" (231). By implication, then, Jewish lesbians "return" to an elemental female existence predating the separations imposed by patriarchy. The novel concludes with a joyous scene in which Elisheva, together with her lover and Israeli lesbian friends, steps into both the historical streets of Jerusalem and a mythical realm of singing and dancing women. Whether in Israel or the United States, the novel suggests, Elisheva and women like her can reconstruct and reconcile their multiple identities by creating supportive and nurturing communities of Jewish lesbians.

The conclusion to Elisheva's journey represents one of the resolutions to the conflicts between (traditional) Judaism and lesbianism or feminism that I suggested above. If the two can be visualized as overlapping circles, then the Jewish lesbian stakes her territory in the area of overlap. Here, surrounded by others of her kind, she can nurture her identity, protected from homophobic Jews and anti-Semitic lesbians. But this solution raises a number of problems that seem relevant to contemporary debates about multiple identities. In the first place, it relies upon images and language drawn from mythology—such as Lilith, Miriam, the Song of Songs—and not the history or contemporary reality of actual Jewish women. Hence, it suggests a nostalgic longing for what might have been (but probably never was) and an idealistic projection of a desired future. The conclusion to the narrative also leaves many questions unanswered. What awaits Elisheva when she reenters the streets of Jerusalem? Will she reenter the world, or only an enclave that exists primarily in myth and dreams? How can she evade the recognition that a "reconstituted" Jerusalem is, in fact, a divided city in which Jews are not merely victims but also oppressors? What, ultimately, will be her relation to the nonlesbian Jewish community and the non-Jewish lesbian community?

I do not wish to be too hard on Alice Bloch's novel. It is an intriguing portrayal of coming out as a Jew and as a lesbian. It identifies many difficult issues that must be addressed, particularly about the status of women and homosexuals in Israel and the impossibility of being both Orthodox and queer. It struggles mightily with attempts to reconcile the conflicts, to create an alternative space in which an unconflicted Jewish lesbian identity might flourish, and to provide models and myths for that identity. It recognizes that creating such a space will require struggle and communication. But I believe that, in the end, the repressed continues to shatter the sphere of wholeness. Lesbianism represents excess within Judaism, and Judaism may still be excessive within the lesbian community. Constructing protected enclaves of Jewish lesbian community may alleviate the tension and alienation for a time, but, I will suggest, it cannot provide a lasting solution.

Where Alice Bloch stops, other Jewish lesbian writers push further. Reading through Irena Klepfisz's *Dreams of an Insomniac*, a collection of essays originally published between 1977 and 1990, for example, I am struck by how often her words evoke danger and conflict, not peace and resolution. As a lesbian within the Jewish community, she identifies herself as both "outsider" and member of her "community": "Enemy and ally. / This is the confusion. . . ."[6] As a lesbian speaking to heterosexual feminists, she warns: "We need to identify conflicts and differences as well as points of agreement and common ground. I have no illusions. Such a dialogue will not be easy, but I believe it is a necessary one" (79). And as a Jew to all other Jews, she notes that "whatever pose we adopt externally, internally we remain lost and confused about what our 'secular' identity consists of and what 'Jewishness' is" (200). Klepfisz also remains resolutely critical of that "dangerous nostalgia" which, for many Jews, results in a single-minded identification with the past (whether the Holocaust, *yiddishkeit,* or Zionism) that ignores contemporary history. That nostalgia can also infect all varieties of feminism and lesbianism, including Jewish lesbian feminism (as I have argued about *The Law of Return*).

Two connected stories by Melanie Kaye/Kantrowitz further illustrate my argument. The first story, "All Weekend No One Mentions Israel" (in *My Jewish Face*), recounts a family barbecue through the point of view of the rebel daughter—lesbian, feminist, leftist—who has grown up and come to uneasy terms with her culture and community. It is a warm and evocative story about family, reconciliation, tolerance, and acceptance. It ends with the presentation of a cake, bearing a simple and innocuous message, HAPPY SUMMER, because the family could not agree on any other, more controversial, words. For the narrator, this cake is the perfect symbol of Jewish family and community: "These are my people. I am their child, not ready for this adulthood, but too bad."[7] In an epilogue to her collected stories, Kaye/Kantrowitz states that "writing the story named something for me"[8]—perhaps the way in which Jewish families and communities (like any family or community that lives, or perceives itself to be living, under seige) suppress discord and dissent in the name of wholeness and harmony. Even the rebel daughter keeps silent, except to mutter cynical comments to her lover under her breath.

This realization, or something like it, caused Kaye/Kantrowitz to write a sequel to the story, one that she calls "a fantasy designed to untrap me" from the comforting ending of "All Weekend" (233). And so she created that disruptive voice in the second story, "In the Middle of the Barbecue She Brings Up Israel." The "she" of the title—Nadine, a younger cousin—has not yet accepted the compromises that have led Vivian, the narrator of the earlier story, to tolerate the "uneasy peace" of the family barbecue. Although Nadine, like Vivian (like myself?), "wants the world to be nice" (232) and the family to be understanding, and the community to be united, she nonetheless breaks the code of silence. The issue that, in fantasy, disrupts the barbecue is Israel and the Palestinians (the issue that Bloch ultimately evades in *The Law of Return*), but it could be homosexuality or feminism. Being a lesbian may not be on a par with the life-and-death matters that constitute Israeli politics, but it is one of the painful conflicts that divide the Jewish community and family, that remind us that being Jewish does not in and of itself guarantee harmony and understanding.

Conclusion

For many lesbian Jews/Jewish lesbians, the parallels between Judaism and homosexuality are obvious and compelling. As Jews lived for nearly two thousand years without a homeland, so lesbians inhabit only a "lesbian nation" hewn from texts, not territory. Twentieth-century lesbian and gay communities embrace the same notion of family that has held the Jews together as a people throughout the centuries of diaspora. As Klepfisz points out, Jews and gays/lesbians "live in every culture and class, reside in every country on this planet."[9] The experience of prejudice and struggle for civil rights, the sustaining of a hidden subculture, the dilemma of "passing" or "coming out," the dual vision produced by living in two worlds—all these, argues Beck, might "provide points of communication and a mutual recognition, perhaps even alliance" between gays and Jews.[10] But, of course, they generally do not. Instead, Jews have been silent in the lesbian community; lesbians and gays, invisible within a Jewish community that, at best, marginalizes us and, at worst, casts us from its midst.

Some Jewish lesbians (and gay men) seek to integrate parts of the self that are often at war: a Jewish tradition that is both theologically and culturally hostile to homosexuality and a gay/lesbian ethos that can minimize cultural differences. Many yearn for a cohesive community in which to harmonize these conflicting influences. Some believe a time will come when, recognizing the errors of its homophobic ways, the larger Jewish community will welcome lesbians and gays into the fold. If not, gay and lesbian Jews will create new congregations and families in which to heal the divisions.

I am less sanguine. I am, in part, influenced by postmodern theories suggesting that it is neither possible nor necessarily desirable to construct seamless, harmonious identities and communities, that, in the twentieth century, the "human condition" is marked instead by multiplicity, contradiction, and incessant transformation. As a number of feminist theorists have argued, concepts like community, identity, and home rely upon the exclusion of that which does not belong to the concept in question.[11] Notions like "the Jewish lesbian community," or even "Jewish lesbian identity," are "essentialist" in that they presume a commonality among various individuals or a unity among the discourses that construct our notions of self. But we have to confront the inevitable realization that even the Jewish lesbian community may not feel like "home," that differences between, for example, Sephardic and Ashkenazic, working-class and middle-class, Zionist and anti-Zionist, or observant and nonobservant remain prominent, indeed desirable, but also potentially divisive. As Evelyn Beck puts it, "Jewish lesbian community—if we are to have it—must be built around more than the fact of our being Jewish and lesbian."[12] What I remain uncertain about is what that something more must be.

We also need to question the relation of the "community" to those outside it, to, for example, non-Jewish lovers or nonlesbian family. Few of us live, or want to live, in exclusively Jewish, let alone Jewish lesbian, worlds. Moreover, while separatist enclaves—and I am a strong proponent of strategic separatism—serve the valuable purposes of renewing energy and reinforcing cultural values, they cannot provide realistic, long-range, political solutions to the oppression and hostility that often generate them. Separatist strategies in and of themselves are unlikely to end homophobia and anti-Semitism, not to mention racism, misogyny, and class bias. Gay seders and synagogues will not overcome Jewish homophobia, nor will nostalgic evocations of Lilith and Miriam mitigate the frustrations of Jewish patriarchy. The points of conflict between Judaism and feminism, between Judaism and homosexuality, are real, painful, and persistent. Only by continuing to struggle as lesbians in the Jewish community, as Jews in the lesbian and gay communities, and as Jewish dykes everywhere, will we create lasting social change.

Hence, I would ask, in the signifier "lesbian-Jew," does one term function as subject and the other as modifier? Or do both function as subjects held together in uneasy union? I believe that the Jewish lesbian who holds these two volatile terms in close proximity lives in a state of constant explosive energy. There is no place of safety, no seamless whole, unless we close our eyes to the conflicts and the tensions. We may need always to live with contradictions. The key may be to stop seeing contradiction as a sign of failure and weakness, and to redefine it as a source of energy and transformation.

There are many reasons why we should consider contradiction a fruitful rather than a debilitating state of being. Recognizing contradiction can be the first step toward deconstructing false or premature notions of unity, notions that eliminate differences in the name of a totalizing sameness. Contradiction works relentlessly to undercut complacency (the idea that everything can be easily unified and harmonized) and nostalgia (the idea that a community once existed in peace and consonance before unity was sundered by external forces). Furthermore, contradiction compels a thinker to reexamine and re-evaluate ideas constantly, preventing simplistic conclusions or formulaic analy-ses. I am drawing in part upon the model of dialectical thinking, in which new ideas are continually generated from the conflict and interplay between opposing forces. Finally, the person who feels herself to be in a conflictual or contradictory relationship to the community serves the valuable role of critic (like the Old Testament Prophets), by insisting that the community rigor-ously investigate its assumptions, motivations, and actions. In short, contra-diction is a necessary source of change and growth. Without conflict and contradiction, we would have no cause for analysis and self-criticism; hence, we would stagnate and die.

As a literary critic who is a feminist, lesbian, and Jew, the conflicts I experience between the different aspects of my identity (or, to be more criti-cally fashionable, different subject positions) necessarily influence my ap-proach to the current debates over identity politics, essentialism, and the postmodern self. The competing pulls of multiple identities make it quite clear that no singular model of identity—Woman, Lesbian, Jew—can possi-bly capture the complexity of subjectivity and individual experience. As theo-rists like Audre Lorde and Gloria Anzaldúa have stated, the subject cannot split herself into fragments or choose one allegiance that excludes all others. But the very real differences that exist between lesbian feminism and Judaism, and the very real differences that exist *within* both lesbian feminism and Judaism, suggest to me that aspects of the self may not always be able to exist in harmony with each other. Hence, my critical stance must reject any simple essentialism that would reduce selfhood to only one position, even the posi-tion of Lesbianfeministjew. And yet, as a lesbian, feminist, and Jew, I can never reject the fundamental insight of identity politics—that categories and labels are not arbitrary and unnecessary constructions, but have a real impact on the formation of consciousness, subjectivity, and critical perspective. I claim a place in the world as a lesbian and as a Jew, and from that place I come to understand the multiple and often contradictory ways in which I speak in society and society speaks through me.

As a Jewish daughter I learned to sidestep conflict through silence. I learned to replace the disputatious style of my immigrant grandparents in favor of a more middle-class politeness and avoidance. I learned not to wash dirty laun-dry in public, not to bring shame upon my family. I learned that family cohesiveness is more important than individual expression. I learned not to speak the truth, because to do so might kill your mother (or father, or grandmother, or the neighbors, or . . .). I learned that you can do just about anything, however, as long as you do not give it a name. As an adult I have learned that homosexuality may be acceptable to some parts of the Jewish community (even to my family) as long as it looks like heterosexuality—

monogamous relationships, conservative style (nothing too butch/femme or leather), professional credentials, middle-of-the-road political views. As an academic, I have learned that being a lesbian or a Jew, or even a Jewish lesbian, is fine as long as fashionable quotation marks are placed around the "identity" in question. It is certainly as much a challenge to be a Jewish lesbian in the 1990s as it was in the 1970s, different as that challenge might be. As Elana Dykewomon writes in *Nice Jewish Girls,* we are all the "fourth daughters" of the Passover story, and we have four hundred (or infinitely more) hard questions to ask of ourselves and our communities. I wish I could end this chapter by indicating what questions we must ask or, better yet, by articulating their answers. But the fact that I cannot do so is the best evidence I can offer of the way I live in a state of fruitful contradiction.

Postscript

My very Orthodox brother shares this story with me: He and my sister-in-law are browsing in a bookstore when they decide to look for Bonnie's book. In the women's studies section, they find it. While they stand there reading through *The Safe Sea of Women*—my brother with his *kipah* and beard, my sister-in-law with her long skirts and covered hair—they joke to each other, wonder what people think about two *frummies* looking at this book. He is amused and very comfortable telling me his tale. I wonder, perhaps there is hope for reconciliation after all.

NOTES

Part of this chapter appeared in a review of *Nice Jewish Girls: A Lesbian Anthology* and *Twice Blessed: On Being Lesbian, Gay and Jewish,* in the *Journal of the History of Sexuality* 2 (October 1991): 326–29. I would like to thank the students in my graduate seminar "Lesbian Literature and Theory" at the University of California–San Diego, fall 1991, for their insights, in particular Karen Raber and Janice Chernikoff.

1. Joan Nestle, "Review: *Nice Jewish Girls,*" *Sinister Wisdom* 43/44 (Summer 1991): *The 15th Anniversary Retrospective,* 204–8.

2. Elana Nachman, *Riverfinger Women* (Plainfield, Vt.: Daughters, Inc., 1974); Nancy Toder, *Choices* (1980; Boston: Alyson Publications, 1984).

3. Bonnie Zimmerman, *The Safe Sea of Women: Lesbian Fiction 1969–1989* (Boston: Beacon Press, 1990).

4. Evelyn Torton Beck, ed., *Nice Jewish Girls: A Lesbian Anthology* (Boston: Beacon Press, 1989), xxxii.

5. Alice Bloch, *The Law of Return* (Boston: Alyson Publications, 1983), 13. The following page references in the text pertain to this source.

6. Irena Klepfisz, *Dreams of an Insomniac: Jewish Feminist Essays, Speeches and Diatribes* (Portland, Oreg.: Eighth Mountain Press, 1990), 67. The following page references in the text pertain to this source.

7. Melanie Kaye/Kantrowitz, "All Weekend No One Mentions Israel," in *My Jewish Face & Other Stories* (San Francisco: Spinsters/Aunt Lute, 1990), 226.

8. Kaye/Kantrowitz, epilogue to *My Jewish Face,* 233. The following page references in the text pertain to this source.

9. Klepfisz, *Dreams of an Insomniac,* 75.

10. Beck, *Nice Jewish Girls,* 173.

11. See Minnie Bruce Pratt, "Identity: Skin Blood Heart," in *Yours in Struggle: Three Feminist Perspectives on Anti-Semitism and Racism,* ed. Elly Bulkin, Minnie Bruce Pratt, and Barbara Smith, 11–63 (Brooklyn: Long Haul Press, 1984); and Biddy Martin and Chandra Talpade Mohanty, "Feminist Politics: What's Home Got to Do with It?" in *Feminist Studies/Critical Studies,* ed. Teresa de Lauretis, 191–212 (Bloomington and Indianapolis: Indiana University Press, 1986).

12. Beck, *Nice Jewish Girls,* xli.

13

Exodus, Discovery, and Coming Home to the Promised Land

Emily Miller Budick

AMERICA IS NOT the first country in which Jews have felt at home. Nonetheless, it has represented an environment so singularly hospitable that for many Jews it has come to seem nothing less than *The Promised Land,* as immigrant Jewish writer Mary Antin entitled her 1911 autobiography. This idea of America-as-Israel inherits a thousands-year-long history of Jewish longing for Zion. At the same time, however, it radically alters and subverts that history. It displaces the literal Eretz Yisrael, the land of Israel, with a figural Zion and thus redefines the nature of Jewish aspiration. In explicit contradistinction to Christianity, Judaism had resisted just this tendency toward the transcendentalization and allegorization of place ("a paradise within thee, happier far," as John Milton put it). The land remained for them literal and concrete. Therefore, while such an act of radical redefinition as Antin's would likely prove traumatic (on some level at least) for any people, for American Jews the idea of an American promised land could not but raise troubling anxieties concerning identity, assimilationism, and disasporism—subjects made famous in contemporary American literature by Philip Roth.

Such anxiety must increase exponentially following the Holocaust (of which many American Jews were survivors only by the accident of their parents and grandparents having recently immigrated to America), and again following the creation/reclamation of a homeland in the biblical Israel. How were American Jews to understand their relationship to America? Were they realizing biblical promise in a new American Israel, thus guaranteeing the survival and flourishing of the Jewish people? Or were they betraying that people, which had already been decimated by a history of unrelenting persecution, pogroms, and genocide, ensuring the end of Jewish history as such?

The situation was even more complex still. For in imagining America as Israel, American Jews (like Antin, Horace Kallen, and others) were by no means importing an alien religious construct into American national identity. Rather, they were borrowing a major trope of American self-representation. Long before American Jews imagined America as Israel, the Puritan settlers of New England had declared themselves new Israelites in a new Canaan, their flight from England an exodus over a desert from the Egypt of their affliction. This Old Testament rhetoric does not terminate with the founding of the nation. For American authors throughout the nineteenth century, male and female, African American and white, America remained a new Israel, a new Jerusalem, a new promised land. The discovery that America was Israel to Christians as well as to Jews could be taken by American Jews as final proof that they had, indeed, come home. But it could also confirm their worst fears—that the only way for Jews ever to be at home in the world was to yield to the Christianization of Jewish ideas, perhaps to Christianity itself.

In engaging these complexities of identity, American Jews have had to confront no less a question than what defines the relationship between society and self or between the sociopolitical and economic conditions of our life in this world and our ideological and religious convictions. Are we the selves we declare ourselves to be, despite the social spheres we inhabit? Or are we always, necessarily, the expression of the time and place in which we live, however much we might want to resist such local determination? How, indeed, does place define itself? Through the raw data of history, sociology, economics, politics, and so forth? Or through some preconception through which a community organizes that raw data?

In experiencing the painful paradoxes and dilemmas of identity and identification, American Jews were not undergoing a crisis unique to them. Rather, they were enacting the essential contradictions of America itself, indeed, of life in any society, including the Jewish national homeland in Israel. But for American Jews, belonging to two histories and two communities, each of which must bring to bear on the individual citizen the powers of its own ideological persuasion, the questions of self-identity, and of whether or not community (and if so, then which community) must determine such identity, could only be severe in the extreme. It could also prove especially creative.

In the following pages I describe one American Jewish odyssey, or perhaps I should say exodus, which confronts the relationship between self-identity and community definition. The journey I record—my own—is not, like Antin's or like John Winthrop's, to America. Rather, it is away from America, to the place named in the Old Testament as Canaan or Israel. It is also not, as in the Old Testament or in the Puritan American adaptation of the Old Testament or even in twentieth-century retellings of that story, an exodus from captivity to freedom or from exile to repatriation. Rather it is a pilgrimage from one home to another, one promised land to another, one freedom to another, which (for me, at least) raises questions concerning what we mean by *home* or land, promised or otherwise, literal or figurative. What constitutes a home, and who makes it, and why, and when, and where, and for whom? And what, then, constitutes our obligation to home, and how can we fulfill such obligation?

Jewish Consciousness in a Christian World: "The American Columbiad"—Seville, 1992

In 1992 the subject for Americanists throughout the world was 1492: the year of the "discovery" of the "New World," the "invention" of "America," an era in world history that seems to us now characterized by unprecedented exploitation, devastation, and the displacements and appropriations of cultures by a white, male, European (and later Euro-American) hegemony.

The year 1492 was a subject for modern-day Israel as well. It marked the expulsion of the Jews from Spain, where Jewish culture had experienced one of its most profound flourishings. That year inaugurated a whole new phase in Jewish history. Diaspora existence brought with it significant cultural and intellectual achievements. It also provided endless persecutions and pogroms, culminating in the Nazi Holocaust.

What was 1492 to me, an American Jew who in 1970 became an Israeli as well? Was 1492 the beginning of the history that would bring my grandparents to America? Was it, therefore, also the beginning of what would become my own involvement in the world's great drive to Judeo-Christian domination? Or was 1492 the end of the possibility of a Jewish hope to flower as a nation in and among the nations of the world? Was it the moment of the exclusion of the Jewish people from the stage of world history, which, following the Holocaust, would necessitate the creation of a Jewish state and thus produce my own emigration from the United States to Israel? Was Zionism an inevitability, forced upon Jews by history, or was it an ideology, internal to Jewish thought, and therefore to be chosen (or not) for reasons completely independent of the persecution of the Jews? Maimonides, who was born in Cordoba, not far from Seville, was not particularly Zionistic. Like many Jews, then and now, he believed that Jews and their culture could grow and develop wherever they found themselves, whether outside or inside the land of Israel. Would the Holocaust have changed his mind about the necessity of Zion? Would the expulsion of the Jews from Spain? Is there anything new in Jewish history after 1492, or 1942, to make one feel differently about a homeland? And did the Jews wander for five hundred years only to complete in Israel (as some would charge) the project of Judeo-Christian domination of victims, which they were once themselves?

I say *Judeo*-Christian advisedly, even resentfully. At this moment of heightened pluralistic consciousness and intense sensitivity to the exclusion of women and ethnic others from positions of power, suddenly it is remembered that Christianity cohabited the arena of world history with other peoples, including the Jews. So now Western society, as it moved ever westward in conquest, is acknowledged to have been not only Christian but also Jewish. Thanks, but no thanks. The forces of conquest that vanquished the Indians were not Jewish, and if Jews are to be incorporated back into world history, I'd rather it not be at the moment of general execration and self-punishment—

unless, of course, such self-recriminations acknowledge Jewish victimization as well. For Christianity treated Judaism as badly, and displaced it as violently, as it did the native cultures it later "discovered" in the "New World." This is not, of course, to say that Jewish history does not contain its own events of conquest or that those moments ought not to be addressed. It is, however, to insist that every human sin does not belong equally to every human being, and that histories of peoples might be as different as peoples themselves.

In one of the keynote addresses of the American Columbiad Conference, a prominent Native American writer, Michael Dorris, created a Columbus intended both to epitomize ethnic diversity and to distribute the blame for the "discovery" of America more equitably. This representative man, according to Dorris, in discovering the Eden of the New World, may well have occasioned the second fall of the human race, as much by introducing the idea of a fall— by importing Old and New Testaments—as by any more visible signs of conquest. And this "Adam" (which, in Hebrew, means simply "man") was, according to Dorris (who was depending on recent scholarship in this area), as much Jew as Christian. But in Christianizing Genesis and Judaizing Columbus, Dorris forgot that, if Columbus (or other of the crew's members) was a Jew (a whisper that has always thrilled American Jewish children), he was a *marrano* or crypto-Jew, forced to keep his Jewish origins and observance secret. And if the Old Testament Genesis seems to record a fall from grace, that interpretation of the Scriptures was itself a Christianization of the text that as much invaded Judaism as any landing on foreign shores. The second Adam is Christian, not Jewish. He would redeem history and crush the serpent beneath his heel through (among other things) the conversion of the Jews. Or their elimination.

It was no accident, then, that attending an American studies conference in Seville as an Israeli participant I should feel myself facing in a direction diametrically opposite to that which defined the conference as a whole. Nor was my choice of paper to present any more of an accident.

The paper was written in the winter of 1991. All of us in Israel were spending our nights in rooms sealed against poison gas attacks and our days warding off international indifference, even discrimination. (Though Israel was one of only three Middle Eastern nations to suffer attack at the hands of the Iraqis, Israelis were not permitted to participate in the international effort to defeat Iraq.) I was putting the final touches on a book entitled *Engendering Romance: Women Writers and the Hawthorne Tradition*. The book dealt with the ways in which male and female writers in a particular genre of American texts were able to accommodate problems of gender difference in order to create a coherent literary tradition. Were problems of ethnic, racial, and religious difference as easily accommodated, I began to wonder (sitting in my sealed room)? I had always assumed that they could be, notwithstanding the powerfully painful and negative example of American racism against blacks. After all, American Jews, among numerous other groups, had successfully integrated into the American mainstream. Certainly in 1991 the problems of Jews in America seemed far less serious than the problems of women. But here we were, Jews in Israel, quite clearly as much on the outside, as much the objects—if not of international persecution, then at least of the international condoning of persecution—as Jews ever were.

The paper that emerged from the war experience was entitled "The Mutual Displacements/Appropriations/Accommodations of Culture in Three Contemporary American Women Writers." It focused on tensions between African Americans and Jewish Americans in the United States. It expressed a (personally) very embattled Jewish point of view. Inevitably it became the paper I would propose to another American Jewish critic, Shelley Fisher Fishkin, an editor of this volume on reconfiguring Jewish American identity, for the panel she was putting together for the Seville conference. My paper was not the only one on her panel to deal with Jewish ideas, though her panel was the only one that dealt with Jewish materials or, for that matter, included African American participants.

In 1992, in Seville, at a European Association of American Studies conference, five hundred years after the expulsion of the Jews from Spain—or was it the discovery of America?—I thought about American Jewish identity and its relationship to American studies in a way that I had never thought about it before.

"American Israelites": Sacvan Bercovitch and the Puritan Origins of the American Jewish Self—Ithaca, New York, 1968

There has been a time when (like many American Jews) I in no way felt myself an alien in America, a Jew in a Christian country. Rather I shared the belief that American culture was staunchly secular, or that, if it did tilt in the direction of one Scripture or another, it was decidedly away from the New Testament and toward the Old—a tilt in my own Jewish direction. This fantasy of an American promised land, with the chosen people accorded a special place in that promised land (rechosen, as it were), long preceded my academic training. But it might well have evaporated along with so much else of my rather assimilated Jewish consciousness were it not for the fact that, just as I was defining myself out of religious identity altogether, I suddenly found myself confronting the American promised land all over again, this time on the higher ground of American cultural history.

One of the first requests made of us by Professor Michael Colacurcio in his undergraduate survey of American literature at Cornell was that we not, please, repeat the error of Sacvan Bercovitch's students at Columbia. Bercovitch's students, Colacurcio reported, were under the strange illusion that the Puritans were Jews. Colacurcio insisted that he himself did not think that they were Roman Catholics. It was not until some years later, after I had heard Bercovitch lecture at Cornell and had read *The Puritan Origins of the American Self* (1975) and *The American Jeremiad* (1978), that I understood just what Colacurcio meant. But by the time we were only a few weeks into Colacurcio's survey, I knew exactly what Colacurcio meant about himself. Colacurcio's Puritans were sacramental symbolists of dazzling incarnationalist powers. They came to inform the whole of my vision of American literature. They weren't, however, to captivate me so completely as Bercovitch's "American Israelites," his "Jewish" Puritans.

The ethnic revivals of the 1960s and 1970s, galvanized by the civil rights movement and black power, might themselves have forced me to rethink my Jewish identity. But it was Bercovitch, sensitive to the ways in which ideology constructs the sociopolitical sphere of everyday discourse (let alone literary texts), who returned me to a specifically Jewish American consciousness, a consciousness, that is, of the inseparability of my American and Jewish identities, as if America were, indeed, the only promised land there ever was, or was ever meant to be. I would only later begin to understand Bercovitch's skepticism and the degree to which, in leaping to the conclusions I was now reaching, I was playing into the hands of the American ideology that Bercovitch would more and more insistently expose.

Bercovitch's insights into what he later came to call "the music of America"[1] were no more separable from the intermeshing of experience and belief in his own life than that music was separable from the play of ideology and politics in America itself. As a Canadian Jew, from a radical leftist immigrant family, who had come from outside America and therefore had to "discover" it as surely as Columbus did, Bercovitch had also interrupted his journey across the border with a detour that bore very specially on my own position vis-à-vis American studies. Even before entering the university in America to learn the national literature that his own critical insights would largely redefine, Bercovitch came to live for several years on a kibbutz in Israel. Was it an accident that, when Bercovitch found (or was it founded?) "America," he perceived in its literary tradition a decided learning toward Zion? I ought to have begun then to think about what Bercovitch himself would later come to make explicit: what it meant that a literary tradition might be so hospitable to the designs we might place upon it. But for the moment, it was nice to find that American literary history was so familiar, so akin to who and what I was. (Perhaps Bercovitch, when he was newly arrived in America, was thus also similarly pleased.) To be made to remember, now with the sanction of scholarly thinking, how right we Jews had been to imagine ourselves at home at last, perhaps even to turn the tables on American hospitality and to discover that it was not America who welcomed the Jews but the Jews who welcomed the Americans—these were glorious discoveries indeed. Here, then, on the academic level, was perfect testimony to what every Jewish child in America (at least of my generation) had most fervently been taught: that America was truly a promised land and always had been.

But I had married a Zionist. And I had moved to Israel.

This was (and still is) a move difficult for any emigrant, especially from the West, and most especially from America. On some level, the problems are purely ordinary—family, friends, money, and the considerable pressures and pain of war. But the real resistance lay elsewhere. It came from the sense that six thousand miles away, on the other side of a continent and an ocean, was a promised land as profoundly blessed and deserving as this one, a promised land that (along with spiritual and moral fulfillment) also offered every manner of self-fulfillment and self-gratification. For the great achievement of America, in the view of many Americans (Christians as well as Jews), was its capacity to break free of the entrapments of the past, to recreate itself anew, generation by generation, if not individual by individual. America was even more a promised land than the original Promised Land. For according to its myth of itself, America was also Eden, Abraham was Adam, and by moving backward out of history to begin history anew, America (it was believed) might just avoid the pitfalls of Christian and Jewish history both. Out of place, out of time, lying somewhere between the imaginary and the real (to quote two great American authors, Edgar Allan Poe and Nathaniel Hawthorne), America was an Israel/Eden of infinite, ahistorical possibility.

This myth of the ahistoricity of America had done much to nurture Jewish hopes. To be an American Israelite was to carry on Jewish history and also be an Adam in a new world (it would take no less than a social revolution for that dream to include being an Eve); it was to perpetuate the Jewish dream of freedom from persecution and, at the same time, to inhabit a paradise of endless personal possibility. To be an Israeli Israelite was good only by half. It was to subordinate oneself to the rigors of an unyielding history: to an identity already created thousands of years in advance of anyone's coming there and defined by millennia of discrimination and persecution. What wouldn't any of us former Americans have given to remove ourselves from this history and go back to the apparent ahistoricity of America?

But, of course, just as I was beginning to feel myself trapped in history in Israel, longing for an American Israel that was eternally prelapsarian, American literary criticism and social thought had begun to discover that America was just as locked in history as any other nation. The fantasy of ahistoricity was apparently just that—a fantasy, and a dangerous, not to mention immoral, one. No scholar was more instrumental to this shift in critical thinking than the very scholar who had given me so accommodating an idea of America in the first place: Sacvan Bercovitch. It was, then, with a satisfaction equivalent to my earlier explorations into the origins of the American Israel outside history that I began to discover Bercovitch's ideological America, the America that was as firmly *in* history as Israel itself was. Just as Bercovitch's earlier work had made American literature as familiar to me as I am to myself (which was his argument concerning the flexibility of the tradition), so his new work paved the way for my growing realization that America was not, and never had been, Israel, neither for Jews nor, for that matter, for Christians.

The book that eventually became *Fiction and Historical Consciousness: The American Romance Tradition* (Yale University Press, 1989) attempted to define the historicity of the New Israel—America—the nation that existed (like all nations) in time but whose existence seemed to be as much predicated (at least in the popular imagination) on a transtemporal, transspatial idea as it was determined by the real events of a real world. From Cooper, Hawthorne, and Melville through a series of writers culminating in Updike and Doctorow, American authors, I began to realize, were hardly pleased with America's conception of itself as a New Israel. They were even less inclined to accept the more dramatic version of that conceit that maintained America as a kind of Eden. Again and again, it seemed to me, American literary texts imagined America as Israel in order to subvert what was, from their point of view, a fatal confusion between sociopolitical reality and transcendental idea. Repeatedly, American writers dramatized the dire consequences of mythologizing America out of its real geographical and historical contexts. Perhaps, these writers seemed to suggest, the only way to be in the world at all was to be in history. Only in history could one conduct the moral business of life.

The American romance writers, therefore, were all along addressing the issue that I was only now grasping: that America and Israel were two separate realities, and that for Americans to confuse them was to distort, perhaps even to unwrite, American history. Rather than resist the idea of history, the classical American canon, I realized, was intensely conscious of it. No wonder, then, that nourished on these texts I had found the idea of the old Israel so congenial and right. The American literary tradition, I concluded, had intended all along for me to come back home, to the only Israel there is—the literal, historical Israel, in time and in place.

I was elated. I was smug. But it wasn't that simple. Because, if America's misstep, according to the tradition of writers who interested me, was to imagine itself as an idea, didn't Israel, the real, literal Israel, exist in much the same way—as an idea as much as or, perhaps, even more than a geopolitical territory? True, contemporary Israel, unlike America, sits on a plot of land that coincides with the boundaries of an ancient place called Israel. Yet, was this difference between the American Israel and the Israeli one more than an accident of borders? I began to realize that in my desire to separate one Israel from another, one promised land from another, I had moved all of "literal" history to one side of the equation (my side, the Israeli side), and the refusal of history to the other side, the American side. And yet, what was the American idea of Israel if not an attempt to retrieve ancient history for present purposes? And what was my real Israel, my historical Israel, if not an idea of a promised land, maintained for millennia in the absence of a literal, geographical place? What, then, if anything, distinguished my one promised land from my other, my one home from my other home?

This Old Yet Unapproachable Israel: Stanley Cavell and Coming Home to the Promised Land—Jerusalem, 1986

" 'I am ready to die out of nature and be born again into this new yet unapproachable America I have found in the West,' " Stanley Cavell quotes Ralph Waldo Emerson.[2] And Cavell continues:

> Why is this new America said to be yet unapproachable? There are many possibilities, three obvious ones. First, it is unapproachable if he (or whoever belongs there) is already there (always already), but unable to experience it, hence to know or tell it; or unable to tell it, hence to experience it. Second, finding a nation is not managed by a landfall; a country must be peopled, and nation speaks of birth. . . . Third, this new America is unapproachable by a process of continuity, if to find it is indeed (to be ready) to be born again, that is to say, suffer conversion; conversion is to be turned around, reversed, and that seems to be a mater of *discontinuity*. "Aversion" is the name Emerson gives to his writing in "Self-Reliance." . . . Then Emerson's writing is (an image or promise of, the constitution for) this new yet unapproachable America: his aversion is a rebirth of himself into it. . . . its present to us is unapproachable, both because there is nowhere *else* to go to find it, we have to turn toward it, reverse ourselves; and because we do not know if our presence to it is peopling it.[3]

Could old Israel be any less unapproachable in Emerson's or Cavell's terms? Could the relationship between citizen and place be any less philosophically complex? any less in need of constant clarification, redefinition, and recommitment?

In 1985–86 Cavell came to Jerusalem as a fellow at the Institute of Advanced Studies at the Hebrew University. This was the first of many journeys to Jerusalem that Cavell would make over the next several years. It was also the beginning of his publishing his serious work on Emerson, some of which he was writing during his stints in Israel. Like many prominent Jewish academics, Cavell had unconcealed Jewish roots. Nonetheless, he was not highly identified as a Jewish critic. Was he, as he was charting America's path back to its philosophical origins, charting his own path back to origins of another kind? Or were these two journeyings, one of mind and soul, the other an actual relocation of place, only accidentally coincidental? And what was the discovery or, perhaps, rediscovery in Cavell's work? Did his (re)discovery of America (in particular of Thoreau and Emerson) proceed in some way (however obscure) from his Jewish background, or did his work on Thoreau and Emerson produce his own return to Zion? And what might I, as a student of American literature and a citizen of Israel, learn from Cavell?

I had already begun to write about the response in the American romance tradition to the myth of the ahistorical America—the America that, in the views of the romance writers, undid historical process and imagined itself first a new Israel and then a new Eden. And yet, insofar as the romancers themselves constituted a tradition of thought, they could also have been understood to function according to an idea or myth of America as opposed to a historically determined geopolitical interpretation of the country. As Bercovitch and others were pointing out (and not only about America), all positions within culture are ideologically or politically informed. They express one set of beliefs rather than another, and they intend to persuade others of the correctness of these beliefs. Romance fiction was no less ideological in this sense. Nonetheless, there might well be a difference between the myth of America/Israel/Eden, popularly conceived, and the myth of America within a particular literary tradition of texts.

A central feature in Cavell's thinking, which became for me the key to differentiating American popular myth and the romance tradition, had to do with philosophical skepticism. It concerned the way in which, by holding open questions of representation and knowledge (as opposed to answering them either in the affirmative or the negative), individuals might create for themselves a place from which to acknowledge, affirm, and take responsibility for the world in which they exist. Because of doubt, and through it, individuals were made conscious of the fact that various choices (of interpretation, belief, action) had no necessary validity, except as expressions of individual, moral will. But precisely for this reason, such decisions as human beings made bore the force of private responsibility. We affirm and acknowledge the events and assumptions of our world not as inevitabilities built into language and culture but as individually mediated choices made by individuals and by nations.

As I began to rethink my position on romance fiction with Cavell in mind it seemed to me more and more the case that the major American romancers wrote from a Cavellian position of acknowledgment and affirmation. What they objected to in the old myths of the American Eden, the American Promised Land, was not the idealism of these myths. Idealism might or might not be a bad thing. Nor was their objection to the ahistoricism of such idealism, though this was a problem. Rather, they objected to the way in which, by mythologizing reality, by understanding it typologically or metaphorically as opposed to factually or historically, people evaded the kind of self-conscious commitment to time and place without which, in the views of Hawthorne, Melville, James, and others, there could be no such thing as a world, no such place as a homeland.

In this light the experience of many an American protagonist (and not a few expatriated writers and critics, of greater and lesser significance) became clear. More than once I myself, "coming home" to America, or "coming home" to Israel for that matter, had felt a little bit like Washington Irving's Rip Van Winkle, or Nathaniel Hawthorne's Robin Molineux. I always seemed to be coming home to a home no longer recognizable or familiar, as a person who was only a version of myself, as if my true self were always in a place (Edenic, perfect) left behind and lost. Perhaps Irving's story is not (as some critics have assumed) about the historical transformation of America, for better or for worse. Perhaps it is about the acquisition of a skeptical self-consciousness as a prerequisite for the birth of a nation, any nation, but especially this nation, which had so much to declare to the world concerning the relationship between the individual consciousness (and conscience) and the world. Hence, the uncertainty of Irving's story, its skepticist consciousness, so like that of the major romances in the American tradition. The experience of Robin in Hawthorne's tale of the American Revolution, "My Kinsman, Major Molineux," would seem to verify this. Locked out of the home of his childhood, repulsed by the home into which he thought himself adopted by his kinsman or kinsmen, Robin, like Melville's Ishmael or Mark Twain's Huck Finn, is one of the many homeless orphans of American fiction who must make a home of a strange and alien world. "Strange things we travellers see," says Robin. "Am I here or there?" he asks, as if it were clear where *here* and *there* are; or which is stranger, the world we remember or the world we discover, Eden, Israel, or just plain old America.

"Travelling is a fool's paradise," writes Emerson in "Self-Reliance." "The soul is no traveller; the wise man stays at home, and when his necessities, his duties, on any occasion call him from his house, or into foreign lands, he is at home still and shall make men sensible by the expression of his countenance that he goes, the missionary of wisdom and virtue, and visits cities and men like a sovereign and not like an interloper or a valet." (I take it that Emerson does not use the word "paradise" lightly.)

Melville, Twain, and especially James will become the American masters of the subject of traveling (two of them actually traveling to the Promised Land). And what their Ishmaels and Clarels, Huck Finns and Connecticut Yankees, Daisy Millers and Isabel Archers will discover, at considerable cost— indeed, sometimes with their very lives—is what Emerson and Thoreau were able to see from the safety of their own backyards: that to found a nation one must find it first, and that home is a constant process of returning home, even if we have never really left home. Only the "traveler" who, never having left his home, comes home to it, can declare that home as his or hers, as Hawthorne does when he says, "*my* kinsman." Only the homebound wanderer can say what home is and tell its story, the story of a homeland.

No wonder, then, that waking up from a twenty-year sleep finally to see America for the first time, Rip becomes the author of its narrative. "Rip Van Winkle," no less than *Walden* or *The Scarlet Letter*, is intended to become a sacred, scriptural, text: I write only to wake my neighbors up, declares Thoreau, directly announcing his scriptural purpose. (There is a *midrash*—i.e., biblical interpretation—that suggests that, when Moses received the law on Sinai, it was accompanied by tremendous noise and thunder lest any of the Israelites remain sleeping.) Irving already knew that, in order to see, one had to awaken to what was always already there. And in order to domesticate the world one first had to see it. In his own story of the American Revolution, Hawthorne also presents his protagonist as waking up from what may or may not be a dream, learning how to see and (perhaps, for the story doesn't say) to stay.

Did I have to go to Israel to learn what Irving and Hawthorne, and Melville and James, and even Robert Frost knew: that home was not a place where, when you went there, they had to take you in; that, quite the contrary, home was a place that one had (Thoreau-fashion) to earn one's right to inhabit? According to Emerson, I didn't have to go so far to learn what was always so near at hand. Nor, according to Emerson, did I need this new yet unapproachable America in order to experience this old/new yet unapproachable Israel. And, perhaps, had I stayed long enough in either place, I would have understood exactly what I came to understand about both of them. But, in the final analysis, Emerson in "Self-Reliance" has "no churlish objection to the circumnavigation of the globe for the purposes of art, of study, and benevolence, so that the man is first domesticated, and does not go abroad with the hope of finding somewhat greater than he knows." And there is a kind of traveling more terrible than the transatlantic shuttle: the vagabond intellect, the fact that "our minds travel when our bodies are forced to stay at home." Might not an airplane, then, as easily as a ship or a train (to pick up some of Emerson's images in *Nature*), serve to change our perspective and give the "whole world a pictorial air," so that we might know that the world is "spectacle," the self is not.

Whether in America or in Israel, I had never left the promised land at all. I had only discovered that such promise as existed, existed only in my coming home, over and over again, in responsibility (Cavell, in the Emerson essay, calls it responsiveness) and commitment, to a place I would call and make my home.

The year 1991 brought Bercovitch and Cavell together in Israel for a workshop, sponsored by an Israel and German research grant, on the subject of the mutual translations of cultures—the way in which cultures exist, not as essentialist expressions of one national character or another, but as dynamic processes of mutual exchanges of individuals and ideologies and beliefs. Not accidentally, both Bercovitch and Cavell wrote on subjects that concerned their identity as Jews—Bercovitch on his discovery of America, from Israeli shores, as a Jewish Canadian; Cavell on the problematical relationship between philosophy and racism, that is, between Emerson and slavery, on the one hand, and between Heidegger and anti-Semitism, on the other.[4] (My own paper, inspired by both of them, was the one written during the Gulf War; I would deliver a version of it at Seville in 1992.) Bercovitch, traveling from Israel to America and back again, and Cavell, traveling from America to Israel, and Israel to America, in a series of frequent voyages, finally came together in the place that was not the stable intersection of their academic lives (it would have been easier for them to get together in Cambridge, Massachusetts, where they both live and teach), but one of many possible fulcrum locations where the continuous processes of cultural translation and, therefore, self-definition occur. Bercovitch and Cavell had both come home. They had both returned to the promised land—though (to paraphrase Hawthorne's "My Kinsman") whether they were "here or there," in this or that

Israel, was impossible to say. But their Israel was my Israel as well, and I learned one more thing from the two of them: coming home was not necessarily something one had to do alone.

Politics and Place—Madrid, 1992

I am on my way home from Spain at last. The different airline companies are lined up, one after the other. Where is El Al? At the Iberia counter I am told to go to the end of the hall. There, the stewardess explains, I will locate El Al. What I find instead are three anonymous booths (generics?), marked *A, B,* and *C.* A small group of vagabond travelers, like myself, is milling around. None of us is particularly concerned. We know that it is only a matter of time until the few tables emerge, the security guards arrive, and the El Al personnel put up the sign. For us, the existence of the state of Israel is a firm enough reality not to be threatened by this sudden vanishing act in (of all places) Spain.

Still, it makes one stop and think. If going home is, finally, an act of mind and spirit, doesn't it nonetheless depend, not only on the minds and spirits of those others with whom one shares one's home, but also on the minds and spirits of those strangers, for whom one's home is not home but on whose good will and generosity such a home depends? And doesn't a home require and deserve a physical, geographical place?

This idea of physical, geographical place is the whole point about Zionism, both as it is expressed in the Mosaic text and in modern political thought. For traditional Judaism, the five books of Moses, which are read out, consecutively, book by book, in the synagogue, on a yearly cycle, constitute more than a code of laws. They inscribe the history of the people, as it moves toward its ultimate goal—its arrival in the land of Canaan, the promised land. Of course, in the five books of Moses the Israelites never do arrive in Israel. This is in part what preserves the idea of Zion as a concept rather than a reality, an aspiration always about to be but never quite fulfilled. It is also what accounts for one school of thinking about Jewish nationalism. For American Jewish writers like Bernard Malamud and Saul Bellow, as for Jewish intellectuals like George Steiner, Jewish consciousness is best expressed (perhaps only possible to express) in the diaspora. But this is to ignore a feature of Jewish observance as significant as the ritual reading of the story of the Jews' nonarrival in Israel. For every passage from the five books of Moses that is read out in synagogue, there is a complementary text from the later books of the Old Testament, the books that record Jewish history after the people do establish themselves in the promised land.

Clearly, however much Zion remains an idea in Jewish consciousness, however much it remains an unfulfillable aspiration, it is nonetheless also a living, breathing, historical, geographical reality, with specific social, political and historical consequences. This is no less true of the contemporary state of

Israel, the reestablishment of an ancient regime as well as an ancient dream in modern times.

And this is the major difference between the state of Israel and the American Israel: whatever its self-definition, the American Israel does not occupy the place of Jewish history. Therefore, though it will produce a history of its own (perhaps as grand, perhaps as hospitable and meaningful to Jews), it cannot carry on the history of that place.

For me "home" is a place called Israel. This statement does not set to rest the questions that prevent an easy consolidation of self-identity. Indeed, the idea of a homeland such as Israel produces questions. What is this Israel? a plot of land? an idea? a promise of an idea? Who promises a land? Who keeps such a promise, and where, and when, and how? on the land? in the mind? and for whom? What about those others for whom this place also represents a home, however differently defined? Who possesses the right of definition to declare what a home is or is not, and for whom? The moral life of the nation depends, not on answering these questions, but on keeping them alive, preserving their capacity to ensure the open spaces of self- and national definition and the free and spontaneous flow of history, ideology, and belief.

But something more is also required, and that is the decision, on the parts of individuals, to declare a place "home" and to accept responsibility for that home. Whatever Israel may be, it is "my" home. It is a home that provides one powerful answer to the condition of homelessness which meant, for six million Jews a mere fifty years ago, extermination. It is a home, however, that can vanish, as thoroughly as (in 1492) that of Native Americans and Jews dissolved and disappeared. Therefore, it is a home that requires more than my affirmation. It requires as well the acceptance of those for whom it is not home, as it requires my acceptance of those who would make it home on terms different from my own. For, as we all know, promises can be made to be broken.

NOTES

1. Sacvan Bercovitch, "Discovering America: A Cross Cultural Perspective," in *The Translatability of Cultures: Figuration of the Space Between,* ed. Sanford Budick and Wolfgang Iser (Stanford: Stanford University Press, 1995).

2. Stanley Cavell, "Finding as Founding," in *This New Yet Unapproachable America: Lectures after Emerson after Wittgenstein* (Albuquerque, N.M.: Living Batch Press, 1989), 90; Emerson's quotation comes from his "Experience."

3. Cavell, "Finding as Founding," 91–93.

4. Sacvan Bercovitch, "Discovering America: A Cross Cultural Perspective", and Stanley Cavell, "Constitutional Amending: Reading 'Fate' "; both in *The Translatability of Cultures,* ed. Budick and Iser.

14

Once More on the Subject of Dostoevsky and the Jews

Michael R. Katz

An anti-Semite is a person who hates the Jews more than is absolutely necessary.
—Hungarian saying

THE JEWISH SOCIETY at Williams College regularly invited junior faculty members to address an audience of students, parents, and siblings at the "Bagels and Lox Brunch" on Fall Parent's Weekend. During my years as an assistant professor of Russian, I attended these gatherings for several different reasons, not the least of which was my fondness for ethnic cuisine.

I remember one talk given by a young philosopher. His title was intriguing: "Being Jewish at Williams." He and I had both been students there during the 1960s; we'd both gone off to graduate school at Oxford; and we'd both accepted teaching positions at our alma mater in the same year—a series of uncanny coincidences. He began his talk asserting that everyone defines himself or herself in terms of a number of categories and then listed those into which he fell: first and foremost, he was an intellectual; next, an American; then, a husband and father; and, somewhere down around number nine, he was a Jew. It wasn't that he denied being Jewish, it was just that in his own opinion it had never seemed all that significant a fact about himself.

I found myself agreeing wholeheartedly with his approach to self-definition and with the conclusion he had reached. He was talking about me; I might have reordered the categories slightly, but Jewishness would certainly have come way down on my list. I had never denied being Jewish, but it had never figured much in my frame of reference. I'd been given a secular upbringing, gone to graduate school in England, where I had tried hard to become English, and was then living in New England, trying hard to become New English. I was lost in these thoughts when I was suddenly startled by a tug on the sleeve. Another of my colleagues, a young astronomer, leaned over and whispered into my ear, "That's so Jewish!" I was dumbfounded, but after a moment's reflection, the philosopher's approach did strike me as being very "Jewish"—both conceiving of one's identity in tidy categories and placing

Jewishness so far down the list. And yet, how could both my colleagues be right? How could I identify with the philosopher's low priority placed on his Jewishness, and at the same time agree with the astronomer's remark that this approach was typically Jewish?

My turn to speak arrived and I chose something I'd been pondering for a while, but hadn't really worked through: "Dostoevsky and the Jews." I began with the Hungarian saying quoted above,[1] and argued that Dostoevsky didn't merely hate the Jews (as so many Russian writers had); instead, I maintained, a study of Dostoevsky's work revealed that he was a genuine anti-Semite, "a person who hates the Jews more than is absolutely necessary." I presented an early version of the argument I'm about to develop here: an investigation of the most prominent manifestations of Dostoevsky's anti-Semitism, including an analysis of his diction, a selection of his fictional characters, his strange rationalizations of his prejudice, and finally my own explanation of its source. I had handouts with lists of Russian words translated; I wrote characters' names and the titles of novels on the blackboard. I read samples of Dostoevsky's prose with appropriate Jewish and/or Russian accents. In short, I gave an entertaining performance (you never know what's going to count when you come up for tenure). At the end of my talk, after a round of polite applause, one student's mother raised her hand. Eager to see how my talk had been received, I nodded. She blurted out: "What's a nice Jewish *boy* like you doing with a subject like that?" I was astounded and mumbled some feeble explanation.

But I found myself getting more and more interested in the topic; the more I read, studied, and taught Dostoevsky, the more perturbed and excited I became. On the one hand, I admired his extraordinary literary talent and his deep humanitarian instincts; on the other, I found myself identifying almost exclusively with the victims of his prejudice.

How does a "Slavist of Russian-Jewish origin" respond to that mother's question? And why have so many Jewish scholars tried to deal with this awkward topic and produced so many works with titles such as *Russian Anti-Semitism and the Jews; Russian Literature and the Jews; Dostoyevsky and the Jews; The Russian Soul and the Jews*—to name only the best known? How can any Jew work on an author and a subject that's so very offensive to his own sense of self (even if his Jewishness is somewhere down on the list of constituents in that self)?

Russian writers have always hated the Jews. But Dostoevsky was different. First of all, we can examine the language he used to describe Jews. In *The Brothers Karamazov* (1881), the narrator takes time out from his preliminary description of the title character of the chapter "The Third Son" to provide some background on Alyosha's father:

> A word or two about Fyodor Pavlovich. For some time before this he'd lived elsewhere. Three or four years after the death of his second wife he set off for the south of Russia and finally turned up in Odessa where he lived for several

years. At first he made the acquaintance, in his own words, "of many Yids, little Yids, dirty little Yids, and Yidkins," But he ended up later being received not only by the Yids, but "even by some Jews too."[2]

The difference between the neutral term "Jew" (*evrei*) and the derogatory word "Yid" (*zhid*) had been apparent for decades before Dostoevsky ever put pen to paper. One of the things that distinguishes this passage is the author's effort to capture that distinction with correlative contrasting phrases, which also involve his attempt to create a lexicon for derogation. Fyodor goes to Odessa and interacts with the dregs of society while the author's imagination provides appropriate "terms of endearment" in Fyodor's "own words." *Zhid* is the simplest form of abuse, "Yid or Kike"; *zhidok* has a diminutive suffix, hence, "little Yid"; *zhidishko* has a suffix that is both diminutive and pejorative, hence, "dirty little Yid"; and last but not least, *zhidenyata*, Dostoevsky's own coinage, has a suffix denoting the plural young of animals, hence "Yidkins," "Yidlings," or "Yidlets." (The obvious analogy is *porosenok/porosyata* = pig/piglets).

Dostoevsky tried to defend his choice of words in his *Diary of a Writer* in the March 1877 issue:

> Am I not accused of *"hatred"* because I sometimes called the Jew a *Yid*? But in the first place, I didn't think it was so abusive; and in the second place, as far as I can remember, I've always used the word *Yid* to denote a certain *idea* . . . a certain conception, orientation, characteristic of our age. One may argue about this idea, and even disagree with it, but one shouldn't feel offended by a *word*.[3]

A word indeed! "A rose by any other name . . ." perhaps, or as Dostoevsky might have said, "A Yid by any other name smells the same."

The point, however, is that in such passages one is dealing with artistic imagination and creativity. These are no conventional, stereotypical traits: this is witty, incisive, brilliant, and very funny language, used both to characterize the variety of "low-down" Yids whom Fyodor encountered in Odessa and to document his "rise" up the social ladder, culminating in his success at being received "even by some Jews." There's no doubt whatever that one is dealing with a case of "more than is absolutely necessary."

Turning from Dostoevsky's lexicon to his cast of characters, we must first note that there are very few Jews among them; however, the ones that do exist merit special attention, not only because they illustrate the author's anti-Semitism, but also because of their extraordinary inventiveness.

Dostoevsky's first (and fullest) portrait of a Jew occurs in the work that heralded his reentry onto the literary scene after his years in exile, namely *Notes from the House of the Dead* (1860–62). There is some evidence that before this Dostoevsky had no direct encounters with Jews (there were very few living in Petersburg); but in Siberia he met a real-life Jewish convict named Isai Bumstehl, who is transformed in the prison memoirs into the remarkable Isai Fomich Bumstein.[4]

The diversity of critical opinion on Isai is astounding: on the one hand he's been described as "devoid of human traits"; on the other, his portrait's been said to be "free of animosity, malice or contempt."[5] David Goldstein, in his comprehensive study *Dostoyevsky and the Jews*, argues *both* sides of the question. He maintains that Isai's portrait lacks depth and human dimension, that it is mere caricature intended to provoke derision; yet at the same time, he says that flashes of "warmth and good will" can be detected, especially on the part of the narrator.[6]

In *Taras Bulba*, Gogol had created a caricature of a Jew in the figure of the pitiful Yid Yankel. Dostoevsky, in a letter to his brother dated January 1844, refers to a play he was working on by the title "Yid Yankel," clearly borrowed from Gogol. In fact, in *Notes from the House of the Dead*, Dostoevsky's narrator makes the connection explicit:

> Every time I looked at him [Isai Bumstein] I was reminded of Gogol's little Yid Yankel in *Taras Bulba*, who, when he undressed to betake himself with his Yiddess to some closet for the night, looked awfully like a chicken. Our little Yid, Isai Fomich, was the spit and image of a plucked chicken.[7]

Dostoevsky's portrait is pure caricature: Isai's name speaks for itself; he is "small and puny," "cunning and yet distinctly stupid," "impudent" yet "terribly cowardly." He's a jeweler and "of course" a money-lender; he "lived like a rich man" even in prison. The other prisoners "amused themselves by teasing him"—he provides entertainment and perpetual diversion. Everyone was really "almost fond of him":

> Luka, who had known many Yids in his time, often teased him, quite without malice and simply for fun, exactly as one amuses oneself with a dog, a parrot, a trained animal, or something of that kind. Isai Fomich knew this and took no offense.[8]

He is the comic foil and a source of amusement in the midst of despair, but he is also a perverse breath of life in this "house of the dead," precisely because he manages to flourish while others merely endure:

> The expression of his face revealed unwavering, unshakeable self-satisfaction and even beatific happiness. He felt apparently not the slightest regret at having landed in prison . . . .[9]

Dostoevsky describes Isai's "Sabbath" as an extraordinary combination of sobbing and howling, punctuated by mad bursts of laughter—a display "deliberately" staged for the benefit of other prisoners. Isai's behavior in the bathhouse is similarly bizarre: while others perceive the bath as a miniature hell, he sees it as the approximation of paradise.[10]

The following repartee between Isai Fomich and the other prisoners shows the treatment Bumstein received, his mechanisms for survival, and the essence of his "philosophy":

"Hey, Yid, I'll run you through!"

"You hit me once, and I'll hit you ten times," answered Isai Fomich boldly.

"Scabby Yid!"

"What if I am?"

"Dirty Yid!"

"Perhaps I am. I may be dirty, but I'm rich; I've got money!"

"You sold Christ."

"So you say."

"Hey, Yid, you'll get whipped and sent to Siberia."

"I'm in Siberia already."

"You'll get sent still farther away."

"Well, is God there?"

"Of course He is."

"Well then, that's all right; if God's there, and money too, it's all right anywhere!"[11]

Bumstein represents *antithesis;* as such he fulfills an important role in the lives of the other prisoners and in the work as a whole. In an obscure footnote to a footnote, the critic Robert Louis Jackson defined Bumstein's role in Dostoevsky's ideological design; that is, the Jew is juxtaposed with the Tatar Alei, the chaste embodiment of a moral ideal, a Christ-like figure loved and cherished by everyone, a man who is intelligent, delicate, and good.[12] This contrast between Jew and Christian gains in significance in Dostoevsky's later fiction, where the sources of his anti-Semitism become more apparent. Here it is merely an indication of the abyss that separates the caricature of the Jew from the idealized Christian Tatar.

Dostoevsky's second "Jewish character" makes only a cameo appearance in *Crime and Punishment* (1865): he is almost invisible and as a result frequently overlooked in analyses of the novel. Nevertheless, the Jewish fireman, or "Achilles" as he has come to be called, provides valuable evidence of Dostoevsky's attitude toward the Jews. The episode in which he appears occurs quite late in the novel: all of Svidrigailov's intellectual arguments have been rebuffed by Raskolnikov; Svidrigailov's last attempt to end his isolation by winning Dunya's love has failed; he has been plagued by nightmares and, sinking into despair, has decided to take his own life.[13] He wanders the streets of Petersburg in search of the perfect place to blow his brains out. Dostoevsky's description of his choice is worth quoting at length:

There was a large building with a watch-tower. Near the big locked gates of the house stood a little man, leaning his shoulder against the building; he was wrapped in a grey soldier's overcoat and was wearing a copper Achilles-like helmet. He coldly directed his sleepy gaze on the approaching Svidrigailov. On his face was written that age-old querulous grief which is so sourly imprinted on the faces of all members of the Jewish tribe without exception. Both of them, Svidrigailov and Achilles, stood looking at each other in silence for some time. Finally it seemed to Achilles that something was amiss; here was a sober man, standing only three paces away from him, looking him right in the eye, saying nothing. "Aaa . . . what do you want here, eh?" he uttered, still immobile and without altering his position.

"Not a thing, brother; hello!" replied Svidrigailov.

"This ain't the place. . . ."

"Brother, I'm going off to distant parts."

"To distant parts?"

"To America."

"To America?"

Svidrigailov pulled out his revolver and cocked the trigger. Achilles raised his eyebrows.

"Aaa . . . what? This is no place for such jokes!"

"Why isn't this the place?"

"It just isn't."

"Well, brother, never mind. The place is right; if they come and ask you, tell them I left for—oh, America."

He put the revolver to his right temple.

"Aaa . . . you mustn't here—this isn't the place," Achilles shuddered; his pupils opened wider and wider.

Svidrigailov pulled the trigger.[14]

In *Dostoyevsky and the Jews,* Goldstein describes the symbolism of this passage as "unquestionable but well-nigh inscrutable."[15] He wonders whether "Achilles" is a "real" character or merely a figment of Svidrigailov's imagination or even Dostoevsky's. Favoring the latter explanation, he regards the Jewish fireman as a "pure phantom," an "artificially inspired" hallucination. The scene certainly has a surrealistic dimension.

Dostoevsky's notebooks for *Crime and Punishment* reveal the author's deep satisfaction with his plans for Svidrigailov's suicide. After a sketchy outline of the character's last days and his death, Dostoevsky notes in parenthesis: "This will be magnificent."[16] Indeed it is.

First and foremost, Dostoevsky has engineered another dramatic reversal. Just as Isai Bumstein thrives in a hellish environment while others languish, here the "puny little man" (*nebolshoi chelovechik*) is dressed in a soldier's great coat and a copper Achilles-like helmet: the victim wears the attire of the victimizer, the persecuted is dressed like the persecutor. The scene is one of pure bathos, grotesque in its effect. As Dostoevsky himself correctly intuited, the juxtaposition of these two characters would be magnificent: Svidrigailov's last moments are extraordinarily powerful.

But why did Dostoevsky do it? Was it merely gratuitous, an unnecessary swipe at an already humiliated, anonymous representative of that "age-old querulous grief" and suffering? Isn't it adding insult to injury? If so, it certainly succeeds. But Goldstein sees another motive that deserves exploration: he argues that Achilles represents an eerie challenge to the messianic role conceived by Dostoevsky for the Russian people and that the author was trying to exorcise this Jewish phantom with "the stamp of the eternal on his brow." Whereas before the "Christ-killer" Isai Bumstein was juxtaposed with the Christ-like Alei in *Notes from the House of the Dead,* so now the ghostlike Achilles' survival is contrasted with Svidrigailov's suicide and, even more important, with Raskolnikov's conversion to Christianity and "resurrection" in the Epilogue. Once again, Dostoevsky's Jewish characters play a crucial role in the author's religious scheme.

The third and last Jewish character Dostoevsky portrays is Lyamshin,[17] the "pickpocket, windbag, and scoundrel," who belongs to "the group of five"— the nihilist conspirators in *Devils* (also known as *The Possessed*) (1871–72). There he plays the fool:

> And if things became really unbearably boring, Lyamshin, the little Jewish post-office clerk, sat down at the piano and played, or else did imitations of a pig, a storm, or a childbirth (including the newborn's first cry), etc.—which was mostly why he was invited.[18]

Alternatively, Lyamshin could demonstrate an enormous capacity for self-hatred, when on demand he would gladly impersonate "all sorts of Jews."

His role in the novel is slight, but extremely important. Immediately following Shatov's murder, Lyamshin loses his head and begins howling uncontrollably. He has to be overpowered by the other conspirators because his hysterics threaten to betray the entire plot. In the end it is Lyamshin's failure as a revolutionary that results in the ultimate unraveling of the conspiracy.[19] Judas reincarnated, Lyamshin confesses all and betrays his comrades.

In addition to his role in the narrative, Lyamshin, like Bumstein and Achilles, also occupies a place in Dostoevsky's ideological scheme; but, unlike in the previous two works, the confrontation between Jewish infidel and Christian believer in *Devils* is direct and explicit. When a strange woman appears in town going door to door selling Bibles,

> . . . Lyamshin, while feigning an interest in buying some Bibles from her, filled the woman's bag with a collection of foreign pornographic photographs; later in the shopping arcade, when the poor woman reached into her bag for Bibles, the obscene pictures fell out and scattered all over the place. People started to laugh, to protest, then to swear. A fight broke out and the police arrived.[20]

This Jew is guilty of outrageous sacrilege; he defiles everything that is holy. It is all the more significant that this same woman reappears at the end of the novel, where she divulges her own "speaking" name (Sophia Ulitina— "wisdom" proceeding at a "snail's" pace) and reveals the truth to Stepan Trofimovich Verkhovensky, the spiritual father of all nihilist devils and demons, while he makes his first and last confession to her on his deathbed. Once again the Jew is depicted as a threat to the true faith, to Dostoevsky's Russian Orthodox Christianity.

These three characters, the only Jews in Dostoevsky's fiction, have a number of attributes in common. First they all display *subhuman traits:* Isai Bumstein is compared to "a dog, a parrot, a trained animal, or something of that kind"; Achilles is a caricature of a hero dressed in great coat and helmet, a pathetic replica of a human being; Lyamshin performs like a clown, does imitations of pigs and newborn babies, and when, after Shatov's murder, he loses all self-control, his howling reveals a primitive, animalistic instinct, and foreshadows his screeching and crawling during his confession to the authorities.

Secondly, Dostoevsky uses all three of these Jewish characters for *humorous effect:* Bumstein provides diversion and comic relief in the "house of the dead" and is an object of derision and ridicule; the portrait of Achilles introduces a note of black humor into Svidrigailov's chilling last moments, as his heavily accented and awkward Russian and his wide-eyed incomprehension contrast with the decisive and desperate act of suicide; and Lyamshin provides both music and entertainment to accompany the deadly serious machinations of the conspirators in *Devils*. Bathos, false or overdone pathos, seems to capture most accurately the essence of Dostoevsky's portrayals of Jews.

Finally, in the author's ideological scheme, each of the three Jewish characters provides evidence of *survival* and constitutes a genuine "threat" (implicit or explicit) to Dostoevsky's own faith: Isai Bumstein thrives in prison while others suffer, and his obscene behavior is contrasted with the morally pure and chaste Christ-like Tatar Alei; Achilles outlives Svidrigailov's despair, and undermines the lasting significance of Raskolnikov's conversion in the Epilogue; finally, Lyamshin defiles sacred icons, humiliates the Gospel-woman, and subverts the Christian universalist message of Stepan Verkhovensky's final confession. Dostoevsky's Jews (Yids) steadfastly refuse to vanish; they withstand both inclusion and assimilation.

In the March 1877 issue of *Diary of a Writer*, Dostoevsky provides a fascinating defense against all accusations that he was an anti-Semite. Entitled "The Jewish Question," it begins with the following disclaimer:

> Oh, please don't think I mean to raise "the Jewish question!" I wrote that title in jest. To raise a question of such magnitude as the status of the Jew in Russia, and the status of Russia which among her sons has three million Jews—is beyond my power. The question exceeds my limits.[21]

What follows is an essay on that very subject in which he responds to charges that he was a Jew-hater. His argument is too elaborate to summarize here, but certain key themes deserve to be highlighted. First Dostoevsky asserts that

> . . . among our common people [Russians] there is no preconceived, *a priori,* blunt religious hatred of the Jew, something along the lines: "Judas sold out Christ." Even if one hears it from little children or drunks, nevertheless our people as a whole look upon the Jew, I repeat, without a preconceived hatred.[22]

This is a splendid example of self-contradiction, inasmuch as Dostoevsky's own novels contain numerous examples of scenes in which little children and drunks, almost without exception, speak the "truth"—precisely because they have yet to learn restraint or have managed to shed the inhibitions and restrictions governing normal adult discourse. The novelist knew all too well that "if one hears it from little children or drunks": then it must be commonly purported to be true!

The overall strategy Dostoevsky pursues in his "rationalization" can be characterized as blaming the victim. If there exists no "preconceived hatred" for Jews, he argues, then the "strong dislike" he acknowledges must arise as a result of things for which the Jew himself is guilty. Jews "reign in Europe," "direct the stock-exchanges and therefore the politics, domestic affairs, and the morality of states"; yet there is no other people who complain as much about their lot, "their humiliation, their suffering, their martyrdom." Jews insist on preserving their *status in statu,* the symptoms of which are alienation and estrangement in religious dogma, the impossibility of "fusion" or inclusion, and "the belief that in the world there exists but one national entity—the Jew." Blame therefore rests "infinitely less on the Russian than on the Jew himself." It is Jews who harbor "a boundless and haughty prejudice against Russians." Russians are willing to accept the Jew in the fullest brotherhood—but "for complete brotherhood—*brotherhood on the part of both sides is needed"* (emphasis in the original).[23]

So the "Jewish question" has been transformed into the "Russian question," and Dostoevsky's solution is simple: Jews should relinquish their claim to be the chosen people, the "one national entity" in the world; they should end their insistence on exclusivity and accept the Russians' generous offer of full brotherhood in exchange for "fusion," that is, total assimilation and presumably conversion.

This line of reasoning finally leads us to the true source of Dostoevsky's anti-Semitism. In the second paragraph of this article, the author makes the following assertion: ". . . a Jew without God is somehow inconceivable; a Jew without God cannot be imagined."[24] Dostoevsky never returned to what he himself calls this "vast theme," but in *Devils,* Shatov offers two closely parallel statements pertaining, not to Jews, but to Russians: "An atheist cannot be a Russian; an atheist immediately stops being a Russian. . . . Someone who is not Orthodox cannot be a Russian."[25] Without distorting the meaning of these statements, we are entitled to reformulate Shatov's sentiment in the following way: A *Russian* without God is somehow inconceivable; a Russian without God cannot even be imagined. The extraordinary similarity between these two claims has led more than one critic to use Shatov's pronouncements as an indication of the author's own views, a conclusion which I also share.

In *Devils,* Shatov goes to great lengths to explain what it is that makes a nation great:

If a great nation does not believe that it alone possesses the truth . . . if it does not believe that it alone is capable of and destined to resurrect and save everyone else by means of that truth—then it immediately ceases to be a great nation and becomes merely an ethnographic designation.[26]

He further explains this claim and makes explicit the comparison between the Jewish nation and the Russian nation:

Every nation is a nation only as long as it possesses its own particular God—and as long as it excludes all other Gods as irreconcilable—and as long as it believes that with the help of its own God, it will conquer and expel all other Gods from the earth. All great nations have believed this from the beginning of time . . . : The Jews lived only in anticipation of the true God, and they bequeathed the true God to the world.[27]

Physicists tell us that two physical bodies cannot occupy the same space at the same time. It seems perfectly clear that in Dostoevsky's view two nations could not fulfill the same spiritual role at the same historical moment.

Then Shatov declares in no uncertain terms:

But there is only one truth, and therefore, only one nation can possess the true God, although other nations have had their own special gods—the single god-bearing nation is the Russian nation.[28]

Clearly the Jewish claim to be the "chosen people" and to possess the "true God" could not possibly coexist with the Russian claim to be the "chosen people" and to possess the "true God."

Russian medieval writers who argued for the centrality of Eastern Orthodoxy in the Christian world devised a theory known as the doctrine of the Third Rome. It held that after Rome had fallen and Constantinople had been overrun by Turks,[29] Moscow became the sole bastion of true, pure, Orthodox Christianity—the "third Rome"—and "a fourth there shall not be." Dostoevsky not only accepts this theory but also expands it with the further claim that Moscow also inherited the Judaic mantle of "the chosen people." As A. Z. Shteinberg once wrote, Dostoevsky sees "the Russians as the God-chosen people, *the reincarnation of Israel*" (emphasis added).[30] The torch had been passed; the Jewish nation was now, in Shatov's words, "merely an ethnographic designation." It must be noted, however, that, unlike the Jewish claim, the Russian assertion was universalist and meant to include everyone. The Russian people had inherited the messianic mantle from Israel and now promised to lead all humankind (including *even* the Jews, if they would agree to "fuse") toward a new truth—in Christ, of course.

But the fly in the ointment, the thorn in the side, is the stubborn perseverance of the Jews. They simply weren't willing to accept the role assigned to them and to leave gracefully, to "quit the scene." Isai Bumstein thrives in prison; Achilles outlives Svidrigailov; Lyamshin confesses and recants his crime. Those Jews just won't go away.

So, what *is* a nice Jewish boy like me doing with a subject like this? How does a Slavist of Russian-Jewish origin deal with such a disturbing prejudice in one of the major figures of classical Russian literature (and one of his own personal favorites)? Before I reveal my own answer to these questions, let's review the way Slavists of similar background have chosen to resolve the issue.

Goldstein's monograph (1976) has been described both as an "implacable indictment" of Dostoevsky's anti-Semitism and as a "bold, but crude attack" on the author.[31] Whatever its faults, it is the first exhaustive study of this aspect of Dostoevsky's thought, and provides many compelling readings of his fiction and nonfiction. But how did Goldstein cope? By careful clarification followed by resounding condemnation. He examines the evidence, analyzes the characters and their arguments, arrives at a hypothesis to explain the cause of the author's antipathy, and then, as it were, condemns Dostoevsky to hell.

It is somewhat bizarre that in the brief but intriguing Foreword to Goldstein's English translation of his own book (1981), the eminent Slavist Joseph Frank attempts to soften the critic's blow. Eager to see Dostoevsky in a more sympathetic light, Frank pursues two quite different strategies. The first takes us back to the Hungarian saying quoted at the start of the chapter. Frank argues that Dostoevsky wasn't really an anti-Semite at all, merely a conventional Jew-hater. He bases his conclusion on two assumptions: (1) Dostoevsky followed in the time-honored Russian tradition of uncomplimentary depiction of Jews from Pushkin to Chekhov—no more, no less. (2) Dostoevsky's anti-Jewish attitude "should be placed in the larger context of a more general xenophobia. . . . he was just as anti-French, anti-German, anti-English and, particularly, anti-Polish—indeed, anti-everybody who was not Russian, and Great Russian at that.[32] So it seems Dostoevsky hated the Jews no more than he hated everyone else. Why single out the Jews?

Frank's second strategy is even more ingenious. He accuses Goldstein of ignoring those passages where Dostoevsky expresses genuine sympathy for his Jewish characters, his positive arguments in favor of extending legal rights to Jews, and his "profoundly ambiguous and divided sensibility." In fact, says Frank, "what distinguishes Dostoevsky's anti-Semitism from all his other national, ethnic and religious hatreds is that, here and here alone, he appears to betray a certain sense of guilt."[33] Thus, if one persists perversely in seeing Dostoevsky as an anti-Semite, it is necessary to invent a new category for him—"the guilty anti-Semite"! Dostoevsky was unable to reconcile his own anti-Semitism; thus the contradictions that emerge in his fictional portrayal of Jews and in his journalistic writings on the Jewish people reflect the "struggle within himself." After reading Frank's Foreword one almost feels sorry for the "tormented genius" whose anti-Semitism caused *him* so much suffering.

Goldstein's book and Frank's Foreword have provoked other responses as well. In a review article entitled "Dostoevsky's Anti-Semitism and the Critics" (1983), Gary Saul Morson criticizes Goldstein's monograph for being "ahistorical" (providing no analysis of the social origins of Dostoevsky's anti-Semitism), and "abiographical" (including no discussion of the evolution of Dostoevsky's anti-Semitic attitude). He accuses Frank of "special pleading"; turning Frank's formulation on Frank himself, he calls him a "guilty apologist" for Dostoevsky. Morson also dismisses the strategy of identifying two Dostoevskys—the compassionate novelist and the chauvinist ideologue—exonerating the former and condemning the latter, since it reflects not so much a bifurcation in Dostoevsky as the difficulties his admirers face when dealing with his views. Thus, "when texts cannot be given a favorable reading, they are ascribed to the other Dostoevsky."[34] Morson then admits to having conceived a "hatred" of Dostoevsky; the author's "repugnant opinions" (political messianism, Russian Orthodox chauvinism, intellectual obscurantism, and anti-Semitism) have "contaminated his novels" once and for all, and displaced the love Morson once felt for his "old friend."[35]

The most recent contribution to the debate, a response to Morson's review, is an essay entitled "Dostoevsky's Kike" by Felix Dreizin, published posthumously in the collection *The Russian Soul and the Jew* (1990). Dreizin accuses Morson of reducing "two incompatible attitudes to a single image" of the author, of being reluctant to consider "the emotional factor in Dostoevsky or his critics," and of refusing to acknowledge that Dostoevsky's "organic aversion" to Jews may be explained by "the intimate needs of his pathological personality." Dreizin argues that the origin and function of Dostoevsky's anti-Semitism must be sought in his "psychology and psychopathology." Modifying Frank's formulation, he maintains that Dostoevsky must be considered a "compulsive anti-Semite," rather than a "guilty" one.[36]

Well, how many Dostoevskys are there really—*one* or *two*? And is he (or they?) a conventional Jew-hater or an anti-Semite? And how do I, yet another Slavist of Russian-Jewish origin, respond to this extraordinary phenomenon?

Of course there is only *one* Dostoevsky, a very complex one, whose views evolved over the course of his life and whose attitudes must be studied in the context of Russian history and literature. That one Dostoevsky *was* an anti-Semite—who hated the Jews "more than was absolutely necessary"—as the evidence of his fiction and nonfiction clearly demonstrates. But how *does* one respond—with condemnation (Goldstein), apologetics (Frank), hatred (Morson), psychologizing and/or psychopathologizing (Dreizin)?

Well, every reader has to cope as best he or she can. My own solution is as follows: I resort to what some may view as cliché; others, as a play on words; and others, merely as an escape. I believe in the idea of a "love-hate relationship," one that characterizes some of our closest emotional bonds: the feelings of a child for its parent, a parent for his or her child; a husband for his wife, a wife for her husband; a teacher for his or her student, a student for his or her teacher; and so on. I hereby confess to harboring such love-hate for

Dostoevsky: he is a complex writer and I am a complex reader. Just as he frequently portrays characters who experience two (or more) emotions at the same time, I, too, can feel several things simultaneously. I neither condemn him outright, nor apologize for him, nor replace love with hatred, nor psychologize. I can appreciate his creativity, originality, and profundity, as well as the sheer power of his language, characters, and convictions—even when he is being his most anti-Semitic. But at the same time I can abhor his prejudice, point out the difficulties and contradictions to my students, and privately ponder the mysteries of the human personality—Dostoevsky's and my own. In one sense then, I suppose, it was reading Dostoevsky that really made me become a Jew.

NOTES

1. Quoted in Gordon W. Allport, *The Nature of Prejudice* (New York: Doubleday and Co., 1958), 4.

2. F. M. Dostoevsky, *Polnoe sobranie sochinenii v tridstati tomakh*, 30 vols. (Leningrad: Nauka, 1976), XIV, 21 (henceforth cited as *PSS*). The quotations from this source are my own translations.

3. Dostoevsky, *PSS*, XXV, 75.

4. See David Goldstein, *Dostoyevsky and the Jews* (Austin: University of Texas Press, 1981), 14–15; originally published as *Dostoïevski et les Juifs* (Paris: Editions Gallimard, 1976).

5. Quoted in Felix Dreizin, *The Russian Soul and the Jew* (Lanham, Md.: University Press of America, 1990), 84.

6. Goldstein, *Dostoyevsky and the Jews*, 14–31.

7. Dostoevsky, *PSS*, IV, 55.

8. Dostoevsky, *PSS*, IV, 94.

9. Dostoevsky, *PSS*, IV, 93.

10. Dreizin, *The Russian Soul*, 88.

11. Dostoevsky, *PSS*, IV, 94.

12. Robert Louis Jackson, "A Footnote to Selo Stepančikovo," *Ricerche Slavistiche* 17 (1970):250.

13. See Katz, *Dreams and the Unconscious in Nineteenth-Century Russian Fiction* (Hanover, N.H.: University Press of New England, 1984), 103–4.

14. Dostoevsky, *PSS*, VI, 394–95.

15. Goldstein, *Dostoyevsky*, 51.

16. *The Notebooks to Crime and Punishment*, ed. and trans. Edward Wasiolek (Chicago: University of Chicago Press, 1974), 225.

17. Lyamshin is generally thought to be a converted Jew. See Goldstein, *Dostoyevsky*, 68 and n. 186.

18. Dostoevsky, *PSS*, X, 30–31.

19. Goldstein argues unconvincingly that Dostoevsky illustrates Lyamshin's profound humanity "in spite of himself" (*Dostoyevsky*, 83).

20. Dostoevsky, *PSS*, X, 251.

21. Dostoevsky, *PSS*, XXV, 74.

22. Dostoevsky, *PSS*, XXV, 80.

23. Dostoevsky, *PSS, XXV,* 74–80.

24. Dostoevsky, *PSS, XXV,* 75.

25. Dostoevsky, *PSS,* X, 197.

26. Dostoevsky, *PSS,* X, 199–200.

27. Dostoevsky, *PSS,* X, 199.

28. Dostoevsky, *PSS,* X, 200.

29. Dostoevsky talks elsewhere in *Diary of a Writer* about the inevitability that Russia will retake Constantinople (see entry for June 1876).

30. A. Z. Shteinberg, "Dostoevsky and the Jews," *Versty* 3 (Paris, 1928).

31. Joseph Frank's Foreword to Goldstein, *Dostoyevsky,* x; Gary Saul Morson, "Dostoevsky's Anti-Semitism and the Critics: A Review Article," *Slavic and East European Journal* 27 (1983):316.

32. Frank's Foreword to Goldstein, *Dostoyevsky,* xiv.

33. Frank's Foreword to Goldstein, *Dostoyevsky,* xii, xiv.

34. Morson, "Dostoevsky's Anti-Semitism," 312.

35. Morson, "Dostoevsky's Anti-Semitism," 316.

36. Dreizin, *The Russian Soul,* 112, 113.

15

Yom Kippurs at Yum Luk
Reflections on Eating, Ethnicity, and Identity

Doris Friedensohn

I SIP CHARDONNAY and study the menu at Asia, a trend-setting Upper East Side restaurant where Chinese, Indian, Indonesian, Thai, and Japanese specialities peaceably cohabit. It is difficult to suppress my amusement. Asia invites worldly New Yorkers, familiar with all the aforementioned cuisines, to take a break from Oriental food connoisseurship and enjoy the upscale, multicultural food-mall approach to lunch.

My friend Jane and I order a spicy Szechuan "salad" of pork, chicken, and red peppers and Pad Thai, noodles with bean sprouts, chopped peanuts, and whole jumbo shrimp. We chat about recent travels and future plans, including a visit to our Buddhist offspring who are married to one another and living in Kathmandu; and we speculate about whether the kids, with their passion for authenticity in things Asian, would even set foot in the place. No matter. Colorful platters of food sail past us, my gastronomical batteries charge, and the day's "research"—an offshoot of other projects in immigration studies—is well launched.

Everything about Asia, the restaurant, intrigues me: The ethnically balanced, transnational menu with its politically correct focus on pasta and vegetables; the spectacular, free-standing fish tanks, stocked with brilliantly hued "designer" fish, which compete with the food for center stage; the impeccably costumed global villagers speaking in a medley of tongues; and the seductiveness of strange smells in a distinctly Americanized olfactory idiom. Clearly, Asia is an artifact of affluent, multicultural New York and a response to late twentieth-century American tastes in eating and restaurant-going; it signals the dramatic impact of immigration, world travel, prodigious cosmopolitanism, and consumer restlessness on contemporary American foodways. The book I am writing grows out of an effort to tell that story.

I had hardly begun when another narrative intruded: a leaving-home story in the form of a food lover's voyage of discovery. Thinking about the "foreign" restaurants I frequent and the "forbidden" foods I crave, I found myself retracing the route from my mother's modified kosher kitchen to my own postethnic larder and table: the early seductions of Chinese, French, and southern Italian cuisines; the lure of Mexican, Greek, North African, northern Italian, and Japanese fare; and my recent pursuit of Korean, Caribbean, Lebanese, Portuguese, and Turkish delights. Call me a fickle food fanatic. My inconstancy is the wry side of a lifetime of eating as rebellion and self-creation.

Here were two related stories, vying for attention: a history of sophisticated, middle-class American eating habits in the last decades of the twentieth century and the autobiography of an eater (responsive to the trends of her class and peers) born in 1936 in New York's gilded ghetto. At the core of both stories is food as a yardstick of consciousness: a reflection of choices made among a multiplicity of options, choices which define communities of meaning and configurations of identity.

Could I convincingly combine the public chronicle and the personal narrative? I wasn't sure. But to get a handle on the former I gave free rein to the latter, and I temporarily set aside problems of genre and method. The work got off to a fast start. When the first half dozen autobiographical pages came bouncing out of my Image Writer II, the book already had a title, "Delicious Acts of Defiance," a theme and a voice I recognized as my own. Some months later, by way of clarification, I added the obligatory subtitle, "Tales of Eating and Everyday Life."

The essays I have been writing on eating, ethnicity, and identity utilize the rebel eater's odyssey as subject or vantage point. My mother and father, husband, children, other close relatives, dear friends, and even some casual acquaintances appear on stage, seize the time, and play out scenes I have not plotted in advance: there are steamy food wars and ritualistic gatherings of the clan, culinary peccadillos and surreptitious adventures, the bliss of good booze and sex after lunch. In the realm beyond the domestic, there are investigations of ethnic restaurants, immigrant food shops, and multiethnic supermarkets; forays into kitsch ethnic, mixed ethnic, and nouvelle cuisines; and meditations on pizza and kim chee, feijoada and couscous, suckling pig and egg foo young.

Writing about food is primal and confrontational, like looking in the mirror and discussing drugs with one's children. It generates an embarrassment of revelations. For example, I eat pork whenever possible; therefore, I am . . . profane, secular, obsessive and oppositional, liberated but not quite autonomous, myself. When I began this project, I did not know what encounters with the past awaited me or how the ground of diurnal doings might tremble under inspection. Nor did I imagine, having circumvented the matter for most of my adult life, the degree to which writing about eating would lead me to review my experience of Jewishness.

I say "review" rather than "rethink" advisedly—as a way of announcing that my Jewish self is elusive, conflicted, and ill defined, and that I grab hold of it best through indirection. This is an embarrassing confession for a self-conscious academic whose constant concern over three decades has been the question of identity in contemporary America. Since the early 1960s, in courses in English, American studies, and women's studies, I have pressed my students to explore the origins and development of their sense of self. During class discussions, I have offered countless autobiographical illustrations of the inevitable struggles with family, society, and personal demons. To encourage students to use their own life tales as data for cultural analysis, I have written about my schooling, my mother and grandmother, my Upper West Side neighborhood, and my illegal abortion. But not about religion or the universe of being Jewish. Not until the food project, that is. And even there, difficult questions about conviction and commitment take a back seat to family psychodramas and irrepressible celebrations of *treif.*

In this chapter, therefore, I draw upon four anecdotal pieces from "Delicious Acts of Defiance"—on violating Yom Kippur, Ramadan in Tunisia, my son's Buddhist-Jewish wedding, and the slow death of Passover—in an effort to unpack some new understandings of my identity as an American and a Jew.

The first section opens with a dutiful but faithless synagogue-going girl who lunches at Yum Luk on the Day of Atonement. There, in that dissonant image of involvement, ambivalence, and undercover resistance, is my quintessential growing-up-Jewish story. And there, in a Jewish nutshell, is my American figure in the carpet: a veneer of easy conformity masking habits of mockery and subversion. The portrait reverberates into the present. While the dutiful girl has long ceased going to the synagogue, the adolescent rebel against conventional Jewishness is alive and well and no less irreverent at fifty-seven.

My favorite egg foo young is one I ate religiously, in an ammonia-scented Cantonese dive on upper Broadway, every Yom Kippur during my high school years. At Yum Luk, three crunchy omelettes, neatly stacked and bulging with bean sprouts, onions, and diced roast pork, rose high above a sea of gluey brown sauce. Sweet and salty, crisp and moist, garlic and pungent: the tastes fused in my nose before the first bite reached my mouth. When we initiated the ritual, about forty years ago, my friend Ruth and I devoured the exotic concoction in a record three-and-a-half minutes. I can still see us, giggling and fussing with our chopsticks, shoveling it in.

The moment and the meal were heavy with meaning. After a morning in the synagogue obediently mouthing prayers, we had opted to violate the cardinal rule of the Day of Atonement: THOU SHALT NOT EAT. More than mere hunger impelled us. To appease a growling stomach, a hot fudge sundae or a chocolate malted would have served quite nicely. But no. The occasion awakened the devil within. While the rest of the Jewish community was suffering through the obligatory fast, we would feast on Forbidden Foods.

Of course, we were desperately afraid of being caught. Supposing a friend of our parents, out for a breath of air between prayers, chanced to pass Yum Luk just as we were emerging from the restaurant. Supposing my chopsticks slipped and some of that sticky sauce stained the pale yellow Orlon sweater I was wearing. There would be hell to pay. Not from the all-knowing god of our ancestors, whose being and behavior were matters of indifference to us. But from our parents, who would not fail to appreciate the enormity of their daughters' rebellion. God might avert his eyes or remain silent, but we would hear from Them and feel the fullness of Their wrath.

No risk, no gain, the saying goes. As a teenager I assumed that fighting the family was as natural and necessary as going along with it. Wasn't growing up about questioning received values and rejecting the parochialism of one's parents and community? Wasn't growing up (even for girls) about separation and leaving home? And didn't we, so many of us, begin packing our bags long before we ever walked out the front door?

My leaving home story begins with my mother: a modern, educated believer, not exactly god-fearing or pious in style but punctilious to the core. For my mother, life as a Conservative Jew was the best of all possible worlds: adaptation and tradition in harmonious embrace. I admired her stance against her parents' Orthodoxy and her commitment to balance American manners and Jewish mores. But I railed against her unwillingness to explain why one traditional practice was important while another was not. Why did my mother insist that we buy meat from the Jewish butcher when we used the same dishes for meat and dairy meals? Why, on Passover, did she lose her Conservative cool and harrass us with two sets of pots, silver, and plates of every conceivable size? Why wouldn't she and my father, who always followed her lead in these matters, confess, just once in a while, to the absurdity of some of their compromises?

For example, there was the "innocent" bacon, lettuce, and tomato on toast in which we all indulged when eating out as opposed to the "corrupt," categorically more gentile, ham. While my mother would occasionally allow me to order a very clean-looking ham and cheese sandwich at Chock Full O' Nuts, frowning darkly when I did, she never permitted herself even a taste. How is it that some forbidden foods were less evil than others? What delusion or double standard accounted for the BLT exemption? Could it be that bacon strips are so removed in their cooked form and appearance from the corpus of the pig as to sever their connection with the "unclean" animal? Is it that the cooked-to-a-crisp strips are obviously beyond contamination by trichinosis? Perhaps for my mother, observing the spirit of *kashrut* at home allowed for "rewards" in restaurants, where the modern Jew could, on occasion and in moderation, relax for a moment and be cheerfully naughty.

A liberal society posits dissent. My mother and father, New York born and college educated, rejected their parents' Orthodoxy as Old World and hidebound. The same self-determination that my parents exhibited propelled me one step further: toward a secular idea of the Jew as intellectual, humanitarian, and conscience of the race.

I do not know when I ceased believing—assuming that as a youngster I actually did believe—or what role my family's emphasis on form over faith might have had in the process. But I do know that by the time I would have been bar mitzvahed (bat mitzvahs were just about unheard of in 1949), I had merged my Jewish self with a more capacious New York persona.

"Real" New Yorkers, I liked to argue, inhabited an immensely alluring terrain beyond neighborhood, community, and birthplace. In an era before the concept of "roots" took hold, real New Yorkers "passed." We spoke standard English, appeared to transcend religious, class, and ethnic origins, and could, like the Great Gatsby, invent ourselves at will. Real New Yorkers celebrated the polyglot city, and the city was generous to its Jewish denizens. But the city also subverted Jewishness. While synagogue-going and ritual practices, from the Yom Kippur fast to the Passover seder, marked us as separate and other, New York certified us as ordinary Americans and citizens of the world.

Sleazy Yum Luk was both a New Yorker's entitlement and my personal antidote to required attendance at Yom Kippur services. Yum Luk signified: "no" to God, "no" to my parents and their Jewish holidays, "no" to piety, parochialism, and the protective custody of Jewish law and observance. Yum Luk beckoned, like a way station for the outward bound. In an era and environment in which so many risks were unthinkable or much too dangerous, food was my frontier of choice. Yom Kippurs at Yum Luk were delicious acts of defiance: the beginning of a long history of infidelities to the religious tradition in which I was raised.

I have always been greedy for travel. And when I travel I am shamelessly preoccupied with food—not only the whereabouts of the next meal and a critique of the last, but also the logistics of grocery shopping, the rituals of restaurant-going, and the aesthetics of street snacking. I collect sensations and snippets of information, turn inward, ponder my reactions, and wait for meanings to suggest themselves. If I am lucky, other people's foodways open up their cultural landscape for me; and sometimes, unexpectedly, they open me up as well—the way Ramadan did in the late spring of 1979 when I was teaching American studies at the University of Tunis.

From the rooftop of 4, rue Djamaa ez Zitouna, six stories above the darkening medina, I train my husband Eli's binoculars on a Tunisian family in the throes of their Ramadan feast. They have taken to their terrace on this sultry June evening, hoping to catch a breeze while they eat and party, as is customary, at the end of another day of mandatory fasting. Their rickety wooden table is covered with food: round flat breads, little dishes of olives, a salad, grilled meat on skewers, a couscous, and a bowl of apricots and peaches. Also a pitcher of water, two bottles of red wine, and a liter-sized bottle of Coke. Four children and three adults huddle around the table. Intent on the food, they eat silently while a velvet-voiced Egyptian pop singer croons on the cassette deck.

Our hosts and good friends, Umberto and Mariu, Italians who have lived their entire lives in Tunisia, are uncharacteristically irritable during Ramadan. Food shopping is particularly difficult because Tunisians, 98 percent of whom are Muslim, counter their acts of religious abnegation during this month with a manic greed: they buy in vast quantities, depleting the stores of eggs and chicken, beef, figs, and cheese. After giving Allah his due during the daylight hours, they generously reward themselves at nightfall.

At a deeper level, the Ramadan rituals of fasting and feasting, which seem to bind the Tunisian people as one family, are bitter reminders to Umberto and Mariu of their abiding outsidership and their vulnerability as Jews. All the more reason, perhaps, that the couple have made their handsome, meticulously cared for house into an emotional fortress. At Djamaa ez Zitouna, in the shadow of the oldest mosque in Tunis, they lavish their warmth and hospitality on a select few. We visit often during my Fulbright year and allow Umberto to pamper us with Johnny Walker Black Label and Mariu to follow suit with tart homemade sorbets and honey-drenched filo pastries.

If it can be made at home, Mariu will make it: preserves and liqueurs, yogurt and mayonnaise, fruit pies according to the season. On the shelves of her pantry, process reigns: *eau de fleur* and rose water are slowly distilled; in two enormous jars, black and green olives are curing; and fine pasta waits to be cut or dried or filled. Only when it comes to bread—truly wonderful French baguettes baked several times a day all over the city—does Mariu allow basic foodstuffs to travel directly from Tunisian hands to her table.

Fear of contamination and disease obsesses her. Each morning she positions three impeccably white towels on three white hooks next to the sink: one for silver and utensils, one for plates, and one for pots. Mariu's purification rites, including the meticulous washing of each leaf of lettuce and the scrubbing of each tomato and carrot, even each orange and lemon, had not been enough to save her son from cancer; but perhaps they can still protect the living whom she loves. Around these domestic rituals and a shared understanding of the links between suffering and Jewish victimization, we bond for life.

Mariu and Umberto's Jewishness, rather like Eli's and mine, is a passion apart from faith or observance. They speak no Hebrew, Yiddish, or Ladino, never visit the synagogue or celebrate the holidays, but they are fiercely proud of the achievements and genius of Jews, both ancient and modern. They also know the pain and helplessness of watching as family properties were confiscated during World War II or as Jewish children were elbowed off the narrow sidewalks of the medina by Tunisian bigots. While they identify themselves as Italians and bearers of Italian passports, they never forget that Umberto's Jewish birth defines who in Tunis is to be trusted and who is not.

Living among Arabs in inflammatory times, our friends are compulsively vigilant—especially when it comes to Israel, which they cherish as a Jewish homeland even though they themselves, should they need to leave Tunisia, would surely take refuge in Italy or France. We learn from Umberto and

Mariu to refer to Israel in code—as *le pais de pamplemousse*, "the land of grapefruits." Anxiously, we follow the venom which spews forth in the daily press against the Zionist demon and its American co-conspirators on Wall Street, and we worry about unremitting threats to Israel's security.

We are warned not to identify ourselves as Jews; nothing good can come of it. I consider removing the "made in Israel" label from the suede jacket which lies on my desk when I lecture. Predictably, Tunisians claim not to be anti-Semitic, just anti-Zionist, and certainly not racist. However, our dark-skinned housekeeper, Mounira, whose father is southern African and black, effectively dispels the myth of equality under Allah. When students inquire about my origins during a unit on "patterns of immigration to the United States," I mention Austria-Hungary during the Great Migration and count on my Nordic looks and German name to bar further inquiries. I "pass" easily but feel compromised. Being Jewish preys on my mind as never before. So does Israel.

I realize in Tunisia how little has been asked of me as a New York Jew. There, no sacrifices are required to enjoy a community of like-minded Jews or to draw sustenance from the record of Jewish distinction. I may fear for my safety as a woman or as a comfortable white person in a "transitional" neighborhood, but not as a Jew. In Tunis, however, intelligence dictates alertness and a healthy modicum of fear. When we go to renew our visas and Eli is queried about his father's identity ("Isn't Abraham a Jewish name?") panic clutches at my stomach. Eli banters with the wily official, and the panic passes. But I remember it. Vividly. I may wear my Jewishness lightly or keep it well under wraps, but if "they" really want to know, they certainly will.

Forced into hiding during nine months in North Africa, our Jewish selves seek expression. Eli and I make plans to fly from Tunis to Jerusalem via Rome. (In Tunisia in 1979, no one, not even a diplomat, is permitted to purchase plane tickets to Israel.) Our enthusiasm for this first visit catches us by surprise: we can hardly wait to give Israel our money, attention, and unstinting affection.

My son, Adam, and his wife, Laura, telephone from Kathmandu just as I am putting their wedding story into the computer. I tell them about this piece and their place in it and wait for a response. Buddhism, Adam hastens to assure me, is not a far road from home. Especially his particular Tibetan Buddhist lineage and practice. The Tibetan Buddhists, he claims, are just like Jews: "rabbinical" in their handling of ideas and consumed by ethical concerns. Does my son think I need this kind of assurance? Perhaps I do. More to the point, perhaps he does, too.

The connection stays with me. As I write I can "hear" Adam and Laura doing one of their regular Buddhist practices, chanting in full voice on the third floor of our house. The words are unfamiliar but the music is Kol Nidre: the soulful, reiterative liturgy of lamentation. The irony is almost too obvious to remark. Adam, who has been given neither faith nor ritual, was fated to find both by himself. When he was drawn to Buddhism during his first year in college we were not unhappy. Adam had hungered for discipline, purpose, and a spiritual life, and Buddhism filled his cup again and again. It even left room for an unlikely Jewish wedding.

September 1990. The rabbi with his guitar, embroidered silk Rastafarian beanie, flowing white robe, and rainbow-colored *tallit* leads the wedding party up the grassy hillock. Adam and Laura, who were married privately five months earlier, are about to repeat their vows in the presence of family and friends. They stand beneath a ceremonial *chuppa*—a bright blue silk "flag," resplendent with male and female symbols and icons from the Jewish and Buddhist traditions—made especially for the occasion by Max, Adam's Indonesian martial arts teacher and dear friend.

Behold, Buddha's children at their Jewish wedding, seeking blessings wherever they are able to be found. Adam, Laura, and the guitar-playing Woodstock rabbi have a common idiom. They invoke the primacy of spirit, the unending quest for wisdom, openness to God, and devotion to the manifold aspects of creation. The parts of the marriage ceremony flow and fit together: harmonies of the psyche powered by celestial energy.

When Adam and Laura informed us that they were willing to let Laura's parents make a big Jewish wedding, we anticipated difficulties. So we were not exactly surprised when Adam broached the subject of Indonesian hors d'oeuvres with us. "It's important to have the Palar family make the hors d'oeuvres," he announced. "You'll appreciate the extraordinary food," he assured us, "but it's more than that. When Indonesians cook for you it's like a gift. They do it with such love." Of course, the notion of Indonesian hors d'oeuvres upset Laura's observant father. He insisted that the laws of *kashrut* be honored: no pork, no seafood, and, when he considered it further, no unkosher meat.

I know about food wars, and I certainly wanted no part on the front lines of this one. The wedding belonged to Adam and Laura, and to Laura's parents by virtue of the power of the purse. Eli and I relished our role as celebrants on the sidelines. But how could we fail to recognize ourselves in Adam's defiant spirit? How could we not enjoy his rebellion, support his need for a symbolic statement—one that gave the foods which nourished his soul a place alongside the foodways enshrined by his father-in-law. Yes, we would be delighted to locate ourselves on the Buddhist-Indonesian side of the family and contribute to the nuptial festivities by paying for the hors d'oeuvres along with the music.

After the ceremony, the hors d'oeuvres are presented on two huge groaning boards, each about twenty feet long—one for their side (smoked trout and baked salmon, warm brie en croute, and five varieties of tempura vegetables), one for ours. On the Indonesian table, a staggering quantity of alluring foods awaits us: chicken curry, spicy beef stew, fine noodles with onions and bean sprouts, cabbage in a hot vinaigrette sauce, lettuce salad with a peanut dressing, and thin, freshly fried lotus-seed crisps. Several of our friends, adventurous eaters all, mistake the Indonesian fare for the wedding dinner and return to it for seconds and thirds. Later, at the round tables under the tent, they give short shrift to attractive plates of grilled fish, pasta salad, and tomatoes with feta cheese. I give three cheers for the upstart appetizers.

Modern weddings are generational struggles. Against parents' assertions of faith and community, the nuptial couple seek their own connections to the past and their separate path. Perhaps Eli and I deprived Adam and Laura of some longed-for struggle with us because we give so little obeisance to tradition. We remember all too well our own unconventional marriage in Mexico and the gala country club party, sans ceremony, that my mother made for us some months later. Yet ceremony is important to Adam and Laura. Buddhist rituals shape their daily lives and give coherence to the community they have chosen to live in. Adam, like so many of his friends, has replaced our secularism with his own perfervid spiritualism—a spiritualism which is more akin to the traditional Judaism of Laura's parents than to our stubborn anticlerical creed.

Thinking back on the ceremony, I am unexpectedly grateful to Laura's parents for mandating a Jewish presence at the wedding and to Adam for ferreting out the exotic Woodstock rabbi for the occasion. Why? I worry about the absence of ceremony in our family's life. What excuses will we use to guarantee future gatherings of the clan once the remaining frail members of the older generation cease to orchestrate ritual celebrations for us?

My parents and their parents and all our ancestors understood that ritual maintains a people, creates identity. Indeed, they understood that food is one of the critical disciplines of difference. The decision not to eat at the tables of "others" is one they made (my parents, albeit, with some flexibility) to keep their covenant with God. I inherited the proscription without the faith to sustain it. In the absence of faith, I anchored myself in the liberal ideology of pluralism. When, as an adolescent, I turned my back on the foodways of my family and the Jewish community, it was not out of Jewish self-hatred or an angry denial of roots. Rather, I had learned from school, from the tolerant culture of New York, and to some extent from my parents to eschew ethnocentrism in favor of cosmopolitanism and global citizenship.

My cosmopolitanism is most visible and steadfast in the realm of food. I glory in choice, and my expansive pattern of choices, rather than providing a new discipline, has doubtless made a glutton of me. Or a fool. I want to choose without losing: divest myself of ritual holiday festivities, for example, yet still hold fast to some pleasurable, tangible evidence of Jewishness in family and community life. The final section, on Passover, is a case in point.

I can always count on that early March phone call to bring out the worst in me. This year once again it was Gerry, my eighty-eight-year-old aunt, announcing plans for the forthcoming family seder. Yes, she was having the usual, "very interesting" group at her house, and she certainly hoped that Eli and I would join them. The older she gets, the more elaborately Gerry spins out the requisite forms of politesse, gentility cloaking her command to participate in the holiday ritual. It is hard to respond graciously to such directives from on high with their subtexts of filial piety and Jewish survival. Still, my tone in accepting the invitation is perky enough, for I am off the hook. My mother, for so many years a stalwart seder-maker but ailing now at eighty-six, will have a seder to go to, and I am spared the burden of providing for her.

Of course, my mother's seders were also unwelcome events: occasions for endless fussing over food, prayer, and the prescribed order of drinking, eating, and washing. We were frequently twenty or more at the table, and feeding this crowd represented at least a week of concentrated activity: first, the planning, cleaning, storing of the regular dishes, silver, and pots, making room for the two sets of each used during Passover; then the shopping and cooking. My mother, who did most of this work herself, commissioned me as her lieutenant for the final stages of preparation and serving.

At our seder table the Party of Tradition and the Party of Modernization negotiated for primacy. The tradition, as once practiced by my maternal grandparents and championed by my mother, required that prayers be chanted in Hebrew—an arcane skill possessed only by (some few) males of my mother's generation. Generally, my mother's youngest brother presided. He would wend his way through the story of the Exodus from Egypt, murmuring for stretches in his old-fashioned Hebrew. Then as if seized by the occasion, he would pour his rich voice into laments of pure anguish and hymns of exaltation. Try as I always did, it was difficult to resist joining him for the moment of release represented by his final, operatic hallelujahs.

The Party of Modernization, aggressively captained by Gerry, advocated a participatory ethos and practice. So the chanting I did not understand and therefore did not mind was balanced by a round of readings in English, an English so convoluted as to confound its revelations of God's mysterious and wondrous ways. How was it, I would inquire of no one in particular, that he who had been so vigilant on behalf of the Jews when they were slaves in Egypt could have slept so soundly during our darkest hours in twentieth-century Europe?

Actually, I was usually too busy during my mother's seders, dashing in and out of the kitchen, checking on the chicken soup and potato pancakes, carrying, fetching, and gossiping with cousins whom I rarely saw to fret too much about God. I was more likely to fret about my mother, his unfortunate surrogate. Had I not been so faithless I might have been more tolerant of her seder stress: anxieties about propriety and hospitality and control. Had I not been so faithless, I might also have been more tolerant of her dependence on me, for labor I did not relish coupled with unfailing cheer and unflappable grace under fire.

Let Gerry worry now. At least at her seder I am free to be a guest and an onlooker. Almost free. My duties this year are to bring the chopped chicken liver for hors d'oeuvres and the *charoseth*—apples, walnuts, cinnamon, and red wine mixed together (like mortar for bricks) symbolizing the Israelites' "labor of affliction" under the pharaohs of Egypt. "Do you know how to make *charoseth?*" Gerry asks me, preparing to dictate instructions in the event that my half-century of sedering should have left me without this very basic skill. Concerning the chicken liver, she credits me with being able to find the right kind of ready-made product.

I give some thought to both assignments. There is an intriguing recipe I have seen for Sephardic *charoseth* using dates instead of apples. I imagine the deep sweetness of the chewy mixture and know how stubbornly it will cling to the teeth. Will this innovation work for Gerry's seder? Or will the two finnicky old ladies and even the laid-back younger folks feel cheated if their familiar apple and nut snack is not available to stave off hunger halfway through the predinner service. Uncertain, I take the path well trodden. Ditto for the chopped chicken liver. After contemplating duck pâté, mousse of *foie gras,* and *pâté dé campagne,* I settle for Squire's rabbinically supervised kosher classic.

Perhaps I am weary of testing the muscle of tradition. Perhaps I am appalled by the recognition that, in our family, the muscle is flabby indeed. My octogenarian mother and aunt have frail bones and failing eyesight. They are making their separate peace with Passover.

At eighty-eight, Gerry's age, the mere act of making a seder is blessing enough. So I ought not to have been surprised by the rather gentle white wine, Israeli and kosher, which was pured into our glasses for the opening *kiddush* ceremony. True, we had liberated ourselves in the late 1960s from Manischewitz's deadly sweet burgundies—but white wine for the Passover seder is something else. Had nobody been assigned to bring a red for the occasion? Had one of my younger cousins decided that a kosher white would be welcomed by our perpetually up-to-date hostess as chic and newly correct? Or had Gerry herself opted for the "lighter" version, especially since she no longer drinks red and since she, rather than one of her brothers, is presiding? To think that I hesitated to bring a Sephardic *charoseth.*

Without an old-school male to chant the prayers, democracy wins by default. The reading of the service will be shared: a paragraph per person of the awkward English text, around the table again and again. Gerry, who is awaiting cataract surgery, struggles to read but gives up. My mother, who has left her glasses at home, reads poorly. I have left my glasses at home, too, but borrow Gerry's and read theatrically, as if to my students. Eli, who has no need of reading glasses, claims to have left his at home and declines to read. The others, more relaxed than Eli and I about their roles in this gathering, take their turns without editorial comment.

We are reaching the end of the line. Gerry's 1990 seder meal carves the message in stone. The chicken soup, which looks lusty, is not only salt, pepper, and fowl free but also seems to have been infused with an unfortunate broth of carrots. The main course, proudly presented as Chicken Hawaiian, has been left in the oven an extra hour so that the requisite golden glaze covers a dozen desiccated breasts. Dessert, traditionally Gerry's forte, is a leaden homemade nut cake topped with a distressed-looking layer of impossibly bitter chocolate.

It used to be that the family gathered for the seder to do God's work and also its own. That edifice has crumbled. When Passover comes, Eli and I seat our bodies at the table of the older generation, drink wine, make entertaining dinner conversation, and wait to be released from our filial obligations. Nine parts cynicism, one part piety. Our demeanor more dramatically dishonors the occasion than honors the family. In fact, we spare our children the burden of this duplicity, and they are grateful to be protected and elsewhere.

Gerry has hosted two more seders since the white wine and Chicken Hawaiian affair, and I have missed them both. Two years ago, Eli was receiving chemotherapy, and we marked the holiday with sushi in his hospital room. He died four months later. Last year, my mother was hospitalized for congestive heart failure, and I left her bedside about the time that the ten plagues were being intoned at Gerry's to eat Singapore noodles alone and in silence. The defiance continues. But I am more mellow now. Wistful. Even a trifle melancholic. My unsettled questions about Jewish identity are confronting the finality of aging and impermanence.

There will come a time soon when this deathwatch is over, and I shall be forced to add up my losses. When the last Passover has come and gone, will I dissolve into nostalgia and embark on a frenzy of ritual cooking? When spring arrives and Passover products appear in the market, will I find myself researching the seder meal of the Venetian ghetto in the seventeenth century? When these ladies are laid to rest, what shall I do with a lifetime of resistance to the bully power of religious ritual and family authority?

Turn my swords into plowshares perhaps. Say yes to history and family without confusing family with deity and piety. Do the ritual work that pleases me most: repeat the gala Thanksgiving family feast in the season of the paschal lamb and in memory of the Israelites' departure from Egypt. The menu will be open to discussion. Adam and Laura will propose a pair of Thai and Nepalese dishes. My nephew Eric and his wife, Gul Ruk, may offer us curries from her native Bangladesh. If my niece Paula and her husband Luis fly up from Guatemala, they will almost certainly have a bean stew to contribute. My niece Laura and her Salvadoran husband, Carlos, may recommend a spicy fish with chili peppers. My stepdaughter, Shola, will wish to complement this intensely flavored Third World fare with an assortment of fresh berries or a delicate soup. And Marsha and Cy, my sister-in-law and brother-in-law, world travelers who now live in Reno, Nevada, will entertain us with a campy "western" creation. If the *New York Times* runs another feature on the subject of Passover around the world, someone may even suggest a Sephardic date, fig, and nut compote or a bitter salad of dandelions.

Religious celebrations are not required to cement our ebullient family. Neither is a common religion nor a common cuisine. But the passion for cooking and eating, and creating beautiful foods, is a powerful force among us. We all relish the necessary union of handwork and headwork; we relish the juxtaposition of the exotic and the familiar, the idiosyncratic and the classical, the fluid process and the unpredictable products. In this doing, invested as it is with the special histories and individual commitments of each of us, will reside our newly minted ritual.

PART IV

EXPLORATIONS

As a spice box contains all sorts of spices, so should a scholar be full of all branches of learning.

—Midrash (on Canticles Rabbah 5:13)

16

The Story of Ruth, the Anthropologist

Ruth Behar

"They broke into weeping again, and Orpah kissed her mother-in-law farewell. But Ruth clung to her. So she said, 'See, your sister-in-law has returned to her people and her gods. Go follow your sister-in-law.' But Ruth replied, 'Do not urge me to leave you, to turn back and not follow you. For wherever you go, I will go; wherever you lodge, I will lodge; your people shall be my people, and your God my God. Where you die, I will die, and there I will be buried.' "
—*Tanakh: A New Translation of
the Holy Scriptures,* chapter 1,
verses 14–17

I SIT WRITING on an old square table in the middle of a bedroom where farmers who knew what it was to earn their rest used to sleep long winter nights, short summer nights. The half-beige, half-mustard walls tilt back as though slumping against cushions. Behind me, an antique painting of Nuestra Señora de los Dolores hangs between the pair of double beds. Before me, the two wardrobes, with their foggy mirrors, reflect the plastic bags and suitcases that have not been totally unpacked. In one of the suitcases I have hidden away postcards of the abandoned synagogues at Toledo and Cordoba, now turned into tourist sites.

On the night table that dips toward the door stands a clay cross set into a clay pedestal. I have moved the cross over to the edge and made a pile of all the books I brought with me. The books form a human tower: Albert Memmi's *The Pillar of Salt* stands atop of Elias Canetti's *The Tongue Set Free,* which stands atop of Margo Glantz's *The Family Tree,* which stands atop of Sandra Cisneros' *Woman Hollering Creek,* which stands atop of Toni Morrison's *Playing in the Dark,* which stands atop of Miguel Barnet's *Rachel's Song,* which stands atop of Amy Tan's *The Kitchen God's Wife.* At the very bottom, undergirding the structure, I have Roberto Fernández Retamar's *Caliban and Other Essays.* And freefloating downstairs, to read a paragraph at a time whenever things are a little quiet, I have Anton Shammas' *Arabesques* (in which, weeks later, I will become so immersed that I will sit reading and reading, totally oblivious to the church bells calling the village to rush to put out a fire in the threshing grounds). These books, carried across the ocean, stand as reminders of all the identities I want to claim in the place I am visiting, but cannot, except in the solitude of this room.

Out of embarrassment, I have hesitated to tell you that between Margo Glantz and Sandra Cisneros there is another book. I am not sure how it fits into my chapter or the image I'd like you to have of me, this book that's become a kind of talisman. It's by a psychologist named Dr. Wilson and the title on the binding, *Don't Panic,* is written in red letters against a black background. On the front cover, in big letters, they've printed the word "PANIC," as though trying to bring it on. I've brought it along on this summer trip to Turkey and Spain in case I need it. I haven't needed it, thankfully, but I'm glad it's there between Glantz and Cisneros.

In the year when Columbus' bones were being rattled, I embarked on a journey in reverse of that taken by my family, my father's family, the family which gave me my surname. I traveled from the New World back to the Old.

The year 1992 began for me in Cuba, where I was born. I brought in the new year dancing with the family of the black woman who reluctantly worked as a maid for my newlywed parents until the day we left Cuba in 1961.

It had not been easy for me to get to Cuba. A month before I was due to leave, I began to experience heart palpitations and loss of breath. I became afraid to get out of bed. When they heard I was going to Cuba, my parents told me to write out a will, because I might not return. "With all the trouble we had escaping from that hell, you want to go back?" they asked me, as if I were insane. Yes, I wanted to go, desperately—but secretly I feared not being able to return to my Wedgwood blue house in the Midwest, with my books, my pantry full of soothing teas for a nervous world, my Mexican pottery, and my oak furniture acquired secondhand at antique fairs. In the midst of being torn one way and another, I found a remaindered copy of Dr. Wilson's *Don't Panic.* Dr. Wilson went with me to Cuba. Dr. Wilson brought me back, safe and sound, to my quiet house and my mug of tea. That is how Dr. Wilson earned his trip to Europe.

Cuba always symbolized for me a place left behind, a point of departure, a place that would turn you into salt for looking back. And yet it was also a point of arrival for my grandparents on both sides of the family, who came, young and hopeful, searching for their America. On my mother's side they were Ashkenazic Jews from Poland and Byelorussia; on my father's side they were Sephardic Jews from Turkey, expelled from Spain centuries ago. Both sides of the family landed in Cuba because of the 1924 Immigration and Exclusion Act, which set severe limits on Eastern and Southern European (and thereby Jewish) immigration to the United States; they had to look for America on the other side of the border.

My mother's extended family, which included my great-grandparents and their younger unmarried children, settled in the Cuban countryside, hoping to build up enough capital to one day open a business in Havana. In a backwater town named Agramonte, where sugar was the main crop, my grandparents and great-grandparents ran a general store; they were the only Jews in the town. I had dreamed of going to Cuba to find out if anyone remembered these *polacos,* as they were called. Several of the old men still remembered. In Agramonte, as 1992 drew near, I heard them utter the names of my great-grandparents, my grandparents, my great-aunts and great-uncles: Abraham, Hannah, Esther, Maximo, Jaime, Dora, Irene. . . .

My father's family settled in Havana from the start, in a tenement by the docks, where everyone came from the same town in Turkey. My grandfather peddled men's suits and Beacon-brand blankets; my grandmother stayed home with the four children and cooked okra with lemon. I had promised my father a photograph of the house he describes sardonically as their condominium with an ocean view. So when I went to Havana I climbed the slick stone stairs to the second floor, and in the darkness I saw that the door to his family's old apartment is sealed off, padlocked. Nothing to discover. No picture.

Of the fifteen thousand Jews who lived on the island, one thousand are left, but I am told there are only thirteen couples in which both partners are Jewish. There, still, is the Patronato synagogue in the new Vedado section of Havana, in front of which I was photographed as a small child, my face contorted into a half-smile, my legs squeezed together holding in the pee. The rich Ashkenazic Jews who financed the building of the Patronato, completed a year before the revolution, never expected that socialism would come to their nice little island. They had their names engraved in gold on placards by the synagogue entrance, not knowing they were leaving behind memorials to their disappearance. The huge main auditorium is as despondent as a deserted lover; the roof is leaking, the cushioned seats have sprouted mold. The Jews have gone and the doves have come to pray for them.

I am in Cuba not just to search out the traces of Jewish life, but also to find real live Jews. In search of Jews, I go to the daily service held at the small but well-preserved Shevet Ahim synagogue in the old section of Havana. I find six shabby elderly men wearing threadbare *guayaberas.* These are Jews? None of them can agree on how the service should be read. They argue and argue and the time passes, each finally praying in his own way by himself. When they are done, a woman in a white apron appears and sets a table in the parlor, where the men are served bread with a gloppy mayonnaise and a dark tea. Two of the men are Sephardic: one wears a beret and reminds me of the peasant men I have known in Spain; the other, who is named Isaac, like my grandfather, whispers into my ear that some of the men just come to the service for the breakfast. They both turn out to be from Silivri, the same town in Turkey my grandparents came from.

Silivri. Another mythical place the granddaughter will come to feel her feet must stand upon in this Columbian year, imagining it bears some secret, some knowledge, some deep truth, about herself.

I have my father's last name, my father's thick, dark brown eyebrows and frizzy hair, my father's hands, my father's calves, and, as my mother always reminded me when she was angry, my father's temper. I take after the Sephardic side of the family, and yet I grew up in the nest of my mother's Yiddish family.

Ashamed of his family's poverty, my father struggled, I think, to forget his origins and be accepted within the Ashkenazic circle into which he had married. Within this circle, whenever my father lost his temper (and he lost it often), they'd shake their heads like the rational Jews they thought they were and say, "What can you expect from a Turk?" But when we came to the United States my father refused to live in Brooklyn, where his family and other Cuban Sephardim had settled, preferring Queens, where my mother's family lived and the milieu was thoroughly Ashkenazic. We spent our first years in the United States in the same apartment building on the outer edges of Queens Boulevard as my maternal grandparents and my mother's older sister.

Like my father, I too came to regard Brooklyn as inferior, primarily because we always went there for the second night of Passover, never for the first, which we celebrated with my mother's family. Gefilte fish, matzoh ball soup, and boiled chicken, one night; egg-lemon soup, grape leaves and tomatoes stuffed with lamb, a special honey cake with an almond pressed into each diamond-shaped chunk, and tiny cups of puddinglike coffee, the next night. I much preferred the sensual richness of my Sephardic grandmother's cooking, but I consumed each bite with fear. My Turkish grandmother, with her beautiful moon-shaped eyes, was very fat; she waddled when she walked. On the drive back to Queens from Brooklyn, my mother would remind me that Abuela had paid a price for eating so much of that wonderful food dripping with olive oil, honey, and almonds. And so I dreamt of platters of my Sephardic grandmother's food, but I knew early on that my Yiddish grandmother's blander and duller diet kept your hips from spreading.

My father bore a lifelong grudge against his own father for having forced him to go to work to support the family in Cuba. He had no choice but to attend night school, where he could study only accounting, not architecture, as he had hoped. After marrying my mother, he went to work for my mother's rich uncle, Moises Levin, in Havana, doing the accounting for his business machine shop. Had it not been for Fidel Castro, my father says he'd still be working for Moises Levin. In his new life in New York he has ended up working for other Ashkenazic Jews instead. Aided by his flowing Spanish and Latin charm, he sells their last year's fabric to buyers in Panama, Mexico, Ecuador, and Argentina.

My father adored his mother. One night she awoke, told my grandfather she needed ice cubes right away, and died. For years she had scolded my father for acting as though she were already dead by not visiting her more often. After she was truly gone, my father began to listen to Sephardic music. In the basement of the brick house in Queens—the house which I never had growing up—he'd play the songs he remembered her singing, and cry and cry. I never told him, but in the first years after Abuela's death that music had the same effect on me. Not until the summer of 1992, when I played the tapes in our rented car while we drove through Spain, could I listen again to those laments, sung in a Spanish of unbearable tenderness.

It was my great-uncle Moises Levin who managed to become even richer in Miami than he had been in Havana, not just a millionaire, but a multimillionaire, my great-uncle who barely reaches five feet, my great-uncle for whom my Sephardic father would still be working if Fidel Castro had decided to play baseball rather than start a revolution, who'd tell me that he didn't understand why I had chosen to travel to Spain as an anthropologist. Didn't I realize the Spaniards had thrown out the Jews and sent all the ones who converted to Catholicism to the Inquisition anyway? At the very least, I should be saving Jewish lives for posterity by studying the Inquisition. But wouldn't there be more for me to do as an anthropologist in Israel, where there is so much history, and so many ruins, and where I would be among my own people?

A fly is buzzing around, banging its head against the window, as I remember these questions that somehow my Sephardic relatives never asked me. I keep the shades open to let in sunlight so I can see to write, even though everyone here keeps them closed, like a shield pressed against the onslaught of summer heat.

I am back in the village in northern Spain that I first visited fourteen years ago when I was intent on becoming an anthropologist. I have returned in this year of *las vacas gordas*, "the fat cows," when Spain has taken on the World's Fair, the Olympics, and the second annual encounter of Iberoamerican Nations. Spain is going for broke, people say, and they add that they'll be paying for it over the next thirty years. It isn't the "discovery" of America that is being commemorated but the awareness that Spain, the new Spain, rightfully belongs in Europe. People greet us in the village, saying, "Ya somos europeos," with a chuckle (We're Europeans now). Later, when I mention this to a friend from the village who now lives in Malaga, he says to me, "We were always part of Europe, but the difference was that they didn't view us as being European. They thought Spain was part of Africa."

I have returned to the village, as I usually do, with a project. This time my aim is to learn whether all the official hoopla about the quest for reconciliation during the five-hundreth anniversary of the expulsion of the Jews from Spain has had any impact on the consciousness of the farmers, and the children and grandchildren of the farmers, from this village that is named after the most Holy Virgin Mary. Now that I am in the village the project seems hopelessly absurd. Back home, in Ann Arbor, I had imagined myself asking people what they knew of the Jewish past in Spain and what they thought of

Jews in general. Then I imagined making a dramatic announcement: that half of my family had its origins here, and that I am a descendant of those people that Spain didn't want, but that it's okay, we survived to sing love songs in Spanish eroded by longing, and here I am, five hundred years later, and, as you've known all these years, I've respected your crucifixes and your saints and your priests and your fiestas, learning to cross myself and recite the rosary and get on my knees and feel the presence of the body and the blood and the suffering.

I have been in the village for a month and I haven't been able to ask my questions or make my announcement. For fourteen years I've been returning to this place and I've never said anything about being Jewish. Only one family that asked me my religion the first day I arrived knows the truth. And yet when this family brought up the subject again recently, I quickly brushed it aside. I was suddenly afraid to be different, to call attention to myself. In the village people tell me I pass for Spanish and I like that, even if I wince to hear string beans being called *judías* (literally, Jewish women). Here I become this entity called an anthropologist, open to all forms of life and thought, my mission to absorb everything and change nothing. It doesn't seem possible or relevant to assert all the contradictions of my identity. What I want is to seem familiar, ordinary, just like everyone else. So I check my inconvenient identities at the door. I imitate the bristling confidence of the Castilian accent so well that I lose my Cuban accent. And I don't refuse the homemade pork sausages that stain your fingers with red pepper, or the ham smoked in the old kitchens where families once ate around an open fire.

Silivri, an hour away from Istanbul, is a town in which no Jews live anymore. The Jews have all left for Istanbul or Israel or taken to the open sea and gone to America. Not a trace remains of the Jewish cemetery, erased by a road.

I am snapping the last pictures of the facade of my grandmother's old house when a young man with bad teeth and chipped nails suddenly orders me to stop. After some discussion with my father's cousin, who is my guide on this trip, the man agrees to let us into the house. As we enter, my cousin whispers to me, in Ladino, not to demand to take photographs of anything, because the man is not *bueno de la cabeza*. I remove my shoes and leave them at the doorstep of the house in which Abuela was born and bred and to which she never returned. I see the dark kitchen that is below the main floor and the bright parlor upstairs and the little bedrooms with their curving floors, which seem to want to bring on astigmatism. My Turkish cousin, who now lives in Israel, assures me the rooms were bigger and more beautiful when they lived there.

In Istanbul, I try to learn how the Jews are handling the quincentenary of their exile in Turkey. When I ask the lead singer of a Sephardic folk group what he thinks, he tells me that a few events are going on, but nothing very dramatic. We prefer not to be too loud, he says; it's better for us, he adds, if we speak softly, quietly, *calladicos*.

At home I never observe the Jewish day of rest, but in Istanbul I decide I must attend a Shabbat service at the Neve Shalom synagogue. Since the bombing of this Orthodox synagogue several years ago, a security guard stands posted at the door. I leave my husband, David, and five-year-old son, Gabriel, downstairs and go upstairs alone to the women's section. Encouraged by the woman next to me, I follow the service.

When I next look down to see what is happening on the main stage, I notice David and Gabriel up at the *bima*. I can barely believe it: David, the stranger, the guest, arriving late, has been asked to carry the Torah. Gabriel takes hold of the edge of the cloth covering the scrolls and in his most ceremonious self walks alongside slowly, entranced to see grown men kiss their fingers and touch the heavy words his father is carrying. From above, with the women holding their hands out to the presence of the holy, I gaze at this scene, knowing what I know and what they don't know. David, a convert to Judaism from Methodism, who grew up in a Dallas suburb on leftover turkey stews rewetted with creamed corn, is carrying the Jewish Book with his son, blond and lanky like him, come out of my Jewish womb. From my position on the balcony, I hover above them, far away. As a woman there is no place for me in the scene below. We have come to Turkey in search of my Jewish roots, but I am allowed to clasp them only vicariously, through my husband and son. I imagine, for one crazy moment, a room gasping in horror as I leap from my seat and splatter to the ground.

Two weeks later we are at another Shabbat service, this time in a synagogue in Madrid. Again, we arrive late. Again, a security check. Again, I am sent upstairs, David and Gabriel downstairs. But this time, no honors, no special welcome. A dull mumbled service.

I see the Sephardic families from Morocco, the women in stylish silk dresses, stockings, and high heels, the men in well-cut gray suits, the children in proper shoes, not in grimy sneakers, like Gabriel. I ought to approach them, say something about my project, but in my wrinkled Indian rayon dress and dusty sandals I am not feeling up to being the anthropologist. I've gone to the synagogue in Madrid. I've seen that it's like the Sephardic Jewish Center in Queens. Now I want to go on to the Prado Museum for the afternoon, have lunch there, and take a look at Goya's black paintings.

And then an invitation comes from a small energetic man with a thin red beard who is surrounded by a flock of elfish boys in three-piece suits. A Lubovitcher. "Will you come to our house for a Shabbat lunch?" Neither David nor I can think how to refuse politely. As we walk the few blocks to the man's house, I tell myself it might be worth it, anthropologically speaking.

We climb an endless series of stairs and end up in a stuffy apartment. Several more children, in different stages of growth, crowd around and stare at us as we enter. A visiting rabbi and his wife and baby son, American Jews who now live in Israel, another rabbi from New York, and a young English Jew are also guests for lunch. The dining room table is set with paper plates, plastic forks, a *challah*. We are all invited to wash our hands ritually in the kitchen and say the appropriate prayers. Then the mother and eldest daughter serve the food; a kind of warm gefilte fish comes first, followed by boiled chicken with potatoes.

I keep trying to count the children (are they six or nine?), who sit at two low tables, eating hungrily. Each child devours his or her tiny piece of *challah* and asks for more, only to be told it's all been eaten. The children seem unnaturally pale and both hyperactive and listless at the same time. I ask if they have grown accustomed to speaking Spanish. The Lubovitcher smiles patiently and tells me that the children speak only Yiddish and English. None of them attends school in Madrid: they are taught at home by their mother, who is a teacher.

Soon the questions are addressed to me: where am I from and what am I doing in Spain? I explain about my family, the Yiddish background, the Turkish background, the Cuban background, the New York background. I explain about my years of visits to a Spanish village, carried out in the name of anthropology. I vaguely allude to my plan to return to the village and learn whether the official quincentenary commemorations—the repeal of the edict expelling Jews from Spain, the ceremonial visits of the king and queen to the old synagogues of Toledo and Cordoba, the return of thousands of Sephardic Jews to Spain for 1992—have had a positive effect on Spanish people's consciousness of Jews and Jewish life.

The Lubovitcher shakes his head: "Good luck," he says, "Come back and tell me if you learn anything new." Then he asks, "So tell me, where do you live in the States?"

"In Ann Arbor," I say.

"Oh, then you must know my brother," he replies. "He heads the Lubovitch community there."

I do, sort of, know his brother. He and his family live a few streets away from us, in the same neighborhood. I have watched them often from a distance, afraid of getting too close. One Saturday morning, driving to a meeting of Latinas on campus, I caught sight of the Lubovitcher father and his two daughters. I remember that his long black coat fluttered joyfully as he strode down the street, certain of where he ought to be, as a Jew, on a Saturday morning. I remember the two girls walking briskly alongside him, the hems of their flowered dresses protruding from their too-short coats.

A long year of meetings and seminars and searches is finally coming to an end. A student has blocked the door to ask me a pointed question: how do I feel about being associated with the Latina/Latino Studies Program? For the past year that I have been codirecting the program with a Puerto Rican colleague, she has assumed I'm not a Latina. I, on the other hand, have assumed that she is.

"I'm half Philippine, half Anglo," she tells me. "And I work on Puerto Rico. I'm dark, so I sort of look Puerto Rican."

I tell her that I'm Cuban.

"Oh, so you're a Latina?" she says, obviously surprised.

I don't give her a chance to ask about my name or any of the other things that make my Latina identity suspect. I go ahead and complete my confession. "But I'm also Jewish," I say, and quickly add, "So I never feel totally authentic."

Plans are made for a Latina potluck dinner to celebrate our survival of the academic year. A date is chosen, a Friday night. I start looking forward to the event. And then I notice that it's been scheduled for the first night of Passover, one of the few holidays I celebrate. I hesitate to say anything about changing the date, because I'm the only Latina who is Jewish. When I mention it, I'm told that no other date is convenient. Someone tells me that it's also Good Friday and people are still going to the potluck.

Am I willfully choosing to isolate myself? Isn't that what Jews have always done—refused to eat at the tables of others? Christ is on the cross and Jews are remembering their own bread of affliction. When I bite into my first piece of matzoh on that night which is different from all other nights, the limits of my Latina identity curl up around the edges and shrink a little.

I have a colleague in the Judaic Studies Program, an Ashkenazi American from Detroit, who has written on the history of Latin American Jews. Around her, I sometimes feel like an anthropological specimen. One evening she stops by my house. Walking in the door, she starts laughing, and says "*Mazel tov?*" I have no idea what she finds so hilarious. At last, she points to "La Ofrenda," a lithograph by the Chicana artist Ester Hernandez, hanging in my living room. In the picture, a contemporary Chicana, her hair cut extremely short, has the Virgin of Guadalupe surrounded by rose blossoms radiating from her naked back. Images of Christ make me uneasy; however, the Virgin of Guadalupe, whom I got to know intimately during years spent in a Mexican town, won my heart. But I don't try to explain my feelings about La Guadalupana to my colleague; I know she wouldn't understand.

Another American-Ashkenazi colleague, a fellow anthropologist, laughed out loud and also said "*Mazel tov*" to me when he heard I'd become codirector of the Latina/Latino Studies Program. I was denied a "target of opportunity" position intended for minority scholars at the University of Michigan because my Jewish background disqualified me from being Latina enough. American Jews always have trouble accepting the Cuban part of my identity. They think it's a joke. They want me to stop kidding myself. To grow up. To realize I'm no Latina. A Latina is someone who recites a rosary, has dark skin, doesn't do so well in school. If only they could hear, as I do, how silly my father sounds when he says, "*Mazel tov, mazel tov,*" trying to imitate the Yiddish accent in English of his New York City bosses.

And so my life seesaws back and forth, back and forth. When I'm left out of the Latina potluck because it is Passover, I eat my matzoh with more affliction. But when American Jews scoff at my Latin roots, I want to curse them out, call them *comemierdas* (sorry, but this I won't translate). My childhood was lived in a Cuban Spanish soaked in diminutives and scatology, and I have been translating myself ever since.

When David and I first went to the village of Santa María del Monte we were not quite twenty-one. It was 1978. We had been lovers for a year and couldn't bear to be separated for a summer.

The professor who invited me to go to "the field" after my first year of graduate school, so I could experience the rite of passage that would make me an anthropologist, was angry and disappointed that I wanted to bring my boyfriend along. With dismay, he told me he had thought I was a serious student. I, who had not gone to a single party all through college, suddenly felt like a whore. Only after David convinced him that he too dreamed of becoming an anthropologist did we get permission to go together. But we needed to tell people in the village we were married.

I invented a story about our wedding in 1977, where it had been, what I had worn, and, yes, we had been very young. That was the first lie.

And there was a second lie. My parents had tried to bar David from my life because he wasn't Jewish, but I continued to see him secretly. That first summer I went to Spain without telling my parents David was going with me. We met at the airport and "eloped."

The third lie: my fieldnotes. I wrote them in the first person, to hide David's existence, and sent my mother the carbon copies.

I don't think this is a lie. It should be viewed as a sign of my professionalism, or as an occupational hazard. In Santa María, I learned to get down on my knees at the appropriate parts of the mass and cross myself as the others did. What else could I do? My professor had placed me in a village where everyone went to mass without fail each Sunday. At first, I hesitated to participate so fully in Catholic practices, but after all, wasn't participation what was expected of me as an anthropologist? They'd never had any problems doing it in New Guinea or Africa. So long as I didn't confess and take communion, I imagined I wasn't breaking any rules of respect toward Catholicism or threatening the integrity of my own Jewish identity. So what if I felt like a liar?

Our professor had arranged for us to live with a peasant family that still worked the land. That way we'd get an "authentic" view of the traditional Spanish countryside. We were given a bedroom above the pig sty. It didn't smell until August. Above our bed there was a cross. I don't know how we dared, but we took it down and put it away in the closet. I can't remember if we thought to put it back before we left. At lunch we'd drink too much wine, then go upstairs, make love, the bed creaking painfully, and sleep long, long siestas. We had a pile of used condoms and crumpled tissues lying by the bedside all that summer.

We never got to sleep in the bedroom above the pig sty again. The following summer, when we tried to rent the room, we were asked for an exorbitant amount of money that far exceeded my student stipend. I always wondered if the real reason we were denied our first bedroom in the village was because we had been too noisy or too messy. I also feared it had something to do with taking down the cross over the bed.

The next two summers we stayed at the schoolteacher's house. Later, when we stayed in Spain for a year, we rented the house of a family that had abandoned the countryside for Bilbao. They locked up their brooms so we wouldn't use them; when the house flooded while we were away, the brooms became fossils in mud. Another summer we rented an old adobe farmhouse that belonged to the village blacksmith and has been crumbling ever since we moved out.

But no arrangement has been stranger than the one we've continued to have since our return visit in the summer of 1987. By then David and I were officially married and our son, Gabriel, was nearly a year old. A major social change had taken place in those ten years: people who had formed part of the rural exodus to the city in the 1960s were increasingly returning to the village for their summer vacations. All the houses, even those that stood empty all winter, were suddenly coveted. So we found ourselves having to accept the invitation of a rich village family, who forbade us to pay rent. We were guests, friends of the family, and from then on would have "our" own room in the house, whenever we wished to return.

The house, to which we again returned in 1992, is huge and filled with antique furniture, tools, and ceramic pots. It has been meticulously restored by the Galician architect and engineer sons-in-law of its owner, a woman named Polonia, who left the village for Madrid in the 1940s after her marriage to a Francoist military man. Polonia was perhaps the first person to use the village as a vacation site; she'd return every summer with her two daughters and her son, so they would get to know their peasant grandparents and learn to wipe mud and dung from their shoes. It is her big-hearted daughter, Rufi, who lives in the city of León with her engineer husband and two teenage sons, who invites us, the anthropologists, to stay with them during the summer. I'm not sure exactly why. We're not such good company. David, at least, does the dishes, but I sit writing on the old table upstairs most mornings, and I don't help very much with the cooking. Maybe the spirits of a farmhouse kept so dutifully antique require the presence of an anthropologist who has written in such detail about "the presence of the past in a Spanish village."[1]

I rush down to eat my breakfast when I wake up, hoping I'll get there before Polonia. It is the height of summer. With all the demand for water among the families vacationing in Santa María, there is now a shortage, and the pipes are turned on for one or two hours a day. I flush the toilet with a bucketful of water and sneak into the kitchen.

I find Polonia seated at the table dipping chunks of bread into warm milk. It is too late to escape. Now I'll have to listen to her harangues about what she heard on the radio that morning. She adores repeating the latest criticism of Felipe González, the Spanish prime minister, and his band of *socialistas*. She refuses to admit that no criticism was permitted during the Franco period, but it's impossible to say this to her. "The *socialistas* used to laugh at Franco, but look at all the hospitals he built, and he didn't collect taxes from anyone. These *socialistas* do nothing but make us pay taxes, and they haven't built a single hospital yet." Hospitals mean a lot to Polonia. Her son is an important cancer doctor in Madrid. It was thanks to him that she was moved up in the line to receive a youthful kidney from a twelve-year-old boy who died in a motorcycle accident. Both her own kidneys had withered up.

Polonia has a tremendous sense of largesse. She feels that half the village owes their life to her family. Not that anyone is grateful. Or even remembers. But they know that if her father hadn't been so generous with food from his harvest and money he'd saved while others squandered theirs, many of the people walking around the village today wouldn't be here. From Polonia's perspective, the anthropologists are probably direct descendants of the needy of days past.

I listen, knowing that the price I pay to stay in the village is to suffer and be still when Polonia grabs my ear. But I can't help wincing when she launches again into her complaints about the Latin Americans who come to Spain in search of work. "They get treated so well in our houses, those people, and still they have the nerve to pick up and leave, without even saying goodbye, just because somewhere else they can earn another hundred *pesetas*."

I feel hurt to the bottom of my Latin American soul when I hear this. Or when I hear, too, as Rufi later tells me, that in the nearby village of Barrio de Nuestra Señora (The Neighborhood of Our Lady) there is now a whorehouse filled with young women from my part of America. Or when Polonia's son-in-law, the architect, whispers to his nephew, when his wife isn't listening, that he must go with him to Cuba on his next business trip: "They have women however you want them, mulatas, everything, all you have to do is ask."

There is pain being in the mother country.

It is cruel of me to write like this about people who were charitable enough to house and feed us for two summers. I ought to be grateful. I know I'm acting like those Latin Americans who never say thank you. The fatal mistake made by the Jews and Arabs who got thrown out of Spain all those centuries ago: they didn't say *gracias* often enough.

The fourth lie; years ago, while I stood in the kitchen chopping garlic with Rufi, she asked me if we were Catholic, and I said yes. She asked me the question as though it were impossible for us to be anything else. After all, I came from a country that had been conquered by the cross of Spain. For a split second I wavered, almost told her the truth, but I couldn't. I didn't know how. The next day she asked me to accompany her to the city to pick up party favors for the first communion of her niece and nephew. They were miniature church bells made of white sugar and silver place cards with tiny crosses engraved on them. Rufi asked me if I too thought the party favors were cute; for the second time, I said yes to her.

In the summer of 1992 I'd confess: "No, Rufi, actually I'm Jewish. I was afraid to tell you. You see, the Inquisition lives on. In my heart. Can you understand?" I'd show her the essay I wrote about death in Santa María, in which I interwove the story of my Yiddish grandfather's death in Miami Beach.[2] I'd show her the new paperback edition of my book, where in an afterword I tell how my parents' refusal to accept David made me not only ashamed of being Jewish but also unable to understand fully the place of Catholicism in the lives of Spanish people. And I'd explain that it wasn't just my parents who were to blame for my uncertainty about how to position myself in so thoroughly Catholic a country. Some of the blame, I'd tell her, has to be borne by the discipline of anthropology, which taught me everything about the symbolism of "primitive religion" and the rationality of witchcraft in the former colonies of Europe while keeping silent about the "Jewish problem" to be faced in studying the Christian European world. I'd play the Sephardic tapes I got in Turkey, so Rufi might hear the voices of Jews who feel so deeply the loss of their beloved Spain that they still sing of their exile in the tongue of the ones who banished them.

Every day, I want to offer these revelations to Rufi. I feel heavy with the weight of my confession. Instead, I find myself hiding the evidence of my Jewishness—the books, the cassettes, the postcards, the posters—deeper within my suitcases. I become a *conversa,* the kind of Jewish convert the Inquisition didn't trust; that's why the other name for such a convert was *marrano,* "pig." Like a *conversa,* I'm outwardly Catholic, inwardly Jewish. When I leave I know my stern Jewish god won't forgive me, but I hope Rufi's sweet-faced Christian god, who so understood suffering, will pardon my sins.

"Jews use the blood of Christian children for matzohs. My Grandpa was a Jew. He had a long white beard, and he wore a kaftan, like Sister Catherine. He wore a striped shawl and he prayed to God all day. I don't think he would eat that kind of matzohs. . . . Jesus knows that I love him. He doesn't mind that I am Jewish."

So wrote Elza Frydrych Shatzkin, a Holocaust survivor. As a child of six, she was hidden with a Polish family and later spent time in a Catholic orphanage. Her parents were killed, but she went on to Cornell University, where she majored in American and British literature. She must have decided that

273

perhaps Jesus did mind, because shortly before her twenty-sixth birthday she committed suicide.[3]

I am taking a walk to the village dam with a young woman who has come of age during my years of visits to Santa María. She is telling me she hopes to finish her studies in three years and then get married, but not have children right away. I ask, What about feminism? She doesn't say anything. So I clarify: I mean, do men and women both do the housework and cooking? Oh no, she says, that doesn't happen.

The afternoon is cool, the light soft, you can see the peaks of the Cantabrian Mountains up ahead. We get to talking about two recent rape cases that have been heavily publicized in the press, and I ask if she isn't afraid to be walking out here alone. No, nothing happens here, she says. We hear the clinking bells of the sheep in the valley.

In the intimacy of our solitude, I decide to try asking her my project questions. I ask, What do you think of the Arabs and Jews who used to live in Spain? Nothing, she says. She doesn't have any prejudices. It's all okay with her. I push her further: What does she know of the expulsion of the Jews and Arabs from Spain? She studied that a long time ago, in elementary school, she replies. And adds that she thinks they did the right thing. If not, Spain wouldn't be what it is today. Anyway, the Jews have their own country now. I persist: But some of them thought Spain was their country. She shrugs, and we keep walking.

Ruth, the anthropologist, is at the solemn mass for the village fiesta, standing by the door. The little church is full to bursting. There is no room left on any of the benches. Everyone is dressed in his or her best.

Two Sundays ago, at the end of the mass, as I crossed myself self-consciously, I watched while the men filed down from the choir loft. An old sense of order still exists in that little church: the children sit in front, the teenage girls behind them, the married women in the middle, the men up in the loft. The men leave first, the children next, the teenage girls and the women last.

Each man comes down, glances rapidly at the altar, and crosses himself. I know every single man, young and old, know each of their stories, know who is happy in marriage, who is sad, who is indifferent, who will remain a bachelor.

Carlos, a teenager whose age is the same as the number of years I've been going to Santa María, crosses himself with his left hand. His right hand, disfigured since birth, is in a perennial cast. But it may well yet be fixed. I remember Carlos as a small child in a wheelchair, his two legs in casts. Now, many operations later, he swaggers, plays soccer, and rides a special motorcycle shaped like a dune buggy. Watching him cross his heart with his left hand, I feel pride that he is a son of the community, as if I were a daughter of the community.

Suddenly my name is being called from the altar. In a falsetto voice, the visiting friar Padre Martín is saying, "Ruth, where are you? Raise your hand please." I hide my head and pretend not to hear. Fortunately, he doesn't seem to see me. Aging Padre Martín, a son of the pueblo who usually spends his summers in England subbing for vacationing priests, fell apart from overwork not too long ago, and he's still recovering. People say he's not all there. But I can vouch for his English; it is impeccable. I hear him rambling on. People can barely keep from chuckling.

"As many of you know, I've been serving as the resident priest at the Women's Psychiatric Center. Do you all know what a psychiatric center is?"

People are working hard to keep from laughing out loud.

"It's a place where people who have mental problems go. They're all women, but that doesn't mean there are no crazy men in the world."

He pauses, steps closer to the children, nearly tripping over the microphone. People begin giggling wildly. His relatives are the only ones keeping a straight face.

"And what are we celebrating today? The village is named for the Virgin, but there was a monastery in the woods named after Saint Pelayo. Talking to Ruth the other day. . . . Ruth, aren't you here?"

I sink into the ground.

"Well, as you all know, Ruth has investigated the history of the pueblo, and she told me the village was founded by Saint Pelayo."

Don Laurentino, the regular priest, clears his throat and Padre Martín gets the message. He quickly wraps up his sermon, saying "The Church is joy. The fiesta is joy. Let's be solemn, but let's also be joyous."

With skill and efficiency Don Laurentino, a younger priest, brings the mass to a close. "You can go in peace," he says briskly, then adds that he needs to make an announcement. He decides, then, to correct Padre Martín.

"Padre Martín has just told you part of the history of the pueblo. Actually, it was impossible for Saint Pelayo to have founded the village, because Saint Pelayo had been dead a few hundred years by then. Poor Saint Pelayo, he preferred to die than to be forced to have homosexual relations with an archbishop who had his eyes on him. Pelayo was a young boy when he died, some time around the year of 700. This pueblo didn't exist yet. But later on they named a monastery here in these woods after Saint Pelayo. When the monastery disappeared, the people who had worked for the friars came and founded this pueblo. If you want to hear this history in detail, ask Ruth, because she's the one who's investigated all of this more fully than anybody from here."

My name is invoked during a Catholic mass by two priests who've given me responsibility for the village histories they've invented—two priests who have no idea I'm a Jew descended from those who were told to convert or leave. I, this odd twentieth-century *conversa,* am to be the historian of the village, the memory of the village, the scribe of the village. When we come out of church, a woman rushes over to me and says, "Ruth, you're an institution around here. The priests can't stop talking about you."

A few days later I am packing up to leave. In one summer so little and so much has happened. Hundreds of rabbits, the lifelong savings of two village brothers, were burned to a crisp in a blazing midsummer fire while I read *Arabesques*. In the dawn hours of the last day of the fiesta a teenager from Madrid, who had come for the festivities with a friend from the village, accelerated too quickly around one of the nearby curves on the highway and killed himself, marking forever the 1992 fiesta as the fiesta that was cut short by a stranger's death. The questionnaire I had hoped to distribute, inquiring about people's views of Jews and Jewish life, never left my desk. Fidel Castro made a stop in his father's hometown in Galicia, but decided not to retire yet. I read some books in my tower; the others went back to my suitcase unread. In the end, I didn't call upon Dr. Wilson.

The desk on which I wrote all summer is as clear as I found it. I return the clay cross set in the clay pedestal to its place on the center of the night table. I take a last look at the Virgin who's been behind my back, radiating her power, and say goodbye to Santa María del Monte.

As we drive away, the village mass is beginning for the teenager from Madrid who came to Santa María to die. I don't feel ready to leave. I stop the car at house after house, giving out hugs, reporting on our itinerary, taking the last photographs in my camera, and promising to write more often, though I know I won't. And then, finally, we face forward and set our eyes on the road ahead.

We have planned on spending two days in Madrid. When we arrive at the motel near the Barajas airport, all I want to do is cry, but I hold back my tears. The room is cramped, stuffy, and smells of regret. But we are too hot and tired to get in the car again and look for another place to stay. So we shower in the strange stall set up on the edge of the room and try to get some rest on the sinking mattresses. At dusk we cross the deserted and dusty plaza to the side opposite the motel in hopes of having a good dinner in the Chinese restaurant located there. The dinner is terrible, but we eat it anyway. I sleep that night without dreaming.

As soon as I wake up, I announce to David that I will not spend my last day in Spain in a depressing motel perched at the airport entrance. He dutifully agrees and we silently pack everything into the car again and drive to the old section of Madrid. At Calle Cervantes, we pull up in front of the familiar entrance to the third-floor hostel named Dulcinea. The room is clean, and though it is also small, at least it smells of nothing more distressing than fresh paint. In the afternoon, after returning our rental car, we take a walk to the Retiro Park, full of memories for me of my first visit to Spain in 1975, when it didn't scare me to travel alone. Near an ice-cream stand run by an African emigrant, I stop to rest at the foot of a huge monument to José Martí, the Cuban independence leader who formulated his ideas about the need for freedom in his native land while living in exile in the United States.

I can tell my departure from Spain is going to be difficult. When I leave the Dulcinea, I get into an argument with the owner because he won't give me a receipt for the cost of my lodging unless I pay an additional state tax. The two of us, who a day ago had exchanged pleasantries about the beauty of northern Spain, part angrily.

Calle Cervantes is usually bustling with taxis, but on the Sunday morning when we need to get to the airport not a single cab passes. I leave David and Gabriel standing by the suitcases and wander around the block to the Ritz. I hail the cab in front of the line, telling the driver we are going to the airport and have a lot of luggage. He tells me there's no problem. As we approach the Dulcinea I feel a sense of accomplishment. But when he opens the trunk of his cab, I become livid with rage. The trunk is filled with several clunky orange gas containers. Where is our luggage to go? I accuse him of tricking me, of lying. The driver, in turn, becomes furious and accuses me of trampling his honor. David tells me to calm down and remember that the clock is ticking and no other cab is in sight. I keep bickering with the driver, who throws our bags onto the roof and straps them in place with a thin piece of rope. I complain loudly, in Spanish, all the way to the airport, deliberately trying to infuriate the man. I half wish, half fear, he will dump us and our ten suitcases in the middle of the highway.

At the airport we learn that our flight has been delayed two hours. We feel so lucky not to be charged for overweight luggage that for the next two hours we wander about the airport distractedly looking for "X-Men" comic books to buy for Gabriel. With David leading, we end up in a distant part of the airport. After we fail to locate any comic books, I insist we start walking back toward our gate because the check-in time is drawing near.

Before I know it, David and Gabriel have crossed to the other side of the X-ray area. I am still fumbling with my bags. I pull out a large plastic tupperware container of exposed film and approach one of the civil guards. In my most formal and Castilianized Spanish I ask him please not to X-ray my film. The guard replies gruffly that everything has to be X-rayed, and that they make no exceptions. I calmly respond that I am a professor and an anthropologist and that the film is extremely important to my work. The guard laughs and says that the whole crew of photographers for the Olympics put their film through this machine, so why shouldn't I? As my pulse starts to quicken, I tell him that I use low-speed film that could be hurt by the X-rays. When he still won't budge, I add that I've been in Spain doing research on a Fulbright award funded by the Spanish government, and that I can't afford to lose an entire summer's worth of photographs. Looking at me with a smirk, he asks for proof of my status. I begin sifting through the papers in my briefcase, but I can't find the letter stating the terms of my award. I manage to pull up something with the letterhead of the Fulbright office in Madrid, a brief note that was paired up with an enclosure. The guard is unimpressed. Anyway, it's in English, he says.

By this time the tears I have been holding back are flowing out of me like blood from a fresh wound. I feel as if I am viewing the world through a screen, and the guard, with his three-cornered hat, embodies all the evils of Spain—the Inquisition, Francoism, religious orthodoxy. He is Haman incarnate. I am possessed by a single wish: to protect my film from his evil X-rays. I seem to know, somehow, that every picture will be destroyed if the film goes through the machine. What is it I really fear? Am I afraid of being seen through? I have spent an entire summer trying to claim all my identities in the Spanish village where I became an anthropologist and a professional liar. And I have failed. The only truth in my life is in those pictures. Is that what I am thinking? I don't know what I am thinking. I am on one side of the X-ray machine standing in a pool of my tears, and David and Gabriel are on the other side waiting for me.

I dry my tears, take a deep breath, and return to the ticket counter, but before I can begin to tell my story I burst out crying again. When I, at last, explain my problem, the agents at the counter sigh and tell me they can't intervene with the civil guards. They tell me to speak to the flight manager, who will be back from a coffee break shortly. When I am about to give up and return to the X-ray gate, the flight manager appears. He walks me back to the gate while I repeat my story again, this time angrily. He glances at my Fulbright letter and says there is nothing indicating that the film cannot be put through the machine. I repeat that I am a professor, an anthropologist, a scholar on a Fulbright award funded by his own government. Nothing makes an impression. I start crying again but the manager is no more moved by my tears than the guard. The tears just seem to convince them further that I must be hiding something terrible inside my film canisters.

And then, overcome with a grief that feels as ancient as the desire of Lot's wife, and all her exiled descendants, to look back, I take my bag of film, my briefcase, and my purse, place them on the X-ray machine, and cross over. Recovering my things on the other side, I cry and cry and cry. I refuse to leave the X-ray area. I spill loud, bitter, madwoman tears. I am crying the salty tears of Lot's wife. I am crying the tears of thousands of Sephardim, who took the keys to their old houses with them in case they ever returned. I am crying the tears of Ruth, the anthropologist, who tried so hard to adapt to other people's gods, to lodge where they lodged. Everyone who crosses through the X-ray machine stops to stare at La Llorona, "the Weeping Woman." Someone asks if I have been hurt or assaulted by the guards.

The guards ignore me for a long time. Then, finally, the guard in his three-cornered hat plants himself in front of me and yells in my face that it's enough already, that if I don't get out of there he's going to have me arrested. I move out of his way, but I cry myself dry all the way to New York.

NOTES

1. Ruth Behar, *The Presence of the Past in a Spanish Village: Santa María del Monte* (1986; rev. ed., Princeton: Princeton University Press, 1991).

2. Ruth Behar, "Death and Memory: From Santa María del Monte to Miami Beach," *Cultural Anthropology* 6 (1991): 346–84.

3. Elza Frydrych Shatzkin, "Przemysl—December 1942," in *The Tribe of Dina: A Jewish Women's Anthology,* ed. Melanie Kaye/Kantrowitz and Irena Klepfisz, 165–67 (Boston: Beacon Press, 1989), quotation is from 167. Elza's life story is told by Irena Klepfisz.

17

The Pastry Shop and the
Angel of Death
What's Jewish in Art History

Eunice Lipton

We had barely stepped into his house, when smiling and filling our glasses, our host said: "I'm so tired of the American press talking about how Jewish this writer is and that writer is. Who cares really?"

Now, this man *looked* Jewish, and to be honest that's why we'd sent him an inquiring note in the first place—that, plus the name Hofenberg on *someone's* mailbox in the hallway. I glanced at Ken and Carol, they at me: Maybe we made a mistake. Always the quickest to take offense, I was ready to leave. But soon the wine and fireplace did their work, and we found that we were excited to be having this conversation here in Paris—this *type* of conversation. Nonetheless, we set to disabusing our host. *We* had not noticed such discussions in the press. Yes, there were many Jewish-American writers and they were regularly reviewed, but any special calling attention to their—what shall we call it, ethnicity?—that wasn't the case.

Francis Hofenberg, our dapper sixty-one-year-old, half-English, half-French host, backed off, but a half-hour later, his eyes hard, his lips white, he said: "Look, my friends, Hitler accomplished what he set out to accomplish. He destroyed European Jewry. What does it mean to be a Jew now? Forget about it."

Forget about it?

—Paris, January 1992

I'VE OFTEN WONDERED why I became an art historian, such a glamorous profession for a working-class Jewish girl born in the Bronx to Communist parents in 1941. Art didn't figure in my childhood; we never went to museums. My mother did have some Mexican things she loved—a plump orange vase, a carved wooden tray. And, yes, there was a brownish print of ballet dancers by someone named Degas and another picture drenched in burgundy by Renoir. But I don't remember where they came from, and no one ever talked about them. It was music and literature we loved with a fervor that would matter all my life—Bizet's *Carmen*, Tchaikovsky and Rachmaninoff's piano music, Dostoevsky, Turgenev, Gorki. So how did it happen that I became expert in the pleasures of seeing? I, along with so very many other Jews—Bernard Berenson, Walter Friedlaender, Sidney Freedberg, Erwin Panofsky, Meyer Schapiro, Linda Nochlin, Irving Lavin, Robert Rosenblum, Carol Duncan, Al Boime, Leo Steinberg, James Ackerman, Clement Greenberg, Harold Rosenberg, Linda Seidel, Rosalind Krauss?

It's winter 1946, Hurleyville, New York. The white-haired grandpa pulls the little girl along, his ruddy, smiling face a talisman. He roars, she giggles through the snow, up the main road of the village, this quiet town in the Catskills, where Jews and Gentiles live together. Rushing by the houses and the hills, the old man pulls the sled filled with the child's merriness and the pristine beauty of the day. The girl, holding tight, loves the wind nipping at her cheeks, her silken hair coaxed out of hiding. She's four years old, and today she's a queen, her grandpa's warm expanse of back her guardian.

"How are you doing, *mein kind?*"

"I'm dreaming, Grandpa. I'm dreaming of Mommy and Grandma's soup and Lucky kissing me and. . . . "

All the white snow and silence.

As their house drifts into view, the girl is imagining the thick soup and warm bread on the table, but suddenly something cold slips around her heart. Something about her grandma by the gate, her hair loose, her soft mouton coat flapping in the wind, a thin housecoat pulled tightly around her legs and hips and breasts.

"Grandma?"

But Grandma looks at Max, her husband, and pushes a newspaper into his hands.

"*Nem* a look, Mendel," she cries, half in English, half in Yiddish, tears running down the creases of her face, her blue eyes gone to gray.

"Max. Max. *Was kennen mir tun?*" What can we do? The grandma, Anna, moans. The child throws her hands up to her ears. The newspaper slips to the snow, and the two old people stand there weeping.

The girl's eye wanders the vista near and far, back and forth, left and right; everything's gone gray and still. Her glance lingers on the newspaper at their feet—some pictures, stick figures like chicken bones eaten clean, black and white striped pajamas. She pulls at Max's hand, but he ignores her. She pulls again, this time smiling up at him. He lifts her, his arms so all-around that she can see his hands on both sides.

"Chanaidl," he says—Anna—"let's eat. We've been dreaming of your nice soup with the barley and carrots and noodles. Come inside Chanaidl." As he says this, Max brushes tears from his face and hers and gently pushes a stray lock of hair behind his wife's ear, "Come, *meydele.*"

They eat their meal together silently. Afterward the little girl sits down in a corner of the big kitchen; she's waiting for her grandma to finish the dishes. Near her are the red geraniums that come in for winter; their orangey velvet transfixes her. But just as she reaches to touch their soft friendly parts, she notices a story-picture on the wall and falls instead to staring at it. In the picture, there's another little girl who is stretched out on two wooden chairs. She is half under a blanket with one arm hanging down. Her lips burn a red spot in her face, her golden hair spreads along a pillow. A kindly man in a black suit sits nearby, leaning toward her, worried. There's a table to his left with a small glass bottle, a lamp with tilted green shade, a cup with a spoon resting in it. On the other side of the child's head is a low rough-hewn bench with a large bowl and pitcher. Behind her hover dark figures, a woman weeping, a man standing alongside. The little girl gazing at the picture is not sure what's happening. Over and over again she scrutinizes every detail. Her eye wanders the light and dark surfaces; the colors—now gold, now green, now black—absorb her; she repeats this activity endlessly. It calms her.

Winters are long in Hurleyville, and although the little girl loves her grandparents, she wishes she had some children to play with. For instance, she wishes she could play with Pearl across the street. Every day lately she says, "Grandma, can I play with Pearl?" And every day Grandma says: "No, it's too late today"; or, "No, I can't come to get you later"; or, "No, they were hollering this morning." But on the day when the newspaper falls to the snow, Grandma looks at her and says, "*Kind,* they're Gentiles over there; they're not Jewish like us. You don't want to play with them."

This makes the girl angry. What's "Jewish"? She's heard this word before, and she's seen the two pretty white buildings in town with the towers and the colored windows and the crosses, and she knows she can't go inside them; she even has a feeling she would die if she did, that some witch would eat her up. She also knows that her grandparents shop on one side of the road in town and not the other. And there's a bakery she thinks Grandpa described as "Jewish." It's from that pastry shop that the old man brings her the wonderful warm cakes with the white sugar stripes and raisins.

Certainly many a Jew of my background—first-generation American, parents born in Eastern Europe, whose first language was Yiddish—chose professions that took them far, far away from the chill and memories of murdered Jews. Indeed, we were legion as we fastidiously stepped out of earshot of the centuries-old moan: "What did we do to deserve this? Why do they hate us so?" Just as the child in Hurleyville threw herself into the painting of the doctor contemplating the dying girl (Fig. 1), so did I, the grown woman, turn a habit of my heart into professional expertise—and armor. Somewhere, unconsciously, I decided never to make a spectacle of myself—a *shanda fur de goyim* (an embarrassment in front of the Gentiles). I would try to dress and sound like everyone else. I would enter a profession where they would least expect to find me. Then they couldn't kill me. They wouldn't know who I am. So, I wound up all my pain and fear, everything I saw that day in my grandpar-

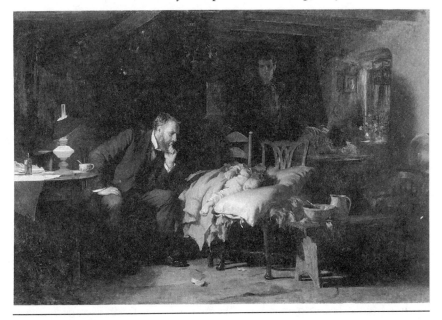

Figure 1. *The Doctor,* by Sir Luke Fildes, 1891. Tate Gallery, London/Art Resource, NY.

ents' aching hearts and sorrow-filled faces, and threw it through the trajectory of my gaze into the contemplation of pictures. I pushed away—pressed way, way down—all the horrors the cold-blooded murder of Jewish people held for me, not least of which was that I might lose the only people who loved me, that my grandparents' hearts would turn to stone, that their eyes would never look upon me with tenderness again. I pressed this terror, sublimated this hurricane, into aesthetic wonder and intellectual perusal. In this I found the pleasure of my senses and my mind. And respectability. I became an art historian.

I attended the City College of New York between the years 1958 and 1962. I was studying history and literature when I fell under the influence of a history professor who came from Riga, the same city where my father was born. This professor, a Jew, was a big balding man, of embarrassing pretensions, who liked me and encouraged me to do research on art. So, at eighteen I started writing about Sienese and Florentine painters, Christian artists of the late Middle Ages. That same year I took my first trip to Europe, the highlight of which was Florence. I remember coming home from the Uffizi late one afternoon, throwing myself upon the bed and weeping desperately. Why? Because I couldn't understand the art. And I couldn't understand it because I was Jewish. The Christian symbolism confounded me, made me an outsider. I returned to New York with the decision to study art history. Through my professor's urgings, I went to graduate school in a mansion on Fifth Avenue, my Bronx-Jewish accent and City

College habits in tow. It wasn't easy. I wrote a dissertation about Picasso, but more specifically about the making of his reputation; it was a skeptical piece of work that at heart challenged the absoluteness of the artist's fame. Then I moved on to Manet and Degas. By that point my work was committedly feminist, and it was 1975.

To this day I find it hard to admit to myself, as well as to others, that I wrote several articles and a book about Degas, and never addressed his rabid and, as Linda Nochlin put it, his ordinary anti-Semitism.[1] I admitted it, but brushed it aside. What *I* was interested in, I would say to myself, were his images of women. My concerns were beyond, superior to, any considerations of racism; art held aloof from such issues: "I'm not Jewish, I'm an art historian."

A number of experiences in the winter of 1992 made me rethink these certitudes. One was the incident described in the epigraph to this chapter. Another was this: I learned one afternoon that many European Jews after World War II did not tell their children they were Jewish. This repulsed me. How *could* they? Were they ashamed? Why would they be? Hadn't the war "vindicated" them? Wasn't the world horrified by what Jews had suffered? Didn't everyone think Germany was a sick, evil society, and Jews innocents? Then a French friend married to a French Jew who hadn't learned he was Jewish until he was twenty-four turned to me angrily and said, "Don't you realize how afraid they were? They knew it could happen again." Afraid? Why it had never occurred to me. Or, rather it had "occurred" to me and so terrified me that I "forgot" it. That's why, I finally understood, I had ignored Degas' anti-Semitism. I couldn't tolerate the thought that I could be that vulnerable; I simply could not admit—was incapable of admitting—this terror to myself. Perhaps Letty Cottin Pogrebin explains it when she says, "I felt so at home in America as a Jew that I was able to concentrate on feeling displaced . . . as a *woman*."[2] But I think a truer explanation was the mechanism of repression facilitated by the permission the distance from Europe gave us; we all "knew" very well what destiny could be ours. So, I held to my respectability and, I hoped, my disguise.

Nonetheless, and contradictorily, I was proud of being Jewish. I'd often embellish my speech with the little Yiddish that I knew. I always *said* I was Jewish. But it was *I* who said it, not others. I thought I couldn't be caught off guard, that the disclosure was my choice, a product of my autonomy. But I always lived and worked among Jews, first in the Bronx in the 1940s and 1950s, then in Washington Heights, then on the Upper West Side of Manhattan. I went to the High School of Music and Art, which I considered Jewish, and then to City College and New York University. I taught at city and state universities in New York. Looking back on it, I realize now that I "saw" Jewish everywhere—not a hard thing to do in New York—but that unbeknownst to myself I was constantly constructing a ghetto for myself in which to feel safe and protected from the gentile world; where Gentiles existed in my world I simply didn't notice them, even when they became my friends.

Becoming an art historian was part of this delusional and protective strategy. The Angel of Death of my title urged me toward this haven.

On the face of it art history seemed a gentile profession. For one thing, the study of Christian art was at its center. In addition, there was an ancient Jewish injunction against making a graven image. But the fact is, the field was filled with Jews. One might even say it was shaped by them. Art history is characterized in this century by studies in connoisseurship, formalist analysis, the study of iconography and iconology, and social analyses. Jews have been prominent in all categories. Bernard Berenson was the most influential of the original connoisseurs. Almost single-handedly, and autocratically, he organized masses of uncatalogued paintings and drawings of northern and central Italy, separating out local schools and the hands of individual artists. Through the penetration and shrewdness of his eye, he shaped the very terrain of Renaissance studies, not to mention the market for what became its masterpieces. He was a sought-after adviser.

Outstanding formalist scholars and critics among Jews are Walter Friedlaender, Robert Rosenblum, Clement Greenberg, Rosalind Krauss, Meyer Schapiro, and Leo Steinberg. Friedlaender's book *From David to Delacroix* is an excellent example. Its mission was to chart the sensuous difference between and among the works of austere neoclassicism and blustery romanticism. A measured approach characterizes the book, but passages of visual delight spill over its pages too. Describing Delacroix's painting *Sardanapalus,* Friedlaender writes: "Delacroix rendered a pandemonium of passions, a whirling mixture of human and animal forms, the brilliant flesh of women, dark Negroes, caparisoned horses, rich stuffs, smoky clouds. . . . "[3]

Robert Rosenblum, Friedlaender's student, did something similar with that most hermetic of styles, cubism, in his *Cubism and Twentieth Century Art.* Rosenblum takes the reader on a never-to-be-forgotten trip through the silver, browns, and mauves of the canyons and crevices of early cubism. Never will those small and puzzling drawings and paintings look the same again: " . . . the syntax has achieved an infinite sophistication revealed . . . in the endlessly intricate shifting of planes within a hairbreadth, or in the equally rich variations of light and dark that make this gossamer scaffolding quiver in unpredictable ways upon the white surface of the paper."[4]

Among the formalists, Schapiro is the most enthralling with his always-synthesizing intelligence, erudition, and appetite for visual pleasure. Of a Van Gogh painting, he writes:

> The enclosed field—the space of the artist himself, a world of luxuriant growth and warm light, spotted with poppies, blue flowers and whites . . . a region of pure happiness—is steeply inclined, permeated by chaotic forces, and cut off from the world around it by a powerful rushing band of lavender-blue. . . . the far distance is . . . acid in places, and the yellow sky rising above the cold mountains is of a famished yellow. . . . [5]

Almost a delirium of pleasure dances across these formalist pages. The study of iconography and iconology was a more austere but no less passionate endeavor developed by Erwin Panofsky and practiced by Jewish scholars like Leo Steinberg, Irving Lavin, and Linda Seidel. Panofsky's studies of particular works of art are so intricate that they are difficult to excerpt. I offer a small and admittedly circumscribed piece of his analysis of Titian's *Sacred and Profane Love*, a depiction—to put it simply—of both a clothed and a naked woman seated in a landscape at either end of an ancient sarcophagus-turned-fountain whose water a putto stirs:

> Not only in the Bible but also in Roman literature actual nudity was often thought objectionable, because it indicated either poverty, or shamelessness. In a figurative sense, however, it was mostly identified with simplicity, sincerity and the true essence of a thing as opposed to circumlocution, deceit and external appearances. All things are "naked and opened unto the eyes" of God. . . . *Nuda virtus* is the real virtue appreciated in the good old days when wealth and social distinction did not count. . . . [6]

There is constant dialectical play in Panofsky's writing.

Linda Seidel puts a feminist twist on iconographical study in her analysis of Jan van Eyck's *Portrait of Giovanni Arnolfini and Giovanna Cenami*. Indeed her entire essay is a reading not only of the portrait itself but also of her teacher Panofsky's reading of it. Where Panofsky focused on the religious meaning of details, Seidel looks for their social and gendered significance. For example, she writes,

> . . . a groom's gifts were bought on credit against the sum he expected to realize in his wife's dowry. Sometimes they were only "loans": the fancy dress and the hangings "to make the bed chamber" were returned soon after the ceremony. Giovanni's gifts, then, may be temporary manifestations of display meant to put his mark on Giovanna. No wonder that she has seemed so "idealized," so absent and unfocused in gaze. She is shown here, in even the most straightforward reading of the panel, not in her own right but as the pawn in men's games. [7]

As a feminist, a Marxist, and a specialist in nineteenth-century French art, I was most influenced by the art historians—and Jews—Meyer Schapiro, Linda Nochlin, and Carol Duncan. We might call Schapiro the American poet laureate of art history. His rhetorical locutions and wit, his breadth of knowledge and attention to detail, are breathtaking. Whether he was writing about the romanesque sculpture of Souillac or French impressionism, his mind wrapped around a subject, burrowed into it, and examined it with a mixture of delicacy, stubbornness, and brilliance. On impressionism:

> It is remarkable how many pictures we have in early Impressionism of informal and spontaneous sociability, of breakfasts, picnics, promenades, boating trips, holidays and vacation travel. These urban idylls not only present the objective forms of bourgeois recreations in the 1860's and 1870's; they also

reflect in the very choice of subjects and in the aesthetic devices the conception of art as solely a field of individual enjoyment, without reference to ideas and motives, and they presuppose the cultivation of these pleasures as the highest field of freedom for an enlightened bourgeois detached from the official beliefs of his class.[8]

No one before Schapiro contemplated meaning in impressionism other than in its formal beauty: the disintegration of form, the play of light, the invention of color. Cézanne's comment about Monet—"Monet is only an eye, but good Lord, what an eye!"[9]—applied to all our contemplation of those pleasure-saturated canvases. Until Schapiro.

Nochlin, in part following Schapiro's lead, but otherwise turning corners only a feminist could, exposed art history's most cherished myths: masterpieces and geniuses began to stumble forth stripped of their special charms. Here she is in her groundbreaking essay, "Why Have There Been No Great Women Artists?":

> Underlying the question about woman as artist . . . we find the myth of the Great Artist—subject of a hundred monographs, unique, godlike—bearing within his person since birth a mysterious essence, rather like the golden nugget in Mrs. Grass's chicken soup, called Genius or Talent, which, like murder, must always out, no matter how unlikely or unpromising the circumstances. . . .
>
> . . .
>
> . . . There *are* no women equivalents for Michealangelo or Rembrandt, Delacroix or Cézanne, Picasso or Matisse . . . any more than there are black American equivalents for the same. . . . [T]hings as they are and as they have been, in the arts as in a hundred other areas, are stultifying, oppressive, and discouraging to all those, women among them, who did not have the good fortune to be born white, preferably middle class and, above all, male. The fault lies not in our stars, our hormones, our menstrual cycles, or our empty internal spaces, but in our institutions and our education. . . .[10]

In this momentous piece Nochlin eliminated the guilt women artists and art historians dragged around with them about the evident absence of great women artists of the past. By so doing she also cleared a space for a new discourse: the social meanings of women's lives *outside* the ideologically shaped histories that paraded as universal truths. In addition, she opened up the possibility of questioning the ways in which male artists constructed the meaning of women and men in their art. Nochlin's generosity to hundreds of women also went far to producing a feminist art historical presence in both Great Britain and the United States.

Carol Duncan added rage to feminist exegesis. In her "Virility and Domination in Early Twentieth-Century Vanguard Paining," she describes nudes by the artists Ernst Ludwig Kirchner and Kees van Dongen this way:

> [Each] stands above the supine woman. Reduced to flesh, she is sprawled powerlessly before him, her body contorted according to the dictates of his

erotic will. . . . One sees an obedient animal. The Artist, in asserting his own
sexual will, has annihilated all that is human in his opponent.[11]

A little further on, she writes:

> But while we are told about the universal, genderless aspirations of art, a deeper
> level of consciousness, fed directly by the powerful images themselves, compre-
> hends that this "general" truth arises from male experience alone. We are also
> taught to keep such suspicions suppressed, thus preserving the illusion that the
> "real" meanings of art are universal. . . . In this way we have been schooled to
> cherish vanguardism as the embodiment of "our" most progressive values.[12]

Duncan daringly put her finger on men's stake in keeping things just exactly
as they are. Politeness is eschewed. No more nice girls, not even in academe.

Several things strike me about my history of art history practiced by Jews. One
is the extent to which Jewish art historians have studied Christian art. Connoisseurs and iconographers involved themselves in the world of high gentile
culture. Only a truly assimilated Jew would even think of this world as a
legitimate subject of study. *Or,* a Jew who *wanted* to assimilate. *Or* perhaps a
self-aware Jew who was ingenious about using his or her marginality. So, in
part, becoming a scholar of art history can be construed within a general desire
to assimilate, to journey into a gentile world and perhaps be invited to stay.
(Ah, a Jew furious to be gentile, what better place than shrouded in the mysteries of art *and* Christianity?) But as my friends, art historians James Saslow and
Carol Zemel, insisted to me, there is a relentless subversion of Christian art that
proceeds in the work of many Jewish art historians. For example, Zemel points
out that Rudolf Wittkower didn't offer courses at Columbia in just humanist
and Christian architecture of the Italian Renaissance; he also taught courses in
non-Western influences on European art, for example, the impact of Islamic
and Judaic cultures on the Middle Ages. And Panofsky's interest in Northern
European art, which was so much more secularized than Italian, was iconoclastic in the face of pervading art historical interests. And, as Saslow puts it, "As
professors in the academy . . . rather than priests in the church, we *secularize*
and denaturalize, demystify Christianity. . . . "[13]

Another striking characteristic of much writing by Jews in art history is the
writing voice. Shall I call it Worried? Dialectical? Talmudic? Zemel says she
hears the chants of the *cheder,* the reading of the Talmud in the cadence of
Schapiro's sentences. I hear the same in Panofsky, Steinberg, Goldwater,
Nochlin. And then Saslow reminds me, "You mention the 'Talmudic' Panofsky,
but can this be pushed further? . . . [Mightn't you] consider the common
stereotypes: we are very literary, text-oreinted (Am Ha-Sefer, 'the People of the
Book'), and at the same time iconophobic (no graven images)."[14]

Then among art historians there is the attachment to the temporal world
and pleasure—the Pastry Shop of my title. And what pleasure there is in
sinking into the lush surfaces of oil painting or savoring the steady glow of

white marble or the sweep of transcendent arches. I once heard a young Jewish curator say while gazing at the autumnal curtains of a Morris Louis painting, "I would love to eat that painting."

It is a commonplace that an abiding and secularized aspect of Jewish tradition is its valuing of sensual satisfaction. Jewish law acknowledges appetite; one is even told how often one should make love. Judaism emphatically rejects the Christian body-soul dichotomy. As Paul Johnson has said, "The Christian idea that, by weakening the body through mortification and fasting, you strengthened the soul, was anathema to Jews."[15] There is no monastic tradition in Judaism. One might also say that Jewish validation of the senses results from the emphasis on human life in the present as opposed to any interest in an afterlife.

But how very skeptical, and oh so Jewish, to adore the cornucopian pleasures of art and then search out its betrayals. That's what the Marxists and social art historians do. This tendency is most striking among historians studying impressionism. Ever dialectical, we observed our own nervous twinges, and had to express our never-far-away cynicism that pleasure can't be just that. We analyzed the role of class and gender in, and on, the delicious canvases by Monet, Renoir, Cassatt, Manet, Morisot, and Degas. Who, we wondered, paid for the pleasures? The working classes and women, we answered. Walter Benjamin, I do believe, was our conscience:

> Whoever has emerged victorious participates . . . in the triumphal procession in which the present rulers step over those who are lying prostrate. . . . The spoils are carried along in the procession. They are called cultural treasures, and a historical materialist views them with cautious detachment. For without exception the cultural treasures he surveys have an origin which he cannot contemplate without horror. They owe their existence not only to the efforts of the great minds and talents who have created them, but also to the anonymous toil of their contemporaries. There is no document of civilization which is not at the same time a document of barbarism.[16]

I wanted two things at once when I became an art historian. I wanted to be where Jews were—that is, I wanted a profession that would allow me tacitly to acknowledge my Jewishness through the company I kept—but I also wanted to hide, to be gentile. I wanted to assimilate, but on my own terms and ambivalently. I didn't give up my singsong, my gesticulating, my haggling, my appetite. I don't think I ever fooled anyone but myself.

So when it came to writing about Degas, I simply didn't notice his anti-Semitism. I excised from my mind the anti-Semitic facts of his life, the many references in the literature to his hatred of Jews: for example, Camille Pissarro, an impressionist painter who was a Jew, casually referring to him as that "ferocious anti-Semite."[17] I never even wrote about his overtly anti-Semitic *At the Stock Exchange* (Fig. 2).[18] In a corner of a bargaining hall which has thick, square, marble, interior supports and a floor littered with pieces of paper, a group of men in dark coats and top hats peer over each other's shoulders at a thin scroll of white paper held by one of them with what presumably is the value of a commodity. The central figure has a red beard and moustache and an unmistakably long, curving, and pointy nose. In the left-hand corner, a nasty twosome with similarly caricatured features scheme. In the painting, grasping, grabbing hands proliferate, reaching for shoulders, clutching pieces of paper, writing furiously. If this picture doesn't equate secretive, clever, and vulgar financial scheming with "Jew," then I've never seen a picture that does.

In my book, *Looking into Degas: Uneasy Images of Women and Modern Life,* I dealt with paintings, drawings, and prints of ballet dancers, washerwomen, milliners, and prostitutes. I wrote from the position of a Marxist and a feminist. I analyzed the relationship between a near-aristocratic man like Degas and his working-class female subjects. That is, I detailed how he transformed his class and psychological experience—which I often noted was a mixture of contempt and admiration toward these women—into pictures. I was particularly interested in Degas' bather paintings, which I interpreted as transformations of a prostitutional motif. Women in government-surveyed brothels were required to wash between customers to prevent the spread of sexually transmitted disease. Degas even occasionally drew the women bathing in front of their customers.

The details of these pictures varied slightly. The contents were some mixture of a towel, water pitcher, and basin, plush chaise longue or easy chair, occasionally a maid tendering a luxurious towel or vigorously brushing the bather's hair or offering a steaming hot chocolate. I was drawn by the pleasure of the pictures: women's bodies cared for and caressed, sometimes by themselves, sometimes by others; the delights of wildly mingled colors— pink-oranges against salmon against silver-blue, greens speckled with rose; cramped, compressed spaces where swirling lines, curves, and angles met. How Degas could miraculously transform the traces of pastel excess and their unsteady path across the paper into forms my eye desired!

There was a painting, however, which bore evident similarities to the bathers, but which I assiduously avoided. Not that I didn't look at it and wonder about it, but I always stopped short of writing about it. Titled *The Pedicure* (Fig. 3), it represents a little girl seated on a daybed in a child's room, a rich child's room. She is wrapped in a sheet out of which protrudes one little hand and one leg from the knee down. The pedicurist is partly hidden by a spindle-backed, straw-bottomed chair that in turn is obscured by another white sheet on which the girl's leg rests. In the background is a dresser on which is a small water pitcher and bowl, and this is abutted by one end of the daybed, at the corner of which some garments hang, presumably what the little girl was wearing before she undressed for her pedicure. In the bottom right corner of the picture is a large washbasin.

Figure 2. *At the Stock Exchange,* by Edgar Degas, 1879. Musée d'Orsay, Paris. © Photo R. M. N. (Réunion des Musées Nationaux).

The Pedicure is a suggestive and muted painting. The washbasin and removed clothing plus the little girl's languor, even stupor, suggest vulnerability. Though nothing precisely threatening is happening, an atmosphere of malaise pervades the canvas.

Another provocative painting of Degas' that I ignored is called alternately *The Interior* and *Rape* (Fig. 4). It is a puzzling nocturnal picture with a man in

Figure 3. *The Pedicure,* by Edgar Degas, 1873. Musée d'Orsay, Paris. © Photo R. M. N. (Réunion des Musées Nationaux).

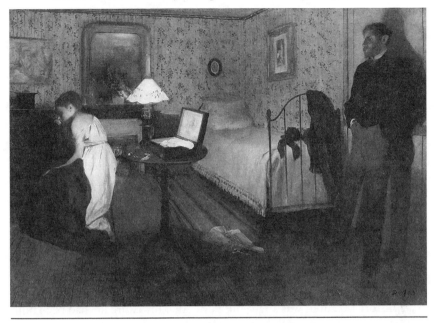

Figure 4. *Interior* or *Rape,* by Edgar Degas, ca. 1868–69. Philadelphia Museum of Art: The Henry P. McIlhenny Collection in memory of Frances P. McIlhenny.

shadow leaning against the door of a bedroom, his legs spread, his hands in his pockets. Across an eerily lighted room sits a woman, who like the man is partly in shadow; she is three-quarters turned away from us. Her white chemise slips off her left shoulder; on her lap she holds some sort of covering; her other hand supports her face. Between the man and the woman is a shimmering, silken bed with iron bedstead, across which is thrown what looks like a woman's street clothes. A corset lies on the floor. A small, round, wooden end table is near the middle of the painting with a lighted, shaded lamp and open vanity box or small suitcase. It is a hot painting, and a mean painting. Both psychological and physical danger pulsate in it.

These works would seem to have fitted easily into my consideration of Degas' art. Class issues are formative in them, and the style is the realist one that interested me all my professional life. I think now that I avoided these paintings because they reminded me too much of *The Doctor* by Luke Fildes, the painting that had so riveted me as a child in Hurleyville. In fact, the stylistic and literal similarities between *Rape* and *The Doctor* are breathtaking: the almost identical diagonals of the beds in each; the nearly interchangeable pose of the seated figures both resembling Rodin's *Thinker;* the table with particularized and emotion-laden objects, the triangular lampshades. A major emotional difference, however, is that the sad but powerful doctor in one is transformed into a vulnerable woman in the other.

The Pedicure and *Rape*, like Fildes' *The Doctor*, show a man and a woman, or girl, together. The women are in jeopardy; death, violation, destruction are possible in all three works. I now believe that I became an art historian because I happened on a picture onto which I projected my deepest terrors. I hid *and* sublimated my fright in this painting. It is where I buried the Holocaust. Is it mere coincidence that this solace also became the form of my assimilation?

I made the subject of my work as an art historian the contempt and admiration that rich and powerful men felt toward the working classes and women. I wrote about laundresses, dancers, milliners, prostitutes. I knew that I had experienced those feelings both as a woman *and* as a person with working-class roots in a field of men who were largely upper class or at least upper middle class and Ivy League educated. It never occurred to me that I had experienced *as a Jew* both the contempt and admiration I attributed to Degas' attitude toward women. Nor that I repressed and sublimated those feelings into the socially aware and angry observations I made as a feminist and Marxist. But, that is what I did. I do not mean to say that I was treated poorly in art history because I was a Jew, but rather that my entire life had been built around fears associated with being Jewish.

What might writing as a Jewish art historian look like? We know something about what writing as a woman is.[19] But as a Jew? It might be something like this:

I've always had secret loves in paintings, rather like the pornographic fantasies you never tell anyone for shame. My embarrassment is liking something I construe—and I'm afraid others will—as sentimental and nostalgic. I fear that trusting the pleasures of the past, savoring them, can only get me into trouble. I hear the injunction to move on, don't look back, don't hold onto the past. Or, if you must remember, think about betrayal and abandonment, not pleasure. Otherwise everything will be snatched away from you.

The Hermitage at Pontoise (Fig. 5), by Camille Pissarro, is the first picture you see when you walk into the Thannhauser Collection at the Guggenheim Museum in New York. It's a big green painting inflected with gold, white, and brown. There are solid mauve square houses along a road which mounts the center of the picture. People chat along the path. The green has more yellow than black in it; it's a sunny, friendly green. The mauve is more white than brown. Pissarro has chosen a tranquil, ordinary moment for his painting.

I love the painting, as I do others like it—big, lush landscapes with neither beginning nor end. It enfolds me, draws me in; it loves the road and the quiet joy people can take in each other's company. I see in this picture an emphasis on community and social intercourse. I suppose you could call it French. Or you could call it Jewish. There are peasants in landscapes by Constable and Corot, but they are small and socially inconsequential

Figure 5. *The Hermitage at Pontoise,* by Camille Pissarro, ca. 1867. Solomon R. Guggenheim Museum, New York, Thannhauser Collection. Photo: David Heald, © The Solomon R. Guggenheim Foundation, New York.

figures; they are used only as spots of color. But in Pissarro the figures are important. You can imagine them, a piece of their lives, even the words they speak to each other.

I am reminded here of something Emmanuel Lévinas wrote in *Difficult Freedom: Essays on Judaism:* "The banal fact of conversation . . . quits the order of violence. This banal fact is the marvel of marvels. To speak, at the same time as knowing the Other, is making oneself known to him. The Other is not only known, but he is greeted."[20] This happens in Pissarro's paintings even when the figures are tiny; it does not happen in Monet. Lévinas thinks this conversation, this looking in the face, as he terms it, is quintessentially Jewish. He continues in the same essay:

> The face, for its part, is inviolable; those eyes, which are absolutely without protection, the most naked part of the human body, none the less offer an absolute resistance to possession, an absolute resistance in which the temptation to murder is inscribed: the temptation of absolute negation. The Other is the only being that one can be tempted to kill. This temptation to murder and this impossibility of murder constitute the very vision of the face. To see a face is already to hear "You shall not kill. . . ."[21]

Perhaps this is too much to say about a mere landscape, but I do feel within Pissarro's painting a valuing of human life. And Pissarro happens to have been a Jew. Did I "know" that?

Historically, Jews haven't owned land, although my grandparents did. Was there something about being in America that gave them the idea that they could? And something perhaps in France that said the same to Pissarro? France, after all, had a reputation of being good to Jews. Until Dreyfus. And this painting by Pissarro was done nearly thirty years before the Dreyfus affair.

And the Hurleyville of my childhood? The town, the hill, the people, the sense of community. The Jews. Even if I didn't think about it, I knew who was Jewish and who wasn't, even when I was five years old. Also, I had such a longing to cross the street and climb the hill behind the house where Pearl, the gentile girl, lived. Actually, it resembled a hill like the one in another Pissarro painting, the one called *Jallais Hill, Pontoise.*[22] Then one time when I did climb it with some friends, we stumbled on spectacular views which we never, never found again, mythical views which never can be found again. Does it matter that the hill was behind the house of a Gentile?

I married a Jew, two actually. I became an expert in a field peopled with Jews. I have lived in New York all my life; even when I should have left to get a better job, I never could. I see now that I couldn't tolerate being treated as an outsider. I wanted to live in a world in which being Jewish is normal. So I stayed in New York. I lived where it was safe. I didn't want to pay attention. Jewish? Yes, but let's not talk about it. Get educated, marry up, develop good taste—in everything from food, to clothes, to art. And yet I have the distinct feeling that I passed.

Well, all that is over now.

NOTES

Many, many thanks to my friends Carol Zemel, James Saslow, and Diana Linden for their interest and suggestions.

1. Linda Nochlin, "Degas and the Dreyfus Affair: A Portrait of the Artist as an Anti-Semite," in *The Dreyfus Affair: Art, Truth, and Justice,* ed. Norman Kleeblatt, 96–116 (Berkeley: University of California Press, 1988).

2. Letty Cottin Pogrebin, *Deborah, Golda, and Me: Being Female and Jewish in America* (New York: Crown Publishers, 1991), 146.

3. Walter Friedlaender, *From David to Delacroix,* trans. Robert Goldwater (1930; Cambridge, Mass.: Harvard University Press, 1952), 113.

4. Robert Rosenblum, *Cubism and Twentieth-Century Art* (New York: Harry N. Abrams, 1960), 60.

5. Meyer Schapiro, *Van Gogh* (New York: Harry N. Abrams, 1950), 98.

6. Erwin Panofsky, "The Neoplatonic Movement in Florence and North Italy (Bandinelli and Titian)," *Studies in Iconology: Humanistic Themes in the Art of the Renaissance* (1939; New York: Harper and Row, Publishers, 1962), 155.

7. Linda Seidel, "Jan van Eyck's 'Arnolfini Portrait': Business as Usual?" *Critical Inquiry* 16 (Autumn 1989): 67–68.

8. Schapiro, "The Nature of Abstract Art," *Modern Art: 19th and 20th Centuries: Selected Papers* (1937; New York: George Braziller, 1978), 192.

9. Ambroise Vollard, *Paul Cézanne*, trans. H.L. Van Doren (London: Brentano's, 1924), 117.

10. Nochlin, "Why Have There Been No Great Women Artists?" *Women, Art, and Power and Other Essays* (1971; New York: Harper and Row, Publishers, 1988), 153, 150.

11. Carol Duncan, "Virility and Domination in Early Twentieth-Century Van-guard Painting," in *Feminism and Art History: Questioning the Litany*, ed. Norma Broude and Mary D. Garrard (1973; New York: Harper and Row, Publishers, 1982), 297.

12. Duncan, "Virility and Domination," 308.

13. James Saslow, letter to me, January 23, 1993.

14. Saslow, letter, January 23, 1993.

15. Paul Johnson, *A History of the Jews* (New York: Perennial Library, 1988), 154.

16. Walter Benjamin, "Thesis on the Philosophy of History," *Illuminations,* trans. Harry Zohn, ed. Hannah Arendt (1940; New York: Schocken Books, 1969), 256.

17. Camille Pissarro, letter to his son, Lucien, January 21, 1898; reprinted in Camille Pissarro, *Letters to his Son Lucien,* ed. John Rewald, with assistance of Lucien Pissarro (Santa Barbara, Calif.: Peregrine Smith, 1981), 409.

18. Linda Nochlin brilliantly analyzes this picture in "Degas and the Dreyfus Affair," 99–101.

19. Nochlin, for example, in her astonishing article "Courbet's Real Allegory: Reading the Painter's Studio," writes, "For me, reading as a woman . . . , the Irish beggar woman constitutes not just a dark note of negativity within the bright Utopian promise of the allegory of the *Painter's Studio* as a whole but, rather, a negation of the entire promise. . . . Figuring all that is unassimilable and inexplicable—female, poor, mother, passive, unproductive but reproductive—she denies and negates all the male-dominated productive energy of the central portion." See "Courbet's Real Allegory: Reading the Painter's Studio," in *Courbet Reconsidered,* ed. Sarah Faunce and Linda Nochlin (New York: Brooklyn Museum, 1988), 27.

See also Eunice Lipton, *Alias Olympia: A Woman's Search for Manet's Notorious Model and Her Own Desire* (New York: Charles Scribner's Sons, 1992) for an interpre-tation which puts the author's feminine subjectivity at the center of the story.

20. Emmanuel Lévinas, *Difficult Freedom: Essays in Judaism,* trans. Sean Hand (1963 and 1976; Baltimore: Johns Hopkins University Press, 1990), 7.

21. Lévinas, *Difficult Freedom,* 8.

22. *Jallais Hill, Pontoise,* by Pissarro, is located in the Metropolitan Museum of Art and was painted in 1867.

18

The "Jew" as "Postmodern":
A Personal Report

Raphael Sassower

I

Having lived a dual life in two different cultures—an Israeli *sabra* with German roots and a naturalized American who emigrated from Israel—I have always been at the "margins."[1] But until quite recently I have thought of my experiences in psychological and personal terms only, never connecting them with my academic life. Of course there has been the occasional intersection of the personal and the public, such as making a "political statement" not to attend or hold classes on Jewish holidays; but that posture was more an act of ethnic "duty" than a portrayal of the connection between heritage and professional aspiration. What happened to change this situation?

I remember walking up the stairs with this bearded Jewish professor who had just been hired, with much fanfare, in the English department. While he was being interviewed a couple of months earlier, I was asked by the vice chancellor for academic affairs to speak to this candidate because he was interested in meeting Jewish faculty members. Since the choices on our campus are so limited, I became the token Jew. I told him whatever I knew about Jewish life in Colorado Springs, which was not much, and suggested he talk to my (then) wife, who was a cantor in Denver. Having accepted the job, he now was inviting me, the Jew from the philosophy department, to have coffee with him. (How New Yorkish of him; in Colorado we drink more healthful stuff, so I am told.) We climb the stairs, find a corner table overlooking Pike's Peak, and without missing a beat he turns to me and asks: "What do you think of the hyphen problem?" My English is not so poor that I am unable to comprehend a simple question (even though the editor of this volume has corrected my writing accent liberally), but this one seemed awfully strange to me. "What hyphen problem are you talking about?" I asked, trying to buy some time and not appear ignorant in the eyes of this recent arrival from UCLA. "Well," he said generously, "American–Jewish."

I looked at him with complete amazement, as if the mere fact that both of us are Jewish should in itself suffice, first, for us to know what the hyphen problem is, and second, for us actually to care about it. We discussed some examples from other ethnic minorities, examined the Pollard case, in which espionage for Israel was read as allegiance to Israel, overriding loyalty to the United States, and shared many other stories and cases. For the first time I was confronted with someone for whom personal identity had become an intellectual preoccupation; he even initiated an entire scholarly debate to which this chapter is a contribution.

As an Israeli I was aware that my Jewishness was taken for granted, so much so that I did not have to attend synagogue. The school system took care of our religious education, and the entire state holiday calendar ensured that we celebrated—that is, went to the beach on—all religious holidays. If anything, I was much more concerned about hiding my German identity, being ashamed of my parents' accents and their poor Hebrew. I was an Israeli first and foremost and Jewish only in a minimalist sense. We had Friday night dinners, but they seemed more a social event and a family ritual of control (you cannot go out till after dinner). Yes, we said the Shabbat prayer, but the trick was to see how fast it could be recited, not how well or with how much devotion.

When I immigrated to the United States I was "wearing many hats," and none of them prepared me for or shielded me from what happened. I was an Israeli who spoke English with a bit of a British accent (because my teachers in Israel were trained during the British mandate); I was a son of German-born parents who immigrated to Palestine; I was a nonpracticing Jew; and I was an immigrant with a green card and a student ID. No wonder that I was totally confused when at a college dance one of the "girls" I asked out did not accept my overture because I was Jewish. Would it have been more reassuring if she had told me the reason was that I was from Israel? Or that I had a funny accent? For a while I even enjoyed toying with the alternative narratives that were offered on my behalf by other classmates: he is Spanish, he is an Italian Catholic, he is French. Why did they provide these constructions? Was it because they genuinely were at a loss in placing my accent? Or was it because they liked me and wanted me to be something other than Jewish? Regardless of the "reasons," somehow all these constructs collapsed, and my Jewishness, even more than my Israeli background, began to draw my attention directly.

I recall a studio sculpture class in which one of the students told a microwave joke concerning the "cooking" of Jews. At first I did not know what to say: what is the proper response? Then I realized that I should say something, that it was my duty to speak up. I, of all people, the newcomer, the foreigner, the one with the broken English, who still takes notes in Hebrew. I turned to her and said: "This is an anti-Semitic joke." She apologized, began to cry, and left the studio. The rest of the class was quiet. They all remembered that they too had laughed just a minute ago.

As an Israeli I was invited to speak before the local Rotary Club. I sat at the president's table to have lunch before my talk. The president turned to me and said: "Don't you think these Jews who live in Highland Park seclude themselves from the rest of the North Shore?" At least I knew some of the facts by then, and I answered: "No, not really. It is because of restrictions that were put on them and prevented them from buying homes in all the other suburbs that they found few places where they could live." He turned his head away and began a conversation with the man on his other side. What was amazing to me was not his comment or his insensitivity or even his outright anti-Semitism; instead, it was the way in which he separated my identity as a Jew and an Israeli—a well-founded separation because there are Christian Israelis and Muslim Israelis, but a separation that for him undoubtedly meant something different. For him the diaspora Jew is different from the Israeli, and here, too, I would have to agree. But what he missed, of course, is the simple fact that despite the differences between the diaspora Jew and the Israeli—as Philip Roth so well documents—they are still relatives who have enough affinities to defend each other in misery and expect sympathy from each other.

As you can tell by now, the hyphen question is contextualized differently for me and for the "standard" bearded college professor who is born in New York and puzzles over his Jewishness on the way to a bagel-and-lox brunch. I have to worry about too many hyphens at once, and this situation cannot be illustrated in a properly constructed English sentence. So, in order to avoid this grammatical (read: ethnic-psychological) problem, I ignored my hyphens as much as I could and immersed myself in my abstract-intellectual pursuits. Or, if I did not completely avoid the issue, I felt a certain urgency in not embracing any specific category; that is, I remained *on* the hyphens themselves, balancing my "act" as I interacted with my sociocultural environment. But avoidance was not as successful as I hoped it would be; there were the occasional encounters that reminded me of who I am or might be perceived to be. Half the professors in my department in graduate school were Jewish; one of my graduate colleagues was an Israeli; and yet when I suggested we cancel classes on the Jewish holidays for political reasons, I was overruled by my Marxist-Jewish professor. In fact, my doctoral defense was scheduled for the eve of Yom Kippur (by my three readers, all of whom were Jewish).

Chicago and Boston were congenial environments for hyphen-laden individuals, at least in the sense of being more sophisticated cities where one could partly "blend" in. Living under these conditions did not resolve questions about my identity, but any resolution did not seem urgent there. In Colorado Springs, by contrast, the situation is different. Two changes happened simultaneously. First, there was such a majority of white Christian faces that I felt completely isolated, and second, I became interested in postmodernism.

II

I arrived at the gates of "postmodernism" quite late, in a fourth intellectual wave of my career, having studied philosophy for a decade—first, of science;

second, of economics; and third, of medicine. In some uncanny way, I found (not just rediscovered) my Jewishness in postmodernism, and especially in the writings of Jean-François Lyotard. "Found" here means I became aware of certain connections that go beyond personal confessions or their anecdotal renderings. Emotions can be sublimated, but ideas need explicit statement to be argued away before their importance can be overlooked. It is not only that Lyotard intersperses his work with "jewish" (lower case for him) examples, but that he understands the concept of "jews" to be an exemplar of what a postmodern orientation signifies: the defiance of a unified characterization or representation. As he says:

> I write "the jews" this way neither out of prudence nor lack of something better. I use lower case to indicate that I am not thinking of a nation. I make it plural to signify that it is neither a figure nor a political (Zionism), religious (Judaism), or philosophical (Jewish philosophy) subject that I put forward under this name. I use quotation marks to avoid confusing these "jews" with real Jews. What is most real about the real Jews is that Europe, in any case, does not know what to do with them: Christians demand their conversion; monarchs expel them; republics assimilate them; Nazis exterminate them. "The jews" are the object of a dismissal with which Jews, in particular, are afflicted in reality.[2]

Reading these lines, I feel that Lyotard is talking to me and at the same time talking about me and about my tribal family. To use his terminology, I wondered whether I am a "real Jew" or a "jew." I realized that questions about my identity are not limited to psychological preoccupations, but are quite interesting intellectually as well. My "jewishness" is emerging through my academic life, not so much with encounters with other American-Jewish or American-jewish colleagues, but with texts that presumably have nothing to do with Jewishness proper. If to be jewish is going to be meaningful to me, then it has to be expressed, debated, and analyzed philosophically; it is not just going to a synagogue or eating properly prepared foods or making little comments in Yiddish. And unexpectedly, while seeking my Identity, I found that Lyotard has provided the nexus in which I reconsidered my identity.

The emerging connection—between a personal sense of being a secular, cultural Jew and a professional academic life where being a "jew" is tantamount to being *an* "other"—raises some interesting questions. For example: has the migration from Israel to America heightened a sense of cultural alienation that licenses me to have a different perspective on American culture and on the Jews within that culture? As some of the stories above illustrate, the answer to this question (though I did not know it at the time) follows Lyotard: I see the American-Jew as an "other," but not in the way seen by an established, well-situated WASP (like my Rotary host). It is the otherness of a tradition "where the soul's only concern is with terror without origin, where it tries desperately, humorously to originate itself by narrating itself," perhaps because of the "absence of accumulation of experience" or because this tradition "neglects the world except with regards to its pain" (28).

Lyotard does not present the "other" as pathetic; the otherness of the jews is not a source for pity or for self-pity, but rather, for me, an occasion to consider the different perspective into which I have fallen by tradition, and not by personal circumstance alone. Perhaps living in the American diaspora, as opposed to a European or even an Israeli diaspora (regardless of nationalist verbiage, claims for homeland, and the like), forced me to reconsider my identity in ways I would not have otherwise; perhaps the American "experience" conditioned my concern for the other as a difference. The difference— of the "jews" or of their perspective—is persistent, in Lyotard's terms: "One converts the Jews in the Middle Ages, they resist by mental restriction. One expels them during the classical age, they return. One integrates them in the modern era, they persist in their difference. One exterminates them in the twentieth century" (23).

Lyotard argues convincingly that there is a price to be paid for persistent difference: extermination. But, if that price is not exacted, there is an opportunity for the Jews to use their difference. That is, the difference of the outsider can illuminate problems and ambiguities, raise questions about issues that have been taken for granted, criticize the received notions, or even suggest alternative modes of behaving and/or thinking. This is why the Nazi hates the Jew and this is, exactly, why Simmel and Lyotard appreciate the jew.

Incidentally, I perceive this orientation to be the guiding theme of the attitude of the postmodern condition, namely, one of great skepticism toward the "totality" of discourses, their terror of power and authority, their claim for Truth and substantiated grounding. In merging the otherness of jews and the postmodern suspicion of any "grand-narratives" that pretend to explain the status quo (while quite often ending in a justification of it or in shielding it), I would suggest that my own sense of marginalization can be transformed into a vantage point from which to observe and judge differently.

I should probably clarify an intellectual chronology that may be puzzling at this juncture. My identity was confusing to myself and to others, my studies were shifting from Marx and Popper toward postmodernism, from two quite different foundationalist critiques to a critique of foundationalism. In this process of intellectual maturation I felt comfortable with intellectual alienation and marginalization as a mode of critique and as an orientation. Only after reading Lyotard's passages (quoted above) did I begin to realize (I hope) that the intellectual quest and its resolution has a psychological dimension and a personal one too: it is intellectual-psychological-existential. I would even venture to say that with the Lyotardian vocabulary of postmodernism I have felt more empowered than with that of the Marxists or Popperians and definitely more than with that of the Jews or of any other views around. This suggests that postmodernism gave me some answers about my own jewish (read: marginal-because-critical) identity.

Having suggested that the prescriptions of postmodernity are appealing to me not only on an intellectual level but on a personal-existential level as well, those of multiplicities of voices and interpretations, of differences and delegitimations, I may ponder the following counterintuitive question: Does the American context provide the jew a more hospitable cultural environment (of postmodernity) than the one found in Israel? Israel definitely gives the impression to its citizenry and the rest of the world that it is a monolithic society, where non-Jews are so segregated and marginalized that they can be completely ignored, except when unrest occurs, such as the Intifada uprising. America, by contrast, is viewed by Americans and the world as an unwieldly agglomeration of ethnic minorites, none of which "represents" the American people or its culture. The foreigner knows about the "typical" midwestern, WASPish, heterosexual farmer, but also about the African-American basketball superstar Michael Jordan and the Catholic entertainer Madonna. It seems that the "American" is difficult to characterize, whereas the "Israeli" is relatively easy to characterize as a notorious, mythical *sabra* (native Israeli, meaning "cactus fruit"), prickly on the outside but sweet on the inside.

Two disclaimers come to the forefront at this juncture. First, the conception of outsiders has been an ongoing theme in the different waves of immigration to Israel since before the turn of this century, so no matter how homogeneous Israeli society may appear to an outside observer, it has suffered the pains of integration and discrimination for almost a century. In this respect, then, there is a family resemblance between the American and the Israeli experiences; moreover, in both cases the indigenous people (in Israel's case both the local Muslim and Jewish populations) have been marginalized by a newly formed society and culture. Second, I am fully aware that setting up the binary of outside and inside is problematic and that such a binary presumes too much about a cohesive inside and a fragmented outside. Yet this mode of speaking is defensible if only because there is such a thing as a dominant culture in America, one that adopts the language of postindustrialist corporate capitalism, one that endorses a Christian ideology and a certain set of rugged-individualist values. All these facets of the culture are expressed daily in films and advertisements, in congressional hearings and presidential campaigns.

Postmodernism is a label attached to too many "items" without discrimination, and this, after all, is not such a bad idea. Scholars would like us to define the term narrowly and apply it carefully if and only if all the predetermined criteria have been met. But the term "postmodernism" is too open-ended to be turned into yet another petrified category. Historians have tried to kill it by articulating it in terms of a chronology (something against which Lyotard warns). Architects and art historians have tried to use the historical record to establish set criteria of demarcation. Literary critics have tried to rehabilitate texts through the deconstruction and reconstruction of meanings and of interpretations, so as to justify their involvement with postmodernism. And anyone who does not quite know how to explain a work or an idea comes up, as a last-ditch effort, with the reassurance that the work or idea in question is postmodern. Even when postmodernism is being used and abused so much, some of its insights are bound to remain in our cultural consciousness. (The best anthology on postmodernism, incidentally, is Hoesterey's *Zeitgeist in Babel: The Postmodernist Controversy.*)

In fact the American environment is postmodern—in the sense of "a patchwork of language pragmatics that vibrate at all times," as Lyotard calls it; and it does not have a "history" in the sense of a heritage and commitments, as Baudrillard suggests;[3] and so it can provide a more hospitable environment for the outsider, the foreigner, the other. The issue of alienation mentioned above thus happily recedes to the background or is at least transformed into that of a negotiated reciprocity between insider and outsider, each trying to legitimate his or her respective vantage point. Perhaps only in America can the outsider get away with being an outsider and even be allowed—not to say invited—to criticize the inside and be heard. But is this view overly optimistic? Do Jews have a "home" altogether?

> "The jews" are the irremissible in the West's movement of remission and pardon. They are what cannot be domesticated in the obsession to dominate, in the compulsion to control domain, in the passion for empire, recurrent ever since Hellenistic Greece and Christian Rome. "The jews," never at home wherever they are, cannot be integrated, converted, or expelled. They are also always away from home when they are at home, in their so-called own tradition, because it incudes exodus as its beginning, excision, impropriety, and respect for the forgotten.[4]

I take postmodernism to be an attitude, a frame of mind, some sort of jewish orientation. In this respect, its value is in its ability to help one to "get going," figure out how to proceed. What is disappointing to most about postmodernism is that it does not provide one with specific answers, only with a multiplicity and an order of significance of questions. It is supposed to lack any foundation whatsoever, but in fact it provides a multiplicity of tentative foundations constitutive of particular contexts. The postmodern condition is thus shifty and puzzling, and to the seeker of ultimate foundation it is alas frustrating. So, what's new? Even the most revered of Jewish texts and documents have never been fully taken up as the "last word." If hermeneutics means anything, as so many commentators now agree, it is what it has meant for millennia of talmudic disputations and scholarship (see, for example, a page of Derrida's *Glas*).[5] According to Jewish tradition, even the word of God—*particularly* the word of God—is open to reinterpretation, because we, mere mortals, cannot fully comprehend his word; we need intermediaries and translators who interpret for us, who explain, deconstruct, and reconstruct to fit a situation, a particular context.

Lyotard makes much of this ongoing Jewish debate over texts in contexts when he examines the moral prescription concerning murder (in his discussion of justice), and shows that, while the Christian Orthodoxy remains rigid and strict, the Jewish Orthodoxy accounts for circumstances under which murder takes on a whole different meaning, such as the entire range from assault to self-defense.[6] Here I am, having forgotten my Talmud lessons from high school, being so unreligious as not to care about what the Jewish tradition says about murder, and here is Lyotard, that postmodern hero of mine with whom I have a continuing dispute over the status of scientific discourse, who all of a sudden points out to me that the Jews have a sophistication of analysis, a recognition of subtlety, superior to that of their Christian counterparts. Now, what is his point? Is he a Jew who is trying to add new prestige and luster to a minor literature?[7] This is, after all, what Deleuze and Guattari do when they call Kafka and Kafka's otherness and, by implication, his Jewishness a minor literature.[8] Or is he (Lyotard) merely using Jewish law as an example for his argument about judging everything only *ad hoc*, "case-by-case"? Is the Jew, according to this reading, the ultimate postmodern or the ultimate person engulfed in the "postmodern condition," the one whose difference is threatened in the name of tolerance?

> I do not intend to stir up hatred, but to respect and make understood the differend. . . . Today, hatred comes softly as integration of "the jews" into a permissive collectivity in the name of the "respect for differences," well known and recognized, between the "ethnocultural" components of what remains of the old modern nations.[9]

III

As I read and reread these Lyotardian texts I am provoked to read Levinas. But I refuse, because Levinas is a Jewish theologian who is grouped with the deconstructionists and poststructuralists and postmodernists, not a critic who happens to be Jewish (he is "out," he is Jewish with a vengeance and identifiably so, because he has an explicitly Jewish research program). The Lyotardian texts are all the more fascinating because of their duplicity and disguise; they illustrate themselves without being blatantly identifiable. They provide the medium that Derrida insists on (following the tradition to which a range of semioticians belongs, from Peirce to Eco), one wherein the reader has an opportunity to bring together previous experiences and knowledge with whatever may be offered in the text. Reading Lyotard, then, is a hyphenated experience for me, where ambiguities are reintroduced and where no answer clearly imposes itself.

I am reminded, too, of my sense of what it is to be an ethnic-cultural jew as opposed to a religious-observant Jew; of how I tried to present these distinctions to the Hungarian novelist and intellectual George Konrad when he visited Colorado; and of how he was quite puzzled that a distinction could signify and have a particular significance. Perhaps it is the ongoing problem of identity imposed on Jews by emancipation ever since the Exodus from Egypt and the growth and change of the Jewish diaspora, one whereby the attraction of the German *Bildung* and Enlightenment[10] turned into a European sense of *Angst* that has become Americanized. (This is why Jewish novelists, for example, have impressed Christian America.) The American flavor one adds to *Angst* is anger, the anger of outsiders and minorities, however they define their subcultures. One may argue that this Americanized anger differs from its European counterpart because disappointment over the promise of equality and absorption is linked in America to a Constitution and Bill of Rights and does not depend solely on the benevolence of monarchs (even when such benevolence is traced to the Code Napoléon). This anger, as one of my teachers once told me, should not be lost or given up. It is an anger one can use productively to stimulate debates and bring about change, or if these two options do not materialize, it is an anger that sustains one in a position from which cooption is untenable.

When I reconsider Lyotard's sense of otherness and the jewish tradition and add to it the anger of missing the Promised Land (here, in America), I think of the relations between Jews and Christians and Muslims, and the extent to which the Jews were always considered different, a minority, and always under siege. The Jew/jew was a threat by mere existence: in the difference lies the potential for improvement, and in the potential for improvement lies the threat to the hegemony of the dominant culture. Even when the Jews do nothing, there is a critique and a threat of the jews by their mere hanging around. Thus I see Lyotard's (and Derrida's for that matter) play with the notion of "*differance*" as a reincarnation of the Jewish experience after the establishment of the Jewish people as a diaspora with no home since the destruction of the second temple in A.D. 70.[11] (Homeless cosmopolitans without passports, Stalin called them.)

But with this realization comes a heavy duty and sometimes a dear price. Perhaps the Holocaust is an extreme price paid only every two millennia or so; perhaps pogroms and anti-Jewish and anti-Semitic incidents are costs more common and much easier to tolerate. This is not to say that because the Holocaust is a unique "cost" it does not figure into our cultural calculations concerning identity; on the contrary, the extreme proportions of the Holocaust are such that they must be recognized and foregrounded and can never be dismissed. As such, the Holocaust must figure prominently into the loose definition of an ethnic-cultural jew. Acknowledging one's history as constitutive of one's identity, the jew has a duty to be a critic of one's society. Once again, the role of the Jew/jew as critic in Israel may be more difficult to play because everyone wears this hat, even if it comes in different sizes and shapes and colors. Perhaps in Israel it is the minority non-Jew who has the role of the jew. As to the American-jew, and regardless of European precedence, especially in Germany of the previous and present centuries,[12] it seems that the Jew as a jew may have more opportunities to be a critic because the status of the other is granted often quite willingly. But what should be criticized?

In a word, everything. When there is a debate on abortion, the binary of "pro-life" and "pro-choice" has to be interrupted by the critic who knows all the qualifications and modifications that Jewish law guarantees a pregnant woman. In some bizarre way, these allowances are more liberal than can be expected from a religious perspective. For example, a woman is permitted to have an abortion if she argues that her mental welfare (not to mention her physical welfare) is in danger if she carries the fetus to term. So, psychoanalysis is not the invention of Freud or the refuge of his contemporaneous Jewish doctors in Europe who could not get civil-servant jobs in the Austro-Hungarian Empire, as Thomas Szasz shows,[13] but an ancient talmudic appreciation of social ills and personal pain.

The jew, be she or he a real Jew or not, is a critic by tradition, and at times by default: it comes with the territory. It is a dirty job, as they say, but someone has to do it. Perhaps the jew is more qualified than many others having a tradition, an accumulated experience, and a need to justify being jewish to anyone who bothers to listen. To be a jew, then, is to be a critic; by the same token, to be a critic is to be jewish, no matter what other religious affiliations one holds onto. In this context I can also explain the affinity academic colleagues feel with each other (when they in fact engage in cultural critique), regardless of where they pray (if at all). This also explains the affinity I find almost inevitable between the anger of African-Americans, Hispanic-Americans, gay and lesbian Americans, and, yes, Jews. Yes, "the whole world is jewish," as the Jewish cliché goes, but here in a Lyotardian sense of lowercase jewish and in the sense of critique.

The jew as critic does not have to adopt Jewish law in order to present ideas and alternatives, especially since much of Jewish law is on the face of it sexist, racist, and homophobic. But this law, with all its problems and drawbacks, illustrates an agility of mind and a constant search for alternative answers to well-known questions and puzzles so that it may be fruitfully used as a model. As Lyotard argues convincingly:

> The fact that the sacred is dead is the very beginning of their Law. Expelled, doomed to exodus. Thus their hatred of geophilosophy. And the mother, language, failed, prostituted, which will have died in and through the eructation of Hitlerian will and the *Führung*. A mourning to be repeated over and over. Writing and rewriting according to this mourning.[14]

The critic must be imbued with the culture and yet feel enough distance, that is, feel both inside and outside at once—be a stranger—or feel so confused that the binary itself would be blurred. Both the literal and cultural language that is in use must still be a mystery, not a transparent tool with which to communicate. I still enjoy the occasional slip-of-tongue, the awkward rendering of a familiar cliché, and the ambiguities of emotive expressions, such as "I love you." To me all of these remain words whose comprehension takes time and effort; they resonate with meaning and ambiguity, almost with awe; yet they are simplistic as well, mere words in a foreign language. To be a minority or a foreigner in the land is to appreciate the territorialization of languages and to fight against this process[15]—a process, as indicated above, that through its claims for tolerance involves the dual activity of elevation and repression.

IV

One of the first stories I retold here is about my encounter with another Jewish professor, about the immediate affinity such an encounter with a *landsman*, a member of one's own tribe, produced, but an affinity that is nevertheless interlaced with suspicion and withdrawal. (Who does she or he think I am? Just because we are both Jewish does not mean a damn thing.) What does this narrative contain? What layers of meanings does it transfix and emanate? There is the momentary reassurance that one feels among friends and relatives, even those not so familiar; but there is always the underlying skepticism, cynicism, and irony: the last person I will trust is one of my own. But this story alludes to different things as well.

What does it mean to be an academic in America? Is Umberto Eco correct in his assertion that America is the only country where there is a division of labor between academics and militant culture?[16] And if this is the case, then into what group do we, Jewish academics, fall? Have we lost our militancy of the 1930s, when on both coasts Jews were at the forefront of union organizing, the Communist party, and all things radical? Have we lost our less radical but still revolutionary potential of the 1960s, with sit-ins and other forms of demonstration, where blacks and Jews and feminists marched together in a show of support and alliance? Have we become by the end of the twentieth century merely "tenured professors" (to borrow Galbraith's book title)? Or perhaps all too many of our crowd turned the other cheek and became reactionary militants of the sort that Norman Podhoretz represents. Perhaps we have lost touch with the unionizing, the political radicalism, and the grassroots organizing activities that were our mark of distinction in places like New York City, Chicago, and Los Angeles. Perhaps, to move alongside the upper middle class, we have sold our critical soul to the Republican ideals of lower taxes and supply-side economics. Perhaps the "we" has shifted from real Jews to Lyotard's jews. Have *we* become intellectually bankrupt?

Intellectual bankruptcy can be understood in various ways. It may mean having abandoned the ideals of justice and fairness, charity and modesty, on our way to economic security and upward mobility. It may mean establishing a detachment between "theory" and "practice" for those academics afraid to lose their promotion and tenure. It may also mean losing touch with the social issues that surfaced after World War II or after the 1960s, issues that refocused the question of integration and discrimination in American culture for groups such as African-Americans, Hispanic-Americans, and Asian-Americans, gays and lesbians and bisexuals. Pretending the Jewish phenomenon is unique in some sense prevents an appreciation of similarities that can bridge differences and create stronger political movements. (For example, is it conceivable that Jews can be racists? Alas, yes.)

Intellectual bankruptcy can also mean detachment from Jewish otherness or from jewishness, as understood earlier in postmodern, Lyotardian terms, that is, in the terms that inform the tradition of jews as critics. Not only are noncritical Jews not jewish, but also as academics they have no claims for intellectual status. One can evaluate, for instance, my concern with the bite and interest, the anger and desire, of jewish criticism in the case of Woody Allen. Woody Allen's *Sleeper* qualifies as social and cultural criticism "befitting" a jewish intellectual, while his later film *Husbands and Wives* is so self-indulgent in its self-doubt and melancholia that it is very Jewish but not sufficiently jewish.

My second little story had to do with growing up in Israel and the alienation I felt even in a "homeland." What was my mother's tongue? Literally it was German, not Hebrew, but it was Hebrew nonetheless in a figurative sense. Were my parents Israelis? Yes, according to their passport, but definitely not in their cultural self-understanding. My grandparents were born in Poland and Hungary, but both sets lived in Germany. My parents were both born in Germany but lived in Palestine-turned-Israel. I was born in Israel and live in America. And my daughters were born in America, but where will they live? The wandering Jew is not a phrase for me, but a reality. At times it bewilders me when people trace their family tree hundreds of years, or point to a house or a town and say that their family has lived there for generations. When I hear this, I feel an envy mixed with pity. I envy the pride that comes with such a statement, but I pity this pride for its expressed boredom: Who would want to be born and die in the same village? Who would not want to begin life anew when the opportunity arose? Who would want to accept a status quo even when it means settling for a unique hegemony?

Is it postmodern or jewish to move from country to country, to begin anew at certain junctures of one's existence, to count on one's immediate past only minimally, and to hold to an ancient tradition that teaches one to cherish the moment as well as one can because the future is so unpredictable? Perhaps my own experiences are postmodern—or is it ancient pre-premodern?— without reference to the term and its various interpretations; they are not modern in the sense of the Enlightenment or in the sense of a commitment to reason and rationality, or the advances of science and technology. That is, my experiences do not "fit" the teleological linear progression that leads to a "good life" or "happiness." Perhaps I "know" too much of my ancient tradition and the unexpectedness of misery and suffering.

As Lyotard says: "Postmodern knowledge is not simply a tool of the authorities; it refines our sensitivity to differences and reinforces our ability to tolerate the incommensurable."[17] Given the different cultures in which I have lived in my brief life, it is impossible not to be sensitive to differences or to remain intolerant of incommensurabilities. Lyotard also says: "Let us wage a war on totality; let us be witnesses to the unpresentable; let us activate the differences and save the honor of the name."[18] (I do not quite understand Lyotard's "witnessing the unpresentable," because both the Holocaust and the establishment of the state of Israel are in some sense unpresentable, and yet numerous attempts to articulate their significance have had some cultural impact even on non-Jews.) It is not merely tolerating differences, but also activating them—being fully engaged in them and celebrating their critical existence.

My third anecdote was about dating in America. This story illustrated how resistant American society may remain to any postmodern idea or ideal that embraces minorities. There are boundaries that are very hard to cross. For example, there are country clubs with ethnic-religious qualifications; they belong to a kind of segregation whose power defies all the Supreme Court edicts. And the fact that my Jewishness and my jewishness (both my genealogy and my critical attitude) may stand in the way of someone who would like to know me better hurts in many ways. Perhaps this dating scenario is the counterexample to everything for which postmodernism stands: tolerance is not part of the vocabulary!

The same goes for the fourth story about the anti-Semitic joke, one of many ethnic jokes that we will never stop hearing. What is the moral of this story? Are only Jewish comedians allowed to make fun of Jews? Are there ethical boundaries or rules of etiquette that must be obeyed? Can Woody Allen get away with character assassination, while Philip Roth may be ostracized by his kin-folk as a self-hating Jew? The postmodern condition should convince all of us that a multiplicity of interpretations is bound to unfold regarding any "story," no matter what the author's "intention" may have been. (The author's intention at times may signify but is never privileged.) Regardless of Philip Roth and Woody Allen, their stories are cultural artifacts that are open to interpretations, and one would hope they are of interest enough to all jews, not only to the diaspora-ghetto Jews in America.

The authority of the author is undermined in postmodern critiques so that the identity of the author becomes almost irrelevant. The Rotary Club anecdote becomes interesting in this context because, though I have focused on "my" identity and the way in which I have learned to appreciate it, it has also become clear from Lyotard's texts that this identity is illusive: how Jewish is my jewishness? This WASP spoke to me as if I had no identity or as if he mistook me for a hat (à la Oliver Sachs). He would not have confided in me had he realized who I was. Was his error pursuant to my ignorance of who I was? Or of my having had too many identities? Or perhaps he did not care who I was, or assumed at once too much and too little about my identity.

Encounters like this sharpen one's encounter with one's identity so that a "construction" becomes an urgent task to be undertaken immediately—the confrontation cries for action. And in emergency every inaction is an action of sorts.

My postmodern condition has seemed at times to be without foundations, but nowadays it seems to have a set of foundations, albeit tentative ones, that are formulated for particular purposes at distinct moments. It is neither a condition that I can cure nor one that I wish would disappear. It keeps me alert and emotionally alive; it requires that I answer "real" and painful questions about my identity all the time. So, on the question of being an American-Jew, I cannot fix an origin or a priority, because both categories are secondary, neither taking precedence over the other, neither being more fundamental or meaningful to my sense of self.

At best, then, I feel myself balancing on the hyphens themselves. The best I can do is balance myself somehow with the aid of the concept of jew; I feel alive when I balance myself along this myriad of hyphens with a critical vengeance that threatens imbalance. Perhaps living on the edges of so many hyphens is an enlightening experience, no matter how difficult and painful.

NOTES

I wish to thank Jeffrey Rubin-Dorsky for his continual probing into my identity and his encouragement of my efforts to connect that identity with my scholarly work. I am grateful to Joseph Agassi for his suggestive comments on a previous draft and to Cheryl Cole for her insightful criticism about the topic in general.

1. There is an entire sociological literature on the difference between the "stranger" and the "foreigner" with which I do not deal here at all, but which I presume as a backdrop for my own comments. For example, Georg Simmel claims that the stranger is "the person who comes today and stays tomorrow" in contrast with the foreigner, who comes today and leaves tomorrow (Georg Simmel *The Sociology of Georg Simmel*, trans. K. H. Wolff [New York: Free Press, 1950], 402). Alfred Schutz understands the stranger as "an adult individual of our times and civilization who tries to be permanently accepted or at least tolerated by the group which he approaches" (Alfred Schutz, *Collected Papers*, Vol. 2: *Studies in Social Theory* [The Hague: Martinus Nijhoff, 1964], 91). See also D. V. Segre, *The High Road and the Low* (New York: Allen Lane, 1974), 52–85.

2. Jean-François Lyotard, *Heidegger and "the jews,"* trans. A. Michel and M. Roberts (Minneapolis: University of Minnesota Press, 1990), 3. The subsequent page references in the text pertain to this source.

3. Jean-François Lyotard and Jean-Loup Thebaud, *Just Gaming*, trans. W. Godzich (Minneapolis: University of Minnesota Press, 1985), 94; Jean Baudrillard, *America*, trans. C. Turner (London: Verso, 1988).

4. Lyotard, *Heidegger and "the jews,"* 22.

5. Jacques Derrida, *Glas* (Paris: Editions Galilee, 1974).

6. For example, Lyotard and Thebaud, *Just Gaming*, 63.

7. The only direct reference concerning Lyotard's religious affilliation comes

from his introduction to a Vienna conference in 1989: "As a child, I was raised in Catholicism. It was of course 'a la francaise,' and I know Italy well enough to know that there are differences between Catholicisms" (Lyotard, *Political Writings,* trans. B. Readings and K. Paul [Minneapolis: University of Minnesota Press, 1993], 135). This reference itself is couched in ambiguity, for to be raised "in" Catholicism is not the same as to be raised "as" a Catholic or raised "to be" a Catholic. Is this just a poor translation or a deliberately confusing phrasing?

8. Gilles Deleuze and Felix Guattari, *Kafka: Toward a Minor Literature,* trans. D. Polan (Minneapolis: University of Minnesota Press, 1986).

9. Lyotard, *Heidegger and "the jews,"* 39.

10. George L. Mosse, *German Jews beyond Judaism* (Bloomington: Indiana University Press, 1985), 1–20.

11. See Bernard Lewis, "Muslims, Christians, and Jews: The Dream of Coexistence," *New York Review of Books,* March 26, 1992, pp. 48–52.

12. See Mosse, *German Jews beyond Judaism.*

13. Thomas Szasz, "Psychoanalysis as Religion: Psychoanalytic Theory as Ideology, Psychoanalytic Practice as Cure of Souls," in *Prescriptions: The Dissemination of Medical Authority,* ed. Gayle L. Ormiston and Raphael Sassower, 121–39 (Westport, Conn.: Greenwood Press, 1990).

14. Lyotard, *Heidegger and "the jews,"* 93.

15. Lyotard and Thebaud, *Just Gaming,* 95.

16. Ingeborg Hoesterey, ed., *Zeitgeist in Babel: The Postmodernist Controversy* (Bloomington: Indiana University Press, 1991), 250.

17. Jean-François Lyotard, *The Postmodern Condition: A Report on Knowledge,* trans G. Bennington and B. Massumi (Minneapolis: University of Minnesota Press, 1985), xxv.

18. Lyotard, *The Postmodern Condition,* 82.

19

Perceptions of "Otherness"

Isaac de Pinto, Voltaire, and a Personal Interpretation of Jewish Experience

Oliver W. Holmes

SHABBAT SERVICES in 1951, and 1953, and 1955, and 1957, and 1961, in New York City, Rochester, New York, and Chicago, at Orthodox and Conservative *shuls*. They glance and stare at the young black youth wearing a *kipah* in the fourth or eighth row, accompanied by adults who are regular synagogue members; they whisper and gesture, revealing the question: "Who is the *schwarze?*"

Shabbat and *hagim* services in 1965, and 1967, and 1971, and 1975, in New York City and Paris, at Orthodox and Conservative *shuls*. They glance and stare at the young black man wearing a *kipah* and *tallit* in the fourth, eighth, or tenth row; they whisper, point (for in Europe it is not always considered indiscreet to point in public). They question: "Who is the *schwarze?*" After the services it is followed by: "What are you, a sociologist?"

Shabbat services in 1967 in Madrid, at a small apartment which serves as the Orthodox synagogue for the Spanish community. There is security at the door. They shout a question: "¿Qué quiere usted?"
"Estoy aqui para el servicio de Shabbat." I am permitted to enter.
The next question: "¿De donde viene usted?"
"Soy Americano."
¿De que parte de América del Sur viene usted?"
"Soy de los Estados Unidos."
"¡No me diga!"

The notion, perception of "otherness," comprises a mode of analysis with which I have been concerned for several years. As a child, though the philosophical connotation of the concept surpassed my understanding, I did fully apprehend its implication in everyday life, for I experienced the human significance of the category since my earliest social memories. After I studied the concept during my secondary school and college years, my comprehension of the category converged with an ever-expanding experience. These experiences revolved around the poor preparation American culture provides us for effectively handling the complex terrain of racial prejudice, despite the "melting pot" myth—particularly in view of the fact that, in everyday reality, the social construction of human relationships promotes the physical differences of individuals rather than emphasizes their common humanity. Though general statements concerning the perception and treatment of me as an "other" can oversimplify, they single out a few salient features of these personal experiences. The narrative quality of these experiences invites a discussion that may shed some light on how I became interested in studying the variegated factors that underlie the notion of "the other." More recently, I have drawn upon the concept of "the other" as an analytical tool by which to approach my current study of the complex interrelationship between the ethnic identity of black, Chinese, and Jewish intellectuals and the universal principle of human and natural rights in the French Socialist movement, and how human and natural rights became the foundation upon which efforts to institute societal changes were made.

I became interested in the subject after studying intellectuals and politics at the time of the Dreyfus Affair. The surge of anti-Semitism during the Dreyfus Affair convinced Jean Jaurès of the urgency with which the Socialist party must move in relation to the "Jewish question." Jaurès was known to quote repeatedly the lines from Michelet: "If all, even the humblest, do not enter Heaven, I will remain outside." In an article that appeared in *La Dépêche de Toulouse* (June 2, 1892) Jaurès made his first public statement on the Jewish question: "I have no prejudice against the Jews; in fact, I favor them, since they have long been among my best friends. I do not like racial quarrels, and I adhere to the idea of the French Revolution, however outmoded it may seem today, that there is only one race and it is humanity." Jaurès' observation provided the occasion with which I began to investigate precisely how, if at all, the Socialist movement became concerned with the Jewish question. The early "Socialists" of the eighteenth century were primarily "moralists," or moral reformers. The Socialist "theorists" of the early nineteenth century opposed the prevailing emphasis on the claims of the individual, and stressed the social elements in human relations. In emphasizing the social aspects of human relations, they sought to bring the "social question" to the center of the lengthy debates concerning the rights of the individual throughout the nineteenth century.

This example points both to the character of the problem and to the approach of the inquiry. Deeper interest in these issues stems from personal memories of my grandparents' struggle to live in a society that was unwilling to tolerate interracial marriages easily, and their commitment to make the principles of humanity and justice realizable in everyday experience. A few years after the Dreyfus Affair, they were politically active in fostering such ideals and in combating anti-Semitism and racism in American society.

These memories drew my attention to the problem and to the politics of "otherness."

The concept of the "other" as the intermediary agent through whom the individual attains self-consciousness derives from a fundamental principle in existential phenomenology. From the point of view of this principle, the "objectifying power" of the other as intervenor signifies that it is the other who "teaches me who I am." This position further posits a necessary condition to become reflectively aware of oneself, as an individual, and implies that consciousness of others should have intended this very individual self as an object. Sartre claims that "the Other is the indispensable mediator between myself and me."[1] Sartre bases this claim on the proposition that, when another intends me as an object, I am as certain of his or her existence as I am of my own existence, for the very reason that such intentionality heightens self-awareness insofar as I have an "objective" self, that is, a "self-for-others." From this standpoint, I cannot have a social self for myself. "I am for myself," Sartre argues, "only as I am a pure reference to the Other."[2]

The social self becomes a form of existence of myself that I discover through the necessary mediation of the other the moment he or she intends me as an object. Through a gaze, or what Sartre calls "the Other's look," I may become an alien, an "outsider," to others who attempt to appraise my behavior with no knowledge of my personal history.[3] In short, my existence as an object in relation to another's purpose may be explained on the basis of others in my community. "The other," he reasons, "accomplishes for us a function of which we are incapable and which nevertheless is incumbent on us: *to see ourselves as we are*" (emphasis added).[4]

The presence of the autobiographical self, in my work, represents an unfamiliar enterprise for me, yet I will attempt to craft certain ideas concerning crucial points at which my personal experiences and work intersect. Individual self-understanding through interpersonal interaction eventually becomes the process by which we understand human experiences. The complexity of human world experiences may, in turn, become comprehensible through historical understanding of individual experiences. In this sense, historical understanding through autobiography provides the genre by which an individual perceives a meaningful pattern of his or her own "lived experiences." The self becomes located in a context sufficiently historical to account for autobiography as a human and cultural activity. Thus, as Dilthey has pointed out, "an autobiography is the highest and most instructive form in which the understanding of life confronts us. Here is the outward phenomenal course of a life which forms the basis for understanding what has produced it within a certain environment. The man who understands it is the same as the one who created it."[5]

The analysis of an individual human life in conjunction with social "lived relations" constitutes the focus of this study. This form of analysis reflects the position that historical knowledge may provide the individualistic facets of human experience. Individuality and the historical process combine to signify the sense in which Dilthey's notion of autobiography becomes relevant for human knowledge and understanding and, hence, for the reflections in this chapter. For among these very experiences are those which help explain how I have approached, developed, and interpreted historical analysis from a personal perspective. This approach will assist in paving the way for attending to autobiography as subjective self-reflection upon past experiences.

The autobiographical perspective entails a certain mode of analysis in relation to one's self and to one's scholarly activity. In my study of Jews in France during the eighteenth century, I investigated relations among the Sephardic and Ashkenazic communities. Some scholars of Jewish history have discussed at length the less than fraternal relations between the two communities.[6] These discussions often characterized the Sephardim as having considered themselves superior to the Ashkenazim and concluded that such proud claims rendered mutual respect and "toleration" of each other difficult, if not impossible. As a consequence of these observations of hostile relations between the groups, I decided to explore the issue in greater detail with the view of gaining a perspective on the problem through my own personal experience in Sephardic communities in France and in Spain, and of interpreting the cultural significance of the issue.

One of the classic historical examples of the issue involves Voltaire's virulent attack on the Jews and the Sephardim's responses to these hostile remarks. Specifically, Isaac de Pinto, an intellectual Sephardic Jew from Bordeaux and later of Amsterdam, formulated a reply to Voltaire in 1762 in defense of the Jews. Pinto responded directly to the article "Juifs," which had appeared in Voltaire's *Essai sur les moeurs* in 1756, and argued on behalf of the Jews by making the curious distinction between the "good" Sephardim from Spain and Portugal and the "bad" Ashkenazim from Germany and Poland:

> If M. de Voltaire had on this occasion referred to that soundness of argument which he professes, he would have begun by singling out from other Jews, the Spanish and Portuguese Jews who have never intermingled with or been incorporated into the masses of the other children of Jacob. He should have pointed out this great difference. I am aware that it is little known in France generally speaking and that this has harmed the Portuguese nation of Bordeaux on more than one occasion. But M. de Voltaire cannot be unaware of the scrupulous fastidiousness of the Portuguese and Spanish Jews not to mix, by marriage, alliance or in any other way, with the Jews of other nations. He has been to Holland and knows that their Synagogues are separate and that although their Religion and articles of Faith are the same, their ceremonies are frequently not alike. The customs of the Portuguese Jews are quite different from those of other Jews. The former do not wear beards and do not affect any peculiarity in their dress, the well-off amongst them carry refinement, elegance and display in this respect as far as the other nations of Europe, from whom they differ only in their form of worship. . . . The idea they quite generally hold that they are

descendants of the Tribe of Judah, the main families of which were sent to Spain at the time of the Babylonian captivity, cannot but lead them to make these distinctions and contribute to that loftiness of feeling that one observes in them, and which even their brethren of other nations appear to recognize. . . .

. . .

Those [people] who know the Portuguese Jews of France, Holland and England are aware that, far from having *an invincible hatred of all the nations who tolerate them,* as M. de Voltaire says, they themselves so identified with these same nations that they consider that they form part of them. Their Spanish and Portuguese origin has become a pure ecclesiastical discipline which the harshest criticism would accuse of pride and vanity, but in no way of greed and superstition. . . . [7]

The conflicts within and between the Sephardim, Ashkenazim, and Avignonese communities continued, in varying degrees of intensity, from the eighteenth to the twentieth century. Surprisingly, contemporary scholars focus upon Pinto's argument on behalf of the Spanish and Portuguese Jews to underscore the feeling of loftiness described in the letter and to demonstrate a kind of irreparable breach between the Sephardim and Ashkenazim. At this point, I should like to compare this historical example, which has been exaggerated when taken out of historical context, with my personal experience with the Sephardic community.

During the course of several years I had the occasion to live and to *daven* amongst the Sephardim, first as a student and later as a professor. My initial sustained contact with the Sephardic community began during my two-year residency in Madrid as a Fulbright scholar in the late 1960s. Prior to this visit to Spain, my only contact with the Sephardic community consisted in occasional visits to Shearith Israel Congregation, known as the Spanish and Portuguese Synagogue in New York City, throughout my childhood and adolescence to observe the manner in which "they," the "other Jews," *davened* and chanted "exotic" melodies. They, in turn, tolerated the curious gazes coming from me and my cohort—all of us Ashkenazim—and carried on their services without much fanfare. To be sure, they were accustomed to the gaze of "outsiders" and curiousity-seekers in their synagogue. The fact that a young black Jew was in their midst did not faze them in the least, for they responded to me as they responded to any other Jew—with a refined aloofness. This perception of aloofness contributed, in part, to an earlier attitude and acceptance, on my part, that the Sephardim considered themselves superior to the Ashkenazim.

In Madrid, my choices of synagogues to attend, Sephardic or Ashkenazic, were limited to one. The sole synagogue in Madrid, located on Calle de Cardinal Cisneros, was founded after World War II. The 1950s were a period when Sephardic Jews were "returning" to the Iberian Peninsula in increasing numbers, particularly after Morocco became independent from Spain in 1957. However, the Jewish community was unable to obtain legal recognition as a religious body until 1967, when Jews and Protestants were permitted to demonstrate their faiths publicly. Before that time, the Sephardic community of Madrid was registered as a corporation, in the feudal sense of the term, under the law and privilege of private associations. In December 1968 a new synagogue was inaugurated officially, in the ceremonial presence of ecclesiastical and governmental authorities, which included Franco and members of the Opus Dei. To symbolize the historic importance of the event, the Franco regime issued a formal repeal of the edict of the expulsion of 1492.

Between 1965 and 1967, the period during which this important historical event was in the making, I was researching and writing my doctoral dissertation on José Ortega y Gasset's philosophy of history. It was also a period in which I was introduced to the Jewish community of Madrid. Though I observed the holidays in London or in Paris, I spent several Shabbatot at the synagogue on Calle de Cardinal Cisneros. The synagogue was located in an apartment because of the legal restrictions imposed on non-Catholic faiths. The Yiddish expression *shtiebel* (small house of prayer) accurately describes the size and atmosphere of the synagogue.

One of the multifaceted ways in which I have been perceived as a black Jew often has occurred during my visits to a *shul* outside my immediate community. Within the secure and unambiguous "boundaries" of the Jewish community of my grandmother, I was a welcomed "insider." Whenever I ventured beyond these invisible walls, I became the "outsider," the other. Throughout my childhood, I was often perceived as a curiosity in town or in the neighborhood, as someone who was the friend of "liberal" hosts. When I was a teenager and young adult, various members of the congregation would sidle up to me and discreetly ask: "What are you, a sociologist?" Invariably, an indiscreet member would whisper loudly, "Who is the *schwarze?*" For some, I represented a cultural reality that was incongruous with their expectations. In spite of the counterintuitive cultural realities of racially mixed marriages, both within American society and Jewish communities throughout the world, some displayed tremendous dismay over the prospect that a *schwarze* could indeed be "one of us." Fortunately, I developed a keen sense of how to traverse arbitrary community boundary lines and deflect the hostile gaze of the other's look.

The various occasions where I have been subjected to the experience of otherness were not confined to the issue of race or to the Jewish community. Projections, on the part of other people, that I ought to be someone other than who I am also revealed instances where unsuitable anti-Semitism emerged.

In 1962 at a distinguished private university in the Midwest where the number of black students can be counted on both hands, a professor of international reputation, chair of the history department, invited all first-year graduate students to his office.

"I invited all the first-year students here to have the opportunity to speak with each of you individually, and to find out how you are adjusting. I am particularly interested in hearing how you are doing."

"Fine. I enjoy the courses I have taken thus far."

"In general, how are things for you?"

"Fine."

"What I had in mind with that question: Most of our student *clientele* here is Jewish. You attended a college where the majority of students were Jewish. I suppose you are probably more comfortable here than most of the first-year students because of this."

"It is difficult to say."

"What do you mean?"

"It is difficult to say whether I am more comfortable here because the majority of the students where I attended college were Jewish, or whether it is because *I am Jewish*."

SILENCE. Then the question: "What courses are you taking?" . . .

The intention may have been good, but the effect could have been devastating.

By contrast, in Spain, whenever I ventured through smaller cities and towns, Spaniards often pointed, shouting, "Un Moro, un Moro." When I first visited the synagogue in Madrid, in 1965, the Sephardim approached me as a Jew who could conceivably be Sephardic. They asked me from which country I came. I answered that I was an American. Since my Spanish was fluent, invariably they would speculate that I came from either Curaçao or somewhere else in South America, but no one would believe I came from North America, not even New York City. Whereupon their logic carried them to recall, "Of course, there is a Spanish-Portuguese community in New York City." When I explained to them that my Jewish origins were Ashkenazic, they became dumbfounded. Personally, for them, the fact that I am *moreno,* or black, was insignificant; for the Sephardim, as a culture, skin pigmentation was hardly an important issue. Culturally, they perceived me as a "kinsman" who was familiar with Jewish observance and fluent in their language. Consequently, the commonality of language and our shared cultural experiences signified that we belonged in the same community. This shared sense of cultural values signified more to them than the fact that I was American and of Ashkenazic background.

However, what appeared incongruous to them was the fact that I spoke fluent Castilian Spanish rather than the Andalucian accent that has come to characterize Ladino, South American and Caribbean Spanish. When I explained how I learned to speak Castilian while living with a Basque family in San Sebastián on the student exchange program Experiment in International Living, they accepted what to most seemed odd. The oddity consisted in the fact that a Jew speaking Castilian Spanish was foreign to them, more so, perhaps, than a black Jew whose origins were Ashkenazic. After having sorted out these curiosities and peculiarities in my background, the Sephardic community embraced me as one of their own.

The Sephardic community was quite familiar with foreigners either passing through or living in Madrid, and yet several members opened their homes to me (and later to me and my spouse) from the outset. They were more welcoming to me, as someone from outside their regular community, than most of the American-Jewish communities I visited throughout the years. Conceivably, their collective experiences as a community in exile since 1492 in Casablanca, Tetuán, and elsewhere may explain the sense of empathy they felt for me as a "stranger" at the gates of a foreign city. Whatever their reasons, the community's warmth and openness were immediate and sincere.

The Madrid to which I returned was not the same city I had visited thirteen years earlier. When I left Madrid as a student in 1967, the Jewish community was approximately three thousand in number. When I returned to Madrid in 1980, to pursue research on a project concerning Spanish intellectuals and the "generation of 1898," the Jewish community had increased to fourteen thousand. This demographic rise was due, in part, to the surge of Jews leaving Morocco after the Israeli-Arab Six-Day War, and the large wave of Jews from Argentina and other South American countries after the death of Franco. The features of the Jewish community changed after this influx of Jews from different corners of the world. By 1980, there were as many Ashkenazim as there were Sephardim in Spain.

Such was the Jewish Madrid to which I returned, accompanied by my spouse. There were a few old-timers who remembered me from my student days, but, for the most part, the majority of the congregants of Communidad Israelita de Madrid, located at Balmés 3, had arrived in Spain after 1967. Nonetheless, my background was as curious to them as before, and, of course, the issue of my speaking Castilian Spanish never ceased to amaze. My wife and I were invited to many a Shabbat meal throughout the course of our stay in Madrid. In contrast with my earlier visit, we remained in Spain for all the holidays and, interestingly, had to draw upon all our diplomatic acumen to handle the generous invitations to lunches and dinners. The warmth and positive feeling with which we were received by the community remain with us to this day. Our close friendships with several of the Sephardic families have endured since our eight-month stay in Madrid. Fortunately, we have had the opportunity to extend our hospitality to some of them who were in the United States during the past few years.

In reflecting upon Isaac de Pinto's response to Voltaire concerning the differences between Ashkenazic and Sephardic, "ceremonies," I am reminded that, despite these differences, our "religion and articles of faith" remain identical. The Sephardic community in Madrid was interested less in the eighteenth-century concern of distinguishing between "rationalism" and "superstition" than in the twentieth-century concern, among the worldwide

Jewish community, of combining an enlightened way of thinking with being an observant Jew. We were able to identify with the latter concern. Moreover, we were able to share a common language and culture beyond our common Jewishness: Spanish culture. Because of these shared perceptions and traditions, the community related to me as a person whose uniqueness failed to hamper our interpersonal interaction.

The "lived relations" I experienced among the Sephardic community contributed significantly to my self-understanding as a Jew and as a historian. As a black Jew whose personal history encompasses the alternating experiences of inclusion and exclusion within Jewish communities, the openness with which the Sephardic community in Madrid embraced me, despite my Ashkenazic background, taught me the value of individual differences and how they contribute to any community. Moreover, the ease with which the Sephardic community was able to live and function in both Jewish and non-Jewish worlds proved instructive to my ability to live as an observant Jew in the modern world. The Sephardim taught me that the boundaries of the Jewish community extend beyond the immediate surroundings of the neighborhood. Through the cumulative effect of their collective experiences over the centuries, I was able to derive a positive sense of individual differences by recognizing, at once, the uniqueness and the collectiveness of my identity as a Jew. A Jew who is perceived as an "outsider" by other Jews becomes an "alien" to the community. A Jew who is perceived as a "kinsman" by other Jews becomes a member of the community through common ties. After Madrid, whenever someone has imposed the category of "otherness" on my person, I have not had to retreat into subjective experience to reclaim my Jewishness.

The experience has afforded me the rare opportunity to apprehend the importance of being able to define myself as Jew solely on the basis of my ability, behavior, and commitment as a Jew, rather than on the willingness of others to accept me accordingly. In this sense, affiliation through "culture" proved to be stronger than affiliation through "blood." A repertoire of cultural convictions has engendered a network of tacit human relationships. Through this experience, I have obtained the feeling of solidarity with *every* Jew everywhere in the world, putting aside political differences.

As a historian, I have come to understand the complexities surrounding general interpretations of history and life, to emphasize concepts of individuality and individual development, and to recognize the historical quality of human existence. When I draw upon this form of historical understanding, I come to read Pinto's *Apologie* differently from his critics, who claim he assumed a posture of superiority with respect to the Ashkenazim. Rather, I tend to emphasize the earlier sections of his *Apologie* in which Pinto cites Montesquieu to demonstrate how all individuals, Jews and non-Jews, are fundamentally the same, attributing the differences between them to "climate."[8] To the notion of climate, I add "culture."

Insofar as there are cultural differences, individual characteristics often result in classification born out of comparisons with Others. However, as an individual who shares in similar cultural traditions, I am the *same* as the Others. In this regard, I am reminded of Sartre's postulate: I become an authentic self when I make myself become recognized by the Other, and when I recognize the Other in an indentical manner. This form of reciprocity has become an important process for me within human relations.

NOTES

1. Jean-Paul Sartre, *Being and Nothingness: An Essay on Phenomenological Ontology,* trans. with an introduction by Hazel E. Barnes (New York: Philosophical Library, 1956), 222.

2. Sartre, *Being and Nothingness,* 260.

3. Sartre, *Being and Nothingness,* 261.

4. Sartre, *Being and Nothingness,* 264.

5. Wilhelm Dilthey, *Pattern and Meaning in History: Thoughts on History and Society,* ed. with an introduction by H. P. Rickman (New York: Harper and Row, 1962), 85–86.

6. For example, see Zosa Szajkowski, "Relations among Sephardim, Ashkenazim and Avignonese Jews in France from the 16th to the 20th Centuries," *YIVO Annual of Jewish Social Science,* 10 (1955): 173, 179–84.

7. Isaac de Pinto, *Apologie pour la nation juive ou réflexions critique sur le premier chapitre du VIIe tome des oeuvres de Monsieur de Voltaire, au suject des Juifs,* in *Lettres de quelques Juifs portugais, allemands et polonais à M. Voltaire . . . ,* the Abbé Antoine Guéneé, seconde édition (Paris: Chez Laurent Prault, 1769), 14–16, 19; the translations are my own.

8. Pinto, *Apologie pour la nation juive,* 9–10.

20

Historians and the Holocaust

Allan M. Winkler

THE HOLOCAUST has been with me all my life. Born in early 1945, I am a child of World War II, still trying to understand the changes that monumental struggle brought. Although my life has been peaceful, and I have been spared the ravages my Jewish forebears endured, I have known of Hitler's Final Solution for as long as I can remember. I was too young to see the newsreels that first showed Americans the horrors of liberated concentration camps, but somewhere in my early years I stumbled upon haunting pictures of haggard survivors, living skeletons with hollow faces and helpless eyes. Only as I have grown older, however, have I learned about the full impact of Nazi policy and about how American commentators have dealt with the horrible results.

My own growing awareness of the Holocaust reflects the increased attention of the broader intellectual community. In the immediate aftermath of World War II, we had little substantive evidence of the destruction of the European Jews. Grim tales told by survivors made us painfully aware of what had happened, but it was a number of years before scholars documented the details of Nazi policy. Their record underscored the systematic German genocide that left six million Jews dead, and also revealed a staggering insensitivity on the part of the American government while the decimation occurred. Our knowledge of that halfhearted reaction helps us better understand our nation's aims in the war and the broader contours of American policy.

My father introduced me to the Holocaust. He had a premonition of things to come while he traveled in Europe on a university fellowship on the eve of the war. He was troubled by what he saw, worried that no one in this country or in Great Britain seemed willing to stop relentless German aggression. After the United States entered the war, he volunteered his services to the American effort. He first joined the Office of War Information, then entered the navy, where he trained and worked as a Japanese language officer. Though his focus was the Pacific, he was doing his part in the monumental military struggle.

At the war's end, he brought home an unwavering bitterness about the Jewish annihilation that had occurred in Europe. Though we had no close family members who perished in the camps, he mourned the extermination of distant relatives he had never known, and felt even more passionately about the blatant disregard for human life. I remember trying unsuccessfully to comprehend the number six million when I was learning to count, when smaller digits had a concrete reality, but larger figures were beyond my capacity to grasp.

All this took place in a family that was not particularly religious. My grandfather (my father's father) was an Orthodox Jew, ordained as a rabbi in Palestine, who had fled to the United States to avoid serving in the Turkish army, and then made his way in this country as a Hebrew school principal. My father grew up within the Jewish tradition, attending Hebrew school every afternoon, only to reject the formality of the faith when he left home to go to college. But the cultural connection remained strong, even while he attempted to live a more secular life.

In our household in the 1950s, the legacy of the Holocaust was a hatred of all things German. My father permitted no German goods at home, so our purchases excluded cars and cameras from that part of Europe, even when they were the best made or most economical. Occasionally we traveled abroad—on a Fulbright in 1954—but while we spent time in England, France, and Switzerland, we avoided postwar Germany.

From time to time, I managed to smuggle in occasional items despite my father's boycott of German products. Once I bought a loden coat made in Germany, and wore it quietly without acknowledging its origin. I'm sure my father found out where it came from, but he said nothing to me at all. I also watched his resistance crumble ever so slowly in other ways. When a group of foreign exchange students came to our New Jersey town, we agreed to host one of them, and ended up with a German boy. I can still recall my father gradually warming up to the student, talking to him about the German past, finally conceding that he was not one of the compliant culprits who had allowed the unspeakable horrors to take place.

While I grew up, my sense of the Holocaust was occasionally heightened by the unwitting actions of the outside world. In my first year of high school, I remember a classmate singing a little ditty as he undressed for gym class at a locker next to mine. It went:

> Riding through the Reich,
> In a black Mercedes Benz,
> Killing all the Jews,
> Saving all my friends.

He meant no harm, at least not consciously, and we remained friends for the next four years. But even to an adolescent, the verse seemed extraordinarily tasteless and crude. Perturbed, as all members of my generation were, by the problem of winning acceptance in the non-Jewish world while still maintaining a sense of Jewish identity, I said nothing, and simply cringed internally at what I heard.

Even as I tolerated that vulgar song, I was learning more, perhaps, than I

324

wanted to know about the mechanics of Nazi policy. My father was a European historian who taught for thirty years at Rutgers University. Among other things, he shared responsibility for the huge Western civilization course, and became something of a campus celebrity for his lecture about Hitler's Germany. As word got out, it became one of those presentations attended by faculty members and students throughout the university, a performance that sometimes brought listeners to tears and always resulted in applause at the end. Lampshades made from human skin, obscene medical experiments performed on unwilling twins—my father spared nothing in his litany of Nazi horrors. One year, thinking I was old enough to understand, my mother took me out of school to attend the famous talk. I felt awkward about being somewhere I didn't belong, uncomfortable at the back of the room with a poor view of the distant lectern, yet proud of my father for his honesty in confronting this awful event.

That lecture created a compelling need to know more, but it went unsatisfied. My high school taught no European history, and my religious school skirted the Holocaust with but passing references to the monstrous Nazi crimes. Conversations at home provided a bit more background, and I saw occasional accounts written with a different audience in mind. Yet even after browsing through random books I still knew very little about the dynamics of modern German history, and even less about the details of the American response.

I learned a bit more about the Holocaust when I went away to college in the 1960s. Harvard had a summer reading program for incoming students, and one of the books we were required to read and then discuss was Alan Bullock's *Hitler: A Study in Tyranny*. "A brilliant, forceful and terrifying biography of the monstrous genius who nearly conquered the world," the *Saturday Review* proclaimed in an excerpt on the cover of the paperback edition we used. First published in 1953, and subsequently abridged and revised, the book was the first full account of the madman who had such a powerful impact on our age. It was also was my first entrance into European history, my father's specialty notwithstanding, and gave me a glimpse of the powerful tides of twentieth-century affairs. It was more about Hitler than about the Holocaust—the index does not even mention the term—but it did contain several pages on extermination plans and policies, and, above all, put them into the larger context I needed. Bullock was intent on testing the degree to which Hitler's will governed the Third Reich, and I savored his biographical focus. I also appreciated the chance to begin to understand the chain of events that resulted in six million deaths.

Recognizing the need to learn more about my European roots, I took a course in Western civilization my first year at Harvard. The course was probably no different from the one my father taught, and in all likelihood less exciting, but because I had chosen it myself, it had a certain legitimacy. I relished finding out about people and events I had heard of but couldn't place. In addition to reading Plato, Aristotle, Hobbes, Locke, and Rousseau, we read *Mein Kampf* and other modern works, and in that class and others, I began to reflect for myself on the troubled history of the contemporary world.

At the same time, Jewish fiction provided an even broader context for the Holocaust. In an English course my freshman year, we read Philip Roth's *Good-bye, Columbus,* which had recently won the National Book Award. I was overwhelmed by Roth's devastating portrait of the Patimkins, equally taken by his explorations of Jewish identity in short stories like "Defender of the Faith" and "Eli the Fanatic" included in the same volume. At the same time I read *The Assistant,* which my father had once claimed was Bernard Malamud's best book, and wondered, as I would later in my life, about the implications of interfaith relationships. Although I felt Jewish, had been bar mitzvahed, and was slowly learning about my European origins, I was struggling with what it meant to be a Jew at Harvard and, more broadly, in the United States. What did assimilation entail? How much of a sense of Jewish identity could survive the process? Roth and Malamud helped me address those questions. André Schwartz-Bart, a French novelist, focused the questions for me on the Holocaust.

The Last of the Just, published in English in 1960, a year after its appearance in French, began with "The Legend of the Just Men." Schwartz-Bart wrote, "the world reposes upon thirty-six Just Men, the Lamed-Vov, indistinguishable from simple mortals; often they are unaware of their station. But if just one of them were lacking, the sufferings of mankind would poison even the souls of the newborn, and humanity would suffocate with a single cry."[1] Beginning with a twelfth-century pogrom and ending with a twentieth-century gas chamber, the novel told of Jewish suffering, and strength, in the face of relentless assault. At the end of the tale, Ernie Levy, the Last of the Just, found himself ravaged in a concentration camp, trying to comfort frightened children and the woman he loved, while the Nazi engine of destruction ground on. In the gas chamber, with all hope of survival gone, his voice entwined with the voices of the rest of those around him in the chant that has sustained Jews for centuries: "SHEMA YISRAEL ADONOI ELOHENU ADONOI EH'OTH . . . Hear, O Israel, the Lord is our God, the Lord is One" (373). That blessing, perhaps the most important chant in Jewish ritual, had always seemed stale and lifeless in the past. Schwartz-Bart's account of Ernie's end brought the blessing to life and made the Holocaust more real for me than it had ever been before.

After college, I did a stint in the Peace corps, where I witnessed a more modern form of genocide in Southeast Asia. Napalm burning the skin of Vietnamese peasants, fragmentation bombs ripping off human flesh—these new methods of torture and death forced me to think again about the wholesale destruction that had occurred in Europe just twenty-five years before. There were profound political differences between World War II and the

Vietnam War, to be sure, but the senseless slaughter of innocent Vietnamese civilians created echoes of the Holocaust.

In the early 1970s, I had a chance to travel to Israel for the first time. There, in Jerusalem, I visited Yad Vashem, the nation's Holocaust memorial, and learned still more of the details of the Final Solution. It was a revelation. Grimly curious, I now found out just what the Nazis had done. I spent hours reading deportation lists, looking at yellow stars, gazing at the gaunt faces of liberated victims in the camps. Such materials existed elsewhere, of course, but I had not seen them. Now they were right in front of me, and I took the time to think about what they meant. I realized that had my relatives not left Europe I might very well have been among the victims. Moved both by the historical exhibits and the quiet testimonials to Jewish survival, I felt pride in the resistance and sorrow for the scapegoats. I also felt more Jewish than I had in the past.

On my return home, I continued the graduate education I had already begun. My foreign travels drew me into American history as I found myself forced to answer questions about my own nation posed by friends and neighbors abroad. So I focused on the United States in the twentieth century. In the process, I became intrigued with World War II, perhaps because of its impact on my father and my major professors, all of whom had reached maturity during the struggle. I therefore embarked on a study of American propaganda during the war, and spent months wading through archival materials in libraries and depositories. In the mid-1970s, I completed first a dissertation, then a book based on that work.

In *The Politics of Propaganda: The Office of War Information, 1942–1945,* I described how the United Sates sought to explain its aims and expectations to both domestic and foreign audiences. I argued that, since President Franklin D. Roosevelt wanted to be his own spokesman, he viewed propagandists as peripheral players in the government, and gave them far less latitude than they thought they needed. Only when they circumscribed their efforts and agreed to work squarely within the confines of diplomatic policy could they make the contributions they had long anticipated. The propaganda they produced was most successful when it supported the maneuvers of military commanders and portrayed the United States as policy makers viewed it. With its image of a powerful and righteous nation, I concluded, "American propaganda reflected American policy, and indeed America itself."[2]

This was a story about the single-minded pursuit of victory and the compromises that pursuit entailed. Yet nowhere did I elaborate on the larger compromise the nation made. I neglected even a passing reference to the incarceration of more than a hundred thousand Japanese-Americans, many of whom were citizens of this country. And I avoided mention of the unwillingness to do anything, in either policy or propaganda, about the Nazi aim of extermination, even when it might have been possible to save some of the victims.

Why those omissions? In part, I think, I was trying to be as careful as possible in my first full-length work of historical scholarship. I sought to follow my sources as closely as I could and to keep to the narrow confines of my story. I was reluctant, at this point in my career, to make the inferences—the larger leaps—that mark the very best historical accounts. And I was cautious about writing publicly on a Jewish issue at a time when I was still working out my own sense of identity as a Jew. Like many members of my generation, I wanted to compartmentalize my Jewishness, to keep religious observance separate from the rest of my life, and so to feel fully assimilated into American life. Being Jewish was peripheral to most other concerns.

Once I began my teaching career, I found myself coming back to America's wartime response to the Holocaust while I continued to explore the question of Roosevelt's leadership. On my trip to Israel, at the suggestion of a tour guide, I had read Arthur D. Morse's angry account *While Six Million Died: A Chronicle of American Apathy*, first published in 1967. Morse made a persuasive case for the ability of the American government to have done something to stop the extermination of the Jews. While Hitler moved relentlessly forward, Morse wrote, "the government and the people of the United States remained bystanders. Oblivious to the evidence which poured from official and unofficial sources, Americans went about their business unmoved and unconcerned. Those who tried to awaken the nation were dismissed as alarmists, cranks or Zionists."[3] Though gripping, the book had a shrill quality. It lacked what I considered adequate scholarly detachment. Perhaps even more important for me as a fledgling academic, Morse was a journalist, not a historian, and although he had waded through official sources as extensive as those I had used in my dissertation, I was inclined to view his work with caution.

Soon, however, I found other books that amplified the charge of American callousness. While a number of my students worked on questions of foreign policy in the 1930s and 1940s, I delved into a growing literature about both the Holocaust and the American reaction to it. I found Raul Hilberg's monumental history, *The Destruction of the European Jews*, which appeared in 1961, and Lucy S. Dawidowicz's equally compelling volume, *The War against the Jews, 1933–1945*, published a decade and a half later. They provided me with the dispassionate documentation of the atrocities I found myself thinking about more and more.

But I was most interested in those works that focused on the United States. One useful treatment was Henry L. Feingold's 1970 book, *The Politics of Rescue: The Roosevelt Administration and the Holocaust, 1938–1945*. Feingold, a historian whose family had fled Germany when he was still a child, noted how "the agencies and departments responsible for administering the various elements which made up the rescue program found themselves in the unceasing conflict of overlapping authorities following divergent policies" and so managed little of substance. He pointed to "the listless manner in which the State Department approached the rescue problem." And he observed how Roosevelt's "own apprehensions and assumptions, especially about ethnic politics," kept him from giving the issue of rescue greater priority during the war.[4]

Even more useful to me was the work of David S. Wyman. *Paper Walls: America and the Refugee Crisis, 1938–1941* appeared two years before Feingold's account and dealt with the same issue in the period before Pearl Harbor. Exhaustively researched, Wyman's book concluded that the years before American entrance into the war could only be seen as "a vast lost chance."[5] The United States did accept more refugees than other nations, yet the "American ability to absorb immigration was vastly greater than that of the small European countries or the little-industrialized, though spacious and less populated, areas of Latin America and Africa" (209). Wyman deplored the "dismal record" of the State Department (212), resulting from the obstructive tactics of the anti-Semitic assistant secretary Breckinridge Long, yet argued, finally, that while one could criticize both FDR and the Congress for not having done more, "the accuser will find himself simultaneously pointing at the society which gave American refugee policy its fundamental shape" (213).

Sixteen years later, Wyman completed his sequel, *The Abandonment of the Jews: America and the Holocaust, 1941–1945*. This account was even more devastating than the first. "This book has been difficult to research and to write," Wyman noted in his preface.[6] "One does not wish to believe the facts revealed by the documents on which it is based" (p. ix). He concluded that, while millions of Jews perished between 1941 and 1945, several hundred thousand of them could have been saved. Had the United States seized the initiative, more might have been done, "but America did not act at all until late in the war, and even then, though it had some success, the effort was a very limited one" (p. ix). Despite authenticated information about Nazi extermination policy, Roosevelt did nothing for fourteen months, and eventually moved only because of political pressures. "Franklin Roosevelt's indifference to so momentous an historical event as the systematic annihilation of European Jewry," Wyman wrote, "emerges as the worst failure of his presidency" (p. xi). Less acerbic than Arthur Morse's *While Six Million Died*, the book was all the more persuasive for its restraint. Wyman, writing as "a Christian, a Protestant of Yankee and Swedish descent" (p. xii), provided incontrovertible evidence of the bankruptcy of America's effort to help the Jews.

There have been other books, of course. But these are the ones that established for me the basic contours of the Holocaust. They provided the background about the atrocities that occurred and documented shortcomings in American policy that changed my own perception of what was possible and what was preferable in the world of public affairs.

The searching accounts of America's response to the Holocaust altered my assessment of the role of FDR. Like many students who came of age before the turbulence of the 1960s, I went through college with an inflated notion of Democratic policy in the New Deal and World War II. I accepted the revolutionary aspects of the New Deal without questioning its shortcomings and endorsed the idea of the war as a selfless struggle for world freedom. William E. Leuchtenburg, Arthur M. Schlesinger, Jr., and John Morton Blum, my adviser in graduate school, were far too skillful historians to have sketched such a one-dimensional view, and I understood that warts and blemishes existed, but still I accepted as conventional wisdom the naive appraisal shared by most Americans.

The work on the Holocaust I had been reading complemented the emerging radical critique of the United States in depression and war. As Barton Bernstein and others challenged both the assumptions and accomplishments of American policy in the 1930s and 1940s, David Wyman and the historians studying the Holocaust added an important dimension to the new analysis that was emerging. They too identified the compromises Roosevelt made, and questioned whether all were necessary or worthwhile. I now found myself critically examining the American search for stability, the effort to maintain economic and political hegemony, and the willingness to make concessions—even those with profound human consequences—in pursuit of national ends. Compromise is always necessary in public affairs, I understood. But now I asked whether some compromises didn't go too far.

Slowly I came to see Roosevelt as a skillful politician juggling numerous constituencies, without a passionate commitment to many of those who tendered their support. Like blacks, Jews hailed him and voted for him out of gratitude for his general support for the disenfranchised, even when specific policies undermined their own aims. Now the important question became whether the compromises Roosevelt made again and again were necessary for him to accomplish his larger goals. Roosevelt was hardly anti-Semitic, but some of his advisers were, and during the war they persuaded him to respond passively to Nazi extermination policy in a way generally consonant with American attitudes toward Jews. That approach, which implicitly regarded the European victims as expendable, was not entirely necessary to win the war. In this area, as in others, Roosevelt clearly could have done more.

By the time I wrote about World War II again, I had a more balanced view of America's role in the conflict. In *Home Front, U.S.A.: America during World War II*, published in 1986, I examined the limitations of American policy toward minorities and women. I noted how military necessity was sometimes used, or misused, to justify American policy, particularly to avoid what administration officials viewed as excessive social change. Again, though, I said nothing about the Jewish experience. John Morton Blum had addressed the role of American Jews in his important volume *V was for Victory: Politics and American Culture during World War II*, published in 1976, and, as I have done throughout my career, I paid careful attention to his work. Nonetheless, in my own short hundred-page book, I neglected the topic altogether.

I believe I can explain that continuing omission in terms of my developing Jewish identity. Despite my reading and reflection on the Holocaust, I was still not ready to confront my perceptions publicly in my academic work. I still kept separate the writing I was doing and my reading about Jewish issues.

But my own self-awareness as a Jew was growing all the time. I wrote *Home Front, U.S.A.* during a year abroad in the Netherlands. Living in Europe made World War II seem more immediate, and I found myself reflecting on what it must have been like to have been Jewish there forty years before. I taught at the University of Amsterdam, with an office on Jodenbreestraat (Jews Broad Street) in what was once the old Jewish quarter. I often wandered by the old Portuguese synagogue, located around the corner. I also visited the Anne Frank house, and, like millions of visitors, was moved by the stark simplicity of her surroundings as well as by her account.

The bat mitzvah of my daughter Jenny in 1985, like the bar mitzvah of my son David in 1989, helped me embrace my Jewish identity more openly. I loved learning the Kaddish for the first time and chanting it during Jenny's preliminary service, reciting the priestly blessing as conclusion to my comments during David's ceremony. I enjoyed watching my children perform in front of my community, Jewish and non-Jewish alike, and for the first time felt at ease in this public declaration of my own Jewishness.

As a result, I finally felt comfortable addressing the Holocaust more openly. Even before David's bar mitzvah, the principal of the Cincinnati Reform Jewish High School, which Jenny attended, learned that I was a historian and asked me to teach a course to ninth and tenth graders on the Holocaust and its effects. For three semesters, I taught the class, and learned an enormous amount in the process. I had a chance to use everything I had read and to think carefully about just what I wanted my students to grasp. We examined documents together, watched excerpts from a dramatization of *The Diary of Anne Frank* and from the documentary *Shoah,* and listened to a recording of Elie Wiesel reading *Night.* Working with young high school pupils required a different approach from the one I used in teaching university students, and forced me to put materials in a form my students could understand.

Thanks to that experience, and to my more open acceptance of my own Jewish identity, the Holocaust is now a logical part of my university teaching. When I address the American role in World War II, I seek to convey as fully as I can what happened and what failed to happen in that monumental struggle. I hope to show my students how American policy was made, and to help them understand its limitations. Examining our response to the Holocaust is one way of identifying shortcomings in the American approach. Our inability to react quickly enough or fully enough to the extermination taking place in Europe tells us as much about American priorities as the confinement of Japanese–Americans or the continuing segregation of blacks in the armed forces during the war. In such cases the claims of Roosevelt and his advisers that they were only concerned with victory ring hollow, for the policies followed were hardly necessary to win the war but were followed instead for partisan ends. Despite the enormous efforts that finally vanquished the German, Italian, and Japanese dictators, there were political trade-offs that sometimes tarnished the American Dream.

At the same time, I have felt more comfortable in the past five years playing an active Jewish role in my community and on campus. I have joined a temple—the same one to which my parents belong—and have involved myself in its activities. I have served for a number of years as a board member of Miami University's Hillel, and worked with the Jewish Federation and other organizations to raise money for its needs. I have also drafted a proposal for a Jewish studies program, and continue to participate in the ongoing effort to secure the funds to establish it.

The Holocaust has played an important role in making me comfortable with being Jewish in America today. My effort to grapple with the Holocaust, intellectually and emotionally, has enhanced my own sense of Jewish tradition and all it includes. It has made me feel much more a part of the migration my ancestors made from Europe and the Middle East, and has helped me understand what they endured, both there and here. My odyssey has been intertwined with my father's struggle to comprehend the savage behavior of the Nazis during World War II. His horror at the genocide sparked my own morbid fascination with it and, in later years, fueled my effort to come to terms with the policy issues it provoked when I began to write about American affairs. My father's ultimate endeavor to make peace with the war also helped frame my own assessment of the struggle. A dozen years ago, while he served as president of the University of Cincinnati, business brought him to Hamburg on a European trip. Although reluctant, he entered Germany for the first time in forty years, and in so doing put the past behind him. I have, in turn, sought to use that circumscribed past to understand my own response to the Holocaust, drawing on his insights and those of other scholars who finally have the distance to wrestle with one of the most troubling events of modern times. Their efforts have helped me embrace my Jewish background, and have given me a better sense of what it means to be marginal and what it means to survive.

NOTES

1. André Schwarz-Bart, *The Last of the Just* (New York: Atheneum Publishers, 1961), 4–5. The subsequent page reference in the text pertains to this source.

2. Allan M. Winkler, *The Politics of Propaganda: The Office of War Information, 1942–1945* (New Haven, Conn.: Yale University Press, 1978), 157.

3. Arthur D. Morse, *While Six Million Died: A Chronicle of American Apathy* (1967; New York: Ace Publishing Corporation, 1968), 309.

4. Henry L. Feingold, *The Politics of Rescue: The Roosevelt Administration and the Holocaust, 1938–1945* (New Brunswick, N.J.: Rutgers University Press, 1970); quotations are from xii, xiii, and xii, respectively.

5. David S. Wyman, *Paper Walls: America and the Refugee Crisis, 1938–1941* (Amherst, Mass.: University of Massachusetts Press, 1968), 209. The subsequent page references in the text pertain to this source.

6. David S. Wyman, *The Abandonment of the Jews: America and the Holocaust, 1941–1945* (New York: Pantheon Books, 1984), ix. The subsequent page references in the text pertain to this source.

21

Using Proust's Jews to Shape
an Identity

Seth L. Wolitz

TWENTY YEARS AGO I wrote The *Proustian Community,* which was a study of Marcel Proust's novel, *Remembrance of Things Past.* I treated the taxonomy of the Jews.[1] It was one of the first treatments of Jews in the masterpiece since the post–World War II period. I studied Jews as individuals and as a caste in French society without resorting to explanations of behavior on "racial" grounds, which heretofore plagued so many earlier interpretations of Proust.

It is hard to believe that scholarly writing on Jewish characters in a French novel might have been unusual in the late 1960s, but in fact there was an element of daring and poignancy in my work, especially because it was written by a young Jewish-American French scholar. It carried a certain implication of undesirable empathy and an implicit hint of possible provinciality, and even of a hidden questioning or doubting of the universality of French culture and civilization. The "Jewish question" was always a vexing one for French scholars, given France's war record and the institutional prejudices current in the American university system at the time.

To a certain extent, any American scholar of French of whatever origins was drawn into the French cultural hegemonic practices of the age, which implied that we had committed ourselves to the absorption of a superior culture, and that any interest departing from the mainstream of French culture was almost traitorous. We did not know the term "cultural imperialism" and other Marxist terminology, but in my later reading of African Francophone writers, it became clear to me that the colonialist model imposed on them was operative even in the Yale French department. The semivoluntary act of cultural assimilation tended to amuse those American-gentile French scholars who were not actively seeking to escape their social condition. They were comfortable in their American ambience, the surrounding majority culture. When I studied at Yale in the mid-1960s, it still preserved a cultivated New England Yankee tone.

We, fresh Italian-American or Jewish-American French scholars, were working at accommodating and absorbing two cultures: French culture and the Anglo-American culture. An Italian-American had the psychological benefit of at least having his own family's cultural origins recognized by the presence of an Italian department and the appreciation of the masterpieces of Italian culture. The Jewish-American was an orphan with absolutely no recognition of his cultural past in a milieu and institution to which he had committed himself totally, assured by his family, peers, and scholars that the "university" is indeed a universalistic entity which privileges only the highest quality of human production. What was a young Jew to think? Not only was Jewish culture totally absent from the curriculum, but also anything Jewish was at best looked upon as quaint and usually dismissed as unworthy of concern. The few professors of Jewish origin in the Yale French department were disturbing role models, for they maintained a stony silence or a feigned ignorance about anything Jewish, even in the privacy of their offices. They were good subalterns of French culture, ignoring Vichy and the reason for their refuge in America, but spouting the universal glories of *Les droits de l'homme* (the Rights of Man). Anything Jewish was kept in a conspiracy of silence.

Although Yale in those days still had a rigid quota system, at least in the undergraduate program, it was acceptable to be of Jewish origin but preferably in not more than a Reform way. We were to be unobtrusive, for our task was to gain a "universal" education and the proper gentile manners and culture of America. As Jack Zipes recently put it in his Introduction to *The Operated Jew:* "Normalization, whether it be in the West or the Middle East, has meant for Jews changing oneself to fit in, becoming anonymous, or more nationalistic than the so-called natives of a nation with the expectation that whatever is Jewish about one's identity will eventually be eliminated."[2]

An Italian-American friend at Yale, when we were students together, once said to me, "What I like about you, Seth, is that you are not kikey like so many of the New York Jews at Yale." He, significantly, had altered his external identity so that the telltale final Italian syllable "lo" had fallen away from his name. (He later became well-known as the commissioner of baseball after giving up the presidency of Yale University: A.[ngelo] Bartlett Giamatti!) Identity was an important matter, for it affected one's future. I was flattered then by his casual remark; it soothed a sad urge to be able "to pass," a not inconsequential concern given this century of the Shoah. On the other hand, did it not prove how pejorative it was to be "identifiable"? How much of my dream to be a *uomo universale* was motivated by the darkest fear of being pointed out?

My Jewish past, a melange of religious rituals, warm family remembrances, the delights of hearing Yiddish and being taken to Yiddish theater, and the pained knowledge of what had happened in the extermination camps in Poland, belonged to me viscerally, and I refused to abandon this unappreciated Ashkenazic inheritance. I should have both *my* East and the West; French literature was, to play on Heine's witticism, "my entrance ticket to European culture." I enjoyed "passing" as French in France and understood that identity has both an external and internal meaning. My French landlady at first mistook me for French, but when I said I was American, she was not displeased (she gained a tax reduction for renting to foreigners); however, when she asked if my family was Protestant and I responded slyly that it was Orthodox, she shouted, "No wonder you speak French so well! All Slavs have a talent for languages" (*le don des langues*). But later when I revealed that I was a Jew (or should I say "Jewish"?), farewell to being French, American, or Slavic. I was unadulteratedly and inescapably in the same boat with Proust's Jews, Swann, Nissim Bernard, Albert Bloch, and all the House of Israel. Good Mlle Richard, a last survivor of the *belle époque,* aided me enormously in understanding allusions to social mores, customs, and prejudices in Proust's novel.

Is it any wonder that being Jewish is a double bind in this century? To the harassing anti-Semite, if one is too Jewish (whatever that means), one is attacked as tribal, exclusive, or provincial; but if one seeks to pass, one is accused of "rootless cosmopolitanism" or hiding what is unassimilable. While I was seeking my own identity, my inner core, and attempting to control my external identity *quae* Jew and American, it was inevitable that, given my Jewish-American situation, I should be drawn to Proust's remarkable study of the social psychology and cultural realities of the Jewish condition. I did not understand then the central role of identity in the novel. I was too fascinated with the strategies of Jewish upward mobility and adaptability to be really appreciative of the "colonial" implications of absorption.

Studying the Proustian novel led me to recognize the meaning of assimilation (indicating here both total acculturation and intermarriage) and to redirect my life to a greater knowledge of my Jewish inheritance. The Holocaust played its role, too, for I realized that Proust and all his Jewish characters could have been gassed with all the other French Jews. Reading Proust's novel, I appreciated little by little the historical failure of the options and strategies chosen by French Jews in their search to be good Frenchmen, even at the cost of denying their authenticity or fleeing their origins. Yet it was just such an option I saw all about me among young Jewish-Americans at Yale. I was forced to confront myself and contemplate, if not make, significant life decisions. To enter further into the fictional world of Proust and to study it as a reflection of the *belle époque* was to use Proust's life and novel as a screen to examine my own novelty and to plot my own future.

The French *belle époque,* in which the major portion of Proust's novel takes place, glowed in a brilliant cultural and social world riddled with class and creedal prejudices. Yet the social world was negotiable for a skilled French Jew, particularly one who was determined to enter the Faubourg St. Germain, the aristocratic and atavistic pinnacle of high society. Proust, raised a Catholic but whose mother was Jewish, sought to achieve this goal and he eventually succeeded. This autobiographical material later served as the matter for his novelistic transmutation. From his observations in the Faubourg St. Germain and his inner experience as an upwardly mobile figure whose maternal Jewish origins hardly aided his ascension, Proust constructed the complex mutations of the French-Jewish applicant moving through arcane social realities in order to win acceptance. This pattern is represented in his major Jewish characters. Swann is the completed and seemingly thoroughly assimilated French Jew, who later backslides, whereas Albert Bloch and his family are at the beginning of their pilgrimage toward acceptance and oblivion. Obviously, I should have wished to be the worldly and elegant Swann, but in fact I was closer to Bloch. Proust placed his own social gaffes on Bloch and made his Marcel, the narrator, the smooth social climber. As the Faubourg St. Germain was Bloch's first encounter with the French aristocracy, so Yale offered me my first real encounter with Americans of the white Protestant Yankee elite. In both cases, there was the excitement of having penetrated a magical world, but both of us were not fully aware of its myriad codes of behavior.

When two groups encounter one another for the first time they do not face one another neutrally. Each has its own expectations. In the case of the Jews entering the world of the Faubourg St. Germain, they expected to find and fulfill at least three aspirations: the attainment of acceptance and its psychological sense of security; the intoxication of participating in the most superior cultural life in the world; and a sense of entitlement, that is, an empowerment of belonging and participating in the governance. To accomplish these aspirations, the Jew in the Proustian novel is willing to forgo totally his historical past without regret and is even prepared to accept that past as contemptible and surely insignificant. Even one's personal self-history can be lost by a willed "amnesia" and reconstructed so as to emerge with a new persona in order to enter the Faubourg.

The Faubourg St. Germain is the fetishized materialization of finally being "at home" and "at ease," a status that is impossible in a social process of continuous reformulation and in which the Jew is a guest and never an arbiter. The Jew, like a colonized figure, therefore presses his luck to solicit recognition and acceptance from those who hold the sociocultural hegemony and who can thereby confer legitimacy which, simply stated, is Frenchness. I felt at Yale that same irresistible attraction to the social, cultural, and political power that surrounded me. Yale and its Yankee culture and Anglo elite accepted me insofar as I conformed to its appealing culture, but I always felt I was, in an anthropological sense, a visitor. Did I wish, however, to deny my Jewishness in order to flatter ambitions which I could in part legitimize and which received support from the Great Neck–Scarsdale Jewish world out of which I came?

The act of seeking to blot out one's Jewish genealogy leaves the individual with the need to hide his nakedness. His past is an embarrassment which must be disguised. In Proust's novel, a Jewish social climber necessarily fills the void with his projected desires: a longing for all things French of historical value. Is it any wonder that Swann lives on the Ile Saint-Louis, the very heart of old Paris, in a fine old house loaded with French antiques, as some ancient *seigneur*? Nor is it surprising that Bloch has written his thesis on Philip II (1165–1223), better known as Philip-Augustus, one of the greatest medieval kings of France, who not only aggrandized his kingdom but also admitted bourgeois into advisory councils. Frenchness, as defined by the French social-climbing Jew, meant a total immersion into all that carried French historical prestige. In this sense, there is even an aesthetic act in wishing to join the Faubourg St. Germain: to hobnob with individuals named Clermont-Tonnerre, La Rochefoucauld or, in more precisely Proustian terms, the reigning aristocrats, the Guermantes.

How pleasant it was at Yale to live and breathe French history, to be at last on the winning side. Talking with Dean Acheson, George Kennan, and others was to feel the heady perfume of power and prestige so absent in the Jewish world, and to enjoy from afar, in American circumstances, something approaching the delight of Swann and Bloch in their access to the Faubourg. It was also to realize that French citizenship, therefore, was insufficient for the French-Jewish social climber. He needed, craved, not only *de jure* acceptance, but also the fullest *de facto* acceptance from the very enemy caste which had once ghettoized him and which looked upon him as the very metaphor of the new, the revolution, that which had deprived the aristocrats of their real interests and historical right: power. Frenchness for the Jew, then, was a psychological empowerment which propelled Swann and Bloch to their dizzy performances.

Frenchness for a prince de Guermantes means not only French spiritual values and history but also race and genealogy. Whereas the Jewish *arriviste* consciously embraces the French inheritance as his own by education, citizenship, and pride, the Guermantes derive and manipulate their interpretation of Frenchness through their genealogy and by invoking their race. The spiritual inheritance of France is merely a corollary to the basic fact of their blood. The cultural accomplishments which intoxicate the French-Jewish *arriviste* are not only secondary; they are also at best the decor necessary to maintain the aura of their legitimacy as *"la vieille France"* in the socially restricted salons. Frenchness, then, for the Guermantes clan can only be what they define it as, and that *je ne sais quoi* must be composed of race, genealogy, and correct opinions.

When Bloch foolishly seeks to discuss seriously the Dreyfus affair in a minor Guermantes salon, the young duc de Chatellerault, in a swift verbal assault, teaches exactly what his Frenchness is all about and just what Bloch's place should be (at best) in the Faubourg St. Germain: " 'You must not ask me, sir, to discuss the Dreyfus case with you; it is a subject which, on principle, I never mention except to Japhetics' " (Japhet, Shem, and Ham: the sons of Noah from whom descend the three races of man).

By foregrounding Bloch's descent from Shem, the young aristocrat underscores how elusive Frenchness can be for the Jewish *salonnard* who, in spite of himself and his own definition of things French, always cedes (in Proust's novel) to the aristocrat the privilege of defining the terms of Frenchness. The duke has stripped Bloch of his French persona and revealed his nakedness and shame: Bloch has not passed; he remains just a Jew for the aristocrat: " 'But how on earth did you know? Who told you?' as though he were a convict. Whereas, given his name, which had not exactly a Christian sound, and his face, his surprise argued a certain simplicity of mind" (P 2:247).[3]

Lacking a repartee, Bloch swallows the insult and thus accommodates himself to an inferior social condition as defined by the Other. The very qualities of Frenchness which Bloch espoused, on the basis of his perception of the spiritual accomplishments of France, yield, in the salon, to a racist aristocrat's reactionary evaluation of Frenchness, which, outside the salon, the Jewish *salonnard* would reject! This cleavage in principle affects the stability of his identity.

Proust himself was an ardent Dreyfusard, and Bloch's pro-Dreyfus stance is the aesthetic translation of his creator's political activism. Even the assimilated Swann found himself affected by the Dreyfus affair, for the Dreyfus affair threatened the legitimacy of the Jew as a part of France and placed in question his identity and even his citizenship.

What the Dreyfus affair was to Proust and his characters, the the civil rights movement of the 1960s was politically and culturally to me. I found myself participating in the earliest sit-ins on the Eastern Shore of Maryland and Virginia, influenced no doubt by Proust's example and by my own growing Jewish consciousness that to defend civil rights is to defend civil rights for all the minorities, and the majorities, in the United States. I felt I was fusing my identity as American Jew and young French scholar in a morally pleasing and rich whole. If this seems naive and overblown today, it reflects, nevertheless, a more innocent era where Jewish activism, after the passive McCarthy era, was new, refreshing, and daring. Like Bloch in the novel, I wished to preserve the best of the old world of the Other and yet pursue what I believed to be my moral duty.

In America, as distinguished from France, I wanted to believe that the Anglo elite, in both North and South, could evolve and accept me without my being obliged to pay the price of the French Jews in Proust's novel.

Swann's and Bloch's emotional need for status and psychological validation of their Frenchness could not be obtained from the republic. The French Revolution in 1791 had conferred citizenship but it did not—could not—confer French "communal rights" on the the historical, aesthetic, social, nationalist, and emotional levels. This aura of total French "authenticity" was guarded and rarely dispensed by the salons of the Faubourg St. Germain. Proust learned this truth and transmuted it in his art, but his Jewish characters remained drawn desperately to the glittering lights of the salons.

I could appreciate such delusions, for I found myself delighted visiting the homes and restricted clubs of my Anglo friends in Wilton and New Canaan. At the same time, I experienced a growing appreciation of my own often maligned "New York Jewish inheritance": museum expeditions every week-end, seats at the "Met" (Metropolitan Opera) and at the "Symphony," attending theater and new gallery shows, debating the meaning of being Jewish in a Chinese restaurant, smelling the aromas of a Jewish delicatessen or bakery (gastronomic Judaism!). What an emotional richness I felt still remained at Jewish family gatherings on Jewish and American holidays, with those groaning tables satirized by Philip Roth surrounded by the wonderous free expression of feelings I witnessed between the generations. New York was seemingly a Jewish polis and I enjoyed belonging to its clan. I did envy the grass tennis courts in a restricted club to which I was invited as a guest; I wanted to copy that Yankee tradition of dinner by candlelight, but I was becoming aware that the Yankee elite were trying quite as much to imitate aristocratic Britons as we Jewish-Americans were in aping our Anglo-American peers. Were we Jewish-Americans not running after a chimera? Our grief was with the restrictive clauses in their clubs and housing areas, as well as with the *numerus clausus* at the universities. But once that world was breached, and the novelty passed, was it not as banal as Marcel the narrator's discovery that the Guermantes were magical in his eyes alone? I, too, had followed the same path. Only now do I realize that I was just beginning the task of decolonizing my mind and accepting myself *quae* Jew and American. Wasn't this precisely the same task that Marcel the narrator relates in the novel in order to find his vocation? Marcel repeats what Proust the author had accomplished earlier.

The "Friendship" proffered by the Guermantes was an abusive contract which exploited real talent in exchange for the "honor" of being in their august presence, which the *Hofjuden* hoped could magically transsubstantiate them into true friends and coequal associates. Blind to their objective condition, as Sartre would have put it, these Jewish social climbers were functioning in "bad faith." Yet they needed to function thusly, for their identity was at stake. Watching their sad performance reinforced my need to turn back to my Jewishness as an act of authenticity.

When my best friend, a Jewish-American, agreed to be married in a church, I refused to be his best man. I rejected his position that we were now "universalists," free and detached from our biological ascendants, and able to choose our destiny without observing our "objective condition" or admitting any responsibility to our historical inheritance, particularly when it was considered negatively by the "significant other" he was espousing. My position cost me a friendship, but I could not accept this willful act of assimilation, the source of which was the shame of being Jewish.

Proust believed in and wanted the ultimate assimilation of the Jews into France and throughout Europe (P 1:738–39). His vision of the melding of the "races" assumes the disappearance of a Jewish nationality. Somehow, Jewish "bad manners" would be cleaned up when mixed with other elements. I found his thinking offensive and realized it was an argument based on his own condition as a child of a mixed marriage and the liberal position of the age. He had no appreciation of a renewed Jewish peoplehood and certainly no patience with Zionism (P 2:620) and its legitimizing a sovereign Jewish nation.

Nevertheless Proust had enough artistic integrity and moral conviction to ridicule Jewish self-hatred, particularly in the case of Albert Bloch, where Proust captures this horrid condition:

> "You can't make a step without meeting them," said the voice. "I am not in principle irremediably hostile to the Jewish nationality, but here there is a plethora of them. You hear nothing but, 'Oy, Abe, guess vot? Jake I just saw!' You would think you were in the Rue d'Aboukir [street of small commercial wholesalers particularly of yard goods in the second arrondissement in Paris]." The man who thus inveighed against Israel emerged at last; we raised our eyes to behold this anti-Semite. It was my old friend Bloch. (P 1:738)

In these unguarded moments, Bloch becomes psychologically close kin to the dominant aggressive Other and thereby tastes ever so briefly its power to deny, denigrate, and dismiss a despised group. By daring to imitate the immigrant accent, he seeks to increase further the distance between himself and his immediate forebears. At the same time, his self-hating mockery serves the spurious argument of the Other to maintain Jewish marginality in French society and to justify Jews' excision from the French "nationhood."

How often did I hear such imitations by Jews so desirous to fawn on the gentile society and to escape their Jewish condition. Thanks to the screen of Proust's novel, my growing sense of my own Jewish dignity permitted me to recognize that our attempts at obsequiousness only earned us greater alienation and disrespect. Unlike my friend, who found the baptismal font the means to obtain his wholeness and fulfillment, I had to turn away and assert my dignity as a Jew and demand my rights as a human being such as I was. At last I understood the powerful statement of Proust's artist, Elstir, who said that wisdom is a point of view on things that can be gained only by one's own efforts, without any help from anyone else (P 1:864).

I finally had to recognize that even Proust, or at least his narrator, Marcel, harbored both racist and naive notions about the Jews and ultimately considered them outsiders. In an offensive scene in which the anti-Semitic Baron de Charlus inquires if Bloch has a Jewish first name, "out of simple aesthetic curiosity and love of local color" (P 2:191), the narrator states in seeming innocence, "An hour later Bloch went about believing that it was out of anti-Semitic malevolence" (P 2:190–91). And yet this Baron de Charlus tells the narrator:

> "Perhaps you could arrange some amusing events. For example, a fight between your friend [Bloch] and his father in which he would wound him as David did Goliath. That would be an amusing farce. . . . since we love exotic spectacles and beating up an extra-european creature would deliver a well-deserved lesson to an old dog." (P 2:288)

("Old dog," in French, is *chameau,* which means both "camel" and, in slang, "old dog" or "scoundrel." Proust's use of *chameau,* therefore, captures both meanings to emphasize that an "extra-european" creature is both foreign and a scoundrel like the *chameau!*)

Marcel, the narrator, is shocked, but a few pages later states quite easily: "Bloch thought he had arrived at his pro-Dreyfus stand by logic, [but] he knew, nonetheless, that his nose, his skin, and his hair had been imposed upon him by his race" (P 2:297).

Race for Proust is an aspect of the natural origins of the world and reflects natural law. Biologically determined, our presumed race forces itself upon the character no matter how much he seeks to shield himself. In Proust's mind, the idea of racial distinction was especially applicable to the Jews. Proust was obsessed with the noses of Jews. When Swann is in his better days, his nose is elegant, but when his Jewish "race" reemerged, the nose became "enormous, swollen, reddened, rather like one of an old Jew, than of a Valois [read: French Aryan]" (P 2:690). When Bloch frenchifies his name to Jacques du Rozier, his nose becomes more refined and makes one think of Mascarillio rather than Salomon (P 2:190). Marcel's thoughts regarding race and the Jews differ little from those of the anti-Semites in the novel.

I well remember the rash of nose jobs in the 1950s among Jews who wished to enter the mainstream of American society and to conform to images of physical correctness set forth in the popular media. How many of my own generation stared at their faces in the mirror to decide if their noses looked too Jewish and needed the operation? How many friends, determined to get into the Ivy League, thought to outsmart the academic trufflehounds by changing their names from Horowitz to Haarewood? Proust's jaunty treatment of noses and racial identity could only be antipathetic to me.

Nevertheless, in the Proustian novel, I was introduced to the rich and complex world of European culture and was able to use the novel as a mirror of my own weaknesses, strengths, and flawed ambitions. It was thanks to this novel that I was able to enter contemporary life and participate in the civil rights movement and to define myself as a Jew and an American. I had emancipated myself of the thought that I wanted to be a Frenchman and live in French culture or pass myself off as a Yankee. It was a good feeling and intellectually satisfying to read the Song of Songs and to listen to a recitation of Sholem Aleichem's *Tevye the Dairyman* in the Yiddish original, as well as to read Saul Bellow or Philip Roth and hear my own community, both past and present, express the values and feelings which were mine by inheritance and now by choice. Thanks to the Proustian novel, I could enjoy the splendors of French literature without needing to sell my soul.

My critical reading of Proust's work taught me to view assimilation as a temptation which must be resisted. Swann and Bloch, for all their intelligence, culture, and worldliness, were no more sophisticated than Emma

Bovary in reading French society. They were seduced as she was by a seemingly superior culture and lifestyle.

Later I wrote a book on Proust's novel. I then further explored my Jewish inheritance. It developed into my life's vocation: the study and recovery of Yiddish literature and culture, that almost forgotten and tragic territory from which modern Jewry emerged.

Proust's novel serves therefore as a milestone in my life. His masterpiece forced me to encounter myself and to redirect my life. To this day, I continue to acknowledge the work's insights and artistry. I find myself agreeing more and more with the words that Proust cleverly put into the mouth of Elstir the artist: "I understand that the image of what we have been in an earlier period may no longer be recognizable and may be in any case disagreeable. It should not be, however, disavowed for it is the evidence that we have truly lived" (P 1:864).

NOTES

1. Seth L. Wolitz, *The Proustian Community* (New York: New York University Press, 1971).

2. *The Operated Jew: Two Tales of Anti-Semitism,* trans. Jack Zipes (New York: Routledge, 1991), 41.

3. All quotations from Proust's novel are from the following edition: Marcel Proust, *A la recherche du temps perdu,* ed. Pierre Clarac and Andre Ferre, 3 vols. (Paris: Librarie Gallimard, 1954). These are cited parenthetically in the text with "P," standing for the original Pleiade edition. The English quotations are my own translations of this edition; however, in some instances I've adapted them on the basis of C. K. Scott Moncrieff's translation of Proust: *Remembrance of Things Past,* 2 vols. (New York: Random House, 1934).

22

"Juifemme"

Elaine Marks

Preface

My work over the past thirty years includes research, writing, and teaching on late-nineteenth-century and twentieth-century French literature with a special emphasis on women writers, on questions relating to the feminist inquiry and critical theory, on autobiographical and biographical texts. My administrative duties with the Women's Studies Program and the Women's Studies Research Center at the University of Wisconsin–Madison from 1977 to 1984 brought me into contact with biological and social scientists working on questions that overlapped with some of mine. Their formulations of these questions and other changes within the intellectual scene in the United States and Western Europe have obliged me to rethink one of the central areas of debate within the humanities: the relative weighting of discursive practice and the status of the referent, the importance accorded on the one hand to language and on the other to lived experience and to history.

During the summer of 1987, I completed work on two articles: one, "1929, *L'histoire de la littérature féminine* by Jean Larnac," for the *Harvard Dictionary of French Literature;* the other, " 'Sapho 1900': Imaginary Renée Viviens and the Rear of the *belle époque,*" for an issue of *Yale French Studies.* The books and journals I consulted for these articles dealt with the rhetorical, ideological, and material effects of late-nineteenth-century nationalist, sexist, racist, and anti-Semitic discourses on the question of *littérature féminine.* I was fascinated by the ways in which these discourses and the theories and ideology that nourish them overlap. I became particularly interested in exploring further the Jewish question as a constitutive element within French literature and culture. I soon realized that the terms and the tenor of the Jewish question in French writing had changed considerably since the end of the nineteenth century. From the time of the Dreyfus affair until 1940, it was the coupling of "La France" and "Le Juif," in which the positive term "La France" defined itself in relation to the negative term "Le Juif," that dominated the anti-Semitic ideology. Since 1945, it is rather "Le(s) Juif(s)" in the form of ashes, absence, and writing that raises simultaneously the specter of nihilism and the glory of the "Book." In a sense it could be said that I came to the Jewish question and presence not through Judaism but rather through "Auschwitz" and the extermination of European Jewry, that is to say, through mourning, loss, death, and absence.

At the same time as I was moving toward an intellectual and affective interest in the Jewish question and presence in French writing, I was also moving toward new dissatisfactions with women's studies and feminisms as they are theorized and practiced in the United States, dissatisfactions that I expressed in my essay "Feminisms' Wake" in *Boundary II* (1985), and in my contribution to "Conference Call" in *differences* (1990). These dissatisfactions found an echo in Harold Bloom's descriptions of "Fundamentalism" in his book of religious criticism, *The American Religion* (1992).

My title, "Juifemme," is taken from a subheading in Hélène Cixous' essay "Sorties" (Ways Out), the second part of *La jeune née* (The Newly Born Woman), written in collaboration with Catherine Clément and published during the *annus mirabilis* of theoretical writing by women in France: 1975. I understand the word "Juifemme" as used by Hélène Cixous to be a conscious attempt to write against the fixed ethnic and gender meanings of fundamentalist or identity politics, to undercut the many dogmas and pieties that inform being "Jewish" or being "woman," and to propose other ways of figuring identity. For my purposes, "Juifemme" displaces being Jewish from the domain of religious questions to the domain of philosophical, or political, or literary, or linguistic questions. In order to do justice to my title, I have divided my chapter into three parts that correspond to three different modes of engaging, in an autobiographical approach, the reconfiguring of (my) Jewish (European and) American identity: the personal, the political, and the poetical.

Part 1. The Personal

Since childhood, Sigmund Freud has been a constant figure in my affective and my intellectual life, a figure associated with family members, particularly one uncle, interminably analyzed, who was my first mentor. For most members of my secular Jewish family, Freudian psychoanalysis played the role of governing principle, frame of reference, and endless source of Jewish pride. This role continued through my own analysis, from age thirteen to seventeen, and beyond adolescence into my young adult life. It colored my encounters with religion, socialism, and feminism on the one hand, anti-Semitism and racism on the other, not to mention my work in French language, literature, and culture and my engagements with people whom I have loved. I would like to explore briefly different moments of this relationship with Sigmund Freud in an attempt to understand why I continue to find it so exciting, and how Freud's Jewish atheism and my own, how being, like Freud, a secular, godless Jew, is central not only to my Jewishness but also to my sense of Who and What I "am."

First of all, my awareness as a child that only boys and men were really Jews: boys were circumcised, some boys wore *yarmulkes*, some boys had bar mitzvahs. You could see, if you looked at their penises, that boys and men were Jews. I could hear that my maternal grandmother was Jewish, because every morning and every evening she recited prayers in Hebrew and Yiddish. But hearing is not seeing. On my mother's side of the family the women, my mother and her sisters, had all been on the stage: acting, singing, playing the piano, and dancing. Not one of them "performed Jewishness," that is to say, dressed or talked or behaved like the Jewish mothers and relatives of my Jewish friends on the south shore of Long Island or on Riverside Drive in New York City. And most important for my understanding, we were not Christians. We did not observe Christian holidays, we were different from, superior to, the *"goyim"* (the word applied exclusively to Christians), who were, in spite of much evidence to the contrary, blonde and dumb. If in my imagination Jews were men, *goyim* were women. This curious binary opposition was reinforced by my "phallic" mother's talent for telling stories, Jewish stories that were often dirty jokes, with the punch line in Yiddish. At gatherings of family and friends, my mother, as storyteller, was the central figure. Her stories, which provoked howls of laughter from most listeners, were usually at the expense of ridiculous, impotent, henpecked Ashkenazic Jewish men, whether Litvaks or Galitzianers. The "little yiddle" (my mother's word) was the focus and the butt of her humor. And then there were the rabbis, whom my mother referred to as the wild ones, in their long coats and wide-brimmed fur hats, who presided over the seders we attended during Pesach with my maternal grandmother at Jewish hotels in the Rockaways. Their performances were commented on with denigrating humor by my mother, next to whom I sat during the meals. Until I encountered Sigmund Freud in my uncle's library and overheard whispered comments about my uncle's analysis, Jews were all pathetic, comic, slightly repulsive male characters. The picture becomes clearer: Jews are unattractive men; we are not Christian; *goyim* are dumb, blonde women; we are Jewish. To be a Jew is not the same as being Jewish. Sigmund Freud was Jewish.

To be Jewish like Freud was to be intelligent, liberal, generous, talented, bright, superior, European, cosmopolitan, and irreligious. *The Future of an Illusion* (1927) was the Torah in our house. My mother frequently repeated Karl Marx's slogan "Religion is the opiate of the masses," but it was Freud, not Moses and not Marx, who was the giver of laws. And if Freud, rather than Marx, was the central figure in our household, it is in great part because, as Yosef Hayim Yerushalmi has understood so well in *Freud's Moses: Judaism Terminable and Interminable,* for both Freud and my mother, " 'Jewishness' can be transmitted independently of 'Judaism,' [because] the former is interminable even if the latter be terminated."[1]

And so this transmission of Jewishness continues through me, with occasional eruptions of Judaism. I transmit Jewishness by saying and repeating "I am Jewish" in social situations when I consider it appropriate to mark a difference or raise the question. This is, in the groups within which I move in the United States and in France, a frequent occurrence. And the reaction I hear most often is: How can you be Jewish without being a practicing Jew or even believing in God? My response is not simple, nor is it usually convincing to my interlocutors. I am Jewish precisely because I am not a believer, because I associate from early childhood the courage not to believe with being Jewish; I am Jewish because of familial ties and loyalties; I am Jewish because of the memory, transmitted to me by members of my family, of suffering and pain. My mother died in October of 1981 and was buried in my father's family plot, the Jacob Marks plot, at Beth El Cemetery in Paramus, New Jersey. The rabbi, hastily found for the occasion and coached by me on what not to say, called for someone to read the graveside Kaddish. I am an only child, divorced and unmarried, and I stepped forward with the righteous gentile woman with whom I live, and we read together the transliterated version of the prayer. "Juifemme" indeed.

Part 2. The Political

During the summer of 1987 in France, the trial of Klaus Barbie took place in Lyons, and Claude Lanzmann's nine-hour film *Shoah* was shown for the first time on public television. The "Question Juive" was receiving considerable attention in the media from all sides of the political spectrum. I had noted with some surprise in early June that, when I went to the movies with friends and the credits appeared on the screen, someone would inevitably say something like: Look at all the names that are not French. The names that were not French were recognizably Jewish names. What interested me then, and continues to fascinate me, is the French preoccupation with what it means to be French, and the manner in which Frenchness is defined in relation to what is not French. What is not French, in France, is frequently Jewish. What's in a name? In France, a fixed, unchanging identity is thought by some to be "revealed" in names.

Jewish names continued to play a leading role during the summer of 1987. At the trial of Klaus Barbie, the French-Jewish lawyer Serge Klarsfeld, who with his German wife, Beate Klarsfeld, was largely responsible for bringing Klaus Barbie to trial, read aloud the names of the Jewish children who were in hiding as refugees at an orphanage in Izieu, not far from Lyons, and whose deportation to Auschwitz Barbie had ordered. For the first time, in the course of this same summer, I held in my hands at the Centre de Documentation Juive et Contemporaine in Paris, the lists of names, carefully noted by the Gestapo, of the Jews deported from France, mostly from Drancy, in eighty-six convoys between 1942 and 1944. (These lists, which people still come to the Centre de Documentation to consult, have been reprinted in the *Memorial to the Jews Deported from France 1942–1944* [1978], edited by Serge Klarsfeld.)

And in a neo-Fascist bookstore in Paris, called significantly La Librairie Française, (The French Bookstore), I picked up a volume called *Les Juifs dans la France d'aujourd'hui* (Jews in France Today) (1985). The author's name, Gygès, is clearly a pseudonym. In all the anti-Semitic books sold publicly in France since the mid-1980s, there is always a preface disavowing any intention of anti-Semitism, and insisting on the need to be fair about the Jewish question, to say both the good and the bad. This kind of preface also regularly states that it is important to write about the Jews because their numbers are increasing in France and because Jews are everywhere (read: they are taking over) in important places. The reader is forewarned.

The purpose of Gygès' book is to identify Jews living in France today. It lists Jewish writers, Jews in the liberal professions, the government, the film industry, journalism, the theater. It lists Jewish organization, synagogues, and cultural groups, and it tells the reader how to recognize modified Jewish names. Moreover when these categories and groups are exhausted, there are lists of names, Jewish names, in alphabetical order—just family names. It is a frightening exercise to juxtapose the list of names of the children of Izieu, or the much longer lists of the *Memorial to the Jews Deported from France,* with the list of names in *Jews in France Today.* Many of the names are, of course, the same.

Here is a brief example of the tone and the intention of Gygès:

> In order to have an idea of the importance of Israelites in the French capital, all you have to do is to open the telephone book at the letter L, to look at Lévi or Levy and to count the number of subscribers listed in the phone book who have one or another of these surnames. You will discover that there are hundreds upon hundreds of them, four times more of them than there are Duponts.[2]

The preoccupation of the anti-Semites with identifying Jews is matched by the preoccupation of some French Jews with "coming out" as Jews and "outing" other Jews. If many anti-Semites in France want to know who is and who isn't Jewish, so do some French Jews. The question of identity has become a central factor in cultural and social as well as political and religious life in France, as it has in the United States. If anti-Semites have *their* favorite stereotype of what constitutes Jewishness, so do some "French" Jews. And *their* stereotype frequently includes the obligation to be a practicing Jew.[3] An active relation to the religion of Judaism is tending to become a sine qua non of Jewishness. Thus far I have spoken of France, but I would now like to give two brief examples from the United States that are equally disturbing, at least for those whose Jewishness resembles mine.

The first example is from a course I taught at the University of Wisconsin–Madison during the spring semester of 1991, through the Women's Studies Program and cross-listed with our nascent Jewish Studies Program, titled "Jewish Women: Writers, Intellectuals, Activists." Most of the Jewish women in the class, about twenty-eight of the forty-five students, were unwilling to accept Rosa Luxembourg, Hannah Arendt, and Simone Weil as "Jewish." Any serious questioning of Judaism by nonpracticing, nonobservant, nonreligious Jews—the students' criticisms did not cover the work of Judith Plaskow, for example—was considered anti-Semitic and was immediately and categorically rejected.

The second example comes from an article that appeared in the *Capital Times* of Madison, Wisconsin, October 19–20, 1990, on the efforts of Rabbi Ephraim Buchwald "to bring the non-religious and the unaffiliated . . . the marginal Jews . . . back into active faith" (9A). In this sentence "non-religious," "unaffiliated," and "marginal" are synonyms. I do not contest the desire to proselytize. But once again, as with my Jewish students, I challenge (and I resent) the refusal to recognize nonreligious, unaffiliated, marginal Jews as Jewish, the refusal even to consider the possible coexistence of Jewishness and "assimilation" (a word which is on its way to becoming the epitome of evil in Jewish studies).

In a letter to Kurt Blumenfeld about the assimilationist position, Hannah Arendt wrote: "In a society on the whole hostile to the Jews—and that situation obtained in all countries in which Jews lived, down to the twentieth century—it is possible to assimilate only by assimilating anti-Semitism also."[4] This is an ironic and a profound comment, and it is essential to my understanding of assimilation. I do not think that it is possible to live in any contemporary Western society without assimilating anti-Semitism, whatever one's religious beliefs and practices may be. Anti-Semitism is too pervasive, in overlapping areas of language and culture, not to become part of discourses and feelings. But at the same time it is, as least for Jews, the coming to terms with the existence of anti-Semitism outside and inside that is an important component of "being" Jewish in the late twentieth century.

"Juifemme" puts into motion "I," "Jew-Jewish," and "woman." What and Who am I? Is the difference only between "Jew-Jewish" and "woman," or is it also between Jews, between women, and between competing theories of the subject? Are we, if we insist on one of these terms alone, "Jew" or "woman," running the risk of reproducing, as Jean-François Lyotard suggests (in the words of Eric Santner), those narcissistic patterns that are partly responsible for nazism as is any attempt to refuse nomadism and fragmentation and to insist upon a return to roots?[5]

In a 1991 issue of *Tikkun*, Ilene Philipson, in an essay entitled "What's the Big I.D.? The Politics of the Authentic Self," "attacks" (the editors' word) identity politics: "At the foundation of identity politics is a fundamental belief in the necessity of expressing an identifiable 'authentic self,' and this belief increasingly has become the means through which individuals interpret their own experience and give it social expression."[6] Ilene Philipson is in turn attacked (or at least severely criticized) by Henry Louis Gates, Jr., Ellen Willis, David Biale, and Arthur Waskow. I am interested in changing the terms of this debate and in investigating what happens when we create, as

Hélène Cixous has, a portmanteau word that attempts, poetically and ironically, to transcend the separate strands that constitute contemporary identity politics by producing a new word: for example "Juifemme."

Part 3. The Poetical

"Juifemme" is, at first glance, the coming together of two French words, *Juif* (Jew) and *femme* (woman). In "Juifemme," depending on how you look at it, there is either a lost *f* or only one *f* that belongs to both words. If the *f* belongs to *Juif* then it is *âme* (the soul) that follows. If the *f* belongs to *femme* then there is a drift toward words that mean "I am, I have pleasure, I hear." Both *Juif* and *femme* are words with a troubled history. *Juif* was the word stamped by the Vichy government on the identity cards of Jews in France, making it easier for the Nazis to round them up. *Juif* in exotic lettering, parodying the letters of the Hebrew alphabet or Gothic script, also appeared on the yellow star that Jews were required to wear sewn onto their outer garments in the Occupied Zone. *Femme,* meaning both "woman" and "wife" in French, may be interpreted as incorporating the subservient and the property status of woman into the assignment of sex and gender.

The French-Jewish writer Albert Cohen, in a text entitled *O vous, frères humains* (Oh You, Human Brothers), tells the story of his encounter in Paris with an anti-Semitic street hawker who verbally harasses him. At the end of his narrative Cohen writes:

> From the day of this encounter, I could not look at a newspaper without immediately noting the word "Juif," immediately at the first glance. And I even notice the words that resemble this terrible word, this sad and beautiful word, I notice immediately "juin" [June] and "suif" [suet, mutton fat] and, in English, I notice immediately "few," "dew," "jewel."[7]

For Albert Cohen, paronomasia and rhyme expand the possibilities of making visible the inner obsession with the word *Juif,* "Jew."

Hélène Cixous' delight in the play of the signifier, in portmanteau words, is of another kind, and echoes the delight of her major intertextual reference, James Joyce, whose famous coupling in *Ulysses* "Jewgreek is greekjew. Extremes meet"[8] is quoted by Jacques Derrida at the end of his essay "Violence and Metaphysics" (1966), on the French-Jewish philosopher Emmanuel Lévinas. In Cixous' "Sorties" (Ways Out), the heading "Juifemme" is preceded by the heading "L'aube du phallocentrisme" (The Dawn of Phallocentrism) and two quotations from Sigmund Freud's *Moses and Monotheism,* and it is followed by references to Kafka's *Before the Law,* a parable through which Cixous reads the birth of phallocentrism and its devastating effects on Jew and woman. The beauty of the portmanteau word is not that it brings together what has been separate (as in "Jewgreek," "Greekjew"), and not, as I interpret it, that it makes a synthesis. "Juifemme" is more than, different from, Jew and woman, or

Jewoman. It is a rich poetic word in which the sounds of *je*, "I," and *jouir*, "to have pleasure," and *ouïr*, "to hear" (*je suis femme* and *je jouis* and *j'ouïs*) as well as the visual juxtaposition of *Juif*, "a Jewish man," and *femme*, "woman," prevent any one-way meaning of sex, gender, subjectivity, or religious belonging, any coincidence of hearing and seeing. As Jean-François Lyotard proposes in his essay "Jewish Oedipus," hearing rather than seeing occupies a primary position both in Hebrew ethics, in which representation is forbidden, and in psychoanalysis. What one hears in "Juifemme" does seem to open more possibilities than what one sees.[9]

If I have chosen a portmanteau word, in French, to carry my deliberately ambivalent messages, it is because, like Jacques Derrida, I suffer from a *mal de l'appartenance*, a "belonging sickness." Let me begin to end with a quotation from *Circonfession* (Circumfession), a text on Jacques Derrida by Geoffrey Bennington *and* Jacques Derrida.

> It is undoubtedly during those years (1942–1943 in Algeria, North Africa) that J.D. was stamped as "belonging" in this curious manner to Judaism: a wound, certainly, a painful sensitivity schooled in anti-Semitism as in all forms of racism, the response of a flayed victim to xenophobia, but also an impatience with gregarious identification, with the militantism of belonging in general, even with Jewish belonging. In short, a double refusal, of which we have so many signs, and much before *Circonfession*. (Let me say in passing that J.D. surprised me less than he believed or pretended to believe in exhibiting his circumcision in these pages: for a long time, he has been speaking only of his circumcision, I can prove this with supporting quotations from such places where he names it as *Glas*, *La carte postale*, *Schibboleth* (in particular), *Ulysse gramophone*. As to what can tie "this is my body and I give it to you" of the Eucharist to the exhibiting of the circumcised body, we can add to the above texts the seminar that J.D., so they tell me, is devoting to "the rhetoric of cannibalism," to what he refers to as "the loving" of "the loving–eating–the other" and, of course, to the big question of transsubstantiation.) This belonging sickness, one might almost say identification sickness, affects the entire corpus of J.D.'s work in which "the deconstruction of one's own" is, it seems to me, at the heart of his afflicted thought.[10]

Geoffrey Bennington's J. D. suffers from the xenophobia of the anti-Semites and the racists and suffers also from the injunction to be Jewish by accepting inclusion in a group already constituted and defined as Jewish. "Identification sickness" may, however, be a misnomer, or at any rate an improper analogy for "belonging sickness." One might identify, one might recognize similarities, without wishing to belong or accepting inclusion. Identifying and recognizing—and these are not the same—are psychological, philosophical stances, whereas belonging is a social position, and involves an obligation to follow preexisting discourses, institutions, and practices. This "belonging sickness," which I and others seem to share with Jacques Derrida as diagnosed by Geoffrey Bennington, is the refusal of identity politics and ultimately of stereotypes. It is the acceptance of being Jewish and being assimilated, of being Jewish and being other at the same time.

Two recent books which I read with a certain ethnic intensity but little intellectual pleasure and one book which I read with ethnic intensity and enormous intellectual pleasure will help me make my points in another mode. The books are Letty Cottin Pogrebin's *Deborah, Golda, and Me: Being Female and Jewish in America;* Alan M. Dershowitz's *Chutzpah;* and Yirmiyahu Yovel's *Spinoza and Other Heretics.* Differences in genre and intention notwithstanding, the autobiographical texts by Pogrebin and Dershowitz inevitably tend toward narcissism and exhibitionism, whereas the philosophical tome on Spinoza maintains a very different style level throughout. I found Pogrebin's account particularly disturbing because she seems to know intuitively how women and Jews should think and behave. Nothing could be further from Hélène Cixous' "Juifemme" than Pogrebin's search for "a comfortable collective identity" that includes being female and Jewish in America. Dershowitz is considerably more open than Pogrebin to differences—political, philosophical, ethnic—and to questions that challenge any simple answers. His sixth chapter, "Visiting Synagogues around the World: Exploring the Different Meanings of Jewishness," repeats in varying formulations "that the Jewish way is not a singular road, but rather an almost endless series of interconnecting paths with a common origin and an uncertain and unknowable destination— or destinations." My preference for Yovel's *Spinoza and Other Heretics* will come as no surprise for the readers of this chapter. Spinoza is represented by Yovel as a heretical Jew who abandoned the normative Jewish practices of his time and refused to convert to Christianity. Spinoza is the Jew who, according to Yovel, prefigures contemporary Judaism, which is determined by the way Jews live rather than by an obligatory model which all Jews must follow.[11] Yovel's Spinoza resembles my Freud.

"Before Auschwitz," two of the main protagonists in European narrative fiction were assimilated Jews, Leopold Bloom and Charles Swann, distinguished by their cultural and "racial" differences from the Christian cultures in which they lived. "After Auschwitz," in texts by Paul Celan, Edmond Jabès, Jacques Derrida, and Hélène Cixous, the trope of the wandering marked Jew and the poet as wanderer erases the racial connotations in favor of estrangement, so that anyone, in Hélène Cixous' words, "can be a Jew, anyone who is sensitive to the cut, to what by marking a limit, produces otherness."[12] We are not by law or by nature "Juifemme," but we may choose to be so.

What remains most important for me is the construction of a discourse that sustains both the particular and the general, the political and the poetical, the social and the ontological, that is, the question of being Jewish and being a woman, and the question of being. At the beginning of this chapter, I noted that I came to questions of Jewishness through the Shoah. It would be more accurate to state that in the beginning was an obsession with death and absence, to which the Jewish story became attached.

The earliest ontological experience that I remember occurred at the age of four at the time of my maternal grandfather's death. I was sitting at the piano and saying over and over again, "Dead forever and ever," and trying to comprehend "forever." The second revelation was occasioned by the taste of bacon (not a neutral food in this context), for which I had an inordinate fondness, and my attempts at comprehending where the taste went when it was no longer in my mouth, the complete absence of what had been so overwhelmingly present. Before I was consciously aware of "being" Jewish or "being" a woman, I was aware of "being" and the possibility of not "being." This has remained over the years as the most constant of my experiences and of my intellectual concerns.

During my years at college, when I was free from the turmoils of adolescence, the literary and philosophical texts that most deeply affected my intellectual growth and my affective life were passages from François Villon's *Testament* (1461), from Blaise Pascal's *Pensées* (1670), French lyrical poetry from Baudelaire to Bonnefoy, Tolstoy's "Death of Ivan Illych" (1886), the long passage on the death of the grandmother in Marcel Proust's *Remembrance of Things Past* (1913–27), passages in Colette's first-person writings on old age, and, in general, novels and biographical writing that tell the story of a life in and through time.

This has not changed, but the specific areas of inquiry have. I am therefore obliged to admit that, had it not been for World War II and the Shoah, I would not have turned my research efforts so passionately to the Jewish question and the Jewish presence in French writing and, by extension, in other languages, literatures, cultures, and in myself. In all honesty I must conclude that the *je suis* (I am) which we hear in "Juifemme" matters more to me now, and always has, than what we see in "Juifemme."

NOTES

1. Yosef Hayim Yerushalmi, *Freud's Moses: Judaism Terminable and Interminable* (New Haven: Yale University Press, 1991), 90.

2. Gygès, *Les Juifs dans la France d' aujourd'hui* (Paris: Documents et Témoignages, 1985), 86.

3. "Les 100 Juifs qui comptent en France," *Passages* 14 (February 1989).

4. Arendt is quoted in Elizabeth Young-Bruehl, *Hannah Arendt: For Love of the World* (New Haven: Yale University Press, 1982), 92.

5. Eric Santner, *Stranded Objects* (Ithaca, N.Y.: Cornell University Press, 1990), 8–9.

6. Ilene Philipson, "What's the Big I.D.? The Politics of the Authentic Self," *Tikkun* (November-December 1991): 51.

7. Albert Cohen, *O vous, frères humains* (Paris: Gallimard, Folio #1915, 1972), 73–74; my translation.

8. James Joyce, *Ulysses* (New York: Random House, Modern Library, 1964), 493.

9. Jean-François Lyotard, "Jewish Oedipus," trans. Susan Hanson, *Genre* 10 (Fall 1977): 395–411.

10. Geoffrey Bennington and Jacques Derrida, *Jacques Derrida: Derridabase circonfession* (Paris: Seuil, 1991), 300–301; my translation. (This text has also been published as *Jacques Derrida*, trans. Geoffrey Bennington [Chicago: University of Chicago Press, 1983].)

11. Letty Cottin Pogrebin, *Deborah, Golda, and Me: Being Female and Jewish in America* (New York: Crown, 1991), xiv; Alan M. Dershowitz, *Chutzpah* (Boston: Little, Brown, 1991), 206; Yirmiyahu Yovel, *Spinoza and Other Heretics*, 2 vols. (Princeton: Princeton University Press, 1989).

12. Hélène Cixous, *Readings: The Poetics of Blanchot, Joyce, Kafka, Kleist, Lispector, and Tsvetayeva*, ed., trans., and intro. Verena Andermatt Conley (Minneapolis: University of Minnesota Press, 1991), 147.

PART V

MEDITATIONS

Thou hast chosen us from among all nations—
what, O Lord, did you have against us?
                                    —Yiddish saying

23

Between Texts

From Assimilationist Novel to
Resistance Narrative

Herbert Lindenberger

INTERLOCUTOR: To get back to this identity question—

AUTHOR: Listen, all my life I've not thought consciously what my identity was supposed to be. You are imposing a totally recent concept—something that dates back at best to the late 1950s[1]—on somebody whose "identity," shall we say, was shaped long before the term was invented.

INTERLOCUTOR: But surely you must feel something inside you corresponding to what people call their Jewish identity.

AUTHOR: If the word wasn't there I'm sure I never felt a thing. What I feel comes from words I've learned.

INTERLOCUTOR: Then we'll scrap the word "identity." Just tell me in what ways you see yourself being Jewish-American.

AUTHOR: I assume this to be a recent term coined on the analogy of Asian-American and Afro-, pardon me, African-American.

INTERLOCUTOR: Let me assure you, people have been calling themselves Jewish-American ever since the big immigration began.

AUTHOR: Not Jewish-American. I never heard that word until the last decade or two. In the old days you said "American Jew," or, for those too coy to make a noun out of their Jewishness, it was simply "American Jewish."

INTERLOCUTOR: You are making a joke out of people's honest attempts to situate themselves.

AUTHOR: And you are sanctifying a hybrid new concoction based on some fashionable model.

INTERLOCUTOR: Your defensiveness has made it hard to communicate.

AUTHOR: Then let me approach this thing another way: I recognize that a certain glamour nowadays adheres to those who see themselves as marginalized. But I for one never learned to see myself in any such categories. When I was growing up in the 1930s and '40s, the thing that mattered for most of us was what linked you to other people, not what made you different or ethnically distinct—and this is precisely the reverse of what it is today.

INTERLOCUTOR: You saw yourself as, shall we say, a universalist?

AUTHOR: Call it what you will. We thought of ourselves (to use the favored cliché of those days) as "brothers under the skin." It was frankly an embarrassment to talk of being Jewish, though of course you always admitted that you *were*. Looks, speech, customs—these were accidentals hiding an essential, unchanging humanity we supposedly all shared. And that was still the way we thought during my undergraduate days at Antioch—and we certainly considered ourselves advanced thinkers for our time. The black students we recruited, including the one who later married Martin Luther King, all these people became homogenized with the rest of us—lost their accents, dated us, and, as far as I could tell, expected to make it in the white world. It was a very nice little Utopia.

INTERLOCUTOR: I'll start from another angle. To what extent were you conscious of your Jewishness during those years?

AUTHOR: Not particularly, but that was probably because I'd grown up in Seattle, which had so few Jews, at least in my neighborhood, that I played mainly in non-Jewish houses. My parents had to send me to the Reform Jewish Sunday school so I'd meet some Jews my age, but I saw them mainly on Sundays from ten to twelve. The difference between Seattle and the East came home to me as soon as I got to Antioch and found there were all sorts of tribal signals among the big-city Jewish kids who'd also just arrived—signals I couldn't immediately understand any more easily than the non-Jewish students could.

INTERLOCUTOR: So you *weren't* all such brothers under the skin?

AUTHOR: On the contrary. The Jews quickly shaped up and commingled with everybody else. In fact, it seemed the exception at Antioch when Jews actually dated one another.

INTERLOCUTOR: I'm sure you can come up with lots of little anecdotes to buttress your claims to universalism. It makes one wonder if maybe you've been using these claims to escape your Jewishness. Do I perhaps sense a trace of anti-Semitism in your attitude?

AUTHOR: I've always resisted any pressures to act like a member of a tribe, theirs or ours. As you will see, I don't much like what happens to people when they function in a group.

INTERLOCUTOR: Is it possible you don't much care for people?

AUTHOR: I like them one to one, above all when you choose them as individuals, not because of the group they happen to belong to.

INTERLOCUTOR: I think I hear the clichés of a rather antiquated ideology you've invoked to justify yourself. So I'll take off from still another angle. Your last book sports a dedication page that sticks out at the reader:

> In memory of my cousin
> Hanni Lindenberger Meyer,
> active in the Herbert Baum resistance group,
> executed in Plötzensee Prison, Berlin,
> 4 March, 1943, age 22[2]

Now I ask you what you see this dedication telling readers about your Jewish identity.

AUTHOR: Nothing in particular. My cousin belonged to a group which, though largely Jewish, was made up of left-wingers intent on political protest. They were caught and executed for trying to sabotage an outdoor exhibition the Nazis staged in May 1942 to satirize life in Soviet Russia. But I can't connect this in any significant way with my being Jewish.

INTERLOCUTOR: Then I'll start from one more angle. Have you been aware of discrimination as a result of your Jewishness?

AUTHOR: Absolutely not. In the world in which I live, being Jewish is a badge of honor, though somewhat less so nowadays than being of color.

INTERLOCUTOR: I don't mean your current world. We all know about the Jewish presence in academia. I'm speaking of the world you grew up in.

AUTHOR: I knew there were a couple of housing developments in Seattle built around golf courses with what they used to call restricted covenants—legal clauses saying Jews and god knows how many other groups weren't allowed to buy in.

INTERLOCUTOR: Surely you were outraged.

AUTHOR: Minority groups had not yet been trained to experience outrage. Let's say the idea made me a bit uncomfortable. One certainly didn't talk about it. Furthermore, I couldn't imagine even *wanting* to live around a golf course.

INTERLOCUTOR: And weren't you aware of the quotas that prevailed those days for Jews applying to college?

AUTHOR: Quite aware, and it meant I didn't get into the two Ivy League places I tried for.

INTERLOCUTOR: And even that did not outrage you?

AUTHOR: I *was* outraged, but not at the quota as such. We were somehow conditioned to accept those things as natural. What outraged me was not being included *within* the quota of students they happened to accept.

INTERLOCUTOR: And weren't you concerned that this same sort of discrimination would follow you when you competed for a job?

AUTHOR: Absolutely not.

INTERLOCUTOR: Surely you'd heard the famous stories of how Lionel Trilling's and Harry Levin's careers nearly got aborted.

AUTHOR: Those stories didn't circulate on my particular grapevine, and anyway that had all happened long before I started in the profession. I was certainly aware that these were problems for an earlier generation, since in the late 1930s a retired biologist came to speak to my Sunday school class—my Jewish indoctrination class—

INTERLOCUTOR: Do I perceive a bias here?

AUTHOR: Let me finish. He told us he'd sweated out a measly career at Oregon State and warned us there'd never be a decent place for any of us in the university world.

INTERLOCUTOR: And this didn't deter you?

AUTHOR: I knew things had changed by the 1950s. I never gave it a thought—except once my first year into my first job, so this must have been 1954 or 1955, when my uncle Fred, the plastic surgeon, took me to lunch at his country club (no special place, let me add, but distinctly the less illustrious of the two Jewish ones then in West Los Angeles). I noticed him staring at my face from a strange angle, and next thing I knew he was stroking his finger up and down my nose. "I'll fix that," he said. "It's bad for your career the way it is." He'd desemitized hundreds, probably thousands, of noses in his time, including those of his former wife, both his daughters, and also my aunt his sister, so I knew my turn was next. Uncle Fred, let me add, was a true artist who, in a less abstract-minded age, would have been sculpting the most classical faces. "Nothing doing," I said to him, "I like my nose the way it is." He wouldn't believe me—after all, patients were paying high fees for his services, and here he was offering me a new nose for nothing—so then I added that in my particular field people usually took you for bright if they also took you for Jewish.

INTERLOCUTOR: So you asserted your Jewish identity?

AUTHOR: Heavens no! I simply had to say something to escape his net.

INTERLOCUTOR: And you are doing your utmost to escape *my* net. Let's approach this from yet another angle: did it ever occur to you how Jewish it was of you to make Wordsworth the subject of your first book?

AUTHOR: What do you mean?

INTERLOCUTOR: Don't pretend you weren't aware of it. Could it be accidental that romanticism, and often Wordsworth in particular, was the favored subject upon which Jewish scholars such as Trilling, Abrams, Hartman, and Bloom lavished their attention at the time?

AUTHOR: So that's what you're getting at—romanticism as displaced Judaism, "Wordsworth and the Rabbis," and all that![3] Yes, I was quite aware of the connection, or should I say the *lack* of connection, between their work and mine. In my case there was simply no Judaism to displace, since there was no way to absorb religion in a Reform Jewish Sunday school. My own book straddled the formal and the historical.[4] I went out of my way, in fact, to avoid the whole moral and religious dimension that was central for these other people.

INTERLOCUTOR: Always escaping from something, avoiding something! Let me put it another way. If you weren't into "displacing," did it ever occur to you to treat any *overtly* Jewish texts in your courses or even (God forbid!) to write about them?

AUTHOR: It never occurred to me, especially since I don't know Hebrew or Yiddish.

INTERLOCUTOR: I was thinking of modern Jewish writing, the existence of which you are surely aware, even if you have chosen to keep your distance. If you wrote a book on Trakl, why couldn't you just as easily have done one on Celan, who after all was influenced by Trakl?[5]

AUTHOR: If I'd come across his writing at the time I discovered Trakl's in 1952, I might very well have wanted to work on Celan, but of course he'd written relatively little poetry by then. Let me assure you it wouldn't have been because he was Jewish or because he wrote on Jewish themes, but rather simply because Celan, like Trakl, was doing fabulous things with language, and it was literary language that interested me at the time. Please, your questions keep implying I'm anti-Semitic or not quite actively Jewish enough to suit some present-day standard. I want you to know I once wrote my own Jewish novel.

INTERLOCUTOR: Your own *what?*

AUTHOR: Jewish novel. There was no such genre at the time I wrote it—at least I never knew of any. It wasn't till many years later that I came across that book from the 1930s by the other Roth.[6]

INTERLOCUTOR: Let's get back to *you,* now that you've revealed yourself to be an ethnic after all.

AUTHOR: Quite the contrary! My Jewish novel—or rather novel manuscript, since it was never published—portrayed an ethnic world which it then firmly rejected.

INTERLOCUTOR: So what motives stand behind all this?

AUTHOR: I was fresh from reading *Ulysses* just before my senior year at Antioch. Seattle became my Dublin, Judaism my Catholicism, except of course my immersion in Judaism was nothing like Joyce's in Catholicism. It was Jewish *life,* Jewish *attitudes* that concerned me while drafting what I called—at least in the first version—"The House of Endenberg."

INTERLOCUTOR: Endenberg, Lindenberger! It must have been shamelessly autobiographical.

AUTHOR: Yes and no. Of my family, yes. Of myself, distinctly not.

INTERLOCUTOR: How so?

AUTHOR: I appeared briefly in it and even called myself Samuel, my actual middle name. But I had myself born a spastic and then killed myself off at age four. I was not about to emulate a thousand other authors who set out to write a portrait of the artist as a sensitive young *shmuck.*

INTERLOCUTOR: You show a positive horror at appearing to be like anybody else. So how did you proceed to reject Jewish life in your book?

AUTHOR: I portrayed a tightly enclosed Jewish community that sought to reproduce the forms of the genteel gentile world they observed around them. Their religious services, with its organ belting out Christian-like hymn tunes, could virtually have passed for those in some liberal Protestant church. Their social life, built around a country club called Glendale, of all things—

INTERLOCUTOR: So what would you have had it called?

AUTHOR: Zion or Sinai would have sounded more honest.

INTERLOCUTOR: Those are names better suited to hospitals.

AUTHOR These people were caught between an Anglo community whose style they imitated but whose life they could not share and the overtly ethnical

Jews (mainly of an older generation) with whom they dreaded being identified. Like Milton's devils, they were busily, ridiculously imitating what they took to be a better world with whatever resources they had at their disposal.

INTERLOCUTOR: Aren't you being unduly hard on people who hadn't the slightest notion they were offending anybody, or even the slightest desire to offend?

AUTHOR: They seemed to me—if you'll permit me to use a now-archaic word—they seemed to me to be "inauthentic." That was the term we used during my college years. But remember it's been well over forty years since I finished the novel, and I don't know if I can fully recapture what my "own" attitudes were at the time. Do we really have attitudes of our own? Can it be that the attitudes we think we hold dear at any age are merely those we get from the books we read and the people we trust at the time? Or the terms we hear being mouthed around us, like "identity" these days? As I reread the two versions of my novel during the past month—and this was my first full reading in all these forty years—it occurred to me that the negative attitudes I expressed toward Jewish life likely derived from the attitudes toward middle-class life in general that I'd picked up from my friends and from the modernist novels they and I had been reading. I suspect it was books and people—above all people who also read books—that shaped what I took to be my own point of view at the time.

INTERLOCUTOR: And you now make these pronouncements about your distant past through the eyes of a current-day literary scholar. Hindsight is not necessarily insight. But let me ask how you feel about this early effort of yours. Was it embarrassing to read? I ask this only because most people find it difficult to confront their early attempts at writing.

AUTHOR: The two versions were entirely different reading experiences. In the first version, which I did in a small workshop group at Antioch with three others, one of them Rod Serling—

INTERLOCUTOR: Did he also write a Jewish novel?

AUTHOR His was about prize-fighting, which I'm sure he found a more gripping part of his past than his Jewishness. He'd been a bantam-weight fighter, in fact. As I said earlier, nobody I knew about in 1949 thought about writing Jewish novels, though there were of course lots of novels that neutered what were really Jewish characters with the blandest of Anglo names and backgrounds. My novel, I can assure you, was as overtly Jewish as it possibly could be. But let me go on: we were all four making our first serious tries at fiction, and I let myself go in imitating whatever modernist techniques seemed appropriate. As I read it today, it looks by turns brilliant and appalling. I was sometimes amazed to find sentences like this one that ends the first chapter: "And Jane, jabbering, homely, striding, leaning over her little father, their backs to the lake, up the path, bath-house, firs, long lawn, home."[7] That same chapter, in the second version, had become hopelessly bland: "He coughed and started up the path past the high firs to the house."[8] This second version, as I reread it, was wholly different—not uneven, like the first, but neatly smoothed out, discomfortingly well plotted. It positively reeked of competence, the sort that creative writing classes inspire, though I didn't precisely do it in class but as a tutorial at the University of Washington during my first year of graduate school, where the writer they assigned to tutor me turned out to be a moonlighting local novelist, very much the regionalist type, and I stupidly allowed him to tell me how to rewrite it.

INTERLOCUTOR: So you gutted the Jewish detail?

AUTHOR: Not in the least, since local color was the sort of thing he liked, though he hadn't the slightest idea there was so much Jewish color to be found in Seattle. No, what he pushed me away from was my wanting to fool around with language—everything, in other words, that reading Joyce and the like had inspired me with in the first place. The Jewish stuff remained intact, like this image of an aging Jew—actually a portrait of my own father— sitting through a Reform Rosh Hashanah service that he disapproves of. I quote from the first version, though most of this passage was left as is:

> The choir broke out in the *bor'chu.* The rabbi carefully translated into English, Praised be his name forever and ever, and when the singing began again Herman joined in, not loud enough to offend, but only in order to give a semblance of the participation he was accustomed to in the orthodox service.
> Herman, sweetheart, shhh! she [his wife] whispered.
> He continued, pretending not to have heard her by singing even louder. The choir extended the six Hebrew words in the verse into a full choral number, repeating each word as many times as it would fit the music. God never wrote an opera, not even *Faust,* Herman asserted to himself.[9]

INTERLOCUTOR: So you were writing from the Orthodox point of view! That's scarcely the impression you sought to give me earlier.

AUTHOR: It was my *character's* point of view, not mine. I never gave a hoot about traditional Judaism, about which I still know next to nothing. In fact the few Orthodox ceremonies I ever witnessed struck me as barbaric Oriental rites, though if I'd known anything about the anthropology of religion at the time, probably my reaction would have been a bit more sophisticated. No, the only thing I shared with my father, or rather the character I modeled after my father, was the sense that Jewish communal life, at least as I'd observed it in Seattle, had something distinctly inauthentic about it. Please excuse my using that word again. I wouldn't be caught dead uttering it today, but the term, plus the whole range of poses it helped one strike, seemed made to order for the world of 1950.

INTERLOCUTOR: Let's get back to that passage in the temple. Whatever you take your own attitude to be—or to have been at the time—your writing displays a greater immersion in Judaism than you seem to let on.

AUTHOR: Absolutely. It's full of ethnical detail—all sorts of things I'd observed, or heard people talk about, or even read. I remember consulting a Reform Jewish prayer book to write that particular scene. In fact, rereading the manuscript, I'm amazed how much Jewish detail I'd managed to cram in. All sorts of things—for example, the horror that German Jews had of being mistaken for Russian Jews. My family kept me so sheltered from the Russian-Jewish world that I didn't learn the word *chutzpah* till many years later when I was living in St. Louis, which was so much more Jewish than Seattle. But I also managed to expose my family's snobbery, like the fact that—except for one branch whose roots go back centuries in East Prussia—their Germanness was only a generation or two deep. My grandmother back in Berlin supposedly spoke a Yiddish-flavored German, and I made a lot out of that sort of detail.

INTERLOCUTOR: So you didn't confine yourself to Seattle?

AUTHOR: I allowed myself some brief flashbacks, like Joyce with Leopold Bloom's ancestors. But I'd not been outside North America when I wrote the novel, and I feared venturing beyond what I thought I knew at first hand. You see how tied I felt to what's been called the "cult of experience" guiding American writing. I set the novel in 1940, precisely a decade before I wrote it, in order to build the action around my family's need to get their relatives out of Germany before it was too late.

INTERLOCUTOR: So it's a Holocaust novel you were writing.

AUTHOR: Hardly. I didn't go beyond 1941, which was before people had been killed in large numbers. And remember, there wasn't much of a sense of the Holocaust in 1950 when I was writing. There wasn't even a name for it, as far as I know, though of course I knew that all my relatives had been killed. The word we used then was "genocide." We'd learned from the International Red Cross about where each of them had died, so with hindsight I could make something dramatic out of the quarrels I'd witnessed among my Seattle family—pretty bitter quarrels about how we could possibly bring people out in time, or who was to provide the money—all sorts of grubby details that the reader, with historical hindsight, was to recognize as matters of life and death.

INTERLOCUTOR: So you were able to bring in the story of your cousin who was executed?

AUTHOR: My Cousin the Communist? The story would have made a sensational novel in the hands of some other writer, but I didn't know enough of what had happened when I was writing my own book. After the war we heard she'd been a member of a spy ring (not true, it turned out), had been listening to British broadcasts (this *was* true), and had helped guide British bombers over Berlin (not true, alas). In any event the conventions of writing I was following would have prevented my trying to apprehend anything so far removed from my own observed experience. But then if I'd known at the time all the details I found out soon after about my cousin's ring, maybe I'd have chucked all those conventions and said to hell with the notion that writing has anything to do with personal experience.

INTERLOCUTOR: So how did you manage to tie the Holocaust matter to the life in Seattle you were depicting?

AUTHOR: Quite simple—by concentrating on the guilt some of my characters felt about not doing enough to get their closest relatives out. And when they didn't show enough guilt, I'd have the other characters work on them to make sure they felt guilty enough.

INTERLOCUTOR: How quintessentially Jewish!

AUTHOR: That's the sort of detail I knew I could catch right, and I made the most of it, though not of course in the comic way that later Jewish novels managed to deal with Jewish guilt. In fact, my book was unrelievedly earnest, untouched by humor or even irony. Everything was designed to capture the disgust I felt for the claustrophobic world in which I'd grown up and which I knew I had to escape.

INTERLOCUTOR: And so how *did* you escape?

AUTHOR: By entering academia. Forty years ago it was the only world in which I wouldn't be ghettoized.

INTERLOCUTOR: Except of course in the academic ghetto. But you said earlier that Jews were few enough in Seattle that you could circulate freely in a non-Jewish world.

AUTHOR: As a child I could. But I was always aware that past a certain point the prison house would close in on me. It's not that way anymore, I'm sure, but it *was* in 1950. The Jews I'd met in Sunday school mostly never left Seattle, where they—the males, that is—went into law or medicine or business, as often as not their father's business (though I never had that particular option), with their social life built securely around the golf club—

INTERLOCUTOR: Glendale, you mean?

AUTHOR: Yes, that's where you spent your Sundays seeking out your prospective clients, patients, or customers. It was a thoroughly self-referential world in which you could only be defined as a *Jewish* lawyer, never a lawyer as such.

INTERLOCUTOR: And you're not a *Jewish* academic?

AUTHOR: Certainly not! Not only is my work separate from whatever Jewishness you can ascribe to me, but also if you look at the alliances I've made, at the various people who have helped shape my career, or the ones whose careers I've participated in, if you look at these ties, you won't find anything that follows ethnical lines.

INTERLOCUTOR: So you sought to homogenize yourself? Then how do you explain that portrait of a Jewish academic you created in *Saul's Fall* in the person of Milton J. Wolfson?[10] He was surely the archetypal Jewish academic by anybody's reckoning.

AUTHOR: I suspect I was creating somebody the opposite of what I thought—or wanted—myself to be.

INTERLOCUTOR: Another attempt to escape yourself! Did it ever occur to you, you might have been depicting an underside of yourself that you sought to cast off?

AUTHOR: Don't confuse me with the psychological thrillers you've read.

INTERLOCUTOR: All right, so you've managed to avoid involvement in a

Jewish Mafia, with whatever benefits or burdens that might have entailed.
But you have yet to convince me that your Jewishness—

AUTHOR: I hate being essentialized.

INTERLOCUTOR: Well, call it your *particular* Jewish background. You have yet
to convince me that your background hasn't affected the topics you've
chosen, the sorts of texts you've focused on.

AUTHOR: We've been through this already with Wordsworth, and the answer
is clearly no.

INTERLOCUTOR: That was a question of religious attitude, and I was willing
to accept your denial there. But let's look at another side of you: your whole
adult life you've lived with the knowledge of the Holocaust (whatever you
chose to call it earlier) and what it did to your relatives here and in Europe.
You grew up surrounded by people feeling guilty for what they had failed to
do or making those around them feel guilty. You took pride enough in the
martyrdom of a cousin whom you never met to dedicate a book to her as
recently as six years ago. You've even admitted that, if you'd known when you
set out on your novel what you later knew about her, this might have inspired
the breakthrough you needed to create a new mode of fiction. Surely there
must be some connections between your work and your Jewishness that I've
not yet heard about. Now what do you have to say?

AUTHOR: If there are connections to be made, rest assured I was unaware of
them when I chose to work on whatever it was I picked out. In retrospect, I
know I've kept hovering around history—the idea of history, the workings of
history, the intersections of events, and the textual accounts to which others
have subjected these events. It seemed only appropriate to collect my essays of
the late 1980s under the title *The History in Literature.* I've been attracted
(morbidly, some might say) to absolute, end-of-the-world, utterly dire
situations—the kind you see in the poetry of Trakl, or in Wordsworth's
"Resolution and Independence," in the tyrants and martyrs that people my
study of historical drama,[11] in the cataclysmic dénouements of nineteenth-
century opera,[12] in my austere hermit-hero Orlando Hennessy-García from
Saul's Fall. As I look back at what has obsessed me over the years, I note how
Büchner's *Danton's Death*—above all the ironic, macabre tone of its prison
scenes—has haunted three of my books composed at widely spaced inter-
vals.[13] So if you force me to make connections, let's say I can trace all this back
to the pressures of history I felt upon the life of my family in the course of
growing up.

INTERLOCUTOR: So when was it you learned the details of your cousin's
execution?

AUTHOR: Soon after finishing my novel manuscript, as a matter of fact. I was
still a graduate student and visiting Germany for the first time, hoping to find
what traces I could of my family's past. I saw the debris of what had been my
grandparents' house in Berlin near the Alexanderplatz, though the family had
been long since removed by the time the house was destroyed as the Russian

army entered the city in 1945. A non-Jewish employee of my grandfather who had stayed with the family till they were all deported traveled in from East Germany to see me and to explain how they had gone to their respective fates. The story of my cousin's activities and execution turned out to be the center of his tale.

INTERLOCUTOR: So how would this information have affected the writing of your novel?

AUTHOR: What I was hearing from Herr Weber, the old family employee, demanded some new form not available to me at the time, something on the order of what we call postmodern: appropriations of documents, of eyewitness accounts, something to jar all one's moral and one's literary expectations. For one thing, Herr Weber roundly condemned what my cousin Hanni had done.

INTERLOCUTOR: I suppose Germans of his generation weren't much used to supporting rebels.

AUTHOR: It wasn't just that. I'd been used to thinking of her as a heroine even if it turned out not to be true that her group helped the British bomb Berlin. But Herr Weber was opening up another perspective that was new to me. Yes, here he was condemning her in my presence for causing her mother to be killed as a result of her grand political act (my Cousin the Matricide, he wanted me to think). "How could she have done such a stupid thing?" he kept asking me. "But she would have been killed anyway," I replied. "They were all going to be killed. Wasn't it better to stage an act of defiance, to face a trial (even if it was rigged), and then die with dignity, wasn't this better, surely, than to be herded onto a train and be marched into the gas chamber?"

INTERLOCUTOR: Most any Jewish-American would feel that way.

AUTHOR: Most any American, Jewish or not. I was speaking my best heroic language and getting immense satisfaction from vicariously assuming Hanni's role, until Herr Weber complicated the plot by revealing something I had been wholly unaware of. "Didn't you know your family would have been saved?" he insisted, and he told me that my uncle Nathan—the same uncle whose pleas to emigrate had been central to my novel—had gone to school with the man who was chief of police in Berlin during the war. This man, he assured me, had been quietly protecting the whole family until Hanni's group was caught for bombing the anti-Soviet exhibit. Even though Herr Weber had the bad luck to be working for Jews, it was clear that he very much relished the status that a "protected" family could confer.

INTERLOCUTOR: The damned generally prefer the higher circles in hell.

AUTHOR: As it turned out, Hanni's arrest meant the end of all protection for everybody (my Cousin the Murderer), though my uncle's personal protection at least got *him*, unlike my other relatives, assigned to Theresienstadt, the most benign of the camps (Herr Weber was even allowed to visit him there and in fact witnessed him in his assigned job of carrying buckets of water all day), where he died not by violence but because the officials withheld the iron pills he needed for his long-standing anemia. The others in the family, lacking even those privileges, all went to Auschwitz and the like.

INTERLOCUTOR: From the point of view of a simple German of his time, Herr Weber obviously got things right.

AUTHOR: From that point of view the consequences were even worse than he told me at the time. Recent research has linked the first major slaughter of German Jews directly to the sabotage perpetrated by Hanni's group, which was known by the name of its leader, Herbert Baum.[14] The first arrests after the sabotage included five Jews, after which the Nazis announced a policy of arresting a hundred additional Jews in reprisal for each member of the group that they had caught. A few days afterward the Gestapo rounded up 154 hostages from a list of Jews who in one way or another had excited suspicion or had elicited accusations, and they brought them to the Sachsenhausen concentration camp just outside Berlin and promptly killed them. To these they quickly added another 96 hostages to complete the first installment of 250. It took another day or two to find the second installment; details are lacking about precisely how these other 250 were located, but in any case one can credit the Nazis with a keen eye for numerology.

INTERLOCUTOR: Is that how you make sense of history, by making wit out of the direst events?

AUTHOR: Doubtless that's how I put some space between myself and what might threaten to engulf me. In any case it's been the ambiguities, the uncertainties, the ironies, the very difficulties you encounter in seeking any meaning to history, that I've let plague me and also attract me all these years. Here was a real-life historical drama to parallel the historical plays I was reading for a genre exam as a graduate student, plays that fed into the book I did on historical drama many years later. And it was always the indeterminacies, the multiplicity of points of view that I looked for, whether in literature or life. Just consider the variety of judgments I've heard voiced about what Hanni and her group did. It wasn't just Herr Weber who objected. A few years ago I told a cousin in Frankfurt—somebody who himself had fled to Israel, then after the war returned to Germany—I told him that while in Berlin I'd be visiting the execution chamber (it's now a public museum) where Hanni and others in the German resistance were decapitated.

INTERLOCUTOR: With what sort of instrument?

AUTHOR: It was a small guillotine they used at Plötzensee, though it's no longer exhibited there. When there were too many executions at a time they hanged their victims from hooks that you can still see in the chamber. This way they could kill eight at a time. But from the evidence I've come across, it looks as though they used the guillotine on the members of the group executed on March 4, 1943.[15] But to get back to my Frankfurt cousin—though he'd known Hanni during adolescence he quickly said he wanted to hear no more about her, not because he bought Herr Weber's argument about the many deaths she had supposedly caused, but simply because sabotaging an exhibit couldn't lead anywhere anyway (my Cousin the Fool). The Baum group—and what we know of their intentions came from some three or four who somehow escaped arrest and survived the war[16]—had hoped that the bombing would send the world a message that there *was* a resistance active in Germany. They first went to the exhibit on a Sunday night but found so large a crowd there that they decided to do the job the following, weekday, night when, showing a humanity that their enemies never reciprocated, they knew they would injure relatively few spectators.

INTERLOCUTOR: So how did the world hear about it?

AUTHOR: They didn't hear—that was the awful thing. As one might have expected, the press reported nothing, and even the reprisal killing of the five hundred hostages was long thought to have been a response to the assassination in Czechoslovakia of the prominent Nazi Reinhard Heydrich just a few days after the Baum group's act of sabotage. In fact, I remember as a child reading in the Seattle papers about what were taken to be the reprisals for Heydrich's murder. My Frankfurt relative's attitude was pretty typical of how Jews in the West reacted to Hanni's story: the last thing they wanted was any sort of left-wing association. Though a good bit of research has been published on the group in the past decade, the standard histories pay little if any attention. Raul Hilberg's massive and influential Holocaust history has only two brief footnotes on them.[17] In this respect, Jewish attitudes simply mirror Western attitudes in general.[18] The resistance museum founded by the Stauffenberg family in Berlin (the Stauffenberg of the aborted anti-Hitler coup in 1944) allots them an insultingly small amount of space. I've been told that even that much was granted only as a result of pressure.

INTERLOCUTOR: In view of all you've said for years about how historical narrative responds to political pressure, you should scarcely seem surprised.

AUTHOR: I'm not in the least surprised, just dismayed. And I was also not surprised that, after I'd told people in East Berlin I was related to a member of the Baum group, I was immediately treated as somebody extra special (my Cousin the Heroine). Schoolchildren in East Germany had been forced to read about them; there's a Herbert Baum street leading straight to the largest Berlin Jewish cemetery, which in fact has a collective gravestone inscribed with the names of each member[19] (their bodies, after execution, had been sent to the University of Berlin medical school). Yet who knows what reinterpretations of their actions will result from German reunification? By now Herbert-Baumstraße may even have reverted to its prewar name, and the heroic aura that had long been attached to the group may become obscured, perhaps even be destroyed as Germans in the east once again rewrite their history.[20]

INTERLOCUTOR: But I assume you yourself are firmly committed to the heroic image.

AUTHOR: Well, I'm certainly proud of what she did, and I like to imagine that I'd have done the same thing, but somehow I flinch from saying I'm wholly committed to any image, heroic or otherwise. Let me repeat that it's the ironies and uncertainties that grab my imagination, whether in the form of personal events, or in what we call public history (the story of my cousin straddles both of these), or in the fictions that people have later made of history. And the closer I look at this supposed heroic story I've been telling you, the more difficulties I find, not just in the varying ways it's been processed, but also in the way I myself confront the events. There's a moment in the narrative that I'm not even sure I know how I would want to process—

INTERLOCUTOR: Since your narrative has no author, there's obviously nobody asserting control over the reader.

AUTHOR: But I'm dependent on particular narrative accounts from the survivors as well as from the researchers, who were themselves reproducing and reinterpreting these accounts.

INTERLOCUTOR: So what's the particular moment that so bothers you?

AUTHOR: A few weeks before the sabotage the group was thinking up ways to raise money for their activities. Until then they'd mainly been mimeographing propaganda statements to distribute to German soldiers. Their own resources were limited, since they were all (except for a couple of non-Jewish members) doing forced labor in various factories in Berlin, so they decided to take up robbery. We know of only a single incident. Several of the men dressed up as Gestapo agents and went to the house of a well-to-do Jew named Felix Freundlich, from whom they commandeered a bunch of Oriental rugs, two cameras, two pairs of opera glasses, a man's watch, a typewriter, and an oil painting (my Cousin the Bandit, or at least the Bandit's Accomplice).[21] How am I to deal with this incident? Should I see it as comic: rich Jew outwitted by poor Jew, and poor Jew donning the archenemy's outfit to gull his fellow victim? This is the stuff of Jonsonian comedy, I tell myself. Or should I see the robbery as a necessary though discomforting moment within a larger chain of tragic events? And then I see the significance of the victim's name: Mr. Happy Friendly, and I wonder if he or any of his descendants survived deportation. If so, I think how much I'd like to meet one of them.

INTERLOCUTOR: Whatever would you want to do *that* for? To apologize for your cousin?

AUTHOR: Nothing that dramatic. Just to make human contact.

INTERLOCUTOR: A little genre scene, in other words. You are now sketching out what, in your critical work, you would have called a sentimental historical drama, one that you'd castigate as being much too unknowing about the larger movements of history.[22]

AUTHOR: You've got me wrong. It's precisely this mixture of private and public, of individual human fallibilities rubbing against these grand movements of history, of comic gesture undermining heroic stance, that has kept my imagination fueled all these years.

INTERLOCUTOR: So—the real-life sufferings of real people, *your* people, caught in those end-of-the-world situations that you so admire—these become transformed in your mind to yield you the highest possible aesthetic pleasure. I now see the unsalutary effects of that academic culture in which you've participated these many years—from the New Critical irony in which you were trained to those deconstructive indeterminacies to which, I assume, you've had to accommodate yourself.

AUTHOR: Then let's rewrite the script altogether and do away with all contingencies. Let's say the Baum group had been given sufficient funds—

INTERLOCUTOR: From whom? What possible source?

AUTHOR: From their favorite Jewish charity!

INTERLOCUTOR: All right, if you insist on being facetious, I won't stop you.

AUTHOR: So they were given sufficient funds to make a whole stack of bombs instead of the pathetic few they put together in one of the members' basements. Then they go en masse with their bombs—on Sunday, not a weekday when everything is empty—to the anti-Soviet exhibit, spread out in the Lustgarten in the center of Berlin. Ten or eleven go to each of the three tents housing the exhibit. They steel themselves against all possible compassion for the onlookers, who after all would never have gone there if they hadn't been hardened Nazis in the first place. The bombs go off like clockwork (my Cousin the Terrorist), hundreds lie dead in the tents, among them perhaps some members of the group (my Cousin the Martyr). The world takes note, resistance groups throughout Europe feel inspired to act, the Holocaust gets nipped in the bud, the course of history is forever changed, and out of all this my early family novel would have burst its seams to make the term "novel" permanently obsolete.

INTERLOCUTOR: Some new verbal form perhaps, but what you now describe would make for the sort of history play you'd never have much patience with.

AUTHOR: Or the sort that could ever happen, whether in literature or in life. That's because there's another contingency I haven't mentioned that would have stopped the whole thing in the first place. Can you imagine anything so conspicuous as thirty Jews (carrying packets of bombs, no less) so much as trying to gain admission to a Nazi exhibit? Of course they knew better and they sent only seven—the two non-Jews and the five others who looked the least Jewish, which included Hanni's husband but not Hanni herself (my Cousin the Jewess). These were the five whose arrests set off the reprisals against the five hundred hostages.

INTERLOCUTOR: So they knew their identity was as much Jewish as Communist.

AUTHOR: And the two strains came together in the fact that they sang Jewish songs as well as the Internationale while being transported from prison to the execution chamber. But that introduces another little irony: they weren't even nominally Communists, since the German Communist party refused to accept Jewish members after the Hitler-Stalin pact. You may accuse me of reading real-life situations as literary texts, and I can only reply that these interjections, these interpenetrations between what we call literature and what we call history, are central to what I've been thinking and writing and, do I also dare say, living?

INTERLOCUTOR: So this is the connection you were trying to establish between calling your book *The History in Literature* and dedicating it to your cousin's memory. Not just history and literature, but history, literature, and life at once!

AUTHOR: I suppose so, but put that way it sounds pretty banal. Maybe I should admit another small motive for the dedication. The time for me to choose a dedication came at the height of all the discussion surrounding Paul de Man's wartime writings. So I set up a little allegory that was meant to imply—privately, of course, since I'm sure nobody caught on—that even in their early twenties people are quite capable of making moral choices. Paul de Man, who was only two years older than my cousin, carried on *his* activities during precisely the same couple of years, 1940 to 1942, as she did hers. Now what are we to make of their respective choices?

INTERLOCUTOR: A most obscure allegory and a most loaded comparison! Your cousin never had the option of collaborating or even of being tempted to do anything we could call wrong.

AUTHOR: She had the option of doing nothing, like nearly everybody else, and then, dying as she would inevitably after being loaded on a train to the gas chambers, she could have offered living proof to support Hannah Arendt's celebrated passivity theory. And at least then Herr Weber would have felt no need to castigate her posthumously. But that's not the option she happened to choose. And did Paul de Man have the option of being a Jew? Yet come to think of it, let's say he *had* been a Jew: he was surely a charismatic enough opportunist to be among the few who would have managed to survive. I say that from personal knowledge after watching him preside over a faculty seminar—and this was long before his ideas had started to circulate— yes, he charmed a whole room of professors into believing themselves a chosen elite pitted against a benighted wooly world outside.

INTERLOCUTOR: And did you find yourself charmed as well?

AUTHOR: For an hour or two. I extricated myself soon after I left the room. But I recalled this experience nearly two decades later once his early work was exposed.

INTERLOCUTOR: Paul de Man would have accused you of resistance to theory.

AUTHOR: I call it resistance to being manipulated. But I won't push my comparison any further. You were right—the cases of Hanni Lindenberger Meyer and Paul de Man do not lend themselves to easy comparison.

INTERLOCUTOR: But I don't want you dropping this matter quite yet. You've tried to create a contrast based on moral issues, yet once we leave out the moral element, we can concentrate on what appears a stark and absolute contrast: two utterly diverse personality types caught in their youth within the Europe of 1940, each with a distinct set of possibilities and restraints to contend with. You have presented your cousin as somebody naive, zealous, desperate. Whatever you may say of Paul de Man, he was none of those things, else he could not have been the deft survivor he turned out to be. And look at the contrast in their subsequent histories. Your cousin had no later history except for the widely divergent interpretations that others have made of her acts. Paul de Man at least went on to make history of another sort; otherwise nobody would be paying the least attention to what he did in the early 1940s.

AUTHOR: That *too* has its widely divergent interpretations—and shamefully so. In fact, whenever I hear a Jew defending Paul de Man—whether it's the early de Man or even the later one—whenever I hear a Jew do that, I can tell you I absolutely bristle. They should know better after all the manipulation they've allowed themselves to be victimized by. And don't think this has anything to do with whatever feelings I have about Paul de Man's ideas. I assure you I don't feel nearly as hostile when I hear the same defense coming from a Gentile.

INTERLOCUTOR: Say that again, I'm not sure I got you correctly.

AUTHOR: I simply said that I feel quite different if it's Jews or non-Jews defending Paul de Man.

INTERLOCUTOR: You put it more bluntly the first time round. In any case, let me offer you my congratulations.

AUTHOR: For what?

INTERLOCUTOR: I congratulate you for coming to terms with your Jewish identity.

AUTHOR: I didn't mean to speak out so tribally.

INTERLOCUTOR: Sorry to have put that universalism of yours to the test. I know one's old biases die hard.

AUTHOR: I don't much care to have this outburst revealed.

INTERLOCUTOR: I shall treat it in utmost confidence.

NOTES

1. See Philip Gleason, "Identifying Identity: A Semantic History," *Journal of American History* 69 (1983): 912–13.

2. Herbert Lindenberger, *The History in Literature: On Value, Genre, Institutions* (New York: Columbia University Press, 1990), v.

3. Lionel Trilling, "Wordsworth and the Rabbis," in *The Opposing Self* (New York: Viking, 1955), 118–50.

4. See Herbert Lindenberger, *On Wordsworth's "Prelude"* (Princeton: Princeton University Press, 1963), vii–xiv.

5. Herbert Lindenberger, *Georg Trakl* (New York: Twayne, 1971). On Trakl's influence on Celan, see 142–43.

6. Henry Roth, *Call It Sleep* (New York: Robert O. Ballou, 1934).

7. Herbert Lindenberger, "The House of Endenberg," unpublished novel (1949–50), 12.

8. Herbert Lindenberger, "The House That Jacob Built," revised version of "The House of Endenberg" (1950–51), 9.

9. Lindenberger, "House of Endenberg," 91.

10. Herbert Lindenberger, *Saul's Fall* (Baltimore: Johns Hopkins University Press, 1979).

11. Herbert Lindenberger, *Historical Drama: The Relation of Literature and Reality* (Chicago: University of Chicago Press, 1975), especially the section entitled "Tyrant and Marter Plays," 38–53.

12. Herbert Lindenberger, *Opera: The Extravagant Art* (Ithaca: Cornell University Press, 1984).

13. Herbert Lindenberger, *Georg Büchner* (Carbondale: Southern Illinois University Press, 1964), 19–53; Lindenberger, *Historical Drama*, 3, 4, 6, 8–9, 11–12, 37–38, 41, 51, 53, 65, 67, 68, 75, 102, 103, 107, 123, 124, 136, 138–39, 146, 150, 154, 157, 161, 164, 180–81n.; Lindenberger, *The History in Literature*, 109–28.

14. See Wolfgang Scheffler, "Der Brandanschlag im Berliner Lustgarten im Mai 1942 und seine Folgen: Eine quellenkritische Betrachtung," in *Berlin in Geschichte und Gegenwart*, ed. Hans J. Reichhardt (Berlin: Siedler, 1984), 106–12; and Simone Erpel, "Struggle and Survival: Jewish Women in the Anti-Fascist Resistance in Germany," in *Leo Baeck Institute Year Book XXXVII* (London: Secker and Warburg, 1992), 409.

15. Lucien Steinberg, *Not as a Lamb: The Jews against Hitler,* trans. Marion Hunter (Farnborough: Saxon House, 1974), 37.

16. See Eric Brothers, "On the Anti-Fascist Resistance of German Jews," in *Leo Baeck Institute Year Book XXXII* (London: Secker and Warburg, 1987), 371; and Erpel, "Struggle and Survival," 408–10.

17. Raul Hilberg, *The Destruction of the Jews,* rev. ed. (New York and London: Holmes and Meier, 1985), 448n., 465n.

18. On the neglect of the Baum group in Western historical accounts, see Wolfgang Wippermann, *Die Berliner Gruppe Baum und der jüdischer Widerstand,* Beiträge zum Thema Widerstand 19 (Berlin: Gedenk-und Bildungsstätte Stauffenbergstraße, 1981), 2–3.

19. See Peter Melcher, *Weißensee: Ein Friedhof als Spiegelbild jüdischer Geschichte in Berlin* (Berlin: Haude und Spener, 1986), 90–93. For a photo of the gravestone, see 92.

20. For a full-length study of the Baum group from a postwar Communist point of view, see Margot Pikarski, *Jugend im Berliner Widerstand: Herbert Baum und Kampfgefährten* (Berlin: Militärverlag der Deutschen Demokratischen Republik, 1978). Pikarski includes photos of the group and discusses the role played by each member. On Hanni Lindenberger Meyer, see pages 126, 129, 139–40, 146. For a statement on Communist interpretations that ignore the group's Jewish ties, see Wippermann, *Die Berliner Gruppe Baum,* 3–4.

21. See Konrad Kwiet and Helmut Eschwege, *Selbstbehauptung und Widerstand: Deutsche Juden im Kampf um Existenz und Menschenwürde 1933–1945* (Hamburg: Christians, 1984), 124–25.

22. See the section entitled "The Public and the Private" in Lindenberger, *Historical Drama,* 118–30.

24

Word-*landslayt*

Gertrude Stein, Allen Ginsberg, Lenny Bruce

Maria Damon

(*for Linda*)

> Jewish, the question which does not stop questioning itself in the reply it calls forth. . . . How is what I *say* or *write* like what, as a Jew, I *should have said* or *written*? . . . Ah, what in my words or actions entitles me to consider myself Jewish?
>
> —Edmond Jabès, "The Solitude of
> the Question," *The Book of Dialogue*

> I neologize Jewish and goyish. . . . Dig: I'm Jewish.
>
> —Lenny Bruce, *The Essential
> Lenny Bruce*

I. I WAS A TEENAGE REEFER-SMOKING PREGNANT YORTSITE CANDLE in a Modernist Nightmare[1]

When I was a child my father's fear of modernism evinced itself in the limerick he recited in response to my question, "Who was Gertrude Stein?"

> There once were three people named Stein
> There's Gert and there's Ep and there's Ein;
> Gert's poems are bunk
> Ep's statues are junk
> And nobody understands Ein.

He cited "pigeons on the grass alas" and "a rose is a rose is a rose" as exemplary bunk, meaningless pablum if not downright harmful on the order of Pound's *Cantos,* which were not allowed in the house because of Pound's Fascist affiliations. To my ears, the two examples of Steinian nonsense seemed no less accessible or cryptic than "to be or not to be," "to sleep perchance to dream" or "through a glass darkly," but he delivered his verdict with unambiguous disgust. Nonetheless, it was clear that, though he had little respect for the content of his recitation, he delighted in reciting both the verse and the little Stein he knew. He delighted in his own ability to recite. And for my part I delighted in the little piece of doggerel I now understand as anti-Semitic as well as antimodernist; suspending my secret conviction that I would one day love Gertrude when able to pursue her on my own, I derived immense pleasure from cracking the code to get "Gertrude Stein," "somebody (Jacob, it turned out) Epstein," and "Albert Einstein." Since my father's name was Albert too, and since we all knew that Einstein's inaccessibility signaled his consummate smartness rather than the incoherent pseudo-aesthetics of the former two, I let the approval of Einstein which I projected onto the limerick shine retroactively and covertly on his two co-Steins.

Because I loved my father, and I loved codes.

In ninth grade a watershed event took place: a soulmate came into my life. Leah was to bring me deeper into my Jewishness, though I didn't know it at the time. Here is a story I wrote about her much later, in graduate school:[2]

My best friend Essie showed up when I was fourteen. In the middle of the school year she came to Miss Cobb's School for girls and I was the one they asked to show her around. English class, Latin class, chicken croquettes with pale translucent gravy at lunch. She'd been kicked out of her other school for trying to commit suicide. I thought that was the coolest thing. She actually went ahead and did it, instead of just thinking about it between Math and Latin homework. She introduced me to Kafka, Proust, Allen Ginsberg. Once we announced to our English teacher that we intended to marry Allen Ginsberg. "You'll have to get past Peter Orlovsky first," Miss Homans said with a mysterious smile, and a peculiar little flame of recognition sparked in me. "What's that supposed to mean?" I pressed, but she only smiled. A few months later, when I discovered the great gay writers, I also discovered something else. Very occasionally, I would find *Giovanni's Room* or *Our Lady of the Flowers* missing from my underwear drawer, and would have to retrieve them from my father's underwear drawer.

At Miss Cobb's School we had a Poetry Reading Contest which was judged for diction and clarity, not for choice of poem or comprehension thereof. Essie mumbled Ginsberg's "America" in a breathy, emotional voice, her blonde hair swinging over her face, pudgy hands trembling. The only audible line was: "Go fuck yourself with your atom bomb." Afterwards a few girls said shyly, "That was really good, Essie—you wrote that, didn't you?" Laura Cabot, who had also won the Posture Prize several years previously, took first place for declaiming on the subject of yellow daffodils, but my friend stole the show. For my fifteenth birthday Essie gave me a woodcut she'd done of the crucifixion, inscribed "Don't let them do this to you," a dozen huge, chewy meringues, and a cake with five different-colored layers.

In the summer I invited Essie down to the house my mother rented on the Cape, a consolation for my father's long and recurring absences in the name of science. The house was right by the ocean and had its own rocky, unswimmable little beach. The bright whiteness of sunshine brought out the whiteness in everything else—the ocean's white-blue glare, the white-green leaves of the scruffy, dense little trees and the grass, everything dazzled. It hurt.

"Essie Peretz!" snorted my mother in her German accent. "She can't appreciate the outdoors. Why not Joy Richardson or Tracy Coolidge? They appreciate the outdoors. They know how to talk to me like a normal person. They don't cringe and flutter. Essie never looks me in the eye." To her credit, she did not suggest Laura Cabot. Even she knew there were limits.

When Essie arrived she gave me New Directions' *Artaud Anthology*. She had bought it for herself but found it kind of creepy. After Essie went to her own room that night, I looked at the photos of Antonin Artaud as a patient at a place called Rodez. In one he was sitting with his doctor on a bench in the bright sunshine in his street clothing, a short woolen coat of elegant cut, a tie and high white collar. He looked like an overly sensitive person trying to hold it together, fragile and dignified and deeply grateful for his own intelligence. The doctor wore a white coat—he looked more like an inmate than his client did. Even his body hunched toward Artaud's, which confidently faced full forward. A funny intellectual affection hovered between them. Artaud must be a person of great honor; his captors themselves looked up to him, seemed to yearn for him.

That night I dreamed a dream of which I can still remember every detail, fifteen years later. Yesterday someone was telling me about a poem in which the ghost of Rousseau appears and tells the poet about Life. I remembered Artaud, and felt a rush of desire to make my dream into a story, and then I remembered all those things about Essie, and I got lost in my life. Anyway here's the dream:

I went to a psychiatric hospital to hear a lecture given to the public by Antonin Artaud, the famous French poet who lived the last years of his life there. He wore a big winter overcoat, although through the huge wall-sized window behind him you could tell it was summer—the sea turned its white-blue over and over just beyond the lawn, and the light was blinding. Artaud talked about giving: "When we give a gift, we really mean to be giving a part of our bodies. I've never seen a man give his skin to another man, but that's what we're really doing when we inscribe the fly-leaf of a book we present to a friend." It was hot and smoky in the hall: everybody fell asleep except me, so Artaud was addressing me alone, standing right in front of me with tears glinting on his thin face. Then while everyone was sleeping we escaped from the hospital. By the time we got out it was winter, snowing, so he had been right about the big overcoat. The institution had metamorphosed into Miss Cobb's School, dark red bricks and cement sidewalks and all. We walked through the sludge until the storm cleared. We met my sisters and pelted each other with snowballs, then lay down and made angels in the snow.

Leah, like me, was a half-breed whose mother was of Nordic descent and whose father was a crypto-Jew. Her paternal grandfather took her out in the woods and did things to hurt her, and then said, "Don't ever tell anyone I'm Jewish, because if you do they'll hurt you." This, also, is part of my story. But neither of us knew these things about ourselves until decades later. Our early friendship was mediated by Allen's bawdy literalness, Marcel's convoluted and delicate semi-self-disclosures, and Franz's demonic conundrums of naked victimization.

And Lenny? Lenny Bruce? I came to Lenny very late, through studying

Stein in graduate school, and he is the subject of my current research. All the Yiddish phrasebooks I read in my pursuit of Stein's Jewishness quoted Lenny. "Kiki, you *nafke* you."[3] "The judge—Aram Avermitz, a red headed junkyard Jew, a real *ferbissiner* with thick fingers and a homemade glass eye. . . ."[4] "Wong, take my mezzuzzah. . . ."[5] Before that, my first and only encounter with him occurred when another high school classmate, Ady, took me to see the movie *Lenny*. "Lenny, Lenny," she murmured with grief-struck affection, as she had moaned, "Otis, Otis," during Otis Redding's sequence in *Monterey Pop*. Dustin Hoffman *shpritz*ed, fumed, pleaded to a jury that "fuck you" was a compliment, and died; Valerie Perrine metamorphosed from a voluptuous red-haired G-stringer to a strung-out and stringy-haired junkie in the space of two hours. The black and white movie left me unmoved, except for the sequence when Lenny yells at Honey for "doing it" with other women. Her face got all squinched up and ugly with tears and snot. "But you made me." Yuck/Wow. Who was Lenny Bruce? A wild skinny guy whose elliptical rapid-fire wordarrows made Yiddish hip, forced people to talk about sex, and embodied a strange and uncomfortable link between Jewishness, sexuality, and social critique—before he degenerated into the utter pathology of his multiple addictions and gave way to the effects of what Phil Spector (half-rightly) termed an "overdose of police."

No—it's not quite true, on reflection, that seeing *Lenny* was my first exposure to the world of Leonard Alfred Schneider. (Memory in this century is an impossible game of losing and regaining loss.) Paul Simon and Art Garfunkel had carefully grafted the news report of Lenny's death into the fade-out of their haunting "Silent Night" on one of my favorite albums: "*Comedian Lenny Bruce died today in his home in Los Angeles . . .* / Sleep in Heavenly Peace. . . ." For these two Jewish boys raised in Queens the comedian was clearly a Christ figure, and they were turning a lullaby celebrating the birth of Christianity into a dirge for a Jewish death—arguably the death of Jewish humor itself[6]—at the hands of a morally obsessed majority (Christian) culture. For me in my adolescence, Lenny was someone who had died. More mysterious was "A Desultory Phillipic," another track on the same album that also memorialized Lenny Bruce: "I learned the truth / From Lenny Bruce / And all of your wealth won't buy me health / . . . and so I smoke a pint of tea a day." I knew what tea was in the jargon of the day; I knew an attack on Ben Franklin when I heard it, though I thought the rhyme childish; but I didn't know Lenny Bruce, and I didn't know "desultory" or "philippic," though I, like my whole family, prided myself on my extensive vocabulary; that is, I thought it was all I had going for me.

I dreamed, at the time, that I looked up those two words in the dictionary: both definitions read simply, "An adult word," meaning, in the logic of the dream and of the society Bruce railed against, a world with sexual and thus secret meanings. I asked my father (who, despite growing evidence to the contrary, I continued to regard as the source of all knowledge, if not insight) who Lenny Bruce was: "A vulgar, crude comedian" was the answer. "How did he die?" "Drugs." (He said the same thing, with the same laconic authority, about Otis Redding.) So before I heard or read a single word of Bruce's he was already implicated in the hotbed of sex, death, language, and Jewishness that made up the underlife of my family mind. No wonder then, that when I met him in my thirties, it was a perfect fit.

By the time I cried over "Kaddish" and became Allen's lovers' lover, my father had died; by the time I broke into Gertrude's language world with "Yet Dish" = "Yid-dish"—a high point in my exegetical career—I had tried hypnotherapy, ethnotherapy, and psychotherapy to get my father back; by the time I picked up Lenny's 1962 trial transcript from his defense lawyer at Fantasy Studios I was a fully grown-up woman with a rental car, a real boyfriend, and a condominium on the way. Leah became a therapist working with street people in New York; Ady, my Otis-and-Lenny-crooning friend, now Adrienne, became the heartthrob of many wild women coast to coast. I earned a doctorate in modern thought and literature, wrote that story about Leah in a burst of by-then rare inspiration and a thesis dedicated to Jean Genet and my father, and still live by the logic of dreams.

II. The Little Abstract and How It Grew (Not)

Subversive Tongues: Jewish-American Verbal Di/s/pla/y/cement in Gertrude Stein, Allen Ginsberg, and Lenny Bruce

Gertrude Stein, Allen Ginsberg, Lenny Bruce, all represent maverick sexuality and language use; all three have been on trial either literally or figuratively, as iconoclasts in both sexual and linguistic arenas. I want to explore how their ethnicity is imprinted in this outlaw stance. As they straddle three linguistic traditions (languages)—Hebrew, English, Yiddish—these artists playfully deconstruct linguistic models of monoculturalism. Furthermore, all three of these wayward verbalists have become icons of gender and sexual "difference" resisting the norms of the dominant culture: Jewish ideals of masculinity prize verbal legerdemain and wit over physical prowess; Jewish ideals of womanhood embrace enterprise and authority over dependency and passivity. As Jewish Americans, these artists shatter and reinvent language and sexual relations as their diasporic psyches and traditional family lives have been shattered and reinvented. These three figures have served me as guideposts in the development of my own relation to language use and Jewishness.

This was the abstract I worked out with Shelley Fisher Fishkin over the telephone, the chapter to whose development I committed myself in contributing to this volume. Periodically I would receive letters from her and from Jeffrey about the progress of the volume. Each communiqué would begin "Dear Contributor," with the latter word crossed out and my name, Maria, handwritten above it. The generic greeting was still legible but superseded and delegitimized by the invocation of my first name, itself a disguise for the Jewishness of my family heritage. Likewise, the official genericism of the lit-crit essay I promised must necessarily be displaced and rewritten—though not rendered invisible—by my endless need to mourn in public. And the object of that mourning is not simply my father or my language but also my Jewishness, which I have at times tried to reassemble as if it were some thing that had been shattered, and at other times justified as a priori fragmentary: an essence characterized by evanescence, an entity defined by its indeterminacy. I wince when I read that abstract now—especially that word "playfully," predictably right next to "deconstruct." I deployed all the right clichés, the academic formulae we know by rote, designed to hold the euphoria of annihilation in suspension, the pain of ethnocide in abeyance. What the abstract promises would be betrayed by its own delivery. If I could neatly grind out the performance I outlined I would be denying the legacy of my models. And denying the wrenching experience this chapter has been. Formulating a sentence often seems impossible; the closure, not even of any argumentative conclusion, but of the basic unit of coherent construction, comes to feel like an act of unimaginable aggression, grandiosity, self-delusion and, simultaneously, like an act of utter necessity. Fragments are more honest—maybe—but doom me to a decentered un/ process that is beyond the nomadism currently so celebrated in cultural studies. I want to make some initiatory notes, if possible, toward elucidating this dynamic between the deconstructive and the reconstructive in my thinking about Jewishness—my Jewishness—invoking the names of three guiding elders (my *schizanalystes*), Gertrude, Allen, and Lenny, for strength, creativity, and sustenance. Their howls and Kaddishes, their Orphic girl-talk and meandering *shpritzes* are the coded vowels and broken syllables that flicker along the path of words, the path that leads me to the home of the imagination.

III. Excursus: "A Greater Sense of Their Richness"

We interrupt this tale of heroic survival thru exegesis to fulfill, at the request of one Jeffrey Rubin-Dorsky, the imperative—suggestion, really—to "broaden your discussion so that we have a greater sense of their richness."[7] That is, Stein's, Ginsberg's, Bruce's. Of course, anyone can see that he's right, but immediately he becomes Daddy, and I defiant. My first impulse is to defend my method of exposition experientially: I came to Stein, Ginsberg, and Bruce, as I have outlined here, through clues, obliquely. Out of these shards of language and reference, and with the twisted logic of my desperate adolescence, I created ladders of lace, slippery significances, fantastically fragile and always touch-and-go, to climb out of the catacombs of my encrypted suburban non/ Jewishness. Nobody helped me, I protest; why should I make this easy for "others (lots, we hope) who have only a cursory knowledge of their work."[8]

Lost, I hope, as I was back then, cursing the language in which we learned to curse ourselves, I want these others to listen to the clues in *their* word-ambiences, their kitchens and family scrapbooks and the closed doors of their parents' bedrooms. (I always assumed my 'rents were talking about me and my sisters.) What words in *your* families were landmines? Did *your* father, ever the gentle, unassuming scholar, unaccountably snap at you to shut up when you stuck out your tongue at the concept of "stuffed cabbage"? No? Well, what, then? Does your body come alive at the smell of stuffed cabbage because of the loving and *haimish* dinners inscribed into your nerve endings? Or do you blush and quiver at the sound of Mickey Katz on those rare and cutesified *klezmer* specials on listener-sponsored radio? What names are household items or resonate with special used-once-a-year sanctity? What rhymes and catchphrases and secret family jokes provided you with the footholds you needed to survive? Because any one of us postwar Jew-babies has a tale to tell, and it's a tale of hanging onto words as if they were our wire-monkey mothers. Jeffrey suggests "defiance" as the model these "performers in language" offered me: of course he's right (you're right of course, Jeffrey). Defiance, and a certain extravagance. And a sense of mystery and deviance. But these three magi came to me with their verbal gifts not entirely intuitively: they have never peopled my dreams like Artaud or, more embarrassingly, Virginia Woolf. (In those dreams, a group of women artists is always waiting in her vestibule to have tea with her; she never shows up, but in the meantime we all get to know and admire each other.) No, they didn't come to me, I went to them—had to follow them; words were both guiding stars and their final gifts. In real time rather than dream time, that is, over the course of about thirty years, I followed words about them, in limericks, Leah/Essie-talks, and snatches of popular songs, all the way to their words about themselves and, ultimately, to their words about words.

I followed Allen from the famous description of what seemed to me my inner self aprowl in my inner landscape—"starving hysterical naked . . . angelheaded hipsters burning for the ancient heavenly connection"—to the breakdown of language in grief over his crazy mother's death—Lord Lord Lord caw caw caw Lord Lord Lord caw caw caw Lord."[9] I followed him to Naropa Institute and found a middle-aged Jewish man preoccupied with boys and mortality, generous, narcissistic, nervous, and (incredibly, to me) jealous of my transient love for his transient loves. I followed his readings across the country and heard him, at age sixty, triumphantly belt out "SH'MA YISRAEL, ADONAI ELOHEYNU, ADONAI EHOD" to an audience of postbeat derelicts and poets, neo-beat teens and college students, and incongruously well-heeled speaker-series season-ticket subscribers at the San Francisco Jewish Community Center. He was pretty well-heeled himself, on the outside—but he was still shocking the bourgeoisie with that voice, and that sensibility.

I followed Gertrude from the *Autobiography of Alice B.* to "Lifting Belly" to "Yet Dish" to *How to Write*. I caught Gertrude, who publicly distanced herself

from Jewishness, who survived World War II in France, and who never even
acknowledged the Holocaust all around her, enumerating the languages embedded in the language my father and I were not allowed to master:

XLVIII
Polish polish is it a hand, polish is it a hand or all. . . .
XLIX
Rush in rush in slice.
L
Little gem in little gem in an. Extra.
LI
In the between egg in, in the between egg or on.[10]

Covertly, she was egging me on. I caught her defending the Old Testament as
ideal model for American avant-garde writers to emulate; it was, she said,
"permanently good reading" because "really in a way in the Old Testament
writing there really was not any such thing there was not really any succession
of anything and really in the Old Testament there is really no sentence existing
and no paragraphing, think about this thing, think if you have not really been
knowing this thing and then let us go on telling about what paragraphs and
sentences have been what prose and poetry has been."[11] Let us go on telling.
And more: I found fat and rapturous representations of eros (anagram of
"rose"):

> A violent luck and a whole squeezing and even then quiet. Water is squeezing,
> water is almost squeezing on lard. Water, water is a mountain. . . . A question of
> sudden rises and more time than awfulness is so easy and shady.
>
> . . .
>
> Wet crossing and a likeness, any likeness
>
> . . .
>
> A blaze, a search in between, a cow, only any wet place, only this tune.[12]

(All that wetness with a likeness—Yuck/Wow.) She made things happen in
language I didn't know could happen. She told me to use my own language;
I'm just now taking seriously her imperative to "A[u]th[o]r a Grammar."[13]
This chapter is my first attempt.

And Lenny? Wild, skinny Lenny Bruce? Gertrude led me right to him,
though publicly she swore she found him distasteful. Sexually ambiguous—
straight but queer—locked in with his mother in suffocating symbiotic friendship, tripped up in and tripped out on his own verbal brilliance, derailing his
senses in every direction, he was as absolutely modern as any teenage poet
plaintively exulting that "je est un autre."[14] In my hunt through Yiddish phrasebooks to crack Gertrude's code (before I realized that, as a German Jew, she had
never been a Yiddish speaker and used the concept only metaphorically—and
before I realized that cracking the code wasn't the point) I found that all the
best examples derived from Lenny. And, when I started taping his records, the
dissociative, broken patter of his Yiddish-inflected hipster argot moved around

in my sensorium in ways that felt like home, like the starry dynamo in the machinery of night. And anyway, he was always already there, like the others, there at the end of the road of glittering syllables, when I came back to where I began. With my father. Where I begin again. And there my studies began. And yours? Happy hunting.

We now regress to our standard programing.[15]

(back to) II. The Little Abstract Gets More So

Elsewhere, and in an era in which I felt more confident of my right to an un-pin-downable, fragmented postmodern Jewishness, I opened an essay with Lenny Bruce's brilliant drug-phrase, "the idiomatic fog that veils the user," as a trope for the glamour and Veil (in W. E. B. Du Bois' sense of socially divisive marker) hovering around the speaker of a despised vernacular.[16] In that and other essays, my objective was to seize on the downtrodden and rejected aspects of this vernacular and its popular reception, in order to redeem it in a defiant, in-your-face spirit. I imagined that my project resonated with some of the principles of the Négritude movement, with all its critically vulnerable history, in which writers such as Aimé Césaire and Léopold Sédar Senghor, while maintaining a certain essentialism (the black soul is this, the white soul is that), reversed the common Western valuation of racial characteristics and celebrated the heretofore devalorized. I have understood the seeming acceptance of limiting dichotomies (linear/nonlinear, civilized/primitive, head/heart) as part of a performance strategy of the Négritude poets, rather than as their naive belief in these binarisms as mutually exclusive sociobiological givens. Wole Soyinka's famous dismissive quip about Négritude—"the tiger doesn't announce its tigritude, it just pounces"[17]—seemed and still seems to me, despite its wittiness, a disingenuous refusal to acknowledge the importance of this performative aspect of self-announcement. First, his metaphor is ill-considered: many nonhuman animals do engage in ritual self-display, announcing and performing their specific speci-ality (both words having origin in "species" > L. a *seeing*) before killing, fighting, or copulating. Second, though the utility of self-reflection and phatic self-definition is certainly open to critique, these human (social and individual) occupations are so much a part of our lives that even Soyinka's criticism is simply part of that self-reflective discourse. One could even accuse his anti-self-reflective position as an attempt to out-primitive the primitivism of the Négritude poets (i.e., let's assume that the exotic tiger doesn't think, and then let's try to be more like that tiger), without their ironic self-consciousness—thus exacerbating the grounds for the other, far more trenchant critique of primitive essentialism. However, even the second and more powerful criticism of Négritude's essentialist dichotomies (and its privileging of the more "primitive" poles of these dichotomies), I believe, overlooks the ways in which the movement's performative, phatic aspect can be dramatized by these seemingly crude appropriations.

I wanted to do this with, as it were, "Yidditude," celebrating as nonlinear, deconstructive, and quintessentially postmodern the incoherence, the pastichelike, nomadic[18] indeterminacy attributed to Yiddish consciousness—sometimes derogatorily and sometimes affirmatively—by the dominant white Christian culture and by some Yiddishists. In underscoring the multiple origins of Yiddish, I used and affirmed the trope of bastardy and bestiality.[19] I intended it in the spirit of Deleuze and Guattari's valorizing trope "becoming-animal" for the process of the re/de/in-formation of minority subjectivity, though I also criticized Deleuze and Guattari for romanticizing the "other" by using "animal" as a valorizing metaphor just as others have, with no doubt unintentional insensitivity, used "woman" or "nigger." On occasion I would receive criticism from generally supportive readers: "What about real Jews, who use Yiddish to communicate with each other rather than to get in the face of the overlords? What about real Jews, whose context is a Jewish community rather than a dominant gentile one, for whom Jewishness is not a defiant display but simply a daily way of life?" To this question I would, in the venerable (vulnerable?) tradition, pose another (defiant, in-your-face) question: "So who gets to be Jewish? Who are these 'real Jews,' and what makes them realer than the Jews I study and the Jew I am?"

The deliberate provocativeness of these questions—indeed, the high premium I placed on indeterminacy—concealed and revealed the fundamental insecurity they triggered. Who is the Jew I am? I was raised by a Jewish father and a Nordic (Danish farmgirl, yet) mother, both of whom had complicated and contradictory feelings about Jewishness; these feelings, needless to say, included anti-Semitism as well as attraction and allegiance. It wasn't until into my late twenties that, after an extraordinary experience of seeing some Hebrew lettering come to life—literally begin to vibrate three-dimensionally with life—on a sympathy card my Jewish grandmother had received, I began to take on the identity that so much of my upbringing—including, of course, my conception (my genetic constitution) itself—had been carefully designed to erase. I was part of my father's fantasy of "hybrid vigor" (as a medical anthropologist he used such terms to affirm his children's good qualities), and only his death in my late teens permitted my escape from this agenda. I was raised with no Jewish ritual, no Jewish religion, very little secular Jewish culture even—in an atmosphere of patronizing tolerance of Yiddish ("an inherently comical language," my father said), contempt for "materialism" and fixation on worldly prestige (which, we were told, were undesirably "Jewish" characteristics); and with a sense that World War II was something that had happened to my mother (who had lived through the German occupation of Denmark) rather than my father (an American Jew who served in the air force in primarily a research capacity). Random information, such as the line that my great-grandparents' village ("Smargón, near Vilna"—the word *shtetl* was not used) no longer existed, was not connected to genocide; it "no longer existed" in the same way that my Danish grandfather no longer used a horse and plow to sow his vegetable garden. One day my father pointed out the Smargón Pharmacy as we drove through Cleveland Circle in Brookline. "Must be owned by some other people from there." We never went in there; never heard the word *landsman,* though I now understand the coded meaning of that observation: "There's an invisible community; we could find each other and help each other; I don't want you to know; I want you to know." The clues were in the words, I learned. Smargón. Or these ones, with which a friend at his twenty-fifth Harvard reunion doubled him over with laughter: Q: Whaddya think I said to my Chinese cab driver this morning? A: Don't *hak* me a *chaynik.* Or

> *pesach-time in Dixieland*
> *can't you here them shofars grand. . . .*
> *Pesach time in Dixie —*
> *Pesach with a shiksie —*
> *Pesach time in Dixiela-a-and —*
> *tsei-dei-dei-dei-dei*

he sang once. When my father died, we were not permitted to sit *shivah* with Grandma. My mother expressed scorn for empty rituals that involved having to "play hostess" to "people I don't even know"—people she didn't know because whole branches of the Jewish family had cut him (us) off when he married her. And he had cut them off.[20]

So, what kind of Jew am I? Other Jews are "real Jews." Even Isaac Deutscher's famous "non-Jewish Jews," the secular Jews, are more Jewish than I.[21] No matter how many *tallitot* I weave for my friends and my friends' children's bar/bat mitzvot, no matter how many Yiddishisms have come to adorn my speech, no matter how many essays I write in which I "problematize" "identity" by taking "the Jew" as the archetypal identity-problematizer (Reb Coyote-shmoyote), everyone knows I'm not real, not authentic, and hence my ardent overvaluing of inauthenticity, performance, and indeterminacy. This, as I explain to my mostly gentile students, is my "Jewish paranoia." "When you guys don't talk or ask questions, I think, 'It's because I'm Jewish.' See, I'm a paranoid Jew; when I'm not paranoid about being too Jewish, I'm paranoid about not being Jewish enough." The few Jews and the Third World students laugh with recognition; the (straight) white Christian students sigh with compassion and embarrassment, and charges of essentialism begin to bubble up from the more sophisticated ones.

Since the clues are in the words, I found the word that opened up these criticisms in a way that I could internalize. The word "philo-Semitic" got me beyond the comfort of defiance, because it captured, in its clinical categoricalness, my "attitude." I heard the word first in a lecture by David Biale and again encountered it in Jack Zipes's *The Operated Jew.*[22] Zipes uses it to describe postwar Germany's official and compensatory stance toward Jews—ostensibly approving and supportive, covertly (and possibly unintentionally) setting Jews up for further resentment and blame. For me the word illuminated the subtext of the criticism I had been receiving for my valorization of hyperverbal defiance and nonlinearity, as if these were intrinsic Jewish traits—or arguably worse, as if the reactive, oppositional tactics of Jewish culture were its most valuable contributions to the modern world. The romance of oppositionality, my critical friends implied, took precedence in my delineation of Jewishness over the quotidian rhythms, joyous or troubled, of Jewish community. Because of my own inherited conflicts, I valued the entanglements of cultural conflict over opportunities to enjoy community and ritual as part of the sustaining fabric of my daily life. And this philo-Semitism marked me, further, as an outsider both to gentile cultures and to the multiple Jewish cultures I had been programatically excluded from. Was there, under and alongside my self-declarations of Jewishness, an anxiety that to be Jewish is to be socially and emotionally disoriented, pathological, sexually ambiguous and ambivalent? Because Jewishness, in my childhood household, was a kind of shameful open secret, it became linked to other sources and causes of discomfort and loud silence. A friend tells me that, *gemisht* as I am, I look at my own Jewishness with a "majority-culture eye," and that "Jews . . . don't do this."[23] When she says this, I feel as if I'm looking at my own eye through the wrong end of a telescope, impossibly and perpetually turned inside out and upside down, irretrievably trapped in the modernist nightmare of my adolescence—which nightmare is, of course, my own body, my own self. I want there to be more "to" Jewishness than what I have, than what I am. Constructing my Jewish identity means disentangling this matrix of claustrophobic *mésalliances* and convolutions so the Jewishness can emerge clean and naked, vulnerable and becoming.

For me (as for all Jews, I believe), Jewishness isn't a comfortable background against which I can play out other complex dramas of subjectivity and identity. Because I have had to construct my own Jewishness in the world, and continue to have to do so, I also constantly have to deconstruct my Jewishness. The kind of Jew I am is the kind who isn't sure what kind of Jew she is. And who resists sureness as stasis, who embraces indeterminacy so that, as a floating signifier, I can sting like a bee when I need to. This doesn't mean dwelling in permanent inadequacy, performance anxiety, and self-erasure, though these can be useful if uncomfortable temporary conditions. Rather, by looking for the clues, the words, I move, not toward a whole picture, but further into the complexities of "becoming-Jewish," which means "unbeing and becoming," which means "becoming-becoming" as well as "unbeing-unbeing."

IV. Family Soul

One story among many remains to be told; it's the story of another soulmate. Some months before I moved to California to undertake my graduate studies, the house I lived in had an opening for a third housemate. The two of us who lived there interviewed a number of people and finally asked a woman to move in. She had long, long braids like my sisters; like me, she wove on a big floor-loom; she was an acupuncturist who treated me for my TMJ in exchange for a needlepoint rose I made for her. Her father was a prominent musician, and her mother had died mysteriously en route to joining him on tour, when my friend had been in her early teens. When she came out to visit me in California we attended the first Jewish Feminist Conference in Berkeley: another turning point for me, though it would be another year before I saw those Hebrew letters undulate and shimmer like gilded fish on that sympathy card at Grandma's house. A year later, by the same glinting summer bay that Leah/Essie had made bearable over a decade earlier, Linda and I discovered, through piecing together the names we'd heard each other say, which resonated oddly and increasingly with names we'd heard from other lives, that our grandparents Henry Diamond/Damon and Sonia had been each other's first loves, that my grandmother Bessie and Linda's great-aunt Bashka the sculptress had been best friends from 1905 to Bashka's death in the 1970s, and that our families had been closely joined by friendship, across the class differences that made Grandma afraid, as a teenaged girl, to cross the barroom to the stairway that led to Linda's great-grandparents' apartment upstairs, and to remark to me eighty years later, "They were so poor they kept their coal in the bathtub in the kitchen! But so talented!" Grandma took piano lessons from Sonia, Bashka's older sister. Sonia was in love with Henry. Years after Henry and Sonia broke up, Henry married Bessie: "I didn't steal him away from her," said Grandma. Linda's father had known my father. My father's sister had had a girlhood crush on Linda's father. But Linda and I had known nothing of each other; the pain of Jewishness drove my father away from the community and took us away from history. The connection was reestablished by coincidence in my generation.

I'm writing this chapter at Linda's apartment in Jamaica Plain during a six-week stay here in Boston. Grandma Bess, 103 years old, lives a few miles to the west. I haven't gone to see her yet. My father's sister lives a few streets over. I haven't called her to tell her I'm in town. My mother and sisters still live in the house I grew up in; in the six weeks I've been in Boston, I haven't been to the house. Gertrude in Paris discovering eros is aroused by a rose named Toklas; Allen lying forlorn on his Columbia dorm bed, his sexual pain transfigured into grace by the voice of William Blake reciting "Ah Sunflower," and then again in Bellevue with Carl Solomon ("My name is Prince Myshkin, and who are you?"); Lenny in his pauper's mansion on the hill, or pleading to a jury, "Just let me do my bit, so you'll get it," could not feel more exiled, more at home. Show me my language, Gertrude, Lenny, and Allen, to untell the tale anew.

V. We Triggered Insecurity by These Questions

As we drove through Cleveland—my valorization of indeterminacy by some other people from there. We triggered insecurity by these questions.

Word*landsman,* though I now understand an anti-Semitic Jewish pharmacy and an anti-invisible community—we—mother—it wasn't until
into my late twenties I don't want you to know; I want you mother of
seeking some Hebrew lettering come to Life learned. *Smargón.* Don't *hak*
me a *chaynik.* dimensionally on a sympathy card the defiance of these
questions—indeed I take on identity concealed and revealed—a fundamental conception (my genetic constitution)—Who is the Jew I am? erase. I
was part of my father's fantasy to erase. yet in my late teens permitted to
escape life, after an extraordinary experience Jewish ritual, no Jewish religion, my Jewish grandmother had received life literally began to vibrate
three— contempt for Yiddish inherently my upbringing, including, of
course, itself, had been carefully designed to circle in Brookline. materialism and fixation on the world. hybrid vigor and only his death never went
in there. must be owned from this agenda. I was raised with no never
went in there; never heard the prestige (which, we were told, were to
know, and could find each other and help each other). To know. The clues
were in the words, he sang once. When my father died, *smargón,* near *vilna,*
not connected to *genocide,* my mother expressed *scorn* the word *shtetl* it no
longer whole *branches* of the Jewish family. grandfather no longer used a
horse and comical language my father said. And he had cut them off.

VI. Coda: A Final Epigraph

in the hopes that someone who writes music will read this and want to set it:[24]

November 19, 1941
How sad to think that at 30 Mazeppa Street, where I spent so many lovely
hours, no one will be left, all of it will become mere legend. I don't know why I
feel guilty toward myself, as if I had lost something and it was my own fault.
                                              —Bruno Schultz, *Letters and*
                                              Drawings of Bruno Schultz

NOTES

1. See *The Essential Lenny Bruce,* ed. John Cohen (New York: Random House,
1967), 158.
2. Maria Damon, "Artaud in Massachusetts," *Sequoia* 31 (Spring 1987): 15–16.
3. Lenny Bruce, "prison break" (elsewhere titled "Father Flotsky's Triumph"),
The Essential Lenny Bruce, 180. See also Arthur Naiman, *Every Goy's Guide to Common
Jewish Expressions* (New York: Ballantine Books, 1981), s.v. *nafke.*
4. Lenny Bruce, *What I Got Arrested For* (the skit "Blah-Blah-Blah"), Fantasy
Records, 1971.
5. Bruce, *The Essential Lenny Bruce,* 181.
6. See Ioan Davis, "Lenny Bruce: Hyperrealism and the Death of Jewish Tragic
Humor," *Social Text* 22 (Spring 1989): 92–114.

7. Jeffrey Rubin-Dorsky, letter to me, January 8, 1993.

8. Rubin-Dorsky letter.

9. Allen Ginsberg, "Howl," in *Howl and Other Poems* (San Francisco: City Lights, 1956), 9; and Ginsberg, "Kaddish," in *Kaddish and Other Poems* (San Francisco: City Lights, 1961), 36.

10. Gertrude Stein, "Yet Dish," in *The Yale Gertrude Stein,* ed. Richard Kostelanetz (New Haven, Conn.: Yale University Press, 1981), 61.

11. Gertrude Stein, "Lecture 2: Narration," in *The Poetics of the New American Poetry,* ed. Donald Allen (New York: Grove Press, 1973), 106.

12. Gertrude Stein, "Sugar," in *Tender Buttons, Selected Writings of Gertrude Stein,* ed. Carl Van Vechten (New York: Random House, 1962), 485.

13. Gertrude Stein, "Arthur a Grammar," in *How to Write* (New York: Dover Publications, 1975), 37.

14. Arthur Rimbaud, letter to Paul Demeny, May 15, 1871.

15. Was that okay, Jeffrey? Our senses richer yet?

16. Lenny Bruce, *The (Almost) Unpublished Lenny Bruce* (Philadelphia: Running Press, 1984), 63; Maria Damon, "Talking Yiddish at the Boundaries," *Cultural Studies* 5 (1991): 14–29.

17. Wole Soyinka, Kampala African Writers' Conference, 1962; subsequently revised in Berlin 1964 ("I was trying to distinguish between propaganda and true poetic creativity").

18. Nomadism is just about my favorite trope circulating in the contemporary theoretical imagination, since "nomad" is "damon" backwards.

19. See Maria Damon, "Women, Dogs and Jews: Gertrude Stein's Doggerel 'Yiddish,' " in *The Dark End of the Street: Margins in American Vanguard Poetry* (Minneapolis: University of Minnesota Press, 1993).

20. My father's story will never be told except through others. I do not speak for him here, nor at this point will I publicly hazard guesses at why Jewishness was so painful for him in particular. I expect to learn more about this in my process.

21. Isaac Deutscher, "The Non-Jewish Jew," in *The Non-Jewish Jew and Other Essays* (Oxford: Oxford University Press, 1968), 25–41.

22. David Biale, "Haskalah and Jewish Sexuality," University of Minnesota, November 1991; Jack Zipes, *The Operated Jew* (New York: Routledge, 1991), 17.

23. Martha Roth, March 1993. Thanks to Martha, Riv-Ellen Prell, Linda Hillyer, Joanna O'Connell, Valerie Miner, Susan Welch, and Helen Hoy for their close readings of this chapter.

24. This is the last extent letter of Bruno Schultz; a year later he was shot on the street by a Gestapo officer. *Letters and Drawings of Bruno Schultz,* ed. Jerzy Ficowski, trans. Walter Arndt with Victoria Nelson (New York: Harper and Row, 1988), 213.

25

Cheder as Chaos and *Chazon*

The Example of *Call It Sleep*

Joel Porte

Where there is no vision [*chazon*], the people perish. . . .
—Proverbs 29:18

The history of the genesis or the old mythology repeats itself in the experience of every child. He too is a demon or god thrown into a particular chaos, where he strives ever to lead things from disorder into order. Each individual soul is such, in virtue of its being a power to translate the world into some particular language of its own. . . .

—Emerson, "The Method of
Nature"

It is worth the expense of youthful days and costly hours, if you learn only some words of an ancient language, which are raised out of the trivialness of the street, to be perpetual suggestions and provocations.

—Thoreau, *Walden*

I

I might as well call it sleep—those soporific late-afternoon sessions in the stuffy basement room of a *shul* on East Third Street in Brooklyn. This was *cheder*, the Hebrew school where I and other boys my age were supposed to learn the sacred language of our tribe in preparation for becoming bar mitzvah. It would have been easy to doze off, with the droning of (mostly) incomprehensible Hebrew at the low point of my circadian rhythm, had it not been for the sting of an occasional spitball or a kick under the desk. Then, too, the ever-threatening hypnagogia was periodically dispelled by sharp outbursts from the *melamed*, cursing and correcting some boy or other for a faltering pronunciation or wayward accent. What had any of this to do with my *real* life, I wondered—with the hot passages I loved to read in *The Amboy Dukes* or with the radio theory I was teaching myself as I looked forward to studying electrical engineering?

As things turned out, neither the bar mitzvah nor the career as an electrical engineer materialized. But the experience of the *cheder*, as a scene of pedagogy and (however scrappy) of linguistic and literary lore, seems to me now to have prefigured my career as an English professor who would one day circle back imaginatively from the canonical Protestant-Christian world of Emerson and Thoreau and Dickinson officially sanctioned in graduate school and, so to speak, return to Hebrew school—as, for example, in Henry Roth's *Call It Sleep,* with its powerful use of the topos of the *cheder.* Coming to teach Roth's great novel, I would find myself sitting with David Schearl in the rank *cheder* of his immigrant world and sharing his fascination with the Haphtorah to Jethro from the sixth chapter of Isaiah, which, in my reading, forms the center of *Call It Sleep.*[1]

I have used the phrase "topos of the *cheder*" as if it were itself a commonplace of literary analysis; but so far as I know it has not been employed before. Viewed more generally under the rubric of a child's confrontation with religious indoctrination, it might be taken back at least as far as Emerson's angry complaint, in "Spiritual Laws," about Sunday schools being "yokes to the neck"—scenes of constraint where young people are shut up "against their will" and made to respond to impertinent questions. More recent versions of this motif, such as one finds in John Updike's "Pigeon Feathers" or in Philip Roth's "The Conversion of the Jews," involve a heated confrontation between an uncomprehending youngster and a complacent liberal minister or Reform rabbi. In both these cases, we are dealing with a struggle between nascent theological concern and establishment pieties that thwart the burgeoning religious sensibilities of the young.

The "topos of the *cheder*" as I use it here, however, has a somewhat different focus and belongs to a different tradition—one that is nicely capped and ragged, for example, by Herman Wouk in chapter 29 of *Inside, Outside,* where we are introduced to the popular Jewish-American writer Peter Quat and his scandalous novella, *The Smelly Melamed.* The Hebrew teacher in question, Shraga Glutz, is noted for "his bad breath, garlicky body odor, thundering belches, and celebrated habit of picking his nose and parking the snot crusts under the seat of his chair."[2] Covering his flanks, Wouk has the narrator insist that Quat made up Shraga Glutz "out of thin air." But the knowledgeable reader will not be fooled by Wouk's disclaimer, for Rabbi Glutz has a tolerably long history in Jewish-American writing. In the 1930s especially, when left-leaning Jewish authors were eager to follow Marx and reject the opiate of their ancestors, we find a number of smelly fictive *melamdim* designed to heap ridicule on religion and its practitioners.

Perhaps the best-known example prior to the publication of *Call It Sleep* can be located in chapter 5 of Mike Gold's *Jews without Money,* where little Mikey is sent to *cheder* to be tortured by the unspeakable Reb Moisha. This man, we are told,

> was a walking, belching symbol of the decay of orthodox Judaism. What could such as he teach any one? He was ignorant as a rat. He was a foul-smelling, emaciated beggar who had never read anything, or seen anything, who knew absolutely nothing but this sterile memory course in dead Hebrew which he whipped into the heads and backsides of little boys.[3]

Clothed in black alpaca "green and disgusting with its pattern of grease, snuff, old food stains and something worse" (65), Reb Moisha blows his nose on the floor and wipes it on his "horrible sleeve." Leaning over his students as they practice their *alef-beyz,* he lets loose "the sirocco blast of a thousand onions" (65) from his polluted beard, thereby dampening, one assumes, his charges' inchoate interest in Hebrew learning.

Mikey is appalled by this chaotic scene, where he "beheld thirty boys leaping and rioting like so many tigers pent in the one cage" (66). Some are spinning tops, others playing tag or wrestling; in a corner, a group of boys are shooting craps. Through it all Reb Moisha sits with a minyan of "surly boys," including Mikey, who are forced to howl "the ancient Hebrew prayers for thunder and lightning and bread and death; meaningless sounds to us" (66). These sounds are not conveyed to the reader. We are not allowed to overhear any scrap of prayer or Scripture in the sacred tongue that might confer a modicum of dignity on this "bedlam" (Mikey's word). Instead, our young hero broods "on the strange man in the sky who must be addressed in Hebrew, that man who had created everything on earth" (67), and muses over why a "God of Love" would put bedbugs, pain, and poverty into the world. We are left to conclude that a God capable of making Reb Moisha in his own image must be a very strange God indeed. Little wonder that by the end of the novel Mikey has traded the Jewish messiah for the workers' revolution, which he calls "the true Messiah." Presumably, in the "garden for the human spirit" (309) which this messiah brings, there will be no room for chaotic *chederim* or smelly *melamdim.*

I think it is likely that Henry Roth knew *Jews without Money.* He would certainly have been interested in the career of an older Jewish writer who had already discovered communism (as Roth himself would) and made a name for himself in leftist circles as an editor of the *New Masses.* Gold's book also provided a kind of model for Roth's semiautobiographical novel about immigrant Jewish life in New York. But whether or not *Jews without Money* played a direct part in the composition of *Call It Sleep,* we may observe that Roth's attitude toward Hebrew school and *melamdim* in his college years did seem to resemble Gold's. In an autobiographical fragment that reconstructs the period, Roth describes his relationship with a high school chum named Lester Winter, who, though Jewish, knew even less than Roth about Jewish practice and tradition. So, for example, when Roth announced whimsically that he was at heart "a *malamut,*" provoking a laugh from Lester and the question, "What's that? An Alaskan husky?" Roth records that he replied, "Oh, no. He's the old guy who slaps you around in the cheder—the little dump where you learn Hebrew."[4]

We may, accordingly, be tempted to conclude (as some critics have) that Roth's Yidel Pankower is cut from the same cloth as Reb Moisha.[5] Indeed Reb Pankower's cloth does not appear to be much cleaner than that of Reb Moisha: "His trousers were baggy and stained, a great area of striped and crumpled shirt intervened between his belt and his bulging vest. The knot of his tie, which was nearer one ear than the other, hung away from his soiled collar."⁶ Like Reb Moisha, Yidel Pankower blows his nose on the ground, though he has the delicacy to use a handkerchief after; and his breath is foul, though from tobacco, not onions. Reb Pankower curses his students (brilliantly), threatens them with a cat-o'-nine-tails, and cuffs and pinches them when he is displeased.⁷

It is also clear, however, that Roth is after bigger game than Gold is in his portrait of the rabbi, for when he reappears in a late chapter (book 4, chapter 16) entirely devoted to the rabbi, Pankower takes on some of the ruined majesty of Faulkner's Dilsey or the comitragic dignity of Joyce's Bloom. As he makes his way through the streets of the city to David's tenement, Reb Pankower's musings are a grab bag of high and low. He thinks of his walking stick, broken when it caught in a manhole cover that morning; remembers the pleasures of administering a good beating to a bad boy's buttocks; and laments the selling of *treif* even by butchers claiming to be kosher. But when he observes the ghetto youth crowding the stoops and sidewalks of this "Golden Land"—these Yiddish-speaking offspring turning into citizens of a so-called New World—Reb Pankower begins to sound more portentous, like some latter-day Crèvecoeur or Tocqueville trying to understand a phenomenon unprecedented in history: "What would become of this new breed? These Americans? . . . brazen, selfish, unbridled."⁸

As Walter Allen observes, though Reb Pankower is "dirty, irascible, a petty sadist, a Dickensian character conducting what appears to be an almost Dickensian parody of religious education," he also is a credible representative of the mind and spirit of traditional Jewish Europe.⁹ Faced with what he calls a "corrupt generation" of Sammy and Sally Glicks in the making, Reb Pankower certainly has the right to wonder if the God of Abraham and Isaac will be remembered in the melting-pot/jackpot of the New World. His interior monologue is a minijeremiad that unwittingly echoes a good deal of American preacherly rhetoric about the dangers lurking in the collective historical amnesia characteristic of an opportunistic young nation. Jews in particular, released from the rabbinical constraints and political tyrannies of the Old World, may feel especially tempted to create new identities—to shake off the names, clothes, habits, and languages of their tradition. Why should the little boys in Reb Pankower's *cheder* be tortured into learning an ancient priestly tongue so apparently foreign to the common life of their new land—a language of strange letters and queer sounds that seems to move against the very tide of progress and logic?

This question—a question that sits squarely at the heart of *Call It Sleep*—is evidently quite different from the one posed by Updike's "Pigeon Feathers" or Philip Roth's "Conversion of the Jews." In these stories our young protagonists feel compelled to engage their liberal ministers in "meaningful" religious dialogue—to drag them back, so to speak, from their cheap answers to the more strenuous terms provided, say, by a Karl Barth or a Martin Buber. But the question implicitly posed by David Schearl is stranger, more basic: can there really be a *sacred* language—"God's tongue," a language in which you can "talk to God"? David hardly seems more prepared than any other child to grasp such a concept. At the start Hebrew strikes him as simply incomprehensible jargon: "First you read, Adonoi elahenoo abababa, and then you say, And Moses said you mustn't, and then you read some more abababa and then you say, mustn't eat in the traife butcher store."[10]

Abababa: merely a child's version of patriarchal prattle (*abba*-babble) that tells you what you mustn't do. But amidst the chaos and confusion of Reb Pankower's *cheder* David learns a different Hebrew—the mysterious and curiously powerful story of a man named Isaiah who had a vision (*chazon*): "Beshnos mos hamelech Uziyahu vaereh es adonoi . . ." (225). Since the boys are beginners, reading by rote, Reb Pankower offers them a paraphrase and translation: "In the year that King Uzziah died, Isaiah saw God. And God was sitting on his throne, high in heaven and in his temple—Understand?" (226–27). David does indeed seem to understand: "—Gee! And he saw Him. Wonder where? (David, his interest aroused, was listening intently. This was something new.)" (227). The "something new" that David is attempting to grasp concerns the irruption of the sacred into the ordinary universe and secular history. Could one actually say, credibly, in English, "In the year in which Woodrow Wilson was elected president I saw God"? David does not put it to himself that way. But what he vaguely comes to feel as Reb Pankower continues to tell the story of Isaiah's vision—of the "blessed angels" with their "Kadosh! Kadosh! Kadosh—Holy! Holy! Holy!"; of God's majesty and "His terrible light"; of the prophet's unclean lips and the cleansing coal—is that this amazing experience ("Gee! It's God") can *only* be paraphrased in English. Somehow, its actuality is *in* the Hebrew—in "that blue book," on page 68.

Later, after David's mother has reinforced for him the notion that God is light, "brighter than the day is brighter than the night" (241), and he has had his own experiences—at the waterfront, in the car tracks—of an apocalyptic radiance "complete and dazzling" (248), totally brilliant, which he associates with the "terrible light" of Isaiah's God, David returns to page 68 of the blue book several times to repeat the Hebrew ("Beshnas mos hamelech Uziyahu vawere es adonoi yoshav al kesai rum venesaw . . ." [255]), and each time he undergoes a kind of linguistic orgasm, his own *chazon*, in and through the *ipsissima verba* of the Hebrew text:

All his senses dissolved into the sound. The lines, unknown, dimly surmised, thundered in his heart with limitless meaning, rolled out and flooded the last shores of his being. . . . (255)

Not as a drone this time, like syllables pulled from a drab and tedious reel, but again as it was at first, a chant, a hymn, as though a soaring presence behind the words pulsed and stressed a meaning. (367)

David's experience of what Longfellow calls "the grand dialect the prophets spake" transfigures the *cheder* for him, so that it ceases to be merely "the little dump where you learn Hebrew" and finally becomes a place of deliverance.[11]

II

In 1971, asked by the *New York Times* to explain his silence after the publication of *Call It Sleep,* Henry Roth wrote a piece called "No Longer at Home," in which he asserted that, for him, "continuity was destroyed when his family moved from snug, orthodox Ninth Street, from the homogeneous East Side to rowdy, heterogeneous Harlem."[12] Lamenting the loss of "the tenets, the ways, the faith [that] were discarded too drastically, too rapidly," Roth speculated that this loss "may have been what he sensed when he wrote his novel," that it "may have been a kind of subliminal theme, dominating him without his knowing it" (168). Unlike Mike Gold, who was content to dismiss his Hebrew school experience in one searing, satiric chapter of *Jews without Money,* Roth insisted that that experience was fundamental for him; it was "that which informed him, connective tissue of his people, inculcated by *heder,* countenanced by the street, sanctioned by God . . ." (170). In letters and taped conversations Roth stressed and denigrated the loss of his ancestral symbols:

> Fact is they were the important ones, however lightly I seemed to part with them. They transmuted themselves into a kind of pervasive mysticism that infused the youth, gave him a kind of singular vision all the years of poverty and worse in Harlem's 119th Street. (170)

Lacking his "symbolic home," Roth (to use his own language [170]) became a "galoot"[13] in *galut*[14]—indeed, doubly in *galut,* since in his consciously cultivated detachment he felt exiled even from his own people's "exilic struggle."[15] Fitfully he identified with James Joyce, the modernist exile par excellence, and later he would wonder whether he might conclude as a wandering "Jewlysses"[16] self-condemned to write a "Portrait of the Artist as an Old Fiasco."[17] But that would happen only if he gave himself totally to the *via dolorosa* of "creative writing"[18] and ended up, like his "great master," Joyce, "in that blind alley coruscating with his genius."[19]

Roth would need to remind himself repeatedly that he was, in fact, radically different from Joyce, because his own "singular vision"[20] was rooted not in the religion of art but rather in the historical realities of an ongoing Jewish experience that he simply couldn't shake. Working in the early 1980s on a memoir entitled "Weekends in New York," Roth explained that his own process of maturation took "the form of a violent negation of Joyce, not of all that he contributed, his virtuosities and innovations, but of what he stood for, or more precisely the direction he faced, what proceeded from his monstrous detachment and artistic autonomy. I move uncertainly in a new reality" (260). One wonders, however, whether that reality was in fact totally new, for despite the profound influence that Joyce had exercised over the author of *Call It Sleep,* Roth's vision was always quite distinct from Joyce's. We may take the measure of that distinctness by comparing Roth's use of the topos of the *cheder* in *Call It Sleep* with Joyce's treatment of young Stephen Daedalus' religious training in *Portrait of the Artist* (for I believe it is *Portrait,* much more than *Ulysses,* that bears directly on the central issues developed by Roth in his own *Bildungsroman*).[21]

One of the most powerful scenes in *Portrait* (chapter 3) occurs in the chapel of Stephen's Jesuit college, where the impressionable young student is subjected to an utterly terrifying and very long sermon on the agonies of Hell. Joyce has the priest exercise considerable rhetorical skill—greater even, one might say, than that of Jonathan Edwards—in making vivid for his charges the full horror of this abysmally dark place that is totally removed from God:

> Hell is a strait and dark and foulsmelling prison, an abode of demons and lost souls, filled with fire and smoke. . . . the fire of hell, while retaining the intensity of its heat, burns eternally in darkness. It is a neverending storm of darkness, dark flames and dark smoke of burning brimstone, amid which the bodies are heaped one upon another without even a glimpse of air. Of all the plagues with which the land of the Pharaohs was smitten one plague alone, that of darkness, was called horrible. . . . The horror of this strait and dark prison is increased by its awful stench. All the filth of the world, all the offal and scum of the world, we are told, shall run there as to a vast reeking sewer. . . . Every sense of the flesh is tortured and every faculty of the soul therewith: the eyes with impenetrable utter darkness, the nose with noisome odours, the ears with yells and howls and execrations, the taste with foul matter, leprous corruption, nameless suffocating filth, the touch with redhot goads and spikes, with cruel tongues of flame. And through the several torments of the senses the immortal soul is tortured eternally in its very essence amid the leagues upon leagues of glowing fires kindled in the abyss by the offended majesty of the Omnipotent God and fanned into everlasting and ever increasing fury by the breath of the anger of the Godhead. . . . [22]

Even a lengthy quotation cannot convey the immense force of the reduplicative images with which poor Stephen's imagination is bombarded as the reality of eternal damnation is made vivid for this beleaguered young believer. While attempting to sustain his faith in a Christian deity usually described—in contradistinction to the presumptively wrathful Jehovah of Hebraic tradition—as a God of love, Stephen is dragged mercilessly into the pit and left to wallow in spiritual darkness, where his brain explodes in an apocalypse of linguistic torment: "—Hell! Hell! Hell! Hell! Hell!"

What is especially interesting about this episode for a student of *Call It Sleep,* with its markedly different experience of religious school, is that Joyce's infernal tour de force is built on a text from the chapter of Isaiah just preceding the one that contains David Schearl's cherished Haphtorah reading: "*Hell has enlarged its soul and opened its mouth without any limits*—words taken, my dear little brothers in Christ Jesus, from the book of Isaias, fifth chapter, fourteenth verse. In the name of the Father and of the Son and of the Holy Ghost, Amen" (117). It seems to me obvious that Roth chose his own text from Isaiah calculatedly, so as to mark the sharp difference between the religious worlds of Stephen Dedaelus and David Schearl. The priest, enlarging relentlessly on his brief text, rubs Stephen's nose over and over again in the loathsomeness of damnation and its attendant demons; the rabbi, on the other hand, enchants and inspires David's fancy with his loving description of "God's blessed angels. How beautiful they were you yourself may imagine."[23] To offset Stephen's agonized "—Hell! Hell! Hell! Hell! Hell!" we have the rabbi's "Kadosh! Kadosh! Kadosh—Holy! Holy! Holy!" Balancing the priest's transcendently filthy burning brimstone, we have the fiery coal that cleanses Isaiah's lips. Rabbi Pankower delivers David from the coal cellar that torments him early in the novel by offering him a specifically Jewish vision of divine glory. The priest, so to speak, delivers Stephen to eternal darkness through a Jansenist version of Catholic Christianity that overlooks the splendor of the *shekhinah* and its power to dispel the gloom of Sheol. "Where is God's cellar I wonder?" David muses. "How light it must be there. Wouldn't be scared, like I once was in Brownsville. Remember?" (231).

In order to achieve his epiphanies—his enchanting glimpse, for example, of the young woman wading in the Liffey—Stephen must turn away from the Church and redefine St. Thomas' *claritas* in terms of his private aesthetic of worldly beauty.[24] The "wild angel" (172) who appears to him and sets his cheeks aflame is not the gift of his religious training; rather, she is "the angel of mortal youth and beauty, an envoy from the fair courts of life" (172) capable of throwing open "before him in an instant of ecstasy the gates of all the ways of error and glory" (172). David, on the other hand, can build on what he has learned in *cheder*, extrapolating from the splendor of Isaiah's divine vision to the theophanies of ordinary experience:

> . . . vivid jets of images—of the glint on tilted beards, of the uneven shine of roller skates, of the dry light on grey stone stoops, of the tapering glitter of rails, of the oily sheen on the night-smooth rivers, of the glow on thin blond hair, red faces, of the glow on the outstretched, open palms of legions upon legions of hands hurtling toward him. He might as well call it sleep.[25]

We might as well call it the product of the visionary gleam that David found out about from Reb Pankower in the *cheder*.[26] His "strangest triumph," perhaps, issues from his "strangest acquiescence"—to the reconfigured traditions and language of his ancestral religion.[27]

III

I observed at the outset that my return, as a student of American writing, to the *talmud torah* of my childhood in the works of Jewish authors required a kind of circling back from the standard canon of American literature to which

I devoted myself in graduate school. I would need to reconfigure my own identity as a scholar and teacher in order to be able to include the work of my coreligionists as part of my professional life, since (as we all know) twenty or more years ago little premium was placed on the "ethnic" in the academy, and we were all effectively taught to suppress traces of it in our lives and work. Isn't that what many of us wanted to do anyway?

A role model such as Lionel Trilling was a crucial case in point. When I met Trilling in 1959, at the end of my second year as a graduate student at Harvard, I thought of him almost purely as the Matthew Arnold redivivus of Morningside Heights. He did not strike me as a Jewish English professor, but rather as the rarefied essence of English professorness, and that is what I thought I wanted to be also. Of Trilling's own struggle with his Jewish identity, his search for a "positive Jewishness," I knew very little until my friend Mark Krupnick began the research that culminated in his *Lionel Trilling*. Now, in Krupnick's incisive study, I could see how the young Trilling "had earlier [before his experience as a writer for the *Menorah Journal*] associated Jewishness with awkwardness and vulgarity."[28] And he hadn't even grown up in pathetically provincial Jewish Brooklyn! My years there seemed to me, as I lived them, impoverished in every sense of the word. I wanted to put all that firmly behind me.

With the passage of time, however, things have changed. The academy and the academic literary canon have, for the most part, become friendly to "ethnicity," and I myself have progressively (predictably?) mellowed in regard to my Brooklyn-Jewish past and its place in my cultural formation. Now, in fact, I wonder whether the sharp opposition I maintained previously between my two worlds—the mainly WASP world of my Harvard training, the "ethnic" Jewish world of my Brooklyn upbringing—was really faithful to my actual experience. I find myself, for example, not entirely sharing Irving Howe's sentiment when he speaks of the "barriers of sensibility that separated Concord, Massachusetts from the immigrant streets of New York"; or when he asks what Emerson could "mean to a boy or girl on Rivington Street in 1929, hungry for books, reading voraciously, hearing Yiddish at home, yet learning to read, write, and think in English? What could the tradition of American romanticism, surely our main tradition, mean to them?"[29]

The truth is that more than one immigrant author responded positively to Emerson (I think of Anzia Yezierska) and not, it seems to me, because he represented the possibility of intellectual and cultural assimilation to Anglo-Saxon gentility, but rather because of his almost Hebraic spiritual intensity. It was Emerson, after all, whose citation of Proverbs 29:18 ("Where there is no vision, the people perish") in the exordium to one of his most passionate addresses set me to thinking about *chazon*. And his insistence, further, that "the wit of man, his strength, his grace, his tendency, his art, is the grace and the presence of God. It is beyond explanation. When all is said and done, the rapt saint is found the only logician," struck a responsive chord in my Jewish soul.[30] This is the same Emerson who would praise his step-grandfather, the Reverend Ezra Ripley, at his death, for being "a modern Israelite, a believer in the Genius or Jehovah of the Jews to the very letter," who nobly represented "the antique Hebraism and customs" that Emerson continued to respect even as he struggled against them (as I did).[31]

Thoreau, too, has always seemed to me inspired by more than a touch of the Hebraic spirit. Undoubtedly, there was no *cheder* in the Concord of his day, but little David Henry (as he was originally named) might well have relished the opportunity even to expend some "youthful days and costly hours" in the acquisition of a few words of that ancient tongue that raises David Schearl "out of the trivialness of the street."[32] When Thoreau asks, "May we not *see* God?" the question strikes me as being put in the spirit of David Schearl's Isaiah. And that seems to me equally true of Thoreau's desire to experience a "vision, or dream"—a desire so fierce that he adds: "I would give all the wealth of the world, and all the deeds of all the heroes, for one true vision." Thus, when Thoreau insists that "our truest life is when we are in dreams awake,"[33] I feel myself drawn forward to the ending of Roth's novel and David's sense that it is only "toward sleep," when the imagination has the Wordsworthian "power to cull again and reassemble" the fragments of ordinary experience into a more triumphant whole, that life begins a little to transcend itself.[34]

I find it helpful to hear Henry Roth saying, in 1968, that "the American people have finally caught up with [the Jew], in the sense that they have assumed some of his characteristics. . . . He has now become the trope of the other exiled, the Americans. Hence the vogue of Jewish writers in the U.S.A. and the revival of *Call It Sleep*."[35] I wonder if Roth ever considered that the Puritans themselves took on a strongly Hebraic identity in their holy exile. So that, for example, the Harvard College curriculum, in the first century or so after its founding, distinguished itself from that of Oxford and Cambridge because of "the attention given to Hebrew and allied languages" (perhaps, as Samuel Eliot Morison suggests, owing to the fact that two of the great early presidents, Dunster and Chauncy, "were Hebraists"). The Italian-Jewish scholar Judah Monis was given a Harvard master's degree in 1720 (a thing unheard of at Oxford or Cambridge); and two years later was named "Instructor of the Hebrew Language" (to be sure, after his conversion to Christianity!), a position he held until 1760, though by then the study of Hebrew had ceased to be required for Harvard undergraduates.[36]

Is it too fanciful of me, then, to think that, in a manner of speaking, Harvard had also been a *cheder*—not just a place where Hebrew was taught along with Latin and Greek (that was the case, too, in the classics department at City College of New York during my undergraduate years), but also a place devoted, with an almost talmudic fervor, to learning in general? It was the same Harvard that would nourish my quasi-Hebraic masters, Emerson and Thoreau, and that, over the years, would open its doors, willy-nilly, to many

Jewish scholars and writers, enabling them (in Emerson's words) "to translate the world into some particular language of [their] own." I can even imagine David Schearl going on, as I did, from New York to Cambridge, Massachusetts, in order to extend and refine his visions without losing his Jewishness. Call that America.

NOTES

1. On Roth and the Bible see Leslie Field, "Henry Roth's Use of Torah and Haftorah in *Call It Sleep*," *Studies in American Jewish Literature* 5 (1979): 22–27. Among the critical works that have enriched my understanding of *Call It Sleep* I want to single out the following: Bonnie Lyons, *Henry Roth: The Man and His Work* (New York: Cooper Square Publishers, 1976); *Studies in American Jewish Literature* 5, 1 (1979)—a special issue devoted to Roth and edited by Bonnie Lyons; Mario Materassi, ed., *Rothiana: Henry Roth nella critica italiana* (Firenze: Editrice La Giuntina, 1985); Naomi Diamant, "Linguistic Universes in Henry Roth's *Call It Sleep*," *Contemporary Literature* 27 (1986): 336–55; Guido Fink and Gabriella Morisco, eds., *Il recupero del testo: Aspetti della letteratura ebraico-americana* (Bologna: Cooperativa Libreria Universitaria Editrice Bologna, 1988); Stephen J. Adams, "'The Noisiest Novel Ever Written': The Soundscape of Henry Roth's *Call It Sleep*," *Twentieth Century Literature* 35 (1989): 43–64.

2. Herman Wouk, *Inside, Outside* (Boston: Little, Brown, 1985), 180.

3. Michael Gold, *Jews without Money* (1930; New York: Carroll and Graf Publishers, 1984), 65. The subsequent page references in the text pertain to this source.

4. Henry Roth, *Shifting Landscape,* ed. Mario Materassi (Philadelphia: Jewish Publication Society, 1987), 207.

5. An extreme example is Gordon Poole ("David in America: Dalla etnicità ebraica all' americanismo cristiano," in *Rothiana*, ed. Materassi, 119–42), who speaks of the "abusive Reb Yidel Pankower, a caricature of the Old World Jew, slovenly and malodorous . . . who is nonetheless a religious authority in the local Jewish-American community. What could have driven Roth's pen—anticlericalism or anti-Semitism?" (126).

6. Henry Roth, *Call It Sleep* (New York: Avon Books, 1964), 212.

7. Pankower's evident pleasure in whipping his students is taken by some critics as a sign that he is little more than a sadist and not a proper teacher of the young. But it is interesting to note what Abraham Cahan has to say on this point in regard to his own experience of *cheder:* "It is not a simple thing to withdraw a youngster from a despotic melamed. The cheder, even with its cat-o'-nine-tails, is a holy place. The children dare not tell of the punishments and the parents dare not interfere with the melamed's authority. How can that authority be effective without slaps, pinches, and blows? To end punishment would be to end the discipline that insures that a youngster will grow up with learning and self-control. It was not easy to differentiate between necessary discipline and sadism." See *The Education of Abraham Cahan*, trans. Leon Stein, Abraham P. Conan, and Lynn Davison (Philadelphia: Jewish Publication Society, 1969), 26.

8. Roth, *Call It Sleep*, 374.

9. Walter Allen, Afterword in Roth, *Call It Sleep*, 445.

10. Roth, *Call It Sleep,* 226. The subsequent page references in the text pertain to this source.

11. Roth, *Shifting Landscape,* 207. Richard J. Fein ("Fear, Fatherhood, and Desire in *Call It Sleep,*" *Yiddish* 5 [1984]: 54) asks: "Can the inadequately grasped and fragmentary Hebrew offer a magic realm of redemption beyond the street brutalities of English and the family turmoil of Yiddish?" The answer would seem to be yes. Bonnie Lyons observes, "David's childlike belief that Hebrew is literally God's language parallels a belief traditionally held by Jewish mystics," and she cites Gershom Scholem on this point: "To them [the Kabbalists], Hebrew, the holy tongue, is not simply a means of expressing certain thought, born out of a certain convention and having purely conventional character, in accordance with the theory of language dominant in the Middle Ages. Language in its purest form, that is, Hebrew, according to the Kabbalists, reflects the fundamental spiritual nature of the world; in other words, it has a mystical value." See Lyons, *Henry Roth,* 71.

12. Roth, "No Longer at Home," in *Shifting Landscape,* 168. The subsequent page references in the text pertain to this source.

13. Roth, "Itinerant Ithacan," in *Shifting Landscape,* 204.

14. Roth, "The Meaning of *Galut* in America Today," in *Shifting Landscape,* 113–15.

15. Roth, "No Longer at Home," 170.

16. Roth, "Intinerant Ithacan," 219.

17. Roth, "The Eternal Plebeian and Other Matters," in *Shifting Landscape,* 301.

18. Roth, "Prolog im Himmel," in *Shifting Landscape,* 179.

19. Roth, "Kaddish," in *Shifting Landscape,* 189.

20. Roth, "No Longer at Home," 170. The subsequent page reference in the text pertains to this source.

21. Bonnie Lyons, for example, devotes a chapter of her *Henry Roth* to the influence of Joyce (117–23) but does not mention *Portrait* at all. William Freedman, in "Henry Roth and the Redemptive Imagination" (*The Thirties: Fiction, Drama, Poetry,* ed. Warren French [Deland, Fla.: Everett Edwards, 1967], 112), claims that *Portrait* is "the book to which *Call It Sleep* is perhaps most frequently compared," but I have not found any really detailed comparisons of the two texts.

22. James Joyce, *A Portrait of the Artist as a Young Man* (New York: Viking Press, 1956), 119–22. The subsequent page reference in the text pertains to this source.

23. Roth, *Call It Sleep,* 227. The subsequent page reference in the text pertains to this source.

24. Joyce, *A Portrait of the Artist,* 213. The subsequent page references in the text pertain to this source.

25. Roth, *Call It Sleep,* 441.

26. As Elena Mortara observes ("Scrivere con il carbone d'angelo: L'arte di Henry Roth," in *Rothiana,* ed. Materassi, 45–75), "In spite of the impudent ignorance of the other boys and the ill-tempered rudeness of the rabbi, in spite of the realism of the context and the representation, it is precisely in the noisy *cheder* that David arrives at his fundamental revelations" (56).

27. Roth, *Call It Sleep,* 441.

28. Mark Krupnick, *Lionel Trilling and the Fate of Cultural Criticism* (Evanston, Ill.: Northwestern University Press, 1986), 22. I actually began to find out about

Trilling's work on the *Menorah Journal* when Andrew Delbanco, Paul Marx, and I gave a course on Jewish-American writing at Dunster House, Harvard, in 1977. Andy dug out a number of Trilling's contributions to the *Journal,* and we discussed them in the seminar.

29. Irving Howe, *Celebrations and Attacks* (New York: Horizon Press, 1979), 12–14. Alfred Kazin reacted differently to Emerson, naming him, along with Blake, Whitman, Nietzsche, and Lawrence, as one of the "rebels of literature, the great wrestlers-with-God," whom he loved. See *Starting Out in the Thirties* (1965; Ithaca, N.Y.: Cornell University Press, 1989), 4.

30. From Ralph Waldo Emerson, "The Method of Nature," in *Essays and Lectures,* ed. Joel Porte (New York: Library of America, 1983), 115–17.

31. Joel Porte, ed., *Emerson in His Journals* (Cambridge: Harvard University Press, 1982), 262–63.

32. Henry David Thoreau, *Walden,* ed. J. Lyndon Shanley (Princeton: Princeton University Press, 1971), 100.

33. Henry David Thoreau, *A Week on the Concord and Merrimack Rivers,* ed. Carl F. Hovde, William L. Howarth, and Elizabeth Hall Witherell (Princeton: Princeton University Press, 1980), 382, 140, 247.

34. Roth, *Call It Sleep,* 441.

35. Roth, *Shifting Landscape,* 177.

36. Samuel Eliot Morison, *Three Centuries of Harvard* (Cambridge, Mass.: Harvard University Press, 1936), 30, 57–58.

26

Shoah as *Shivah*

Michael S. Roth

> I had no concept; I had obsessions,
> which is different. . . .
> —Claude Lanzmann

THE ROOM WAS not a holy place, no Torah, no prayer books, no candles. We may have called it an auditorium, but it resembled a basement playroom, or a place where socials—not quite dances—could take place when the school hours were finished. There may have been an American flag in one corner, an Israeli flag in the other; but perhaps I am condensing rooms here to lend the scene of this memory more sociological specificity than it had, as a room, at the time. Religious school on suburban Long Island. Reform. Assimilated. I now know how hard it is for communities to perpetuate a sense of their collective identities without rituals of some kind, without a dogma that goes without saying. Then, I just liked going to temple for religious school. By the time I was sixteen it had become a place to see other Jews, friends with whom I felt something in common. There were very few Jews in my large high school, and at temple there was some undefined sense of commonality. Where did this commonality come from? Was it simply the case that I knew my parents had *only* Jewish friends, and so I adopted their feelings of connection ("we are more comfortable with Jews, that's all") despite my protests about them? Or was there something else that not only set me and the kids at this school apart but also bound us together? (I knew I was set apart; my gentile friends gently—and not so gently—and frequently reminded me.) We had all by this time completed the rudimentary education that allowed us to perform the bar and bat mitzvah rituals. We had that much. But what connected us with one another? What made us Jews? Why, at least for me at this time, did being a Jew have to do with being connected with (tied to?) other Jews?

The room was not a holy place, no Torah, no prayer books, no candles. We gathered there sometimes to sing, to hear talks about the attractions of Israel, or about the dangers of the conspiratorial Jews-for-Jesus, or simply to "get together." That night there would be a film. I remember no other specific occasion of our gathering in this room; indeed, I have no other memory of religious school as powerful as my memory of this film. I imagine that we sat talking, flirting, fooling around just before the projector began to flash. But then I remember (that's right, I don't imagine, I remember) the tears of rage, of sadness, of impotent anger, that burned my eyes in that darkness. What to do with this film?

Alain Resnais' *Night and Fog* remained locked in my memory as a fixed point of Jewish consciousness, of consciousness of what it meant for me to be Jewish. The mountains of eyeglasses, of shoes, of hair—these were Jewish glasses (they were mine), these were Jewish shoes (they were mine), this was Jewish hair (it was mine). *That's* what it meant to be a Jew—to have some connection to the people (were they still people?) whose skeletons were being shoveled into pits; whose empty eyes stared out from behind the barbed wire fences. An adolescent response, to be sure; an identification that was totally "unearned." And yes, I know there was surely an ideological function to this identification. I was being shown that I belonged to the Jewish people, and the Jewish people could be constituted by its enemies (at any time) and annihilated. One does not have to be Sartre to see that. The moral was clear. Vigilance! Never again! Assimilation was not protection. Look at the screen. What made us, in this banal room, so like any other social hall, Jews? We could be *them*. Look at the screen. Now, when I look at this film on the screen, when I discuss it with my students, I also screen this memory of that room in the basement of the synagogue. But what does this memory screen? Look at the screen.

Night and Fog remains one of the most startling, powerful films made about the Nazi period. Recently, when the charges of crimes against humanity were dropped in the case of Paul Touvier, Minister of Culture Jack Lang asked French television channels to show *Night and Fog*. In the early 1950s its director, Alain Resnais, was asked to make a film to mark the tenth anniversary of the liberation of the concentration camps. The result was *Nuit et Bouillard,* a short film whose stark images of mutilated bodies are juxtaposed with a text warning viewers of the omnipresent threat of the *mentalité concentrationnaire.* Its visual, musical, and verbal languages are aggressive in the extreme. There is no place to hide from its assault. In writing about *Night and Fog,* Robert Benayoun recalls Paul Strand's film, *Heart of Spain,* in which we are shown a nurse dressing a horrible wound as the voice-over tells us: "You must not look away." The events obscured by the night and fog are to be revealed by the piercing gaze of the camera. We get to see the camps *en pleine lumière* as a warning against the politics and culture which made them possible.

Resnais seemed to think that he could burn his lesson into the minds of his viewers. He was asked to commemorate the liberation of the camps, but what would count as a "proper" memory of these places? What would the appropriate images be with which to mark this past and our present relation to it? Resnais insisted that he work together on this project with a deportee, since he himself had no authority to speak on this subject. Thus, the text was written by Jean Cayrol, who had been imprisoned in Oranienburg.[1] The authors of the film did not aim to make a memorial to the dead but "a warning signal." Intolerance and racist militarism were no strangers to France in the middle 1950s, and Resnais meant to remind his viewers about the dangers of the culture of totalitarianism.

The connection of horror and memory has recently been given much attention, and what I want to suggest here is that already in *Night and Fog* Resnais is making that connection problematic. He does so by acknowledging and exploring the impossibility of ever representing the reality of the camps. And if the camps cannot be represented, what does that say about our capacity to remember them? How does memory depend on representation? I quote from the film's text:

> How to discover the reality of these camps, when it was despised by those who made them and eluded those who suffered here? These wooden blocks, these tiny beds where one slept three, these burrows where people hid, where they ate furtively and where even sleep was a threat? No description or shot can restore their true dimension, that of an uninterrupted fear. One would have to have the very mattresses where they slept, the blanket which was fought over. Only the husk and shade remain of the brick dormitory.

We are shown the "husk and shade," we are shown the skeletons, but we are ceaselessly reminded that we are seeing nothing of the reality of the camps. In the language that Duras used so successfully in Resnais' *Hiroshima mon amour:* You have seen nothing of the camps. And we are told this as we see on the screen pictures which are almost impossible to look at. For Resnais, the history that is written in *Night and Fog* does not capture the past, but it can provoke us into an awareness of present dangers. And this is certainly part of the reason that a religious school in an assimilated community would show the film. The danger for this school was that "we" were losing Jews all around us. We were being blended into a deceptively hostile environment, an environment hostile to our Jewishness. The familiar message was that we had to protect ourselves from contamination by outsiders. Our effort to preserve a collective identity was not the only sign of our Jewishness, but it often seemed to me the essential component of what it meant to *be* a Jew.

Although Resnais' montage and rhetoric do provoke fear, *Night and Fog* concludes with the impossibility of a history adequate to these places and events of the horrific past. Be that as it may, a sense of the past may still be necessary for an effective politics in the present. When work began on *Night and Fog,* the cold war dominated the international scene, and French intellectuals felt trapped between the sparring superpowers. The threat of massive confrontation was real, and politics offered little to be hopeful about. France was in the midst of the violent struggle of decolonization. What had changed since World War II? Had the world learned anything from this experience? How *could* one learn from it if this past experience could not be represented?

But I cared nothing about the problems of representation, or even about

French decolonization when I first saw this film. These thoughts came much later, when I tried to understand (publicly) Resnais' achievement, and when I tried to come to terms (privately) with my memory of the film. I recall the film as imposing my Jewishness on me. "So, this is what it means to be a Jew," I thought, "and yes, this is what I am." Jews are those who must remember these events. Jews are those who must carry this loss with them, to abide this loss. This is not quite an identification with the victims. No, it even prohibits such an identification. The burden of living with this loss, of bearing it but not suffering it, was the task I took from *Night and Fog,* and it is a task I have been trying to acknowledge and understand ever since.

Until very recently, there seemed to me nothing particularly Jewish about this task; or rather, I had not yet come to think about it in relation to my being a Jew. As my intellectual interests began to form, they centered on problems that were shared among philosophy, psychology, and history. These problems all concerned the status of the abnormal, and the ways in which one's past could make one sick, or could provide one with the capacities for change. My first book (which I began as my senior thesis project in college), *Psycho-Analysis as History: Negation and Freedom in Freud,*[2] is an attempt to read Freud's work as a theory of history which aims at freedom through a self-consciousness of the presentness of the past. In retrospect, I can see that I had two agendas in undertaking this study. The first was clear and somewhat familiar: to show that Freud's work is compatible with radical politics—that it leads not only to accommodation but also to a self-consciousness which can initiate fundamental change. The second was to insist that radical change carries the past along with it. Freedom can be found only in acknowledging the scars of one's history, not in escaping from it. In Freud I had found (and constructed) a thinker who rejects reconciliation, redemption, and forgiveness: "the dialectic [in psycho-analysis] is not resolved; knowing is not resolution" (132). The thinker I'd found (and constructed) allowed me to retain a hope in and commitment to change without having to abandon the effort to dwell with loss, to sustain the memory of loss. *Jews are those who must remember these events. Jews are those who must carry this loss with them, to abide it.* The Freud I found (and constructed) transforms living with loss into "creating a past with which one could live": "The reading of Freud presented here forecloses any escape from our histories and our desires, and instead aims to make a clearing in which the acknowledging and creation of a meaningful past will enable us to find the effects of our freedom in the present" (189).

Hegel was the philosopher I set off against Freud. Hegel, who wrote "the wounds of Spirit heal, and leave no scars behind,"[3] insisted that there are some things that are just too painful to be preserved, worked through, negated. The great miracle of Spirit (a miracle that can be apprehended by the dialectical philosopher, who in all other respects insists on the presentness of the past) is the "reconciling affirmation" that redeems the past—the appear-

ance of God on earth, the disappearance of senseless suffering from consciousness. Those things that are just too traumatic to be integrated into a coherent
whole can be let go without trace, without scars. The Hegel of increasingly
unfashionable totality, the philosopher of hyper-narrative coherence (which
for me meant living with loss, living with what Hegel called the pain of the
negative), was the other thinker who most attracted me. The philosopher's
description of the disappearance of wounds was for me the disappearance of
loss—a failure of nerve, a giving in to (Christian) redemption. Freud corrected this. He made his territory the scars that did not heal; only by dwelling
within this territory could real change occur. Or so I argued. And it is an
argument I would return to at length in my next book, *Knowing and History:
Appropriations of Hegel in Twentieth-Century France.*[4]

Why was this landscape so important to me? It was, I think, the same place
where *Night and Fog* led me. A place where redemption seemed obscene, but
where authentic representation was impossible. Freud called this place the
unconscious, and although he usually thought of it in individual terms, one
can also consider it on a historical level. The unconscious does not disappear
through enlightenment or revelation. Psycho-analysis aims only at transforming misery into unhappiness, and makes no claim that the interpretations
offered are authentic representations of what really occurred in the past.
Instead, Freud insisted on the importance of acknowledging ineradicable
ambivalence, and creating possibilities for change out of the meanings one
finds in the past (the "husk and shade"?) in relation to one's desires in the
present. This was a Freud who thought through the dialectics of fundamental
change without leaving the past behind: "Negation through acknowledge-
ment and action is not an escape from the past, but like all negations, a form
of preservation as well. This hard fact of dialectical awareness must be an
essential part of any self-conscious effort at change."[5] Is there anything Jewish
about this "hard fact of dialectical awareness"? Or perhaps the better question
is the following: Is there anything about my life as a Jew that made this
question important to me?

Only one ritual was observed without fail in my family. My mother would
buy the little drinking glasses with candles in them well in advance. She
would light them silently, I think; in any event, without ceremony. The candle
would be set on top of the refrigerator, and I would see its flickering light if I
came out of my room at night. I remember this flickering light, and I knew
that one candle was for my grandfather and that one was for my brother, both
of whom died not long before I was born. I knew many stories about my
grandfather, but very little about my brother, whose sudden death at five
years of age cut a wedge through my parents' life. The balm for this pain was
pregnancy: and I was born about a year after Neil's death. I was to fill the
void left by this loss; or was I to create a place for myself and my family to put
alongside this loss? I was "given" a special role: to be both the hero who
would set the family right again, who would heal the wounds caused by the

death of that beautiful little boy, whose pictures still haunt my memories; and to be the sign of those wounds, their trace.

Perhaps my own relation to loss, to the preservation of a sign of loss and the refusal to think this sign an adequate representation of what is absent, is part of what lies behind the screen of my reaction to *Night and Fog*. The film's refusal to function as a documentary and its insistence nonetheless on the political importance of remembering have continued to resonate with me as I pursue my investigations of how people make sense of, live with, and deny their pasts. I only began to connect this work with themes in Judaism when I wrote a review essay of Josef Yerushalmi's brilliant book, *Zakhor: Jewish History and Jewish Memory (1982)*. Yerushalmi shows that although an intense attachment to the past was a crucial part of daily life for premodern European Jewry, historiography played little or no role for Jews trying to make sense of their past after the biblical age and until the nineteenth century. History writing gained importance only with emancipation and assimilation, that is, when the lived memory of the past was in crisis. And history was a weak substitute for daily rituals and faith, which had been the vessels that perpetuated the past in the present. How can the past of a community be carried over into the present, especially when that past is a trauma?

Claude Lanzmann's *Shoah* is an attempt to speak to this problem of memory, its transmission, and what he calls its incarnation. The film seeks to portray this living with loss, and at times to perform this mode of life as well. But to "perform this mode of life" means somehow to convey a silence, an absence, at the heart of these events:

> The Holocaust is first of all unique in that it constructs a circle of flames around itself, the limit not to be broken because a certain absolute horror is not transmittable: to pretend to do so, on the other hand, is to become guilty of the most serious transgression. One must speak and be silent at the same time, to know that here silence is the most authentic mode of speech, to maintain, as in the eye of the cyclone, a protected, preserved region in which nothing must ever enter.[6]

The problem is to screen loss, to make present in the film the absence of the dead, yet without representing this lost object, the world destroyed with the murdered Jews.

"I began precisely with the impossibility of telling this story," Lanzmann told the *Cahiers du cinema* (295). His view of this impossibility is very different from Resnais' in *Night and Fog*. Resnais took powerful, arresting archival images and juxtaposed them with a voice-over which told us, "Even this is not enough . . . even this is just husk and shade of a reality which remains inaccessible to us." Lanzmann shows us no archival material; he presents us with no gruesome images from the past. He aims at the silence and the absence:

> That convoy—there was no way of knowing that it was the first earmarked for extermination. Besides, one couldn't have known that Sobibor would be used for the mass extermination of the Jewish people. The next morning when I came here

to work, the station was absolutely silent, and we realized, after talking with the other railway men who worked at the station here, that something utterly incomprehensible had happened. First of all, when the camp was being built, there were orders shouted in German, there were screams, Jews were working at a run, there were shots, and here there was silence, no work crews, a really total silence. Forty cars had arrived, and then . . . nothing. It was all very strange.

It was the silence that tipped them off?

That's right.

Can he describe that silence?

It was a silence . . . a standstill in the camp. You heard and saw nothing; nothing moved. So then they began to wonder, "Where have they put those Jews?"[7]

Shoah must create that silence in order to open a clearing in which the past can become present. The past must *be* in the present. As Anny Dayan-Rosenman has said, the silence created in the film allows the past to emerge now, for us:

Above all we needed silence.
To create in us a hole, to distance us from the exterior world, to separate the words of Shoah from other everyday, profane, words.[8]

For Lanzmann, this does not mean that the past is represented in the present, but that the past is incarnated in the present. He insists that this is a problem neither of history nor of memory:

The film was not made with memories, I knew it immediately. Memory horrifies me: memory is weak. The film is the destruction of all distance between past and present, I relived this history in the present. (301)

It is not a historical film: it is a kind of originary event since I filmed it in the present, since I was obliged myself, to construct it with the traces of traces, with that which was strong in what I had filmed. (303–304)

The traces of traces had to be put together in just such a way as to open the clearing in which the past could emerge. There are times when Lanzmann insists on the fact that he is responsible for these occasions: he is the director, the *auteur* who does not find past material in the archives but creates it in front of the camera:

There is much *mise en scène* in the film. It is not a documentary. The locomotive, at Treblinka, it is *my* locomotive, I rented it at the Polish Railways, which was not simple, as it was not simple to insert it into the traffic. (298)

Even in what is probably the film's most emotional scene and the one which seems the most spontaneous—the interview with the barber, Abraham Bomba—the director insists on his role:

This is the reason why I rented the barber shop. I tried to create a setting where something could happen. I was not sure. You have to understand me, I did not know what would happen during the scene. But I knew what I wanted from him, what he had to say.[9]

In a moving essay on *Shoah,* Shoshana Felman underlines how Lanzmann's function is to be a silent narrator, even as he creates possibilities for narration as an interviewer and an inquirer:

> It is only in this way, by this abstinence of the narrator, that the film can in fact be a narrative of testimony: a narrative of that, precisely, which can neither be reported nor narrated, by another. The narrative is thus essentially a narrative of silence, the story of the film maker's *listening.*[10]

By assembling the conditions for this kind of listening, by opening this clearing in which the past can be embodied in voices in the present, Lanzmann has created the conditions for *shivah.*

Shivah, the Jewish ritual observed for seven days after the burial of the mourned person, seemed to me as I grew up to be a strange, powerful sign of Jewishness. In the assimilated, almost areligious context of my childhood, *shivah* was still observed in my family and among the Jews that I knew. I was struck by what seemed to me to be the injunction to talk about the dead. Was this because my brother's brief life was thereafter to be guarded in silence? Was this because of my own fear of breaking this silence with my parents or older brother? I imagined *shivah,* and perceived it when I participated in the ritual, as an incessant talking about the deceased. In religious school this was given a psychological explanation: by talking about the mourned, the mourners work through their own feelings of loss. The point is not simply, however, to dissipate these feelings but also to heighten and share them. The absence is made present for the community of mourners through a ritual which brings the dead to mind, to voice.

Lanzmann's film creates the conditions for this experience of loss when we become the witnesses of the losses of those talking on the screen. We sit with them (there is nothing we can do) while they describe the horrors of *not* dying with their brethren; we sit with them (there is nothing we can do) while they describe watching their loved ones go to their deaths; we sit with them (there is nothing we can do) while their torturers explain in gruesome detail the mechanics of murder, the technical problem of killing so many so quickly without leaving too many traces. But there are traces, and they speak to us; they are made to speak to us, and we must force ourselves to stay, to remain seated with them. Often throughout the nine and a half hours of the film we want to turn away, walk away, stop the talking. It is, after all, very repetitive: the cold, the screams, the cold, the beatings, the trains, the trains. . . . But we stay seated with them. There is nothing we can do. The absence is made present for the community of mourners through a ritual which brings the dead to mind, to voice.

How different this message is from that delivered by Resnais' film. Although *Night and Fog* was made as a "warning signal," we should be clear that the warning is not what Jews have in mind with the deceptive phrase "never again." There is no attention to Jews as such in *Night and Fog,* and this is one of the curiosities about its becoming the Holocaust film for American religious schools. The word "Jew" does not occur in the film, although we do see people with stars of David sewn on their clothes. Resnais' film is to remind us of the dangers of racist fascism; the *mentalité concentrationnaire* can return. As the narrative of the film proclaims, "War nods but has one eye open. The skill shown by the Nazis would be child's play today." It also tells us to beware:

> Who is on the lookout from this strange observation post for the new executioners? Are their faces really different from ours? Somewhere among us lucky *kapos* survive. . . .
> There are those who look sincerely at these ruins as if the old concentration camp monster was dead underneath them. Those who hope as the image fades that we have been healed of the old *concentrationnaire* plague, who pretend that all this happened only one time and in one country, who do not think to look around us, who are deaf to the endless deafening cry.

By awakening us to this cry, *Night and Fog* puts its viewers on alert, in a position to defend themselves against any revivals of the mentality which made the camps possible.

Shoah does not put us into a position of alert. Its goal is to allow us to assume a posture of receptivity. We must become ready to listen to the past emerge from the people on the screen; we must become ready to see the past become present. How do we become ready? We are silent before all this testimony, as the film itself opens with silence—written paragraphs on the screen to be read silently by the viewers and not spoken by a narrator. The Shulkhan Aruk (chap. 207, par. 1) tells us in the laws of mourning: "The comforters are not permitted to open [conversation] until the mourner opens first." No one speaks to Job before he begins to tell of his misery. They await the words. Thus the film attempts to put its viewers in proper relation to the past being (re)experienced by the people on the screen. It presents the past on film but a past manifested in the present. The events of the Shoah happened thirty-five years before the interviews were done, and yet under the persistence of Lanzmann's questioning the people being interviewed at times seem to be *right there* with the past. And this is why Lanzmann insists on his claim that the distance between past and present is abolished in the film, a claim that is at the heart of a historian's effort not merely to represent the past but to *bring it back.* Michelet called his nineteenth-century histories "resurrections."

Resnais' film has the problem of trying to confront us with an exceptional experience, an experience of ultimate horror and absolute evil, so as to remind us of what human beings are capable. The difficulty here is that in showing us something exceptional he may so distance us from the event as to make it almost irrelevant for us. Lanzmann's film, on the contrary, gives us small, recognizably ordinary human beings: people with whom you can identify, people whom you can hate. Lanzmann's interviews—on the farm, in a living room, in a barber shop or a restaurant—are *everyday;* they are scenes which we are to imagine as taking place right next door. Both films use shots of the train lines, but in *Shoah* the railway track is a commuter line; we should imagine ourselves going down it, or at least traveling down the track of memory until we get to the black hole of the camps. The track in Resnais' film is of a very different order. He is taking us to another planet, or at least that is part of what he wants us to feel. It is true that there are areas of the other planet that we can recognize: it has its orphanage, its home for the handicapped, its hospital, and its prison. It is the world, perhaps, of our nightmares, a landscape both foreign and familiar. We are to feel, not the small steps that led the old gentleman to being a sadistic beast, but the leap into a world of total fear. We are to be afraid of what we see. Now, one of the responses we have to fear is flight. We may view these images and mentally leave the theater, or physically close our eyes. This is *too much;* is there any real possibility of relating to the mountain of hair, or to the skin and soap? Resnais' gamble is that we will not turn away mentally or physically, but that instead we will have the other response to fear: we will want to fight. Fight against what? Not just Nazi war criminals or collaborators, but against the human propensity for evil that is nakedly displayed in the film. This propensity is usually hidden beneath the cover of night and fog. Lanzmann has a very different agenda. He takes us slowly into this night, or at least into the darkness of his subjects' memories. He is willing to navigate in the fog. Resnais, on the other hand, shines his light into this obscure evil. Look at it, he says, and beware!

The dilemma for both film-makers is a problem with all historical representation. Let me call that problem the dialectic between connection and otherness. All historical representation must indicate that the subjects being referred to are of another time; they are not simply *just like us.* This is clear if you study the history of a culture not your own, but it is always the case insofar as the time you study is not your own. Historical representation, properly so-called, must communicate this distance, this otherness. At the same time, the representation cannot be confined to difference or otherness. All history is history of the present, and a successful representation must convey something of the way we connect to this otherness. When Lanzmann is carried away by the fantasy of obliterating the distance between present and past, he neglects an important quality of his own achievement. This fantasy helped him make his extraordinary film, and the desire to unite with the past lends the work enormous energy. I think I recognize this fantasy and can acknowledge the energy it sometimes provides. But uniting with the past, taking the place of the dead or even being in their place, is only a fantasy.

Lanzmann's interviews show us *the distance* the survivors must travel to have the past return to them; we witness them making the connection to the past. Lanzmann is also at times fascinated by this distance, by the difference between those things which stay the same and those which change (and thus have a past different from the present). "But the tracks? I show them to him, I ask him: 'Are these the same ones?' 'Yes,' he tells me, 'absolutely the same.' I needed that: a permanence of iron, of steel. I needed to attach myself to it."[11] Lanzmann struggles to find the line dividing the world of the camp from the rest of the world, and he wants to record the ramp over which the Jews passed from one to the other. Here is the series of questions the director poses to Jan Piwonski at the Sobibor Station:

> The station building, the rails, the platforms are just as they were in 1942? Nothing's changed?
> Exactly where did the camp begin?
> So I'm standing inside the camp perimeter, right?
> Where I am now is fifty feet from the station, and I'm already outside the camp. This is the Polish part, and over there is death?[12]

You can see some of the people he interviews cross that line, and struggle against doing so. The distance between present and past cannot be obliterated for the survivors. They can cross over, but neither they nor we are anywhere but in the present. This is something we must learn from *Shoah*, and from *shivah*. Mourning, or the historical consciousness that results from it, is not a reparation; it is not replacing the dead but making a place for something else to be in relation to the past. This is a crucial part of the pain of surviving the dead, of consciously coming after them. It is a lesson that Lanzmann continues to wrestle with:

> The idea which was always the most painful for me, it was that all these people died alone. . . . When I say that they died alone, it is in relation to me that this phrase has meaning. For me, the most profound and at the same time most incomprehensible meaning of the film, is in a way . . . to resuscitate these people, and to kill them a second time, with me; in accompanying them.[13]

This is the language of mourning, of *shivah*. In accompanying these people, in passing with them through the past, Lanzmann performs what Jewish law calls a "highly meritorious act." He comes to dwell with those who suffer loss, and with some who are lost in their suffering. The absence is to be made present for the community of mourners through a ritual which brings the dead to mind, to voice.

The community helps one to make a connection to loss, to cross the line from the past and return to the present. *Shoah*, like *shivah*, is an act of piety. The point of the repetitive details of the film, of all those hours sitting with the people on the screen and in the theater, is not just to understand the past correctly (although that is part of the project); nor is it just to arm people against future outbursts of racism (although that, too, may be a result); it is also to dwell with loss, to suffer one's poverty, to be linked together in the presence of those absent and to give them, as Lanzmann quotes from Isaiah, an everlasting name.

Shivah reminds us in the midst of our pain that we are not alone. Two of Lanzmann's survivors related to him that as they struggled to stay alive each had the fantasy that he was the last Jew or the last person in the world. *Shoah* reminds us that they and the survivors of the Holocaust were not and are not alone. But one does not have to identify with them—to assume their place—to be connected to them. The painful work of mourning enables one to find one's own place, to find a way of living with the dead as the past in the present. During *shivah* we bring the past to the present, we allow ourselves to experience what we have lost, and also what we are—*that* we are—despite this loss. Neither *Shoah* nor *shivah* attempts to replace the past, to offer compensations for loss. They allow us to incarnate the past, to name it, and to remain in the present. They are acts of connection and of otherness. Acts of piety.

In my life, such acts recall me to my Jewishness.

NOTES

1. Robert Benayoun, *Alain Resnais, arpenteur de l'imaginaire: De Hiroshima à Mélo* (Paris: Stock, 1980), 52.

2. Michael Roth, *Psycho-Analysis as History: Negation and Freedom in Freud* (Ithaca, N.Y.: Cornell University Press, 1987). The subsequent page references in the text pertain to this source.

3. Georg Hegel, *The Phenomonology of Spirit,* trans. A. V. Miller (Oxford: Oxford University Press, 1977), 407.

4. Michael Roth, *Knowing and History: Appropriations of Hegel in Twentieth-Century France* (Ithaca, N.Y.: Cornell University Press, 1988).

5. Roth, *Psycho-Analysis as History,* 133.

6. *Au sujet de* Shoah: *Le film de Claude Lanzmann* (Paris: Belin, 1990), 310. The subsequent page reference in the text pertains to this source.

7. Claude Lanzmann, *Shoah: An Oral History of the Holocaust* (New York: Pantheon, 1985), 67. The director's questions are in italics.

8. *Au sujet de* Shoah, 188. The subsequent page references in the text pertain to this source.

9. Claude Lanzmann, "Seminar on *Shoah,*" *Yale French Studies* 79 (1991): 95.

10. Shoshana Felman, "The Return of the Voice: Claude Lanzmann's *Shoah,*" in Shoshana Felman and Dori Laub, M.D., *Testimony: Crises of Witnessing in Literature, Psychoanalysis and History,* 204–83 (New York: Routledge, 1992), quotation is from 218.

11. *Au sujet de* Shoah, 290.

12. Lanzmann, *Shoah: An Oral History of the Holocaust,* 38–39.

13. *Au sujet de* Shoah, 291.

27

"The Master of Turning"

Walter Benjamin, Gershom Scholem, Harold Bloom, and the Writing of a Jewish Life

Norman Finkelstein

LIVES ARE LIKE literary works: we live as we read, experiencing the life and the text with an ineluctable doubleness. The life and the text stretch before and behind; the result, if not narrative, is at least linearity, allowing forward and backward movement over time. But the life and the text also present themselves as momentary: we encounter an uncanny simultaneity of events that defies narrative, forbids reduction to cause and effect, challenges even the simplest stretching of occurrence over time's linear frame. I feel this way about literature most acutely when, after reading and rereading a poem or a story, I begin to write about it. My encounter with the text constitutes a single instant, and however rationally I perceive movement and development, something in me always protests the act of criticism as a clumsy misrepresentation of the reading process.

How much more loudly that voice speaks out when I attempt to write not criticism but autobiography, to write my life, that text with which I am most intimate, since it is supposedly the record of my truest self. From the *Pirke Avot:* "Turn it and turn it again, for everything is in it."[1] From Edmond Jabès: "Thus the Jew bends over his book, knowing in advance that the book always remains to be discovered in its words and in its silences."[2] So I study my life as a series of tropes, which, taken altogether, make up the text of the self. And so I attempt to represent that text here, in this text. But though I am the subject of the text, of the life lived, this is by no means the authorized version; that is to say, in writing a life, no one speaks with authority.

Poet, critic, Jew: by now, the three terms are so intermingled in my consciousness that I surprise myself when I look back to a time, not so long ago, when I regarded them as more or less discrete aspects of my identity. To be sure, since graduate school I had thought of my poetry and my criticism as the sum of my literary activity. But though I claimed them to be a totality, understanding my criticism as a commentary on my poetic concerns, however oblique, I harbored doubts as to what I can only call the lived truth of that claim. My poetry has always been something of a scholar's art, while my criticism, even if it had to be cast in an academic mold, consistently sought for some degree of more personal investment. The lines of communication were there, but they were often experienced rather abstractly. "Hammer your thoughts into unity," Yeats advises.[3] Yet even in considering modern poets (as poetic influences, as the subjects of criticism), there were times when I sensed that my efforts were not of a piece.

All along, Judaism—as cultural heritage, as world view, as personal history—stood behind the scenes, as if waiting for the occasion to come forward and . . . unify the work? Energize it? Provide it with a trajectory that it had heretofore failed to achieve? None of these terms feels quite right. Simply put, there came a time when I began to read, to think, to feel, and to write through Judaism—through my Jewishness—in a way that I had not done previously. We think of such turns or changes in a life as parts of a narrative, as narratives in themselves. But their facticity, the being we grant them, undermines any tale we might tell, any analysis we might construct.

"Critics, in their secret hearts, love continuities," says Harold Bloom, "but he who lives with continuity alone cannot be a poet."[4] If I were just a critic and not a poet as well, writing a literary autobiography would be an easier task. My identity as a commentator would be more straightforward. The line that I can trace from my early studies of modern poetry, through my interest in Marxism and literary theory, to my rediscovery of Jewish authors and Jewish ways of reading, would not be overshadowed by a more compelling, more dramatic, and more intimate narrative. Yet both narratives are equally literary and Jewish.

My poetic identity begins with voices and with books, in public declamation and closeted reading that thrilled the impressionable child. In my youthful imagination, the words of the Rosh Hashanah service were strangely intertwined with those of Coleridge's "Kubla Khan":

> The great shofar is sounded, and a still, small voice is heard. . . .

> I would build that dome in air,
> That sunny dome! those caves of ice!
> And all who heard should see them there,
> And all should cry, Beware! Beware!
> His flashing eyes, his floating hair!

On the deepest level, poetry and prophecy, reading and ritual, were all part of the same enchantment, the same arrival at the authoritative beauty of speech. It seemed to be a truth that could be recognized on special occasions by the entire community, but could be sustained, could be lived daily in the imagination, only by the solitary devotee.

Yet such a devotee is never truly solitary: the young reader beginning to imagine himself as a writer sees before him a visionary company which he both envies and admires. Again, Bloom:

For the poet is condemned to learn his profoundest yearnings through an awareness of *other selves.* The poem is *within* him, yet he experiences the shame and splendor of *being found by* poems—great poems—*outside* him. To lose freedom in this center is never to forgive, and to learn the dread of threatened autonomy forever.[5]

This gnosis, founded, of course, on that of Freud, impressed me deeply when I first encountered it, for I had already been living it for some time. I first read *The Anxiety of Influence* in 1975, when I was beginning my graduate studies and writing poetry at a furious pace. But in learning from it, I also defended myself against it through fierce idealization: it was Marxism rather than any version of psychoanalytic criticism which was beginning to excite me then, and which would occupy my intellectual development for several more years. Coming of age between the enthusiasms of the 1960s and the solipsism of the 1970s, I built a strange identity for myself, part engaged critic, part symbolist poet, altogether driven by a force which Ernst Bloch and other Marxist thinkers call utopian desire.

Then as now, my thinking was volatile and dialectical. When the young Marx writes that "free, conscious activity is the species-character of human beings," I thought of poetry as the highest form of that praxis.[6] In the tradition of Marxist criticism and in literary theory generally, I was most attracted to those writers for whom the text becomes the site of a struggle between the forces of historical contingency and the activity of subjective human desire. Against what Georg Lukács calls "the sterile power of the merely existent" could be posited a utopian horizon that was always receding into the future.[7] As Ernst Bloch teaches, art and literature maintain that horizon, and it is criticism's task to keep it in view. "The essential function of utopia is a critique of what is present," Bloch tells us. "If we had not already gone beyond the barriers, we could not even perceive them as barriers."[8] And because I wanted to be on the forefront of the struggle, my criticism was aimed at contemporary American poetry: those poets of my own time and place through and against whom I was writing my poetry.

Yet for all my commitment to a poetry of the present moment ("It has to face the men of the time and to meet / The women of the time" says Stevens of modern poetry[9]), I felt increasingly estranged from most of the poetic currents around me. Even those contemporary poets whose work I most admired, and who may well have influenced me in terms of the Bloomian agon, could not provide me with the intellectual key that I felt would open my richest storehouse of poetic material. The same is true for the romantics and modernists with whom I felt the strongest affinities. Thinking back to my poetry of the late 1970s and early 1980s (almost none of which has been published), I realize that, however much I had learned from the Anglo-American tradition—indeed, however much that poetry *had called me into being as a poet*—that tradition in itself could not have made me the poet I wanted to be. Ironically, it was the *criticism* I was reading and that was shaping my own prose that would lead me to the poetic matter I sought, no matter how much I traveled in the realms of gold.

The authors who mean the most to us arrive with an uncanny inevitability. I do not recall when I first began to read Walter Benjamin—it may have been in graduate school—but by the mid-1980s he was as important to me as any of the poets whom I had studied earlier with such devotion. If poetry had given me birth and raised me as a writer, then Benjamin's work, as the chief representative of a different constellation, confirmed me as I came of age. First I had seen myself as affiliated with the traditions of American and British poetry. Now, largely because of Benjamin, I also saw myself in terms of Jewish and central European modes of critical speculation and prose narrative. The notorious volatility of Benjamin's thought, the tragedy of his career, and the enigma of his personality led me into these traditions and continue to haunt me today. The tension in his work between dialectical materialism and kabbalistic messianism fascinated me; and I came to appreciate how such an apparent contradiction bore fruit in his literary criticism. As I brooded over Judaism's various transformations through the forces of modernity, Benjamin seemed to me the very type of the modern Jewish intellectual: his struggles with the appropriations of Judaism came to represent modern Jewish identity in itself.

Like Kafka, whom he understood so well, Benjamin knew that modern Jews, suffering "the decay of wisdom," still had to pay attention to "a sort of theological whispered intelligence dealing with matters discredited and obsolete."[10] This whispered intelligence, of course, was still largely bound up in textual traditions, involving inspired scribal faith and insistent hermeneutic rituals. But to an even greater extent than Kafka (perhaps because of his more flagrant status of commentator), Benjamin recognized that the Jew's subservience to the text, which had always been richly problematic, took on, under modern conditions, a heretofore unknown historical resonance. Taking his cue from Kafka, and perhaps from Freud as well, Benjamin universalized the dilemma of modern Judaism, for in the dynamics of Jewish textuality he saw the fate of modern culture itself.

In one of the most famous passages in his work, Benjamin describes Kafka's writings as raising "a mighty paw" against *halakhah,* a paw that consists of their rebelliously Aggadic quality. Because Kafka "sacrificed truth for the sake of clinging to its transmissibility," truth, wisdom, or doctrine (these terms are often interchangeable in Benjamin) *decays,* leaving us only with that theological whisper, and with folly, which seems to characterize any benevolent human act.[11] The decay of wisdom places it irrevocably in the past. Midrashically conflating a number of Benjamin's ideas, we can say that the removal of wisdom into the past transforms it into a *ruin* and ritually invests it with *aura,* that is, the power of a thing as it ceases to be, or when its historical validity is called into question.

The pattern of wisdom in decay, which simultaneously recedes into the past and is handed on in some dubious form, can be found again and again in Benjamin's work. In his considerations of Kafka (1934, 1938), it is *halakhah*, Jewish law itself, which undergoes this passage. In the essay on Leskov (1936), it is the figure of the storyteller, whose value as a counselor is recognized only when modernity silences him; whereas in the study of Baudelaire (1939), the poet pointedly renounces his aura in order to become modernity's voice. In "The Work of Art in the Age of Mechanical Reproduction" (1936), one of his most vociferously Marxist pieces, it is the task of revolutionary culture to unmake the artwork's aura through modern means of reproduction, detaching it from the "domain of tradition" by bringing it across the ritual distance to be examined close at hand. Yet in one of Benjamin's most personal essays, "Unpacking My Library" (1931), the old-fashioned book collector as a social type is celebrated, however ambivalently; his private library, ritualistically gathered by this ironically named "man of leisure," is seen not only as the most honorable setting for books but also the one which allows for the highest degree of *transmissibility*. While public collections are less "objectionable socially," personal ownership is still "the most intimate relationship one can have to objects" (67). There is something more chilling here than in any of his other works when Benjamin states that "only in extinction is the collector comprehended" (67).

How could these motifs fail to move me? For if it is true that in Benjamin's work the fate of Judaism (or at least of Judaism's culture of the Book) is congruent with the fate of modern culture in general, then I had discovered that in brooding about my own relationship to Judaism I was also brooding about my relationship to modernity. Ineluctably modern and ineluctably Jewish, I realized that both of those dimensions of my self embodied an uncertain longing for versions of an idealized past which I had never really experienced, for to a great extent they were imaginative constructs. Yet these constructs inspired my best writing; indeed, it was in some of that writing that these image-worlds came to be constructed. In reading Benjamin, I realized that this strangely productive version of nostalgia—what Susan Sontag calls Benjamin's "analytical way of relating the past"—was built into the forms and experiences of modern culture, and that a secular Jewish sensibility is particularly suited to recognize and articulate its significance.[12]

Furthermore, in studying Benjamin's work and appropriating it for my own purposes, I was enacting but also resolving—insofar as it can be resolved—the crisis of transmissibility with which he was so concerned. Because I had always read it as a kind of secular wisdom literature, Benjamin's writing itself took on an auratic quality, and its meaning seemed to recede from me even as I tried to claim it for my own. It became a modern version of that "sort of theological whispered intelligence," and like an inspired but not altogether faithful scribe, I wondered if my own work was a distortion, a fragmented reiteration of some original that could never be fully recovered.

Perhaps the decay of Benjamin's wisdom resulted in the same bifurcation as that of the Law in Kafka's work. If so, was I listening hard to a disappearing rumor of truth? Or was I, in following such whispers, only another Sancho Panza, another scholarly *schlemiel*?

Then again, there have always been risks involved in seeking wisdom, some of them greater than the possibility of becoming a *schlemiel*. How often in Jewish history has wisdom been lost, how often has it been recovered in what suddenly appears to be a different form? Perhaps this is a less personal way of describing the anxiety of influence: What are we beside those who have come before us? What do we know compared with what they knew? How can we write in the shadow of what they wrote? There has always been an answer, even one that obviates such questions, at least for the observant Jew: there is a timeless wisdom that remains as accessible to you as to your predecessors. Return to the text, for "revelation comprises everything that will ever be legitimately offered to interpret its meaning."

These are the words of Gershom Scholem from his great essay "Revelation and Tradition as Religious Categories in Judaism."[13] Scholem, hardly the model of the observant Jew, revolutionized the historical study of Jewish texts and, in doing so, discovered (or created) a new paradigm for the modern Jew's relationship to textual wisdom, one which maintains, in form if not substance, the traditional Jewish attitudes toward reading and writing. Through the process of innovative commentary, the authority of revelation unfolds and is maintained through history. This crucial dialectic of authority and innovation, which is the sine qua non of traditional Jewish textuality, is displaced, after the crisis of the Haskalah or Jewish Enlightenment, onto modern (i.e., secular) Jewish writing. Still seeking the "revelation" of legitimating texts, modern Jewish writers experience a dizzying but exhilarating power in the production of work which, as inspired commentary, seems to share equally in the sacred and the profane.

By the time I turned toward Scholem, directed toward him, naturally enough, by my reading of Benjamin and Bloom, I was consciously seeking my own niche in the complex and often contradictory world of Jewish modernity—which meant, to a large extent, the world of modern Jewish letters. For Jewish writers, there is something both familiar and alienating in William Blake's insistence that he invent his own system or be enslaved by another man's. Even the most rebelliously self-reliant Jewish writers are aware on some level that such head-on confrontations with tradition will not win them the expressivity they seek—and in writing as a Jew, I did not necessarily think of myself as rebellious. Scholem declares what most of us already intuit: "Not system but *commentary* is the legitimate form through which truth is approached," a statement which certainly confirmed me in my practice as both critic and poet.[14] Yet the word "legitimate," which recurs so often in "Revelation and Tradition," is bound to create misgivings among Jewish writers today.

If the crisis of modern Jewish culture is a crisis of loss, it is also, as I have been implying, a crisis of legitimation. The decay of halakhic wisdom is only the first episode in an old tale, the tale of the secularization of Jewish life. As Scholem darkly observes, "Like all destruction, secularism is both liberation and risk."[15] Indeed, despite what is by now a secure record of intellectual and artistic triumphs—and not only those which are destructive or critical in nature— generation after generation of secular Jews regard themselves and their labors with doubt and regret. Cut free from religious tradition but still haunted by its erstwhile authority, secular Jewish intellectuals endure what Jacques Derrida brilliantly names "the necessity of interpretation as an exile."[16]

These feelings often emerge over questions of canonic authority, since even today, after all its vicissitudes, Jewish culture remains, as Bloom says, "text-centered." What texts, then, can secular Jewish writers acknowledge as legitimate and authoritative? Again I consider my own situation: emerging from a second-generation Jewish-American milieu, grounded in English and American literature rather than the Jewish classics, I returned only quite recently to a world of Jewish culture, which I have discovered to be far richer (and more personally empowering) than I had previously imagined. Writing poetry and criticism in a Jewish context, I vacillate endlessly between assertive confidence and vexing doubt. I yearn for authority even as I seek to subvert it, and my ambivalence is confirmed every time I open a work of modern Jewish literature. Perhaps it is the very desire for legitimating texts, nostalgic as it might be, which actually defines the Jewish writer when all other aspects of Jewish identity have been lost or cast into doubt.

If Scholem's position can create such anxieties, it can also ease them, and this double effect is one of the reasons that I value it so highly. In a crucial passage from an interview in *On Jews and Judaism in Crisis,* Scholem speaks of his own religious and cultural attitudes and the impact of his work on his "secularist listeners":

> I don't consider myself a secularist. My secularism fails right at the core, owing to the fact that I am a religious person, because I am sure of my belief in God. My secularism is not secular. But the fact that I addressed myself to *kabbalah* not merely as a chapter of history but from a dialectical distance—from identification and distance together—certainly stems from the fact that I had the feeling that *kabbalah* had a living center; it expressed itself according to the time, and that in another form it could, perhaps, have said something to another generation. Something unknown of this sort must have motivated me beyond all the philological games and masquerades at which I excel. I can understand that something of this sort inspired my secularist listeners the way it inspired me.[17]

Scholem is correct in assuming that secularism depends upon doubt (at least) in a belief in God, and that is why his understanding of *kabbalah's* "living center," its relevance as an inspiring historical phenomenon to modern, secular Jews, is so important. Scholem's own secularism may "fail" because of his religious faith, but his dialectical attitude toward his subject—"identification and distance together"—can serve as a model for contemporary Jews seeking a stance that somehow reconciles tradition and secular culture. The vexed relationship of today's secular Jews to their religious and cultural heritage proves to be a consistent and formative feature in Judaism's long history, different perhaps in the degree of tension, but not in kind. Like *kabbalah* itself, which Scholem demonstrates to be a force of both conservation and innovation in Jewish history, Scholem's dialectic reassures us that the aura of tradition, which so concerned and inspired his friend Walter Benjamin, need not simply vanish or contract into itself, like some historical version of the kabbalistic *tzimtzum,* the divine self-withdrawal that was necessary to make a space for Creation. As Scholem declares in "Revelation and Tradition," "tradition undergoes changes with the times, new facets of its meaning shining forth and lighting its way."[18]

If reading Scholem historicizes the problems and opportunities of my secular Jewishness, then reading Bloom, now as in the past, returns me to literary matters—though of late these matters appear to coincide with what Bloom calls, in his essay "Jewish Culture and Jewish Identity," "the central question of American Jewish culture." That question is, of course, "What is the identity of the secular American Jew?" and it is a question that is intimately bound up with the evaluation of Jewish-American literature.[19] For Bloom, the cultural memory of tomorrow's secular Jewish elite will be composed of Kafka, Freud, and Scholem; indeed, they already shape mature Jewish-American imaginations, such as that of Philip Roth. But American Jewry has produced no figure of their stature, nor have we produced someone who compares with the greatest gentile American writers: an Emerson, a Melville, a Dickinson, or in this century, a Faulkner or a Stevens. Jewish-American identity depends on Jewish-American cultural achievement. What does Bloom, the theorist of belatedness, prophesy in this regard?

> Whatever the future American Jewish cultural achievement will be, it will become Jewish only *after* it has imposed itself as achievement. And because it will not bear the stigmata of *Galut,* it will be doubly hard for us to recognize it as Jewish, even after it has imposed itself. But by then it will be very difficult for us to recognize ourselves as Jewish anyway, unless an achievement will be there that revises us even as it imposes itself upon us. (357)

The burden this places on the aspiring Jewish-American writer is heavy indeed; it is a weight that is even more difficult to bear than the usual anxiety of influence. According to Bloom, today's Jewish-American writer lacks the traditional cultural context, the context of Jewish achievement in diaspora, upon which the European-Jewish modernists could rely even as they drastically revised it. "The old formulae of *Galut* simply do not work in the diffuse cultural contexts of America," declares Bloom, since the Jews are like all Americans, "survivors of an Election Theology" (357), "a religion that became a people" (356). The diffusiveness of American life threatens the "text-centeredness" that sustained and enriched the diaspora. Thus, to write in a Jewish context in modern America is to attempt the complete re-creation of Jewish culture, despite the ambiguous force of traditional Jewish textuality which one would expect to find behind the writer. The Jewish-American writer must impose his or her vision upon our culture in general, which will in turn lead to the recognition of a specifically Jewish achievement.

It is an odd formulation, and one that seems to be refuted by the course of Bloom's own intellectual career, at least as I read him and as his work has affected my own. Bloom certainly did not begin his career as the eccentric spokesman for Jewish culture that he has since become. This is not to say that such is his only role today, but it is a crucial element in his persona of universal cultural critic, "the Yiddisher Dr. Johnson." From *Shelley's Mythmaking* (1959) to *The Book of J* (1990), the appearance of explicitly Jewish ideas, terms, and texts has been a gradual but accelerating phenomenon in Bloom's work. Arguably, the more Bloom has stressed Jewish cultural difference, the more authority he has claimed for himself in the American literary and intellectual world at large. In this case, "cultural achievement" and "Jewish cultural achievement" have imposed themselves *simultaneously:* they are integrated into one immensely ambitious critical project.

There is a lesson here for the aspiring Jewish-American writer, and it is one that I have gradually taken to heart. Reading Bloom since the beginning of my formal literary education, watching him integrate more, and more audacious, Jewish ideas and modes of thought into his cultural criticism, I realize now how intimately and complexly a Jewish literary sensibility can be intertwined with American culture. Some, like George Steiner, would argue that America has no real culture, that it merely appropriates what other cultures, including that of the Jews, have produced. Others, like Cynthia Ozick, regard "the Jewish Idea" as a hedge against the dubious attractions of paganism, most recently made manifest in contemporary American arts and letters. But Bloom, however gloomy his pronouncements might be, has a more nuanced and dialectical attitude. A true heir of Scholem and Benjamin, Bloom understands how the historical tensions within Judaism, as well as those between Jewry and the gentile world, continually remake the Jewish mind in every generation. There is no telling what we will draw from that immense and ancient reservoir of Jewish beliefs, texts, and cultural forms, and how we will combine that matter with what we have gained from other traditions. Even the apparent dissolution of Jewish material, as Benjamin observed in Kafka's writing, can take place through enduring Jewish forms and processes; and that which is denied or repressed, as Scholem learned in studying *kabbalah,* can actually reinspire Jewish life. In this context, even Bloom's anxiety of influence may be taken as a sign of Jewish cultural vitality.

My last turn returns me to my self, the text I have been interpreting by interpreting the texts of those who have come before me. For Jews in particular, "the Vale of Soul-making" (Keats's term for the world as the place of imaginative self-discovery) is composed of others' texts. This making of the self through others, a process which entails both the acknowledgment of authority and the insistence upon autonomy, comes to us as a Jewish cultural paradigm, one which Freud universalized when he began to treat the psyche as a book, a sequence of tropes. Bloom wryly comments that Freud's Family Romance "might be called the only poem that even unpoetical natures continue to compose";[20] it may also be the only Jewish practice in which all human beings engage, regardless of nation or creed. Freud may have made Jews and poets of us all, but these metaphors can hardly satisfy an actual Jewish poet sitting down to write a poem.

At the beginning of this chapter, I mentioned that my poetry has always been something of a scholar's art. To put this in more specifically Jewish terms, I could say that, although much of my poetry, like most lyric poetry, is about the self, what I am moved to declare about that self is mediated by the strong and frequently explicit presence of other texts within the zone of poetic utterance. In short, my poetry is *always already a commentary*, as much as my criticism is. Regardless of genre, my vehicle of written expression is charged through its contact with other writing; and it is through such contact that I gain access to what I have to say about myself and the world. And while I cannot psychoanalyze myself, and thus cannot know against which poetic precursors I truly defend myself, the concept of influence anxiety in itself does not cause me anxiety. Indeed, to hear it articulated came as no surprise, but brought instead an uncanny sense of deja vu.

A similar sense of deja vu came to me when I began reading deeply in Jewish literature and scholarship. However remote and forbidding the work seemed, there were spaces in the text into which my own words could be fitted, passages which seemed to be waiting for commentary. If I could write both with and against the work, write with audacity and respect in equal measure, then the matter of my Jewish identity would no longer remain in the abstract; it would become a practice, and a relatively traditional practice at that. Some of my writing of this sort naturally took the form of expository prose, but just as much proved to be a matter of lyrical expression, becoming a part of my ongoing project in poetry. Eventually, I found myself writing two books simultaneously: a volume of poems, *Restless Messengers,* and a critical study, *The Ritual of New Creation.* In regard to my Jewish identity, the impulse behind the two works is the same.

Meanwhile, the climate of the academic and literary world was changing as writers and intellectuals became more disposed to thinking in terms of cultural difference. I realized that there were others around me, Jewish-Americans from backgrounds much like my own, who were making similar discoveries regarding their heritage, and incorporating those discoveries into their literary and scholarly activities in an unprecedented fashion. Perhaps they would understand the enthusiasms and doubts that were reshaping my writing—and perhaps my awareness of a potential community of readers and writers inspired me to keep working, despite what was by now a long-standing vision of myself as a solitary devotee. If it is true that we are in the midst of a renaissance of Jewish studies, in which varied and often contradictory voices speak of the past and future of Jewish culture, then perhaps there is a place for such lines as these, from my poem "Braids":

> All things called into being
> share in this one quality:
> as they were spoken, so do they speak;
> the world perceived as a texture of sound,
>   revealed fold upon fold.
> The days too form nodes of meaning:
> strands of time come bearing events,
> weaving themselves into elaborate coincidences
> until the past is gathered into a single moment,
>   waiting to be understood.
>   But it is never complete,
>   never to be finished,
> and history proves as inadequate as biography
>   as a telling of the tale.
>   None of this is meaningful;
> it hovers in the void that precedes utterance,
> bearing within it a multitude of lights
>   waiting to be lit.

> The candle is burning;
>   its three wicks are formed
>   in the light of a single flame.
> The Shekinah uncoils her braids
>   and her hair covers the page.
> The Sabbath of memory is over:
>   an invisible hand unbinds the past
>   and the words fall away.[21]

NOTES

1. *Sayings of the Fathers,* trans. Jospeh H. Hertz (New York: Behrman House, 1945), 103.
2. Edmond Jabès, "The Key," in *Midrash and Literature,* ed. Geoffrey H. Hartman and Sandford Budick (New Haven: Yale University Press, 1986), 350.
3. W. B. Yeats, "If I Were Four-and-Twenty," in *Explorations* (New York: Collier Books, 1962), 263.
4. Harold Bloom, *The Anxiety of Influence* (New York: Oxford University Press, 1973), 78.

5. Bloom, *The Anxiety of Influence*, 26.

6. Karl Marx, *Early Writings*, trans. T. B. Bottomore (New York: McGraw-Hill, 1963), 127.

7. Georg Lukács, *The Theory of the Novel*, trans. Anna Bostock (Cambridge: MIT Press, 1971), 153.

8. Ernst Bloch, *The Utopian Function of Art and Literature*, trans. Jack Zipes and Frank Mecklenburg (Cambridge: MIT Press, 1988), 12.

9. Wallace Stevens, *The Collected Poems* (New York: Knopf, 1954), 240.

10. Walter Benjamin, *Illuminations*, trans. Harry Zohn (New York: Schocken, 1969), 144.

11. Benjamin, *Illuminations*, 144. The subsequent page references in the text pertain to this source.

12. Susan Sontag, *Under the Sign of Saturn* (New York: Farrar, Straus and Giroux, 1980), 115.

13. Gershom Scholem, *The Messianic Idea in Judaism* (New York: Schocken, 1971), 289.

14. Scholem, *The Messianic Idea*, 289.

15. Gershom Scholem, *On Jews and Judaism in Crisis*, ed. Werner J. Dannhauser (New York: Schocken, 1976), 34.

16. Jacques Derrida, *Writing and Difference*, trans. Alan Bass (Chicago: University of Chicago Press, 1978), 292.

17. Scholem, *On Jews and Judaism in Crisis*, 46.

18. Scholem, *The Messianic Idea in Judaism*, 296.

19. Harold Bloom, *Poetics of Influence*, ed. John Hollander (New Haven: Henry R. Schwab, 1988), 356. The subsequent page references in the text pertain to this source.

20. Bloom, *The Anxiety of Influence*, 63.

21. Norman Finkelstein, "Braids," in *Restless Messengers* (Athens, Ga.: University of Georgia Press, 1992), 74–75.

28

Cynthia Ozick's Paradoxical Wisdom

Marilyn Yalom

FOR MOST OF my adult life, the writers I identified as Jewish-American were men. Saul Bellow, Bernard Malamud, Philip Roth, and Herbert Gold formed a constellation of stars shining from afar. But increasingly during the past decade, the words "Jewish-American writers" have become associated with women—Grace Paley, Tillie Olsen, Kim Chernin, Vivian Gornick, Rebecca Goldstein, Adrienne Rich, and Cynthia Ozick—all of whom illuminate my life like candles in my own room.

Most of these women represent a secular Jewish tradition concerned with the social problems that beset Jews and other minority peoples in a multicultural nation. Moreover, they also share a feminist world view that confronts the patriarchal nature of Judaism. I have no trouble identifying with this kind of Jewishness.

But among these writers one stands apart from the rest, for she is neither secular nor feminist, and never "politically correct." Cynthia Ozick's first allegiance is to traditional Judaism, a religion whose male deity has no divine wife, mother, or daughter and whose practices both exclude and segregate women (for example, in limiting the *minyan* to ten men, and in separating the women from the men during Orthodox services). Although Ozick has herself suffered from sexism within Judaism, she refuses to compromise her religious affiliation through political bonds with other women.

Her characters, Jewish to the marrow, continually test their faith in the Hebrew God, and agonize over the moral responsibility of having been born a Jew. Few of them are thoroughly likable, and there are even fewer with whom I can identify. What have I to do with all those misfits querulously surviving in New York City or Miami Beach? (And in my inner ear Kafka whispers: "What have I in common with the Jews?")

Yet in spite of, or perhaps because of, the challenges encountered in Ozick's landscape, it has begun to occupy more and more space in my imagination, Proustian meadows and salons ceding territory to make room for ugly concrete buildings that house unkempt rabbis and unfashionable women. A female *golem* takes up residence in my thoughts alongside Kafka's cockroach man. Ms. Puttermesser, that Jewish overachiever, appears regularly on the stage of my mind, originally with her magically created daughter, Xantippe, more recently with Ozick's literary mentor, George Eliot ("Puttermesser and Xantippe," "Puttermesser Paired").[1] Ozick herself rises in my dreams like some irritating archangel with wings outstretched guarding the Promised Land. It is with her I must struggle to find my own Jewish truth.

Why is Ozick's world simultaneously attractive and repellent to me? Is there a way to reconcile her sometimes testy pronouncements on feminism with her personal sensitiviy to the female condition? Could I follow her into the dark recesses of faith? Would I want to? The feature of her work that most intrigues me is its ambiguity: its ability to encompass the rational and the irrational, good and evil, forms of femininity and masculinity, contemporary and past historical moments, high culture and low culture, Orthodoxy and disbelief.

Ozick expresses the contradictory mysteries of human existence, which are always more complex than our theories about existence. She recalls the paradoxes intrinsic to the fiction of Kafka, I. B. Singer, and the rabbinical tales of Eastern Europe, from which (not incidentally) her parents and mine immigrated to America. Her modern Jewish parables have subterranean connections with the world of dreams and fantasy, where life's polarities form secret alliances.

A good example of these antinomies is found in the story "Bloodshed." Here a modern, skeptical Jew named Bleilip comes in contact with the rabbi of a Hasidic community living in the New York suburbs.

> "Sometimes," the rebbe said, "even the rebbe does not believe. My father when he was the rebbe also sometimes did not believe. It is characteristic of believers sometimes not to believe. And it is characterisitic of unbelievers sometimes to believe. Even you, Mister Bleilip—even you now and then believe in the Holy One, Blessed Be He? Even you now and then apprehend the Most High?"
>
> "No," Bleilip said; and then "Yes."[2]

We hear in this interchange the echoes of a Jewish verbal tradition that always encompasses two answers, that resists a monolithic world view. Judaism contains a self-critique, a questioning of Orthodoxy, an endless progression of textual commentaries that opens the door to multiple interpretations. Perhaps because Jews have lived for so long in the diaspora and have been obliged to straddle both minority and majority cultures, they have come to appreciate more keenly than other peoples the ironic contradictions inherent in human existence.

Nowhere is this dichotomous world view more apparent than in one of Ozick's early stories, "The Pagan Rabbi." Reduced to its story line, it recounts the baffling suicide of a young rabbi, exemplary in his scholarship and reputation for holiness, as well as for his marriage to a Holocaust survivor, with whom he has had seven daughters. The plot follows the detective work performed by the rabbi's friend, a former seminary classmate who had abandoned religion in favor of atheism and a gentile wife. As in many of Ozick's stories, this investigation takes the narrator into totally unexpected terrain—first, the Trilham's Inlet at the end of the subway line, where the rabbi, Isaac Kornfeld, had hanged himself on a lone tree in a meadow near the bay; thence to the home of the widowed *rebbitsin* Kornfeld, who astonishes the narrator with an unexpected picture of her rabbi husband given to lengthy hikes, picnics, and outings; and finally, into the mind of the dead man through the medium of the notebook and letter he had left behind. What emerges is the picture of a devout Jew drawn away from Judaic law by the pull of nature, and inevitably destroyed by his pantheistic fornications with a plantlike nymph. The disillusioned wife passes succinct and unforgiving judgment: "He was a pagan."[3]

What are we to make of this tortured tale of polar contradictions? Reduced to its philosophical content, it incarnates the opposition between pantheism—the belief that God exists in Nature—and the Jewish concept of God as the creator of nature. Scheindel, the *rebbitsin*, irrevocably bound to Judaism, is the *porte parole* for Ozick's condemnation of the Hellenic-Christian strain of American culture—a condemnation so passionately felt that Ozick has personally experienced it as "a revulsion . . . of the surrounding culture itself: a revulsion against Greek and pagan modes."[4] From this perspective, "The Pagan Rabbi" is a cautionary tale of what can happen to even an exemplary Jew who founders in what Ozick has called "the ancient and eternal rift between the Jewish idea and the world at large."[5]

But if it were only a cautionary tale, only an expression of ideology, I should have put it down after a first reading, however enjoyable, and thought no more about it. That was not the case with "The Pagan Rabbi"; it is not the case now, years later. I am still fascinated by the pagan rabbi, still intrigued by the conflict he represents. Jewish law, the life of the mind and spirit, the mandate of texts and covenants—these line up on one side of my brain in an awesome brigade. They glower across a cerebral landscape toward the enemy on the other side, a powerful opponent conducting warfare under the cover of trees and flowers. And like the pagan rabbi, what is to keep me from hiding out in the woods and copulating with a nature spirit, preferably male or androgynous? Surely not the "cautionary" message of Ozick's tale. For in the telling, Ozick has made that pagan experience so alive, so inviting, that it lures the reader as much as it repels. We are tempted. And here I see Ozick in the line of those great writers—Dante and Milton, Goethe and Camus—for whom the temptations of an evil spirit rivaled the joys of salvation.

Still, I wonder how we are to read the epigraph that precedes "The Pagan Rabbi." Are we to take Ozick seriously in her citation from *The Ethics of the Fathers,* that the person who breaks off study to remark, " 'How lovely is that tree!' . . . hurts his own being" (3) ? Must we repudiate nature and the wisdom that comes directly from the senses? And even as I ask that question, I know the answer. Ozick represents an absolute position against which my relativism will always be tested. In the antithesis between Kierkegaard's aesthetic and ethical life (first articulated in *Either/Or* [1843]), Ozick stands firmly on the side of the latter, construing it as synonymous with Jewishness and relegating aesthetics to an amoral, irreligious, all-pervasive Hellenism in the Western world. By forcing me to question my own propensity toward aesthetic solutions (my tendency to choose style over substance, grace over goodness) and to ponder the ethical-aesthetic dichotomy in the terms of her unequivocal adherence to Judaism, she raises a standard for which I and other Jews have reason to be grateful.

I am reminded of a question I was often asked in the late 1970s and early 1980s when I headed a university research center on women. Members of the surrounding community, even some of the faculty, would come to me and decry what they considered excessive in the women's movement. They complained that radical women wanted to push men off the face of the earth, quickly adding, "But you're not like that." Lesbian women were upsetting the "natural order" of things. (You're not like that.) Women libbers were destroying the family. (You're not like that.) At first I sat silently not knowing how to respond. Did I want to be identified with women more politically radical than myself? In time, I developed a feminist consciousness large enough to encompass the grievances of separatists and lesbians and women of color whose differences from my heterosexual, white (albeit Jewish), mainstream concerns were very real indeed. And I learned to say to my interrogators that, if radical feminists were not at the barricades, the rest of us would be even further behind in our search for social justice.

Ozick, too, is at the barricades, and her defense of Jewishness brooks no other cause. Art—the idol of her youth; Nature—the beguiling Spinozan heresy; Feminism—a gendered icon: these are perceived as distractions, if not enemies, of the Jewish spirit. Art, nature, feminism, humanism, universalism are all viewed with suspicion, not because they are intrinsically bad, but because their very attractiveness threatens an exclusive commitment to Judaism. Ozick, like Yahweh, is a jealous master.

I am struggling now to extend my Jewish feminist consciousness so as to make peace with Cynthia Ozick. Take, for example, her pronouncements on the "woman writer," a juxtaposition of words which she abhors. In her view, the label "woman writer" marginalizes and denigrates the woman artist, and places her in a lesser category then the simple word "writer." Ozick stresses sameness in the writerly mission of both women and men, and refuses to segregate the former from the latter for fear of ghettoization, with its attendant negative consequences; in her words, "the term 'woman writer' has shut out, damaged and demeaned writers."[6] Ozick's vision of creative men and women follows an Enlightenment ideal, in which the qualities of "mind" or "personhood" subsume gender difference.

Ironically, as has been noted by several Ozick commentators, this universalist position is set aside in relation to religion.[7] Ozick considers herself a

"Jewish writer" and takes issue with those identifying themselves, like Roth and Bellow, as writers who just happen to be Jews. The urgency of her commitment to Judaism does not tolerate divided loyalties, although she often refers to the term "Jewish writer" as an oxymoron because writing can be seen as a form of creative rivalry with God. This strict interpretation of the second commandment forbidding the construction of graven images has, however, given way to a somewhat softer stance in some of Ozick's later pronouncements.[8] Whatever tension Ozick experiences between art and religion (i.e., between aesthetics and ethics) is theoretically resolved by putting one squarely in the service of the other. In principle, "Jewish art" serves Jewish ideals; in practice, Ozick's art often strays from an unambiguous vision of Jewish liturgical morality, and certainly cannot be accused of parochialism.

Her embrace of the term "Jewish writer" and her refusal of the term "woman writer" derive from a system of loyalties that ranks Judaism far above sisterhood. This is undoubtedly her right, yet I am nonetheless troubled by her ambivalent relationship to feminism. Or perhaps I am troubled mainly by the kind of feminism she embraces, the kind that pursues equality between men and women, without validating feminine differences. Mind—pure mind—is for Ozick without sex or gender. Railing against "the Ovarian Theory of Literature," she pleads for the imaginative freedom that art can confer upon both women and men,[9] a position few would want to contest.

If Ozick and I disagree on the use of the term "woman writer," it is not only because I believe that women's gendered experiences usually influence the content and sometimes the sensibility of their work, but also because the term is politically expedient as a means of calling attention to women in courses, scholarly publications, and textbooks, where women's cultural contributions are still often neglected. In truth, I would not have been able to teach Ozick during the 1980s had she not been a "woman writer." Today she is where she should have been all along—in courses on American literature, as well as in courses in women's studies and Jewish studies.

Turning from Ozick's polemics to her art, one finds narrative forms that belie her more intransigent pronouncements. Ozick admits as much in the delightful introduction to her last collection of essays, *Metaphor and Memory.* There she warns against assuming that stories are "illustrations" of ideas or that her essays express "the ideational (or even at times the ideological) matrix of the stories." By now, she allows that "nearly every essay, like every story, is an experiment, not a credo," and certainly "never a tenet."[10]

Thus forewarned, I plunged into her essay "Ruth."[11] Here I found a combination of autobiography and textual exegesis illuminated by Ozick's passion for the Jewish idea. The story of Ruth begins in Ozick's childhood house, where "there were only two pictures on the walls"—that of her stern-looking paternal grandfather and that of Ruth gleaning in the fields of Boaz (240). The Orthodox grandfather and the figure of Ruth the Moabite, which coexisted in Ozick's childhood imagination, were literally brought together on the holiday of Shavuot, when her grandfather read the Book of Ruth. A retelling of this biblical story constitutes the spine of Ozick's essay, allowing her to reflect on the meaning of exogamy within Jewish law, the qualities of mercy and normality, and the singularity of the Jewish covenant.

I read this essay for the first time as if it were a piece of fiction, marveling at Ozick's ability to juxtapose biblical text, commentary, and speculative versions of Ruth's history within a spellbinding narrative. Instead of asking how Ruth's story would unfold, for I knew that already, I followed with fascination the turns of Ozick's mind, asking myself: How will she resolve the contradiction between the Jewish injunction against marriage with a stranger and the honored position of Ruth the Moabite? Why does she spend several pages on Orpah, Ruth's noncanonical sister-in-law? What will Ozick do when she comes to the hallowed moment when Ruth declares her loyalty to her Jewish mother-in-law, Naomi?

Three times Ozick tells the story of Ruth's declaration to Naomi, first as imagined in the language of personal relations, then according to a vision of ideal conduct, and finally as it is told in the Bible: "Do not urge me to leave you, to turn back and not follow you. For wherever you go, I will go; wherever you lodge, I will lodge; your people shall be my people, and your God my God" (258; originally spoken in Ruth 1:16).

The biblical words take on new depth and meaning when retold after the more modern and more prosaic versions of the same tale. They resound with the language of the sacred even in my secular ears, and I nod in assent at Ozick's poetic affirmation: "Her words have set thirty centuries to trembling" (252). For me, it would have been sufficient for the recently widowed Ruth to have declared to her mother-in-law: "Whither thou goest, I shall go" (to quote the version on which I was raised). That declaration established a standard of human loyalty I have tried to maintain, literally, with my family and, figuratively, with close friends. But Ozick goes further; for her, the crucial words are "Your God shall be my God." It is Ruth's commitment to Israel, to "the One Universal Creator," that earns her the right, in Ozick's eyes, to an exalted place within the Jewish temple (258).

Ozick seems to believe in this Creator of the universe. My own beliefs are less certain. Is the God of the Jews my God? Is the God of the Jews also the God of non-Jews? Where does a doubting Jew, like me, find sustenance? And, once again, even as I ask the last question, I know the answer. In the text.

The words of Scripture sustain me. "Whither thou goest, I shall go." "By the rivers of Babylon, there we sat down, yea, we wept" (Psalms 137:1). "Surely goodness and mercy shall follow me all the days of my life" (Psalms 23:6). ". . . and they shall beat their swords into plowshares" (Micah 4:3). My Jewishness is wedded to writing; it is a portable religion adapted to a people in exile. And what people are not in exile? As the Israeli scholar Sidra Ezrahi maintained in a lecture at Stanford University, though three million Jews have found a homeland in Israel, even they are still (inevitably?) in metaphysical exile. The kingdom of God, the land of milk and honey, is always far from human habitation. Fortunately, however, there is the permanent refuge of the text, which, as Kafka reminds us, is "unchangeable," despite its changing interpretations. What Ozick has accomplished in her essay on Ruth is to intensify the beauty and meaning of a story familiar to me since childhood, first by recasting it in two secular versions, then by resacralizing through an expression of faith in the story's original meaning. Though I cannot embrace the faith of the biblical Ruth, Ozick's re-vision (following the spelling and meaning first deconstructed by Adrienne Rich)[12] allows me to see her story anew and to reclaim it as a part of my heritage.

Central to Ozick's retelling of Jewish history are the stories, novellas, novels, and essays that take their impetus from the Holocaust. Few other American-born writers (if any) have persevered so courageously in confronting the enormity of the Holocaust. From her first book, *Trust* (1966), to her last book, *The Shawl* (1989), Ozick's preoccupation with the Holocaust has produced a literary legacy that American Jews ignore at their peril.[13]

Like many Jews born in the generation of World War II, I approach the literature of the Holocaust in a spirit of dread. I could have been one of those children gassed at Auschwitz like my cousin, who perished with her mother in a concentration camp. In my mother's album I have often stared at the faded photo of a girl with braided dark blonde hair, similar to my own at that age.

As a teenager, I saw the documentaries of the camps, the gas chambers, the cadavers—both dead and alive—that greeted the invading American armies. In the 1950s and 1960s, I read *The Last of the Just* and *Treblinka*,[14] and then could read no more. Later, movies like *Sophie's Choice* and *Europa, Europa* seemed to me to be patently false; films of the Holocaust should be made only in black and white, if made at all.[15] I watched *Schindler's List* with a hand over my eyes.

But as Ozick's reader, I found it impossible to avoid a cohort of Holocaust victims obstinately surviving in New York, in the Florida hinterlands, in the Midwest. The *rebbitsin* Kornfeld in "The Pagan Rabbi," members of the Hasidic community in "Bloodshed," Joseph Brill in *The Cannibal Galaxy*[16] are all European transplants destined to prick the moral imagination of comfortably assimilated Jewish-Americans like myself. Their outlandish presence reminds us of the mandate not to forget.

Ozick's survivors are by no means paragons of goodness and rectitude, somehow exempt from normal human foibles because of their transfiguring past. Even Scheindel the *rebbitsin,* with her tatooed arm and religious intransigence, is occasionaly undercut by the narrator's ironic humor. Miraculously, Ozick grants her characters unexpected attributes and incomprehensible acts, for, as A. Alvarez has noted, "her flair as a writer is for the oddities of people, their contradictions, depths, and sudden passions."[17] Ozick does not make them any more likable, comprehensible, or all-of-a-piece than characters from the world of Dostoevsky, with whom she shares a spiritual kinship.

Nowhere is her ability to convey the monstrous tragedy of the Holocaust more powerful than in her short story, "The Shawl," and her novella, *Rosa,* which first appeared separately in the *New Yorker* and then together in book form. In the words of Michiko Kakutani, "The two stories stand, at once, as dazzling philosophical meditations and beautifully crafted works of fiction."[18]

"The Shawl" is barely eight pages long, scarcely more than an extended metaphor. Its plot follows the history of Rosa, her baby daughter, Magda, and her fourteen-year-old niece, Stella, sent together to a concentration camp where Magda is initially hidden and then brutally murdered. Given the fate of Jews during the Holocaust, a baby's murder should come as no surprise, yet, as in Greek tragedy, the apprehension of doom intensifies the observer's horror. The reader is never lulled like Madga by the shawl in which she is hidden, the magic shawl with the flavor of milk that "could nourish an infant for three days and three nights."[19] Like Rosa, we foresee that Magda is going to die, but we do not yet know the manner of her death. So we anxiously watch her "little pencil legs scribbling this way and that" as she takes her first steps, and then her last (7).

At this stage of commentary I am loath to continue. I do not want to analyze this text. Why break apart a tale whose tragic power lies in its implosive concentration? I imagine Ozick's compulsion to create a written equivalent for her terrible inner vision, the hours and days devoted to elusive phrases and recalcitrant sentences, the emerging web of words never quite perfect but, finally, good enough. And when finished, when set in print, Ozick's words fly on the wings of the shawl to readers thirsty for their magic milk. We drink them in a state of beatific horror, wondering if, in Magda's sacrifice, there can be some tiny spark of redemption.

Redemption for whom? For Magda, an innocent baby? For Rosa, doomed to suffer the loss of her child for a lifetime? For Stella, whose "borrowing" of the shawl led directly to Magda's death? For the German murderer and the German people, tainted for generations by Nazi butchery? For humankind, which has committed genocide on Jews and Gypsies, Armenians and Cambodians, to mention only some of the victims of our century? Redemption—can such a word still have meaning?

If redemption means the cleansing of sin, as one understands it within the Judeo-Christian tradition, then I am asking "The Shawl" to provide what is conventionally found in rituals performed by priests, ministers, and rabbis. That is surely asking too much from a text. Yet, at the least, "The Shawl" and a few comparable short works of literature (think of Tolstoy's "Death of Ivan Ilych") force confrontation with ultimate concerns, with the meaning of life and death, and good and evil. As the central reference point for evil in the twentieth-century Western world, the Holocaust swallows us up by its sheer magnitude. We need some small piece of it to meditate upon, some memento mori that encapsulates Hitler's hell on earth.

I remember something my father said to me when I was a teenager. When asked why he, a nonbeliever, a progressive member of the NAACP, a lover of Whitman and the brotherhood of man, continued to practice Jewish rituals, he answered that he would always be a Jew as long as Jews were persecuted. Over the years, that answer has resonated with the words of myriad other Jews, most eloquently those of Elie Wiesel and Cynthia Ozick. While persecution is surely not the only reason for Jews to preserve their heritage, it has indeed heightened the obligation for living Jews to remember the victims of the Holocaust and to maintain a sense of Jewish community.

Turning from "The Shawl" to *Rosa* is like moving from the sacred to the profane, from the sanctity of ritual to the banality of daily existence. Rosa, thirty years later, lives like a resident bag lady in an old people's building in Miami. Her squalid surroundings interest her no more than the people around her. She is totally obsessed with her memories and fantasies of her daughter, Magda, who appears in her imagination in different stages of the life cycle—sometimes as a teenager, sometimes as an accomplished young woman. Yet this tragic tale of obsessional madness is by no means devoid of humor, especially after Rosa's encounter with the seventy-one-year-old laundromat Romeo, Simon Persky.

> "Your name?" her companion said.
> "Lublin, Rosa."
> "A pleasure," he said. "Only why backwards? I'm an application form? Very good. You apply, I accept." He took command of her shopping cart. "Wherever is your home is my direction that I'm going anyhow."
> "You forgot to take your laundry," Rosa said.
> "Mine I did day before yesterday."
> "So why did you come here?"
>
>] . . . [
>
> "All right, so I go to have a visit with the ladies. Tell me, you like concerts?"
> "I like my own room, that's all."
> "A lady what wants to be a hermit!"
> "I got my own troubles," Rosa said.
> "Unload on me."[20]

Rosa does not prove to be an easy pickup. Her most vivid reality lies elsewhere, in the internal world haunted by the wraith of her daughter. As in the case of most survivors, the Holocaust continues to ravage her psyche decades after its official end, despite the admonitions of those like Persky, who tell her "it's finished" and that "forgetting is necessary" (58).

The difference between Rosa and Persky, both born in Warsaw, are legion. Having left Poland in 1920, he escaped the Holocaust and lived most of his life as a member of the Jewish-American working class. Rosa separates herself from him not only by virtue of her personal suffering during the war but also because of class differences. She came from the Polish-Jewish bourgeoisie; her parents mocked the Yiddish that Persky still reads in his daily newspaper; her Warsaw, as she continually tells him, was not his Warsaw. Ozick plays upon

Rosa's sense of cultural superiority with comic indulgence; after all, it represents a small measure of self-worth salvaged from a life stripped of all amenities. Persky, with his "long rows of glinting dentures" (19), his life compared to an insignificant button, his good-natured persistence and Yiddish-inflected humor, succeeds in making a connection with the half-mad Rosa. The novella ends with the suggestion that she may yet find a way to live in the present, beyond the prison of the past. The mandate not to forget the dead, Ozick implies, must not be interpreted as an excuse to forget the living.

Rosa draws me into the Jewish Miami I knew from my mother's long residence there. It is a world I would prefer to avoid because, like Rosa, I am a cultural snob. Every time I flew across the country to visit my mother, I prepared myself for the accents of the people around her, their endless photos and stories of children and grandchildren, their myopic vision informed by a single question: Is it good for the Jews? I learned that it was pointless to question their uncritical allegiance to Israel or to suggest they think more generously of Latinos or blacks or, God forbid, Arabs.

For the most part, they were old and infirm. Those who were mobile walked with the aid of canes or on the arms of companions barely more mobile than themselves. Miniature couples aiding each other in the last steps of life. When my mother and I greeted them in the elevator or by the pool, they looked at me with Munchkin-like wonder, as if I were Dorothy in the company of the Good Witch of the West. Surely I should have found friendlier words to meet their hunger for kinship. Had I learned nothing in the way of compassion from a half-century of lived and literary experiences?

For most of my academic career, it was fashionable to assume that literature really has little to do with life. Texts were viewed as the self-generated products of language crafted solely for aesthetic purposes. To suggest that literature emerges from real-life passions and moral concerns was often treated as naïve. How well I remember the disdain expressed by a colleague summing up my views at a conference: "Well, Marilyn still believes that literature has something to do with life." Yes, that was my position then, as it is now. I believe that every work of literature springs from an autobiographical source, from an "unconscious memoir" as Nietzsche phrased it in *Beyond Good and Evil* (1886). No matter how disguised or undisguised, no matter how well or poorly crafted, the work of literature—and especially the significant work of literature—expresses a personal truth.

Now that the pendulum of literary criticism has begun to swing in the opposite direction, to embrace context as well as text, it has become almost trendy to affirm the twin relationship between life and art. This is the position taken by Elaine M. Kauvar and Victor Strandberg in their recent books on Ozick.[21] Following Ozick's lead, critics have begun to question T. S. Eliot's influential divorce between biography and art. Strandberg, in particular, insists that it is necessary to examine Ozick's personal history if one is to understand her conflicted art. But Ozick herself (as always) is of two minds on this issue. "The life on the page," she argues in her essay on Saul Bellow, "resists the dust of flesh, and is indifferent to external origins."[22] Her own biography counts, and does not count, when we confront the creations of her fictive imagination.

The narratives that have emerged from Ozick's life as a Jewish-American woman writer resonate with the tensions and ambiguities of truly great art. While rooted in the specifics of her historical moment and milieu, they speak to any sensitive human of any time and place, overcoming cultural and ideological differences. My own quarrel with Ozick's antifeminism bows before her genius. It dwindles away as I am drawn more closely into a Jewish circle of her making, one that provides a reference point for my own sense of Jewish identity and community. I shall never again go to Miami without the thought that Rosa may be one of the crazed-looking women pushing her laundry cart in the street. Nor can I ever forget the fate of her daughter, Magda, thrown like a ball against an electrified fence. These are my people.

Postscript. Passover, 1994. Once again the communal supper that punctuates our history as a people. Once again the eternal drama of persecution and liberation. Ozick's presence infiltrates my mind alongside the characters in the Haggadah. Would she be comfortable with the egalitarian seder we have devised, with nonsexist terms like "the Eternal One" and "the Holy One," rather than the traditionally masculine "Lord of the Universe"? Would she be satisfied with our nontheistic, ethical-cultural approach, with our lack of belief in the supernatural?

I marvel at Ozick's ability to believe. I marvel even more at the abiding faith of Elie Wiesel, a Holocaust survivor. All the old questions of God's existence, goodness, and omnipotence remain, like so many unlocked doors in the cavern of my psyche. Faith does not seem to me, as it does to my husband, to be a comforting illusion, but merely beyond my reach. It comforts me to know that others believe, that Ozick and Wiesel believe.

Yet even more than the solace I find in their faith is the pride I feel in identifying with them as Jews. Ozick, in particular, because she is a Jewish-American woman like myself, draws me into the fold, allows me to experience by choice a sense of sisterhood with the people of my birth.

NOTES

I wish thank to Marcia Falk, John and Mary Felstiner, Susan Bell, Walter Sokel, Alice Kaplan, and Irvin Yalom for helpful comments on this chapter.

1. Cynthia Ozick, "Puttermesser and Xantippe," in *Levitation: Five Fictions* (1982; New York: Dutton, 1983); and Cynthia Ozick, "Puttermesser Paired," *New Yorker,* October 8, 1990, pp. 40–52.

2. Cynthia Ozick, "Bloodshed," in *Bloodshed and Three Novellas* (1976; New York: Dutton, 1983), 73.

3. Cynthia Ozick, "The Pagan Rabbi," in *The Pagan Rabbi and Other Stories* (1971; New York: Dutton, 1983), 22.

4. Cynthia Ozick, *Art and Ardor: Essays* (1983; New York: Dutton, 1984), 156.

5. Ozick, "The Pagan Rabbi," 161. The subsequent page reference in the text pertains to this source.

6. Ozick, *Art and Ardor*, 262.

7. For example, see Bonnie Lyons, "Cynthia Ozick as a Jewish Writer," *Studies in American Jewish Literature* 6 (Fall 1987): 13–23.

8. An account of changes in two of Ozick's major theoretical positions can be found in Michael Greenstein, "The Muse and the Messiah: Cynthia Ozick's Aesthetics," *Studies in American Jewish Literature* 8 (Spring 1989): 50–65.

9. Ozick, *Art and Ardor*, 266.

10. Cynthia Ozick, *Metaphor and Memory* (New York: Vintage, 1991), ix–xii.

11. Cynthia Ozick, "Ruth," in *Metaphor and Memory*, 240–64. The subsequent page references in the text pertain to this source.

12. Adrienne Rich, "When We Dead Awaken: Writing as Re-vision" (1971), in *On Lies, Secrets, and Silence: Selected Prose 1966–1978* (New York: W. W. Norton, 1979), 33–49.

13. Cynthia Ozick, *Trust* (New York: New American Library, 1966); and Cynthia Ozick, *The Shawl* (New York: Knopf, 1989).

14. André Schwarz-Bart, *The Last of the Just*, 1st American ed. (New York: Atheneum, 1960); Jean François Steiner, *Treblinka* (New York: Simon and Schuster, 1967).

15. For a fuller discussion of criteria for judging films on the Holocaust and Holocaust literature in general, see Joel Shatzky, "Creating an Aesthetic for Holocaust Literature," *Studies in American Jewish Literature* 10 (Spring 1991): 104–14. Two fine book-length studies of film and the Holocaust are Annette Insdorf, *Indelible Shadows: Film and the Holocaust* (Cambridge: Cambridge University Press, 1983; 2d ed., 1989); and Ilan Avisar, *Screening the Holocaust: Cinema's Images of the Unimaginable* (Bloomington: Indiana University Press, 1988).

16. Cynthia Ozick, *The Cannibal Galaxy* (1983; New York: Dutton, 1984).

17. A. Alvarez, "On *The Cannibal Galaxy*," in *Cynthia Ozick*, ed. Harold Bloom (New York: Chelsea House Publishers, 1986), 135.

18. Michiko Kakutani, "Cynthia Ozick on the Holocaust, Idolatry and Loss," *New York Times*, September 5, 1989, p. C17.

19. Ozick, *The Shawl*, 5. The subsequent page reference in the text pertains to this source.

20. Ozick, *Rosa*, in *The Shawl*, 21–22. The subsequent page references in the text pertain to this source.

21. Elaine, M. Kauvar, *Cynthia Ozick's Fiction: Tradition & Invention* (Bloomington: Indiana University Press, 1993); and Victor Strandberg, *Greek Mind/Jewish Soul: The Conflicted Art of Cynthia Ozick* (Madison: University of Wisconsin Press, 1994).

22. Ozick, *Metaphor and Memory*, 51.

29

"Crazy, of Course"

Spiritual Romanticism and the Redeeming
of Female Spirituality in
Contemporary Jewish-American Women's Fiction

Miriyam Glazer

I

There is an incident in Anne Roiphe's novel *Lovingkindness* that has haunted me, as a Jew, a woman, and a scholar, ever since I read it. The incident functions as an epiphany for me, illuminating the ambivalence toward modern Judaism inscribed in the novels of contemporary Jewish-American women writers and intimately echoing my own experience. At the same time, it also suggests a particular kind of "spiritual romanticism," as I have come to call it, which, eroding the borders of that Judaism, infuses these writers' work.

The incident takes place in a "sane synagogue" in New York. Bewildered by her postmodern-punk daughter Andrea's sudden commitment to Orthodoxy and troubled by her own intense, recurrent dreams of the charismatic Hasidic mystic Nachman of Bratslav (1773–1810), narrator Annie Johnson visits the rabbi of the "sane synagogue." In sharp contrast with the all-encompassing religiosity of the Jerusalem *yeshiva* in which Andrea has ensconced herself, this modern American synagogue, Annie comments,

> made no excessive demands on its congregation. It allowed them to attend infrequently. It supplied services for weddings and funerals. It was a discreet synagogue with a board of trustees and a monthly bulletin and a sisterhood that had luncheons twice a year. This synagogue was not pushing its ways into the daily life of its congregants, separating them from others, confining them to certain streets, denying them the pleasures of philosophy and Hollywood.[1]

In short, for American Jews it is familiar territory, resembling the synagogues many of us know—and the Conservative temple in which I grew up.

Annie has not gone to the synagogue to pray. She has gone because the head of the *yeshiva* has asked her to supply documents proving that she (and therefore Andrea) is Jewish. Efficiently, the synagogue supplies them. But when the documents are in hand, Annie doesn't leave: she lingers at the door of the rabbi's office, for she is restive, spiritually confused. Secular feminist though Annie believes herself to be, the unruly Nachman is bedeviling her dreams, exhorting her to pay attention to his vexatious, perplexing tales.[2] Abruptly, Annie now confronts the rabbi with the question really on her mind. "What do you think of Rabbi Nachman from Bratslav?" Annie asks. Here is his reply:

> "Wonderful storyteller. Precursor of Kafka and Max Brod. I have an excellent commentary on him by Steinsaltz; gifted man, but crazy, of course."
> "Of course," [Annie says], shaking his hand and walking to the elevator without deliberate haste.[3]

In *A Weave of Women*, Esther Broner describes the act of reading as "feeding a book through yourself."[4] When I "feed" this moment of *Lovingkindness* through myself, I feel in my bloodstream my own long quest to find my place, my home, within Judaism; to come into vital relation with this faith and this people to which I have always been fiercely drawn or from which, with equal ferocity, withdrawn. I relive the pain I felt knowing that neither my spiritual thirst nor my intellectual hunger was discernable to the learned rabbi of our home congregation, for whom all girls were future housewives only, "Mothers in Israel." Like Annie, who earlier in *Lovingkindness* suggests her hurt as a girl-child when she is deprived of a significant spiritual-intellectual relation to Judaism, I turned away from Judaism, toward secular culture, for intellectual nourishment/encouragement. But like Annie's daughter, Andrea, life in the churning melting pot—in my case, of the 1960s—overwhelmed me, and in 1968 I left the chaotic rebellion of my generation in the States for Jerusalem, in search of something more. I imagined a brief and romantic expatriation: Jerusalem after the Six-Day War would be my version of Paris in the 1920s. I would sip espresso in left-wing cafes, writing poems and an occasional dispatch for the underground Liberation News Service while waiting for the Vietnam War to end. And then I would be an exile returned.

But Israel for me was more than a respite; it was an awakening, a revelation. In the radiant air of Jerusalem, the biblical past felt as alive in me as in the stones. Perhaps most important of all, among the vastly varied, pied beauty of the Jewish people—the wiry Yemenites, dark North Africans, blond-haired, broad-hipped Europeans, sari-clad Indians—my own American-bred internalized stereotype of who Jews are dissolved. I felt I belonged. My very body felt different.

Several months after my arrival, I was offered a position at the fledgling English department of the University of the Negev, later Ben Gurion University, in Be'ersheva. To me that offer meant a beckoning to participate in the pioneering national dream of "building the state": I would help the desert culturally to bloom. I would bridge my world of English literature with the destiny of the Jews. I ceased being an "American expatriate," and stayed at Ben Gurion for eleven years.

Those years in Jerusalem and Be'ersheva fostered a new vision of myself as a Jew. With Hebrew as my everyday tongue and an Israeli identity card in hand, I could buy pork from the Christian butcher in the Old City on Yom Kippur to defy the religious authorities, and still consider myself living fully as a Jew. Living in Israel freed me of the diaspora choices among religious commitment, dejudaicized assimilation into the gentile mainstream ("gentilization"?), or nostalgic reliance on bagels and lox to remind me I was vestigially a Jew.

The voice of both my religious defiance and my own personal quest, the subject on which I passionately lectured and to which I devoted my scholarship, my hero, soul-brother, guru, became the romantic poet-prophet-artist William Blake. As I suspect he was for many a 1960s-generation Jewish-American scholar positioned on the margins of both Judaism and American society, Blake in his raging pronouncements against the hegemony of a repressive "Urizen" articulated the intuitions that were born out of my own sense of marginalization as an American woman Jew. Too, like Emerson's quintessentially Protestant-American "self-reliance," Blake's radical individualism gave voice to the U.S.-bred-and-educated part of me, so alien to the collectivist Israeli-Judaic self; but at the same time, rich with the rhythms and tropes of the Hebrew Bible, his poetry bridged the English-language literary scholar in me and the Jew. And, finally, with only shadowy intuitions of the social construction of gender, I was enthralled by the power he imagined in "holy Generation, Image of regeneration!",[5] his portrayal of the power of sexuality both in itself and as symbolic energies at once of history and of the individual psyche, to be reconciled ultimately in a Sacred Marriage. In those years, inspired by his work and living as an entirely secular Israeli Jew, I never thought to consider whether his cry, "Everything that lives is holy!" might also be found in Jewish tradition. It took a return to diasporic consciousness for me to seek out Jewish texts and thus one day to come upon Nachman of Bratslav's parallel spiritual vision. "How wonderful it would be," says Nachman, "if one could only be worthy of hearing the song of the grass."[6] It took diasporic consciousness for me to probe the resemblances between Blake's "Jerusalem" and the kabbalistic *shekhinah*.

It is impossible to overestimate the impact the birth of the women's movement—in the States and later in the mid-1970s in Israel—had on our lives. Esther Broner's *Weave of Women* fictionalizes, even mythologizes, the energy and intensity of those days; Marcia Freedman's *Exile in the Promised Land* tells some of the story.[7] For me, the women's movement brought a visceral upheaval in consciousness. Naming and grasping the pervasive sexism that women had suffered meant at last bearing a language to articulate the life-long dis-ease I had experienced in religious and secular, social, cultural, intellectual, political, institutional life. An activist in the movement in Israel, I found that everything in my life—personal and professional—changed, changed utterly. Eventually, the hero of my intellectual world toppled as well: for while it was not difficult to recognize the similarities between Blake's critique of eighteenth-century reason and culture on the one hand, and the argument of feminism with patriarchy on the other, I was, in the 1970s, unforgiving of the androcentric limits of his vision. My scholarly articles of that period harp on those limits, pointing out how "the first female form now separate" terrified him; how, for Blake, the true imaginative function of the female was to serve as midwife to the male creative process; and how his concept of androgyny really meant the incorporation of the female in the male.[8] I despaired; even Blake could not speak for me. Like Annie throughout *Lovingkindness,* Judith in Nessa Rapoport's *Preparing for Sabbath,* and Lillywhite in Rhoda Lerman's *God's Ear,*[9] once I disengaged from Blake, I had to ask what a restively spiritual, intellectual, Jewish woman could believe in.

There are thousands of Jewish-Americans who choose to cast off their diaspora selves like an unwonted/unwanted cloak and become "absorbed" into Israeli life. I was only ephemerally one of those. Being a religiously rebellious "Blakean" while safeguarding my Jewish identity by living in Israel began dissolving as an existential and spiritual solution. I wanted to contribute to the women's movement and so edited *Burning Air and a Clear Mind,*[10] the first (and only) collection of Israel's contemporary women poets to appear in English. But then, disenchanted by the changes in Israeli life that accompanied the rise of the right-wing settler movement, uncertain now of my purpose in Israel, or even my purpose as a scholar, I left Israel and my tenured position, and returned to the States.

And, predictably, I eventually found myself back in that liminal state before the "rabbi's office" of American Judaism. Almost literally so: for in 1988, I ended my self-chosen exile from academia by joining the faculty of the University of Judaism, established by rabbinic scholars of the very Conservative movement I had fled from years before. But by now feminism had impacted us both: it was neither the same movement nor the same I. The door of the male "rabbi's office" had opened a crack: in Conservative Judaism, women were now counted in the *minyan,* accepted for ordination as rabbis. To push that opening wider, I established "The Timbrels of Miriam," an annual campus event celebrating the new rituals and renewed spirituality of Jewish women, and evolved a ceremony in which to assume my Hebrew name, Miriyam, and "A Ritual of Healing" to exorcise the sexism of traditional Jewish Divorce.[11]

When I had set out as a scholar, I had had to reach out to a voice crying in the wilderness of late-eighteenth- and early-nineteenth-century England to find validation for my own restless, angry, impassioned search; upon my return I came to realize that a new and very different romanticism was flowering, one whose roots were buried deep in the local ground of my own life. For after the shock of coming face to face with anti-Semitism within the international women's movement, feminists who had been only incidentally Jews were driven to look again at their Jewishness, while Jewish-identified women, empowered by the feminist critique, were beginning to challenge the profound marginalization of women within Judaism. I came to see that, of the many still very mobile outcomes of the Jewish feminist movement, one was and is an emerging fiction that probes the psychic consequences of that marginalization which had so marked my own early life. For me, the particular fascination of this literature is severalfold. First, unlike so much of the American fiction produced by Jews in the past, the narratives of Jewish women's spiritual searching are not being written with the "gentile reader over the shoulder"; that is to say, these novels are not about the problematics of bourgeois "gentilization" for characters who are only uncomfortably, peripherally, or nostalgically Jewish. To the contrary: Esther Broner's *Weave of Women*, Rhoda Lerman's *God's Ear*, Nessa Rapoport's *Preparing for Sabbath*, Tova Reich's *Master of the Return*,[12] and Anne Roiphe's *Lovingkindness*, are all written from *within* Jewish identity, and they are all possessed with spiritual questions they are asking of Judaism.

Second, just as Annie Johnson's nascent spiritual life is egged on by the Hasidic rabbi Nachman of Bratslav, so, reflecting the consciousness that is a consequence of women's long marginalization within Judaism, these novelists are drawn to what, since the Jewish Enlightenment, have been marginalized Judaisms. Thus, while the dominant denominations of contemporary, rationalist, American Judaism have become religiously egalitarian, the narratives of spiritually searching Jewish-American women have turned away from this rationalist-based egalitarianism, implicitly perceiving it as what Luce Irigaray calls the "service of the same";[13] they have chosen, rather, to explore the Judaisms of the outback territories, the Judaisms that, like the rabbi in *Lovingkindness*, "sane" rationalists consider "crazy, of course." For one of the riches of mystical Judaism is its cognizance of the power of gender, and the sense—needing to be reinterpreted by contemporary women—of the anguish of the Absent Female, the exiled *shekhinah*. That in their search for a recomprehension of that Absent Female these narratives are evolving a new spiritual romanticism, rooted at once in the experience of Jewish womanhood and in a mystically imaginative Judaism, has brought my own quest full circle.

II

What is it about this encounter between Annie Johnson and the rabbi of the "sane synagogue" that has such resonance, such impact? I imagine Annie self-conscious, ill at ease, troubled, clumsily struggling to integrate her secular, scholarly, skeptical, single-mother, American-born self with the Judaic self in turmoil. The best she can do at this stage is to linger at the rabbi's door and blurt out a question that barely evidences the real issue of her soul. And then I imagine the rabbi, who does not ask this woman at the edge of his office (with what sort of expression on her face? speaking in what tone of voice?) why she is so abruptly asking him about Nachman. And last, there is his urbane, academic, intellectually remote, derivative response: in Roiphe's construction, the rabbi is as blind to Annie's (urgent, hidden) need as he is to the provocative spiritual intent of Nachman's tales.

To be fair: perhaps we can read (as some of my older male students have read) the rabbi's answer as his attempt to relate to Annie in the terms in which she is outwardly presenting herself: assimilated, sophisticated, literary, intellectual. In that scenario, just as his synagogue accommodates American life, so he, as rabbi, adjusts to her self-presentation. But the words "crazy, of course" preempt dialogue and force closure, tacitly requiring Annie's assent, which he assumes that she, as a "reasonable" being, will give. And Annie does assent, for she is unable to integrate her secularly educated, assimilated self with that nagging voice of her dreams, the voice aroused by the loss of her daughter, the voice of her own unrealized spiritual life. In the face of what Emily Dickinson called "the Danger to be Sane," Annie allows the rabbi to believe she too is a member of the (Jewish) intellectual mainstream ("Of course," she says); but then, like Lilith of myth, she flees, though as inconspicuously as possible ("without *deliberate* haste"; emphasis added), for Annie is assenting at the price of denying the inchoate inner life that has insisted upon her attention through the Hasidic Nachman. In structuring this incident, Roiphe's narrative suggests that to dismiss the storytelling spiritual intensity of the mystic as mad is to consider a writing, dreaming, spiritually searching woman, struggling with issues of motherhood, daughterhood, Judaism, and the sacred, "crazy, of course," as well. Perhaps no other single moment in contemporary Jewish-American women's narratives so vividly encapsulates that sense of alienation—indeed, of exile—from the dominant rationalist Judaisms that these novels as a whole reveal.

III

But why is it the male rabbi Nachman who serves as the psychopomp, the guide to the underworld, of Annie's dreams? Or—a related question—why is it that, to try to hear the silenced voice of women's spirituality, Jewish women turn to the Judaism that sets the most rigid limits on the ritual participation of women, mystical Hasidism? Partly, as I suggested earlier, it is because, like women, Hasidism—described by one disapproving critic as "the seductive underbelly of Judaism"[14]—has been the discounted Other of rationalist post-Enlightenment Judaism. As Susan Handelman points out, Gershom Scholem, the rationalist pioneering scholar of the nonrational, spoke of mystical Judaism as consigned to the " 'cellar' of Jewish history: a subterranean, suppressed, subversive, esoteric tradition that [ran] 'counter' to the official version of Judaism created by the Rabbis . . . irrational, destructive, heretic, [possessing] demonic impulses."[15] Reacting against established rabbinic authority, Hasidim, says Scholem, defended individual "inner reality," "spontaneity of feeling," and "emotional enthusiasm," all of which, from the perspective of the "reason and knowledge" of the rabbis, were "bound to seem absurd and paradoxical."[16] But the subsequent reaction against Hasidism, the "emancipation" of Judaism from mystical inwardness and intense emotionality—its rationalization—also diluted its spiritually imaginative power: who among us, for example, in our Americanized synagogues, with their Protestant-inspired architecture, singing (in English!) "Come Thou O Sabbath Queen," really believed there was a spiritual Queen? "I wasn't comfortable in Conservative synagogues," says a character in Rapoport's *Preparing for Sabbath,* "although some of them gave women rights, because there was equality but no life, no heart in the buildings I saw."[17]

Equality—but within the Economy of the phallocentric Same. The dominant rational "emancipated" Judaisms that emerged in the United States let the Jewish bride's hair grow, let her sit beside males in the synagogue, but suppressed the energy of gender: in the absence of rituals of their own, women became eunuch males; the *shekhinah,* Fairy Godmother. For contemporary writers wrestling with women's role, one of the imaginatively and emotionally compelling aspects of Jewish mysticism lies in its infusion of gender with theurgic spiritual and symbolic significance. Rabbi Nachman of Bratslav essentially abandoned his wife and daughters to make his spiritual trek to the Holy Land, but the recurrent motif of his numinous tales—like those the imagined Nachman tells in the dreams of *Lovingkindness*—is the pain of *spiritual* separation of male and female. Psychic and spiritual wholeness for the individual, redemption for the Jewish people, and cosmic harmony itself can exist only when male and female are reconciled in the *hieros gamos,* the Sacred Marriage. In the Zoharic tradition, "blessings reside only in the place where male and female are together."[18]

If wholeness is the Sacred Marriage, the condition of this world is division, duality. The iconic symbol of the exile of the individual from God, of the Jewish people from the homeland, of cosmic dissonance, is the exile of the *shekhinah,* a profoundly complex, multivalent symbol reminiscent for a literary scholar like myself of Blake's Jerusalem. In the mystical texts, the *shekhinah* undergoes metamorphoses. She is variously conceived of as the liminal "matrix and guardian of Israel's physical and spiritual existence," the "Rose of Sharon, the terrestial Garden of Eden . . . the Temple, the *Sukkah* [Canopy] of Peace, the Sea into which all rivers flow."[19] For the mystics, the *shekhinah* is Jerusalem. She is the "primordial mother," the Sacred Bride, Daughter, Divine Presence, mystical Community of Israel, Lover of the Holy One, source of compassion, the "quasi–independent feminine element" within God.[20] The Zohar teaches that "all the females in the world exist in her mystery."[21]

And, on Shabbat, may even come to embody her. In his brilliant study *The Sabbath in the Classical Kabbalah,* Elliot K. Ginsburg offers a cogent analysis of the way in which kabbalistic Shabbat serves as a means of furthering the divine-human nexus. The Shabbat becomes "a marriage festival," as husband

and wife come to embody the "holy union of the masculine and feminine aspects of God. . . . In the rich and fluid Kabbalistic imagery Male and Female become the archetypal Bride and Groom donning evershifting masks and personae."[22] But though on Shabbat the *shekhinah* emerges from exile and becomes embodied in woman, and though the Zohar imagines all females in the world existing in her mystery, males alone were privy to the study of *kabbalah,* and women were rigidly excluded from communal spiritual life. The significance of the exile of the *shekhinah* at its core, then, may well be the intuition of the spiritual exile of females within Judaism six days of the week and the absence of a fully envisioned female spirituality. Or as Natalie, the so-called Nut of Rhoda Lerman's *God's Ear,* declares to the Hasid Yussel Fetner, "You guys have a romance with God, who am I supposed to have it with? What do I have to circumcise?" Admitting at last that "Natalie was right," Yussel confronts a fellow Hasid:

> "Women can't read Torah. They can't welcome the Sabbath Bride. They can't be part of a minyan. They can't go to the Wailing Wall. They can't say Kaddish for their parents. They can't carry the Torah at Simchas Torah. Maybe that's why there are so many Catholic women . . . at least they can take communion."[23]

"We are . . . fiction writers until we can change circumstances," one of the women of Broner's *A Weave of Women* remarks.[24] The narratives of contemporary Jewish-American women writers wrestle with those "circumstances." Entering the gendered spiritual landscape of the outback regions of Judaism, attending to the plangent voice of women's exile, contemporary Jewish-American women writers are transforming it even as they record it, and in the process suggesting the possibility of a reconceived, and thus redeemed, home.

IV

Up until the present moment, the predictable *mise-en-scène* of most Jewish-American literature has been the secular world and the social, cultural, political arenas of that world. But for these Jewish-American women writers, the secular landscape is chaotic or empty, barren, bleak. In *Lovingkindness,* Annie half-expects to hear that Andrea was found "dead of an overdose in a pickup truck with a Hell's Angel" or "naked hallucinating on the L.A. freeway,"[25] and she herself despairs of the limits of psychology to unravel questions of the spirit. In *Master of the Return,* Golda, a "mathematics prodigy from MIT," longs for a way to widen the spectrum of the "black and white, orderly, lifeless, world of the rational intellect."[26] In the same novel, after Ivriya, a self-described "wild and rebellious daughter," falls off a horse she was riding proudly bare-breasted, her legs are paralyzed. But the secular world can offer no solace for her loss. Sophisticated, assertive, and antireligious, even her doctor-mother cannot minister to Ivriya's dis-ease: "Her mother, her friends—all of them collaborated in the pretense that nothing essential had changed: Hey, it's all right if paralysis is your thing, as horses once were, as travel, as poetry, as dancing, as relationships; hey, so now you're into wheelchairs" (183).

The narrative encoding of this rejection of secularity is a parallel rejection of the conventions of realism. Broner, Lerman, and Reich in particular present landscapes and experiences in which the doors of perception open, the ordinary alchemizes into the holy, and the borders of the "real" grow slippery. "Robin," in *A Weave of Women*, turns into a bird, perching herself on the Western Wall, and Mickey, in that same novel, is possessed by a dybbuk. The aged midwife of *Master of the Return* metamorphoses into a young woman as she attends the birth of a baby. The souls of the dead awaken and dance when Lillywhite of *God's Ear* chants the Kaddish for her father.

But it is the anguish of woman's assigned position within both secular and religious culture that these narratives uncover as most devastating. Annie Johnson remembers her Hasidic grandfather's dismissal of secular culture as well as his simultaneous refusal to pass on to her—a mere girl-child but the only member of the family hungry to hear—the tales of Nachman so precious to him, tales, he claimed to the entranced child, that "made the stars come into your mouth so you could taste them."[27] In *A Weave of Women*, the woman possessed by a dybbuk is a battered wife whom the rabbinate refuses to grant a divorce, while the tormented dybbuk is Magda, a spirit who herself was refused a divorce; Deedee, a young American, is stoned by a *yeshiva* student; the British Jew Joan remembers her "teachers" as "the rabbis who trained me . . . and who tried to kill me."[28] *Master of the Return* at once satirizes *ad absurdum* the oppression of women within Bratslaver Hasidism and at the same time, with almost painful sensitivity, probes the psyche and soul of its female protagonist Ivriya, who nearly loses her son to the zealous messianism of her husband. Lerman's *God's Ear* is a whimsical and poignant *midrash* on the marginalization of women in Hasidic Judaism—and the spiritual price paid by both sexes for that marginalization. In *Preparing for Sabbath*, the young and religiously fervent protagonist, Judith, argues that "women have a spirituality that hasn't been tapped. . . . what women know about relationships and love can transform Judaism, even the way we think about God."[29]

In challenging the painful androcentrism, these novels are drawn into undertaking a spiritual guest. Or as Esther Broner has written, "Somewhere, we are all looking to remake our mythic past."[30]

V

That in four of these novels Jerusalem is the center of the renewed spiritual quest is not merely fortuitous, for the city has always possessed a womanly spiritual aura of its own, an engendered romantic "correspondent breeze," a *ruach*. Partly it is the sheer topography: the hills, I wrote in my first Hebrew

poem, are "round / like a woman's stomach."[31] The mystics imagined the
visible city fashioned detail by detail on the model of her heavenly Mother; in
time, they said, spiritual Jerusalem will descend, the Mother will join the
Daughter, and "the two [will] become as one." "Palestine is the land of the
Godbook, Jerusalem—God's veiled bride," the poet Else Lasker-Schuler
wrote in the pre-state days.[32]

Living in this mystically compelling landscape affects one. One late spring
evening of 1969, in the old Talbieh section of the city, as the redolence of
jasmine and honeysuckle lay heavy in the air, a woman friend and I were
intently conversing under a canopy of bougainvillea in her garden. As the
moon rose, I confessed a secret of my soul: I was the Shulamith, I told her
shyly, the "dark and comely" woman of the Song of Songs "who sought him
whom my soul loveth" (3:1).

My friend was taken aback. "You can't be," she responded. "*I* am."

In Los Angeles years later, I recounted this conversation to my sister. "Ah,"
she sighed, "in those days, we were all Daughters of Jerusalem."

"Something about The Land makes this possible." Esther Broner writes in
A Weave of Women:

> In the Judean Hills one walks on stilts. Prophets come to this city to preach, or
> people, after a sojourn in this city, decide they *are* prophets.
> In the North prophets live in caves. Elijah lived in a cave at the base of
> Mount Carmel. A street, not far from Girls Town, is named for him, Street of
> the Prophet. It would be unthinkable to shirk such ancestry and responsibility.[33]

That sense of ancestry and responsibility infuses the language and the tenor of
these narratives through their evocation of the dissolution of ego-boundaries
and experiences of self-transcendence, their nexus of the earthy and the
numinous, and their theurgic energy. In a brilliant analysis of contemporary
women's fiction, critic Marilee Lindemann calls attention to the recurrent
inscription of "fluid, sexual/mythical selfhood" in women's novels, position-
ing women readers "to hear in the narrative echoes of our own lost powers, to
see in its vision selves from which we seem so separated."[34] A Judaic version
of that same phenomenon weaves its way through these Jewish women's
novels. In *Lovingkindness*, Annie Johnson's final dream of Rabbi Nachman
takes place in Jerusalem, where her psychopomp relentlessly insists that she
help him find the "lost Queen." Her intellect rejects the possibility of any
such spiritual reality. But, later, when her daughter, Andrea, now living in the
Jerusalem *yeshiva* and renamed Sarai, lights the Sabbath candles, Annie feels
pulled back "into a moment when the valor of women burned with the
Sabbath candle and we thought of ourselves as covered with jewels, wandering down from eternity, dispensing favors, waving gentle hands like the
Sabbath queen bringing rest to the weary."[35]

In *Master of the Return*, Ivriya—whose name, paradigmatically, means
"Hebrew woman" and, from the Hebrew *la'avor* (to pass through, to cross),

"a boundary-crosser, a maker of transition"—yearns to overcome the claims of her (now half-paralyzed) body and to "launch her soul," and she thus becomes a penitent in an extremist sect of Bratslaver Hasidism. She marries a fellow penitent, the former drug dealer, rock musician, and egomaniac, Shmuel Himmelhoch (Shmuel=God hears; Himmelhoch=High Heaven). But driven by an androcentric, fanatical, and messianic faith, Shmuel disappears, and later apparently arranges to have their son, Akiva, kidnaped, so that, with Akiva in the role of Isaac, Shmuel can attempt to reenact the *akedah* on what the mystics believed to be the spiritual center of the world, the Even Hashettiyah, the *omphalos mundi* of Mount Moriah—also, in the tradition, the dwelling place of the *shekhinah*.[36] Imagining himself a herald of the Messiah, Shmuel tests God by binding and trying to sacrifice his and Ivirya's son.

The disappearance of Akiva had left Ivirya "heart-crippled." Now, evoking the story of Sarah, whose death is announced in Genesis directly after the telling of the Binding of Isaac, the narrator of *Master of the Return* relates that the return of Akiva from his near-sacrifice on Moriah bursts Ivirya's "woman's soul."[37] A "high-heavened" faith rooted in rejection of the female body is dangerous to children and women. Yet *Master of the Return* does not reject spiritual transformation as a desirable possibility for women; rather, it suggests an alternative model, one based, not on secrecy, grandiosity, challenge, and sacrifice, but rather on a gynocentric affirmation of life.

Named for the biblical midwives Shifra and Puah, who defied the pharaonic edict to murder all male Hebrew newborns, the novel's Shifra-Puah is presented as an "ancient Bokharan midwife" summoned to attend the birth of the baby of a woman called Tikva—Hebrew for "hope." "Listen to the push song inside you, my love," croons the midwife to Tikva. "Sing out loud with it . . . my soul!" Shifra-Puah herself sings through the birthing. As she sings, time dissolves. Age glides off her "like oil." Reaching through the birth canal into "the dark rocking womb" of Tikva, Shifra-Puah becomes "like a woman in the full power of strength of her thirty years." As she delivers the "tethered-at-the-naval, blood-and-paste-smeared, wrinkled, ancient baby," she herself arises "white and rose, radiant and triumphant, like a young girl" (124–25). The baby is a girl, among whose many given names is Geula, "redemption."

All through the novel, religious males have guarded their own sanctity by insisting on the silence of women. But "achingly close to Mount Moriah," the site of the *akedah* but also the *omphalos mundi* and the site of the dwelling of the *shekhinah,* the promise of a living redemption has come through birth, spiritually envisioned as a transformative, self-transcending woman's space that soul-sings in reverence to the energies of life and that honors the transtemporal spirit of woman as newborn, young girl, mother, and crone.

The power of woman's soul-song and its celebration of life is reiterated at the end of the novel, after the nearly sacrificed Akiva is restored to Ivirya. Ivirya nourishes the child with "milk and honey," those ancient symbols of the "plenitude and fructification" of the Land. Milk and honey are what the narrator calls "mother food": "Each time the child drew the mother food away from his face, the down above his upper lip was filmed in white, and his breath dripped sweetness. Flowing with milk and with honey."[38]

Like the *shekhinah* encompassing "all the females of the world" in her mystery, the sweetness of the song of the milk-and-honey "mother food" comes from its possession within itself of "all of the individual melodies" of "each blade of grass" in the land. The agent of true spiritual power is revealed as woman in harmony with the variousness of individual souls and the healing and nourishing energy of the land.

VI

> In the evening we wait,
> we daughters of Jerusalem.
> We smell of nana and cinnamon.
> We smell like the gardens of the king.
> Between our thighs is the grotto of Ein Gedi.
> The ascent of our breasts is like unto
> the hills of Judea.
>
> —Esther Broner, *A Weave of Women*

Reich, in *Master of the Return,* restores richness and strength to female spirituality by connecting redemption to self-transformation through the honoring of the energies of life in individuals, in the female body, and in the land. Despite the differences between the novels, a similar impulse informs Broner's *Weave of Women.* Her "tribe" of women, "who are born or arrive in the land," who were all "travelers before settling down in each other's friendships," reconceive themselves as "daughters of Jerusalem" by writing "The Women's Song of Songs." The amniotic fluid of the birthing mother Simha is likened to the Dead Sea, the River Jordan, the Nile; like the stones of Jerusalem, the women turn golden in the evening light. When one of them searches for women's words to sing, and finds only a heritage of wordless melody, her sounds give voice to the "trills of landscapes, ululating Judean hills, a song of sounds women make, lullabies and cries."[39]

The power of female spirituality is thus reclaimed not because the women invoke the *shekhinah* in their prayers. Rather, they become her agent, engaging in communal acts of a healing lovingkindness through which they themselves are transformed. They enter a mythic dimension as "Temple Priestesses, renewing themselves and saving lives" (88). When the women become trapped in their grief over the death of Simha's baby, when "the depth of the well is dry . . . as are all streams and brooks, even the river coming from Eden" (137), they journey together to the Dead Sea, where "every bruise is cut by salt" (141). Moved by compassion, love, and a profound sense of sisterhood, they chant prayers of healing evolving from the fleeting objects they perceive—the screech of a passing eagle, grains of sand, the whisper of the waves. As in *Master of the Return,* the natural world, infused with spirit in this "Holy Land," becomes the visionary space of women, affirming life.

Master of the Return ends with the image of the mother nourishing her recovered son; *Weave of Women* concludes with marriage, the promise of a future marriage, and with a question: "What will happen to . . . this caravan of women that encircles the outskirts of the city, that peoples the desert?" (294). Both books, each in its own way, celebrate woman's spirituality, but with both, as well, the reader is left still distrusting the spirituality of men. Of all these novels, in fact, only *God's Ear* holds out the promise that the redemption of female spirituality can lead to a new visionary space for both women *and* men, to a Judaism renewed through a new Sacred Marriage, in which the roles of both male and female are transformed and enriched.

Set in an eccentric vagabond community of Hasidim in the midwestern United States, *God's Ear* is a wildly comic *tour de force* rich with mysticism, *midrash,* and Hasidic lore. At the heart of the story is the charged relationship of the Hasid Yussel Fetner and the forceful Lillywhite Stevie, an empassioned "Ivriya," that is, a boundary-crossing woman haunted by her estrangement both from Judaism and from her late father, a woman who has spent years wandering from London to Annapurna to Kathmandu, avoiding Israel. Yussel is the scion of a long line of rabbis, but he "wanted no part of the soul, the law, the rabbinate, the lineage, the blood"; he wanted "only to be a wealthy Jew, sell insurance, live in his house by the ocean in Far Rockaway, be comfortable."[40] His comfort is disrupted when his father dies—and he soon finds himself responsible for leading the Rabbi Fetner's ragtag congregation of Hasidic "shmegeggies" in the wilderness of Kansas. But Yussel is by Hasidic standards no true rabbi; he is too much like the rabbi of Roiphe's "sane synagogue"; he *isn't* "crazy, of course":

> "Yussele, maybe for a nice Reform synagogue in Sante Fe for nonobservant Jews, maybe for them you're a rabbi, do a little service, a lot of weddings, talk politics on Shabbas. But for us you have an uncircumcised heart. You aren't attached. . . . When your heart is broken, then you'll be a rabbi." (114)

Yussel's heart *is* broken in the course of the novel. He is forced to face the truth that anesthetizing his heart against God also means being numb to the energy of women, ignoring and thereby belittling them, living life oblivious of their strength, intelligence, and profound spiritual needs. The catalyst for his transformation is his obsession with Lillywhite, a woman he cannot dismiss, a woman who seems to him "filled with light":

> . . . cut with such swells, prisms, curves, facets, she was fire herself. . . . Yussel thought of the Shabbas candles burning, the white shoulders of the candles, the blue flame, the hot blue center of her eyes, the flaming face of Sabbath. . . .

He'd never seen a woman with so much fire in her eyes. Except for his mother when she battled with his father. (152)

The imagery associates Lillywhite with the fiery light of the Sabbath, with the *shekhinah* herself. But the light of this *shekhinah* flames with anger—like that of Yussel's mother—for being ignored. For Lillywhite, Yussel is the male who has undermined and erased her. "I know who you are," Lillywhite confronts him. "You're five thousand years old. You won't look at me. I see you every place I go and you won't look at me" (208). In despair over his own obsession, he tries to dismiss her: "This one was a sexpot, a whore," he tells himself, "the work of the Yetzer Hara [the evil impulse]"; but, at the same time, "also maybe possibly Lillywhite and he were fragments of the same soul. . . . Why else would he be in agony without her? Someone, for good or evil, had put in front of him a woman he couldn't dismiss" (274). But Lillywhite won't let him off the hook: "You can't see my soul for my tits, can you?" she says (275).

Lillywhite doesn't want love from Yussel. She wants acknowledgment. She wants to mourn her father's death, and she wants Yussel to teach her the words to the Kaddish. By the end of the novel, Yussel has suffered too much—including the possible death of his own daughter—to continue to refuse Lillywhite's demand. He agrees to accompany her to the cemetery. And it is there they discover that they have both descended from the same Old Country *shtetl*, that they share the same ancestral roots. In a visionary flash, Yussel perceives how their souls are inextricably linked, and he experiences "the agony of this awesome soul who had no words because the men in the generations behind him had kept the words for themselves" (304).

Lillywhite and Yussel begin to sing the *kaddish* together, and then she sings alone "so loud and strong, [that] leaves rose and tumbled around her boots" (305). The voice of Lillywhite awakens the graveyard of the past into living presence, for hers is the voice of all Jewish women disempowered by a Judaism that has ignored them, a voice that embraces the confused Annie Johnson, the troubled Ivriya, as well as the longings of Judith Rafael, all the women of *A Weave of Women*. It is the collective voice of the Daughters of Jerusalem, containing "all the females in the world . . . in her mystery." When, at last, Lillywhite sings, the universe itself "holds its breath."

As her song rises, the ancient rabbis of the past awaken from their graves, singing, dancing; "drunk with grief, glory, knowledge"; their limbs, "so sanctified in the circle, each step weds worlds together" (307). The song dissolves the boundaries that separate past and present, life and death, male and female. Singing out the long-silenced voice of Jewish women, Lillywhite calls back the people from exile in the healing music of the *shekhinah*. In the presence of this voice, the male who has lived, as Blake would say, "without a female counterpart," is also changed: the stoney heart of Yussel Fetner becomes a heart of flesh. And it breaks. "The angels can hear it," says the late but present rabbi Fetner. For now "your ears hear what they should hear and your mouth speaks what it should speak and your heart feels what it should feel. . . . Mazel tov" (304–8).

Just as in *Master of the Return*, throughout *God's Ear*, the voices of Jewish women raised in prayer had been treated as a sexual distraction to be shunned by religious men intent upon their own holiness. But in Broner's words, we are "fiction writers till we can change circumstances." Although as I write these words, women's voices are still being silenced by the religious authorities at the Western Wall in Jerusalem so as not to "distract" praying men, the stories woven by Jewish-American women envision the spiritual power that would be invoked by ending that silence. At its most glorious, it is the spiritual power of the transformed and transformative, redeemed and redeeming, *shekhinah* come home.

NOTES

Parts of this chapter have appeared in "Orphans of Culture and History: Gender and Spirituality in Contemporary Jewish-American Women Writers," *Tulsa Studies in Women's Literature* 13 (Spring 1994): 127–41.

1. Anne Roiphe, *Lovingkindness* (New York: Warner, 1987), 141.

2. The tales of the imagined rabbi in Annie's dreams bear a provocative resemblance to the thirteen spiritual tales told by the actual Nachman. Over the years, there have been many translations and renditions of those tales, which are still studied by Bratslaver Hasidim as sacred texts. For a modern accurate translation, see *Nachman of Bratslav: The Tales,* translation, introduction, and commentaries by Arnold J. Band (New York: Paulist Press, 1978). For an analysis of the narrative significance of Annie's dreams, see my "Male and Female, King and Queen: The Theological Imagination of Anne Roiphe's *Lovingkindness,*" *Studies in American Jewish Literature* 10 (1991): 81–92.

3. Roiphe, *Lovingkindness*, 142.

4. Esther Broner, *A Weave of Women* (New York: Holt, Rinehart and Winston, 1978).

5. William Blake, *Jerusalem*, in *The Complete Writings of William Blake: With All the Variant Readings,* ed. Geoffrey Keynes (London: Nonsuch Press; New York: Random House, 1957), 626.

6. Nachman of Bratslav, *Outpourings of the Soul* (Jerusalem: Bratslaver Research Institute, 1980), 42.

7. Marcia Freedman, *Exile in the Promised Land: A Memoir* (Ithaca, N.Y.: Firebrand Books, 1990).

8. See my essay, "Why the Sons of God Want the Daughters of Men: William Blake and D. H. Lawrence," in *William Blake and the Moderns,* ed. Robert Bertholf and Annette Levitt (Albany, N.Y.: SUNY Press, 1982).

9. Rhoda Lerman, *God's Ear* (New York: Henry Holt and Company, 1989).

10. Miriyam Glazer, ed., *Burning Air and a Clear Mind: Contemporary Israeli Women Poets* (Athens, Ohio: Ohio University Press, 1981).

11. See Miriyam Glazer, "Exorcising the *Get:* A Ritual Healing," in *A Ceremonies*

Sampler: New Rites, Celebrations, and Observances of Jewish Women, ed. Elizabeth Resnick Levine, 61–67 (San Diego: Women's Institute for Continuing Jewish Education, 1991).

12. Nessa Rapoport, *Preparing for Sabbath* (1981; Sunnyside, N.Y.: Biblio Press, 1988); Tova Reich, *Master of the Return* (San Diego: Harcourt Brace Jovanovich, 1988).

13. Luce Irigaray, "Any Theory of the 'Subject' Has Always Been Appropriated by the Masculine,' " in *Speculum of the Other Woman,* trans. Gillian C. Gill (Ithaca, N.Y.: Cornell University Press, 1985), 135.

14. Peter Eli Gordon, "Imagining Hasidism," *Tikkun* (September-October 1990): 49–51; the quotation is from 48.

15. Susan A. Handelman, *The Slayers of Moses: The Emergence of Rabbinic Interpretation in Modern Literary Theory* (Albany, N.Y.: SUNY Press, 1982), 198.

16. Gershom Scholem, *On the Kabbalah and Its Symbolism,* trans. Ralph Manheim (New York: Schocken Books, 1965), 348, 334, 388.

17. Rapoport, *Preparing for Sabbath,* 146.

18. Zohar I, 182a; Isaiah Tishby, *The Wisdom of the Zohar: An Anthology of Texts,* vol. 1, arranged by F. Lachower and Isaiah Tishby, trans. David Goldstein (1989; Oxford: published for the Littman Library of Jewish Civilization by Oxford University Press, 1991), 410.

19. Elliot K. Ginsburg, *The Sabbath in the Classical Kabbalah* (New York: State University of New York Press, 1989), 33.

20. Scholem, *On the Kabbalah and Its Symbolism,* 106–7, 141; Raphael Patai, *The Hebrew Goddess* (1967; New York: Avon, 1978), 117.

21. Zohar I, 228b; Tishby, *The Wisdom of the Zohar,* 464.

22. Ginsburg, *The Sabbath in the Classical Kabbalah,* 101.

23. Lerman, *God's Ear,* 71.

24. Broner, *A Weave of Women,* 78.

25. Roiphe, *Lovingkindness,* 3.

26. Reich, *Master of the Return,* 130; the subsequent page reference in the text pertains to this source.

27. Roiphe, *Lovingkindness,* 11.

28. Broner, *A Weave of Women,* 242.

29. Rapoport, *Preparing for the Sabbath,* 242.

30. Esther Broner, interview, "Of Holy Writing and Priestly Voices," *Massachusetts Review* 24 (1983): 254–69; the quotation is from 255.

31. Miriyam Glazer, "Journey to Bethlehem" (in Hebrew), in *B'gvulam* (Tel Aviv: Eked, 1970), 22.

32. Dennis Silk, ed., *Retrievements: A Jerusalem Anthology* (Jerusalem: Israel Universities Press, 1968), 78; Else Lasker-Schuler, *The Land of the Hebrews,* in *Retrievements,* ed. Silk, 153.

33. Broner, *A Weave of Women,* 285.

34. Marilee Lindemann, " 'This Woman Can Cross Any Line': Power and Authority in Contemporary Women's Fiction," in *Engendering the Word: Feminist Essays in Psychosexual Poetics,* ed. Temma F. Berg et al. (Urbana: University of Illinois Press, 1989), 121.

35. Roiphe, *Lovingkindness,* 179.

36. Ginsburg, *The Sabbath in the Classical Kabbalah,* 86.

37. Reich, *Master of the Return,* 220, 239; the subsequent page reference in the text pertains to this source.

38. Ellen Golub, "Honey from the Rock: The Function of Food, the Female, and Fusion in Jewish Literature," Ph.D. dissertation, State University of New York at Buffalo, 1978, pp. 33, 240.

39. Broner, *A Weave of Women,* 9, 239, 38; the epigraph is from 261. The subsequent page references in the text pertain to this source.

40. Lerman, *God's Ear,* 3; the subsequent page references in the text pertain to this source.

30

Perversion or Perversity?
Woody and Me

Jeffrey Rubin-Dorsky

> Jewishness is a private institution.
> —Philip Roth, 1993 NPR interview
> with Terry Gross

I TRACE THE reassessment of my identity as a Jew to the echoes of an old Jewish joke. Here it is: A janitor is sweeping the back of the sanctuary when the rabbi walks up to the *bema* (altar) and begins to pray: "O Lord, King of the Universe, Mightiest of the Mighty, You are everything, I am nothing." When he finishes, he takes a seat and reads from the Torah. The janitor, who has been observing, nods in approval. Then the *khazan* (cantor) enters, goes to the *bema* and begins to pray: "O Lord, Ruler of the Heavens and the Earth, Mightiest of the Mighty, You, O Lord, are Everything; in Your eyes I am nothing." Completing the prayer, he sits next to the rabbi. The janitor nods again, then puts down his broom, walks to the front and begins to pray: "Lord of the Universe, King of kings, You are everything and I am nothing." The rabbi looks up, and upon seeing the janitor turns to the *khazan* and says, "*Nu,* look who thinks he's nothing!"

About ten years ago, while I was living in Los Angeles and teaching at UCLA, I became separated from my first wife. One day I got a call from her saying that she had just quit her lucrative consulting job, and that she was going to enroll at the University of Judaism in order to become a rabbi. She also told me that I would have to support her while she was studying.

My first thought: "*Nu,* look who thinks she's Jewish."

My second thought: "I wonder if 'support' includes making the payments on the BMW." (It did.)

Now R., like me, had never denied being Jewish, but we were little more than cultural Jews, proud of secular Jewish achievement, (irregularly) observant on holidays. So her announcement took me somewhat by surprise— "somewhat," because I was aware that she felt the big M (MEANING) was missing from her life. Maybe this decision was part of a quest. But I was hardly prepared for what followed: first, she decided to observe the Sabbath, then to keep kosher, then, after leaving the UJ, to become completely Orthodox.

"What happened to being a rabbi?" I asked.

"The Orthodox don't ordain women," she answered.

"I know," I responded with a sarcastic edge. "I meant that ironically."

"I've given up irony," she said calmly.

"This is no way for a 'nice Jewish girl' from the Bronx to be Jewish," I said. "Besides," I pointed out, "if you really follow through with this, you won't be able to have sex again until you remarry."

"What's it your business?" she said (echoing—or so it seemed to me—the young Alvy Singer's mother in *Annie Hall*), with what I could have sworn was an ironic smile.

(It wasn't until a few years later, when we were already divorced, that a friend helped me put this episode into perspective. I was having dinner in a Northampton restaurant with Don and Barbara Weber and Amy Kaplan and her husband, Harvey Weiss, and I was telling the story of how R. had become a *baal tshuve* [a Jew who has turned religious]. "It makes perfect sense," Harvey said. "You left, and who could take your place but God?")

So how was I going to be more significantly Jewish than my estranged wife? As always, I needed a model. I knew as a young man that I would have to look outside my family for mentors, since my father was a self-confessed professor of profanity, and I wanted to be a professor of poetry. When I first went to graduate school in New York, it was Jack Salzman who provided the inspiration, with his blend of the sacred and the profane—a sacred love of books expressed through a profane use of language. At Chicago, I chose Jim Miller and Bob Streeter to emulate: Jim for his sense of humor and enormous productivity, Bob for his equally fine appreciation of the absurd and his prodigious reading. As a beginning assistant professor I found my models on UCLA's radical fringe, in the historian Gary Nash and my English department colleague Ken Lincoln, both of whom had dedicated their scholarly careers to writing about the marginalized and the vanquished, and their personal lives to living well and decently in Los Angeles; in the Nowhere City they were definitely somewhere.

But who was going to nurture in me a deeper regard for Jewishness? At first I thought it might be my colleague Max Novak, a shrewd and nuanced reader of texts, a man learned in Jewish law and tradition. Max, however, had long ago figured out his relationship to Judaism, and while he willingly shared his wisdom, I discovered that I needed as a guide someone still struggling for definition; someone, like myself, uncomfortable within institutions, suspicious of affiliation, distrusting of authority; someone, that is, who understood his birthright to be alienation and whose preferred means of expressing loyalty was irreverence. After sifting through the possible candidates, I narrowed my choice to two: Henry Kissinger and Woody Allen. But because of my own birthplace, my model Jew also had to be born in Brooklyn. So it was bye-bye Henry, hello Woody.

Over the last several years, Woody Allen has become seriously interested in exploring Jewish history and values, though he has not embraced the collective culture, observed the honored rituals, or participated in communal institutions, and he never will. (For those of you troubled by events in Allen's recent past, do not put this essay aside just yet. I will explain further on about values versus Soon-Yi, about the writer-director versus the man.) In earlier films, Jewishness and the Jewish family were subjects of humor and mockery, spirits to be exorcised, and neuroses to be dealt with in therapy. When Allen ludicrously appeared in Hasid's garb in *Take the Money and Run* (1969) and *Bananas* (1971), or when he outrageously parodied Jewish family conversation around the dinner table in *Sleeper* (1973), his comic—and irreverent—intentions were clear. In this vein, the scenes that viewers tend to remember most are the contrasting portraits in *Annie Hall* (1977) of Annie's and Alvy's families (again seated at the dinner table), with the WASPs in Chippewa Falls making the politest of small talk about local events and neighbors while the Jews in Brooklyn exchange heated and overlapping words about the follies of their friends; and then the split-screen image of the two attempting to converse across a gulf of ethnic incomprehension. This double-edged satiric moment is preceded by Alvy's aside to the audience about "Grammy" Hall being a "classic Jew hater." In Grammy's eyes Alvy resembles an Eastern European ghetto-dweller, and thus Allen once again takes the opportunity to don the long black coat and wide-brimmed hat of the ultra-Orthodox Jew.

In a middle period of his career (overlapping somewhat with earlier and later phases), from *Annie Hall* to *Crimes and Misdemeanors* (1989), Jewishness was encoded in a search by Allen's fictional alter egos for *mentshlekhkayt* (a vision of moral living), a desire—and often a claim—to occupy the moral high ground. Being a *mentsh,* striving for the particular qualities Ashkenazic Jews valued in a human being—uprightness, honorableness, trustworthiness; in a word, *dignity*—cannot be achieved through either yearning or faith, but through the highest moral and intellectual values. Thus, from Alvy Singer through Cliff Stern, the Woody persona in the films in which Allen appears takes the role as moral guide, the figure on whom the audience can rely, in the midst of uncertainty and confusion, to articulate the ethical issues and problems, if not actually solve them.

In spite of the endless descriptions of Allen's alter egos as neurotics, *nebbishes,* and *schlemiels,* and in spite of Allen the director's at times unflattering camera focused satirically on Allen the actor, the primary quality of the Woody persona that audiences respond to is that of the would-be moral man in the, at best, indifferent universe (a version, it should be noted, of the "Jew as conscience of society"). Time and again we see him reaching—or struggling to reach—the difficult decision that we would all like to make in similar circumstances, the one that rejects self-interest for the greater goal of honesty or loyalty or moral clarity. Or we see him challenging characters whose actions have been based on self-gratification, willful blindness, and/or easy rationalizations. These latter figures generally get what they are after, while the Allen character stands puzzled, chagrined, angered, or overwhelmed in the face of deceit and betrayal. Here are four scenes that illustrate these situations: from *Manhattan* (1979), *Stardust Memories* (1980), *Broadway Danny Rose* (1984), and *Crimes and Misdemeanors* (1989). In each case, although the Allen character articulates the ethically right choice, it is possible to see how his shallow antagonist finds the hero's position romanticized, impractical, unreasonable—even pretentious, holier than thou.

SCENE 1 (from *Manhattan*): Isaac, a television sit-com writer and would-be novelist, confronts the cynical Yale (who has been avoiding this conversation) about dating Mary again without telling him. Demanding honesty and integrity in relationships, Isaac claims that Yale has been duplicitous with himself and his friend. Yale defends himself by accusing Isaac of self-righteousness. Turning metaphysical, Ike points to a skeleton (shades of Hamlet in his "Alas, poor Yorick" speech), saying, "Someday we'll look like him. . . . I want to be well thought of when I thin out."

SCENE 2 (from *Stardust Memories*): Sandy, the celebrated director attending a retrospective honoring his work, returns to his room where a young woman lies waiting in his bed. This groupie's goal is to "make it" with him, although he abruptly rejects the idea as basically mechanical sex with a stranger. The flaky woman won't accept his refusal, insisting that Sandy will enjoy himself if he just releases some tension and relaxes his resistance. Instead, he takes the high moral road and worries about the betrayal of her husband.

SCENE 3 (from *Danny Rose*): Danny, the patient, long-suffering talent agent, accompanies Lou and Tina after Lou's successful nightclub comeback, only to learn that Lou has made plans to change management. Shocked, Danny reminds Lou of his loyalty and all they have accomplished together, but to no avail. Danny's a big boy, says Tina, he'll get over it; Lou tells him, vulgarly, that he's "in for a taste" if things go well. Instead of responding, Danny storms off, hurt and offended. Nevertheless, he keeps the faith with his other clients who depend upon him, and goes on to give his annual Thanksgiving dinner for these dispossessed souls.

SCENE 4 (from *Crimes and Misdemeanors*): Cliff, a moderately successful documentary movie-maker, at the film's conclusion hears Judah's plot for a perfect murder in which the protagonist goes unpunished (just as Judah has). But for the epilogue Cliff proposes a Dostoevskian twist where the hero turns himself in and achieves moral stature. Judah dismisses this as mere fiction; in the real world, he says somewhat smugly, we live with sins on our conscience.

In these scenes the audience would like to identify with the Allen character's rejection of the foils' self-serving (and perhaps all-too-human) behavior. But in terms of recognizable everyday fragility, weakness, and defensiveness, their actions are more nearly our own. Not that we're supposed to approve of their justifications—Yale's "we're just people," the midnight groupie's "empty sex is better than no sex," Lou Canova's "I gotta do what's right for my career," and Judah Rosenthal's "in reality we rationalize"—or that we would find ourselves in those precise situations, but rather that we understand their self-protectiveness, recognize that in comparable dilemmas we might explain, deny, and even accept our ethical failings much as they do.

In fact, Allen himself shows some ambivalence over the moral imperative by undercutting his persona's high ideal with low-brow humor; in *Manhattan*, when Yale accuses Isaac of moral presumption, of thinking he's God, Ike quips that he has to model himself after someone. In *Stardust Memories*, the groupie tells Sandy not to be so angry, and the film then cuts to a sequence from one of Sandy's own movies where *his* persona's hostility, comically and satirically embodied as a furry monster, has escaped in order to avenge old wounds by attacking his mother, his brother, his ex-wife, and even her alimony lawyer. In *Crimes*, Judah responds to Cliff Stern's (he's much too strict, too stern, for this morally lax world) redemptive vision by telling him that he watches too many films: "If you want a happy ending, you should see a Hollywood movie." (The camera then leaves Cliff isolated in sad silence.) The undermining is gentlest in *Danny Rose:* Danny speaks passionately about his personal attachment and his devoted attention to Lou and his career, then slips into his humorous but digressive and irrelevant vaudeville *shtick*, this time about his uncle Meyer who sold apples. Moreover, by the time this scene occurs, Allen has already played—actually caricatured—Danny so broadly as a misfit (using the most exaggerated hand and facial gestures of any of his alter egos) that we can hardly locate anything of ourselves in his character.

These scenes are individually effective because each embodies emotional complexity: Allen encourages his viewers to project themselves as Ike, Sandy, Danny, and Cliff in their moments of moral clarity or righteous outrage, yet through various forms of jesting and mockery he also enables the audience to accept the fact that they rarely if ever achieve such elevation. His genius as director-actor here is to make viewers feel good about themselves even as they fall short of the standard his persona has set. Metaphorically, he assures them that "you would behave ideally if you could, and though [like Yale] you're often too easy on yourselves, it's still acceptable if you don't." "And besides," the Woody character seems to reassure us, "I'm your surrogate; despite all my other social and psychological problems, in the realm of moral action you can count on me."

Whether he intended to or not, Allen destroyed this comforting, though ultimately illusory, bond with his audience—who expected the man to behave in the same manner as his screen creations—when he entered into an affair with Soon-Yi Farrow Previn instead of retreating, as the writer-professor Gabe Roth does from his student Rain in *Husbands and Wives*. (He intensified the rupture by insisting that he gave no thought to the social, ethical, and moral implications of his actions.) In their eyes, he was suddenly no different from the Yales and Lous and Judahs; and in the guise of reprobate, he erased the image of both his own and their best selves. Reversing his implied promise, he now said, in effect, "You can't count on me anymore." Their ensuing outrage was comprehensible: having been stripped of their moral hero, either they would have to recognize themselves as deeply flawed (like Allen); or, worse, they would have to fulfill the commandments on their own. And in today's world, with its many readily available temptations, who wants to model himself or herself after God? It may well be that Allen had been preparing us for disillusionment all along, not by diminishing the significance of the hard moral choices over which his alter egos anguish, but by showing us how imperfect even these deeper characters are. In fact, even our hero's hero falls tragically short. Professor Levy in *Crimes and Misdemeanors,* Cliff's philosophical ideal, provides the most extreme example of this gap between the desirable and the possible when he betrays our hope in his life-affirming ideas through his suicide. Because Levy cannot live his own words, Cliff feels cheated; his faith goes out the window.

In later works, Jewish identity has exerted a more profound influence on Allen, providing him with a source of knowledge and a way of framing morally difficult issues. In the highly acclaimed *Crimes and Misdemeanors,* for example, Allen engages issues of sin, guilt, faith, and redemption within a clearly delineated, and respectfully presented, Jewish context. The title suggests Dostoevsky as Allen's source, but the true progenitors are Job and Ecclesiastes; the film is a meditation, if not quite a *midrash,* on Job's questions and Ecclesiastes' doubts. Critics have written a good deal about its concern with whether or not there is a moral structure to the universe—and to be sure, *Crimes and Misdemeanors* asks us to consider these sorts of theological and philosophical issues—but at its heart the problem the film ponders is how an individual can live a moral life in what the movie calls, and we experience as, the "real world."

Not social justice, then, but personal morality is the film's true subject, and through the actions of its central protagonist, the opthamologist Judah Rosenthal, who for most of the movie cannot free himself from the terrifying image of God's watchful eyes, we learn that neither fear, nor guilt, nor anxiety lead to moral choice. And through the seder table conversation—portrayed without humor by Allen the director—which focuses on the conflict between historical accuracy and spiritual truth, as well as the debate over whether the Holocaust may lead to faith or atheism, hope or cynicism, we learn that Aunt May's brutal realism will not get us there either. The voice that ultimately guides us belongs to Judah's radiantly pious father, Sol ("sun" in Spanish), who claims that if he must he would choose God over "truth," since the Almighty demands that degree of faith. His words linger long after they are pronounced, for the film underscores the idea that the moral world that governs the individual is the one he has chosen to accept.

Lingering, too, is the image of Professor Levy, the object of the Allen character Cliff Stern's latest documentary. Even though he appears transcendently calm in the few clips we see, and (seemingly) has the answers people seek about life's dilemmas, Levy fails to sustain his optimistic perspective and throws himself out the window. His wisdom and his disturbing death are supposed to make us think of Primo Levi, and the question that haunts Allen and the film, just as it must every serious reader of Levi's eloquent examinations of the moral condition of the modern world, is: Why did he commit suicide? That question may not have an answer—the film certainly cannot provide one (though Cynthia Ozick has written brilliantly about it in her essay "The Suicide Note"[1])—but to ask it, to insist that the disturbing question *must* be asked, is to engage in the kind of moral inquiry that, for me, distinguishes Jewish intellectual and artistic achievement.

If Allen has been attempting to travel the road to *mentshlekhkayt* in his films, *Crimes and Misdemeanors* shows him moving in the right direction. One reason for his success here is that Cliff Stern is a complicated, troubled character; while still acting as our moral guide, he is nevertheless so deeply flawed that, despite the confusion of some critics who see him as Allen's spokesman, we must question both his judgments and his pronouncements. In addition to being a naïve idealist, Cliff is also somewhat pompous, as well as insecure, hostile, and immature. He misreads Halley's character, underestimates Lester's intelligence (which is why, even though he is a version of the proverbial "good guy," he does not "get the girl"), and in general fails to find the right balance between the economic demands of the world and the moral demands of the soul. Thus, unlike other Allen personae, he has no answers to the questions he poses, which is one reason the film is far more disturbing than anything else Allen has produced. When Cliff tells his wife, Johanna, about his sister's terrible sexual humiliation—her new boyfriend tied her up and then defecated on her—Johanna asks the obvious question, "Why?" In its various incarnations this becomes the question at the heart of the movie: Why does God permit evil? Why do evildoers prosper? Cliff, in a rather helpless way, answers, "Would any explanation be satisfying?" "What can you answer to a 'Why?' " Which is, of course, a recapitulation of the story of Job, and in this way the film resonates with Jewish meaning. As much as sexuality is a mystery, so is the moral life, and Allen, in a far more Hebraic state of mind than ever before, confronts the issue of fashioning a moral identity in the midst of disintegrating values, especially those of Judah, the representative of worldly Jewish accomplishment.

Allen continued in this exploratory vein in *Shadows and Fog* (1992), a much misunderstood and undeservedly maligned film, where he symbolically examines the European anti-Semitism that preceded Hitler's propaganda, the dark and misplaced fear of the "other" shadowing deeper doubts about self that leads to the Final Solution of eradication. Allen's character, Kleinman, the "little man" who is enlisted against his will by a vigilante group tracking down a mysterious murder in a fog-bound city, represents the well-meaning but powerless Jew, respectful of authority (the police, the Catholic church, his employer, the mob itself) but helpless when it turns against him. Becoming the object of the vigilantes' anxiety and wrath when they cannot locate the real villain, whose ghastly deeds connote deep spiritual corruption within the city, Kleinman is nothing less than their scapegoat, referred to at one point as "no better than a piece of vermin, only fit for extermination." This echo of extremist Nazi language, along with other allusions to the Holocaust, reveals another side of Allen's investigation into the conundrums of Jewish history: specifically, why must the innocent suffer persecution, and is there any way to combat such evil? The vicious cycle of paranoia that the film dramatizes and exaggerates will eventually culminate in the victimization of the Jews. Historian Frank Fox called *Shadows and Fog* a "shameful allegory" and deplored its "mixture of sacred and profane,"[2] which is an overreaction to Allen's unsuccessful attempt to blend humor and pathos. Still, despite its defects in execution and its conflicting tone, *Shadows and Fog* should further remove doubt about Allen's commitment to fathoming his Jewish identity.

Unfortunately, it has not, especially in the wake of the Soon-Yi episode. All kinds of Jews—ranging from my mother, who never reads a book (not even mine) and rarely sees a film, to scholars like Samuel Dresner, who writes many books and is schooled in Jewish history and tradition—felt personally betrayed by what they interpreted as Allen's immorality. My mother's reaction was simple and direct: she called him a *mamzer* (literally, a bastard, but she meant he was untrustworthy, a real "lowlife"), and told me that if I continued to write about him I was as *meshugge* as he. Dresner's was more complex and because he purports to speak for Jews and has access to a substantial segment of the Jewish community through his essays, far more insidious. I want to examine it briefly in order to point out why it is both unfair and dangerous to equate Allen the man with Allen the director.

Writing in *Midstream*, Dresner spewed forth his ire, not just at Allen, but at Allen's Jewish fans as well, doing a disservice to both.[3] He first isolated particular incidents, images, or comic routines from Allen's ouevre which he claims signify "perverse behavior" (23; he means perverted, I think); for example, in *Annie Hall*, Rob, the character played by Tony Roberts, asks Allen's Alvy Singer to imagine the "mathematical possibilities" of cohabiting with sixteen-year-old twins. Dresner then magnified these into the total meaning of that body of work, despite the fact that Allen has been writing scripts for over thirty years (*What's New, Pussycat?* appeared in 1963) and directing films for more than twenty-five (*Take the Money and Run* dates back to 1969). He then cited Allen's involvement with Soon-Yi and the *alleged* child abuse of his adopted daughter, Dylan, as confirmation of that meaning. (This logic for Dresner also operates in reverse: the "paganism" of Allen's work proves that he must be guilty of real-life moral turpitude and depravity, as well as of all criminal charges against him.) Thus, for Dresner, Allen's "dramas" appeal to our "savage nature" (21).

Moreover, because Allen's devious intentions are "couched in clever dialogue, sly humor, appealing artistry, and in perverse fantasy" (22; again, he means perverted), Jews have been fooled into uncritical approval; indeed, those (like myself) who have found Allen's work not only entertaining but also morally instructive are obtuse—"and worse" (20). The more Jewish critics praise his films, and the more Jewish film-goers applaud them, the greater the corruption of the Jewish soul. "The accepting Jewish audience of Allen's writings and films," says Dresner, "has not only contributed to a betrayal of Jewish values, but to a betrayal of the Jewish people" (20). "If outrage was expressed for Woody's behavior," he asks, then "why not for his films and writings over the years?" (22), as if life and art were one and the same.

Dresner's desire to see a smooth, uncomplicated fusion of Allen's screen personae and his life as a man in the world is unsophisticated at best. Viewing artistic images as if they were pure representations of reality, he seems never to have encountered the idea that a complex, sometimes convoluted relationship exists between the artist, the work of art, and the society that is both refracted through and reflected in them. As a result, he badly misunderstands Allen's work, believing that every scene or dialogue in a film perfectly mirrors Allen's actions, or precisely echoes Allen's choices, in his private life. Moreover, for Dresner, what a narrator says in a story or a character proclaims in a film must extend and illustrate Allen's deeply held beliefs. He is blind to satire, has no ear for irony, and absolutely no recognition of irreverence. Thus, in the previous illustration from *Annie Hall,* what Dresner fails to see is that Allen is mocking the character who idealizes a "relationship" with sixteen-year-old twins as well as satirizing the West Coast culture that would celebrate such an "ideal." In leaving New York for Los Angeles, not only has Rob abandoned the pursuit of a serious acting career, but also, more problematically, he has willingly suspended his sound judgment and embraced the "hip" mores (read: shallow nonvalues) of Lotus Land, a place scorned by Allen throughout more than one of his films.

Furthermore, in his narrow discussion of Allen's cinema, Dresner gives no hint that there can be and often is an emotional distance between director and actor, so that at times the Woody character is *deliberately* made to appear foolish, immature, hostile, and anxious; in other words, he becomes an object of irony and satire, rather than a paragon of dubious virtue to be adored and emulated. That is in part what makes the films interesting to other people— even Gentiles. Isaac Davis (in *Manhattan*) is one such example: as I have previously said, Director Allen wants his audience to identify with Isaac, played by Actor Allen, when he insists on the need for forthrightness in relationships, but also expects viewers to recognize Isaac's failure—in his self-deception and in his half-truths to teenage Tracy—to live up to his own standards.

It is clear that Allen's Jewish (as well as non-Jewish) audience has enjoyed and celebrated his films over the years. But Dresner gives his fans no credit for critical discernment: because he disregards everything that is positive and uplifting, seeing everywhere instead only the negative and unsavory, he accuses us of "forsak[ing] elemental Jewish values" (23). The charge is without merit. Presumably, we would also be abandoning these values if we were to see in (New York State) Justice Wilk's custody decision on the Allen-Farrow children some of the same excessiveness that characterizes Dresner's comments. According to the *New York Times,*[4] Justice Wilk said Allen exhibited "serious parental inadequacies," such as not knowing the names of his sons' teachers, or the children's best friends, their dentists, their pediatricians. He attended parent-teacher conferences not on his own initiative, but when requested to do so by Mia Farrow. Only occasionally did he dress the children, mostly by helping them put on socks and jackets. Clearly, Allen was not involved in daily "parenting," and these and other omissions probably did disqualify him for the role of custodian.

Still, Allen resembles nothing so much as an old-fashioned father, one like my own, for example, who also could not have answered any of the questions about names of doctors put to Allen by Farrow's lawyer—that was the mother's province. A hard-working man, my father had little time and even less patience for attending to his sons' everyday needs, but like many other fathers of his generation, and like Allen, he loved his children in the way he could—by teaching the example of hard work, by making as good a living as possible, by telling stories, by buying presents, by sometimes fixing a meal. When he wanted to share something with us, he naturally followed his own interests, and he took us to a ball game. To be sure, the outing was fun, but he was generally insensitive to his sons' deeper emotional needs. No one ever accused my father of being an unloving, uncaring, irresponsible father, as the judge labeled Allen, and from this perspective Justice Wilk's opinion seems harsh and mean-spirited.

While Justice Wilk sanctified Mother Mia and scourged Father Woody—Farrow was loving and protective, he declared, whereas Allen was "self-absorbed, untrustworthy, and insensitive"—he did, however, stop short of accusing Allen of sexual perversion; Dresner, on the other hand, did not hesitate. Yet there remains absolutely no evidence of this: Allen was exonerated of molesting his stepdaughter, Dylan; and Soon-Yi, whatever one believes about Farrow's compulsive adopting, is—and was—a consenting adult. In fact, throughout all the controversy, Allen emphatically denied that he had crossed any taboo boundaries; from his perspective, his love for Soon-Yi was neither illicit nor illegal. He was never, "in *any* sense of the word," a father to Mia Farrow's adopted children, he told *Time,* not even a father surrogate. He was not part of "some type of family unit in *any* remote way" ("family" meaning the larger Farrow household). Moreover, he insisted, without discernible irony, that Soon-Yi was a "grown woman . . . probably more mature than I am."[5] Soon-Yi corroborated Allen's views in her own *Time* interview. "To think that Woody was in *any* way a father or stepfather to me is laughable."[6] At twenty-one years old, she claimed to be a fully functioning adult, capable of making independent decisions (and she certainly sounded like one, though the strained way both she and Allen repeated the word "any" in their protestations belied their calm). Her falling for Mia's ex-boyfriend may have been "offbeat," she told *Newsweek*, "but let's not get hysterical."[7]

While most of Allen's audience avoided hysteria, they did get angry, especially over what they perceived as Allen's willful obtuseness. That is, he compounded the problem and provoked further disillusionment, not only by minimizing the significance of his behavior, but also by offering banalities as pseudoexplanations at every opportunity: in *Newsweek*, in *Time*, on "60 Minutes." At times he resembled a politician practicing "deniability," especially when he maintained (in a most unfortunate phrase) that he and Soon-Yi shared "an equal-opportunity relationship."[8] Or, worse, he sounded like a parody of his characters *in extremis*. For example, at one point he described his relationship with Soon-Yi as a "major, major situation," which recalls an anxious Danny Rose, after Lou's girlfriend, Tina, gets troubling advice from a fortune-teller, telling his nostalgic crooner, "We're into a definite type of situation here, Lou . . . a complete type of situation." By contrast, Allen's personae would, at their most insightful, and in their stuttering, fumbling way, manage to articulate the intuitively right—the honest, the genuine—response. Had Allen chosen *those* moments to emulate, he might have avoided the inanity of inanities: "The heart wants what it wants." Or his schoolboy's version of romance: "You meet someone and you fall in love and that's that" (61). Better to have quoted Alexander Portnoy on the workings of lust: "*Ven der putz shteht, ligt der sechel in drerd*" (literally, When the prick stands up, the brains get buried in the ground).[9] Offensive as that phrase may have been to some, it would at least have been an engaged response. It probably would have made his audience laugh. It would, in one way or another, have made a connection with them. Clearly, he did not want one. By perversely giving interviews with no substance—in effect, going public but staying private—he declined to play the thoughtful, intelligent role his fans desired. He refused to live up to their ideals.

Ironically, this refusal to meet his audience's expectations and needs is the very characteristic—indeed, the *perverse* quality—that has made him the independent and inventive artist he has proved himself to be. His achievements warrant our continued open-mindedness, even if we remain skeptical about his past behavior. Above all, disappointment and disapproval must not cloud reason and judgment, so that in our frustration we turn a private episode into the meaning of a public career—one that is far from over, and will surely continue to produce superior work artistically, and perhaps morally as well.

I have defended Woody Allen the film-maker, even though I feel somewhat ambivalent about the man, because he has provided me, as a Jewish academic, with an imaginative model for wrestling with the issue of what it means to be a moral man in contemporary America. There can be, as I see it, no higher individual goal than *mentshlekhkayt*. In addition, Allen's continuous development as a Jewish artist has inspired me to think of myself as a *Jewish* writer in the academy; hence, with the help of my coeditor, the conception for this very book, which is certainly a departure from my usual scholarly activity.

I also admire the way Allen has responded to exigency and circumstance—some, of course, of his own making—by replenishing and renewing his fundamental commitment to his art. Radical changes in his personal life have served as a trigger for his growth as a director. In an earlier period, a split with Diane Keaton marked the end of his physical comedy (his "funny movies" with caricatured Jews) and generated the development, beginning with *Annie Hall*, of personae who muddle through moral conundrums. Most recently, he may have needed the break with Mia Farrow in order to find a new artistic direction, signaled by the unsettling film *Husbands and Wives* (1992), though its future shape (and for that matter, leading lady) is as yet unknown. The end of this nonmarriage brought to a conclusion a twelve-year period of creativity unmatched among American writer-directors, a period comprising such experimentally rich and artistically diverse films as *Zelig* (1983), *Broadway Danny Rose* (1984), *Purple Rose of Cairo* (1985), *Radio Days* (1987), and *Another Woman* (1988)—leading to the climactic fusion of humor and drama in Allen's most fully realized vision of the tragic comedy that is human existence, *Crimes and Misdemeanors* (1989), with its framework of Jewish texts and issues.

Mention of *Husbands and Wives* raises another way in which Allen serves as an influence on me. Writing in the *New York Times*, Vincent Canby wondered whether the form of *Husbands,* producing the sense that we are watching a narrative in which the characters are reticent participant-actors, shows Allen to be working in a "post-modern mode,"[10] and the question is an important one, Jewishly speaking. (Recall that the film is shot with a jerky, hand-held camera, giving the effect of an impromptu home movie that no one wants to be in.) For all its assault on the possibility of shared reality, on absolute truth—there are many realities here and no central truth—and for all its undermining of belief in the stable and knowable self, the film as text shies away from regarding itself as the source of experience rather than its reflection. Though the film-within-the-film's camera may bully the actors and intrude into the characters' lives, it does not create those lives; reality, fragmented and in shards though it may be, is not, as it would be in an early Bergman film, an artifact of imagination. That is because, for Allen, social justice and righteous action in the world still matter, and qualities such as honesty, loyalty, and generosity still define personal success.

Allen thus has not abandoned the search for a meaningful life in the world, has not given up faith—his Jewish faith—in people's ability to grow in moral stature. Rather, what he articulates at the end of *Husbands and Wives* is a desire to be liberated from the contours of an old mask, one that has outlived its usefulness. Gabe's final, self-reflexive words ("Can I go? Is this over?"), signaling the story's end, indicate his reluctance to reveal more of himself, and at the same time show the film-maker's spirit rebelling against the frame of the film, just as Allen the man attempted to escape (albeit somewhat clumsily) from the narrative of the last twelve years of his life with Mia Farrow. Undoubtedly a newer version of his persona will take shape in yet another cinematic form, for as we can see from his films during those years, Allen has found what Philip Roth calls the "disguise of me" enormously energizing and, in spite of his pronouncements to the contrary, a means of exploring, and transcending the intractability of, selfhood.

In fact, one can already see the outlines of this direction in the recent film *Bullets over Broadway* (1994), where a much younger actor (John Cusack, substituting for Allen himself) plays an inexperienced, idealistic playwright struggling with the ethics of Broadway, the purity of Art, and the morality of sexual fidelity—all concerns of paramount importance in both the real and imagined worlds of Woody Allen. (The film even kills off a ditzy blonde actress.) Using a period piece and the added device of a play within the film (titled *God of Our Fathers*) to camouflage, and psychologically distance himself from, the personal, Allen examines the issue of whether an "artist creates his own moral universe," words spoken in the film, interestingly enough, by an untrustworthy figure named Flender (sounds like philanderer, which he is). Yet this idea was championed by Allen during his crisis with Mia Farrow, and in *Bullets over Broadway* the true wordsmith is also a gangster and murderer. A ruthless Nietzchean monster-hero, Cheech prizes direct, vital language above everything, and the contradictions of his character force us to ask such questions as, Who is an artist, and can you separate the artist from the man? What sacrifices does art demand, and what compromises, if any, must the artist make with his society? Continuing in his Jewish mode of inquiry, in *Bullets over Broadway* Allen also ponders the problem of what happens when Art supersedes humanity, when in the modern world (the film is set in the 1920s, the era of Joyce and Hemingway) the Artist replaces the (Hebrew) God of our Fathers.

Regarding my own Jewishness, I see myself in a continuing phase of renewal and regeneration, though still uncertain about definition. My activity is primarily verbal and intellectual: I read widely in Jewish cultural history, seeking to incorporate this material into scholarly and critical projects, foremost a book on Philip Roth, Woody Allen, and the uses of irreverence, as well as this volume on Jewish consciousness among scholars like myself. I study Jewish humor, learning to appreciate the role of comic irony in the resistance to malevolent purpose and tyrannous circumstance. I offer courses on Jewish-American literature, hoping to show my students the extent to which Jews have both embraced and shaped American culture and society. Yet I wonder and ask: Is this enough? Is it not possible to connect to some mode of organized Jewish life?

I know, however, my Jewishness cannot take the form of either institutional participation or communal consciousness. Like Woody Allen, who insists on controlling every aspect of film production (and thus works exclusively with small distribution companies), I cling fiercely—perversely perhaps—to a belief in independence, though at the same time knowing full well the degree to which true "individuality" is illusory. Consequently, I am suspicious of all forms of community, not because, as Allen jokingly claims (following Groucho Marx), "I would never join an organization that would have me as a member," but rather because all my experience of groups and group destiny has been unsatisfying: sooner or later the desire for harmony yields to the need for ego gratification, and what had been peaceful cooperation turns into a war of competing agendas. At some point, order must be imposed, and someone else's idea of order generally feels like coercion to me. This has been true of my contact with the larger Jewish community as well, though I have enjoyed working with the contributors to this collection, who constitute a "community" of Jewish scholars.

Nor does Jewishness, as it does for many others, move me in the direction of Israel, either as a nexus of spiritual existence or as a source of cultural nourishment. I have always believed that America is as much a modern homeland as Israel, more so, in fact, if "home" means a place where Jews can live peacefully, without turbulence and strife, *as Jews*. Like Woody Allen, I have a great regard for the Jewish state, support its striving for harmonious coexistence in the Middle East, yet am troubled by the history of its dealings with the Palestinians in the West Bank and Gaza. That is why I again defend him, this time for having written, in the *New York Times*, at a time of particularly severe Israeli suppression of the West Bank uprising, that although he has "always been outraged at the horrors inflicted on this little nation by hostile neighbors, vile terrorists, and much of the world at large," and while he has "no sympathy for the way the Arabs have treated the Israelis," he is nevertheless "appalled . . . by the treatment of the rioting Palestinians by the Jews" (i.e., "breaking the hands of men and women so they can't throw stones," withholding "food and medical supplies . . . to make a rebellious community 'uncomfortable,'" etc.).[11] The charge against him was moral posturing; his behavior, according to conservative columnist Charles Krauthammer, was like that of other Jews who spoke out in the hope that an American audience would not accuse them of complicity with Israel's repressive policies. "Woody Allen was not writing to move [Yitzhak] Shamir or [Yitzhak] Rabin," Krauthammer sarcastically says, "he was trying to reassure his tablemates at Elaine's: Not me."[12] Unfortunately, Allen's column included among its sincere statements what I take to be attempts at parodic humor; still, I believe he was expressing genuine anguish over the suffering caused, but also experienced, by Israel. The op-ed piece coincided with the making of *Crimes and Misdemeanors,* and serves as yet another indication of Allen's engagement with issues of deep concern to all Jews.

Thus for me, Jewishness focuses on neither congregation nor Zionism. Now, as it did in the beginning, Jewishness centers on texts. When I was a boy attending the local synagogue (which happened to be Orthodox) on Saturdays, I would squirm and fidget all during the service, mumbling the prayers partly in earnest, though mostly in protest. But during the rabbi's sermon, when my friends were escaping the sanctuary, I sat at attention as he explicated the Torah passages, thrilled at how he mined meaning from words that I read but could not penetrate. The characters and events were always vibrantly real to me, and it was doubly pleasing to discover that the stories held profound truths. In fact, exegesis was so satisfying that, although I felt uncomfortable, I did not rebel when interpretation slid inexorably into pre-scription. (It seems logical to me now that a text-centered people like the Jews would expect their books—their Book—to provide moral guidance, both absolutely and temporally.) Though often I had trouble obeying Jewish law, failing to subdue my will to its demands, and had misgivings about a wrathful Authority that even then seemed arbitrary (and too much like my father in an angry mood), I nevertheless understood the necessity for both, knew that how you behave, publicly as well as privately, truly matters.

Rebellion, of course, came later, though recently I have begun to think again about these issues of authority, hierarchy, and structure, codes, prescrip-tions, and laws, mostly because of my developing friendship with a rabbi of an Orthodox synagogue. Considered liberal by Orthodox standards–he runs a Saturday service with mixed seating—and with many secular accomplish-ments to his credit, he nevertheless believes that the survival of Judaism rests solely within the Orthodox community, that, indeed, strict Orthodoxy is the only *authentic* form of Judaism. The Orthodox, he says, have not capitulated to the demands of the social and material world; they have not compromised their religion for worldly rewards. Judaism, he tells me, is not a menu; selecting a law to observe from column A, a ritual to follow from column B, will not, in the end, preserve the heritage of the Jewish people, which, he insists, resides in religious observance. "Jewishness," he claims, is amorphous, little more than a cultural "feeling" that easily dissipates, whereas Judaism, the faith, belief, and *practice* of the Fathers and Mothers (as I said, he tends toward liberalism), is granitelike, of and for the ages.

"But, Rabbi," I protest, "many of the Orthodox remove themselves as much as possible from contact with society; they wish to be left alone. What happens then to *tikkun olam* [the commandment to heal and repair the world]?" "Yes," he responds, "it is of the utmost importance, and cannot be overlooked, which the Orthodox often do." After this paradox, I ask him many other questions: "Who is a Jew?" I want to know. "And why exclude those who proclaim their faith but were not born to a Jewish mother? What about the Jewish Renewal movement that is enlivening and enriching many Jewish lives? Are not these Jews *choosing* a way of being spiritual and, apparently, sustaining it?" As he is both a learned and patient man, he answers fully and generously. We argue and debate; I listen to lectures and presentations at his temple; I even offer a Jewish-American film series there on Sunday evenings, and another forum focusing on Woody Allen! He invites me to Shabbot dinner, and I go, wearing a *yarmulke* and respectfully participating in the prayers. But were he to ask me, I would steadfastly refuse to attend services, would resist his efforts to bring me, as it were, into the fold.

Still, I have my doubts. Can my books and my reading, my research and my writing, continue to nurture me—and sustain my sense of myself—as a Jew? Is it enough to be an individual engaging, and sometimes struggling with, Jewish texts, subjects, and themes? Or is the rabbi right: what matters is only that which has been and can continue to be observed and practiced in a highly codified form? Was my ex-wife right (God forbid!): the only way to be Jewish is to go all the way? How will I know? Where, I ask myself, is the answer?

And then it comes to me:

> Let your Jewish conscience by your guide.
> —Philip Roth, *Operation Shylock*

NOTES

1. Cynthia Ozick, "The Suicide Note," *New Republic* (March 21, 1988): 32–36.
2. Frank Fox, "A Holocaust Parable," *Midstream* (October 1992): 28.
3. Samuel Dresner, "Woody Allen and the Jews," *Midstream* (December 1992): 19–23; the subsequent page references in the text pertain to this essay.
4. Peter Marks, "Allen Loses to Farrow in Bitter Custody Battle," *New York Times*, June 8, 1993, pp. A1, B16.
5. Walter Isaacson, " 'The Heart Wants What It Wants' " (interview with Woody Allen), *Time*, August 31, 1992, pp. 59–61.
6. "Soon-Yi: Woody Was Not My Father" (interview with Soon-Yi Farrow Previn), *Time*, August 31, 1992, p. 61.
7. "Soon-Yi Speaks: 'Let's Not Get Hysterical' " (statement of Soon-Yi Farrow Previn), *Newsweek*, August 31, 1992, p. 57.
8. Isaacson, " 'The Heart Wants What It Wants,' " 61; the subsequent page references in the text pertain to this interview.
9. Philip Roth, *Portnoy's Complaint* (New York: Random House, 1969), 128.
10. Vincent Canby, "Is Life Following Art? It Doesn't Matter" (review of *Husbands and Wives*), *New York Times*, September 18, 1992, p. B4.
11. Woody Allen, "Am I Reading the Papers Correctly?" *New York Times*, January 28, 1988, op-ed page.
12. Charles Krauthammer, "No Exit," *New Republic* (March 14, 1988): 29.

GLOSSARY OF HEBREW, YIDDISH, AND
"YINGLISH" TERMS

NOTES ON CONTRIBUTORS

INDEX

GLOSSARY OF HEBREW, YIDDISH
AND "YINGLISH" TERMS

Contributors to this volume collaborated on these definitions, drawing on family traditions and on reference sources including Leo Rosten's *The Joys of Yiddish*, the *Oxford English Dictionary*, the *New Shorter Oxford English Dictionary*, *Webster's New World Hebrew Dictionary*, Abba Eban's *Heritage*, and Rabbi Joseph Telushkin's *Jewish Literacy*. We have retained the contributors' quirky spellings as a sign of the diverse dialects, pronunciations, and transliteration traditions that existed among Ashkenazic Jewry in the U.S. during the twentieth century—dialects, pronunciations, and traditions that are giving way, in contemporary America, to the more standardized transliteration practices for Hebrew and Yiddish codified by YIVO Institute of Jewish Research in New York and the Library of Congress. The editors also thank Milton Fisher, Itzik Gottesman, Riki and Ezra Greenspan, and Karen King for their help, and contributor Seth Wolitz for his guidance.

afikomen: (Greek) the piece of matzoh that must be eaten by everyone present before the Passover seder is considered finished; family traditions often involve young children hiding or hunting for the *afikomen* at the seder.

akedah: (Hebrew) the binding of Isaac (Genesis 22:1–19).

alef-beyz: (Yiddish, Hebrew) (*alef-bet* in contemporary Hebrew pronunciation) the Hebrew alphabet.

aliyah: (Hebrew) lit.: ascent; "going up" to the Torah (see below) to recite the blessing during the Torah reading; to make *aliyah* means to immigrate to Israel.

allyah: see *aliyah* (above).

alrightnik: ("Yinglish") someone rich and successful; nouveau riche; coined by Abraham Cahan, editor of the most successful Yiddish newspaper in early twentieth-century America and author of *The Rise of David Levinsky*.

am avi: (Hebrew) people of my father.

am avoteinu: (Hebrew) people of our fathers.

Am Yisrael: (Hebrew) the Jewish people.

Ashkenaze: see Ashkenazi (below).

Ashkenazi: (Hebrew, also English) (n.) pertaining to Jews of Central, Northern, or Eastern European descent; a Jew of this descent. (From "Ashkenaz," a Hebrew name for Germany; Ashkenazic Jews originally spoke Yiddish [see below].)

Ashkenazic: the adjectival form of "Ashkenazi" (see above).

Ashkenazim: pl. of "Ashkenazi" (see above).

azoy: (Yiddish) so, very.

baal tshuve: (Hebrew) lit.: one possessed of an answer; a Jew who returns to observant religious life (*t'shuva* means "repentance, a return to God").

Babba Metzia: (Aramaic, Hebrew) lit.: middle gate; name of a tractate of the Talmud (see below).

bar mitzvah: (Hebrew) lit.: son of the commandment; the age (thirteen) at which a Jewish male becomes responsible for fulfilling the commandments, and standing for a *minyan* (see below); usually marked in the synagogue by a young man's first *aliyah* (see above) to the Torah (see below).

bat mitzvah: (Hebrew) female equivalent of bar mitzvah, usually at twelve years of age.

bema: see *bima* (below).

bet midrash: (Hebrew) house of study; usually an institution of Torah learning. In Israel today, often refers to a *yeshiva* (see below).

bima: (Hebrew) lit.: platform or stage on which Torah readers stand.

bissel: (Yiddish) a little.

borchu: (Hebrew) "Let us bless"; leads into the recital of the *Sh'ma* (see below).

brent (Yiddish) burns.

brit: (Hebrew; Yiddish, *bris*) convenant; refers to God's covenant with Israel; *brith milah:* ritual circumcision of the male child, performed on the eighth day of the child's life.

bubbe: (Yiddish) grandmother.

bücher: a Yiddishization of the Hebrew *bachur,* which means "boy"; a *yeshiva-bücher* is a boy who attends *yeshiva,* a schoolboy.

chainik: (Yiddish) see *chaynik* (below).

challah: (Hebrew) lit.: a piece of dough removed from the bread dough before baking, then burned or discarded; *challah* commonly refers to the braided egg bread prepared for the Sabbath meal and festivals.

chalupses: (Yiddish) stuffed cabbage.

Chanukah: (Hebrew) lit.: dedication; Jewish holiday, the Festival of the Lights or the Feast of the Maccabees, celebrated on the twenty-fifth of the month of Kislev. Begun in 165 B.C.E. to celebrate the dedication of the new sacrificial altar in the Temple of Jerusalem, where several years earlier at the same site Antiochus Epiphanes had erected an altar upon which Jews were to offer sacrifices to pagan deities. Legend has it that when the Jews recaptured the temple, there was enough sacred oil to burn in the candelabrum (the eternal light) for one day, but the oil miraculously lasted for eight days and nights, enough time for more sanctified pure olive oil to be readied. In commemoration of this miracle, the holiday of Chanukah lasts for eight days each year.

charoses: (Yiddish) see *charoseth* (below).

charoseth: (Hebrew) (also *charoset*) a mixture of apples, walnuts, cinnamon, and red wine (the Ashkenazic version) eaten at Passover seders to represent the bitter work of captivity (the mortar and bricks made for the pharaohs) and also the sweet deliverance from bondage (the Sephardic version may include dried apricots and other fruits).

chaserei: (Yiddish) lit.: pig stuff; junk, garbage, filth (comes from the Hebrew *chasir,* meaning "pig").

Chasid: (Yiddish) see "Hasid" (below).

chassenes: (Yiddish) weddings.

chaynik: (Yiddish) teapot. ("Don't *hak* me a *chaynik*"—lit., "Don't knock my teapot"—means "Don't keep talking on and on and on like that.")

chazon: (Hebrew) vision.

cheder: (Hebrew, Yiddish) Hebrew: lit.: room; Yiddish: religious elementary school. (Elementary education was given in a room, often the kitchen, of the home of the *melamed,* or teacher.)

chederim: pl. of *cheder* (see above).

cheyn: (Hebrew, Yiddish) charm, grace.

chochma: (Hebrew) wisdom.

chreyn: (Yiddish) horseradish.

chuppa: (Yiddish) the canopy under which a Jewish couple is married.

chusen: a Yiddishization of *chusid,* from the Hebrew "Hasid" (see below).

chutzpah: (Yiddish) nerve, gumption, gall.

chutzpahdik: (Yiddish) having nerve, gumption.

converso: Jew who converted to Christianity in medieval Spain to avoid persecution; many secretly maintained Jewish traditions. See also *marrano* (below).

dalet amot: (Hebrew) lit.: four cubits; used as private space.

daven: (Yiddish) to pray.

davened: ("Yinglish") see *daven* (above). (The Yiddish verb is here conjugated as an English verb, with an -ed ending added.)

Dayenu: (Hebrew) "It would have been enough"; song of praise sung at the Passover seder.

derech erets: (Hebrew) lit.: the way of the country; usually means ethical behavior.

dreidel: see *dreidl* (below).

dreidl: (Yiddish) four-sided top. Each side contains a Hebrew letter representing the sentence, "A Great Miracle Happened There" (or in Israel, "A Great Miracle Happened Here"). Games are played with the top during Chanukah.

Elohim: (Hebrew) a plural appellation for God, indicating a collective being.

El Shaddai: (Hebrew) lit.: Almighty; an appellation for God.

Eretz Yisrael: (Hebrew) the land of Israel.

Even Hashettiyah: (Hebrew) the rock from which God created the world; foundation stone from the primeval waters of the deep.

eyn: (Yiddish) one.

farmisht: (Yiddish) (adj.) confused, mixed up. See also *gemisht* (below).

fayerl: (Yiddish) little fire.

ferbisiner: (Yiddish) bitter one.

ferbissiner: see *ferbisiner* (above).

fleishig: (Yiddish) meat or meat products.

freilach: see *freylach* (below).

freylach: (Yiddish) (also *freylekh*) (adj.) joyful; (n.) a Jewish wedding dance.

frummies: ("Yinglish") nonderogatory slang for observant Orthodox Jews; derives from the Yiddish *frum,* which is an adjective meaning "religious, observant, Orthodox." *Frummies* is the Anglicized plural of the Yiddish *frummer* (a *frum* man) and *frummeh* (a *frum* woman).

Galitzianers: a nineteenth-century term for the Jews of Galicia, an area that became part of the former Soviet Union. In the social hierarchy, Galitzianers were considered less urbane than Litvaks (see below), but both were considered culturally inferior to German Jews.

galut: (Hebrew) diaspora; dispersion of the Jews to the lands outside Israel; a state of alienation.

gefeyrlach: (Yiddish) dangerous, terrible.

gehenna: (Hebrew) (*ge'hinom*) hell.

gelt: (Yiddish) lit.: gold; money; also short for Chanukah-*gelt*, chocolate "gold coins" given to children for Chanukah.

Gemara: (Hebrew) that part of the Talmud (see below) that consists of the commentaries and discussions of the oral law, the Mishnah (see below).

gemisht: (Yiddish) lit.: mixed; often used to mean "confused" or "mixed up." See also *farmisht* (above).

genug: (Yiddish, also German) enough (as in "Stop! Enough already!").

golem: (Hebrew) an artificial figure constructed in the shape of a human and endowed with life.

gonef: see *gonif* (below).

gonif: (Yiddish) thief (from Hebrew *ganav*).

gornisht: (Yiddish) nothing.

goy kadosh: (Hebrew) a holy nation.

goy: (Yiddish) a non-Jew.

goyim: pl. of *goy* (see above).

goyish: (Yiddish) non-Jewish.

goyishe: see *goyish* (above).

goyishe kop: (Yiddish) lit.: a non-Jewish head; to say that someone has a *goyishe kop* means that you think he/she is not very smart.

Gush Emonim: (Hebrew) (also Gush Emunim) movement of right-wing Jewish fundamentalist settlers in Eretz Yisrael (see above), mainly in the West Bank, deriving from the belief that the entire land of Israel was sanctified to the Jews, and its redemption from non-Jewish hands is therefore considered to be a *mitzvah* (see below). *Emunim* means "faithful people."

Ha-Kodesh Barukh Hu: (Hebrew) "The Holy One, blessed be He"; a name for God.

Hadassah: (Hebrew) lit.: Esther. Name of the charitable women's organization founded by Henrietta Szold (1860–1945), the largest Jewish organization in the United States.

hadlakat nerot: (Hebrew) lighting candles for the Sabbath, for holidays, or on the eve of the Sabbath or holidays.

Haftorah: (Hebrew) portion of the Prophets read in the synagogue after the weekly portion of the Pentateuch (see below).

haggadah: (Hebrew) lit.: legend or parable, tale or "telling"; the Passover or Pesach Haggadah is a collection of stories, prayers, parables, and songs read at the seder (see below) that detail the story of the Israel's bondage in and flight from Egypt.

haggadot: pl. of *haggadah* (see above).

hagim: (Hebrew) holidays.

haimish: (Yiddish) homelike or homey; "down-home."

hak: (Yiddish) knock. ("Don't *hak* me a *chaynik*," or "*Hak nit keyn chaynik*"—lit.: "Don't knock my teapot"—means "Don't talk my ears off; don't keep yammering away like that.")

halachah: (Hebrew) lit.: the way; refers to Jewish law and Jewish jurisprudence; a legal decision based on interpretation of the Torah (see below) through the guidance of the oral tradition.

halachot: pl. of *halachah* (see above).

halakhah: see *halachah* (above).

hamentaschen: see *homantashen* (below).

Hanukkah: see Chanukah (above).

Haphtorah: see Haftorah (above).

Hasid: (Hebrew) a pious person; a follower of Hasidic philosophy and a way of life.

Hasidic: the adjectival form of "Hasid" (see above).

Hasidim: (Hebrew) pl. of "Hasid" (see above); lit.: members of a religious movement that began in Eastern Europe in the eighteenth century, founded by the leader known as the Ba'al Shem Tov, regarded at its founding as religiously liberal and revolutionary; term often used today to refer to a range of ultra-Orthodox, pious Jews.

Haskalah: (Hebrew) the movement in eighteenth-century Germany, led by Moses Mendelssohn (1729–86) and his followers, that urged Jews to discard what was viewed as a medieval frame of mind and to enter the modern world; the Jewish Enlightenment; secular education among Jews.

havurot (pl. of *havurah*): (Hebrew) fellowship circles organized for the purpose of spiritual, cultural, and social growth.

heder: see *cheder* (above).

helfin: (Yiddish) to help ("*gornisht helfin*": nothing helps, or can't do anything about it).

heys: (Yiddish) hot.

Hillel: (Yiddish) name of a great rabbi from the first century B.C.E.; name of a national Jewish organization devoted to meeting the needs of Jewish college and university students; also commonly used to refer to the building on any particular campus that houses this organization.

hokhmah: see *chochma* (above).

homantashen: (Yiddish) tri-cornered filled pastries eaten on the holiday of Purim (see below) meant to represent the hat of the villain Haman.

hora, horah: (Hebrew) a traditional Jewish folk dance.

Jahweh: (Hebrew) see "Yahweh" (below).

judenrein: (German) (adj.) cleansed of Jews.

kabbalah: (Hebrew) Jewish mysticism; used to apply to entire range of Jewish mystical activity.

Kaddish: (Aramaic) lit.: an Aramaic prayer of praise and acceptance more than two thousand years old, some version of which is recited at every prayer service. One form of Kaddish is recited in memory of the dead, and the term is often used to refer in general to the mourner's prayer that family members (originally only sons) recite daily during the year after the death of a parent and thereafter on the anniversary of the death.

kashrut: (Hebrew) the system of Jewish dietary laws, including which foods are allowed and which are forbidden, which foods may not be eaten together, and how animals should be slaughtered. The major categories of foods within the laws of *kashrut* are *milchig* (see below), milk products; *fleishig* (see above), meat products; and *pareve,* neither a meat nor a milk product, which therefore can be eaten with either.

kepot: pl. of *kipah* (see below).

ketubot (pl. of *ketuba*): (Hebrew) marriage contracts.

kharoset: see *charoseth* (above).

khazan: (Hebrew) cantor.

khazn: (Yiddish) cantor.

kibbitzing: ("Yinglish") see *kibitz* (below). (The Yiddish verb is here conjugated as an English verb, with an -ing ending added.)

kibbutz: (Hebrew) a communal farming settlement.

kibitz: (Yiddish) to banter, tease, make provocative comments, fool around verbally.

kiddush: (Hebrew) lit.: sanctification; prayer recited over wine before a Sabbath or holiday meal, at weddings, and so forth.

kind: (Yiddish) child.

kinderlach: (Yiddish) little children.

kipah: (Hebrew) a skullcap, religious headcovering.

kleyne: (Yiddish) little.

klezmer: (Yiddish) musician; Eastern European Jewish traditional music played at weddings and celebrations.

kol ishah: (Hebrew) lit.: voice of a woman; a phrase in rabbinic literature which refers to a prohibition against hearing the singing voice of women because it was considered seductive.

krum: (Yiddish) crooked and bent.

kvell: (Yiddish) to take pride in.

la'avor: (Hebrew) to pass through, to cross.

Ladino: (Judeo-Arabic) a language spoken by some Sephardic Jews, based on Old Spanish and written in Hebrew characters.

landslayt: pl. of *landsman* (see below).

landsman: (Yiddish) a person from the same region in the Old Country; a countryman.

landsmanshaft: (Yiddish) an association of *landslayt* (see above).

latkes: (Yiddish) potato pancakes, traditionally served during Chanukah (see above).

le hadlik nerot: infinitive form of *hadlakat nerot* (see above).

lernt: (Yiddish) teaches, studies.

Litvaks: a nineteenth-century term for the Jews that used to live in Lithuania. In the social hierarchy, Litvaks were considered more urbane than Galitzianers (see above), but both were considered culturally inferior to German Jews.

Lubovitch: (Yiddish) a Hasidic (see above) movement begun in Lubovitch, Russia, at the end of the eighteenth century, now headquartered in Brooklyn, New York; a member of the Lubovitcher movement.

Maimonides (RaMbaM): a name by which Moses ben Maimon (1135–1204) was known. Maimonides was a prolific and influential twelfth-century Jewish sage, the author of the first systematic code of Jewish law, as well as an important philosophical statement on Judaism (see *Moreh Nevukhim,* below), and many books on medicine. He was physician to the sultan of Egypt and leader of the Jewish community of Cairo.

mamzer: (Hebrew, Yiddish) lit.: a bastard; someone untrustworthy, a lowlife.

mandelbrot: (Yiddish) cookies cut from an almond loaf made of cookie dough.

Ma nish-ta-naw ha-lai-law hazeh meekawl ha-laylos?: (Hebrew) "Why is this night different from all other nights?" The central question asked by the youngest child in the family at the Passover seder (see below); prompts retelling of the Passover story to assembled group.

maror: (Hebrew) bitter herbs eaten during the Passover seder (see below); symbol of suffering of the Israelites.

marrano: (Spanish) lit.: swine, pig; originally used contemptuously to describe a Jew in medieval Spain who professed to be converted to Christianity to avoid persecution, but who secretly maintained Jewish traditions. (This originally derogatory term is now more commonly used than *converso* [see above], since, as Abba Eban notes in *Heritage,* "history is usually written by the victors.")

matzah: see "matzoh" (below).

matzoh: (Hebrew) unleavened bread eaten to help commemorate the Exodus during Passover week.

maven: (Yiddish) an expert, a knowledgeable person.

maychelach: (Yiddish) delectable morsels.

mazel tov: (Hebrew) lit.: good luck; congratulations.

mazol tov: see *mazel tov* (above).

mehuyev: (Hebrew) obligated; committed, responsible for.

melamdim: pl. of *melamed* (see below).

melamed: (Hebrew) teacher.

mensch: see *mensh* (below).

mensh: (Yiddish) a person who is honorable, upright, trustworthy; a fine person.

mentsh: see *mensh* (above).

mentshlekhkayt: (Yiddish) civility; a vision of moral living; ethical behavior.

meshugas: (Yiddish) craziness (noun form of *meshugge*).

meshugge: (Yiddish, Hebrew) crazy.

meshugenah: (Yiddish) a crazy person.

meydele: (Yiddish) little girl.

mezuzah: (Hebrew) lit.: doorpost. Small case containing parchment inscribed on one side with the texts of Deuteronomy 6:4–9 and 11:13–21, and on the other with the divine name Shadai, attached to the right side of the doorpost in Jewish houses (and sometimes on the doorposts of rooms within the house, as well) as literally commanded in the text.

midrash: (Hebrew) lit.: commentary. An ancient Jewish narrative commentary on some part of the Hebrew scriptures, using allegory, parable, and story.

mikvah: (Hebrew; Yiddish, *mikveh*) ritual bath.

milchig: (Yiddish) milk or other dairy products.

minyan: (Hebrew) quorum of ten adult Jews (over age thirteen) required for Jewish religious services (in the past, and among the Orthodox, ten male adults).

mishigas: see *meshugas* (above).

Mishnah: (Hebrew) a six-volume collection of laws which forms the basis of the Talmud (see below) and embodies the written version of the oral law; portion of the Talmud containing the code of laws; also, an individual law in the Mishnah is called a *mishnah.*

mitzvah: (Hebrew) commandment; act of religious duty or obligation; sometimes understood to mean "good deed."

mitzvot: pl. of *mitzvah* (see above).

mitzvot assey she eyn ha-z'man grama: (Hebrew) commandments of things a Jewish person is required to do at specific times of the day; traditionally Jewish women are not obligated to observe such time-bound positive commandments.

Moreh Nevukhim: (Hebrew) *Guide for the Perplexed,* a book by Moses ben Maimon (also known by his acronym, RaMbaM, or as Maimonides).

Na'asseh ve nishma: (Hebrew) "Let us do and [then] hear [understand]" (Exodus 24:7); refers to the unquestioned acceptance of the commandments.

nachas: (Yiddish) pleasure, satisfaction.

nafke: (Yiddish) prostitute.

nar, narr: (Yiddish) fool.

nebbish: ("Yinglish") a born loser, an unlucky person, or sometimes used to mean "a real nothing."

nem: (Yiddish) lit.: take.

niddah: (Hebrew) condition of a woman's ritual uncleanness during and after menstruation and after giving birth; obligations connected with this condition, including obligation to go to the *mikvah* (see above).

Nu?: (Yiddish) So? What's up?

nudge: (Yiddish) (n., v.) nag.

oy vey: (Yiddish) Oh no!

payos: (Hebrew) long, curly sidelocks worn by some sects of Hasidic Jews (see Hasidim, above); one of the identifying marks of these groups.

Pentateuch: (Greek) the five books of Moses.

Pesach: (Hebrew) Passover. Jewish holiday celebrated the evening of the fourteenth day of the month of Nisan. Commemorates the "passing over" of the Israelites' homes by the Angel of Death when the Egyptians were plagued with the loss of their firstborn, and, more generally, the Israelites' liberation from bondage.

Pirke Avot: (Hebrew) one of the sixty-three tractates of the Mishna (see below), usually translated as *Ethics of the Fathers,* containing moral advice in the form of the most famous sayings and proverbs of leading rabbis and rabbinic scholars.

pripetshik: (Yiddish) broad roof of the hearth in the main room of a Jewish home in the *shtetl* (see below).

Purim: (Hebrew) Feast of Esther, celebrated on the fourteenth day of the month of Adar; commemorates the foiling of a plot by a villain named Haman to kill all the Jews in ancient Persia.

quatsch: (German; Yiddish, *kvatch*) rot, nonsense.

rachmanut: (Hebrew) see *rachmones* (below).

rachmones: (Yiddish) compassion.

Rashi: (1040–1105) a great eleventh-century Jewish scholar and commentator on the Old Testament and Talmud. Rashi is an acronym for *Rabbi Solomon* (or *Shlomo*) bar *Isaac.* Rashi's commentary is printed as part of the Talmud (see below).

rav: see *rov* (below).

rebbe: (Yiddish) rabbi, teacher, Hasidic rabbi.

rebbitsin: (Yiddish) the wife of a rabbi.

Rosh Hashanah: (Hebrew) Jewish New Year, celebrated in the month of Tishrei. One of the two holidays referred to as the High Holy Days, or Days of Awe, a time of ethical and religious reassessment of one's life.

rov: (Hebrew) lit.: majority or head.

ruach: (Hebrew) spirit of life; winds; Ruach Ha Kodesh is the "Holy Spirit," or God.

rugelach: (Yiddish) flaky rolled pastry containing cinnamon and walnuts.

sabra: (Hebrew) an Israeli-born Jew.

sâdû: (Akkadian) mountain.

schiksa: see *shikse* (below).

schlemiel: (Yiddish, "Yinglish") a foolish person, a simpleton, a "fall guy," a hard-luck type; also an uncomplaining victim.

schwarze: (German) see *shvartze* (below).

sechel: (Yiddish, Hebrew) intelligence.

seder: (Hebrew) lit.: order; the ritual of commemorating, at Passover, the story of the Israelites' Exodus from Egypt.

Sephardi: (Hebrew) (n.) pertaining to a Jew of Spanish or Portuguese descent; a descendant of the Spanish Jewry that flourished under the Moors; a Jew of Spanish or Portuguese descent (from "Sefarad," a Hebrew word for Spain). Term is also applied to Jews from the Arab world—Morocco, Iraq, Yemen, and so forth. See also "Ladino" (above).

Sephardic: the adjectival form of "Sephardi" (see above).

Sephardim: pl. of Sephardi (see above).

seychel: see *sechel* (above).

Shabbas: (Hebrew) see "Shabbat" (below).

Shabbat: (Hebrew) Sabbath.

Shabbatot: pl. of Shabbat (see above).

Shabbes: (Yiddish) see "Shabbat" (above).

Shabbos: (Yiddish) see "Shabbat" (above).

shad: (Hebrew) breast.

shanda fur de goyim: (Yiddish) an embarrassment in front of the Gentiles.

Shavuot: (Hebrew) a harvest holiday that also celebrates the giving of the Torah. The Talmud teaches that God gave the Jews the Ten Commandments on the first night of Shavuot.

shekhinah: (Hebrew) lit.: indwelling; an aspect of God's spiritual presence; female aspect in Jewish mysticism.

Sheol: (Hebrew) a biblical term for the netherworld, first used by Jacob; later it came to mean "Hell."

sheyn: (Yiddish) beautiful.

sheyn meydele: (Yiddish) darling, wonderful little girl.

shiker: (Yiddish, Hebrew) drunk.

shiksa: see *shikse* (below).

shikse: (Yiddish) a non-Jewish female.

shivah: (Hebrew) seven-day period of mourning for the dead.

shlufen: (Yiddish) to sleep.

Sh'ma: (Hebrew) lit.: hear; the central watchword of Judaism is *"Sh'ma Yisrael, Adonai Eloheynu, Adonai Ehod"* (Hear O Israel, the Lord our God, the Lord is One); prayer affirming faith in God.

shmuck: (Yiddish) lit.: jewel; vul.: penis; vul.: bastard, fool, chump; malevolent man.

Shoah: (Hebrew) the Holocaust.

shofar: (Hebrew) ram's horn blown during Jewish new year.

shpritz: (Yiddish) (n., v.) spray.

shpritzing: ("Yinglish") see *shpritz* (above). (The Yiddish verb is here conjugated as an English verb, with an -ing ending added.)

shtetl: (Yiddish) town in Jewish communities of Eastern Europe prior to World War II.

shtick: see *shtik* (below).

shtiebel: (Yiddish) a small synagogue or house of prayer.

shtik: Yiddish) lit.: a piece; comic routine, performance of comic routine.

shtub: (Yiddish) room.

shul: (Yiddish) synagogue.

Shulkhan Aruk: (Hebrew) lit.: a table set up for dining; broad code of Jewish laws, compiled in the sixteenth century by Reb Joseph Karo of Safed, considered a definitive authority on legal questions.

shvartze: (Yiddish) (adj., n.) black; black person.

shveyhr: (Yiddish) difficult hard.

Simchat Torah: (Hebrew) lit.: joy of the Torah; holiday on the twenty-third day of the month of Tishrei, celebrating the completion of the cycle of weekly Torah readings, and the recommencement of the cycle from the beginning.

tallis: (Yiddish) see *tallit* (below).

tallit: (Hebrew) long shawl worn by Jews at prayer.

tallith: (Hebrew) see *tallit* (above).

tallitot: pl. of *tallit* (see above).

Talmud: (Hebrew) the body of Jewish oral traditions, scriptural interpretations, and legends of sages who lived between the second century B.C.E. and the fifth century C.E. The Talmud consists of the oral law, the Mishnah (see above); and the commentaries and discussions regarding it, the Gemara (see above).

talmud torah: (Hebrew) lit.: the study of the Torah; also used for a place of Jewish learning, a house of study, a school.

tantzen: (Yiddish) to dance.

tchotchke: (Yiddish) knick-knack, white elephant.

tefillin: (Hebrew, Aramaic) phylacteries; small leathern boxes containing four texts of scripture (Deuteronomy 6:4–9 and 11:13–20, and Exodus 13:1–10, 11–16) written in Hebrew on vellum, and worn by observant Jews as part of the ritual of morning prayers (but not on the Sabbath) as a reminder of the obligation to keep the law.

tikkun olam: (Hebrew) healing and repair of the world; repair of the world through good deeds.

tikvah: (Hebrew) hope ("Hatikvah" [the hope] is the Israeli national anthem).

toches: (Yiddish) rear end; behind.

Torah: (Hebrew) the five books of Moses, the Pentateuch.

treif: (Yiddish) (also *treyf, trayf*) any food that is not kosher, hence forbidden to observant Jews.

tsafon: (Hebrew) the hidden.

tsafoon: see *tsafon* (above).

tsedakah: (Hebrew) justice, righteousness; commonly used to refer to charity.

tsuris: (Yiddish; Hebrew, *tsarot*) trouble, aggravation.

tsvay: (Yiddish) two; two people.

tuches: (Yiddish) see *toches* (above).

tzedakah: see *tsedakah* (above).

tzimtzum: (Hebrew) divine self-withdrawal from the Creation; a term in mystical Judaism.

verml: (Yiddish) little worm.

vorm: (Yiddish) worm.

Was kennen mir tun?: (Yiddish) "What can we do?"

yachad: (Hebrew) lit.: together; currently used to refer to Jewish gay and lesbian social and support groups.

Yad Vashem: (Hebrew) lit.: a hand and a name; Holocaust memorial and museum in Jerusalem.

yahrzeit: (German) anniversary of someone's death. Commemoration includes lighting a candle in the home and/or in the synagogue; the *yahrzeit* candle burns from sunset to sunset.

Yahweh: (Hebrew) in untransliterated form, the four-lettered name for God, which was unutterable by anyone but the early priests.

yarmulke: (Yiddish; Hebrew: *kipah* [see above]) skullcap; religious headcovering.

yekke: (corrupted Yiddish) a vernacular term referring to a German Jew; used to indicate someone who is fastidious and precise.

yeshiva: (Hebrew, Yiddish) Jewish house of study; a rabbinical seminary or college; in the United States, can be a secondary Hebrew school or elementary school.

Yiddish: (English) a language based largely on German and Hebrew, written with Hebrew letters; the language developed by Ashkenazic Jews.

yiddishe: see *yidishe* (below).

yiddishkeit: (Yiddish) Jewishness; also used to refer to the religious (and at times the secular) culture of Yiddish-speaking Jews; the culture of Eastern European Jewry.

yidishe: (Yiddish) (adj.) Jewish.

Yisrael: (Hebrew) Israel, the people and the place.

Yom Kippur: (Hebrew) the Day of Atonement and the only fast day mandated in the Torah. One of the two holidays referred to as the High Holy Days, or Days of Awe, a time of ethical and religious reassessment of one's life.

Yortsite: see *yahrzeit* (above).

yoshev: (Hebrew) (v.) sit, sitting; (n.) settler. (*Yishuv* means "settlement" in contemporary Hebrew.)

zaida, zayda, zayde: see *zeyde* (below).

zees: (Yiddish) sweet.

zeyde: (Yiddish) grandfather.

zeyer: (Yiddish) very.

NOTES ON CONTRIBUTORS

Ruth Behar teaches anthropology at the University of Michigan. She is the author of *Translated Woman: Crossing the Border with Esperanza's Story* (Beacon, 1993), the editor of *Bridges to Cuba/Puentes a Cuba* (Michigan, 1995), and coeditor of *Women Writing Culture* (California, 1995). Having been named a MacArthur Fellow, she recently received a Guggenheim fellowship to undertake new research in Cuba, which will result in a memoir about her Jewish family's immigration to Cuba and her return journeys to the island.

Emily Miller Budick teaches American literature in the department of American studies at the Hebrew University of Jerusalem, Israel, where she is also chair of the department. Her major publications include *Nineteenth-Century American Romance: Genre and the Construction of Democratic Culture* (Macmillan, 1996), *Engendering Romance: Women Writers and the Hawthorne Tradition, 1850–1990* (Yale, 1994), and *Fiction and Historical Consciousness: The American Romance Tradition* (Yale, 1989).

Maria Damon is associate professor of English and American studies at the University of Minnesota. She is the author of *The Dark End of the Street: Margins in American Vanguard Poetry* (Minnesota, 1993), and of a forthcoming book on poetic language and American diaspora cultures.

Rachel Blau DuPlessis has recently published *The Pink Guitar: Writing as Feminist Practice* (Routledge, 1990) and *Tabula Rosa* and *Drafts 3–14* (Potes & Poets, 1987 and 1991). DuPlessis is also the author of *Writing Beyond the Ending: Narrative Strategies of Twentieth-Century Women Writers* (Indiana, 1985) and *H.D.: The Career of That Struggle* (Indiana, 1986), and editor of *The Selected Letters of George Oppen* (Duke, 1990). She teaches English at Temple University.

Norman Finkelstein is the author of a book of poems, *Restless Messengers* (Georgia, 1992), and two works of criticism, *The Utopian Moment in Contemporary American Poetry* (Bucknell, 1988) and *The Ritual of New Creation: Jewish Tradition and Contemporary Literature* (SUNY, 1992). He is professor and chair of the English department at Xavier University.

Shelley Fisher Fishkin, professor of American studies and English at the University of Texas at Austin, is the author of *Was Huck Black? Mark Twain and African-American Voices* (Oxford, 1993) and *From Fact to Fiction: Journalism and Imaginative Writing in America* (Oxford, 1988), and is the editor of *The Oxford Mark Twain* (1996). She is coeditor, with Elaine Hedges, of *Listening to Silences: New Essays in Feminist Criticism*

(Oxford, 1994) and, with Arnold Rampersad, of Oxford's "Race and American Culture" series.

Doris Friedensohn is professor and chair of women's studies at Jersey City State College. She writes and lectures on women's photo and oral history, immigration, and American diversity. With "Delicious Acts of Defiance: Tales of Eating and Everyday Life" (a book manuscript), she indulges her passions for food and travel and her preference for the autobiographical essay as a way of doing American studies.

David A. Gerber is professor of history at the State University of New York at Buffalo. A social historian, his research interests include various ethnic, racial, and religious minorities, disabled veterans and their representation in the movies, and anti-Semitism. He has authored *Black Ohio and the Color Line, 1860–1915* (Illinois, 1976) and *The Making of American Pluralism: Buffalo, New York, 1825–1860* (Illinois, 1989), and has edited *Anti-Semitism in American History* (Illinois, 1986), and with Scott Eberle, *The Rise and Fall of a Frontier Entrepreneur: Benjamin Rathbun, Master Builder and Architect* (Syracuse, 1996).

Miriyam Glazer, chair of the literature department at the University of Judaism, is the editor of *Burning Air and a Clear Mind: Contemporary Israeli Women Poets* (Ohio, 1981) and the forthcoming *Dreaming the Actual: Israeli Women Writers in the 1990s* (SUNY). She has published numerous articles on Jewish American women writers.

Susan Gubar, with her collaborator Sandra Gilbert, has coauthored *The Madwoman in the Attic* (Yale, 1979), and its three-volume sequel, *No Man's Land: The Place of the Woman Writer in the Twentieth Century* (Yale, 1988–94). Together, they also coedited the *Norton Anthology of Literature by Women* (1985), which they are currently revising for a second edition. Distinguished Professor of English and Women's Studies at Indiana University, Gubar is now embarked on a project entitled "White Skin, Black Face: Representations of Racechange in Twentieth-Century Culture."

Oliver W. Holmes is professor of European intellectual history at Wesleyan University. He is the author of *Human Reality and the Social World: Ortega's Philosophy of History* (Massachusetts, 1975), and of numerous essays on phenomenology, philosophy of history, and the politics of culture and modernity. He is completing a book entitled "The Politics of the 'Other': Black, Chinese and Jewish Intellectuals and the Socialist Movement in France, 1789–1950."

Michael R. Katz is chair of the department of Slavic languages and director of the Center for Post-Soviet and East European Studies at the University of Texas at Austin. His books include *The Literary Ballad in Early Nineteenth-Century Russian Literature* (Oxford, 1976) and *Dreams and the Unconscious in Nineteenth-Century Russian Fiction* (New England, 1984). He has also published English translations of novels by Herzen, Chernyshevsky, Turgenev, and Dostoevsky.

Susanne Klingenstein is assistant professor of writing and humanistic studies at the Massachusetts Institute of Technology, and the author of *Jews in the American Acade-*

my, 1900–1940: The Dynamics of Intellectual Assimilation (Yale, 1991). She has published articles on Holocaust literature, Jewish-American history, literature, and culture, and is currently completing a book manuscript entitled "Enlarging America: The Cultural Work of Jewish Literary Scholars, 1930–1990."

Paul Lauter, the Allan K. and Gwendolyn Miles Smith Professor of Literature at Trinity College, is the author of *Canons and Contexts* (Oxford, 1991) and general editor of the *Heath Anthology of American Literature* (Heath, 1990; second edition, 1994). His edited books include *Reconstructing American Literature* (Feminist Press, 1983) and, with Louis Kampf, *The Politics of Literature* (Pantheon, 1972). He served as president of the American Studies Association in 1994–95.

Herbert S. Lindenberger, Avalon Foundation Professor of the Humanities at Stanford University, founded the comparative literature program at Stanford, where he has taught since 1969. Earlier he taught at the University of California, Riverside, and Washington University, St. Louis. He has written books on Wordsworth, Büchner, Trakl, historical drama, opera, and critical theory, and is currently completing a book to be called "Opera in History: From Monteverdi to Cage." He will serve as president of the Modern Language Association in 1997.

Eunice Lipton, a writer and art historian, lives in New York City. Her books include *Alias Olympia: A Woman's Search for Manet's Notorious Model and Her Own Desire* (Scribner's and Penguin/Meridian, 1992) and *Looking into Degas: Uneasy Images of Women and Modern Life* (California, 1987).

Elaine Marks is Germaine Brée Professor of French and Women's Studies at the University of Wisconsin–Madison. Her current research focuses on French and Italian Jewish writers of the twentieth century and the death of God. Among her published works are *Colette* (Rutgers, 1960, 1981) and *Simone de Beauvoir: Encounters with Death* (Rutgers, 1973). Her most recent book, *Marrano as Metaphor: The Jewish Presence in French Writing,* was published by Columbia University Press (1995). She was president of the Modern Language Association in 1993.

Nancy K. Miller is Distinguished Professor of English at Lehman College and the Graduate Center, City University of New York. Her books include *Subject to Change: Reading Feminist Writing* (Columbia, 1988), *Getting Personal: Feminist Occasions and Other Autobiographical Acts* (Routledge, 1991), and *French Dressing: Women, Men, and Ancien Régime Fiction* (Routledge, 1995). She coedits, with Carolyn Heilbrun, the "Gender and Culture" series at Columbia University Press.

Gary Saul Morson, Frances Hooper Professor of the Arts and Humanities at Northwestern University, is the author of several books on Dostoevsky, Tolstoy, Bakhtin, and various problems of literary theory. With Caryl Emerson, he wrote *Mikhail Bakhtin: Creation of a Prosaics* (Stanford, 1990), which won an award for best book in Slavic literary studies. His most recent book is *Narrative and Freedom: The Shadows of Time* (Yale, 1994).

Alica Ostriker is the author of eight books of poetry, and a recipient of the William Carlos Williams Award from the Poetry Society of America (1986). Her most recent book of poems is *The Crack of Everything* (Pittsburgh, 1996). Among her prose works are two books on the Bible, *Feminist Revision and the Bible* (Blackwell, 1993) and *The Nakedness of the Fathers* (Rutgers, 1994). She is professor of English at Rutgers University.

Joel Porte is Ernest I. White Professor of American Studies and Humane Letters at Cornell University. His books include *In Respect to Egotism: Studies in American Romantic Writing* (Cambridge, 1991), *Representative Man: Ralph Waldo Emerson in His Time* (Oxford, 1979), and *The Romance in America: Studies in Cooper, Poe, Hawthorne, Melville and James* (Wesleyan, 1969). He has edited *New Essays on "The Portrait of a Lady"* (Cambridge, 1990) as well as two books on Emerson.

Riv-Ellen Prell, an anthropologist, is associate professor of American studies at the University of Minnesota. She has written *Prayer and Community: The Havurah in American Judaism* (Wayne State, 1989), and coedited, with the Personal Narratives Group, *Interpreting Women's Lives: Personal Narratives and Feminist Theory* (Indiana, 1989). *Fighting to Become Americans: Jewish Women and Men in Conflict in the Twentieth Century* is forthcoming from Basic Books.

Michael S. Roth is assistant director for scholars and seminars at the Getty Center. His most recent books are *The Ironist's Cage: Memory, Trauma and the Construction of History* (Columbia, 1995), a paperback edition of *Psycho-Analysis as History: Negation and Freedom in Freud* (Cornell, [1987], 1995), *Knowing and History: Appropriations of Hegel in 20th Century France* (Cornell, 1988), and two edited volumes: *Rediscovering History: Culture, Politics, and the Psyche* (Stanford, 1994) and, with Ralph Cohen, *History and . . . : Histories within the Human Sciences* (Virginia, 1995).

Jeffrey Rubin-Dorsky teaches English and American studies at the University of Colorado, Colorado Springs. He writes on nineteenth-century American literature and contemporary Jewish-American literature and culture. He has published *Adrift in the Old World: The Psychological Pilgrimage of Washington Irving* (Chicago, 1988); his new book will be titled *Philip Roth and Woody Allen: The Loyal Opposition*.

Raphael Sassower is professor and chair of the department of philosophy at the University of Colorado, Colorado Springs. Among his recent publications are *Cultural Collisions: Postmodern Technoscience* (Routledge, 1995), *Knowledge without Expertise: On the Social Status of Scientists* (SUNY, 1993), and "On Madness in the Academy," *Journal of Higher Education* 65 (1994): 473–85.

Laurence Mordekhai Thomas is professor of philosophy and political science at Syracuse University, where he is also a member of the Jewish Studies Program. He is the author of *Living Morally: A Psychology of Moral Character* (Temple, 1989) and of *Vessels of Evil: American Slavery and the Holocaust* (Temple, 1993).

Notes on Contributors

Allan M. Winkler teaches twentieth-century American history at Miami University of Ohio. He has published eight books dealing with the period from World War II to the present, including *Life under a Cloud: American Anxiety about the Atom* (Oxford, 1993) and *Home Front, U.S.A.: America during World War II* (Harlan Davidson, 1986). He has lectured widely on historical issues in countries around the world.

Seth L. Wolitz, who holds the Gale Chair of Jewish Studies and is professor of French, Slavic, and comparative literature at the University of Texas at Austin, is a specialist in Proust, the European novel, and Yiddish literature. His publications include *The Proustian Community* (NYU Press, 1971), "The Golem Motif in German Expressionist Film," in *Passion and Rebellion* (University Books, 1983), "The Jewish National Art Renaissance in Russia," in *Tradition and Revolution* (Israel Museum, 1987), "The Americanization of Tevye or Boarding the Jewish *Mayflower*," (*American Quarterly* 40 (1988), "Experiencing Visibility and Phantom Existence," in *Russian-Jewish Artists* (Prestel, 1995), and translations of Aimé Césaire, Sholem Aleichem, I. L. Peretz and David Bergelson.

Marilyn Yalom is the senior scholar at the Institute for Research on Women and Gender at Stanford University. Formerly professor of French at California State, Hayward, she is the author of *Blood Sisters: The French Revolution in Women's Memory* (Basic Books, 1993) and the forthcoming *A History of the Breast* (Knopf, 1997), and has published numerous edited books and articles.

Bonnie Zimmerman is professor of women's studies at San Diego State University. She is the author of *The Safe Sea of Women: Lesbian Fiction 1969–1989* (Beacon, 1990), and coeditor, with George E. Haggerty, of *Professions of Desire: Lesbian and Gay Studies in Literature* (MLA Publications, 1995) and, with Toni A. McNaron, of the second edition of *Lesbian Studies* (Feminist Press, 1996).

INDEX

Index

Index

Wisconsin Studies in American Autobiography
WILLIAM L. ANDREWS
General Editor

Robert F. Sayre
The Examined Self: Benjamin Franklin, Henry Adams, Henry James

Daniel B. Shea
Spiritual Autobiography in Early America

Lois Mark Stalvey
The Education of a WASP

Margaret Sams
Forbidden Family: A Wartime Memoir of the Philippines, 1941–1945
Edited, with an introduction, by Lynn Z. Bloom

Journeys in New Worlds: Early American Women's Narratives
Edited by William L. Andrews

Mark Twain
Mark Twain's Own Autobiography:
The Chapters from the "North American Review"
Edited, with an introduction, by Michael J. Kiskis

American Autobiography: Retrospect and Prospect
Edited by Paul John Eakin

Charlotte Perkins Gilman
The Living of Charlotte Perkins Gilman: An Autobiography
Introduction by Ann J. Lane

Caroline Seabury
The Diary of Caroline Seabury: 1854–1863
Edited, with an introduction, by Suzanne L. Bunkers

Cornelia Peake McDonald
*A Woman's Civil War: A Diary with Reminiscences of the War,
from March 1862*
Edited, with an introduction, by Minrose G. Gwin

Marian Anderson
My Lord, What a Morning
Introduction by Nellie Y. McKay

American Women's Autobiography: Fea(s)ts of Memory
Edited, with an introduction, by Margo Culley

Frank Marshall Davis
Livin' the Blues: Memoirs of a Black Journalist and Poet
Edited, with an introduction, by John Edgar Tidwell

Joanne Jacobson
Authority and Alliance in the Letters of Henry Adams

Kamau Brathwaite
The Zea Mexican Diary
Foreword by Sandra Pouchet Paquet

Genaro M. Padilla
*My History, Not Yours:
The Formation of Mexican American Autobiography*

Frances Smith Foster
*Witnessing Slavery: The Development
of Ante-bellum Slave Narratives*

Native American Autobiography: An Anthology
Edited, with an introduction, by Arnold Krupat

American Lives: An Anthology of Autobiographical Writing
Edited, with an introduction, by Robert F. Sayre

Carol Holly
*Intensely Family: The Inheritance of Family Shame and the
Autobiographies of Henry James*

*People of the Book: Thirty Scholars Reflect
on Their Jewish Identity*
Edited, with an introduction, by Jeffrey Rubin-Dorsky
and Shelley Fisher Fishkin